19th Conference on Computational Natural Language Learning

(CoNLL 2015)

Co-located with ACL-IJCNLP 2015

Beijing, China
30 – 31 July 2015

ISBN: 978-1-5108-0938-3

Printed from e-media with permission by:

Curran Associates, Inc.
57 Morehouse Lane
Red Hook, NY 12571

Some format issues inherent in the e-media version may also appear in this print version.

Printed by Curran Associates, Inc. (2015)

Association for Computational Linguistics
209 N. Eighth Street
Stroudsburg, Pennsylvania 18360

Phone: 1-570-476-8006
Fax: 1-570-476-0860

acl@aclweb.org

Additional copies of this publication are available from:

Curran Associates, Inc.
57 Morehouse Lane
Red Hook, NY 12571 USA
Phone: 845-758-0400
Fax: 845-758-2634
Email: curran@proceedings.com
Web: www.proceedings.com

CoNLL 2015

The 19th Conference on Computational Natural Language Learning

Proceedings of the Conference

July 30-31, 2015
Beijing, China

Production and Manufacturing by
Taberg Media Group AB
Box 94, 562 02 Taberg
Sweden

CoNLL 2015 Best Paper Sponsors:

Google

Microsoft Research

Introduction

The 2015 Conference on Computational Natural Language Learning is the nineteenth in the series of annual meetings organized by SIGNLL, the ACL special interest group on natural language learning. CONLL 2015 will be held in Beijing, China on July 30-31, 2015, in conjunction with ACL-IJCNLP 2015.

For the first time this year, CoNLL 2015 has accepted both long (9 pages of content plus 2 additional pages of references) and short papers (5 pages of content plus 2 additional pages of references). We received 144 submissions in total, of which 81 were long and 61 were short papers, and 17 were eventually withdrawn. Of the remaining 127 papers, 29 long and 9 short papers were selected to appear in the conference program, resulting in an overall acceptance rate of almost 30%. All accepted papers appear here in the proceedings.

As in previous years, CoNLL 2015 has a shared task, this year on Shallow Discourse Parsing. Papers accepted for the shared task are collected in a companion volume of CoNLL 2015.

To fit the paper presentations in a 2-day program, 16 long papers were selected for oral presentation and the remaining 13 long and the 9 short papers were presented as posters. The papers selected for oral presentation are distributed in four main sessions, each consisting of 4 talks. Each of these sessions also includes 3 or 4 spotlights of the long papers selected for the poster session. In contrast, the spotlights for short papers are presented in a single session of 30 minutes. The remaining sessions were used for presenting a selection of 4 shared task papers, two invited keynote speeches and a single poster session, including long, short and shared task papers.

We would like to thank all the authors who submitted their work to CoNLL 2015, as well as the program committee for helping us select the best papers out of many high-quality submissions. We are also grateful to our invited speakers, Paul Smolensky and Eric Xing, who graciously agreed to give talks at CoNLL.

Special thanks are due to the SIGNLL board members, Xavier Carreras and Julia Hockenmaier, for their valuable advice and assistance in putting together this year's program, and to Ben Verhoeven, for redesigning and maintaining the CoNLL 2015 web page. We are grateful to the ACL organization for helping us with the program, proceedings and logistics. Finally, our gratitude goes to our sponsors, Google Inc. and Microsoft Research, for supporting the best paper award and student scholarships at CoNLL 2015.

We hope you enjoy the conference!

Afra Alishahi and Alessandro Moschitti

CoNLL 2015 conference co-chairs

Organizers:

Afra Alishahi, Tilburg University
Alessandro Moschitti, Qatar Computing Research Institute

Invited Speakers:

Paul Smolensky, Johns Hopkins University
Eric Xing, Carnegie Mellon University

Program Committee:

Steven Abney, University of Michigan
Eneko Agirre, University of the Basque Country (UPV/EHU)
Bharat Ram Ambati, University of Edinburgh
Yoav Artzi, University of Washington
Marco Baroni, University of Trento
Alberto Barrón-Cedeño, Qatar Computing Research Institute
Roberto Basili, University of Roma, Tor Vergata
Ulf Brefeld, TU Darmstadt
Claire Cardie, Cornell University
Xavier Carreras, Xerox Research Centre Europe
Asli Celikyilmaz, Microsoft
Daniel Cer, Google
Kai-Wei Chang, University of Illinois
Colin Cherry, NRC
Grzegorz Chrupała, Tilburg University
Alexander Clark, King's College London
Shay B. Cohen, University of Edinburgh
Paul Cook, University of New Brunswick
Bonaventura Coppola, Technical University of Darmstadt
Danilo Croce, University of Roma, Tor Vergata
Aron Culotta, Illinois Institute of Technology
Scott Cyphers, Massachusetts Institute of Technology
Giovanni Da San Martino, Qatar Computing Research Institute
Walter Daelemans, University of Antwerp, CLiPS
Ido Dagan, Bar-Ilan University
Dipanjan Das, Google Inc.
Doug Downey, Northwestern University
Mark Dras, Macquarie University
Jacob Eisenstein, Georgia Institute of Technology
James Fan, IBM Research
Raquel Fernandez, ILLC, University of Amsterdam
Simone Filice, University of Roma "Tor Vergata"
Antske Fokkens, VU Amsterdam
Bob Frank, Yale University
Stefan L. Frank, Radboud University Nijmegen
Dayne Freitag, SRI International
Michael Gamon, Microsoft Research

Wei Gao, Qatar Computing Research Institute
Andrea Gesmundo, Google Inc.
Kevin Gimpel, Toyota Technological Institute at Chicago
Francisco Guzmán, Qatar Computing Research Institute
Thomas Gärtner, University of Bonn and Fraunhofer IAIS
Iryna Haponchyk, University of Trento
James Henderson, Xerox Research Centre Europe
Julia Hockenmaier, University of Illinois Urbana-Champaign
Dirk Hovy, Center for Language Technology, University of Copenhagen
Rebecca Hwa, University of Pittsburgh
Richard Johansson, University of Gothenburg
Shafiq Joty, Qatar Computing Research Institute
Lukasz Kaiser, CNRS & Google
Mike Kestemont, University of Antwerp
Philipp Koehn, Johns Hopkins University
Anna Korhonen, University of Cambridge
Annie Louis, University of Edinburgh
André F. T. Martins, Priberam, Instituto de Telecomunicacoes
Yuji Matsumoto, Nara Institute of Science and Technology
Stewart McCauley, Cornell University
David McClosky, IBM Research
Ryan McDonald, Google
Margaret Mitchell, Microsoft Research
Roser Morante, Vrije Universiteit Amsterdam
Lluís Màrquez, Qatar Computing Research Institute
Preslav Nakov, Qatar Computing Research Institute
Aida Nematzadeh, University of Toronto
Ani Nenkova, University of Pennsylvania
Vincent Ng, University of Texas at Dallas
Joakim Nivre, Uppsala University
Naoaki Okazaki, Tohoku University
Miles Osborne, Bloomberg
Alexis Palmer, Heidelberg University
Andrea Passerini, University of Trento
Daniele Pighin, Google Inc.
Barbara Plank, University of Copenhagen
Thierry Poibeau, LATTICE-CNRS
Sameer Pradhan, cemantix.org
Verónica Pérez-Rosas, University of Michigan
Jonathon Read, School of Computing, Teesside University
Sebastian Riedel, UCL
Alan Ritter, The Ohio State University
Brian Roark, Google Inc.
Dan Roth, University of Illinois
Josef Ruppenhofer, Hildesheim University
Rajhans Samdani, Google Research
Hinrich Schütze, University of Munich
Djamé Seddah, Université Paris Sorbonne
Aliaksei Severyn, University of Trento
Avirup Sil, IBM T.J. Watson Research Center
Khalil Sima'an, ILLC, University of Amsterdam

Kevin Small, Amazon
Vivek Srikumar, University of Utah
Mark Steedman, University of Edinburgh
Anders Søgaard, University of Copenhagen
Christoph Teichmann, University of Potsdam
Kristina Toutanova, Microsoft Research
Ioannis Tsochantaridis, Google Inc.
Jun'ichi Tsujii, Aritificial Intelligence Research Centre at AIST
Kateryna Tymoshenko, University of Trento
Olga Uryupina, University of Trento
Antonio Uva, University of Trento
Antal van den Bosch, Radboud University Nijmegen
Menno van Zaanen, Tilburg University
Aline Villavicencio, Institute of Informatics, Federal University of Rio Grande do Sul
Michael Wiegand, Saarland University
Sander Wubben, Tilburg University
Fabio Massimo Zanzotto, University of Rome "Tor Vergata"
Luke Zettlemoyer, University of Washington
Feifei Zhai, The City University of New York
Min Zhang, SooChow University

Table of Contents

Keynote Talks

Long Papers

Short Papers

Conference Program

Thursday, July 30, 2015

08:45-09:00 **Opening Remarks**

09:00-10:10 **Session 1.a: Embedding input and output representations**

Multichannel Variable-Size Convolution for Sentence Classification
Wenpeng Yin and Hinrich Schütze

Task-Oriented Learning of Word Embeddings for Semantic Relation Classification
Kazuma Hashimoto, Pontus Stenetorp, Makoto Miwa and Yoshimasa Tsuruoka

Symmetric Pattern Based Word Embeddings for Improved Word Similarity Prediction
Roy Schwartz, Roi Reichart and Ari Rappoport

A Coactive Learning View of Online Structured Prediction in Statistical Machine Translation
Artem Sokolov, Stefan Riezler and Shay B. Cohen

10:10-10:30 **Session 1.b: Entity Linking (spotlight presentations)**

A Joint Framework for Coreference Resolution and Mention Head Detection
Haoruo Peng, Kai-Wei Chang and Dan Roth

Entity Linking Korean Text: An Unsupervised Learning Approach using Semantic Relations
Youngsik Kim and Key-Sun Choi

Linking Entities Across Images and Text
Rebecka Weegar, Kalle Åström and Pierre Nugues

Recovering Traceability Links in Requirements Documents
Zeheng Li, Mingrui Chen, LiGuo Huang and Vincent Ng

10:30-11:00 **Coffee Break**

11:00-12:00 **Session 2.a: Keynote Talk**

On Spectral Graphical Models, and a New Look at Latent Variable Modeling in Natural Language Processing
Eric Xing, Carnegie Mellon University

12:00-12:30 **Session 2.b: Short Paper Spotlights**

Deep Neural Language Models for Machine Translation
Thang Luong, Michael Kayser and Christopher D. Manning

Reading behavior predicts syntactic categories
Maria Barrett and Anders Søgaard

One Million Sense-Tagged Instances for Word Sense Disambiguation and Induction
Kaveh Taghipour and Hwee Tou Ng

Model Selection for Type-Supervised Learning with Application to POS Tagging
Kristina Toutanova, Waleed Ammar, Pallavi Choudhury and Hoifung Poon

Feature Selection for Short Text Classification using Wavelet Packet Transform
Anuj Mahajan, Sharmistha Jat and Shourya Roy

Do dependency parsing metrics correlate with human judgments?
Barbara Plank, Héctor Martínez Alonso, Željko Agić, Danijela Merkler and Anders Søgaard

Learning Adjective Meanings with a Tensor-Based Skip-Gram Model
Jean Maillard and Stephen Clark

Accurate Cross-lingual Projection between Count-based Word Vectors by Exploiting Translatable Context Pairs
Shonosuke Ishiwatari, Nobuhiro Kaji, Naoki Yoshinaga, Masashi Toyoda and Masaru Kitsuregawa

Finding Opinion Manipulation Trolls in News Community Forums
Todor Mihaylov, Georgi Georgiev and Preslav Nakov

12:30-14:00 **Lunch Break**

14:00-15:30 **Session 3: CoNLL Shared Task**

The CoNLL-2015 Shared Task on Shallow Discourse Parsing
Nianwen Xue, Hwee Tou Ng, Sameer Pradhan, Rashmi Prasad, Christopher Bryant, Attapol Rutherford

A Refined End-to-End Discourse Parser
Jianxiang Wang and Man Lan

The UniTN Discourse Parser in CoNLL 2015 Shared Task: Token-level Sequence Labeling with Argument-specific Models
Evgeny Stepanov, Giuseppe Riccardi and Ali Orkan Bayer

The SoNLP-DP System in the CoNLL-2015 shared Task
Fang Kong, Sheng Li and Guodong Zhou

15:30-16:00 **Coffee Break**

16:00-17:10 **Session 4.a: Syntactic Parsing**

A Supertag-Context Model for Weakly-Supervised CCG Parser Learning
Dan Garrette, Chris Dyer, Jason Baldridge and Noah A. Smith

Transition-based Spinal Parsing
Miguel Ballesteros and Xavier Carreras

Cross-lingual Transfer for Unsupervised Dependency Parsing Without Parallel Data
Long Duong, Trevor Cohn, Steven Bird and Paul Cook

Incremental Recurrent Neural Network Dependency Parser with Search-based Discriminative Training
Majid Yazdani and James Henderson

17:10-17:30 **Session 4.b: Cross-language studies (spotlight presentations)**

Structural and lexical factors in adjective placement in complex noun phrases across Romance languages
Kristina Gulordava and Paola Merlo

Instance Selection Improves Cross-Lingual Model Training for Fine-Grained Sentiment Analysis
Roman Klinger and Philipp Cimiano

Annotation Projection-based Representation Learning for Cross-lingual Dependency Parsing
Min Xiao and Yuhong Guo

Friday, July 31, 2015

09:00-10:10 **Session 5.a: Semantics**

Detecting Semantically Equivalent Questions in Online User Forums
Dasha Bogdanova, Cicero dos Santos, Luciano Barbosa and Bianca Zadrozny

An Iterative Similarity based Adaptation Technique for Cross-domain Text Classification
Himanshu Sharad Bhatt, Deepali Semwal and Shourya Roy

Making the Most of Crowdsourced Document Annotations: Confused Supervised LDA
Paul Felt, Eric Ringger, Jordan Boyd-Graber and Kevin Seppi

Big Data Small Data, In Domain Out-of Domain, Known Word Unknown Word: The Impact of Word Representations on Sequence Labelling Tasks
Lizhen Qu, Gabriela Ferraro, Liyuan Zhou, Weiwei Hou, Nathan Schneider and Timothy Baldwin

10:10-10:30 **Session 5.b: Extraction and Labeling (spotlight presentations)**

Labeled Morphological Segmentation with Semi-Markov Models
Ryan Cotterell, Thomas Müller, Alexander Fraser and Hinrich Schütze

Opinion Holder and Target Extraction based on the Induction of Verbal Categories
Michael Wiegand and Josef Ruppenhofer

Temporal Information Extraction from Korean Texts
Young-Seob Jeong, Zae Myung Kim, Hyun-Woo Do, Chae-Gyun Lim and Ho-Jin Choi

10:30-11:00 **Coffee Break**

11:00-12:00 **Session 6.a: Keynote Talk**

Does the Success of Deep Neural Network Language Processing Mean – Finally! – the End of Theoretical Linguistics?
Paul Smolensky, Johns Hopkins University

12:00-12:30 **Session 6.b: Business Meeting**

12:30-14:00 **Lunch Break**

14:00-15:10 **Session 7.a: Language Structure**

Cross-lingual syntactic variation over age and gender
Anders Johannsen, Dirk Hovy and Anders Søgaard

A Synchronous Hyperedge Replacement Grammar based approach for AMR parsing
Xiaochang Peng, Linfeng Song and Daniel Gildea

Contrastive Analysis with Predictive Power: Typology Driven Estimation of Grammatical Error Distributions in ESL
Yevgeni Berzak, Roi Reichart and Boris Katz

AIDA2: A Hybrid Approach for Token and Sentence Level Dialect Identification in Arabic
Mohamed Al-Badrashiny, Heba Elfardy and Mona Diab

15:10-15:30 **Session 7.b: CoNLL Mix (spotlight presentations)**

Analyzing Optimization for Statistical Machine Translation: MERT Learns Verbosity, PRO Learns Length
Francisco Guzmán, Preslav Nakov and Stephan Vogel

Learning to Exploit Structured Resources for Lexical Inference
Vered Shwartz, Omer Levy, Ido Dagan and Jacob Goldberger

Quantity, Contrast, and Convention in Cross-Situated Language Comprehension
Ian Perera and James Allen

15:30-16:00 **Coffee Break**

Reading behavior predicts syntactic categories
Maria Barrett and Anders Søgaard

One Million Sense-Tagged Instances for Word Sense Disambiguation and Induction
Kaveh Taghipour and Hwee Tou Ng

Model Selection for Type-Supervised Learning with Application to POS Tagging
Kristina Toutanova, Waleed Ammar, Pallavi Choudhury and Hoifung Poon

Feature Selection for Short Text Classification using Wavelet Packet Transform
Anuj Mahajan, Sharmistha Jat and Shourya Roy

Do dependency parsing metrics correlate with human judgments?
Barbara Plank, Héctor Martínez Alonso, Željko Agić, Danijela Merkler and Anders Søgaard

Learning Adjective Meanings with a Tensor-Based Skip-Gram Model
Jean Maillard and Stephen Clark

Accurate Cross-lingual Projection between Count-based Word Vectors by Exploiting Translatable Context Pairs
Shonosuke Ishiwatari, Nobuhiro Kaji, Naoki Yoshinaga, Masashi Toyoda and Masaru Kitsuregawa

Finding Opinion Manipulation Trolls in News Community Forums
Todor Mihaylov, Georgi Georgiev and Preslav Nakov

Shared Task Papers

A Hybrid Discourse Relation Parser in CoNLL 2015
Sobha Lalitha Devi, Sindhuja Gopalan, Lakshmi S, Pattabhi RK Rao, Vijay Sundar Ram and Malarkodi C.S.

A Minimalist Approach to Shallow Discourse Parsing and Implicit Relation Recognition
Christian Chiarcos and Niko Schenk

A Shallow Discourse Parsing System Based On Maximum Entropy Model
Jia Sun, Peijia Li, Weiqun Xu and Yonghong Yan

Hybrid Approach to PDTB-styled Discourse Parsing for CoNLL-2015
Yasuhisa Yoshida, Katsuhiko Hayashi, Tsutomu Hirao and Masaaki Nagata

Improving a Pipeline Architecture for Shallow Discourse Parsing
Yangqiu Song, Haoruo Peng, Parisa Kordjamshidi, Mark Sammons and Dan Roth

JAIST: A two-phase machine learning approach for identifying discourse relations in newswire texts
Son Nguyen, Quoc Ho and Minh Nguyen

Shallow Discourse Parsing Using Constituent Parsing Tree
Changge Chen, Peilu Wang and Hai Zhao

Shallow Discourse Parsing with Syntactic and (a Few) Semantic Features
Shubham Mukherjee, Abhishek Tiwari, Mohit Gupta and Anil Kumar Singh

The CLaC Discourse Parser at CoNLL-2015
Majid Laali, Elnaz Davoodi and Leila Kosseim

The DCU Discourse Parser for Connective, Argument Identification and Explicit Sense Classification
Longyue Wang, Chris Hokamp, Tsuyoshi Okita, Xiaojun Zhang and Qun Liu

The DCU Discourse Parser: A Sense Classification Task
Tsuyoshi Okita, Longyue Wang and Qun Liu

17:30-17:45 Session 8.b: Best Paper Award and Closing

Keynote Talk

On Spectral Graphical Models, and a New Look at Latent Variable Modeling in Natural Language Processing

Eric Xing

Carnegie Mellon University

epxing@cs.cmu.edu

Abstract

Latent variable and latent structure modeling, as widely seen in parsing systems, machine translation systems, topic models, and deep neural networks, represents a key paradigm in Natural Language Processing, where discovering and leveraging syntactic and semantic entities and relationships that are not explicitly annotated in the training set provide a crucial vehicle to obtain various desirable effects such as simplifying the solution space, incorporating domain knowledge, and extracting informative features. However, latent variable models are difficult to train and analyze in that, unlike fully observed models, they suffer from non-identifiability, non-convexity, and over-parameterization, which make them often hard to interpret, and tend to rely on local-search heuristics and heavy manual tuning.

In this talk, I propose to tackle these challenges using spectral graphical models (SGM), which view latent variable models through the lens of linear algebra and tensors. I show how SGMs exploit the connection between latent structure and low rank decomposition, and allow one to develop models and algorithms for a variety of latent variable problems, which unlike traditional techniques, enjoy provable guarantees on correctness and global optimality, can straightforwardly incorporate additional modern techniques such as kernels to achieve more advanced modeling power, and empirically offer a 1-2 orders of magnitude speed up over existing methods while giving comparable or better performance.

This is joint work with Ankur Parikh, Carnegie Mellon University.

Biography of the Speaker

Dr. Eric Xing is a Professor of Machine Learning in the School of Computer Science at Carnegie Mellon University, and Director of the CMU/UPMC Center for Machine Learning and Health. His principal research interests lie in the development of machine learning and statistical methodology, and large-scale computational system and architecture; especially for solving problems involving automated learning, reasoning, and decision-making in high-dimensional, multimodal, and dynamic possible worlds in artificial, biological, and social systems. Professor Xing received a Ph.D. in Molecular Biology from Rutgers University, and another Ph.D. in Computer Science from UC Berkeley. He servers (or served) as an associate editor of the Annals of Applied Statistics (AOAS), the Journal of American Statistical Association (JASA), the IEEE Transaction of Pattern Analysis and Machine Intelligence (PAMI), the PLoS Journal of Computational Biology, and an Action Editor of the Machine Learning Journal (MLJ), the Journal of Machine Learning Research (JMLR). He was a member of the DARPA Information Science and Technology (ISAT) Advisory Group, a recipient of the NSF Career Award, the Sloan Fellowship, the United States Air Force Young Investigator Award, and the IBM Open Collaborative Research Award. He is the Program Chair of ICML 2014.

Keynote Talk

Does the Success of Deep Neural Network Language Processing Mean – Finally! – the End of Theoretical Linguistics?

Paul Smolensky

Johns Hopkins University

smolensky@jhu.edu

Abstract

Statistical methods in natural-language processing that rest on heavily empirically-based language learning – especially those centrally deploying neural networks – have witnessed dramatic improvement in the past few years, and their success restores the urgency of understanding the relationship between (i) these neural/statistical language systems and (ii) the view of linguistic representation, processing, and structure developed over centuries within theoretical linguistics.

Two hypotheses concerning this relationship arise from our own mathematical and experimental results from past work, which we will present. These hypotheses can guide – we will argue – important future research in the seemingly sizable gap separating computational linguistics from linguistic theories of human language acquisition. These hypotheses are:

1. The internal representational format used in deep neural networks for language – numerical vectors – is covertly an implementation of a system of discrete, symbolic, structured representations which are processed so as to optimally meet the demands of a symbolic grammar recognizable from the perspective of theoretical linguistics.
2. It will not be successes but rather the *failures* of future machine learning approaches to language acquisition which will be most telling for determining whether such approaches capture the crucial limitations on human language learning – limitations, documented in recent artificial-grammar-learning experimental results, which support the nativist Chomskian hypothesis asserting that
   - reliably and efficiently learning human grammars from available evidence requires
   - that the hypothesis space entertained by the child concerning the set of possible (or likely) human languages
   - be limited by abstract, structure-based constraints;
   - these constraints can then also explain (in principle at least) the many robustly-respected universals observed in cross-linguistic typology.

This is joint work with Jennifer Culbertson, University of Edinburgh.

Biography of the Speaker

Paul Smolensky is the Krieger-Eisenhower Professor of Cognitive Science at Johns Hopkins University in Baltimore, Maryland, USA. He studies the mutual implications between the theories of neural computation and of universal grammar and has published in distinguished venues including Science and the Proceedings of the National Academy of Science USA. He received the David E. Rumelhart Prize for Outstanding Contributions to the Formal Analysis of Human Cognition (2005), the Chaire de Recherche Blaise Pascal (2008—9), and the Sapir Professorship of the Linguistic Society of America (2015). Primary results include:

- Contradicting widely-held convictions, (i) structured symbolic and (ii) neural network models of cognition are mutually compatible: formal descriptions of the same systems, the mind/brain, at (i) a highly abstract, and (ii) a more physical, level of description. His article "On the proper treatment of connectionism" (1988) was until recently one of the 10-most cited articles in The Behavioral and Brain Sciences, itself the most-cited journal of all the behavioral sciences.

- That the theory of neural computation can in fact strengthen the theory of universal grammar is attested by the revolutionary impact in theoretical linguistics (within phonology in particular) of Optimality Theory, a neural- network-derived symbolic grammar formalism that he developed with Alan Prince (in a book widely released 1993, officially published 2004).

- The learnability theory for Optimality Theory was founded at nearly the same time as the theory itself, in joint work of Smolensky and his PhD student Bruce Tesar (TR 1993; article in the premier linguistic theory journal, Linguistic Inquiry 1998; MIT Press book 2000). This work laid the foundation upon which rests most of the flourishing formal theory of learning in Optimality Theory.

- There is considerable power in formalizing neural network computation as statistical inference/optimization within a dynamical system. Smolensky's Harmony Theory (1981–6) analyzed network computation as Harmony Maximization (an independently-developed homologue to Hopfield's "energy minimization" formulation) and first deployed principles of statistical inference for processing and learning in the bipartite network structure later to be known as the 'Restricted Boltzmann Machine' in the initial work on deep neural network learning (Hinton et al., 2006–).

- Powerful recursive symbolic computation can be achieved with massive parallelism in neural networks designed to process tensor product representations (TR 1987; journal article in Artificial Intelligence 1990). Related uses of the tensor product to structure numerical vectors is currently under rapid development in the field of distributional vector semantics.

Most recently, as argued in Part 1 of the talk, his work shows the value for theoretical and psycholinguistics of representations that share both the discrete structure of symbolic representations and the continuous variation of activity levels in neural network representations (initial results in an article in Cognitive Science by Smolensky, Goldrick & Mathis 2014).

A Coactive Learning View of Online Structured Prediction in Statistical Machine Translation

Artem Sokolov and **Stefan Riezler***
Computational Linguistics & IWR*
69120 Heidelberg, Germany
{sokolov,riezler}@cl.uni-heidelberg.de

Shay B. Cohen
University of Edinburgh
Edinburgh EH8 9LE, UK
scohen@inf.ed.ac.uk

Abstract

We present a theoretical analysis of online parameter tuning in statistical machine translation (SMT) from a coactive learning view. This perspective allows us to give regret and generalization bounds for latent perceptron algorithms that are common in SMT, but fall outside of the standard convex optimization scenario. Coactive learning also introduces the concept of weak feedback, which we apply in a proof-of-concept experiment to SMT, showing that learning from feedback that consists of slight improvements over predictions leads to convergence in regret and translation error rate. This suggests that coactive learning might be a viable framework for interactive machine translation. Furthermore, we find that surrogate translations replacing references that are unreachable in the decoder search space can be interpreted as weak feedback and lead to convergence in learning, if they admit an underlying linear model.

1 Introduction

Online learning has become the tool of choice for large scale machine learning scenarios. Compared to batch learning, its advantages include memory efficiency, due to parameter updates being performed on the basis of single examples, and runtime efficiency, where a constant number of passes over the training sample is sufficient for convergence (Bottou and Bousquet, 2004). Statistical Machine Translation (SMT) has embraced the potential of online learning, both to handle millions of features and/or millions of data in parameter tuning via online structured prediction (see Liang et al. (2006) for seminal early work), and in interactive learning from user post-edits (see Cesa-Bianchi et al. (2008) for pioneering work on online computer-assisted translation). Online learning algorithms can be given a theoretical analysis in the framework of online convex optimization (Shalev-Shwartz, 2012), however, the application of online learning techniques to SMT sacrifices convexity because of latent derivation variables, and because of surrogate translations replacing human references that are unreachable in the decoder search space. For example, the objective function actually optimized in Liang et al.'s (2006) application of Collins' (2002) structure perceptron has been analyzed by Gimpel and Smith (2012) as a non-convex ramp loss function (McAllester and Keshet, 2011; Do et al., 2008; Collobert et al., 2006). Since online convex optimization does not provide convergence guarantees for the algorithm of Liang et al. (2006), Gimpel and Smith (2012) recommend CCCP (Yuille and Rangarajan, 2003) instead for optimization, but fail to provide a theoretical analysis of Liang et al.'s (2006) actual algorithm under the new objective.

The goal of this paper is to present an alternative theoretical analysis of online learning algorithms for SMT from the viewpoint of coactive learning (Shivaswamy and Joachims, 2012). This framework allows us to make three main contributions:

• Firstly, the proof techniques of Shivaswamy and Joachims (2012) are a simple and elegant tool for a theoretical analysis of perceptron-style algorithms that date back to the perceptron mistake bound of Novikoff (1962). These techniques provide an alternative to an online gradient descent view of perceptron-style algorithms, and can easily be extended to obtain regret bounds for a la-

Proceedings of the 19th Conference on Computational Language Learning, pages 1–11,
Beijing, China, July 30-31, 2015.

tent perceptron algorithm at a rate of $O\left(\frac{1}{\sqrt{T}}\right)$, with possible improvements by using re-scaling. This bound can be directly used to derive generalization guarantees for online and online-to-batch conversions of the algorithm, based on well-known concentration inequalities. Our analysis covers the approach of Liang et al. (2006) and supersedes Sun et al. (2013)'s analysis of the latent perceptron by providing simpler proofs and by adding a generalization analysis. Furthermore, an online learning framework such as coactive learning covers problems such as changing n-best lists after each update that were explicitly excluded from the batch analysis of Gimpel and Smith (2012) and considered fixed in the analysis of Sun et al. (2013).

- Our second contribution is an extension of the online learning scenario in SMT to include a notion of "weak feedback" for the latent perceptron: Coactive learning follows an online learning protocol, where at each round t, the learner predicts a structured object y_t for an input x_t, and the user corrects the learner by responding with an improved, but not necessarily optimal, object $\bar{y}_t$ with respect to a utility function U. The key asset of coactive learning is the ability of the learner to converge to predictions that are close to optimal structures y_t^*, although the utility function is unknown to the learner, and only weak feedback in form of slightly improved structures $\bar{y}_t$ is seen in training. We present a proof-of-concept experiment in which translation feedback of varying grades is chosen from the n-best list of an "optimal" model that has access to full information. We show that weak feedback structures correspond to improvements in TER (Snover et al., 2006) over predicted structures, and that learning from weak feedback minimizes regret and TER.

- Our third contribution is to show that certain practices of computing surrogate references actually can be understood as a form of weak feedback. Coactive learning decouples the learner (performing prediction and updates) from the user (providing feedback in form of an improved translation) so that we can compare different surrogacy modes as different ways of approximate utility maximization. We show experimentally that learning from surrogate "hope" derivations (Chiang, 2012) minimizes regret and TER, thus favoring surrogacy modes that admit an underlying linear model, over "local" updates (Liang et al., 2006) or "oracle" derivations (Sokolov et al., 2013), for which learning does not converge.

It is important to note that the goal of our experiments is not to present improvements of coactive learning over the "optimal" full-information model in terms of standard SMT performance. Instead, our goal is to present experiments that serve as a proof-of-concept of the feasibility of coactive learning from weak feedback for SMT, and to propose a new perspective on standard practices of learning from surrogate translations. The rest of this paper is organized as follows. After a review of related work (Section 2), we present a latent percpetron algorithm and analyze its convergence and generalization properties (Section 3). Our first set of experiments (Section 4.1) confirms our theoretical analysis by showing convergence in regret and TER for learning from weak and strong feedback. Our second set of experiments (Section 4.2) analyzes the relation of different surrogacy modes to minimization of regret and TER.

2 Related Work

Our work builds on the framework of coactive learning, introduced by Shivaswamy and Joachims (2012). We extend their algorithms and proofs to the area of SMT where latent variable models are appropriate, and additionally present generalization guarantees and an online-to-batch conversion. Our theoretical analysis is easily extendable to the full information case of Sun et al. (2013). We also extend our own previous work (Sokolov et al., 2015) with theory and experiments for online-to-batch conversion, and with experiments on coactive learning from surrogate translations.

Online learning has been applied for discriminative training in SMT, based on perceptron-type algorithms (Shen et al. (2004), Watanabe et al. (2006), Liang et al. (2006), Yu et al. (2013), *inter alia*), or large-margin approaches (Tillmann and Zhang (2006), Watanabe et al. (2007), Chiang et al. (2008), Chiang et al. (2009), Chiang (2012), *inter alia*). The latest incarnations are able to handle millions of features and millions of parallel sentences (Simianer et al. (2012), Eidelmann (2012), Watanabe (2012), Green et al. (2013), *inter alia*). Most approaches rely on hidden derivation variables, use some form of surrogate references, and involve n-best lists that change after each update.

Online learning from post-edits has mostly been confined to "simulated post-editing" where independently created human reference translations, or post-edits on the output from similar SMT systems, are used as for online learning (Cesa-Bianchi et al. (2008), López-Salcedo et al. (2012), Martínez-Gómez et al. (2012), Saluja et al. (2012), Saluja and Zhang (2014), *inter alia*). Recent approaches extend online parameter updating by online phrase extraction (Wäschle et al. (2013), Bertoldi et al. (2014), Denkowski et al. (2014), Green et al. (2014), *inter alia*). We exclude dynamic phrase table extension, which has shown to be important in online learning for post-editing, in our theoretical analysis (Denkowski et al., 2014).

Learning from weak feedback is related to binary response-based learning where a meaning representation is "tried out" by iteratively generating system outputs, receiving feedback from world interaction, and updating the model parameters. Such world interaction consists of database access in semantic parsing (Kwiatowski et al. (2013), Berant et al. (2013), or Goldwasser and Roth (2013), *inter alia*). Feedback in response-based learning is given by a user accepting or rejecting system predictions, but not by user corrections.

Lastly, feedback in form of numerical utility values for actions is studied in the frameworks of reinforcement learning (Sutton and Barto, 1998) or in online learning with limited feedback, e.g., multi-armed bandit models (Cesa-Bianchi and Lugosi, 2006). Our framework replaces quantitative feedback with immediate qualitative feedback in form of a structured object that improves upon the utility of the prediction.

3 Coactive Learning for Online Latent Structured Prediction

3.1 Notation and Background

Let $\mathcal{X}$ denote a set of input examples, e.g., sentences, and let $\mathcal{Y}(x)$ denote a set of structured outputs for $x \in \mathcal{X}$, e.g., translations. We define $\mathcal{Y} = \cup_x \mathcal{Y}(x)$. Furthermore, by $\mathcal{H}(x, y)$ we denote a set of possible hidden derivations for a structured output $y \in \mathcal{Y}(x)$, e.g., for phrase-based SMT, the hidden derivation is determined by a phrase segmentation and a phrase alignment between source and target sentences. Every hidden derivation $h \in \mathcal{H}(x, y)$ deterministically identifies an output $y \in \mathcal{Y}(x)$. We define $\mathcal{H} = \cup_{x,y} \mathcal{H}(x, y)$. Let $\phi\colon \mathcal{X} \times \mathcal{Y} \times \mathcal{H} \to \mathbb{R}^d$ denote a feature function that maps a triplet (x, y, h) to a d-dimensional vector. For phrase-based SMT, we use 14 features, defined by phrase translation probabilities,

Algorithm 1 Feedback-based Latent Perceptron

Initialize $w \leftarrow 0$
for $t = 1, \ldots, T$ **do**
  Observe x_t
  $(y_t, h_t) \leftarrow \arg\max_{(y,h)} w_t^\top \phi(x_t, y, h)$
  Obtain weak feedback $\bar{y}_t$
  if $y_t \neq \bar{y}_t$ **then**
    $\bar{h}_t \leftarrow \arg\max_h w_t^\top \phi(x_t, \bar{y}_t, h)$
    $w_{t+1} \leftarrow w_t + \Delta_{\bar{h}_t, h_t}(\phi(x_t, \bar{y}_t, \bar{h}_t) - \phi(x_t, y_t, h_t))$

language model probability, distance-based and lexicalized reordering probabilities, and word and phrase penalty. We assume that the feature function has a bounded radius, i.e. that $\|\phi(x, y, h)\| \leq R$ for all x, y, h. By $\Delta_{h,h'}$ we denote a distance function that is defined for any $h, h' \in \mathcal{H}$, and is used to scale the step size of updates during learning. In our experiments, we use the ordinary Euclidean distance between the feature vectors of derivations. We assume a linear model with fixed parameters w_* such that each input example is mapped to its correct derivation and structured output by using $(y^*, h^*) = \arg\max_{y \in \mathcal{Y}(x), h \in \mathcal{H}(x,y)} w_*{}^\top \phi(x, y, h)$. We define for each given input x, its highest scoring derivation over all outputs $\mathcal{Y}(x)$ such that $h(x; w) = \arg\max_{h' \in \mathcal{H}(x,y)} \max_{y \in \mathcal{Y}(x)} w^\top \phi(x, y, h')$ and the highest scoring derivation for a given output $y \in \mathcal{Y}(x)$ such that $h(x|y; w) = \arg\max_{h' \in \mathcal{H}(x,y)} w^\top \phi(x, y, h')$. In the following theoretical exposition we assume that the $\arg\max$ operation can be computed exactly.

3.2 Feedback-based Latent Perceptron

We assume an online setting, in which examples are presented one-by-one. The learner observes an input x_t, predicts an output structure y_t, and is presented with feedback $\bar{y}_t$ about its prediction, which is used to make an update to an existing parameter vector. Algorithm 1 is called "Feedback-based Latent Perceptron" to stress the fact that it only uses weak feedback to its predictions for learning, but does not necessarily observe optimal structures as in the full information case (Sun et al., 2013). Learning from full information can be recovered by setting the informativeness parameter α to 1 in Equation (2) below, in which case the feedback structure $\bar{y}_t$ equals the optimal structure y_t^*. Algorithm 1 differs from the algorithm of Shivaswamy and Joachims (2012) by a joint maximization over output structures y and hidden derivations h in prediction (line 4), by choosing a hidden derivation $\bar{h}$ for the feedback structure $\bar{y}$ (line 7), and by the use of the re-scaling factor $\Delta_{\bar{h}_t,h_t}$ in the update (line 8), where $\bar{h}_t = h(x_t|\bar{y}_t; w_t)$ and $h_t = h(x_t; w_t)$ are the derivations of the feedback structure and the prediction at time t, respectively. In our theoretical exposition, we assume that $\bar{y}_t$ is reachable in the search space of possible outputs, that is, $\bar{y}_t \in \mathcal{Y}(x_t)$.

3.3 Feedback of Graded Utility

The key in the theoretical analysis in Shivaswamy and Joachims (2012) is the notion of a linear utility function, determined by parameter vector w_*, that is unknown to the learner:

$$U_h(x, y) = w_*{}^\top \phi(x, y, h).$$

Upon a system prediction, the user approximately maximizes utility, and returns an improved object $\bar{y}_t$ that has higher utility than the predicted y_t s.t.

$$U(x_t, \bar{y}_t) > U(x_t, y_t)$$

where for given $x \in \mathcal{X}$, $y \in \mathcal{Y}(x)$, and $h^* = \arg\max_{h \in \mathcal{H}(x,y)} U_h(x, y)$, we define $U(x, y) = U_{h^*}(x, y)$ and drop the subscript unless $h \neq h^*$. Importantly, the feedback is typically not the optimal structure y_t^* that is defined as

$$y_t^* = \arg\max_{y \in \mathcal{Y}(x_t)} U(x_t, y).$$

While not receiving optimal structures in training, the learning goal is to predict objects with utility close to optimal structures y_t^*. The regret that is suffered by the algorithm when predicting object y_t instead of the optimal object y_t^* is

$$\text{REG}_T = \frac{1}{T} \sum_{t=1}^{T} \big(U(x_t, y_t^*) - U(x_t, y_t)\big). \quad (1)$$

To quantify the amount of information in the weak feedback, Shivaswamy and Joachims (2012) define a notion of *α-informative* feedback, which we generalize as follows for the case of latent derivations. We assume that there exists a derivation $\bar{h}_t$ for the feedback structure $\bar{y}_t$, such that for all predictions y_t, the (re-scaled) utility of the weak feedback $\bar{y}_t$ is higher than the (re-scaled) utility of the prediction y_t by a fraction α of the maximum possible utility range (under the given utility model). Thus $\forall t, \exists \bar{h}_t, \forall h$ and for $\alpha \in (0, 1]$:

$$\begin{aligned} &\big(U_{\bar{h}_t}(x_t, \bar{y}_t) - U_h(x_t, y_t)\big) \times \Delta_{\bar{h}_t,h} \\ &\quad \geq \alpha\big(U(x_t, y_t^*) - U(x_t, y_t)\big) - \xi_t, \quad (2) \end{aligned}$$

where $\xi_t \geq 0$ are slack variables allowing for violations of (2) for given α. For slack $\xi_t = 0$, user feedback is called *strictly α-informative*.

3.4 Convergence Analysis

A central theoretical result in learning from weak feedback is an analysis that shows that Algorithm 1 minimizes an upper bound on the average regret (1), despite the fact that optimal structures are not used in learning:

Theorem 1. *Let $D_T = \sum_{t=1}^{T} \Delta^2_{\bar{h}_t,h_t}$. Then the average regret of the feedback-based latent perceptron can be upper bounded for any $\alpha \in (0, 1]$, for any $w_* \in \mathbb{R}^d$:*

$$\text{REG}_T \leq \frac{1}{\alpha T} \sum_{t=1}^{T} \xi_t + \frac{2R\|w_*\|}{\alpha} \frac{\sqrt{D_T}}{T}.$$

A proof for Theorem 1 is similar to the proof of Shivaswamy and Joachims (2012) and the original mistake bound for the perceptron of Novikoff (1962).[1] The theorem can be interpreted as follows: we expect lower average regret for higher values of α; due to the dominant term T, regret will approach the minimum of the accumulated slack (in case feedback structures violate Equation (2)) or 0 (in case of strictly α-informative feedback). The main difference between the above result and the result of Shivaswamy and Joachims (2012) is the term D_T following from the re-scaled distance of latent derivations. Their analysis is agnostic of latent derivations, and can be recovered by setting this scaling factor to 1. This yields $D_T = T$, and thus recovers the main factor $\frac{\sqrt{D_T}}{T} = \frac{1}{\sqrt{T}}$ in their regret bound. In our algorithm, penalizing large distances of derivations can help to move derivations h_t closer to $\bar{h}_t$, therefore decreasing D_T as learning proceeds. Thus in case $D_T < T$, our bound is better than the original bound of Shivaswamy and Joachims (2012) for a perceptron without re-scaling. As we will show experimentally, re-scaling leads to a faster convergence in practice.

3.5 Generalization Analysis

Regret bounds measure how good the average prediction of the current model is on the next example in the given sequence, thus it seems plausible that a low regret on a sequence of examples should imply good generalization performance on the entire domain of examples.

[1] Short proofs are provided in the appendix.

Generalization for Online Learning. First we present a generalization bound for the case of online learning on a sequence of random examples, based on generalization bounds for expected average regret as given by Cesa-Bianchi et al. (2004). Let probabilities $\mathbb{P}$ and expectations $\mathbb{E}$ be defined with respect to the fixed unknown underlying distribution according to which all examples are drawn. Furthermore, we bound our loss function $\ell_t = U(x_t, y_t^*) - U(x_t, y_t)$ to $[0, 1]$ by adding a normalization factor $2R||w_*||$ s.t. $\text{REG}_T = \frac{1}{T}\sum_{t=1}^{T} \ell_t$. Plugging the bound on REG_T of Theorem 1 directly into Proposition 1 of Cesa-Bianchi et al. (2004) gives the following theorem:

Theorem 2. *Let $0 < \delta < 1$, and let $x_1, \ldots, x_T$ be a sequence of examples that Algorithm 1 observes. Then with probability at least $1 - \delta$,*

$$\mathbb{E}[\text{REG}_T] \leq \frac{1}{\alpha T}\sum_{t=1}^{T} \xi_t + \frac{2R\|w_*\|}{\alpha}\frac{\sqrt{D_T}}{T} + 2||w_*||R\sqrt{\frac{2}{T}\ln\frac{1}{\delta}}.$$

The generalization bound tells us how far the expected average regret $\mathbb{E}[\text{REG}_T]$ (or average risk, in terms of Cesa-Bianchi et al. (2004)) is from the average regret that we actually observe in a specific instantiation of the algorithm.

Generalization for Online-to-Batch Conversion. In practice, perceptron-type algorithms are often applied in a batch learning scenario, i.e., the algorithm is applied for K epochs to a training sample of size T and then used for prediction on an unseen test set (Freund and Schapire, 1999; Collins, 2002). The difference to the online learning scenario is that we treat the multi-epoch algorithm as an empirical risk minimizer that selects a final weight vector $w_{T,K}$ whose expected loss on unseen data we would like to bound. We assume that the algorithm is fed with a sequence of examples $x_1, \ldots, x_T$, and at each epoch $k = 1, \ldots, K$ it makes a prediction $y_{t,k}$. The correct label is y_t^*. For $k = 1, \ldots, K$ and $t = 1, \ldots, T$, let $\ell_{t,k} = U(x_t, y_t^*) - U(x_t, y_{t,k})$, and denote by $\Delta_{t,k}$ and $\xi_{t,k}$ the distance at epoch k for example t, and the slack at epoch k for example t, respectively. Finally, we denote by $D_{T,K} = \sum_{t=1}^{T} \Delta_{t,K}^2$, and by $w_{T,K}$ the final weight vector returned after K epochs. We state a condition of convergence[2]:

[2]This condition is too strong for large datasets. However, we believe that a weaker condition based on ideas from the perceptron cycling theorem (Block and Levin, 1970; Gelfand et al., 2010) should suffice to show a similar bound.

Condition 1. *Algorithm 1 has converged on training instances $x_1, \ldots, x_T$ after K epochs if the predictions on $x_1, \ldots, x_T$ using the final weight vector $w_{T,K}$ are the same as the predictions on $x_1, \ldots, x_T$ in the Kth epoch.*

Denote by $\mathbb{E}_X(\ell(x))$ the expected loss on unseen data when using $w_{T,K}$ where $\ell(x) = U(x, y^*) - U(x, y')$, $y^* = \arg\max_y U(x, y)$ and $y' = \arg\max_y \max_h w_{T,K}^\top \phi(x, y, h)$. We can now state the following result:

Theorem 3. *Let $0 < \delta < 1$, and let $x_1, \ldots, x_T$ be a sample for the multiple-epoch perceptron algorithm such that the algorithm converged on it (Condition 1). Then, with probability at least $1-\delta$, the expected loss of the feedback-based latent perceptron satisfies:*

$$\mathbb{E}_X(\ell(x)) \leq \frac{1}{\alpha T}\sum_{t=1}^{T} \xi_{t,K} + \frac{2R\|w_*\|}{\alpha}\frac{\sqrt{D_{T,K}}}{T} + R\|w_*\|\sqrt{\frac{8\ln\frac{2}{\delta}}{T}}.$$

The theorem can be interpreted as a bound on the generalization error (lefthand-side) by the empirical error (the first two righthand-side terms) and the variance caused by the finite sample (the third term in the theorem). The result follows directly from McDiarmid's concentration inequality.

4 Experiments

We used the LIG corpus[3] which consists of 10,881 tuples of French-English post-edits (Potet et al., 2012). The corpus is a subset of the news-commentary dataset provided at WMT[4] and contains input French sentences, MT outputs, post-edited outputs and English references. To prepare SMT outputs for post-editing, the creators of the corpus used their own WMT10 system (Potet et al., 2010), based on the Moses phrase-based decoder (Koehn et al., 2007) with dense features. We replicated a similar Moses system using the same monolingual and parallel data: a 5-gram language model was estimated with the KenLM toolkit (Heafield, 2011) on `news.en` data (48.65M sentences, 1.13B tokens), pre-processed with the tools from the `cdec` toolkit (Dyer et al., 2010).

[3]http://www-clips.imag.fr/geod/User/marion.potet/index.php?page=download

[4]http://statmt.org/wmt10/translation-task.html

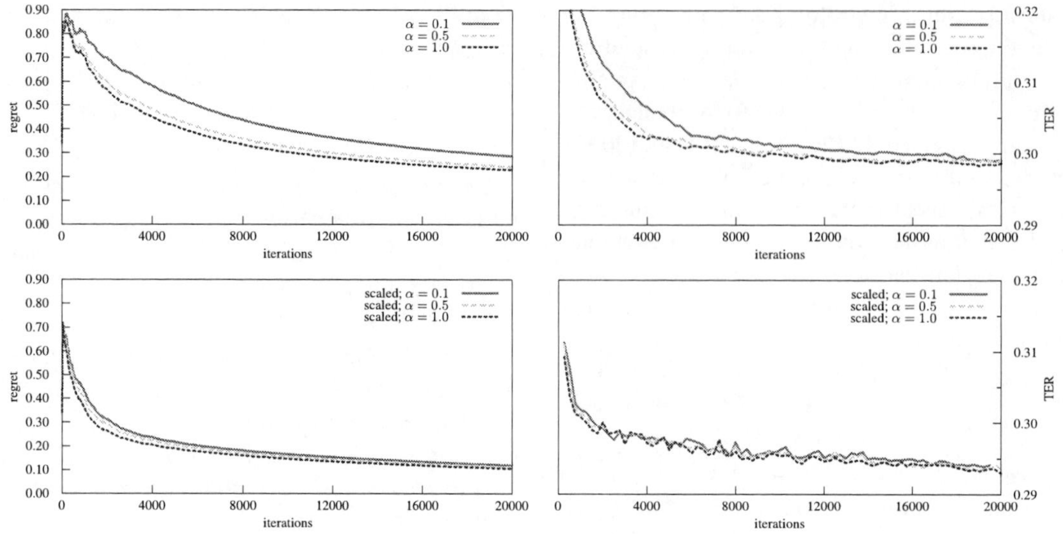

Figure 1: Regret and TER vs. iterations for α-informative feedback ranging from weak ($\alpha = 0.1$) to strong ($\alpha = 1.0$) informativeness, with (lower part) and without re-scaling (upper part).

Parallel data (`europarl+news-comm`, 1.64M sentences) were similarly pre-processed and aligned with `fast_align` (Dyer et al., 2013). In all experiments, training is started with the Moses default weights. The size of the n-best list, where used, was set to 1,000. Irrespective of the use of re-scaling in perceptron training, a constant learning rate of 10^{-5} was used for learning from simulated feedback, and 10^{-4} for learning from surrogate translations.

Our experiments on online learning require a random sequence of examples for learning. Following the techniques described in Bertsekas (2011) to generate random sequences for incremental optimization, we compared *cyclic* order (K epochs of T examples in fixed order), *randomized* order (sampling datapoints with replacement), and random *shuffling* of datapoints after each cycle, and found nearly identical regret curves for all three scenarios. In the following, all figures are shown for sequences in the cyclic order, with re-decoding after each update. Furthermore note that in all three definitions of sequence, we never see the fixed optimal feedback y_t^* in training, but instead in general a different feedback structure $\bar{y}_t$ (and a different prediction y_t) every time we see the same input x_t.

4.1 Idealized Weak and Strong Feedback

In a first experiment, we apply Algorithm 1 to user feedback of varying utility grade. The goal of this experiment is to confirm our theoretical analysis by showing convergence in regret for learning from weak and strong feedback. We select feedback of varying grade by directly inspecting the optimal w_*, thus this feedback is idealized. However, the experiment also has a realistic background since we show that α-informative feedback corresponds to improvements under standard evaluation metrics such as lowercased and tokenized TER, and that learning from weak and strong feedback leads to convergence in TER on test data.

	strict ($\xi_t = 0$)	slack ($\xi_t > 0$)
# datapoints	5,725	1,155
$\text{TER}(\bar{y}_t) < \text{TER}(y_t)$	52.17%	32.55%
$\text{TER}(\bar{y}_t) = \text{TER}(y_t)$	23.95%	20.52%
$\text{TER}(\bar{y}_t) > \text{TER}(y_t)$	23.88%	46.93%

Table 1: Improved utility vs. improved TER distance to human post-edits for α-informative feedback $\bar{y}_t$ compared to prediction y_t using default weights at $\alpha = 0.1$.

For this experiment, the post-edit data from the LIG corpus were randomly split into 3 subsets: PE-train (6,881 sentences), PE-dev, and PE-test (2,000 sentences each). PE-train was used for our online learning experiments. PE-test was held out for testing the algorithms' progress on unseen data. PE-dev was used to obtain w_* to define the utility model. This was done by MERT optimization (Och, 2003) towards post-edits under the TER target metric. Note that the goal of our experi-

	% strictly α-informative
local	39.46%
filtered	47.73%
hope	83.30%

Table 2: α-informativeness of surrogacy modes.

ments is not to improve SMT performance over any algorithm that has access to full information to compute w_*. Rather, we want to show that learning from weak feedback leads to convergence in regret with respect to the optimal model, albeit at a slower rate than learning from strong feedback. The feedback data in this experiment were generated by searching the n-best list for translations that are α-informative at $\alpha \in \{0.1, 0.5, 1.0\}$ (with possible non-zero slack). This is achieved by scanning the n-best list output for every input x_t and returning the first $\bar{y}_t \neq y_t$ that satisfies Equation (2).[5] This setting can be thought of as an idealized scenario where a user picks translations from the n-best list that are considered improvements under the optimal w_*.

In order to verify that our notion of graded utility corresponds to a realistic concept of graded translation quality, we compared improvements in utility to improved TER distance to human post-edits. Table 1 shows that for predictions under default weights, we obtain strictly α-informative (for $\alpha = 0.1$) feedback for 5,725 out of 6,881 datapoints in PE-train. These feedback structures improve utility per definition, and they also yield better TER distance to post-edits in the majority of cases. A non-negative slack has to be used in 1,155 datapoins. Here the majority of feedback structures do not improve TER distance.

Convergence results for different learning scenarios are shown in Figure 1. The left upper part of Figure 1 shows average utility regret against iterations for a setup without re-scaling, i.e., setting $\Delta_{\bar{h},h} = 1$ in the definition of α-informative feedback (Equation (2)) and in the update of Algorithm 1 (line 8). As predicted by our regret analysis, higher α leads to faster convergence, but all three curves converge towards a minimal regret. Also, the difference between the curves for

[5]Note that feedback provided in this way might be stronger than required at a particular value of α since for all $\beta \geq \alpha$, strictly β-informative feedback is also strictly α-informative. On the other hand, because of the limited size of the n-best list, we cannot assume strictly α-informative user feedback with zero slack ξ_t. In experiments where updates are only done if feedback is strictly α-informative we found similar convergence behavior.

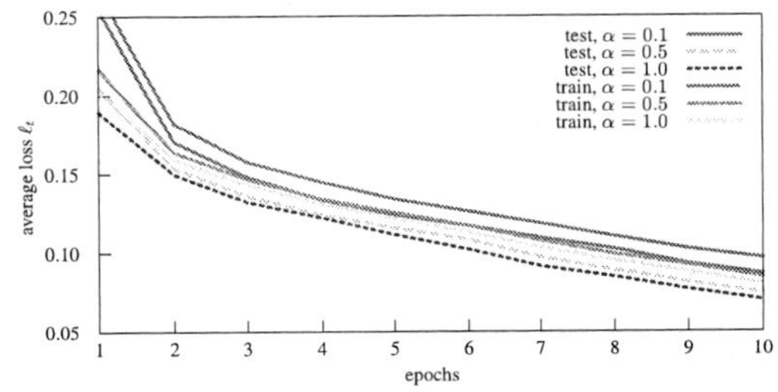

Figure 3: Average loss ℓ_t on heldout and train data.

$\alpha = 0.1$ and $\alpha = 1.0$ is much smaller than a factor of ten. As expected from the correspondence of α-informative feedback to improvements in TER, similar relations are obtained when plotting TER scores on test data for training from weak feedback at different utility grades. This is shown in the right upper part of Figure 1.

The left lower part of Figure 1 shows average utility regret plotted against iterations for a setup that uses re-scaling. We define $\Delta_{\bar{h}_t,h}$ by the ℓ_2-distance between the feature vectors $\phi(x_t, \bar{y}_t, \bar{h}_t)$ of the derivation of the feedback structure and the feature vector $\phi(x_t, y_t, h_t)$ of the derivation of the predicted structure. We see that the curves for all grades of feedback converge faster than the corresponding curves for un-scaled feedback shown in the upper part Figure 1. Furthermore, as shown in the right lower part of Figure 1, TER is decreased on test data as well at a faster rate.[6]

Lastly, we present an experimental validation of the online-to-batch application of our algorithm. That is, we would like to evaluate predictions that use the final weight vector $w_{T,K}$ by comparing the generalization error with the empirical error stated in Theorem 3. The standard way to do this is to compare the average loss on heldout data with the the average loss on the training sequence. Figure 3 shows these results for models trained on α-informative feedback of $\alpha \in \{0.1, 0.5, 1.0\}$ for 10 epochs. Similar to the online learning setup, higher α results in faster convergence. Furthermore, curves for training and heldout evaluation converge at the same rate.

4.2 Feedback from Surrogate Translations

In this section, we present experiments on learning from real human post-edits. The goal of this experiment is to investigate whether the stan-

[6]We also conducted online-to-batch experiments for simulated feedback at $\alpha \in \{0.1, 0.5, 1.0\}$. Similar to the online learning setup, higher α results in faster convergence.

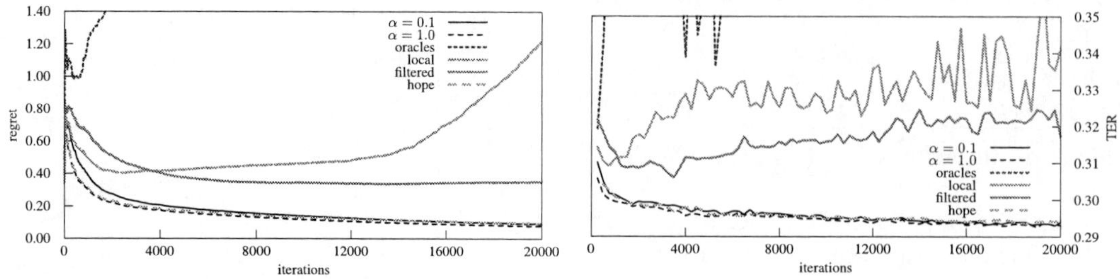

Figure 2: Regret and TER for online learning from `oracles`, `local`, `filtered`, and `hope` surrogates.

dard practices for extracting feedback from observed user post-edits for discriminative SMT can be matched with the modeling assumptions of the coactive learning framework. The customary practice in discriminative learning for SMT is to replace observed user translations by surrogate translations since the former are often not reachable in the search space of the SMT decoder. In our case, only 29% of the post-edits in the LIG-corpus were reachable by the decoder. We compare four heuristics of generating surrogate translations: `oracles` are generated using the lattice oracle approach of Sokolov et al. (2013) which returns the closest path in the decoder search graph as reachable surrogate translation.[7] A `local` surrogate $\tilde{y}$ is chosen from the n-best list of the linear model as the translation that achieves the best TER score with respect to the actual post-edit y: $\tilde{y} = \arg\min_{y' \in n\text{-best}(x_t;w_t)} \text{TER}(y', y)$. This corresponds to the local update mode of Liang et al. (2006). A `filtered` surrogate translation $\tilde{y}$ is found by scanning down the n-best list, and accepting the first translation as feedback that improves TER score with respect to the human post-edit y over the 1-best prediction y_t of the linear model: $\text{TER}(\tilde{y}, y) < \text{TER}(y_t, y)$. Finally, a `hope` surrogate is chosen from the n-best list as the translation that jointly maximizes model score under the linear model and negative TER score with respect to the human post-edit: $\tilde{y} = \arg\max_{y' \in n\text{-best}(x_t;w_t)}(-\text{TER}(y', y) + w_t^\top \phi(x_t, y', h))$. This corresponds to what Chiang (2012) termed "hope derivations". Informally, `oracles` are model-agnostic, as they can pick a surrogate even from outside of the n-best list; `local` is constrained to the n-best list, though still ignoring the ordering according to the linear model; finally, `filtered` and `hope` represent different ways of letting the model score influence the selected surrogate.

As shown in Figure 2, regret and TER decrease with the increased amount of information about the assumed linear model that is induced by the surrogate translations: Learning from `oracle` surrogates does not converge in regret and TER. The `local` surrogates extracted from 1,000-best lists still do not make effective use of the linear model, while `filtered` surrogates enforce an improvement over the prediction under TER towards the human post-edit, and improve convergence in learning. Empirically, convergence is achieved only for `hope` surrogates that jointly maximize negative TER and linear model score, with a convergence behavior that is very similar to learning from weak α-informative feedback at $\alpha \simeq 0.1$. We quantify this in Table 2 where we see that the improvement in TER over the prediction that holds for any `hope` derivation, corresponds to an improvement in α-informativeness: `hope` surrogates are strictly α-informative in 83.3% of the cases in our experiment, whereas we find a correspondence to strict α-informativeness only in 45.74% or 39.46% of the cases for `filtered` and `local` surrogates, respectively.

5 Discussion

We presented a theoretical analysis of online learning for SMT from a coactive learning perspective. This viewpoint allowed us to give regret and generalization bounds for perceptron-style online learners that fall outside the convex optimization scenario because of latent variables and changing feedback structures. We introduced the concept of weak feedback into online learning for SMT, and provided proof-of-concept experiments whose goal was to show that learning from weak feedback converges to minimal regret, albeit at a

[7] While the original algorithm is designed to maximize the BLEU score of the returned path, we tuned its two free parameters to maximize TER.

slower rate than learning from strong feedback. Furthermore, we showed that the SMT standard of learning from surrogate `hope` derivations can to be interpreted as a search for weak improvements under the assumed linear model. This justifies the importance of admitting an underlying linear model in computing surrogate derivations from a coactive learning perspective.

Finally, we hope that our analysis motivates further work in which the idea of learning from weak feedback is taken a step further. For example, our results could perhaps be strengthened by applying richer feature sets or dynamic phrase table extension in experiments on interactive SMT. Our theory would support a new post-editing scenario where users pick translations from the n-best list that they consider improvements over the prediction. Furthermore, it would be interesting to see if "light" post-edits that are better reachable and easier elicitable than "full" post-edits provide a strong enough signal for learning.

Acknowledgments

This research was supported in part by DFG grant RI-2221/2-1 "Grounding Statistical Machine Translation in Perception and Action."

Appendix: Proofs of Theorems

Proof of Theorem 1

Proof. First we bound $w_{T+1}^\top w_{T+1}$ from above:

$$\begin{aligned} w_{T+1}^\top w_{T+1} &= w_T^\top w_T \\ &+ 2w_T^\top(\phi(x_T,\bar{y}_T,\bar{h}_T) - \phi(x_T,y_T,h_T))\Delta_{\bar{h}_T,h_T} \\ &+ (\phi(x_T,\bar{y}_T,\bar{h}_T) - \phi(x_T,y_T,h_T))^\top\Delta_{\bar{h}_T,h_T} \\ &\quad(\phi(x_T,\bar{y}_T,\bar{h}_T) - \phi(x_T,y_T,h_T))\Delta_{\bar{h}_T,h_T} \\ &\leq w_T^\top w_T + 4R^2\Delta^2_{\bar{h}_T,h_T} \leq 4R^2 D_T. \end{aligned} \quad (3)$$

The first equality uses the update rule from Algorithm 1. The second uses the fact that $w_T^\top(\phi(x_T,\bar{y}_T,\bar{h}_T) - \phi(x_T,y_T,h_T)) \leq 0$ by definition of (y_T,h_T) in Algorithm 1. By assumption $\|\phi(x,y,h)\| \leq R, \forall x,y,h$ and by the triangle inequality, $\|\phi(x,y,h) - \phi(x,y',h')\| \leq \|\phi(x,y,h)\| + \|\phi(x,y',h')\| \leq 2R$. Finally, $D_T = \sum_{t=1}^T \Delta^2_{\bar{h}_t,h_t}$ by definition, and the last inequality follows by induction.

The connection to average regret is as follows:

$$\begin{aligned} w_{T+1}^\top w_* &= w_T^\top w_* \\ &+ \Delta_{\bar{h}_T,h_T}(\phi(x_T,\bar{y}_T,\bar{h}_T)) - \phi(x_T,y_T,h_T))^\top w_* \\ &= \sum_{t=1}^T \Delta_{\bar{h}_t,h_t}(\phi(x_t,\bar{y}_t,\bar{h}_t) - \phi(x_t,y_t,h_t))^\top w_* \\ &= \sum_{t=1}^T \Delta_{\bar{h}_t,h_t}(U_{\bar{h}_t}(x_t,\bar{y}_t) - U_{h_t}(x_t,y_t)). \end{aligned} \quad (4)$$

The first equality again uses the update rule from Algorithm 1. The second follows by induction. The last equality applies the definition of utility.

Next we upper bound the utility difference:

$$\begin{aligned} &\sum_{t=1}^T \Delta_{\bar{h}_t,h_t}(U_{\bar{h}_t}(x_t,\bar{y}_t) - U_{h_t}(x_t,y_t)) \\ &\quad\leq \|w_*\|\|w_{T+1}\| \leq \|w_*\|2R\sqrt{D_T}. \end{aligned} \quad (5)$$

The first inequality follows from applying the Cauchy-Schwartz inequality $w_{T+1}^\top w_* \leq \|w_*\|\|w_{T+1}\|$ to Equation (4). The seond follows from applying Equation (3) to $\|w_{T+1}\| = \sqrt{w_{T+1}^\top w_{T+1}}$.

The final result is obtained simply by lower bounding Equation (5) using the assumption in Equation (2).

$$\begin{aligned} &\|w_*\|2R\sqrt{D_T} \\ &\geq \sum_{t=1}^T \Delta_{\bar{h}_t,h_t}(U_{\bar{h}_t}(x_t,\bar{y}_t) - U_{h_t}(x_t,y_t)) \\ &\geq \alpha\sum_{t=1}^T (U(x_t,y_t^*) - U(x_t,y_t)) - \sum_{t=1}^T \xi_t \\ &= \alpha\, T\, \text{REG}_T - \sum_{t=1}^T \xi_t. \end{aligned} \quad \square$$

Proof of Theorem 3

Proof. The theorem can be shown by an application of McDiarmid's concentration inequality:

Theorem 4 (McDiarmid, 1989). *Let $Z_1,\ldots,Z_m$ be a set of random variables taking value in a set $\mathcal{Z}$. Further, let $f\colon \mathcal{Z}^m \to \mathbb{R}$ be a function that satisfies for all i and $z_1,\ldots,z_m,z_i' \in \mathcal{Z}$:*

$$\begin{aligned} &|f(z_1,\ldots,z_i,\ldots,z_m) \\ &\quad - f(z_1,\ldots,z_i',\ldots,z_m)| \leq c, \end{aligned} \quad (6)$$

for some c. Then for all $\epsilon > 0$,

$$\mathbb{P}(|f - \mathbb{E}(f)| > \epsilon) \leq 2\exp(-\frac{2\epsilon^2}{mc^2}). \quad (7)$$

Let f be the average loss for predicting y_t on example x_t in epoch K: $f(x_1,\ldots,x_T) = \text{REG}_{T,K} = \frac{1}{T}\sum_{t=1}^T \ell_{t,K}$. Because of the convergence condition (Condition 1), $\ell_{t,K} = \ell(x_t)$. The expectation of f is $\mathbb{E}(f) = \frac{1}{T}\sum_{t=1}^T \mathbb{E}[\ell_{t,k}] = \frac{1}{T}\sum_{t=1}^T \mathbb{E}[\ell(x_t)] = \mathbb{E}_X(\ell(x))$.

The first and second term on the righthand-side of Theorem 3 follow from upper bounding REG_T in the Kth epochs, using Theorem 1. The third term is derived by calculating c in Equation (6) as follows:

$$\begin{aligned} &|f(x_1,\ldots,x_t,\ldots,x_T) - f(x_1,\ldots,x_t',\ldots,x_T)| \\ &= |\frac{1}{T}\sum_{t=1}^T \ell_{t,K} - \frac{1}{T}\sum_{t=1}^T \ell'_{t,K}| = |\frac{1}{T}\sum_{t=1}^T (\ell_{t,K} - \ell'_{t,K})\,| \\ &\leq \frac{1}{T}\sum_{t=1}^T (|\ell_{t,k}| + |\ell'_{t,K}|) \leq \frac{4R\|w_*\|}{T} = c. \end{aligned}$$

The first inequality uses the triangle inequality; the second uses the upper bound $|\ell_{t,k}| \leq 2R\|w_*\|$. Setting the righthand-side of Equation (7) to at least δ and solving for ϵ, using c, concludes the proof. $\square$

References

Jonathan Berant, Andrew Chou, Roy Frostig, and Percy Liang. 2013. Semantic parsing on freebase from question-answer pairs. In *EMNLP*, Seattle, WA.

Nicola Bertoldi, Patrick Simianer, Mauro Cettolo, Katharina Wäschle, Marcello Federico, and Stefan Riezler. 2014. Online adaptation to post-edits for phrase-based statistical machine translation. *Machine Translation*, 29:309–339.

Dimitri P. Bertsekas. 2011. Incremental gradient, subgradient, and proximal methods for convex optimization: A survey. In Suvrit Sra, Sebastian Nowozin, and Stephen J. Wright, editors, *Optimization for Machine Learning*. MIT Press.

Henry D. Block and Simon A. Levin. 1970. On the boundedness of an iterative procedure for solving a system of linear inequalities. *Proceedings of the American Mathematical Society*, 26(2):229–235.

Leon Bottou and Olivier Bousquet. 2004. Large scale online learning. In *NIPS*, Vancouver, Canada.

Nicolò Cesa-Bianchi and Gàbor Lugosi. 2006. *Prediction, Learning, and Games*. Cambridge University Press.

Nicolo Cesa-Bianchi, Alex Conconi, and Claudio Gentile. 2004. On the generalization ablility of on-line learning algorithms. *IEEE Transactions on Information Theory*, 50(9):2050–2057.

Nicolò Cesa-Bianchi, Gabriele Reverberi, and Sandor Szedmak. 2008. Online learning algorithms for computer-assisted translation. Technical report, SMART (`www.smart-project.eu`).

David Chiang, Yuval Marton, and Philip Resnik. 2008. Online large-margin training of syntactic and structural translation features. In *EMNLP*, Waikiki, HA.

David Chiang, Kevin Knight, and Wei Wang. 2009. 11,001 new features for statistical machine translation. In *NAACL*, Boulder, CO.

David Chiang. 2012. Hope and fear for discriminative training of statistical translation models. *Journal of Machine Learning Research*, 12:1159–1187.

Michael Collins. 2002. Discriminative training methods for hidden markov models: theory and experiments with perceptron algorithms. In *EMNLP*, Philadelphia, PA.

Ronan Collobert, Fabian Sinz, Jason Weston, and Leon Bottou. 2006. Trading convexity for scalability. In *ICML*, Pittsburgh, PA.

Michael Denkowski, Chris Dyer, and Alon Lavie. 2014. Learning from post-editing: Online model adaptation for statistical machine translation. In *EACL*, Gothenburg, Sweden.

Chuong B. Do, Quoc Le, and Choon Hui Teo. 2008. Tighter bounds for structured estimation. In *NIPS*, Vancouver, Canada.

Chris Dyer, Adam Lopez, Juri Ganitkevitch, Jonathan Weese, Ferhan Türe, Phil Blunsom, Hendra Setiawan, Vladimir Eidelman, and Philip Resnik. 2010. cdec: A decoder, alignment, and learning framework for finite-state and context-free translation models. In *ACL*, Uppsala, Sweden.

Chris Dyer, Victor Chahuneau, and Noah A. Smith. 2013. A simple, fast, and effective reparameterization of IBM model 2. In *NAACL*, Atlanta, GA.

Vladimir Eidelmann. 2012. Optimization strategies for online large-margin learning in machine translation. In *WMT*, Montreal, Canada.

Yoav Freund and Robert E. Schapire. 1999. Large margin classification using the perceptron algorithm. *Journal of Machine Learning Research*, 37:277–296.

Andrew E. Gelfand, Yutian Chen, Max Welling, and Laurens van der Maaten. 2010. On herding and the perceptron cycling theorem. In *NIPS*, Vancouver, Canada.

Kevin Gimpel and Noah A. Smith. 2012. Structured ramp loss minimization for machine translation. In *NAACL*, Montreal, Canada.

Dan Goldwasser and Dan Roth. 2013. Learning from natural instructions. *Machine Learning*, 94(2):205–232.

Spence Green, Jeffrey Heer, and Christopher D. Manning. 2013. The efficacy of human post-editing for language translation. In *CHI*, Paris, France.

Spence Green, Sida I. Wang, Jason Chuang, Jeffrey Heer, Sebastian Schuster, and Christopher D. Manning. 2014. Human effort and machine learnability in computer aided translation. In *EMNLP*, Doha, Qatar.

Kenneth Heafield. 2011. KenLM: faster and smaller language model queries. In *WMT*, Edinburgh, UK.

Philipp Koehn, Hieu Hoang, Alexandra Birch, Chris Callison-Birch, Marcello Federico, Nicola Bertoldi, Brooke Cowan, Wade Shen, Christine Moran, Richard Zens, Chris Dyer, Ondrej Bojar, Alexandra Constantin, and Evan Herbst. 2007. Moses: Open source toolkit for statistical machine translation. In *ACL*, Prague, Czech Republic.

Tom Kwiatowski, Eunsol Choi, Yoav Artzi, and Luke Zettlemoyer. 2013. Scaling semantic parsers with on-the-fly ontology matching. In *EMNLP*, Seattle, WA.

Percy Liang, Alexandre Bouchard-Côté, Dan Klein, and Ben Taskar. 2006. An end-to-end discriminative approach to machine translation. In *COLING-ACL*, Sydney, Australia.

Francisco-Javier López-Salcedo, Germán Sanchis-Trilles, and Francisco Casacuberta. 2012. Online learning of log-linear weights in interactive machine translation. In *IberSpeech*, Madrid, Spain.

Pascual Martínez-Gómez, Germán Sanchis-Trilles, and Francisco Casacuberta. 2012. Online adaptation strategies for statistical machine translation in post-editing scenarios. *Pattern Recognition*, 45(9):3193–3202.

David McAllester and Joseph Keshet. 2011. Generalization bounds and consistency for latent structural probit and ramp loss. In *NIPS*, Granada, Spain.

Colin McDiarmid. 1989. On the method of bounded differences. *Surveys in combinatorics*, 141(1):148–188.

Albert B.J. Novikoff. 1962. On convergence proofs on perceptrons. *Symposium on the Mathematical Theory of Automata*, 12:615–622.

Franz Josef Och. 2003. Minimum error rate training in statistical machine translation. In *NAACL*, Edmonton, Canada.

Marion Potet, Laurent Besacier, and Hervé Blanchon. 2010. The LIG machine translation system for WMT 2010. In *WMT*, Upsala, Sweden.

Marion Potet, Emanuelle Esperança-Rodier, Laurent Besacier, and Hervé Blanchon. 2012. Collection of a large database of French-English SMT output corrections. In *LREC*, Istanbul, Turkey.

Avneesh Saluja and Ying Zhang. 2014. Online discriminative learning for machine translation with binary-valued feedback. *Machine Translation*, 28:69–90.

Avneesh Saluja, Ian Lane, and Ying Zhang. 2012. Machine translation with binary feedback: A large-margin approach. In *AMTA*, San Diego, CA.

Shai Shalev-Shwartz. 2012. Online learning and online convex optimization. *Foundations and Trends in Machine Learning*, 4(2):107–194.

Libin Shen, Anoop Sarkar, and Franz Josef Och. 2004. Discriminative reranking for machine translation. In *NAACL*, Boston, MA.

Pannaga Shivaswamy and Thorsten Joachims. 2012. Online structured prediction via coactive learning. In *ICML*, Edinburgh, UK.

Patrick Simianer, Stefan Riezler, and Chris Dyer. 2012. Joint feature selection in distributed stochastic learning for large-scale discriminative training in SMT. In *ACL*, Jeju, Korea.

Matthew Snover, Bonnie Dorr, Richard Schwartz, Linnea Micciulla, and John Makhoul. 2006. A study of translation edit rate with targeted human annotation. In *AMTA*, Cambridge, MA.

Artem Sokolov, Guillaume Wisniewski, and François Yvon. 2013. Lattice BLEU oracles in machine translation. *Transactions on Speech and Language Processing*, 10(4):18.

Artem Sokolov, Stefan Riezler, and Shay B. Cohen. 2015. Coactive learning for interactive machine translation. In *ICML Workshop on Machine Learning for Interactive Systems (MLIS)*, Lille, France.

Xu Sun, Takuya Matsuzaki, and Wenjie Li. 2013. Latent structured perceptrons for large scale learning with hidden information. *IEEE Transactions on Knowledge and Data Engineering*, 25(9):2064–2075.

Richard S. Sutton and Andrew G. Barto. 1998. *Reinforcement Learning. An Introduction*. The MIT Press.

Christoph Tillmann and Tong Zhang. 2006. A discriminative global training algorithm for statistical MT. In *COLING-ACL*, Sydney, Australia.

Katharina Wäschle, Patrick Simianer, Nicola Bertoldi, Stefan Riezler, and Marcello Federico. 2013. Generative and discriminative methods for online adaptation in SMT. In *MT Summit*, Nice, France.

Taro Watanabe, Jun Suzuki, Hajime Tsukada, and Hideki Isozaki. 2006. NTT statistical machine translation for IWSLT 2006. In *IWSLT*, Kyoto, Japan.

Taro Watanabe, Jun Suzuki, Hajime Tsukada, and Hideki Isozaki. 2007. Online large-margin training for statistical machine translation. In *EMNLP*, Prague, Czech Republic.

Taro Watanabe. 2012. Optimized online rank learning for machine translation. In *NAACL*, Montreal, Canada.

Heng Yu, Liang Huang, Haitao Mi, and Kai Zhao. 2013. Max-violation perceptron and forced decoding for scalable MT training. In *EMNLP*, Seattle, WA.

Alan Yuille and Anand Rangarajan. 2003. The concave-convex procedure. *Neural Computation*, 15:915–936.

A Joint Framework for Coreference Resolution and Mention Head Detection

Haoruo Peng **Kai-Wei Chang** **Dan Roth**
University of Illinois, Urbana-Champaign
Urbana, IL, 61801
{hpeng7,kchang10,danr}@illinois.edu

Abstract

In coreference resolution, a fair amount of research treats mention detection as a preprocessed step and focuses on developing algorithms for clustering coreferred mentions. However, there are significant gaps between the performance on gold mentions and the performance on the real problem, when mentions are *predicted* from raw text via an imperfect Mention Detection (MD) module. Motivated by the goal of reducing such gaps, we develop an ILP-based joint coreference resolution and mention head formulation that is shown to yield significant improvements on coreference from raw text, outperforming existing state-of-art systems on both the ACE-2004 and the CoNLL-2012 datasets. At the same time, our joint approach is shown to improve mention detection by close to 15% F1. One key insight underlying our approach is that identifying and co-referring mention *heads* is not only sufficient but is more robust than working with complete mentions.

1 Introduction

Mention detection is rarely studied as a stand-alone research problem (Recasens et al. (2013) is one key exception). Most coreference resolution work simply mentions it in passing as a module in the pipelined system (Chang et al., 2013; Durrett and Klein, 2013; Lee et al., 2011; Björkelund and Kuhn, 2014). However, the lack of emphasis is not due to this being a minor issue, but rather, we think, its difficulty. Indeed, many papers report results in terms of gold mentions versus system generated mentions, as shown in Table 1. Current state-of-the-art systems show a very significant drop in performance when running on system generated mentions. These performance gaps are worrisome, since the real goal of NLP systems is to process raw data.

System	Dataset	Gold	Predict	Gap
Illinois	CoNLL-12	77.05	60.00	17.05
Illinois	CoNLL-11	77.22	60.18	17.04
Illinois	ACE-04	79.42	68.27	11.15
Berkeley	CoNLL-11	76.68	60.42	16.26
Stanford	ACE-04	81.05	70.33	10.72

Table 1: **Performance gaps between using gold mentions and predicted mentions for three state-of-the-art coreference resolution systems.** Performance gaps are always larger than 10%. Illinois's system (Chang et al., 2013) is evaluated on CoNLL (2012, 2011) Shared Task and ACE-2004 datasets. It reports an average F1 score of MUC, B^3 and $CEAF_e$ metrics using CoNLL v7.0 scorer. Berkeley's system (Durrett and Klein, 2013) reports the same average score on the CoNLL-2011 Shared Task dataset. Results of Stanford's system (Lee et al., 2011) are for B^3 metric on ACE-2004 dataset.

This paper focuses on improving end-to-end coreference performance. We do this by: 1) Developing a new ILP-based joint learning and inference formulation for coreference and mention head detection. 2) Developing a better mention head candidate generation algorithm. Importantly, we focus on heads rather than mention boundaries since those can be identified more robustly and used effectively in an end-to-end system. As we show, this results in a dramatic improvement in the quality of the MD component and, consequently, a significant reduction in the performance gap between coreference on gold mentions and coreference on raw data.

Existing coreference systems usually consider a pipelined system, where the mention detection step is followed by that of clustering mentions into coreference chains. Higher quality mention identification naturally leads to better coreference performance. Standard methods define mentions as *boundaries* of text, and expect *exact* boundaries as input in the coreference step. However, mentions have an intrinsic structure, in which mention heads carry the crucial information. Here, we define a mention head as the last token of a syntactic head, or the whole syntactic head for proper names.[1] For example, in "the

[1] Here, we follow the ACE annotation guideline. Note that

Proceedings of the 19th Conference on Computational Language Learning, pages 12–21,
Beijing, China, July 30-31, 2015.

incumbent [Barack Obama]" and "[officials] at the Pentagon", "Barack Obama" and "officials" serve as mention heads, respectively. Mention heads can be used as auxiliary structures for coreference. In this paper, we first identify mention heads, and then detect mention boundaries based on heads. We rely heavily on the first, head identification, step, which we show to be sufficient to support coreference decisions. Moreover, this step also provides enough information for "understanding" the coreference output, and can be evaluated more robustly (since minor disagreements on mention boundaries are often a reason for evaluation issues when dealing with predicted mentions). We only identify the mention boundaries at the end, after we make the coreference decisions, to be consistent with current evaluation standards in the corefernce resolution community. Consider the following example[2]:

> [Multinational companies investing in [China]] had become so angry that [they] recently set up an anti-piracy *league* to pressure [the [Chinese] government] to take action. [Domestic manufacturers, [who] are also suffering], launched a similar body this month. [They] hope [the government] can introduce a new law increasing fines against [producers of fake goods] from the amount of profit made to the value of the goods produced.

Here, phrases in the brackets are mentions and the underlined simple phrases are mention heads. Moreover, mention boundaries can be nested (the boundary of a mention is inside the boundary of another mention), but mention heads never overlap. This property also simplifies the problem of mention head candidate generation. In the example above, the first "they" refers to "Multinational companies investing in China" and the second "They" refers to "Domestic manufacturers, who are also suffering". In both cases, the mention heads are sufficient to support the decisions: "they" refers to "companies", and "They" refers to "manufacturers". In fact, most of the features[3] implemented in existing coreference resolution systems rely solely on mention heads (Bengtson and Roth, 2008).

Furthermore, consider the possible mention candidate "league" (italic in the text). It is not chosen as a mention because the surrounding context is not focused on "anti-piracy league". So, mention

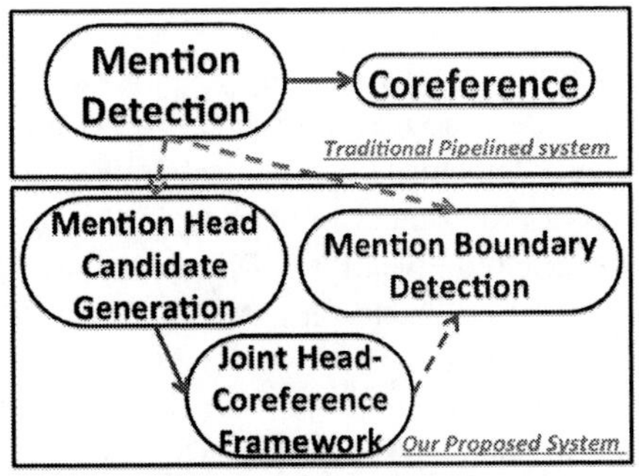

Figure 1: **Comparison between a traditional pipelined system and our proposed system.** We split up mention detection into two steps: mention head candidate generation and (an optional) mention boundary detection. We feed mention heads rather than complete mentions into the coreference model. During the joint head-coreference process, we reject some mention head candidates and then recover complete mention boundaries after coreference decisions are made.

detection can be viewed as a global decision problem, which involves considering the relevance of a mention to its context. The fact that the coreference decision provides a way to represent this relevance, further motivates considering mention detection and coreference jointly. The insight here is that a mention candidate will be more likely to be valid when it has more high confidence coreference links.

This paper develops a joint coreference resolution and mention head detection framework as an Integer Linear Program (ILP) following Roth and Yih (2004). Figure 1 compares a traditional pipelined system with our proposed system. Our joint formulation includes decision variables both for coreference links between pairs of mention heads, and for all mention head candidates, and we simultaneously learn the ILP coefficients for all these variables. During joint inference, some of the mention head candidates will be rejected (that is, the corresponding variables will be assigned '0'), contributing to improvement both in MD and in coreference performance. The aforementioned joint approach builds on an algorithm that generates mention head candidates. Our candidate generation process consists of a statistical component and a component that makes use of existing resources, and is designed to ensure high recall on head candidates.

Ideally, after making coreference decisions, we extend the remaining mention heads to complete mentions; we employ a binary classifier, which shares all features with the mention head detection model in the joint step.

Our proposed system can work on both ACE and OntoNotes datasets, even though their styles of annotation are different. There are two main differ-

the CoNLL-2012 dataset is built from OntoNotes-5.0 corpus.

[2]This example is chosen from the ACE-2004 corpus.

[3]All features except for those that rely on modifiers.

ences to be addressed. First, OntoNotes removes singleton mentions, even if they are valid mentions. This causes additional difficulty in learning a good mention detector in a pipelined framework. However, our joint framework can adapt to it by rejecting those singleton mentions. More details will be discussed in Sec. 2. Second, ACE uses shortest denotative phrases to identify mentions while OntoNotes tends to use long text spans. This makes identifying mention boundaries unnecessarily hard. Our system focuses on mention heads in the coreference stage to ensure robustness. As OntoNotes does not contain head annotations, we preprocess the data to extract mention heads which conform with the ACE style.

Results on ACE-2004 and CoNLL-2012 datasets show that our system[4] reduces the performance gap for coreference by around 25% (measured as the ratio of performance improvement over performance gap) and improves the overall mention detection by over 10 F1 points. With such significant improvements, we achieve the best end-to-end coreference resolution results reported so far.

The main contributions of our work can be summarized as follows:

1. We develop a new, end-to-end, coreference approach that is based on a joint learning and inference model for mention heads and coreference decisions.
2. We develop an improved mention head candidate generation module and a mention boundary detection module.
3. We achieve the best coreference results on predicted mentions and reduce the performance gap compared to using gold mentions.

The rest of the paper is organized as follows. We explain the joint head-coreference learning and inference framework in Sec. 2. Our mention head candidate generation module and mention boundary detection module are described in Sec. 3. We report our experimental results in Sec. 4, review related work in Sec. 5 and conclude in Sec. 6.

2 A Joint Head-Coreference Framework

This section describes our joint coreference resolution and mention head detection framework. Our work is inspired by the latent left-linking model in Chang et al. (2013) and the ILP formulation from Chang et al. (2011). The joint learning and inference model takes as input mention head candidates (Sec. 3) and jointly (1) determines if they are indeed mention heads and (2) learns a similarity metric between mentions. This is done by simultaneously learning a binary mention head detection classifier and a mention-pair coreference classifier. The mention head detection model here is mainly trained to differentiate valid mention heads from invalid ones. By learning and making decisions jointly, it also serves as a singleton mention head classifier, building on insights from Recasens et al. (2013). This joint framework aims to improve performance on both mention head detection and on coreference.

We first describe the formualtion of the mention head detection and the ILP-based mention-pair coreference separately, and then propose the joint head-coreference framework.

2.1 Mention Head Detection

The mention head detection model is a binary classifier $g_m = w_1^\top \varphi(m)$, in which $\varphi(m)$ is a feature vector for mention head candidate m and w_1 is the corresponding weight vector. We identify a candidate m as a mention head if $g_m > 0$. The features utilized in the vector $\varphi(m)$ consist of: 1) Gazetteer features 2) Part-Of-Speech features 3) Wordnet features 4) Features from the previous and next tokens 5) Length of mention head. 6) Normalized Pointwise Mutual Information (NPMI) on the tokens across a mention head boundary 7) Feature conjunctions. Altogether there are hundreds of thousands of sparse features.

2.2 ILP-based Mention-Pair Coreference

Let M be the set of all mentions. We train a coreference model by learning a pairwise mention scoring function. Specifically, given a mention-pair (u,v) ($u,v \in M$, u is the antecedent of v), we learn a left-linking scoring function $f_{u,v} = w_2^\top \phi(u,v)$, where $\phi(u,v)$ is a pairwise feature vector and w_2 is the weight vector. The inference algorithm is inspired by the best-left-link approach (Chang et al., 2011), where they solve the following ILP problem:

$$\begin{aligned} &\arg\max_{y} \sum_{u<v,u,v\in M} f_{u,v} y_{u,v}, \\ &\text{s.t.} \sum_{u<v} y_{u,v} \leq 1, \quad \forall v \in M, \qquad (1) \\ &y_{u,v} \in \{0,1\} \quad \forall u,v \in M. \end{aligned}$$

Here, $y_{u,v} = 1$ iff mentions u,v are directly linked. Thus, we can construct a forest and the mentions in the same connected component (i.e., in the same tree) are co-referred. For this mention-pair coreference model $\phi(u,v)$, we use the same set of features used in Bengtson and Roth (2008).

[4] Available at http://cogcomp.cs.illinois.edu/page/software_view/Coref

2.3 Joint Inference Framework

We extend expression (1) to facilitate joint inference on mention heads and coreference as follows:

$$\begin{aligned}&\arg\max_{y} \sum_{u<v,u,v\in M} f_{u,v}y_{u,v} + \sum_{m\in M} g_m y_m,\\ &\text{s.t. } \sum_{u<v} y_{u,v} \le 1, \quad \forall v \in M',\\ &\sum_{u<v} y_{u,v} \le y_v, \quad \forall v \in M',\\ &y_{u,v} \in \{0,1\}, \quad y_m \in \{0,1\} \quad \forall u,v,m \in M'.\end{aligned}$$

Here, M' is the set of all mention head candidates. y_m is the decision variable for mention head candidate m. $y_m = 1$ if and only if the mention head m is chosen. To consider coreference decisions and mention head decisions together, we add the constraint $\sum_{u<v} y_{u,v} \le y_v$, which ensures that if a candidate mention head v is not chosen, then it will not have coreference links with other mention heads.

2.4 Joint Learning Framework

To support joint learning of the parameters w_1 and w_2 described above, we define a joint training objective function $C(w_1,w_2)$ for mention head detection and coreference, which uses a max-margin approach to learn both weight vectors. Suppose we have a collection of documents D, and we generate n_d mention head candidates for each document d ($d \in D$). We use an indicator function $\delta(u,m)$ to represent whether mention heads u,m are in the same coreference cluster based on gold annotations ($\delta(u,m)=1$ iff they are in the same cluster). Similarly, $\Omega(m)$ is an indicator funtion representing whether mention head m is valid in the gold annotations.

For simplicity, we first define

$$\begin{aligned}u' &= \arg\max_{u<m}(w_2^\top \phi(u,m) - \delta(u,m)),\\ u'' &= \arg\max_{u<m,\delta(u,m)=1} w_2^\top \phi(u,m)\Omega(m).\end{aligned}$$

We then minimize the following joint training objective function $C(w_1,w_2)$.

$$\begin{aligned}C(w_1,w_2) = \frac{1}{|D|}\sum_{d\in D}\frac{1}{n_d}\sum_{m}(&C_{coref,m}(w_2)\\ &+C_{local,m}(w_1)+C_{trans,m}(w_1)) + R(w_1,w_2).\end{aligned}$$

$C(w_1,w_2)$ is composed of four parts. The first part is the loss function for coreference, where we have

$$\begin{aligned}C_{coref,m}(w_2) &= -w_2^\top \phi(u'',m)\Omega(m)\\ &+(w_2^\top \phi(u',m) - \delta(u',m))(\Omega(m) \vee \Omega(u')).\end{aligned}$$

It is similar to the loss function for a latent left-linking coreference model[5]. As the second component, we have the quadratic loss for the mention head detection model,

$$C_{local,m}(w_1) = \frac{1}{2}(w_1^\top \varphi(m) - \Omega(m))^2.$$

Using the third component, we further maximize the margin between valid and invalid mention head candidates when they are selected as the best-left-link mention heads for any valid mention head. It can be represented as

$$C_{trans,m}(w_1) = \frac{1}{2}(w_1^\top \varphi(u') - \Omega(u'))^2\Omega(m).$$

The last part is the regularization term

$$R(w_1,w_2) = \frac{\lambda_1}{2}||w_1||^2 + \frac{\lambda_2}{2}||w_2||^2.$$

2.5 Stochastic Subgradient Descent for Joint Learning

For joint learning, we choose stochastic subgradient descent (SGD) approach to facilitate performing SGD on a per mention head basis. Next, we describe the weight update algorithm by defining the subgradients.

The partial subgradient w.r.t. mention head m for the head weight vector w_1 is given by

$$\begin{aligned}&\nabla_{w_1,m}C(w_1,w_2) =\\ &\frac{1}{|D|n_d}(\nabla C_{local,m}(w_1) + \nabla C_{trans,m}(w_1)) + \lambda_1 w_1, \quad (2)\end{aligned}$$

where

$$\begin{aligned}\nabla C_{local,m}(w_1) &= (w_1^\top \varphi(m) - \Omega(m))\varphi(m),\\ \nabla C_{trans,m}(w_1) &= (w_1^\top \varphi(u') - \Omega(u'))\varphi(u')\Omega(m).\end{aligned}$$

The partial subgradient w.r.t. mention head m for the coreference weight vector w_2 is given by

$$\nabla_{w_2,m}C(w_1,w_2) = \lambda_2 w_2 + \begin{cases}\phi(u',m) - \phi(u'',m) & \text{if } \Omega(m)=1,\\ \phi(u',m) & \text{if } \Omega(m)=0 \text{ and } \Omega(u')=1,\\ 0 & \text{if } \Omega(m)=0 \text{ and } \Omega(u')=0.\end{cases} \quad (3)$$

Here λ_1 and λ_2 are regularization coefficients which are tuned on the development set. To learn the mention head detection model, we consider two different parts of the gradient in expression (2). $\nabla C_{local,m}(w_1)$ is exactly the local gradient of mention head m while we add $\nabla C_{trans,m}(w_1)$ to represent

[5] More details can be found in Chang et al. (2013). The difference here is that we also consider the validity of mention heads using $\Omega(u), \Omega(m)$

the gradient for mention head u', the mention head chosen by the current best-left-linking model for m. This serves to maximize the margin between valid mention heads and invalid ones. As invalid mention heads will not be linked to any other mention head, ∇_{trans} is zero when m is invalid. When training the mention-pair coreference model, we only consider gradients when at least one of the two mention heads m, u' is valid, as shown in expression (3). When mention head m is valid ($\Omega(m) = 1$), the gradient is the same as local training for best-left-link of m (first condition in expression (3)). When m is not valid while u' is valid, we only demote the coreference link between them (second condition in expression (3)). We consider only the gradient from the regularization term when both m, u' are invalid.

As mentioned before, our framework can handle annotations with or without singletion mentions. When the gold data contains no singleton mentions, we have $\Omega(m) = 0$ for all singleton mention heads among mention head candidates. Then, our mention head detection model partly serves as a singleton head detector, and tries to reject singletons in the joint decisions with coreference. When the gold data contains singleton mentions, we have $\Omega(m) = 1$ for all valid singleton mention heads. Our mention head detection model then only learns to differentiate invalid mention heads from valid ones, and thus has the ability to preserve valid singleton heads.

Most of the head mentions proposed by the algorithms described in Sec. 3 are positive examples. We ensure a balanced training of the mention head detection model by adding sub-sampled invalid mention head candidates as negative examples. Specifically, after mention head candidate generation (described in Sec. 3), we train on a set of candidates with precision larger than 50%. We then use Illinois Chunker (Punyakanok and Roth, 2001)[6] to extract more noun phrases from the text and employ Collins head rules (Collins, 1999) to identify their heads. When these extracted heads do not overlap with gold mention heads, we treat them as negative examples.

We note that the aforementioned joint framework can take as input either complete mention candidates or mention head candidates. However, in this paper we only feed mention heads into it. Our experimental results support our intuition that this provides better results.

[6]http://cogcomp.cs.illinois.edu/page/software_view/Chunker

3 Mention Detection Modules

This section describes the module that generates our mention head candidates, and then how the mention heads are expanded to complete mentions.

3.1 Mention Head Candidate Generation

The goal of the mention head candidate generation process is to acquire candidates from multiple sources to ensure high recall, given that our joint framework acts as a filter and increases precision. We view the sources as independent components and merge all mention heads generated. A sequence labelling component and a named entity recognition component employ statistical learning methods. These are augmented by additional heads that we acquire from Wikipedia and a "known heads" resource, which we incorporate utilizing string matching algorithms.

3.1.1 Statistical Components

Sequence Labelling Component We use the following notations. Let $O =< o_1, o_2, \cdots, o_n >$ represent an input token sequence over an alphabet Ω. A mention is a substring of consecutive input tokens $m_{i,j} =< o_i, o_{i+1}, \cdots, o_j >$ for $1 \leq i \leq j \leq n$. We consider the positions of mentions in the text: two mentions with an identical sequence of tokens that differ in position are considered different mentions.

The sequence labeling component builds on the following assumption:

Assumption *Different mentions have different heads, and heads do not overlap with each other. That is, for each $m_{i,j}$, we have a corresponding head $h_{a,b}$ where $i \leq a \leq b \leq j$. Moreover, for another head $h_{a',b'}$, we have the satisfying condition $a - b' > 0$ or $b - a' < 0$ $\forall h_{a,b}, h_{a',b'}$.*

Based on this assumption, the problem of identifying mention heads is a sequential phrase identification problem, and we choose to employ the *BILOU*-representation as it has advantages over traditional *BIO*-representation, as shown, e.g. in Ratinov and Roth (2009). The *BILOU*-representation suggests learning classifiers that identify the **B**eginning, **I**nside and **L**ast tokens of multi-token chunks as well as **U**nit-length chunks. The problem is then transformed into a simple, but constrained, 5-class classification problem.

The *BILOU*-classifier shares all features with the mention head detection model described in Sec. 2.1 except for two: length of mention heads and NPMI over head boundary. For each instance, the feature vector is sparse and we use sparse perceptron (Jackson and Craven, 1996) for supervised training. We also apply a two layer prediction aggregation. First, we apply a baseline *BILOU*-classifier, and then use the resulting predictions as additional features in a second level of inference to take interactions into account in an efficient manner. A similar technique has been applied in Ratinov and Roth (2009), and has shown favorable results over other "standard" sequential prediction models.

Named Entity Recognition Component We use existing tools to extract named entities as additional mention head candidates. We choose the state-of-the-art "Illinois Named Entity Tagger" package[7]. It uses distributional word representations that improve its generalization. This package gives the standard Person/Location/Organization/Misc labels and we take all output named entities as candidates.

3.1.2 Resource-Driven Matching Components

Wikipedia Many mention heads can be directly matched to a Wikipedia title. We get 4,045,764 Wikipedia titles from Wikipedia dumps and use all of them as potential mention heads. The Wikipedia matching component includes an efficient hashing algorithm implemented via a DJB2 hash function[8]. One important advantage of using Wikipedia is that it keeps updating. This component can contribute steadily to ensure a good coverage of mention heads. We first run this matching component on training documents and compute the precision of entries that appear in the text (the probability of appearing as mention heads). We then get the set of entries with precision higher than a threshold α, which is tuned on the development set using F1-score. We use them as candidates for mention head matching.

Known Head Some mention heads appear repeatedly in the text. To fully utilize the training data, we construct a known mention head candidate set and identify them in the test documents. To balance between recall and precision, we set a parameter $\beta > 0$ as a precision threshold and only allow those mention heads with precision larger than β on the training set. Please note that threshold β is also tuned on the development set using F1-score.

We also employ a simple word variation tolerance algorithm in our matching components, to generalize over small variations (plural/singular, etc.).

[7]http://cogcomp.cs.illinois.edu/page/software_view/NETagger

[8]http://www.cse.yorku.ca/~oz/hash.html

3.2 Mention Boundary Detection

Once the joint learning and inference process determines the set of mention heads (and their coreference chains), we extend the heads to complete mentions. Note that this process may not be necessary, since in many applications, the head clusters often provide enough information. However, for consistency with existing coreference resolution systems, we describe below how we expand the heads to complete mentions.

We learn a binary classifier to expand mentions, which determines if the mention head should include the token to its left and to its right. We follow the notations in Sec. 2.1. We construct positive examples as $(o_p, h_{a,b}, dir)$, $\forall m_{i,j}(h_{a,b})$. Here $p \in \{i, i+1, \cdots, a-1\} \cup \{b+1, b+2, \cdots, j\}$ and when $p = i, i+1, \cdots, a-1$, $dir = L$; when $p = b+1, b+2, \cdots, j$, $dir = R$. We construct negative examples as $(o_{i-1}, h_{a,b}, L)$ and $(o_{j+1}, h_{a,b}, R)$. Once trained, the binary classifier takes in the head, a token and the direction of the token relative to the head, and decides whether the token is inside or outside the mention corresponding to the head. At test time, this classifier is used around each confirmed head to determine the mention boundaries. The features used here are similar to the mention head detection model described in Sec. 2.1.

4 Experiments

We present experiments on the two standard coreference resolution datasets, ACE-2004 (NIST, 2004) and OntoNotes-5.0 (Hovy et al., 2006). Our approach results in a substantial reduction in the coreference performance gap between gold and predicted mentions, and significantly outperforms existing stat-of-the-art results on coreference resolution; in addition, it achieves significant performance improvement on MD for both datasets.

4.1 Experimental Setup

Datasets The ACE-2004 dataset contains 443 documents. We use a standard split of 268 training documents, 68 development documents, and 106 testing documents (Culotta et al., 2007; Bengtson and Roth, 2008). The OntoNotes-5.0 dataset, which is released for the CoNLL-2012 Shared Task (Pradhan et al., 2012), contains 3,145 annotated documents. These documents come from a wide range of sources which include newswire, bible, transcripts, magazines, and web blogs. We report results on the test documents for both datasets.

	MUC	B^3	$CEAF_e$	AVG
$Gold_{M/H}$	78.17	81.64	78.45	79.42
$Stanford_M$	63.89	70.33	70.21	68.14
$Predicted_M$	64.28	70.37	70.16	68.27
$H\text{-}M\text{-}Coref_M$	65.81	71.97	71.14	69.64
$H\text{-}Joint\text{-}M_M$	**67.28**	**73.06**	**73.25**	**71.20**
$Stanford_H$	70.28	73.93	73.04	72.42
$Predicted_H$	71.35	75.33	74.02	73.57
$H\text{-}M\text{-}Coref_H$	71.81	75.69	74.45	73.98
$H\text{-}Joint\text{-}M_H$	**72.74**	**76.69**	**75.18**	**74.87**

Table 2: **Performance of coreference resolution for all systems on the ACE-2004 dataset.** Subscripts ($_M$, $_H$) indicate evaluations on (mentions, mention heads) respectively. For gold mentions and mention heads, they yield the same performance for coreference. Our proposed *H-Joint-M* system achieves the highest performance. Parameters of our proposed system are tuned as $\alpha = 0.9$, $\beta = 0.8$, $\lambda_1 = 0.2$ and $\lambda_2 = 0.3$.

	MUC	B^3	$CEAF_e$	AVG
$Gold_{M/H}$	82.03	70.59	66.76	73.12
$Stanford_M$	64.62	51.89	48.23	54.91
$HotCoref_M$	70.74	58.37	55.47	61.53
$Berkeley_M$	71.24	58.71	55.18	61.71
$Predicted_M$	69.63	57.46	53.16	60.08
$H\text{-}M\text{-}Coref_M$	70.95	59.11	54.98	61.68
$H\text{-}Joint\text{-}M_M$	**72.22**	**60.50**	**56.37**	**63.03**
$Stanford_H$	68.53	56.68	52.36	59.19
$HotCoref_H$	72.94	60.27	57.53	63.58
$Berkeley_H$	73.05	60.39	57.43	63.62
$Predicted_H$	72.11	60.12	55.68	62.64
$H\text{-}M\text{-}Coref_H$	73.22	61.42	56.21	63.62
$H\text{-}Joint\text{-}M_H$	**74.83**	**62.77**	**57.93**	**65.18**

Table 3: **Performance of coreference resolution for all systems on the CoNLL-2012 dataset.** Subscripts ($_M$, $_H$) indicate evaluations on (mentions, mention heads) respectively. For gold mentions and mention heads, they yield the same performance for coreference. Our proposed *H-Joint-M* system achieves the highest performance. Parameters of our proposed system are tuned as $\alpha = 0.9$, $\beta = 0.9$, $\lambda_1 = 0.25$ and $\lambda_2 = 0.2$.

The ACE-2004 dataset is annotated with both mention and mention heads, while the OntoNotes-5.0 dataset only has mention annotations. Therefore, we preprocess Ontonote-5.0 to derive mention heads using Collins head rules (Collins, 1999) with gold constituency parsing information and gold named entity information. The parsing information[9] is only needed to generate training data for the mention head candidate generator and named entities are directly set as heads. We set these extracted heads as gold, which enables us to train the two layer *BILOU*-classifier described in Sec. 3.1.1. The non-overlapping mention head assumption in Sec. 3.1.1 can be verified empirically on both ACE-2004 and OntoNotes-5.0 datasets.

Baseline Systems We choose three publicly available state-of-the-art end-to-end coreference systems as our baselines: *Stanford* system (Lee et al., 2011), *Berkeley* system (Durrett and Klein, 2014) and *HOTCoref* system (Björkelund and Kuhn, 2014).

Developed Systems Our developed system is built on the work by Chang et al. (2013), using Constrained Latent Left-Linking Model (CL^3M) as our mention-pair coreference model in the joint framework[10]. When the CL^3M coreference system uses gold mentions or heads, we call the system *Gold*; when it uses predicted mentions or heads, we call the system *Predicted*. The mention head candidate generation module along with mention boundary detection module can be grouped together to form a complete mention detection system, and we call it *H-M-MD*. We can feed the predicted mentions from *H-M-MD* directly into the mention-pair coreference model that we implemented, resulting in a traditional pipelined end-to-end coreference system, namely *H-M-Coref*. We name our new proposed end-to-end coreference resolution system incorporating both the mention head candidate generation module and the joint framework as *H-Joint-M*.

Evaluation Metrics We compare all systems using three popular metrics for coreference resolution: MUC (Vilain et al., 1995), B^3 (Bagga and Baldwin, 1998), and Entity-based CEAF ($CEAF_e$) (Luo, 2005). We use the average F1 scores (AVG) of these three metrics as the main metric for comparison. We use the v7.0 scorer provided by CoNLL-2012 Shared Task[11]. We also evaluate the mention detection performance based on precision, recall and F1 score. As mention heads are important for both mention detection and coreference resolution, we also report results evaluated on mention heads.

4.2 Performance for Coreference Resolution

Performance of coreference resolution for all systems on the ACE-2004 and CoNLL-2012 datasets is shown in Table 2 and Table 3 respectively.[12] These results show that our developed system *H-Joint-M*

[9]No parsing information is needed at evaluation time.

[10]We use Gurobi v5.0.1 as our ILP solver.

[11]The latest scorer is version v8.01, but MUC, B^3, $CEAF_e$ and CoNLL average scores are not changed. For evaluation on ACE-2004, we convert the system output and gold annotations into CoNLL format.

[12]We do not provide results from *Berkeley* and *HOTCoref* on ACE-2004 dataset as they do not directly support ACE input. Results for *HOTCoref* are slightly different from the results reported in Björkelund and Kuhn (2014). For *Berkeley* system, we use the reported results from Durrett and Klein (2014).

shows significant improvement on all metrics for both datasets. Existing systems only report results on mentions. Here, we also show their performance evaluated on mention heads. When evaluated on mention heads rather than mentions[13], we can always expect a performance increase for all systems on both datasets. Even though evaluating on mentions is more common in the literature, it is often enough to identify just mention heads in coreference chains (as shown in the example from Sec. 1). *H-M-Coref* can already bring substantial performance improvement, which indicates that it is helpful for coreference to just identify high quality mention heads. Our proposed *H-Joint-M* system outperforms all baselines and achieves the best results reported so far.

4.3 Performance for Mention Detection

The performance of mention detection for all systems on the ACE-2004 and CoNLL-2012 datasets is shown in Table 4. These results show that our developed system exhibits significant improvement on precision and recall for both datasets. *H-M-MD* mainly improves on recall, indicating, as expected, that the mention head candidate generation module ensures high recall on mention heads. *H-Joint-M* mainly improves on precision, indicating, as expected, that the joint framework correctly rejects many of the invalid mention head candidates during joint inference. Our joint model can adapt to annotations with or without singleton mentions. Based on training data, our system has the ability to preserve true singleton mentions in ACE while rejecting many singleton mentions in OntoNotes[14]. Note that we have better mention detection results on ACE-2004 dataset than on OntoNotes-5.0 dataset. We believe that this is due to the fact that extracting mention heads in the OntoNotes dataset is somewhat noisy.

4.4 Analysis of Performance Improvement

The improvement of our *H-Joint-M* system is due to two distinct but related modules: the mention head candidate generation module ("Head") and the joint learning and inference framework ("Joint").[15] We evaluate the effect of these two modules in terms of *Mention Detection Error Reduction* (MDER) and *Performance Gap Reduction* (PGR) for coreference. MDER is computed as the ratio of performance improvement for mention detection over the original mention detection error rate, while PGR is computed as the ratio of performance improvement for coreference over the performance gap for coreference. Results on the ACE-2004 and CoNLL-2012 datasets are shown in Table 5.[16]

The mention head candidate generation module has a bigger impact on MDER compared to the joint framework. However, they both have the same level of positive effects on PGR for coreference resolution. On both datasets, we achieve more than 20% performance gap reduction for coreference.

Systems	Precision	Recall	F1-score
ACE-2004			
Predicted$_M$	75.11	73.03	74.06
H-M-MD$_M$	77.45	92.97	83.90
H-Joint-M$_M$	85.34	91.73	**88.42**
Predicted$_H$	76.84	86.99	79.87
H-M-MD$_H$	80.82	93.45	86.68
H-Joint-M$_H$	88.85	92.27	**90.53**
CoNLL-2012			
Predicted$_M$	65.28	63.41	64.33
H-M-MD$_M$	70.09	76.72	73.26
H-Joint-M$_M$	78.51	75.52	**76.99**
Predicted$_H$	76.38	74.02	75.18
H-M-MD$_H$	77.73	83.99	80.74
H-Joint-M$_H$	85.07	82.31	**83.67**

Table 4: **Performance of mention detection for all systems on the ACE-2004 and CoNLL-2012 datasets.** Subscripts ($_M$, $_H$) indicate evaluations on (mentions, mention heads) respectively. Our proposed *H-Joint-M* system dramatically improves the MD performance.

5 Related Work

Coreference resolution has been extensively studied, with several state-of-the-art approaches addressing this task (Lee et al., 2011; Durrett and Klein, 2013; Björkelund and Kuhn, 2014; Song et al., 2012). Many of the early rule-based systems like Hobbs (1978) and Lappin and Leass (1994) gained considerable popularity. The early designs were easy to understand and the rules were designed manually. Machine learning approaches were introduced in many works (Connolly et al., 1997; Ng and

[13]Here, we treat mention heads as mentions. Thus, in the evaluation script, we set the boundary of a mention to be the boundary of its correponding mention head.

[14]Please note that when evaluating on OntoNotes, we eventually remove all singleton mentions from the output.

[15]"Joint" rows are computed as "H-Joint-M" rows minus "Head" rows. They reflect the contribution of the joint framework to mention detection (by rejecting some mention heads).

[16]We use bootstrapping resampling (10 times from the test data) with signed rank test. All the improvements shown are statistically significant.

ACE-2004	MDER	PGR(AVG)
Head_M	37.93	12.29
Joint_M	17.43	13.99
H-Joint-M_M	55.36	26.28
Head_H	34.00	7.01
Joint_H	19.22	15.21
H-Joint-M_H	53.22	22.22
CoNLL-2012	**MDER**	**PGR(AVG)**
Head_M	25.04	12.16
Joint_M	10.45	10.44
H-Joint-M_M	35.49	22.60
Head_H	22.40	10.58
Joint_H	11.81	13.75
H-Joint-M_H	34.21	24.33

Table 5: **Analysis of performance improvement in terms of *Mention Detection Error Reduction* (MDER) and *Performance Gap Reduction* (PGR) for coreference resolution on the ACE-2004 and CoNLL-2012 datasets.** "Head" represents the mention head candidate generation module, "Joint" represents the joint learning and inference framework, and "H-Joint-M" indicates the end-to-end system.

Cardie, 2002; Bengtson and Roth, 2008; Soon et al., 2001). The introduction of ILP methods has influenced the coreference area too (Chang et al., 2011; Denis and Baldridge, 2007). In this paper, we use the Constrained Latent Left-Linking Model (CL^3M) described in Chang et al. (2013) in our experiments.

The task of mention detection is closely related to *Named Entity Recognition* (NER). Punyakanok and Roth (2001) thoroughly study phrase identification in sentences and propose three different general approaches. They aim to learn several different local classifiers and combine them to optimally satisfy some global constraints. Cardie and Pierce (1998) propose to select certain rules based on a given corpus, to identify base noun phrases. However, the phrases detected are not necessarily mentions that we need to discover. Ratinov and Roth (2009) present detailed studies on the task of named entity recognition, which discusses and compares different methods on multiple aspects including chunk representation, inference method, utility of non-local features, and integration of external knowledge. NER can be regarded as a sequential labeling problem, which can be modeled by several proposed models, e.g. Hidden Markov Model (Rabiner, 1989) or Conditional Random Fields (Sarawagi and Cohen, 2004). The typical BIO representation was introduced in Ramshaw and Marcus (1995); OC representations were introduced in Church (1988), while Finkel and Manning (2009) further study nested named entity recognition, which employs a tree structure as a representation of identifying named entities within other named entities.

The most relevant study on mentions in the context of coreference was done in Recasens et al. (2013); this work studies distinguishing single mentions from coreferent mentions. Our joint framework provides similar insights, where the added mention decision variable partly reflects if the mention is singleton or not.

Several recent works suggest studying coreference jointly with other tasks. Lee et al. (2012) model entity coreference and event coreference jointly; Durrett and Klein (2014) consider joint coreference and entity-linking. The work closest to ours is that of Lassalle and Denis (2015), which studies a joint anaphoricity detection and coreference resolution framework. While their inference objective is similar, their work assumes gold mentions are given and thus their modeling is very different.

6 Conclusion

This paper proposes a joint inference approach to the end-to-end coreference resolution problem. By moving to identify mention heads rather than mentions, and by developing an ILP-based, joint, online learning and inference approach, we close a significant fraction of the existing gap between coreference systems' performance on gold mentions and their performance on raw data. At the same time, we show substantial improvements in mention detection. We believe that our approach will generalize well to many other NLP problems, where the performance on raw data (the result that really matters) is still significantly lower than the performance on gold data.

Acknowledgments

This work is partly supported by NSF grant #SMA 12-09359 and by DARPA under agreement number FA8750-13-2-0008. The U.S. Government is authorized to reproduce and distribute reprints for Governmental purposes notwithstanding any copyright notation thereon. The views and conclusions contained herein are those of the authors and should not be interpreted as necessarily representing the official policies or endorsements, either expressed or implied, of DARPA or the U.S. Government.

References

A. Bagga and B. Baldwin. 1998. Algorithms for scoring coreference chains. In *In The First International Conference on Language Resources and Evaluation Workshop on Linguistics Coreference*.

E. Bengtson and D. Roth. 2008. Understanding the value of features for coreference resolution. In *EMNLP*.

A. Björkelund and J Kuhn. 2014. Learning structured Perceptrons for coreference resolution with latent antecedents and non-local features. In *ACL*.

C. Cardie and D. Pierce. 1998. Error-driven pruning of Treebanks grammars for base noun phrase identification. In *Proceedings of ACL-98*.

K. Chang, R. Samdani, A. Rozovskaya, N. Rizzolo, M. Sammons, and D. Roth. 2011. Inference protocols for coreference resolution. In *CoNLL*.

K.-W. Chang, R. Samdani, and D. Roth. 2013. A constrained latent variable model for coreference resolution. In *EMNLP*.

K. Church. 1988. A stochastic parts program and noun phrase parser for unrestricted text. In *ANLP*.

M. Collins. 1999. *Head-driven Statistical Models for Natural Language Parsing*. Ph.D. thesis, Computer Science Department, University of Pennsylvenia.

D. Connolly, J. Burger, and D. Day. 1997. A machine learning approach to anaphoric reference. In *New Methods in Language Processing*.

A. Culotta, M. Wick, and A. McCallum. 2007. First-order probabilistic models for coreference resolution. In *NAACL*.

P. Denis and J. Baldridge. 2007. Joint determination of anaphoricity and coreference resolution using integer programming. In *NAACL*.

G. Durrett and D. Klein. 2013. Easy victories and uphill battles in coreference resolution. In *EMNLP*.

G. Durrett and D. Klein. 2014. A joint model for entity analysis: Coreference, typing, and linking.

J. Finkel and C. Manning. 2009. Nested named entity recognition. In *EMNLP*.

J. R. Hobbs. 1978. Resolving pronoun references. *Lingua*.

E. Hovy, M. Marcus, M. Palmer, L. Ramshaw, and R. Weischedel. 2006. Ontonotes: The 90% solution. In *Proceedings of HLT/NAACL*.

J. Jackson and M. Craven. 1996. Learning sparse perceptrons. *Proceedings of the 1996 Advances in Neural Information Processing Systems*.

S. Lappin and H. Leass. 1994. An algorithm for pronominal anaphora resolution. *Computational linguistics*.

E. Lassalle and P. Denis. 2015. Joint anaphoricity detection and coreference resolution with constrained latent structures.

H. Lee, Y. Peirsman, A. Chang, N. Chambers, M. Surdeanu, and D. Jurafsky. 2011. Stanford's multi-pass sieve coreference resolution system at the conll-2011 shared task. In *Proceedings of the CoNLL-2011 Shared Task*.

H. Lee, M. Recasens, A. Chang, M. Surdeanu, and D. Jurafsky. 2012. Joint entity and event coreference resolution across documents. In *EMNLP*.

X. Luo. 2005. On coreference resolution performance metrics. In *EMNLP*.

V. Ng and C. Cardie. 2002. Improving machine learning approaches to coreference resolution. In *ACL*.

NIST. 2004. The ACE evaluation plan.

S. Pradhan, A. Moschitti, N. Xue, O. Uryupina, and Y. Zhang. 2012. CoNLL-2012 shared task: Modeling multilingual unrestricted coreference in OntoNotes. In *CoNLL*.

V. Punyakanok and D. Roth. 2001. The use of classifiers in sequential inference. In *NIPS*.

L. R. Rabiner. 1989. A tutorial on hidden Markov models and selected applications in speech recognition. *Proceedings of the IEEE*.

L. A. Ramshaw and M. P. Marcus. 1995. Text chunking using transformation-based learning. In *Proceedings of the Third Annual Workshop on Very Large Corpora*.

L. Ratinov and D. Roth. 2009. Design challenges and misconceptions in named entity recognition. In *Proc. of the Annual Conference on Computational Natural Language Learning (CoNLL)*.

M. Recasens, M.-C. de Marneffe, and C. Potts. 2013. The life and death of discourse entities: Identifying singleton mentions. In *NAACL*.

D. Roth and W. Yih. 2004. A linear programming formulation for global inference in natural language tasks. In Hwee Tou Ng and Ellen Riloff, editors, *CoNLL*.

S. Sarawagi and W. Cohen. 2004. Semi-Markov conditional random fields for information extraction. In *NIPS*.

Y. Song, J. Jiang, W.-X. Zhao, S. Li, and H. Wang. 2012. Joint learning for coreference resolution with markov logic. In *Proceedings of the 2012 Joint Conference of EMNLP-CoNLL*.

W. M. Soon, H. T. Ng, and D. C. Y. Lim. 2001. A machine learning approach to coreference resolution of noun phrases. *Comput. Linguist.*

M. Vilain, J. Burger, J. Aberdeen, D. Connolly, and L. Hirschman. 1995. A model-theoretic coreference scoring scheme. In *Proceedings of the 6th conference on Message understanding*.

A Supertag-Context Model for Weakly-Supervised CCG Parser Learning

Dan Garrette* **Chris Dyer**† **Jason Baldridge**‡ **Noah A. Smith**†

*Computer Science & Engineering, University of Washington, dhg@cs.washington.edu
†School of Computer Science, Carnegie Mellon University, {cdyer,nasmith}@cs.cmu.edu
‡Department of Linguistics, University of Texas at Austin, jbaldrid@utexas.edu

Abstract

Combinatory Categorial Grammar (CCG) is a lexicalized grammar formalism in which words are associated with categories that specify the syntactic configurations in which they may occur. We present a novel parsing model with the capacity to capture the associative adjacent-category relationships intrinsic to CCG by parameterizing the relationships between each constituent label and the preterminal categories directly to its left and right, biasing the model toward constituent categories that can combine with their contexts. This builds on the intuitions of Klein and Manning's (2002) "constituent-context" model, which demonstrated the value of modeling context, but has the advantage of being able to exploit the properties of CCG. Our experiments show that our model outperforms a baseline in which this context information is not captured.

1 Introduction

Learning parsers from incomplete or indirect supervision is an important component of moving NLP research toward new domains and languages. But with less information, it becomes necessary to devise ways of making better use of the information that is available. In general, this means constructing inductive biases that take advantage of unannotated data to train probabilistic models.

One important example is the constituent-context model (CCM) of Klein and Manning (2002), which was specifically designed to capture the linguistic observation made by Radford (1988) that there are regularities to the contexts in which constituents appear. This phenomenon, known as *substitutability*, says that phrases of the same type appear in similar contexts. For example, the part-of-speech (POS) sequence ADJ NOUN frequently occurs between the tags DET and VERB. This DET—VERB context also frequently applies to the single-word sequence NOUN and to ADJ ADJ NOUN. From this, we might deduce that DET—VERB is a likely context for a noun phrase. CCM is able to learn which POS contexts are likely, and does so via a probabilistic generative model, providing a statistical, data-driven take on substitutability. However, since there is nothing intrinsic about the POS pair DET—VERB that indicates *a priori* that it is a likely constituent context, this fact must be inferred entirely from the data.

Baldridge (2008) observed that unlike opaque, atomic POS labels, the rich structures of Combinatory Categorial Grammar (CCG) (Steedman, 2000; Steedman and Baldridge, 2011) categories reflect universal grammatical properties. CCG is a lexicalized grammar formalism in which every constituent in a sentence is associated with a structured category that specifies its syntactic relationship to other constituents. For example, a category might encode that "this constituent can combine with a noun phrase to the right (an object) and then a noun phrase to the left (a subject) to produce a sentence" instead of simply VERB. CCG has proven useful as a framework for grammar induction due to its ability to incorporate linguistic knowledge to guide parser learning by, for example, specifying rules in lexical-expansion algorithms (Bisk and Hockenmaier, 2012; 2013) or encoding that information as priors within a Bayesian framework (Garrette et al., 2015).

Baldridge observed is that, cross-linguistically, grammars prefer simpler syntactic structures when possible, and that due to the natural correspondence of categories and syntactic structure, biasing toward simpler categories encourages simpler structures. In previous work, we were able to incorporate this preference into a Bayesian parsing model, biasing PCFG productions toward sim-

Proceedings of the 19th Conference on Computational Language Learning, pages 22–31,
Beijing, China, July 30-31, 2015.

pler categories by encoding a notion of category simplicity into a prior (Garrette et al., 2015). Baldridge further notes that due to the natural associativity of CCG, adjacent categories tend to be combinable. We previously showed that incorporating this intuition into a Bayesian prior can help train a CCG supertagger (Garrette et al., 2014).

In this paper, we present a novel parsing model that is designed specifically for the capacity to capture both of these universal, intrinsic properties of CCG. We do so by extending our previous, PCFG-based parsing model to include parameters that govern the relationship between constituent categories and the preterminal categories (also known as *supertags*) to the left and right. The advantage of modeling context within a CCG framework is that while CCM must learn which contexts are likely purely from the data, the CCG categories give us obvious *a priori* information about whether a context is likely for a given constituent based on whether the categories are combinable. Biasing our model towards both simple categories and connecting contexts encourages learning structures with simpler syntax and that have a better global "fit".

The Bayesian framework is well-matched to our problem since our inductive biases — those derived from universal grammar principles, weak supervision, and estimations based on unannotated data — can be encoded as priors, and we can use Markov chain Monte Carlo (MCMC) inference procedures to automatically blend these biases with unannotated text that reflects the way language is actually used "in the wild". Thus, we learn context information based on statistics in the data like CCM, but have the advantage of additional, *a priori* biases. It is important to note that the Bayesian setup allows us to use these universal biases as *soft* constraints: they guide the learner toward more appropriate grammars, but may be overridden when there is compelling contradictory evidence in the data.

Methodologically, this work serves as an example of how linguistic-theoretical commitments can be used to benefit data-driven methods, not only through the construction of a model family from a grammar, as done in our previous work, but also when exploiting statistical associations about which the theory is silent. While there has been much work in computational modeling of the interaction between universal grammar and observable data in the context of studying child language acquisition (e.g., Villavicencio, 2002; Goldwater, 2007), we are interested in applying these principles to the design of models and learning procedures that result in better parsing tools. Given our desire to train NLP models in low-supervision scenarios, the possibility of constructing inductive biases out of universal properties of language is enticing: if we can do this well, then it only needs to be done once, and can be applied to any language or domain without adaptation.

In this paper, we seek to learn from only raw data and an incomplete dictionary mapping some words to sets of potential supertags. In order to estimate the parameters of our model, we develop a blocked sampler based on that of Johnson et al. (2007) to sample parse trees for sentences in the raw training corpus according to their posterior probabilities. However, due to the very large sets of potential supertags used in a parse, computing inside charts is intractable, so we design a Metropolis-Hastings step that allows us to sample efficiently from the correct posterior. Our experiments show that the incorporation of supertag context parameters into the model improves learning, and that placing combinability-preferring priors on those parameters yields further gains in many scenarios.

2 Combinatory Categorial Grammar

In the CCG formalism, every constituent, including those at the lexical level, is associated with a structured CCG category that defines that constituent's relationships to the other constituents in the sentence. Categories are defined by a recursive structure, where a category is either *atomic* (possibly with *features*), or a function from one category to another, as indicated by a slash operator:

$$C \rightarrow \{\mathsf{s}, \mathsf{s}_{\mathsf{dcl}}, \mathsf{s}_{\mathsf{adj}}, \mathsf{s}_{\mathsf{b}}, \mathsf{np}, \mathsf{n}, \mathsf{n}_{\mathsf{num}}, \mathsf{pp}, ...\}$$
$$C \rightarrow \{(C/C), (C\backslash C)\}$$

Categories of adjacent constituents can be combined using one of a set of combination rules to form categories of higher-level constituents, as seen in Figure 1. The direction of the slash operator gives the behavior of the function. A category $(\mathsf{s}\backslash\mathsf{np})/\mathsf{pp}$ might describe an intransitive verb with a prepositional phrase complement; it combines on the right (/) with a constituent with category pp, and then on the left (\) with a noun phrase (np) that serves as its subject.

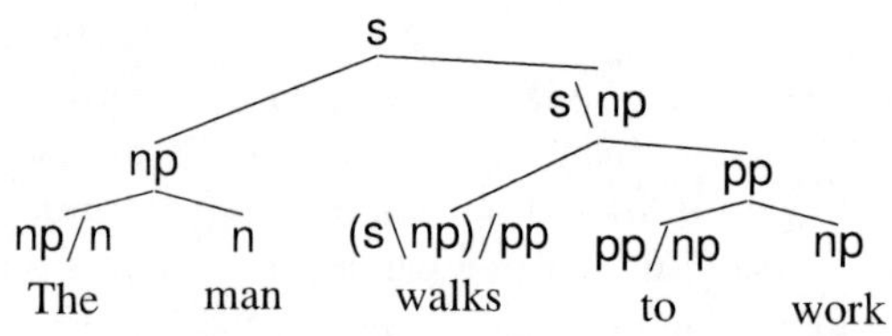

Figure 1: CCG parse for "The man walks to work."

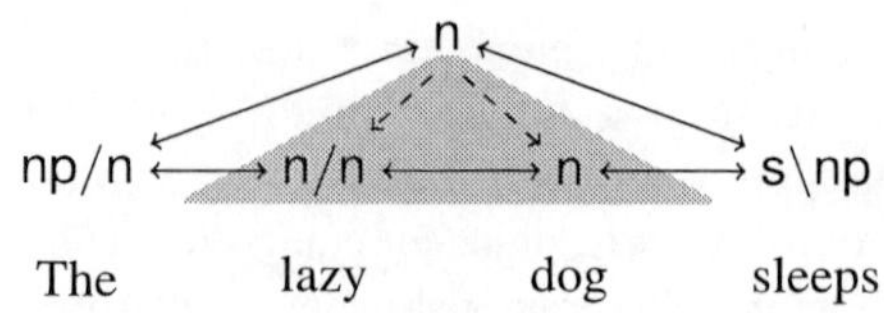

Figure 2: Higher-level category n subsumes the categories of its constituents. Thus, n should have a strong prior on combinability with its adjacent supertags np/n and s\np.

We follow Lewis and Steedman (2014) in allowing a small set of generic, linguistically-plausible unary and binary grammar rules. We further add rules for combining with punctuation to the left and right and allow for the *merge* rule $X \rightarrow X\ X$ of Clark and Curran (2007).

3 Generative Model

In this section, we present our novel supertag-context model (SCM) that augments a standard PCFG with parameters governing the supertags to the left and right of each constituent.

The CCG formalism is said to be naturally *associative* since a constituent label is often able to combine on either the left or the right. As a motivating example, consider the sentence "The lazy dog sleeps", as shown in Figure 2. The word *lazy*, with category n/n, can either combine with *dog* (n) via the Forward Application rule (>), or with *The* (np/n) via the Forward Composition (>**B**) rule. Baldridge (2008) showed that this tendency for adjacent supertags to be combinable can be used to bias a sequence model in order to learn better CCG supertaggers. However, we can see that if the supertags of adjacent words *lazy* (n/n) and *dog* (n) combine, then they will produce the category n, which describes the entire constituent span "lazy dog". Since we have produced a new category that subsumes that entire span, a valid parse must next combine that n with one of the remaining supertags to the left or right, producing either (The·(lazy·dog))·sleeps or The·((lazy·dog)·sleeps). Because we know that one (or both) of these combinations must be valid, we will similarly want a strong prior on the connectivity between lazy·dog and its supertag context: The↔(lazy·dog)↔sleeps.

Assuming $\mathcal{T}$ is the full set of known categories, the generative process for our model is:

Parameters:

$$
\begin{array}{lll}
\theta^{\text{ROOT}} & \sim \text{Dir}(\alpha^{\text{ROOT}}, \theta^{\text{ROOT-0}}) & \\
\theta^{\text{BIN}}_{\mathbf{t}} & \sim \text{Dir}(\alpha^{\text{BIN}}, \theta^{\text{BIN-0}}) & \forall \mathbf{t} \in \mathcal{T} \\
\theta^{\text{UN}}_{\mathbf{t}} & \sim \text{Dir}(\alpha^{\text{UN}}, \theta^{\text{UN-0}}) & \forall \mathbf{t} \in \mathcal{T} \\
\theta^{\text{TERM}}_{\mathbf{t}} & \sim \text{Dir}(\alpha^{\text{TERM}}, \theta^{\text{TERM-0}}_{\mathbf{t}}) & \forall \mathbf{t} \in \mathcal{T} \\
\lambda_{\mathbf{t}} & \sim \text{Dir}(\alpha_{\lambda}, \lambda^{0}) & \forall \mathbf{t} \in \mathcal{T} \\
\theta^{\text{LCTX}}_{\mathbf{t}} & \sim \text{Dir}(\alpha^{\text{LCTX}}, \theta^{\text{LCTX-0}}_{\mathbf{t}}) & \forall \mathbf{t} \in \mathcal{T} \\
\theta^{\text{RCTX}}_{\mathbf{t}} & \sim \text{Dir}(\alpha^{\text{RCTX}}, \theta^{\text{RCTX-0}}_{\mathbf{t}}) & \forall \mathbf{t} \in \mathcal{T}
\end{array}
$$

Sentence:

$$
\begin{array}{l}
\textbf{do } \mathbf{s} \sim \text{Cat}(\theta^{\text{ROOT}}) \\
\quad \mathbf{y} \mid \mathbf{s} \sim \text{SCM}(\mathbf{s}) \\
\textbf{until } \textit{the tree } \mathbf{y} \textit{ is valid}
\end{array}
$$

where $\langle \boldsymbol{\ell}, \mathbf{y}, \mathbf{r} \rangle \mid \mathbf{t} \sim \text{SCM}(\mathbf{t})$ is defined as:

$$
\begin{array}{l}
z \sim \text{Cat}(\lambda_{\mathbf{t}}) \\
\textbf{if } z = \text{B}: \quad \langle \mathbf{u}, \mathbf{v} \rangle \mid \mathbf{t} \sim \text{Cat}(\theta^{\text{BIN}}_{\mathbf{t}}) \\
\quad \mathbf{y}_{\text{L}} \mid \mathbf{u} \sim \text{SCM}(\mathbf{u}), \quad \mathbf{y}_{\text{R}} \mid \mathbf{v} \sim \text{SCM}(\mathbf{v}) \\
\quad \mathbf{y} = \langle \mathbf{y}_{\text{L}}, \mathbf{y}_{\text{R}} \rangle \\
\textbf{if } z = \text{U}: \quad \langle \mathbf{u} \rangle \mid \mathbf{t} \sim \text{Cat}(\theta^{\text{UN}}_{\mathbf{t}}) \\
\quad \mathbf{y} \mid \mathbf{u} \sim \text{SCM}(\mathbf{u}) \\
\textbf{if } z = \text{T}: \quad w \mid \mathbf{t} \sim \text{Cat}(\theta^{\text{TERM}}_{\mathbf{t}}) \\
\quad \mathbf{y} = w \\
\boldsymbol{\ell} \mid \mathbf{t} \sim \text{Cat}(\theta^{\text{LCTX}}_{\mathbf{t}}), \quad \mathbf{r} \mid \mathbf{t} \sim \text{Cat}(\theta^{\text{RCTX}}_{\mathbf{t}})
\end{array}
$$

The process begins by sampling the parameters from Dirichlet distributions: a distribution θ^{ROOT} over root categories, a conditional distribution $\theta^{\text{BIN}}_{\mathbf{t}}$ over binary branching productions given category $\mathbf{t}$, $\theta^{\text{UN}}_{\mathbf{t}}$ for unary rewrite productions, $\theta^{\text{TERM}}_{\mathbf{t}}$ for terminal (word) productions, and $\theta^{\text{LCTX}}_{\mathbf{t}}$ and $\theta^{\text{RCTX}}_{\mathbf{t}}$ for left and right contexts. We also sample parameters $\lambda_{\mathbf{t}}$ for the probability of $\mathbf{t}$ producing a binary branch, unary rewrite, or terminal word.

Next we sample a sentence. This begins by sampling first a root category $\mathbf{s}$ and then recursively sampling subtrees. For each subtree rooted by a category $\mathbf{t}$, we generate a left context supertag $\boldsymbol{\ell}$ and a right context supertag $\mathbf{r}$. Then, we sam-

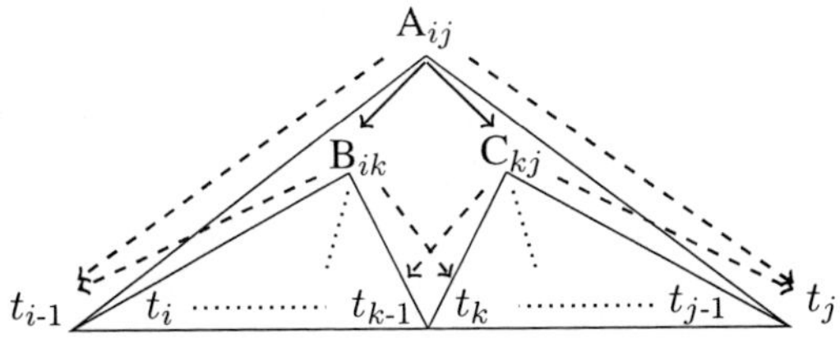

Figure 3: The generative process starting with non-terminal A_{ij}, where t_x is the supertag for w_x, the word at position x, and "A $\rightarrow$ B C" is a valid production in the grammar. We can see that non-terminal A_{ij} generates nonterminals B_{ik} and C_{kj} (solid arrows) as well as generating left context $t_{i\text{-}1}$ and right context t_j (dashed arrows); likewise for B_{ik} and C_{kj}. The triangle under a non-terminal indicates the complete subtree rooted by the node.

ple a production type z corresponding to either a (B) binary, (U) unary, or (T) terminal production. Depending on z, we then sample either a binary production $\langle \mathbf{u}, \mathbf{v} \rangle$ and recurse, a unary production $\langle \mathbf{u} \rangle$ and recurse, or a terminal word w and end that branch. A tree is complete when all branches end in terminal words. See Figure 3 for a graphical depiction of the generative behavior of the process. Finally, since it is possible to generate a supertag context category that does not match the actual category generated by the neighboring constituent, we must allow our process to reject such invalid trees and re-attempt to sample.

Like CCM, this model is *deficient* since the same supertags are generated multiple times, and parses with conflicting supertags are not valid. Since we are not generating from the model, this does not introduce difficulties (Klein and Manning, 2002).

One additional complication that must be addressed is that left-frontier non-terminal categories — those whose subtree span includes the first word of the sentence — do not have a left-side supertag to use as context. For these cases, we use the special sentence-start symbol $\langle \text{S} \rangle$ to serve as context. Similarly, we use the end symbol $\langle \text{E} \rangle$ for the right-side context of the right-frontier.

We next discuss how the prior distributions are constructed to encode desirable biases, using universal CCG properties.

3.1 Non-terminal production prior means

For the root, binary, and unary parameters, we want to choose prior means that encode our bias toward cross-linguistically-plausible categories. To formalize the notion of what it means for a category to be more "plausible", we extend the *category generator* of our previous work, which we will call P_{CAT}. We can define P_{CAT} using a probabilistic grammar (Garrette et al., 2014). The grammar may first generate a start or end category ($\langle \text{S} \rangle$,$\langle \text{E} \rangle$) with probability p_{se} or a special token-deletion category ($\langle \text{D} \rangle$; explained in §5) with probability p_{del}, or a standard CCG category C:

$$
\begin{array}{ll}
X \rightarrow \langle \text{S} \rangle \mid \langle \text{E} \rangle & p_{se} \\
X \rightarrow \langle \text{D} \rangle & p_{del} \\
X \rightarrow C & (1 - (2p_{se} + p_{del})) \cdot P_{\text{C}}(C)
\end{array}
$$

For each sentence s, there will be one $\langle \text{S} \rangle$ and one $\langle \text{E} \rangle$, so we set $p_{se} = 1/(25+2)$, since the average sentence length in the corpora is roughly 25. To discourage the model from deleting tokens (only applies during testing), we set $p_{del} = 10^{-100}$.

For P_{C}, the distribution over standard categories, we use a recursive definition based on the structure of a CCG category. If $\overline{p} = 1 - p$, then:[1]

$$
\begin{array}{lll}
C \rightarrow a & p_{term} \cdot p_{atom}(a) & \\
C \rightarrow A/A & \overline{p}_{term} \cdot p_{fwd} \cdot (\, p_{mod} \cdot P_{\text{C}}(A) \; + & \\
 & \qquad\qquad \overline{p}_{mod} \cdot P_{\text{C}}(A)^2 \,) & \\
C \rightarrow A/B & \overline{p}_{term} \cdot p_{fwd} \cdot \;\; \overline{p}_{mod} \cdot P_{\text{C}}(A) \cdot P_{\text{C}}(B) & \\
C \rightarrow A\backslash A & \overline{p}_{term} \cdot \overline{p}_{fwd} \cdot (\, p_{mod} \cdot P_{\text{C}}(A) \; + & \\
 & \qquad\qquad \overline{p}_{mod} \cdot P_{\text{C}}(A)^2 \,) & \\
C \rightarrow A\backslash B & \overline{p}_{term} \cdot \overline{p}_{fwd} \cdot \;\; \overline{p}_{mod} \cdot P_{\text{C}}(A) \cdot P_{\text{C}}(B) &
\end{array}
$$

The category grammar captures important aspects of what makes a category more or less likely: (1) simplicity is preferred, with a higher p_{term} meaning a stronger emphasis on simplicity;[2] (2) atomic types may occur at different rates, as given by p_{atom}; (3) modifier categories (A/A or $A\backslash A$) are more likely than similar-complexity non-modifiers (such as an adverb that modifies a verb); and (4) operators may occur at different rates, as given by p_{fwd}.

We can use P_{CAT} to define priors on our production parameters that bias our model toward rules

[1] Note that this version has also updated the probability definitions for modifiers to be sums, incorporating the fact that any A/A is *also* a A/B (likewise for $A\backslash A$). This ensures that our grammar defines a valid probability distribution.

[2] The probability distribution over categories is guaranteed to be proper so long as $p_{term} > \frac{1}{2}$ since the probability of the depth of a tree will decrease geometrically (Chi, 1999).

that result in *a priori* more likely categories:[3]

$$\theta^{\text{ROOT-0}}(\mathbf{t}) = P_{\text{CAT}}(\mathbf{t})$$
$$\theta^{\text{BIN-0}}(\langle \mathbf{u}, \mathbf{v} \rangle) = P_{\text{CAT}}(\mathbf{u}) \cdot P_{\text{CAT}}(\mathbf{v})$$
$$\theta^{\text{UN-0}}(\langle \mathbf{u} \rangle) = P_{\text{CAT}}(\mathbf{u})$$

For simplicity, we assume the production-type mixture prior to be uniform: $\lambda^0 = \langle \frac{1}{3}, \frac{1}{3}, \frac{1}{3} \rangle$.

3.2 Terminal production prior means

We employ the same procedure as our previous work for setting the terminal production prior distributions $\theta_{\mathbf{t}}^{\text{TERM-0}}(w)$ by estimating word-given-category relationships from the weak supervision: the tag dictionary and raw corpus (Garrette and Baldridge, 2012; Garrette et al., 2015).[4] This procedure attempts to automatically estimate the frequency of each word/tag combination by dividing the number of raw-corpus occurrences of each word in the dictionary evenly across all of its associated tags. These counts are then combined with estimates of the "openness" of each tag in order to assess its likelihood of appearing with new words.

3.3 Context parameter prior means

In order to encourage our model to choose trees in which the constituent labels "fit" into their supertag contexts, we want to bias our context parameters toward context categories that are *combinable* with the constituent label.

The right-side context of a non-terminal category — the probability of generating a category to the right of the current constituent's category — corresponds directly to the category transitions used for the HMM supertagger of Garrette et al. (2014). Thus, the right-side context prior mean $\theta_{\mathbf{t}}^{\text{RCTX-0}}$ can be biased in exactly the same way as the HMM supertagger's transitions: toward context supertags that connect to the constituent label.

To encode a notion of combinability, we follow Baldridge's (2008) definition. Briefly, let $\kappa(\mathbf{t}, \mathbf{u}) \in \{0, 1\}$ be an indicator of whether $\mathbf{t}$ combines with $\mathbf{u}$ (in that order). For any binary rule that can combine $\mathbf{t}$ to $\mathbf{u}$, $\kappa(\mathbf{t}, \mathbf{u})$=1. To ensure that our prior captures the natural associativity of CCG, we define combinability in this context to include composition rules as well as application rules. If atoms have *features* associated, then the atoms are allowed to unify if the features match, or if at least one of them does not have a feature. In defining κ, it is also important to ignore possible arguments on the wrong side of the combination since they can be consumed without affecting the connection between the two. To achieve this for $\kappa(\mathbf{t}, \mathbf{u})$, it is assumed that it is possible to consume all preceding arguments of $\mathbf{t}$ and all following arguments of $\mathbf{u}$. So $\kappa(\mathsf{np}, (\mathsf{s}\backslash\mathsf{np})/\mathsf{np}) = 1$. This helps to ensure the associativity discussed earlier. For "combining" with the start or end of a sentence, we define $\kappa(\langle \mathsf{S} \rangle, \mathbf{u})$=1 when $\mathbf{u}$ seeks no left-side arguments (since there are no tags to the left with which to combine) and $\kappa(\mathbf{t}, \langle \mathsf{E} \rangle)$=1 when $\mathbf{t}$ seeks no right-side arguments. So $\kappa(\langle \mathsf{S} \rangle, \mathsf{np}/\mathsf{n})$=1, but $\kappa(\langle \mathsf{S} \rangle, \mathsf{s}\backslash\mathsf{np})$=0. Finally, due to the frequent use of the unary rule that allows n to be rewritten as np, the atom np is allowed to unify with n if n is the argument. So $\kappa(\mathsf{n}, \mathsf{s}\backslash\mathsf{np}) = 1$, but $\kappa(\mathsf{np}/\mathsf{n}, \mathsf{np}) = 0$.

The prior mean of producing a right-context supertag $\mathbf{r}$ from a constituent category $\mathbf{t}$, $P^{right}(\mathbf{r} \mid \mathbf{t})$, is defined so that combinable pairs are given higher probability than non-combinable pairs. We further experimented with a prior that biases toward both combinability *and* category likelihood, replacing the uniform treatment of categories with our prior over categories, yielding $P_{\text{CAT}}^{right}(\mathbf{r} \mid \mathbf{t})$. If $\mathcal{T}$ is the full set of known CCG categories:

$$P^{right}(\mathbf{r} \mid \mathbf{t}) = \begin{cases} \sigma \cdot 1/|\mathcal{T}| & \text{if } \kappa(\mathbf{t}, \mathbf{r}) \quad \sigma > 1 \\ 1/|\mathcal{T}| & \text{otherwise} \end{cases}$$

$$P_{\text{CAT}}^{right}(\mathbf{r} \mid \mathbf{t}) = \begin{cases} \sigma \cdot P_{\text{CAT}}(\mathbf{r}) & \text{if } \kappa(\mathbf{t}, \mathbf{r}) \quad \sigma > 1 \\ P_{\text{CAT}}(\mathbf{r}) & \text{otherwise} \end{cases}$$

Distributions $P^{left}(\boldsymbol{\ell} \mid \mathbf{t})$ and $P_{\text{CAT}}^{left}(\boldsymbol{\ell} \mid \mathbf{t})$ are defined in the same way, but with the combinability direction flipped: $\kappa(\boldsymbol{\ell}, \mathbf{t})$, since the left context supertag precedes the constituent category.

4 Posterior Inference

We wish to infer the distribution over CCG parses, given the model we just described and a corpus of sentences. Since there is no way to analytically compute these modes, we resort to Gibbs sampling to find an approximate solution. Our strategy is based on the approach presented by Johnson et al. (2007). At a high level, we alternate between resampling model parameters (θ^{ROOT}, θ^{BIN}, θ^{UN}, θ^{TERM}, λ, θ^{LCTX}, θ^{RCTX}) given the current set of parse trees and resampling those trees given the

[3] For our experiments, we normalize P_{CAT} by dividing by $\sum_{\mathbf{c} \in \mathcal{T}} P_{\text{CAT}}(\mathbf{c})$. This allows for experiments contrasting with a uniform prior ($1/|\mathcal{T}|$) without adjusting α values.

[4] We refer the reader to the previous work (Garrette et al., 2015) for a fuller discussion and implementation details.

current model parameters and observed word sequences. To efficiently sample new model parameters, we exploit Dirichlet-multinomial conjugacy. By repeating these alternating steps and accumulating the productions, we obtain an approximation of the required posterior quantities.

Our inference procedure takes as input the distribution prior means, along with the raw corpus and tag dictionary. During sampling, we restrict the tag choices for a word w to categories allowed by the tag dictionary. Since real-world learning scenarios will always lack complete knowledge of the lexicon, we, too, want to allow for unknown words; for these, we assume the word may take any known supertag. We refer to the sequence of word tokens as $\mathbf{w}$ and a non-terminal category covering the span i through $j-1$ as y_{ij}.

While it is technically possible to sample directly from our context-sensitive model, the high number of potential supertags available for each context means that computing the inside chart for this model is intractable for most sentences. In order to overcome this limitation, we employ an accept/reject Metropolis-Hastings (MH) step. The basic idea is that we sample trees according to a simpler *proposal* distribution Q that approximates the full distribution and for which direct sampling is tractable, and then choose to accept or reject those trees based on the true distribution P.

For our model, there is a straightforward and intuitive choice for the proposal distribution: the PCFG model without our context parameters: $(\theta^{\text{ROOT}}, \theta^{\text{BIN}}, \theta^{\text{UN}}, \theta^{\text{TERM}}, \lambda)$, which is known to have an efficient sampling method. Our acceptance step is therefore based on the remaining parameters: the context $(\theta^{\text{LCTX}}, \theta^{\text{RCTX}})$.

To sample from our proposal distribution, we use a blocked Gibbs sampler based on the one proposed by Goodman (1998) and used by Johnson et al. (2007) that samples entire parse trees. For a sentence $\mathbf{w}$, the strategy is to use the Inside algorithm (Lari and Young, 1990) to inductively compute, for each potential non-terminal position spanning words w_i through w_{j-1} and category $\mathbf{t}$, going "up" the tree, the probability of generating $w_i, \ldots, w_{j-1}$ via any arrangement of productions that is rooted by $y_{ij} = \mathbf{t}$.

$$\begin{aligned} p(w_i \mid y_{i,i+1} = \mathbf{t}) = {} & \lambda_{\mathbf{t}}(\text{T}) \cdot \theta^{\text{TERM}}_{\mathbf{t}}(w_i) \\ & + \textstyle\sum_{\mathbf{t}\to\mathbf{u}} \lambda_{\mathbf{t}}(\text{U}) \cdot \theta^{\text{UN}}_{\mathbf{t}}(\langle\mathbf{u}\rangle) \\ & \quad \cdot p(w_{i:j-1} \mid y_{ij} = \mathbf{u}) \end{aligned}$$

$$\begin{aligned} p(w_{i:j-1} \mid y_{ij} = \mathbf{t}) = {} & \\ & \textstyle\sum_{\mathbf{t}\to\mathbf{u}} \lambda_{\mathbf{t}}(\text{U}) \cdot \theta^{\text{UN}}_{\mathbf{t}}(\langle\mathbf{u}\rangle) \\ & \quad \cdot p(w_{i:j-1} \mid y_{ij} = \mathbf{u}) \\ & + \textstyle\sum_{\mathbf{t}\to\mathbf{u}\ \mathbf{v}} \sum_{i<k<j} \lambda_{\mathbf{t}}(\text{B}) \cdot \theta^{\text{BIN}}_{\mathbf{t}}(\langle\mathbf{u},\mathbf{v}\rangle) \\ & \quad \cdot p(w_{i:k-1} \mid y_{ik} = \mathbf{u}) \\ & \quad \cdot p(w_{k:j-1} \mid y_{kj} = \mathbf{v}) \end{aligned}$$

We then pass "downward" through the chart, sampling productions until we reach a terminal word on all branches.

$$\begin{aligned} y_{0n} \sim {} & \theta^{\text{ROOT}}_{\mathbf{t}} \cdot p(w_{0:n-1} \mid y_{0n} = \mathbf{t}) \\ x \mid y_{ij} \sim {} & \big\langle \theta^{\text{BIN}}_{y_{ij}}(\langle\mathbf{u},\mathbf{v}\rangle) \cdot p(w_{i:k-1} \mid y_{ik} = \mathbf{u}) \\ & \quad \cdot p(w_{k:j-1} \mid y_{kj} = \mathbf{v}) \\ & \qquad \forall\, y_{ik}, y_{kj} \text{ when } j > i+1, \\ & \theta^{\text{UN}}_{y_{ij}}(\langle\mathbf{u}\rangle) \cdot p(w_{i:j-1} \mid y'_{ij} = \mathbf{u}) \quad \forall\, y'_{ij}, \\ & \theta^{\text{TERM}}_{y_{ij}}(w_i) \qquad \text{when } j = i+1 \big\rangle \end{aligned}$$

where x is either a split point k and pair of categories y_{ik}, y_{kj} resulting from a binary rewrite rule, a single category y'_{ij} resulting from a unary rule, or a word w resulting from a terminal rule.

The MH procedure requires an *acceptance distribution* A that is used to accept or reject a tree sampled from the proposal Q. The probability of accepting new tree $\mathbf{y}'$ given the previous tree $\mathbf{y}$ is:

$$A(\mathbf{y}' \mid \mathbf{y}) = \min\left(1, \frac{P(\mathbf{y}')}{P(\mathbf{y})} \frac{Q(\mathbf{y})}{Q(\mathbf{y}')}\right)$$

Since Q is defined as a subset of P's parameters, it is the case that:

$$P(\mathbf{y}) = Q(\mathbf{y}) \cdot p(\mathbf{y} \mid \theta^{\text{LCTX}}, \theta^{\text{RCTX}})$$

After substituting this for each P in A, all of the Q factors cancel, yielding the acceptance distribution defined purely in terms of context parameters:

$$A(\mathbf{y}' \mid \mathbf{y}) = \min\left(1, \frac{p(\mathbf{y}' \mid \theta^{\text{LCTX}}, \theta^{\text{RCTX}})}{p(\mathbf{y} \mid \theta^{\text{LCTX}}, \theta^{\text{RCTX}})}\right)$$

For completeness, we note that the probability of a tree $\mathbf{y}$ given only the context parameters is:[5]

$$\begin{aligned} p(\mathbf{y} \mid \theta^{\text{LCTX}}, \theta^{\text{RCTX}}) = {} & \\ & \prod_{0 \le i < j \le n} \theta^{\text{LCTX}}(y_{i-1,i} \mid y_{ij}) \cdot \theta^{\text{RCTX}}(y_{j,j+1} \mid y_{ij}) \end{aligned}$$

[5]Note that there may actually be multiple y_{ij} due to unary rules that "loop back" to the same position (i, j); all of these much be included in the product.

Before we begin sampling, we initialize each distribution to its prior mean ($\theta^{\text{ROOT}}=\theta^{\text{ROOT-0}}$, $\theta_{\mathbf{t}}^{\text{BIN}}=\theta^{\text{BIN-0}}$, etc). Since MH requires an initial set of trees to begin sampling, we parse the raw corpus with probabilistic CKY using these initial parameters (excluding the context parameters) to guess an initial tree for each raw sentence.

The sampler alternates sampling parse trees for the entire corpus of sentences using the above procedure with resampling the model parameters. Resampling the parameters requires empirical counts of each production. These counts are taken from the trees resulting from the previous round of sampling: new trees that have been "accepted" by the MH step, as well as existing trees for sentences in which the newly-sampled tree was rejected.

$$\begin{aligned}
\theta^{\text{ROOT}} &\sim \text{Dir}(\langle \alpha^{\text{ROOT}} \cdot \theta^{\text{ROOT-0}}(\mathbf{t}) \quad + C_{root}(\mathbf{t}) \rangle_{\mathbf{t}\in\mathcal{T}}) \\
\theta_{\mathbf{t}}^{\text{BIN}} &\sim \text{Dir}(\langle \alpha^{\text{BIN}} \cdot \theta^{\text{BIN-0}}(\langle \mathbf{u},\mathbf{v}\rangle) + C(\mathbf{t}\rightarrow\langle \mathbf{u},\mathbf{v}\rangle) \rangle_{\mathbf{u},\mathbf{v}\in\mathcal{T}}) \\
\theta_{\mathbf{t}}^{\text{UN}} &\sim \text{Dir}(\langle \alpha^{\text{UN}} \cdot \theta^{\text{UN-0}}(\langle \mathbf{u}\rangle) \quad + C(\mathbf{t}\rightarrow\langle \mathbf{u}\rangle) \rangle_{\mathbf{u}\in\mathcal{T}}) \\
\theta_{\mathbf{t}}^{\text{TERM}} &\sim \text{Dir}(\langle \alpha^{\text{TERM}} \cdot \theta_{\mathbf{t}}^{\text{TERM-0}}(w) \quad + C(\mathbf{t}\rightarrow w) \rangle_{w\in V}) \\
\lambda_{\mathbf{t}} &\sim \text{Dir}(\langle \alpha_\lambda \cdot \lambda^0(\text{B}) + \textstyle\sum_{\mathbf{u},\mathbf{v}\in\mathcal{T}} C(\mathbf{t}\rightarrow\langle \mathbf{u},\mathbf{v}\rangle), \\
&\qquad \alpha_\lambda \cdot \lambda^0(\text{U}) + \textstyle\sum_{\mathbf{u}\in\mathcal{T}} C(\mathbf{t}\rightarrow\langle \mathbf{u}\rangle), \\
&\qquad \alpha_\lambda \cdot \lambda^0(\text{T}) + \textstyle\sum_{w\in V} C(\mathbf{t}\rightarrow w) \quad \rangle) \\
\theta_{\mathbf{t}}^{\text{LCTX}} &\sim \text{Dir}(\langle \alpha^{\text{LCTX}} \cdot \theta_{\mathbf{t}}^{\text{LCTX-0}}(\boldsymbol{\ell}) + C_{left}(\mathbf{t},\boldsymbol{\ell}) \rangle_{\boldsymbol{\ell}\in\mathcal{T}}) \\
\theta_{\mathbf{t}}^{\text{RCTX}} &\sim \text{Dir}(\langle \alpha^{\text{RCTX}} \cdot \theta_{\mathbf{t}}^{\text{RCTX-0}}(\mathbf{r}) + C_{right}(\mathbf{t},\mathbf{r}) \rangle_{\mathbf{r}\in\mathcal{T}})
\end{aligned}$$

It is important to note that this method of resampling allows the draws to incorporate both the data, in the form of counts, and the prior mean, which includes all of our carefully-constructed biases derived from both the intrinsic, universal CCG properties as well as the information we induced from the raw corpus and tag dictionary.

After all sampling iterations have completed, the final model is estimated by pooling the trees resulting from each sampling iteration, including trees accepted by the MH steps as well as the duplicated trees retained due to rejections. We use this pool of trees to compute model parameters using the same procedure as we used directly above to sample parameters, except that instead of drawing a Dirichlet sample based on the vector of counts, we simply normalize those counts. However, since we require a final model that can parse sentences efficiently, we drop the context parameters, making the model a standard PCFG, which allows us to use the probabilistic CKY algorithm.

5 Experiments

In our evaluation we compared our supertag-context approach to (our reimplementation of) the best-performing model of our previous work (Garrette et al., 2015), which SCM extends. We evaluated on the English CCGBank (Hockenmaier and Steedman, 2007), which is a transformation of the Penn Treebank (Marcus et al., 1993); the CTB-CCG (Tse and Curran, 2010) transformation of the Penn Chinese Treebank (Xue et al., 2005); and the CCG-TUT corpus (Bos et al., 2009), built from the TUT corpus of Italian text (Bosco et al., 2000).

Each corpus was divided into four distinct data sets: a set from which we extract the tag dictionaries, a set of raw (unannotated) sentences, a development set, and a test set. We use the same splits as Garrette et al. (2014). Since these treebanks use special representations for conjunctions, we chose to rewrite the trees to use conjunction categories of the form $(X\backslash X)/X$ rather than introducing special conjunction rules. In order to increase the amount of raw data available to the sampler, we supplemented the English data with raw, unannotated newswire sentences from the NYT Gigaword 5 corpus (Parker et al., 2011) and supplemented Italian with the out-of-domain WaCky corpus (Baroni et al., 1999). For English and Italian, this allowed us to use 100k raw tokens for training (Chinese uses 62k). For Chinese and Italian, for training efficiency, we used only raw sentences that were 50 words or fewer (note that we did *not* drop tag dictionary set or test set sentences).

The English development set was used to tune hyperparameters using grid search, and the same hyperparameters were then used for all three languages. For the category grammar, we used p_{punc}=0.1, p_{term}=0.7, p_{mod}=0.2, p_{fwd}=0.5. For the priors, we use $\alpha^{\text{ROOT}}=1$, $\alpha^{\text{BIN}}=100$, $\alpha^{\text{UN}}=100$, $\alpha^{\text{TERM}}=10^4$, $\alpha_\lambda=3$, $\alpha^{\text{LCTX}}=\alpha^{\text{RCTX}}=10^3$.[6] For the context prior, we used $\sigma=10^5$. We ran our sampler for 50 burn-in and 50 sampling iterations.

CCG parsers are typically evaluated on the *dependencies* they produce instead of their CCG derivations directly since there can be many different CCG parse trees that all represent the same dependency relationships (spurious ambiguity), and CCG-to-dependency conversion can collapse those differences. To convert a CCG tree into a dependency tree, we follow Lewis and Steedman

[6] In order to ensure that these concentration parameters, while high, were not dominating the posterior distributions, we ran experiments in which they were set much higher (including using the prior alone), and found that accuracies plummeted in those cases, demonstrating that there is a good balance with the prior.

		Size of the corpus (tokens) from which the *tag dictionary* is extracted					
		250k	**200k**	**150k**	**100k**	**50k**	**25k**
English	no context	60.43	61.22	59.69	58.61	56.26	54.70
	context (uniform)	64.02	**63.89**	62.58	61.80	59.44	57.08
	$+P^{left}$ / P^{right}	**65.44**	63.26	**64.28**	**62.90**	**59.63**	**57.86**
	$+P^{left}_{\text{CAT}}$ / P^{right}_{CAT}	59.34	59.89	59.32	58.47	57.85	55.77
Chinese	no context				32.70	32.07	28.99
	context (uniform)				**36.02**	33.84	32.55
	$+P^{left}$ / P^{right}				35.34	33.04	31.48
	$+P^{left}_{\text{CAT}}$ / P^{right}_{CAT}				35.15	**34.04**	**33.53**
Italian	no context						51.54
	context (uniform)						**53.57**
	$+P^{left}$ / P^{right}						52.54
	$+P^{left}_{\text{CAT}}$ / P^{right}_{CAT}						53.29

Table 1: Experimental results in three languages. For each language, four experiments were executed: (1) a no-context model baseline, Garrette et al. (2015) directly; (2) our supertag-context model, with uniform priors on contexts; (3) supertag-context model with priors that prefer combinability; (4) supertag-context model with priors that prefer combinability *and* simpler categories. Results are shown for six different levels of supervision, as determined by the size of the corpus used to extract a tag dictionary.

(2014). We traverse the parse tree, dictating at every branching node which words will be the dependents of which. For binary branching nodes of *forward* rules, the right side—the argument side—is the dependent, unless the left side is a modifier (X/X) of the right, in which case the left is the dependent. The opposite is true for *backward* rules. For *punctuation* rules, the punctuation is always the dependent. For *merge* rules, the right side is always made the parent. The results presented in this paper are dependency accuracy scores: the proportion of words that were assigned the correct parent (or "root" for the root of a tree).

When evaluating on test set sentences, if the model is unable to find a parse given the constraints of the tag dictionary, then we would have to take a score of zero for that sentence: every dependency would be "wrong". Thus, it is important that we make a best effort to find a parse. To accomplish this, we implemented a parsing backoff strategy. The parser first tries to find a valid parse that has either s_{dcl} or np at its root. If that fails, then it searches for a parse with any root. If no parse is found yet, then the parser attempts to strategically allow tokens to subsume a neighbor by making it a dependent (first with a restricted root set, then without). This is similar to the "deletion" strategy employed by Zettlemoyer and Collins (2007), but we do it directly in the grammar. We add unary rules of the form $\langle \text{D} \rangle \rightarrow \mathbf{u}$ for every potential supertag $\mathbf{u}$ in the tree. Then, at each node spanning exactly two tokens (but no higher in the tree), we allow rules $\mathbf{t} \rightarrow \langle \langle \text{D} \rangle, \mathbf{v} \rangle$ and $\mathbf{t} \rightarrow \langle \mathbf{v}, \langle \text{D} \rangle \rangle$. Recall that in §3.1, we stated that $\langle \text{D} \rangle$ is given extremely low probability, meaning that the parser will avoid its use unless it is absolutely necessary. Additionally, since $\mathbf{u}$ will still remain as the preterminal, it will be the category examined as the context by adjacent constituents.

For each language and level of supervision, we executed four experiments. The no-context baseline used (a reimplementation of) the best model from our previous work (Garrette et al., 2015): using only the non-context parameters (θ^{ROOT}, θ^{BIN}, θ^{UN}, θ^{TERM}, λ) along with the category prior P_{CAT} to bias toward likely categories throughout the tree, and $\theta_{\mathbf{t}}^{\text{TERM-0}}$ estimated from the tag dictionary and raw corpus. We then added the supertag-context parameters (θ^{LCTX}, θ^{RCTX}), but used uniform priors for those (still using P_{CAT} for the rest). Then, we evaluated the supertag-context model using context parameter priors that bias toward categories that combine with their contexts: P^{left} and P^{right} (see §3.3). Finally, we evaluated the supertag-context model using context parameter priors that bias toward combinability *and* toward *a priori* more likely categories, based on the category grammar (P^{left}_{CAT} and P^{right}_{CAT}).

Because we are interested in understanding how our models perform under varying amounts of supervision, we executed sequences of experiments in which we reduced the size of the corpus from which the tag dictionary is drawn, thus reducing the amount of information provided to the model. As this information is reduced, so is the size of the full inventory of known CCG categories that can be used as supertags. Additionally, a smaller tag dictionary means that there will be vastly more unknown words; since our model must assume that these words may take any supertag from the full set of known labels, the model must contend with a greatly increased level of ambiguity.

The results of our experiments are given in Table 1. We find that the incorporation of supertag-context parameters into a CCG model improves performance in every scenario we tested; we see gains of 2–5% across the board. Adding context parameters never hurts, and in most cases, using priors based on intrinsic, cross-lingual aspects of the CCG formalism to bias those parameters toward connectivity provides further gains. In particular, biasing the model toward trees in which constituent labels are combinable with their adjacent supertags frequently helps the model.

However, for English, we found that additionally biasing *context* priors toward simpler categories using $P^{left}_{\text{CAT}}/P^{right}_{\text{CAT}}$ degraded performance. This is likely due to the fact that the priors on production parameters $(\theta^{\text{BIN}}, \theta^{\text{UN}})$ are already biasing the model toward likely categories, and that having the context parameters do the same ends up over-emphasizing the need for simple categories, preventing the model from choosing more complex categories when they are needed. On the other hand, this bias helps in Chinese and Italian.

6 Related Work

Klein and Manning (2002)'s CCM is an unlabeled bracketing model that generates the span of part-of-speech tags that make up each constituent and the pair of tags surrounding each constituent span (as well as the spans and contexts of each non-constituent). They found that modeling constituent context aids in parser learning because it is able to capture the observation that the same contexts tend to appear repeatedly in a corpus, even with different constituents. While CCM is designed to learn which tag pairs make for likely contexts, without regard for the constituents themselves, our model attempts to learn the relationships between context categories and the types of the constituents, allowing us to take advantage of the natural *a priori* knowledge about which contexts fit with which constituent labels.

Other researchers have shown positive results for grammar induction by introducing relatively small amounts of linguistic knowledge. Naseem et al. (2010) induced dependency parsers by hand-constructing a small set of linguistically-universal dependency rules and using them as soft constraints during learning. These rules were useful for disambiguating between various structures in cases where the data alone suggests multiple valid analyses. Boonkwan and Steedman (2011) made use of language-specific linguistic knowledge collected from non-native linguists via a questionnaire that covered a variety of syntactic parameters. They were able to use this information to induce CCG parsers for multiple languages. Bisk and Hockenmaier (2012; 2013) induced CCG parsers by using a smaller number of linguistically-universal principles to propose syntactic categories for each word in a sentence, allowing EM to estimate the model parameters. This allowed them to induce the inventory of language-specific types from the training data, without prior language-specific knowledge.

7 Conclusion

Because of the structured nature of CCG categories and the logical framework in which they must assemble to form valid parse trees, the CCG formalism offers multiple opportunities to bias model learning based on universal, intrinsic properties of the grammar. In this paper we presented a novel parsing model with the capacity to capture the associative adjacent-category relationships intrinsic to CCG by parameterizing *supertag contexts*, the supertags appearing on either side of each constituent. In our Bayesian formulation, we place priors on those context parameters to bias the model toward trees in which constituent labels are *combinable* with their contexts, thus preferring trees that "fit" together better. Our experiments demonstrate that, across languages, this additional context helps in weak-supervision scenarios.

Acknowledgements

We would like to thank Yonatan Bisk for his valuable feedback. This work was supported by the U.S. Department of Defense through the U.S. Army Research Office grant W911NF-10-1-0533.

References

Jason Baldridge. 2008. Weakly supervised supertagging with grammar-informed initialization. In *Proc. of COLING*.

Marco Baroni, Silvia Bernardini, Adriano Ferraresi, and Eros Zanchetta. 1999. The WaCky wide web: a collection of very large linguistically processed web-crawled corpora. *Language Resources and Evaluation*, 43(3).

Yonatan Bisk and Julia Hockenmaier. 2012. Simple robust grammar induction with combinatory categorial grammar. In *Proc. of AAAI*.

Yonatan Bisk and Julia Hockenmaier. 2013. An HDP model for inducing combinatory categorial grammars. *Transactions of the Association for Computational Linguistics*, 1.

Prachya Boonkwan and Mark Steedman. 2011. Grammar induction from text using small syntactic prototypes. In *Proc. of IJCNLP*.

Johan Bos, Cristina Bosco, and Alessandro Mazzei. 2009. Converting a dependency treebank to a categorial grammar treebank for Italian. In M. Passarotti, Adam Przepiórkowski, S. Raynaud, and Frank Van Eynde, editors, *Proc. of the Eighth International Workshop on Treebanks and Linguistic Theories (TLT8)*.

Cristina Bosco, Vincenzo Lombardo, Daniela Vassallo, and Leonardo Lesmo. 2000. Building a treebank for Italian: a data-driven annotation schema. In *Proc. of LREC*.

Zhiyi Chi. 1999. Statistical properties of probabilistic context-free grammars. *Computational Linguistics*.

Stephen Clark and James R. Curran. 2007. Wide-coverage efficient statistical parsing with CCG and log-linear models. *Computational Linguistics*, 33.

Dan Garrette and Jason Baldridge. 2012. Type-supervised hidden Markov models for part-of-speech tagging with incomplete tag dictionaries. In *Proc. of EMNLP*.

Dan Garrette, Chris Dyer, Jason Baldridge, and Noah A. Smith. 2014. Weakly-supervised Bayesian learning of a CCG supertagger. In *Proc. of CoNLL*.

Dan Garrette, Chris Dyer, Jason Baldridge, and Noah A. Smith. 2015. Weakly-supervised grammar-informed Bayesian CCG parser learning. In *Proc. of AAAI*.

Sharon Goldwater. 2007. *Nonparametric Bayesian Models of Lexical Acquisition*. Ph.D. thesis, Brown University.

Joshua Goodman. 1998. *Parsing inside-out*. Ph.D. thesis, Harvard University.

Julia Hockenmaier and Mark Steedman. 2007. CCGbank: A corpus of CCG derivations and dependency structures extracted from the Penn Treebank. *Computational Linguistics*, 33(3).

Mark Johnson, Thomas Griffiths, and Sharon Goldwater. 2007. Bayesian inference for PCFGs via Markov chain Monte Carlo. In *Proc. of NAACL*.

Dan Klein and Christopher D. Manning. 2002. A generative constituent-context model for improved grammar induction. In *Proc. of ACL*.

Karim Lari and Steve J. Young. 1990. The estimation of stochastic context-free grammars using the inside-outside algorithm. *Computer Speech and Language*, 4:35–56.

Mike Lewis and Mark Steedman. 2014. A* CCG parsing with a supertag-factored model. In *Proc. of EMNLP*.

Mitchell P. Marcus, Beatrice Santorini, and Mary Ann Marcinkiewicz. 1993. Building a large annotated corpus of English: The Penn Treebank. *Computational Linguistics*, 19(2).

Tahira Naseem, Harr Chen, Regina Barzilay, and Mark Johnson. 2010. Using universal linguistic knowledge to guide grammar induction. In *Proc. of EMNLP*.

Robert Parker, David Graff, Junbo Kong, Ke Chen, and Kazuaki Maeda. 2011. English Gigaword Fifth Edition LDC2011T07. Linguistic Data Consortium.

Andrew Radford. 1988. *Transformational Grammar*. Cambridge University Press.

Mark Steedman and Jason Baldridge. 2011. Combinatory categorial grammar. In Robert Borsley and Kersti Borjars, editors, *Non-Transformational Syntax: Formal and Explicit Models of Grammar*. Wiley-Blackwell.

Mark Steedman. 2000. *The Syntactic Process*. MIT Press.

Daniel Tse and James R. Curran. 2010. Chinese CCGbank: Extracting CCG derivations from the Penn Chinese Treebank. In *Proc. of COLING*.

Aline Villavicencio. 2002. *The acquisition of a unification-based generalised categorial grammar*. Ph.D. thesis, University of Cambridge.

Nianwen Xue, Fei Xia, Fu-Dong Chiou, and Martha Palmer. 2005. The Penn Chinese TreeBank: Phrase structure annotation of a large corpus. *Natural Language Engineering*, 11(2):207–238.

Luke S. Zettlemoyer and Michael Collins. 2007. Online learning of relaxed CCG grammars for parsing to logical form. In *Proc. of EMNLP*.

A Synchronous Hyperedge Replacement Grammar based approach for AMR parsing

Xiaochang Peng, Linfeng Song and **Daniel Gildea**
Department of Computer Science
University of Rochester
Rochester, NY 14627

Abstract

This paper presents a synchronous-graph-grammar-based approach for string-to-AMR parsing. We apply Markov Chain Monte Carlo (MCMC) algorithms to learn Synchronous Hyperedge Replacement Grammar (SHRG) rules from a forest that represents likely derivations consistent with a fixed string-to-graph alignment. We make an analogy of string-to-AMR parsing to the task of phrase-based machine translation and come up with an efficient algorithm to learn graph grammars from string-graph pairs. We propose an effective approximation strategy to resolve the complexity issue of graph compositions. We also show some useful strategies to overcome existing problems in an SHRG-based parser and present preliminary results of a graph-grammar-based approach.

1 Introduction

Abstract Meaning Representation (AMR) (Banarescu et al., 2013) is a semantic formalism where the meaning of a sentence is encoded as a rooted, directed graph. Figure 1 shows an example of the edge-labeled representation of an AMR graph where the edges are labeled while the nodes are not. The label of the leaf edge going out of a node represents the concept of the node, and the label of a non-leaf edge shows the relation between the concepts of the two nodes it connects to. This formalism is based on propositional logic and neo-Davidsonian event representations (Parsons, 1990; Davidson, 1967). AMR does not encode quantifiers, tense and modality, but it jointly encodes a set of selected semantic phenomena which renders it useful in applications like question answering and semantics-based machine translation.

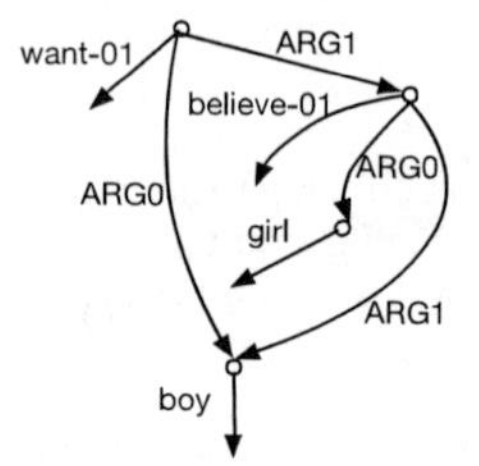

Figure 1: An example of AMR graph representing the meaning of: "The boy wants the girl to believe him"

The task of AMR graph parsing is to map natural language strings to AMR semantic graphs. Flanigan et al. (2014) propose a two-stage parsing algorithm which first maps meaningful continuous spans on the string side to concept fragments on the graph side, and then in the second stage adds additional edges to make all these fragments connected. Concept identification (Flanigan et al., 2014; Pourdamghani et al., 2014) can be considered as an important first step to relate components of the string to components in the graph.

Wang et al. (2015) also present a two-stage procedure where they first use a dependency parser trained on a large corpus to generate a dependency tree for each sentence. In the second step, a transition-based algorithm is used to greedily modify the dependency tree into an AMR graph. The benefit of starting with a dependency tree instead of the original sentence is that the dependency structure is more linguistically similar to an AMR graph and provides more direct feature information within limited context.

Hyperedge replacement grammar (HRG) is a context-free rewriting formalism for generating graphs (Drewes et al., 1997). Its synchronous counterpart, SHRG, can be used for transforming a graph from/to another structured representation such as a string or tree structure. HRG has great potential for applications in natural language un-

Proceedings of the 19th Conference on Computational Language Learning, pages 32–41,
Beijing, China, July 30-31, 2015. ©2015 Association for Computational Linguistics

derstanding and generation, and also semantics-based machine translation.

Given a graph as input, finding its derivation of HRG rules is NP-complete (Drewes et al., 1997). Chiang et al. (2013) describe in detail a graph recognition algorithm and present an optimization scheme which enables the parsing algorithm to run in polynomial time when the treewidth and degree of the graph are bounded. However, there is still no real system available for parsing large graphs.

An SHRG can be used for AMR graph parsing where each SHRG rule consists of a pair of a CFG rule and an HRG rule, which can generate strings and AMR graphs in parallel. Jones et al. (2012) present a Syntactic Semantic Algorithm that learns SHRG by matching minimal parse constituents to aligned graph fragments and incrementally collapses them into hyperedge nonterminals. The basic idea is to use the string-to-graph alignment and syntax information to constrain the possible HRGs.

Learning SHRG rules from fixed string-to-graph alignments is a similar problem to extracting machine translation rules from fixed word alignments, where we wish to automatically learn the best granularity for the rules with which to analyze each sentence. Chung et al. (2014) present an MCMC sampling schedule to learn Hiero-style SCFG rules (Chiang, 2007) by sampling tree fragments from phrase decomposition forests, which represent all possible rules that are consistent with a set of fixed word alignments, making use of the property that each SCFG rule in the derivation is in essence the decomposition of a larger phrase pair into smaller ones.

In this paper, we make an analogy to treat fragments in the graph language as phrases in the natural language string and SHRG rules as decompositions of larger substring, graph fragment pairs into smaller ones. Graph language is different from string language in that there is no explicit order to compose the graph and there is an exponential number of possible compositions. We propose a strategy that uses the left-to-right order of the string to constrain the structure of the derivation forest and experiment with different tactics in dealing with unaligned words on the string side and unaligned edges on the graph side.

Specifically, we make the following contributions:

1. We come up an alternative SHRG-based AMR parsing strategy and present a reasonable preliminary result without additional dependency information and global features, showing promising future applications when a language model is applied or larger datasets are available.

2. We present the novel notion of **fragment decomposition forest** and come up with an efficient algorithm to construct the forest from fixed string-to-graph alignment.

3. We propose an MCMC algorithm which samples a special type of SHRG rules which helps maintain the properties of AMR graphs, which should be able to generalize to learning other synchronous grammar with a CFG left side.

4. We augment the concept identification procedure of Flanigan et al. (2014) with a phrase-to-graph-fragment alignment table which makes use of the dependency between concepts.

5. We discovered that an SHRG-based approach is especially sensitive to missing alignment information. We present some simple yet effective ways motivated by the AMR guideline to deal with this issue.

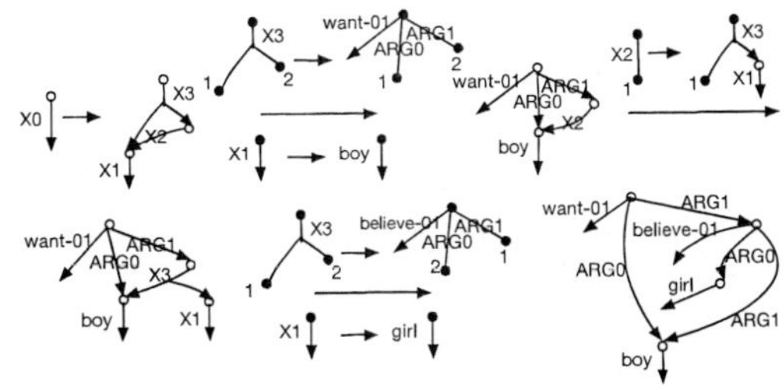

Figure 2: The series of HRG rules applied to derive the AMR graph of "The boy wants the girl to believe him". The first rule is directly shown. The other HRG rules are either above or below each right arrow. The white circle shows the root of each hyperedge. The indexes in each rule show the one-to-one mapping between the attachment nodes of l.h.s. nonterminal edges and the external nodes of the r.h.s. subgraph

2 Hyperedge Replacement Grammar

Hyperedge replacement grammar (HRG) is a context-free rewriting formalism for graph generation (Drewes et al., 1997). HRG is like CFG in that it rewrites nonterminals independently. While CFG generates natural language strings by successively rewriting nonterminal tokens, the nonterminals in HRG are hyperedges, and each rewriting step in HRG replaces a hyperedge nonterminal with a subgraph instead of a span of a string.

2.1 Definitions

In this paper we only use edge-labeled graphs because using both node and edge labels complicates the definitions in our HRG-based approach. Figure 2 shows a series of HRG rules applied to derive the AMR graph shown in Figure 1.

We start with the definition of hypergraphs. An *edge-labeled, directed hypergraph* is a tuple $H = \langle V, E, l, X \rangle$, where V is a finite set of nodes, $E \subseteq V^+$ is a finite set of hyperedges, each of which will connect to one or more nodes in V. $l : E \rightarrow L$ defines a mapping from each hyperedge to its label from a finite set L. Each hyperedge is an atomic item with an ordered list of nodes it connects to, which are called attachment nodes. The *type* of a hyperedge is defined as the number of its attachment nodes. $X \in V^*$ defines an ordered list of distinct nodes called *external nodes*. The ordered external nodes specify how to fuse a hypergraph with another graph, as we will see below. In this paper, we alternately use the terms of hypergraph and graph, hyperedge and edge, and also phrase, substring and span for brevity.

An HRG is a rewriting formalism $G = \langle N, T, P, S \rangle$, where N and T define two disjoint finite sets called nonterminals and terminals. $S \in N$ is a special nonterminal called the start symbol. P is a finite set of productions of the form $A \rightarrow R$, where $A \in N$ and R is a hypergraph with edge labels over $N \cup T$ and with nonempty external nodes X_R. We have the constraint that the type of the hyperedge with label A should coincide with the number of nodes in X_R. In our grammar, each nonterminal has the form of Xn, where n indicates the type of the hyperedge. Our special start symbol is separately denoted as $X0$.

The rewriting mechanism replaces a nonterminal hyperedge with the graph fragment specified by a production's righthand side (r.h.s), attaching each external node of the r.h.s. to the corresponding attachment node of the lefthand side. Take Figure 2 as an example. Starting from our initial hypergraph with one edge labeled with the start symbol "$X0$", we select one edge with nonterminal label in our current hypergraph, and rewrite it using a rule in our HRG. The first rule rewrites the start symbol with a subgraph shown on the r.h.s.. We continue the rewriting steps until there are no more nonterminal-labeled edges.

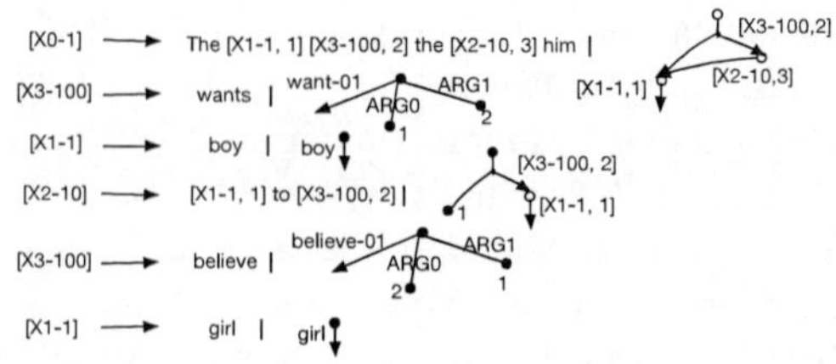

Figure 3: A series of symbol-refined SHRG rules used to derive the AMR graph for the sentence "The boy wants the girl to believe him".

The synchronous counterpart of HRG can be used for transforming graphs from/to another form of natural language representation. Productions have the form $(A \rightarrow \langle S, R \rangle, \sim)$, where $A \in N$ and S and R are called the source and the target and at least one of them should be hypergraphs over $N \cup T$. $\sim$ is a bijection linking nonterminals mentions in S and R. In our case, the source side is a CFG and the target side is an HRG. Given such a synchronous grammar and a string as input, we can parse the string with the CFG side and then derive the counterpart graph by deduction from the derivation. The benefit of parsing with SHRG is that the complexity is bounded by a CFG-like parsing.

2.2 SHRG-based AMR graph parsing

We write down AMR graphs as rooted, directed, edge-labeled graphs. There is exactly one leaf edge going out of each node, the label of which represents the concept of the node. We define this leaf edge as **concept edge**. In Figure 1, for example, the edge labeled with "boy", "want-01", "girl" or "believe-01" connects to only one node in the AMR graph and each label represents the concept of that node. AMR concepts are either English words ("boy"), PropBank framesets ("want-01"), or special keywords like special entity types, quantities, and logical conjunctions. The label of each non-leaf edge shows the relation between the AMR concepts of the two nodes it connects to.

The constraint of having exactly one concept edge for each node is not guaranteed in general SHRG. Our strategy for maintaining the AMR graph structure is to refine the edge nonterminal label with an extra binary flag, representing whether it will have a concept edge in the final rewriting result, for each external node. The basic intuition is to explicitly enforce the one concept edge constraint in each nonterminal so that no additional concept edge is introduced after applying each rule. The graph derived from this type of SHRG is guaranteed to have exactly one concept edge at each node.

Figure 3 shows one example of our symbol-refined SHRG. For each nonterminal $Xi\text{-}b_1 \cdots b_i$, i defines the type of the nonterminal, while each b_i indicates whether the i-th external node will have a concept edge in the rewriting result.[1] The second rule, for example, rewrites nonterminal $X3$-100 with *wants* on the string side and a hypergraph with three external nodes where the root has a concept edge *:want-01* as the first binary flag 1 indicates, while the other two external nodes do not with the binary flag 0. This guarantees that when we integrate the r.h.s. into another graph, it will introduce the concept edge *:want-01* to the first fusing position and no concept edge to the next two.

While this refinement might result in an exponential number of nonterminals with respect to the maximum type of hyperedges, we found in our experiment that most of the nonterminals do not appear in our grammar. We use a maximum edge type of 5, which also results in a relatively small nonterminal set.

3 Sampling SHRG from forests

The fragment decomposition forest provides a compact representation of all possible SHRG rules that are consistent with a fixed string-to-graph alignment. Each SHRG rule in the derivation is in essence the decomposition of larger phrase, graph fragment pairs on the left hand side (l.h.s.) into smaller ones on the r.h.s. and is encoded in a tree fragment in the forest. Our goal is to learn an SHRG from this forest. We first build a forest representation of possible derivations and then use an MCMC algorithm to sample tree fragments from this forest representing each rule in the derivation.

3.1 Fragment Decomposition Forest

We first proceed to define the **fragment decomposition forest**. The fragment decomposition forest is a variation of the phrase decomposition forest defined by Chung et al. (2014) where the target side is a graph instead of a string.

A **phrase** $p = [i, j]$ is a set of continuous word indices $\{i, i+1, \ldots, j-1\}$. A **fragment** f is a hypergraph with external nodes X_f. A string-to-graph alignment $h : P \to F$ defines the mapping from spans in the sentence to fragments in the graph. Our smallest phrase-fragment pairs are the string-to-graph alignments extracted using heuristic rules from Flanigan et al. (2014). The figure above shows an example of the alignments for the sentence "The boy wants the girl to believe him". The symbol $\emptyset$ represents that the word is not aligned to any concept in the AMR graph and this word is called an **unaligned word**. After this alignment, there are also left-over edges that are not aligned from any substrings, which are called **unaligned edges**.

Given an aligned string, AMR graph pair, a phrase-fragment pair n is a pair $([i, j], f)$ which defines a pair of a phrase $[i, j]$ and a fragment f such that words in positions $[i, j]$ are only aligned to concepts in the fragment f and vice versa (with unaligned words and edges omitted). A fragment forest $H = \langle V, E \rangle$ is a hypergraph made of a set of hypernodes V and hyperedges E. Each node $n = ([i, j], f)$ is **tight** on the string side similar to the definition by Koehn et al. (2003), i.e., n contains no unaligned words at its boundaries. Note here we do not have the constraint that f should be connected or single rooted, but we will deal with these constraints separately in the sampling procedure.

We define two phrases $[i_1, j_1], [i_2, j_2]$ to be *adjacent* if word indices $\{j_1, j_1 + 1, \ldots, i_2 - 1\}$ are all unaligned. We also define two fragments $f_1 = \langle V_1, E_1 \rangle, f_2 = \langle V_2, E_2 \rangle$ to be *disjoint* if $E_1 \cap E_2 = \emptyset$. And f_1 and f_2 are adjacent if they are disjoint and $f = \langle V_1 \cup V_2, E_1 \cup E_2 \rangle$ is connected. We also define the *compose* operation of two nodes: it takes two nodes $n_1 = ([i_1, j_1], f_1)$ and $n_2 = ([i_2, j_2], f_2)$ ($j_1 \leq i_2$) as input, and computes $f = \langle V_1 \cup V_2, E_1 \cup E_2 \rangle$, the output is a composed node $n = ([i_1, j_2], f)$. We say n_1 and n_2 are *immediately adjacent* if f is connected and single-rooted.

We keep composing larger phrase-fragment

[1] $X0$-1 is different as $X0$ is the start symbol of type one and should always have a concept edge at the root

Figure 4: The fragment decomposition forest for the (sentence, AMR graph) pair for "The boy wants the girl to believe him"

pairs (each one kept in a node of the forest) from smaller ones until we reach the root of the forest whose phrase side is the whole sentence and the fragment side is the complete AMR graph. We define **fragment decomposition forest** to be made of all possible phrase-fragments pairs that can be decomposed from the sentence AMR graph pair. The fragment decomposition forest has the important property that any SHRG rule consistent with the string-to-graph alignment corresponds to a continuous tree fragment of a complete tree found in the forest.

While we can compose larger phrases from smaller ones from left to right, there is no explicit order of composing the graph fragments. Also, the number of possible graph fragments is highly exponential as we need to make a binary decision to decide each boundary node of the fragment and also choose the edges going out of each boundary node of the fragment, unlike the polynomial numbers of phrases for fixed string alignment.

Our bottom-up construction procedure starts from the smallest phrase-fragment pairs. We first index these smallest phrase-fragment pairs $([i_k, j_k], f_k), k = 1, 2, \ldots, n$ based on ascending order of their start positions on the string side, i.e., $j_k \leq i_{k+1}$ for $k = 1, 2, \ldots, n-1$. Even with this left-to-right order constraint from the string side, the complexity of building the forest is still exponential due to the possible choices in attaching graphs edges that are not aligned to the string. Our strategy is to deterministically attach each unaligned relation edge to one of the identified concept fragments it connects to. We attach *ARG*s and *op*s to its head node and each other types of unaligned relations to its tail node.[2]

Algorithm 1 A CYK-like algorithm for building a fragment decomposition forest

1: For each smallest phrase-fragment pairs $([i_k, j_k], f_k)$, $k = 1, 2, \ldots, n$, attach unaligned edges to fragment f_k, denoting the result as f'_k. Build a node for $([i_k, j_k], f'_k)$ and add it to chart item $c[k][k+1]$.
2: Extract all the remaining unaligned fragments, build a special unaligned node for each of them and add it to unaligned node set $unaligned\_nodes$
3: Keep composing unaligned nodes with nodes in different chart items if they are immediate adjacent and add it to the same chart item
4: **for** $span$ from 2 to n **do**
5:   **for** i from 1 to n-$span$+1 **do**
6:     $j = i + span$
7:     **for** k from $i+1$ to $j-1$ **do**
8:       **for** $n1 = ([start_1, end_1], f_1)$ in $c[i][k]$ **do**
9:         **for** $n2 = ([start_2, end_2], f_2)$ in $c[k][j]$ **do**
10:           **if** f_1 and f_2 are disjoint **then**
11:             $new\_node = compose(n1, n2)$
12:             add incoming edge $(n1, n2)$ to new_node
13:             **if** n_1 and n_2 are not *immediate adjacent* **then**
14:               $new\_node.nosample\_cut$=True
15:             *insert_node*(new_node, $c[i][j]$)

Algorithm 1 shows our CYK-like forest construction algorithm. We maintain the length 1 chart items according to the order of each smallest phrase-fragment pair instead of its position in the string.[3] In line 1, we first attach unaligned edges to the smallest phrase-fragment pairs as stated before. After this procedure, we build a node for the k-th phrase-fragment (with unaligned edges added) pair and add it to chart item $c[k][k+1]$. Note here that we still have remaining unaligned edges; in line 2 we attach all unaligned edges going out from the same node as a single fragment and build a special **unaligned node** with empty phrase side and add it to $unaligned\_nodes$ set. In line 3, we try to compose each unaligned node with one of the nodes in the length 1 chart items $c[k][k+1]$. If they are immediately adjacent, we add the composed node to $c[k][k+1]$. The algorithm then composes smaller phrase-fragment pairs into larger ones (line 4). When we have composed two nodes n_1, n_2, we need to keep track

[2]Our intuition is that the ARG types for verbs and ops structure usually go with the concept of the head node. We assume that other relations are additional introduced to the head node, which resembles a simple binarization step for other relations.

[3]We use this strategy mainly because the alignments available do not have overlapping alignments, while our algorithm could still be easily adapted to a version that maintains the chart items with string positions when overlapping alignments are available

of this incoming edge. We have the constraint in our grammar that the r.h.s. hypergraph of each rule should be connected and single rooted.[4] Lines 13 to 14 enforce this constraint by marking this node with a *nosample_cut* flag, which we will use in the MCMC sampling stage. The *insert_node* function will check if the node already exists in the chart item. If it already exists, then we only update the incoming edges for that node. Otherwise we will add it to the chart item.

For some sentence-AMR pairs where there are too many nodes with unaligned edges going out, considering all possible compositions would result in huge complexity overhead. One solution we have adopted is to disallow disconnected graph fragments and do not add them to the chart items (Line 15). In practice, this pruning procedure does not affect much of the final performance in our current setting. Figure 4 shows the procedure of building the fragment decomposition forest for the sentence "The boy wants the girl to believe him".

3.2 MCMC sampling

Sampling methods have been used to learn Tree Substitution Grammar (TSG) rules from derivation trees (Cohn et al., 2009; Post and Gildea, 2009) for TSG learning. The basic intuition is to automatically learn the best granularity for the rules with which to analyze our data. Our problem, however, is different in that we need to sample rules from a compact forest representation. We need to sample one tree from the forest, and then sample one derivation from this tree structure, where each tree fragment represents one rule in the derivation. Sampling tree fragments from forests is described in detail in Chung et al. (2014) and Peng and Gildea (2014).

We formulate the rule sampling procedure with two types of variables: an edge variable e_n representing which incoming hyperedge is chosen at a given node n in the forest (allowing us to sample one tree from a forest) and a cut variable z_n representing whether node n in forest is a boundary between two SHRG rules or is internal to an SHRG rule (allowing us to sample rules from a tree). Figure 5 shows one sampled derivation from the forest. We have sampled one tree from the forest using the edge variables. We also have a 0-1 variable at each node in this tree where 0 represents the current node is internal to an SHRG rule, while 1 represents the current node is the boundary of two SHRG rules.

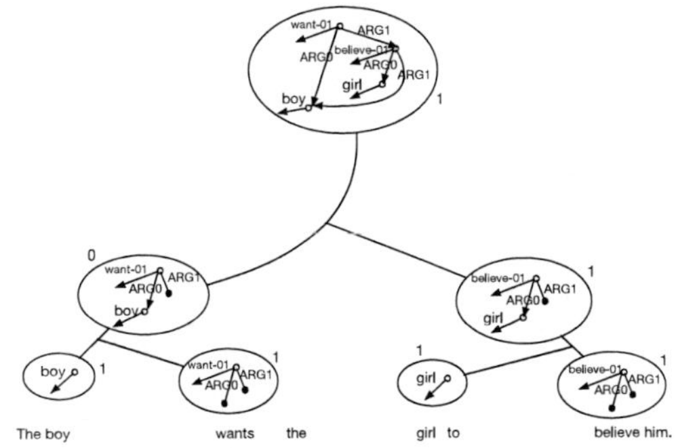

Figure 5: The sampled derivation for the (sentence, AMR graph) pair for "The boy wants the girl to believe him"

Let all the edge variables form the random vector Y and all the cut variables form the random vector Z. Given an assignment y to the edge variables and assignment z to the cut variables, our desired distribution is proportional to the product of weights of the rules specified by the assignment:

$$P_t(Y = y, Z = z) \propto \prod_{r \in \tau(y,z)} w(r) \qquad (1)$$

where $\tau(y, z)$ is the set of rules identified by the assignment and $w(r)$ is the weight for each individual rule. We use a generative model based on a Dirichlet Process (DP) defined over composed rules. We draw a distribution G over rules from a DP, and then rules from G.

$$G \mid \alpha, P_0 \sim Dir(\alpha, P_0)$$
$$r \mid G \sim G$$

We define two rules to have the same **rule type** if they have the same string and hypergraph representation (including order of external nodes) on the r.h.s..For the base distribution P_0, we use a uniform distribution where all rules of the same size have equal probability. By marginalizing out G we get a simple posterior distribution over rules which can be derived using the Chinese Restaurant Process (CRP). We define a table of counts $N = \{N_C\}_{C \in I}$ which memorizes different categories of counts in the previous assignments, where I is an index set for different categories of counts. Each N_C is a vector of counts for category C. We

[4]We should be able to get rid of both constraints as we are parsing on the string side.

have the following probability over rule r given the previous count table N:

$$P(r_i = r|N) = \frac{N_R(r) + \alpha P_0(r)}{n + \alpha} \quad (2)$$

here in the case of DP, $I = \{R\}$, where R is the index for the category of rule counts.

We use the *top-down* sampling algorithm of Chung et al. (2014) which samples cut and edge variables from top down and one at a time. For each node n, we denote the composed rule type that we get when we set the cut of node n to 0 as r_1 and the two split rule types that we get when we set the cut to 1 as r_2, r_3. We sample the cut value z_i of the current node according to the posterior probability:

$$P(z_i = z|N) = \begin{cases} \frac{P(r_1|N)}{P(r_1|N)+P(r_2|N)P(r_3|N')} & \text{if } z = 0 \\ \frac{P(r_2|N)P(r_3|N')}{P(r_1|N)+P(r_2|N)P(r_3|N')} & \text{otherwise} \end{cases} \quad (3)$$

where the posterior probability $P(r_i|N)$ is according to a DP, and N, N' are tables of counts. In the case of DP, N, N' differ only in the rule counts of r_2, where $N'_R(r_2) = N_R(r_2) + 1$.

As for edge variables e_i, we refer to the set of composed rules turned on below n including the composed rule fragments having n as an internal or root node as $\{r_1, \ldots, r_m\}$. We have the following posterior probability over the edge variable e_i:

$$P(e_i = e|N) \propto \prod_{i=1}^{m} P(r_i|N^{i-1}) \prod_{v \in \tau(e) \cap \text{in}(n)} \deg(v) \quad (4)$$

where $\deg(v)$ is the number of incoming edges for node v, $\text{in}(n)$ is the set of nodes in all subtrees under n, and $\tau(e)$ is the tree specified when we set $e_i = e$. N^0 to N^m are tables of counts where $N^0 = N$, $N^i_R(r_i) = N^{i-1}_R(r_i) + 1$ in the case of DP.

After we have sampled one SHRG derivation from the forest, we still need to keep track of the place where each nonterminal edge attaches. As we have maintained the graph fragment it represents in each node of the forest, we can retrieve the attachment nodes of each hyperedge in the r.h.s. by tracing at which graph nodes two fragments fuse with each other. We perform this rule extraction procedure from top-down and maintain the order of attachment nodes of each r.h.s. nonterminal edge. When we further rewrite a nonterminal edge, we need to make sure that it keeps the order of the attachment nodes in its parent rule. As for the unaligned words, we just insert all the omitted unaligned words in the composition procedure. We also add additional rules including the surrounding 2 unaligned words context to make sure there are terminals on the string side.

3.3 Phrase-to-Graph-Fragment Alignment Extraction

Aside from the rules sampled using the MCMC algorithm, we also extract a phrase-to-graph-fragment alignment table from the fragment decomposition forest. This step can be considered as a mapping of larger phrases made of multiple identified spans (plus unaligned words) to a larger fragments made of multiple concept fragments (plus the way they connect using unaligned edges).

Our extraction happens along with the forest construction procedure. In line 1 of Algorithm 1 we extract one rule for each smallest phrase-fragment pairs before and after the unaligned edges are attached. We also extract one rule for each newly constructed node after line 11 if the fragment side of the node is single-rooted.[5] We do not extract rules after line 2 because it usually introduces additional noise of meaningful concepts which are unrecognized in the concepts identification stage.

4 Decoding

4.1 Concept identification

During the decoding stage, first we need to identify meaningful spans in the sentence and map them to graph fragments on the graph side. Then we use SHRG rules to parse each sentence from bottom up and left to right, which is similar to constituent parsing. The recall of the concept identification stage from Flanigan et al. (2014) is 0.79, which means 21% of the meaningful concepts are already lost at the beginning of the next stage.

Our strategy is to use lemma and POS tags information after the concept identification stage, we use it to recall some meaningful concepts. We find that, except for some special function words, most nouns, verbs and, adjectives should be aligned. We use the lemma information to retrieve unaligned words whose morphological form does not appear in our training data. We also use

[5]Here we will also look at the surrounding 2 unaligned words to fix partial alignment and noise introduced by meaningful unaligned words

POS tag information to deal with nouns and quantities. Motivated by the fact that AMR makes extensive use of PropBank framesets, we look up the argument structure of the verbs from the PropBank. Although the complicated abstraction of AMR makes it hard to get the correct concept for each word, the more complete structure can reduce the propagation of errors along the derivation tree.

4.2 AMR graph parsing

We use Earley algorithm with cube-pruning (Chiang, 2007) for the string-to-AMR parsing. For each synchronous rule with N nonterminals on its l.h.s., we build an $N+1$ dimensional cube and generate top K candidates. Out of all the hypotheses generated by all satisfied rules within each span (i, j),we keep at most K candidates for this span. Our glue rules will create a pseudo $R/ROOT$ concept and use ARGs relations to connect disconnected components to make a connected graph.

We use the following local features:

1. StringToGraphProbability: the probability of a hypergraph given the input string
2. RuleCount: number of rules used to compose the AMR graph
3. RuleEdgeCount: the number of edges in the r.h.s. hypergraph
4. EdgeType: the type of the l.h.s. nonterminal. For rules with same source side tokens, we prefer rules with smaller edge types.
5. AllNonTerminalPunish: one for rules which only have non-terminals on the source side.
6. GlueCount: one for glue rules.

As our forest structure is highly binarized, it is hard to capture the *:op*n structure when n is large because we limit the number of external nodes to 5. The most common *:op* structure in the AMR annotation is the coordinate structure of items separated by ";" or separated by "," along with and. We add the following two rules:

$$[X1\text{-}1]- > [X1\text{-}1, 1]; [X1\text{-}1, 2]; \cdots ; [X1\text{-}1, n] \mid$$

$$(.\ \textit{:a/and :op1}\ [X1\text{-}1, 1]\ \textit{:op2}\ [X1\text{-}1, 2] \cdots \textit{:op}n\ [X1\text{-}1, n])$$

$$[X1\text{-}1]- > [X1\text{-}1, 1], [X1\text{-}1, 2], \cdots\ \textit{and}\ [X1\text{-}1, n] \mid$$

$$(.\ \textit{:a/and :op1}\ [X1\text{-}1, 1]\ \textit{:op2}\ [X1\text{-}1, 2] \cdots \textit{:op}n\ [X1\text{-}1, n])$$

where the HRG side is a *:a/and* coordinate structure of $X1$-1s connected with relation *:op*s.

5 Experiments

	Precision	Recall	F-score
Concept id only	0.37	0.53	0.44
+ MCMC	0.57	0.53	0.55
+ MCMC + phrase table	0.60	0.54	0.57
+ All	0.59	0.58	0.58

Table 1: Comparisons of different strategies of extracting lexical rules on dev.

We use the same newswire section of LDC2013E117 as Flanigan et al. (2014), which consists of 3955 training sentences, 2132 dev sentences and 2132 test sentences. We also use the string-to-graph alignment from Flanigan et al. (2014) to construct the fragment decomposition forest and to extract the phrase-to-fragment table.

In the fragment decomposition forest construction procedure, we have experimented with different ways of dealing with the unaligned edges. First we have tried to directly use the alignment, and group all unaligned edges going out from the same node as an unaligned fragment. Using this constraint would take a few hours or longer for some sentences. The reason for this is because the many number of unaligned edges can connect to each branch of the aligned or unaligned fragments below it. And there is no explicit order of composition with each branch. Another constraint we have tried is to attach all unaligned edges to the head node concept. The problem with this constraint is that it is very hard to generalize and introduces a lot of additional redundant relation edges.

As for sampling, we initialize all cut variables in the forest as 1 (except for nodes that are marked as $nosample\_cut$, which indicates we initialize it with 0 and keep it fixed) and uniformly sample an incoming edge for each node. We evaluate the performance of our SHRG-based parser using Smatch v1.0 (Cai and Knight, 2013), which evaluates the precision, recall and $F1$ of the concepts and relations all together. Table 1 shows the dev results of our sampled grammar using different lexical rules that maps substrings to graph fragments. Concept id only is the result of using the concepts identified by Flanigan et al. (2014). From second line, we replace the concept identification result with the lexical rules we have extracted from the training data (except for named entities and time expressions). +MCMC shows the result using additional alignments identified using our sampling approach. We can see that using the phrase to graph fragment alignment learned from our training data can significantly improve the smatch. We have also tried extracting all phrase-to-fragment

	Precision	Recall	F-score
JAMR	0.67	0.58	0.62
Wang et al.	0.64	0.62	0.63
Our approach	0.59	0.57	0.58

Table 2: Comparisons of smatch score results

alignments of length 6 on the string side from our constructed forest. We can see that using this alignment table further improves the smatch score. This is because the larger phrase-fragment pairs can make better use of the dependency information between continuous concepts. The improvement is not much in comparison with MCMC, this is perhaps MCMC can also learn some meaning blocks that frequently appear together. As the dataset is relatively small, so there are a lot of meaningful concepts that are not aligned. We use lemma as a backoff strategy to find the alignment for the unaligned words. We have also used the POS tag information to retrieve some unaligned nouns and a PropBank dictionary to retrieve the argument structure of the first sense of the verbs. +All shows the result after using lemma, POS tag and PropBank information, we can see that fixing the alignment can improve the recall, but the precision does not change much.

Table 2 shows our result on test data. JAMR is the baseline result from Flanigan et al. (2014). Wang et al. (2015) shows the current state-of-art for string-to-AMR parsing. Without the dependency parse information and complex global features, our SHRG-based approach can already achieve competitive results in comparison with these two algorithms.

6 Discussion

In comparison to the spanning tree algorithm of Flanigan et al. (2014), an SHRG-based approach is more sensitive to the alignment. If a lot of the meaningful concepts are not aligned, then the lost information would break down the structure of our grammar. Using more data would definitely help ease this issue. Building overlapping alignments for the training data with more concepts alignment would also be helpful.

Another thing to note is that Flanigan et al. (2014) have used path information of dependency arc labels and part of speech tags. Using these global information can help the predication of the relation edge labels. One interesting way to include such kind of path information is to add a graph language model into our CFG decoder, which should also help improve the performance.

All the weights of the local features mentioned in Section 4.2 are tuned by hand. We have tried tuning with MERT (Och, 2003), but the computation of smatch score for the k-best list has become a major overhead. This issue might come from the NP-Completeness of the problem smatch tries to evaluate, unlike the simple counting of N-grams in BLEU (Papineni et al., 2001). Parallelization might be a consideration for tuning smatch score with MERT.

7 Conclusion

We presented an MCMC sampling schedule for learning SHRG rules from a fragment decomposition forest constructed from a fixed string-to-AMR-graph alignment. While the complexity of building a fragment decomposition forest is highly exponential, we have come up with an effective constraint from the string side that enables an efficient construction algorithm. We have also evaluated our sampled SHRG on a string-to-AMR graph parsing task and achieved some reasonable result without using a dependency parse. Interesting future work might include adding language model on graph structure and also learning SHRG from overlapping alignments.

Acknowledgments Funded by NSF IIS-1446996, NSF IIS-1218209, the 2014 Jelinek Memorial Workshop, and a Google Faculty Research Award. We are grateful to Jeff Flanigan for providing the results of his concept identification.

References

Laura Banarescu, Claire Bonial, Shu Cai, Madalina Georgescu, Kira Griffitt, Ulf Hermjakob, Kevin Knight, Philipp Koehn, Martha Palmer, and Nathan Schneider. 2013. Abstract meaning representation for sembanking. In *Proceedings of the 7th Linguistic Annotation Workshop and Interoperability with Discourse*.

Shu Cai and Kevin Knight. 2013. Smatch: an evaluation metric for semantic feature structures. In *ACL (2)*, pages 748–752.

David Chiang, Jacob Andreas, Daniel Bauer, Karl Moritz Hermann, Bevan Jones, and Kevin Knight. 2013. Parsing graphs with hyperedge replacement grammars. In *Proceedings of the 51st Annual Meeting of the Association for Computational Linguistics (Volume 1: Long Papers)*, pages 924–932.

David Chiang. 2007. Hierarchical phrase-based translation. *Computational Linguistics*, 33(2):201–228.

Tagyoung Chung, Licheng Fang, Daniel Gildea, and Daniel Štefankovič. 2014. Sampling tree fragments from forests. *Computational Linguistics*, 40:203–229.

Trevor Cohn, Sharon Goldwater, and Phil Blunsom. 2009. Inducing compact but accurate tree-substitution grammars. In *Proceedings of Human Language Technologies: The 2009 Annual Conference of the North American Chapter of the Association for Computational Linguistics*, pages 548–556, Boulder, Colorado, June. Association for Computational Linguistics.

Donald Davidson. 1967. The logical form of action sentences. In Nicholas Rescher, editor, *The Logic of Decision and Action*, pages 81–120. Univ. of Pittsburgh Press.

Frank Drewes, Hans-Jörg Kreowski, and Annegret Habel. 1997. Hyperedge replacement, graph grammars. In *Handbook of Graph Grammars*, volume 1, pages 95–162. World Scientific, Singapore.

Jeffrey Flanigan, Sam Thomson, Jaime Carbonell, Chris Dyer, and Noah A Smith. 2014. A discriminative graph-based parser for the abstract meaning representation. In *Proc. of ACL*, pages 1426–1436.

Bevan Jones, Jacob Andreas, Daniel Bauer, Karl Moritz Hermann, and Kevin Knight. 2012. Semantics-based machine translation with hyperedge replacement grammars. In *COLING*, pages 1359–1376.

Philipp Koehn, Franz Josef Och, and Daniel Marcu. 2003. Statistical phrase-based translation. In *Proceedings of NAACL-03*, pages 48–54, Edmonton, Alberta.

Franz Josef Och. 2003. Minimum error rate training for statistical machine translation. In *Proceedings of ACL-03*, pages 160–167, Sapporo, Japan.

K. Papineni, S. Roukos, T. Ward, and W.-J. Zhu. 2001. BLEU: a method for automatic evaluation of MT. Technical Report Research Report, Computer Science RC22176 (W0109-022), IBM Research Division, T.J.Watson Research Center.

Terence Parsons. 1990. *Events in the Semantics of English*, volume 5. Cambridge, Ma: MIT Press.

Xiaochang Peng and Daniel Gildea. 2014. Type-based MCMC for sampling tree fragments from forests. In *Conference on Empirical Methods in Natural Language Processing (EMNLP-14)*.

Matt Post and Daniel Gildea. 2009. Bayesian learning of a tree substitution grammar. In *Proc. Association for Computational Linguistics (short paper)*, pages 45–48, Singapore.

Nima Pourdamghani, Yang Gao, Ulf Hermjakob, and Kevin Knight. 2014. Aligning english strings with abstract meaning representation graphs. In *Proceedings of the 2014 Conference on Empirical Methods in Natural Language Processing (EMNLP)*, pages 425–429.

Chuan Wang, Nianwen Xue, and Sameer Pradhan. 2015. A transition-based algorithm for amr parsing. In *Proceedings of the 2015 Conference of the North American Chapter of the Association for Computational Linguistics: Human Language Technologies*, pages 366–375, Denver, Colorado, May–June. Association for Computational Linguistics.

AIDA2: A Hybrid Approach for Token and Sentence Level Dialect Identification in Arabic

Mohamed Al-Badrashiny, Heba Elfardy[†] and Mona Diab
Department of Computer Science, The George Washington University
{badrashiny,mtdiab}@gwu.edu
[†]Department of Computer Science, Columbia University
[†]heba@cs.columbia.edu

Abstract

In this paper, we present a hybrid approach for performing token and sentence levels Dialect Identification in Arabic. Specifically we try to identify whether each token in a given sentence belongs to Modern Standard Arabic (MSA), Egyptian Dialectal Arabic (EDA) or some other class and whether the whole sentence is mostly EDA or MSA. The token level component relies on a Conditional Random Field (CRF) classifier that uses decisions from several underlying components such as language models, a named entity recognizer and and a morphological analyzer to label each word in the sentence. The sentence level component uses a classifier ensemble system that relies on two independent underlying classifiers that model different aspects of the language. Using a feature-selection heuristic, we select the best set of features for each of these two classifiers. We then train another classifier that uses the class labels and the confidence scores generated by each of the two underlying classifiers to decide upon the final class for each sentence. The token level component yields a new state of the art F-score of 90.6% (compared to previous state of the art of 86.8%) and the sentence level component yields an accuracy of 90.8% (compared to 86.6% obtained by the best state of the art system).

1 Introduction

In this age of social media ubiquity, we note the pervasive presence of informal language mixed in with formal language. Degree of mixing formal and informal language registers varies across languages making it ever harder to process. The problem is quite pronounced in Arabic where the difference between the formal modern standard Arabic (MSA) and the informal dialects of Arabic (DA) could add up to a difference in language morphologically, lexically, syntactically, semantically and pragmatically, exacerbating the challenges for almost all NLP tasks. MSA is used in formal settings, edited media, and education. On the other hand the spoken, and, currently written in social media and penetrating formal media, are the informal vernaculars. There are multiple dialects corresponding to different parts of the Arab world: (1) Egyptian, (2) Levantine, (3) Gulf, (4) Moroccan, and, (5) Iraqi. For each one of these sub-dialectal variants exist. Speakers/writers code switch between the two forms of the language especially in social media text both inter and intra sententially. Automatically identifying code-switching between variants of the same language (Dialect Identification) is quite challenging due to the lexical overlap and significant semantic and pragmatic variation yet it is crucial as a preprocessing step before building any Arabic NLP tool. MSA trained tools perform very badly when applied directly to DA or to intrasentential code-switched DA and MSA text (ex. *Alfryq fAz bAlEAfyp bs tSdr qA}mp Aldwry*, where the words correspond to MSA MSA DA DA MSA MSA MSA, respectively)[1]. Dialect Identification has been shown to be an important preprocessing step for statistical machine Translation (SMT). (Salloum et al., 2014) explored the impact of using Dialect Identification on the performance of MT and found that it improves the results. They trained four different SMT systems; (a) DA-to-English SMT, (b) MSA-to-English SMT, (c) DA + MSA-to-English SMT, and (d) DA-to-English hybrid MT system and treated the task of choosing

[1]We use Buckwalter transliteration scheme to represent Arabic in Romanized script throughout the paper. http://www.qamus.org/transliteration.htm

Proceedings of the 19th Conference on Computational Language Learning, pages 42–51,
Beijing, China, July 30-31, 2015.

which SMT system to invoke as a classification task. They built a classifier that uses various features derived from the input sentence and that indicate, among other things, how dialectal the input sentence is and found that this approach improved the performance by 0.9% BLEU points.

In this paper, we address the problem of token and sentence levels dialect identification in Arabic, specifically between Egyptian Arabic and MSA. For the token level task, we treat the problem as a sequence labeling task by training a CRF classifier that relies on the decisions made by a language model, a morphological analyzer, a shallow named entity recognition system, a modality lexicon and other features pertaining to the sentence statistics to decide upon the class of each token in the given sentence. For the sentence level task we resort to a classifier ensemble approach that combines independent decisions made by two classifiers and use their decisions to train a new one. The proposed approaches for both tasks significantly beat the current state of the art performance with a significant margin, while creating a pipelined system.

2 Related Work

Dialect Identification in Arabic has recently gained interest among Arabic NLP researchers. Early work on the topic focused on speech data. Biadsy et al. (2009) presented a system that identifies dialectal words in speech through acoustic signals. More recent work targets textual data. The main task for textual data is to decide the class of each word in a given sentence; whether it is *MSA*, *EDA* or some other class such as Named-Entity or punctuation and whether the whole sentence is mostly *MSA* or *EDA*. The first task is referred to as "Token Level Dialect Identification" while the second is "Sentence Level Dialect Identification".

For sentence level dialect identification in Arabic, the most recent works are (Zaidan and Callison-Burch, 2011), (Elfardy and Diab, 2013), and (Cotterell and Callison-Burch, 2014a). Zaidan and Callison-Burch (2011) annotate MSA-DA news commentaries on Amazon Mechanical Turk and explore the use of a language-modeling based approach to perform sentence-level dialect identification. They target three Arabic dialects; Egyptian, Levantine and Gulf and develop different models to distinguish each of them against the others and against MSA. They achieve an accuracy of 80.9%, 79.6%, and 75.1% for the Egyptian-MSA, Levantine-MSA, and Gulf-MSA classification, respectively. These results support the common assumption that Egyptian, relative to the other Arabic dialectal variants, is the most distinct dialect variant of Arabic from MSA. Elfardy and Diab (2013) propose a supervised system to perform Egyptian Arabic Sentence Identification. They evaluate their approach on the Egyptian part of the dataset presented by Zaidan and Callison-Burch (2011) and achieve an accuracy of 85.3%. Cotterell and Callison-Burch (2014b) extend Zaidan and Callison-Burch (2011) work by handling two more dialects (Iraqi and Moroccan) and targeting a new genre, specifically tweets. Their system outperforms Zaidan and Callison-Burch (2011) and Elfardy and Diab (2013), achieving a classification accuracy of 89%, 79%, and 88% on the same Egyptian, Levantine and Gulf datasets. For token level dialect identification, King et al. (2014) use a language-independent approach that utilizes character n-gram probabilities, lexical probabilities, word label transition probabilities and existing named entity recognition tools within a Markov model framework.

Jain and Bhat (2014) use a CRF based token level language identification system that uses a set of easily computable features (ex. isNum, isPunc, etc.). Their analysis showed that the most important features are the word n-gram posterior probabilities and word morphology.

Lin et al. (2014) use a CRF model that relies on character n-grams probabilities (tri and quad grams), prefixes, suffixes, unicode page of the first character, capitalization case, alphanumeric case, and tweet-level language ID predictions from two off-the-shelf language identifiers: cld2[2] and ldig.[3] They increase the size of the training data using a semi supervised CRF autoencoder approach (Ammar et al., 2014) coupled with unsupervised word embeddings.

MSR-India (Chittaranjan et al., 2014) use character n-grams to train a maximum entropy classifier that identifies whether a word is *MSA* or *EDA*. The resultant labels are then used together with word length, existence of special characters in the word, current, previous and next words to train a CRF model that predicts the token level classes of words in a given sentence/tweet.

[2]https://code.google.com/p/cld2/

[3]https://github.com/shuyo/ldig

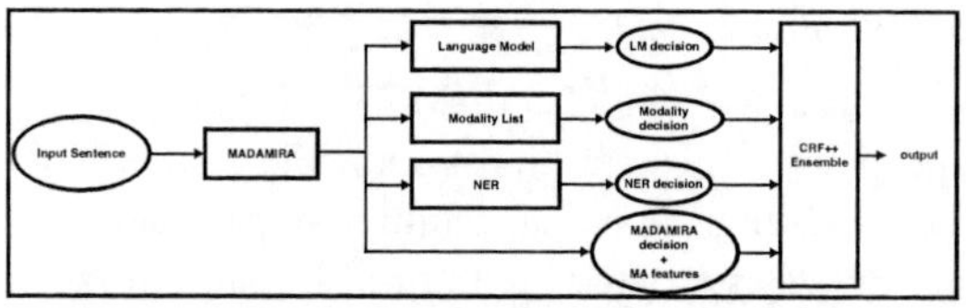

Figure 1: Token-level identification pipeline

In our previously published system *AIDA* (Elfardy et al., 2014) we use a weakly supervised rule based approach that relies on a language model to tag each word in the given sentence to be *MSA*, *EDA*, or *unk*. We then use the LM decision for each word in the given sentence/tweet and combine it with other morphological information, in addition to a named entity gazetteer to decide upon the final class of each word.

3 Approach

We introduce *AIDA*2. This is an improved version of our previously published tool *AIDA* (Elfardy et al., 2014). It tackles the problems of dialect identification in Arabic both on the token and sentence levels in mixed modern standard Arabic *MSA* and Egyptian dialect *EDA* text. We first classify each word in the input sentence to be one of the following six tags as defined in the shared task for "Language Identification in Code-Switched Data" in the first workshop on computational approaches to code-switching [ShTk](Solorio et al., 2014):

- *lang1*: If the token is *MSA* (ex. AlwAqE, "The reality")
- *lang2*: If the token is *EDA* (ex. m$, "Not")
- *ne*: If the token is a named entity (ex. >mrykA, "America")
- *ambig*: If the given context is not sufficient to identify the token as *MSA* or *EDA* (ex. slAm Elykm, "Peace be upon you")
- *mixed*: If the token is of mixed morphology (ex. b>myT meaning "I'm always removing")
- *other*: If the token is or is attached to any non Arabic token (ex. numbers, punctuation, Latin character, emoticons, etc)

The fully tagged tokens in the given sentence are then used in addition to some other features to classify the sentence as being mostly *MSA* or *EDA*.

3.1 Token Level Identification

Identifying the class of a token in a given sentence requires knowledge of its surrounding tokens since these surrounding tokens can be the trigger for identifying a word as being *MSA* or *EDA*. This suggests that the best way to approach the problem is by treating it as a sequence labeling task. Hence we use a Conditional Random Field (CRF) classifier to classify each token in the input sentence. The CRF is trained using decisions from the following underlying components:

- *MADAMIRA*: is a publicly available tool for morphological analysis and disambiguation of *EDA* and *MSA* text (Pasha et al., 2014).[4] *MADAMIRA* uses *SAMA* (Maamouri et al., 2010) to analyze the *MSA* words and *CALIMA* (Habash et al., 2012) for the *EDA* words. We use *MADAMIRA* to tokenize both the language model and input sentences using D3 tokenization-scheme, the most detailed level of tokenization provided by the tool (ex. bAlfryq, "By the team" becomes "b+ Al+ fryq")(Habash and Sadat, 2006). This is important in order to maximize the Language Models (LM) coverage. Furthermore, we also use *MADAMIRA* to tag each token in the input sentence as *MSA* or *EDA* by tagging the source of the morphological analysis, if *MADAMIRA*. analyses the word using *SAMA*, then the token is tagged *MSA* while if the analysis comes from *CALIMA*, the token is tagged *EDA*. Out of vocabulary words are tagged *unk*.
- *Language Model*: is a D3-tokenized 5-grams language model. It is built using the 119K manually annotated words of the training data of the shared task ShTk in addition to 8M words from weblogs data (4M from *MSA* sources and 4M from *EDA* ones). The weblogs are automatically annotated based on their source, namely, if the source of the data is dialectal, all the words from this source are tagged as *EDA*. Otherwise they are tagged *MSA*. Since we are using a D3-tokenized data, all D3 tokens of a word are assigned the same tag of their corresponding word (ex. if the word "bAlfryq" is tagged *MSA*, then each of "b+", "Al+", and "fryq" is tagged *MSA*). During runtime, the *Language Model* classifier module creates a lattice of all possible tags for each word in the input sentence after it is being tokenized by *MADAMIRA*. Viterbi search algorithm (Forney, 1973) is then used to find the best sequence of tags for the given sentence. If the input sentence contains out of vocabulary

[4]http://nlp.ldeo.columbia.edu/madamira/

words, they are being tagged as *unk*. This module also provides a binary flag called "*isMixed*". It is "true" only if the LM decisions for the prefix, stem, and suffix are not the same.

- *Modality List*: ModLex (Al-Sabbagh et al., 2013) is a manually compiled lexicon of Arabic modality triggers (i.e. words and phrases that convey modality). It provides the lemma with a context and the class of this lemma (*MSA*, *EDA*, or both) in that context. In our approach, we match the lemma of the input word that is provided by *MADAMIRA* and its surrounding context with an entry in ModLex. Then we assign this word the corresponding class from the lexicon. If we find more than one match, we use the class of the longest matched context. If there is no match, the word takes *unk* tag. Ex. the word "Sdq" which means "told the truth" gets the class "both" in this context ">flH An Sdq" meaning "He will succeed if he told the truth".
- *NER*: this is a shallow named entity recognition module. It provides a binary flag "*isNE*" for each word in the input sentence. This flag is set to "true" if the input word has been tagged as *ne*. It uses a list of all sequences of words that are tagged as *ne* in the training data of ShTk in addition to the named-entities from ANERGazet (Benajiba et al., 2007) to identify the named-entities in the input sentence. This module also checks the POS provided by *MADAMIRA* for each input word. If a token is tagged as *noun_prop* POS, then the token is classified as *ne*.

Using these four components, we generate the following features for each word:.

- *MADAMIRA-features*: the input word, prefix, stem, suffix, POS, *MADAMIRA* decision, and associated confidence score;
- *LM-features*: the "*isMixed*" flag in addition to the prefix-class, stem-class, suffix-class and the confidence score for each of them as provided by the language model;
- *Modality-features*: the *Modality List* decision;
- *NER-features*: the "*isNE*" flag from the *NER*;
- *Meta-features*: "*isOther*" is a binary flag that is set to "true" only if the input word is a non Arabic token. And "*hasSpeechEff*" which is another binary flag set to "true" only if the input word has speech effects (i.e. word lengthening).

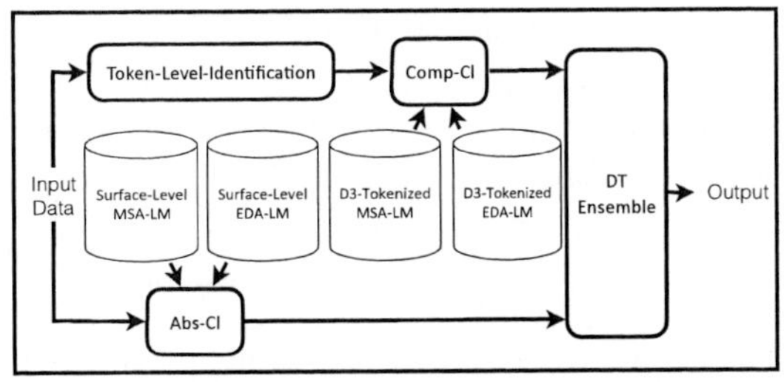

Figure 2: Sentence-level identification pipeline

We then use these features to train a CRF classifier using CRF++ toolkit (Sha and Pereira, 2003) and we set the window size to 16.[5] Figure 1 illustrates the different components of the token-level system.

3.2 Sentence Level Identification

For this level of identification, we rely on a classifier ensemble to generate the class label for each sentence. The underlying classifiers are trained on gold labeled data with sentence level binary decisions of either being *MSA* or *EDA*. Figure 2 shows the pipeline of the sentence level identification component. The pipeline consists of two main pathways with some pre-processing components. The first classifier (Comprehensive Classifier/*Comp-Cl*) is intended to cover dialectal statistics, token statistics, and writing style while the second one (Abstract Classifier/*Abs-Cl*) covers semantic and syntactic relations between words. The decisions from the two classifiers are fused together using a decision tree classifier to predict the final class of the input sentence.[6]

3.2.1 Comprehensive Classifier

The first classifier is intended to explicitly model detailed aspects of the language. We identify multiple features that are relevant to the task and we group them into different sets. Using the D3 tokenized version of the input data in addition to the classes provided by the "Token Level Identification" module for each word in the given sentence, we conduct a suite of experiments using the decision tree implementation by *WEKA* toolkit (Hall et al., 2009) to exhaustively search over all features in each group in the first phase, and then exhaustively search over all of the remaining features

[5]The window size is set empirically, we experimented with window sizes of 2, 4, 6, 8, 12.

[6]We experiment with different classifiers: Naive Bayes and Bayesian Network classifiers, but Decision Trees yielded the best results

from all groups to find the best combination of features that maximizes 10-fold cross-validation on the training data. We explore the same features used by Elfardy and Diab (2013) in addition to three other features that we refer to as "Modality Features". The full list of features include:

- *Perplexity-Features [PF]*: We run the tokenized input sentence through a tokenized *MSA* and a tokenized *EDA* 5-grams LMs to get sentence perplexity from each LM (*msaPPL* and *edaPPL*). These two LMs are built using the same data and the same procedure for the LMs used in the "Token Level Identification" module;
- *Dia-Statistics-Features [DSF]*:
  - The percentage of words tagged as *EDA* in the input sentence by the "Token Level Identification" module (*diaPercent*);
  - The percentage of words tagged as *EDA* and *MSA* by *MADAMIRA* in the input sentence (*calimaWords* and *samaWords*, respectively). And the percentage of words found in a precompiled *EDA* lexicon *egyWords* used and provided by (Elfardy and Diab, 2013);
  - *hasUnk* is a binary feature set to "true" only if the language model of the "Token Level Identification" module yielded at least one *unk* tag in the input sentence;
  - Modality features: The percentage of words tagged as *EDA*, *MSA*, and both (*modEDA*, *modMSA*, and *modBoth*, respectively) using the *Modality List* component in the "Token Level Identification" module.
- *Sentence-Statistics-Features [SSF]*: The percentage of Latin words, numbers, and punctuation (*latinPercent*, *numPercent*, and *puncPercent*, respectively) in the input sentence. In addition to the average word length (*avgWordLen*) and the total number of words (*sentLength*) in the same sentence;
- *Sentence-decoration-features [SDF]*: Some binary features of whether the sentence has/doesn't have diacritics (*hasDiac*), speech effects (*hasSpeechEff*), presence of exclamation mark (*hasExMark*), presence of emoticons (*hasEmot*), presence of question mark (*hasQuesMark*), presence of decoration effects (*hasDecEff*) (ex: ****), or repeated punctuation (*hasRepPunc*).

3.2.2 Abstract Classifier

The second classifier, *Abs-Cl*, is intended to cover the implicit semantic and syntactic relations between words. It runs the input sentence in its surface form without tokenization through a surface form *MSA* and a surface form *EDA* 5-gram LMs to get sentence probability from each of the respective LM (*msaProb* and *edaProb*). These two LMs are built using the same data used in the "Token Level Identification" module LM, but without tokenization.

This classifier complements the information provided by *Comp-Cl*. While *Comp-Cl* yields detailed and specific information about the tokens as it uses tokenized-level LMs, *Abs-Cl* is able to capture better semantic and syntactic relations between words since it can see longer context in terms of the number of words compared to that seen by *Comp-Cl* (on average a span of two words in the surface-level LM corresponds to almost five words in the tokenized-level LM) (Rashwan et al., 2011).

3.2.3 DT Ensemble

In the final step, we use the classes and confidence scores of the preceding two classifiers on the training data to train a decision tree classifier. Accordingly, an input test sentence goes through *Comp-Cl* and *Abs-Cl*, where each classifier assigns the sentence a label and a confidence score for this label. It then uses the two labels and the two confidence scores to provide its final classification for the input sentence.

4 Experimental Setup

4.1 Data

To our knowledge, there is no publicly available standard dataset that is annotated for both token and sentence levels to be used for evaluating both levels of classifications. Accordingly we use two separate standard datasets for both tasks.

For the token level identification, we use the training and test data that is provided by the shared task ShTk. Additionally, we manually annotate more token-level data using the same guidelines used to annotate this dataset and use this additional data for training and tuning our system.

- *tokTrnDB*: is the ShTk training set. It consists of 119,326 words collected from Twitter;

- *tokTstDB*: is the ShTk test set. It consists of 87,373 words of tweets collected from some unseen users in the training set and 12,017 words of sentences collected from Arabic commentaries;
- *tokDevDB*: 42,245 words collected from weblogs and manually annotated in house using the same guidelines of the shared task.[7] We only use this set for system tuning to decide upon the best configuration;
- *tokTrnDB2*: 171,419 words collected from weblogs and manually annotated in house using the same guidelines of the shared task. We use it as an extra training set in addition to *tokTrnDB* to study the effect of increasing training data size on the system performance.[8]

Table 1 shows the distribution of each of these subsets of the token-level dataset.

	lang1	*lang2*	*ambig*	*ne*	*other*	*mixed*
tokTrnDB	79,059	16,291	1,066	14,110	8,688	15
tokTstDB	57,740	21,871	240	11,412	8,121	6
tokTrnDB2	77,856	69,407	46	14,902	9,190	18
tokDevDB	23,733	11,542	34	4,017	2,916	3

Table 1: Tag distribution in the datasets used in our token level identification component.

For sentence level dialect identification, we use the code-switched *EDA-MSA* portion of the crowd source annotated dataset (Zaidan and Callison-Burch, 2011). The dataset consists of user commentaries on Egyptian news articles. The data is split into training (*sentTrnDB*) and test (*sentTstDB*) using the same split reported by Elfardy and Diab (2013). Table 2 shows the statistics for that data.

	MSA Sent.	*EDA* Sent.	*MSA* Tok.	*EDA* Tok.
sentTrnDB	12,160	11,274	300,181	292,109
sentTstDB	1,352	1,253	32,048	32,648

Table 2: Number of *EDA* and *MSA* sentences and tokens in the training and test sets.

4.2 Baselines

4.2.1 Token Level Baselines

For the token level task, we evaluate our approach against the results reported by all systems participating in ShTk evaluation test bed. These baselines include:

- *IUCL*: The best results obtained by King et al. (2014);
- *IIIT*: The best results obtained by Jain and Bhat (2014);
- *CMU*: The best results obtained by Lin et al. (2014);
- *MSR-India*: The best results obtained by Chittaranjan et al. (2014);
- *AIDA*: The best results obtained by us using the older version *AIDA* (Elfardy et al., 2014).

4.2.2 Sentence Level Baselines

For the sentence level component, we evaluate our approach against all published results on the Arabic "Online Commentaries (AOC)" publicly available dataset (Zaidan and Callison-Burch, 2011). The sentence level baselines include:

- *Zidan et al*: The best results obtained by Zaidan and Callison-Burch (2011);
- *Elfardy et al*: The best results obtained by Elfardy and Diab (2013);
- *Cotterell et al*: The best result obtained by Cotterell and Callison-Burch (2014a);
- *All Features*: This baseline combines all features from *Comp-Cl* and *Abs-Cl* to train a single decision tree classifier.

5 Evaluation

5.1 Token Level Evaluation

Table 3 compares our token level identification approach to all baselines. It shows, our proposed approach significantly outperforms all baselines using the same training and test sets. *AIDA*2 achieves 90.6% weighted average F-score while the nearest baseline gets 86.8% (this is 28.8% error reduction from the best published approach). By using both *tokTrnDB* and *tokTrnDB2* for training, the weighted average F-score is further improved by 2.3% as shown in the last row of the table.

5.2 Sentence Level Evaluation

For all experiments, we use a decision-tree classifier as implemented in *WEKA* (Hall et al., 2009) toolkit. Table 4 shows the 10-folds cross-validation results on the *sentTrnDB*.

- "*Comp-Cl*" shows the results of the best selected set of features from each group. (The

[7] The task organizers kindly provided the guidelines for the task.

[8] We are expecting to release both *tokDevDB* and *tokTrnDB2* in addition to some other data are still under development to the community by 2016

Baseline	*lang1*	*lang2*	*ambig*	*ne*	*other*	*mixed*	Avg-F
AIDA	89.4	76.0	0.0	87.9	99.0	0.0	86.8
CMU	89.9	81.1	0.0	72.5	98.1	0.0	86.4
IIIT	86.2	52.9	0.0	70.1	84.2	0.0	76.6
IUCL	81.1	59.5	0.0	5.8	1.2	0.0	61.0
MSR-India	86.0	56.4	0.7	49.6	74.8	0.0	74.2
AIDA2	**92.9**	**82.9**	**0.0**	**89.5**	**99.3**	**0.0**	**90.6**
AIDA2+	**94.6**	**88.3**	**0.0**	**90.2**	**99.4**	**0.0**	**92.9**

Table 3: F-score on held-out test-set *tokTstDB* using our best setup against the baselines. *AIDA2+* shows the the results of training our system using *tokTrnDB* and *tokTrnDB2*

	Group	Accuracy
Comp-Cl	**Perplexity-Features**	80.0%
	Dia-Statistics-Features	85.1%
	Sentence-Statistics-Features	61.6%
	Sentence-decoration-features	53.1%
	Best of all groups	87.3%
Abs-Cl		78.4%
DT Ensemble		89.9%

Table 4: Cross-validation accuracy on the *sentTrnDB* using the best selected features in each group

ones that yield best cross-validation results of *sentTrnDB*. "Best-of-all-groups" shows the result of the best selected features from the retained feature groups which in turn is the final set of features for the comprehensive classifier. In our case the best selected features are *msaPPL, edaPPL, diaPercent, hasUnk, calimaWords, modEDA, egyWords, latinPercent, puncPercent, avgWordLen*, and *hasDiac*.

- "*Abs-Cl*" shows the results and best set of features (*msaProb* and *edaProb*) for the abstract classifier.
- "DT Ensemble" reflect the results of combining the labels and confidence scores from *Comp-Cl* and *Abs-Cl* using a decision tree classifier.

Among the different configurations, the ensemble system yields the best 10-fold cross-validation accuracy of 89.9%. We compare the performance of this best setup to our baselines on both the cross-validation and held-out test sets. As Table 5 shows, the proposed approach significantly outperforms all baselines on all sets.

6 Results Discussion

6.1 Token Level Results Discussion

Last row in table 3 shows that the system results in 24.5% error reduction by adding 171K words of gold data to the training set. This shows that the system did not reach the saturation state yet, which means that adding more gold data can increase performance.

Baseline	*sentTrnDB*	*sentTstDB*	*sentTrnDB + sentTstDB*
Zidan et al	N/A	N/A	80.9
Elfardy et al	85.3	83.3	85.5
Cotterell et al	N/A	N/A	86.6
All Features	85.8	85.3	85.5
DT Ensemble	**89.9**	**87.3**	**90.8**

Table 5: Results of using our best setup (DT Ensemble) against baselines

Table 6 shows the confusion matrix of our best setup for all six labels over the *tokTstDB*. The table shows that the highest confusability is between *lang1* and *lang2* classes; 2.9% are classified as *lang1* instead of *lang2* and 1.6% are classified as *lang2* instead of *lang1*. This accounts for 63.8% of the total errors. The Table also shows that our system does not produce the *mixed* class at all probably because of the tiny number of *mixed* cases in the training data (only 33 words out of 270.7K words). The same case applies to the *ambig* class as it represents only 0.4% of the whole training data. *lang1* and *ne* are also quite highly confusable. Most of *ne* words have another non-named entity meaning and in most cases these other meanings tend to be *MSA*. Therefore, we expect that a more sophisticated NER system will help in identifying these cases.

		Predicted					
		lang1	*lang2*	*ambig*	*ne*	*other*	*mixed*
Gold	*lang1*	55.7%	1.6%	0.0%	0.9%	0.0%	0.0%
	lang2	2.9%	18.9%	0.0%	0.2%	0.0%	0.0%
	ambig	0.1%	0.1%	0.0%	0.0%	0.0%	0.0%
	ne	0.8%	0.2%	0.0%	10.3%	0.1%	0.0%
	other	0.0%	0.0%	0.0%	0.0%	8.2%	0.0%
	mixed	0.0%	0.0%	0.0%	0.0%	0.0%	0.0%

Table 6: Token-level confusion matrix for the best performing setup on *tokTstDB*

Table 7 shows examples of the words that are misclassified by our system. The misclassified word in the first examples (bED meaning "each other") has a gold class *other*. However, the gold label is incorrect and our system predicted it correctly as *lang2* given the context. In the second example, the misclassified named entity refers to the name of a charitable organization but the word also means "message" which is a *lang1* word. The third example shows a *lang1* word that is incorrectly classified by our system as *lang2*. Similarly, in the last example our system incorrectly classified a *lang2* word as a *lang1*.

Sentence	Word	Gold	Pred
tlt twytr mzwr . nSh AkwntAt m$ $gAlh w AlbAqy mblkyn bED تلت تويتر مزور . نصه اكونتات مش شغالة و الباقي مبلكين بعض *One third of twitter is forged. Half of the accounts are not working while the rest block each other..*	bED بعض each other	*other*	*lang2*
kmA Anny mTlE Ely mA tqwmwn bh fy mxtlf AljmEyAt wAlAn$Tp AlAhlyp . mvl rsAlp . كما اني مطلع علي ما تقومون به في مختلف الجمعيات والانشطة الاهلية . مثل رسالة. *Also I know what you are doing in different domains and civil activities like Resala.*	rsAlp رسالة Resala	*ne*	*lang1*
>nA bxyr . SHty wAlHmd llh fy >fDl HAl . انا بخير صحتي والحمد لله في افضل حال. *I am fine. Thank God, my health is in best condition.*	SHty صحتي my health	*lang1*	*lang2*
lm Aqr> AlbyAn w qrrt AEtrD Elyh glAsp لم اقرأ البيان و قرّرت اعترض عليه غلاسة *I did not read the statement and decided to object to it just to be annoying*	AEtrD اعترض object	*lang2*	*lang1*

Table 7: Examples of the words that were misclassified by our system

6.2 Sentence Level Results Discussion

The best selected features shows that *Comp-Cl* benefits most from using only 11 features. By studying the excluded features we found that:

- Five features (*hasSpeechEff*, *hasEmot*, *hasDeceff*, *hasExMark*, and *hasQuesMark*) are zeros for most records, hence extremely sparse, which explains why they are not selected as relevant distinctive features. However, it should be noted that the *hasSpeechEff* and *hasEmot* features are markers of informal language especially in the social media (not to ignore the fact that users write in *MSA* using these features as well but much less frequently). Accordingly we anticipate that if the data has more of these features, they would have significant impact on modeling the phenomena;

- Five features are not strong indicators of dialectalness. For the *sentLength* feature, the average length of the *MSA*, and *EDA* sentences in the training data is almost the same. While, the *numPercent*, *modMSA*, *modBoth*, and *hasRepPunc* features are almost uniformly distributed across the two classes;

- The initial assumption was that *SAMA* is exclusively *MSA* while *CALIMA* is exclusively *EDA*, thereby the *samaWords* feature will be a strong indicator for *MSA* sentences and the *calimaWords* feature will be a strong indicator for *EDA* sentences. Yet by closer inspection, we found that in 96.5% of the *EDA* sentences, *calimaWords* is higher than *samaWords*. But, in only 23.6% of the *MSA* sentences, *samaWords* is higher than *calimaWords*. This means that *samaWords* feature is not able to distinguish the *MSA* sentences efficiently. Accordingly samaWords feature was not selected as a distinctive feature in the final feature selection process.

Although *modEDA* is selected as one of the representative features, it only occurs in a small percentage of the training data (10% of the *EDA* sentences and 1% of the *MSA* sentences). Accordingly, we repeated the best setup (DT Ensemble) without the modality features, as an ablation study, to measure the impact of modality features on the performance. In the 10-fold-cross-validation on the *sentTrnDB* using *Comp-Cl* alone, we note that performance results slightly decreased (from 87.3% to 87.0%). However given the sparsity of the feature (it occurs in less than 1% of the tokens in the *EDA* sentences), 0.3% drop in performance is significant. This shows that if the modality lexicon has more coverage, we will observe a more significant impact.

Table 8 shows some examples for our system predictions. The first example is correctly classified with a high confidence (92%). Example 2 is quite challenging. The second word is a typo where two words are concatenated due to a missing white space, while the first and third words can be used in both *MSA* and *EDA* contexts. Therefore, the system gives a wrong prediction with a low confidence score (59%). In principle this sentence could be either *EDA* or *MSA*. The last example should be tagged as *EDA*. However, our system tagged it as *MSA* with a very high confidence score of (94%).

Input sentence	Gold	Pred	Conf
wlA AElAnAt fY Altlyfzywn nAfEp w lA jrArAt jdydp nAfEp.. w bEdyn. ولا اعلانات في التلفزيون نافعة ولا جرارات جديدة نافعة.. وبعدين. *Neither TV commercials nor new tractors work. So now what.*	*EDA*	*EDA*	92%
Allhm AgfrlhA wArHmhA اللّهم اغفرلها وارحمها *May God forgive her and have mercy on her.*	*MSA*	*EDA*	59%
tsmHly >qwlk yAbAbA? تسمحلي اقولك يابابا؟ *Do you allow me to call you father?*	*EDA*	*MSA*	94%

Table 8: Examples of the sentences that were misclassified by our system

7 Conclusion

We presented *AIDA2*, a hybrid system for token and sentence levels dialectal identification in code switched Modern Standard and Egyptian Dialectal Arabic text. The proposed system uses a classifier ensemble approach to perform dialect identification on both levels. In the token level module, we run the input sentence through four different classifiers. Each of which classify each word in the sentence. A CRF model is then used to predict the final class of each word using the provided information from the underlying four classifiers. The output from the token level module is then used to train one of the two underlying classifiers of the sentence level module. A decision tree classifier is then used to to predict the final label of any new input sentence using the predictions and confidence scores of two underlying classifiers. The sentence level module also uses a heuristic features selection approach to select the best features for each of its two underlying classifiers by maximizing the accuracy on a cross-validation set. Our approach significantly outperforms all published systems on the same training and test sets. We achieve 90.6% weighted average F-score on the token level identification compared to 86.8% for state of the art using the same data sets. Adding more training data results in even better performance to 92.9%. On the sentence level, *AIDA2* yields an accuracy of 90.8% using cross-validation compared to the latest state of the art performance of 86.6% on the same data.

References

Rania Al-Sabbagh, Jana Diesner, and Roxana Girju. 2013. Using the semantic-syntactic interface for reliable arabic modality annotation. In *Proceedings of the Sixth International Joint Conference on Natural Language Processing*, pages 410–418, Nagoya, Japan, October. Asian Federation of Natural Language Processing.

Waleed Ammar, Chris Dyer, and Noah A Smith. 2014. Conditional random field autoencoders for unsupervised structured prediction. In Z. Ghahramani, M. Welling, C. Cortes, N.D. Lawrence, and K.Q. Weinberger, editors, *Advances in Neural Information Processing Systems 27*, pages 3311–3319. Curran Associates, Inc.

Yassine Benajiba, Paolo Rosso, and Jos Miguel Benedruiz. 2007. Anersys: An arabic named entity recognition system based on maximum entropy. In *In Proceedings of CICLing-2007.*

Fadi Biadsy, Julia Hirschberg, and Nizar Habash. 2009. Spoken arabic dialect identification using phonotactic modeling. In *Proceedings of the Workshop on Computational Approaches to Semitic Languages at the meeting of the European Association for Computational Linguistics (EACL), Athens, Greece.*

Gokul Chittaranjan, Yogarshi Vyas, Kalika Bali, and Monojit Choudhury, 2014. *Proceedings of the First Workshop on Computational Approaches to Code Switching*, chapter Word-level Language Identification using CRF: Code-switching Shared Task Report of MSR India System, pages 73–79. Association for Computational Linguistics.

Ryan Cotterell and Chris Callison-Burch. 2014a. A multi-dialect, multi-genre corpus of informal written arabic. In Nicoletta Calzolari (Conference Chair), Khalid Choukri, Thierry Declerck, Hrafn Loftsson, Bente Maegaard, Joseph Mariani, Asuncion Moreno, Jan Odijk, and Stelios Piperidis, editors, *Proceedings of the Ninth International Conference on Language Resources and Evaluation (LREC'14)*, Reykjavik, Iceland, may. European Language Resources Association (ELRA).

Ryan Cotterell and Chris Callison-Burch. 2014b. A multi-dialect, multi-genre corpus of informal written arabic. In *Proceedings of the Language Resources and Evaluation Conference (LREC).*

Heba Elfardy and Mona Diab. 2013. Sentence-Level Dialect Identification in Arabic. In *Proceedings of ACL2013*, Sofia, Bulgaria, August.

Heba Elfardy, Mohamed Al-Badrashiny, and Mona Diab, 2014. *Proceedings of the First Workshop on Computational Approaches to Code Switching*, chapter AIDA: Identifying Code Switching in Informal Arabic Text, pages 94–101. Association for Computational Linguistics.

Jr. Forney, G.D. 1973. The viterbi algorithm. *Proceedings of the IEEE*, 61(3):268–278, March.

Nizar Habash and Fatiha Sadat. 2006. Arabic preprocessing schemes for statistical machine translation. *Proceedings of the 7th Meeting of the North AmericanChapter of the Association for Computational Linguistics/Human Language Technologies Conference (HLT-NAACL06)*.

Nizar Habash, Ramy Eskander, and AbdelAti Hawwari. 2012. A Morphological Analyzer for Egyptian Arabic. In *NAACL-HLT 2012 Workshop on Computational Morphology and Phonology (SIGMORPHON2012)*, pages 1–9.

Mark Hall, Eibe Frank, Geoffrey Holmes, Bernhard Pfahringer, Peter Reutemann, and Ian H Witten. 2009. The weka data mining software: an update. *ACM SIGKDD Explorations Newsletter*, 11(1).

Naman Jain and Ahmad Riyaz Bhat, 2014. *Proceedings of the First Workshop on Computational Approaches to Code Switching*, chapter Language Identification in Code-Switching Scenario, pages 87–93. Association for Computational Linguistics.

Levi King, Eric Baucom, Timur Gilmanov, Sandra Kübler, Daniel Whyatt, Wolfgang Maier, and Paul Rodrigues. 2014. The iucl+ system: Word-level language identification via extended markov models. In *Proceedings of the First Workshop on Computational Approaches to Code-Switching*. EMNLP 2014, Conference on Empirical Methods in Natural Language Processing, Doha, Qatar.

Chu-Cheng Lin, Waleed Ammar, Lori Levin, and Chris Dyer, 2014. *Proceedings of the First Workshop on Computational Approaches to Code Switching*, chapter The CMU Submission for the Shared Task on Language Identification in Code-Switched Data, pages 80–86. Association for Computational Linguistics.

Mohamed Maamouri, Dave Graff, Basma Bouziri, Sondos Krouna, Ann Bies, and Seth Kulick. 2010. Ldc standard arabic morphological analyzer (sama) version 3.1.

Arfath Pasha, Mohamed Al-Badrashiny, Mona Diab, Ahmed El Kholy, Ramy Eskander, Nizar Habash, Manoj Pooleery, Owen Rambow, and Ryan M. Roth. 2014. MADAMIRA: A Fast, Comprehensive Tool for Morphological Analysis and Disambiguation of Arabic. In *Proceedings of LREC*, Reykjavik, Iceland.

M.A.A. Rashwan, M.A.S.A.A. Al-Badrashiny, M. Attia, S.M. Abdou, and A. Rafea. 2011. A stochastic arabic diacritizer based on a hybrid of factorized and unfactorized textual features. *Audio, Speech, and Language Processing, IEEE Transactions on*, 19(1):166–175, Jan.

Wael Salloum, Heba Elfardy, Linda Alamir-Salloum, Nizar Habash, and Mona Diab. 2014. Sentence level dialect identification for machine translation system selection. In *Proceedings of the annual meeting of the Association for Computational Linguistics (ACL)*.

Fei Sha and Fernando Pereira. 2003. Shallow parsing with conditional random fields. pages 213–220.

Thamar Solorio, Elizabeth Blair, Suraj Maharjan, Steve Bethard, Mona Diab, Mahmoud Gonheim, Abdelati Hawwari, Fahad AlGhamdi, Julia Hirshberg, Alison Chang, , and Pascale Fung. 2014. Overview for the first shared task on language identification in code-switched data. In *In Proceedings of the First Workshop on Computational Approaches to Code-Switching. EMNLP 2014, Conference on Empirical Methods in Natural Language Processing, October, 2014, Doha, Qatar*.

Omar F Zaidan and Chris Callison-Burch. 2011. The arabic online commentary dataset: an annotated dataset of informal arabic with high dialectal content. In *ACL 2011*.

An Iterative Similarity based Adaptation Technique for Cross Domain Text Classification

Himanshu S. Bhatt **Deepali Semwal** **Shourya Roy**
Xerox Research Center India, Bengaluru, INDIA
{Himanshu.Bhatt,Deepali.Semwal,Shourya.Roy}@xerox.com

Abstract

Supervised machine learning classification algorithms assume both train and test data are sampled from the same domain or distribution. However, performance of the algorithms degrade for test data from different domain. Such cross domain classification is arduous as features in the test domain may be different and absence of labeled data could further exacerbate the problem. This paper proposes an algorithm to adapt classification model by iteratively learning domain specific features from the unlabeled test data. Moreover, this adaptation transpires in a similarity aware manner by integrating similarity between domains in the adaptation setting. Cross-domain classification experiments on different datasets, including a real world dataset, demonstrate efficacy of the proposed algorithm over state-of-the-art.

1 Introduction

A fundamental assumption in supervised statistical learning is that training and test data are independently and identically distributed (i.i.d.) samples drawn from a distribution. Otherwise, good performance on test data cannot be guaranteed even if the training error is low. In real life applications such as business process automation, this assumption is often violated. While researchers develop new techniques and models for machine learning based automation of one or a handful business processes, large scale adoption is hindered owing to poor generalized performance. In our interactions with analytics software development teams, we noticed such pervasive diversity of learning tasks and associated inefficiency. Novel predictive analytics techniques on standard datasets (or limited client data) did not generalize across different domains (new products & services) and has limited applicability. Training models from scratch for every new domain requires human annotated labeled data which is expensive and time consuming, hence, not pragmatic.

On the other hand, transfer learning techniques allow domains, tasks, and distributions used in training and testing to be different, but related. It works in contrast to traditional supervised techniques on the principle of transferring learned knowledge across domains. While transfer learning has generally proved useful in reducing the labelled data requirement, brute force techniques suffer from the problem of *negative transfer* (Pan and Yang, 2010a). One cannot use transfer learning as the proverbial hammer, but needs to gauge when to transfer and also how much to transfer.

To address these issucs, this paper proposes a domain adaptation technique for cross-domain text classification. In our setting for cross-domain classification, a classifier trained on one domain with sufficient labelled training data is applied to a different test domain *with no labelled data*. As shown in Figure 1, this paper proposes an iterative similarity based adaptation algorithm which starts with a shared feature representation of source and target domains. To adapt, it iteratively learns domain specific features from the unlabeled target domain data. In this process, similarity between two domains is incorporated in the adaptation setting for similarity-aware transfer. The major contributions of this research are:

- An iterative algorithm for learning domain specific discriminative features from unlabeled data in the target domain starting with an initial shared feature representation.
- Facilitating similarity-aware domain adaptation by seamlessly integrating similarity between two domains in the adaptation settings.

Proceedings of the 19th Conference on Computational Language Learning, pages 52–61,
Beijing, China, July 30-31, 2015.

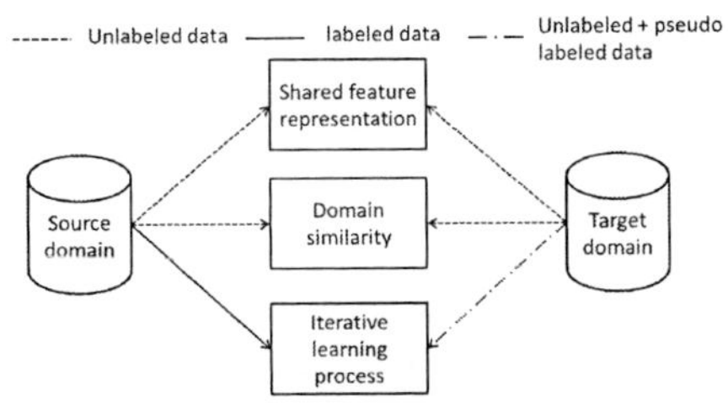

Figure 1: Outlines different stages of the proposed algorithm i.e. shared feature representation, domain similarity, and the iterative learning process.

To the best of our knowledge, this is the first-of-its-kind approach in cross-domain text classification which integrates similarity between domains in the adaptation setting to learn domain specific features in an iterative manner. The rest of the paper is organized as follows: Section 2 summarizes the related work, Section 3 presents details about the proposed algorithm. Section 4 presents databases, experimental protocol, and results. Finally, Section 5 concludes the paper.

2 Related Work

Transfer learning in text analysis (domain adaptation) has shown promising results in recent years (Pan and Yang, 2010a). Prior work on domain adaptation for text classification can be broadly classified into instance re-weighing and feature-representation based adaptation approaches.

Instance re-weighing approaches address the difference between the joint distributions of observed instances and class labels in source domain with that of target domain. Towards this direction, Liao et al. (2005) learned mismatch between two domains and used active learning to select instances from the source domain to enhance adaptability of the classifier. Jiang and Zhai (2007) proposed instance weighing scheme for domain adaptation in NLP tasks which exploit independence between feature mapping and instance weighing approaches. Saha et al. (2011) leveraged knowledge from source domain to actively select the most informative samples from the target domain. Xia *et al.* (2013) proposed a hybrid method for sentiment classification task that also addresses the challenge of mutually opposite orientation words.

A number of domain adaptation techniques are based on learning common feature representation (Pan and Yang, 2010b; Blitzer et al., 2006; Ji et al., 2011; Daumé III, 2009) for text classification. The basic idea being identifying a suitable feature space where projected source and target domain data follow similar distributions and hence, a standard supervised learning algorithm can be trained on the former to predict instances from the latter. Among them, Structural Correspondence Learning (SCL) (Blitzer et al., 2007) is the most representative one, explained later. Daumé (2009) proposed a heuristic based non-linear mapping of source and target data to a high dimensional space. Pan et al. (2008) proposed a dimensionality reduction method Maximum Mean Discrepancy Embedding to identify a latent space. Subsequently, Pan et al. (2010) proposed to map domain specific words into unified clusters using spectral clustering algorithm. In another follow up work, Pan *et al.* (2011) proposed a novel feature representation to perform domain adaptation via Reproducing Kernel Hilbert Space using Maximum Mean Discrepancy. A similar approach, based on co-clustering (Dhillon et al., 2003), was proposed in Dai *et al.* (2007) to leverage common words as bridge between two domains. Bollegala et al. (2011) used sentiment sensitive thesaurus to expand features for cross-domain sentiment classification. In a comprehensive evaluation study, it was observed that their approach tends to increase the adaptation performance when multiple source domains were used (Bollegala et al., 2013).

Domain adaptation based on iterative learning has been explored by Chen et al. (2011) and Garcia-Fernandez et al. (2014) and are similar to the philosophy of the proposed approach in appending pseudo-labeled test data to the training set. The first approach uses an expensive feature split to co-train two classifiers while the former presents a single classifier self-training based setting. However, the proposed algorithm offers novel contributions in terms of 1) leveraging two independent feature representations capturing the shared and target specific representations, 2) an ensemble of classifiers that uses labelled source domain and pseudo labelled target domain instances carefully moderated based on similarity between two domains. Ensemble based domain adaptation for text classification was first proposed by Aue and Gammon (2005) though their approach could not achieve significant improvements over baseline. Later, Zhao et al. (2010) proposed online transfer learning (OTL) framework which forms the basis of our ensemble based domain adaptation. However, the proposed algorithm differs in the following ways: 1) an unsupervised approach that transforms unlabeled data into pseudo labeled data unlike OTL which is supervised, and 2) incorporates similarity in the adaptation setting for gradual transfer.

3 Iterative Similarity based Adaptation

The philosophy of our algorithm is gradual transfer of knowledge from the source to the target domain while being cognizant of similarity between two domains. To accomplish this, we have developed a technique based on ensemble of two classifiers. Transfer occurs within the ensemble where a classifier learned on shared representation transforms unlabeled test data into pseudo labeled data to learn domain specific classifier. Before explaining the algorithm, we highlight its salient features:

Common Feature Space Representation: Our objective is to find a *good* feature representation which minimizes divergence between the source and target domains as well as the classification error. There have been several works towards feature-representation-transfer approach such as (Blitzer et al., 2007; Ji et al., 2011) which derives a transformation matrix Q that gives a shared representation between the source and target domains. One of the widely used approaches is Structural Correspondence Learning (SCL) (Blitzer et al., 2006) which aims to learn the co-occurrence between features expressing similar meaning in different domains. Top k Eigenvectors of matrix, W, represent the principal predictors for weight space, Q. Features from both domains are projected on this principal predictor space, Q, to obtain a shared representation. Source domain classifier in our approach is based on this SCL representation. In Section 4, we empirically show how our algorithm generalizes to different shared representations.

Iterative Building of Target Domain Labeled Data: If we have enough labeled data from the target domain then a classifier can be trained without the need for adaptation. Hence, we wanted to explore if and how (*pseudo*) labeled data for the target domain can be created. Our hypothesis is that certain target domain instances are more similar to source domain instances than the rest. Hence a classifier trained on (a suitably chosen transformed representation of) source domain instances will be able to categorize similar target domain instances confidently. Such confidently predicted instances can be considered as pseudo labeled data which are then used to initialize a classifier in target domain.

Only handful of instances in the target domain can be confidently predicted using the shared representation, therefore, we further iterate to create pseudo labeled instances in target domain. In the next round of iterations, remaining unlabeled target domain instances are passed through both the classifiers and their output are suitably combined. Again, confidently labeled instances are added to the pool of pseudo labeled data and the classifier in the target domain is updated. This process is repeated till all unlabeled data is labeled or certain maximum number of iterations is performed. This way we gradually adapt the target domain classifier on pseudo labeled data using the knowledge transferred from source domain. In Section 4, we empirically demonstrate effectiveness of this technique compared to one-shot adaptation approaches.

Domain Similarity-based Aggregation: Performance of domain adaptation is often constrained by the dissimilarity between the source and target domains (Luo et al., 2012; Rosenstein et al., 2005; Chin, 2013; Blitzer et al., 2007). If the two domains are largely similar, the knowledge learned in the source domain can be aggressively transferred to the target domain. On the other hand, if the two domains are less similar, knowledge learned in the source domain should be transferred in a conservative manner so as to mitigate the effects of *negative transfer*. Therefore, it is imperative for domain adaptation techniques to account for similarity between domains and transfer knowledge in a similarity aware manner. While this may sound obvious, we do not see many works in domain adaptation literature that leverage inter-domain similarity for transfer of knowledge. In this work, we use the cosine similarity measure to compute similarity between two domains and based on that gradually transfer knowledge from the source to the target domain. While it would be interesting to compare how different similarity measures compare towards preventing negative transfer but that is not the focus of this work. In Section 4, we empirically show marginal gains of transferring knowledge in a similarity aware manner.

Table 1: Notations used in this research.

Symbol	Description
$\{\mathbf{x}_i^s, y_i^s\}_{i=1:n_s}$; $\mathbf{x}_i^s \in R^d; y_i^s \in \{-1, +1\}$	Labeled source domain instances
$\{\mathbf{x}_i^t\}_{i=1:n_t}$; $\hat{y}_i \in \{-1, +1\}$	Unlabeled target domain instances and predicted label for target domain
Q	Co-occurrence based projection matrix
P_u, P_s	Pool of unlabeled and pseudo-labeled target domain instances respectively
C_s, C_t ; function from $R^d \rightarrow \{-1, +1\}$	Classifier C_s is trained on $\{(Q\mathbf{x}_i^s, y_i^s)\}$; classifier C_t is trained on $\{\mathbf{x}_i^t, \hat{y}_i^t\}$ where $x_i^t \in P_s$ and $\hat{y}$ is the pseudo label predicted labels by Ensemble E
α	confidence of prediction
E	Weighted ensemble of C_s and C_t
θ_1, θ_2	confidence threshold for C_s and ensemble E
w^s, w^t	Weights for C_s and C_t respectively

3.1 Algorithm

Table 1 lists the notations used in this research. Inputs to the algorithm are labeled source domain instances $\{x_i^s, y_i^s\}_{i=1:n_s}$ and a pool of unlabeled target domain instances $\{x_i^t\}_{i=1:n_t}$, denoted by P_u. As shown in Figure 2, the steps of the algorithm are as follows:

1. Learn Q, a shared representation projection matrix from the source and target domains, using any of the existing techniques. SCL is used in this research.

2. Learn C_s on SCL-based representation of labeled source domain instances $\{Q\mathbf{x}_i^s, y_i^s\}$.

3. Use C_s to predict labels, $\hat{y}_i$, for instances in P_u using the SCL-based representation $Q\mathbf{x}_i^t$. Instances which are predicted with confidence greater than a pre-defined threshold, θ_1, are moved from P_u to P_s with pseudo label, $\hat{y}$.

4. Learn C_t from instances in $P_s \in \{\mathbf{x}_i^t, \hat{y}_i^t\}$ to incorporate target specific features. P_s only contains instances added in step-3 and will be growing iteratively (hence the training set here is small).

5. C_s and C_t are combined in an ensemble, E, as a weighted combination with weights as w^s and w^t which are both initialized to 0.5.

6. Ensemble E is applied to all remaining instances in P_u to obtain the label $\hat{y}_i$ as:

$$E(x_i^t) \rightarrow \hat{y}_i \rightarrow w^s C_s(Qx_i^t) + w^t C_t(x_i^t) \quad (1)$$

   (a) If the ensemble classifies an instance with confidence greater than the threshold θ_2, then it is moved from P_u to P_s along with pseudo label $\hat{y}_i$.

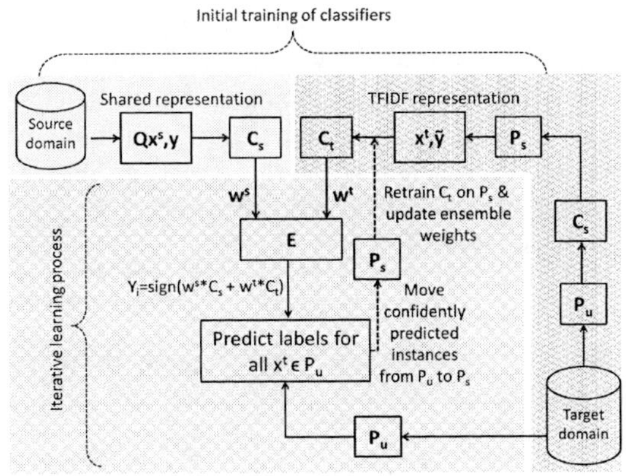

Figure 2: Illustrates learning of the initial classifiers and iterative learning process of the proposed similarity-aware domain adaptation algorithm.

   (b) Repeat step-6 for all $x_i^t \in P_u$.

7. Weights w^s and w^t are updated as shown in Eqs. 2 and 3. This update facilitates knowledge transfer within the ensemble guided by the similarity between domains.

$$w_{(l+1)}^s = \frac{(sim * w_l^s * I(C_s))}{(sim * w_l^s * I(C_s) + (1 - sim) * w_l^t * I(C_t))} \quad (2)$$

$$w_{(l+1)}^t = \frac{((1 - sim) * w_l^t * I(C_t))}{(sim * w_l^s * I(C_s) + (1 - sim) * w_l^t * I(C_t))} \quad (3)$$

where, l is the iteration, sim is the similarity score between domains computed using cosine similarity metric as shown in Eq. 4

$$sim = \frac{\mathbf{a} \cdot \mathbf{b}}{||\mathbf{a}||||\mathbf{b}||} \quad (4)$$

where $\mathbf{a}$ & $\mathbf{b}$ are normalized vector representations for the two domains. $I(\cdot)$ is the loss function to measure the errors of individual classifiers in each iteration:

$$I(\cdot) = \exp\{-\eta l(C, Y)\} \quad (5)$$

where, η is learning rate set to 0.1, $l(y, \hat{y}) = (y - \hat{y})^2$ is the square loss function, y is the label predicted by the classifier and $\hat{y}$ is the label predicted by the ensemble.

8. Re-train classifier C_t on P_s.

9. Repeat step $6 - 8$ until P_u is empty or maximum number of iterations is reached.

In this iterative manner, the proposed algorithm transforms unlabeled data in the test domain into pseudo labeled data and progressively learns classifier C_t. Confidence of prediction, α_i for i^{th} instance, is measured as the distance from the decision boundary (Hsu et al., 2003) which is computed as shown in Eq. 6.

$$\alpha = \frac{R}{|v|} \tag{6}$$

where R is the un-normalized output from the support vector machine (SVM) classifier, v is the weight vector for support vectors and $|v| = v^T v$. Weights of individual classifiers in the ensemble are updated with each iteration that gradually shifts emphasis from the classifier learned on shared representation to the classifier learned on target domain. Algorithm 1 illustrates the proposed iterative learning algorithm.

Algorithm 1 Iterative Learning Algorithm

Input: C_s trained on shared co-occurrence based representation $Q\mathbf{x}$, C_t initiated on TFIDF representation from P_s, P_u remaining unlabeled target domain instances.
Iterate: $l = 0$: till $P_u = \{\phi\}$ or $l \leq iterMax$
Process: Construct ensemble E as weighted combination of C_s and C_t with initials weights w_l^s and w_l^t as 0.5 and sim = similarity between domains.
for $i = 1$ **to** n (size of P_u) **do**
  Predict labels: $E(Q\mathbf{x}_i, \mathbf{x}_i) \rightarrow \hat{y}_i$; calculate α_i
  if $\alpha_i > \theta_2$ **then**
    Remove i^{th} instance from P_u and add to P_s with pseudo label $\hat{y}_i$.
  end if.
end for. Retrain C_t on P_s and update w_l^s and w_l^t.
end iterate.
Output: Updated C_t, w_l^s and w_l^t.

4 Experimental Results

The efficacy of the proposed algorithm is evaluated on different datasets for cross-domain text classification (Blitzer et al., 2007), (Dai et al., 2007). In our experiments, performance is evaluated on two-class classification task and reported in terms of classification accuracy.

4.1 Datasets & Experimental Protocol

The first dataset is the Amazon review dataset (Blitzer et al., 2007) which has four different domains, Books, DVDs, Kitchen appliances and Electronics. Each domain comprises 1000 positive and 1000 negative reviews. In all experiments, 1600 labeled reviews from the source and 1600 unlabeled reviews from the target domains are used in training and performance is reported on the non-overlapping 400 reviews from the target domain.

The second dataset is the 20 Newsgroups dataset (Lang, 1995) which is a text collection of approximately 20,000 documents evenly partitioned across 20 newsgroups. For cross-domain text classification on the 20 Newsgroups dataset, we followed the protocol of Dai et al. (2007) where it is divided into six different datasets and the top two categories in each are picked as the two classes. The data is further segregated based on sub-categories, where each sub-category is considered as a different domain. Table 2 lists how different sub-categories are combined to represent the source and target domains. In our experiments, $4/5^{th}$ of the source and target data is used to learn shared feature representation and results are reported on the remaining $1/5^{th}$ of the target data.

Table 2: Elaborates data segregation on the 20 Newsgroups dataset for cross-domain classification.

dataset	D_s	D_t
comp vs rec	comp.graphics comp.sys.ibm.pc.hardware comp.sys.mac.hardware rec.motorcycles rec.sport.hockey	comp.os.ms-windows.misc comp.windows.x rec.autos rec.sport.baseball
comp vs sci	comp.graphics comp.os.ms-windows.misc sci.crypt sci.electronics	comp.sys.ibm.pc.hardware comp.sys.mac.hardware comp.windows.x sci.med sci.space
comp vs talk	comp.graphics comp.sys.mac.hardware comp.windows.x talk.politics.mideast talk.religion.misc	comp.os.ms-windows.miscnewline comp.sys.ibm.pc.hardware talk.politics.guns talk.politics.misc
rec vs sci	rec.autos rec.sport.baseball sci.med sci.space	rec.motorcycles rec.sport.hockey sci.crypt sci.electronics
rec vs talk	rec.autos rec.motorcycles talk.politics.guns talk.politics.misc	rec.sport.baseball rec.sport.hockey talk.politics.mideast talk.religion.misc
sci vs talk	sci.electronics sci.med talk.politics.misc talk.religion.misc	sci.crypt sci.space talk.politics.guns talk.politics.mideast

The third dataset is a real world dataset comprising tweets about the products and services in different domains. The dataset comprises tweets/posts from three collections, $Coll1$ about gaming, $Coll2$ about Microsoft products and $Coll3$ about mobile support. Each collection has 218 positive and negative tweets. These tweets are collected based on user-defined keywords captured in a listening engine which then crawls the social media and fetches comments matching the keywords. This dataset being noisy and comprising short-text is more challenging than the previous two datasets.

All datasets are pre-processed by converting to lowercase followed by stemming. Feature selection based on document frequency ($DF = 5$) reduces the number of features as well as speed up the classification task. For Amazon review dataset, TF is used for feature weighing whereas TFIDF is used for feature weighing in other two datasets. In all our experiments, constituent classifiers used in the ensemble are support vector machines (SVMs) with radial basis function kernel. Performance of the proposed algorithm for cross-domain classification task is compared with different techniques[1] including 1) in-domain classifier trained and tested on the same domain data, 2) baseline classifier which is trained on the source and directly tested on the target domain, 3) SCL[2], a widely used domain adaptation technique for cross-domain text classification, 4) 'Proposed w/o sim', removing similarity from Eqs. 2 & 3.

4.2 Results and Analysis

For cross-domain classification, the performance degrades mainly due to 1) feature divergence and 2) negative transfer owing to largely dissimilar domains. Table 3 shows the accuracy of individual classifiers and the ensemble for cross-domain classification on the Amazon review dataset. The ensemble has better accuracy than the individual classifiers, therefore, in our experiments the final reported performance is the accuracy of the ensemble. The combination weights in the ensemble represent the contributions of individual classifiers toward classification accuracy. In our experiments, the maximum number of iterations ($iterMax$) is set to 30. It is observed that at the end of the iterative learning process, the target specific classifier is assigned more weight mass as compared to the classifier trained on the shared representation. On average, the weights for the two classifiers converge to $w^s = 0.22$ and $w^t = 0.78$ at the end of the iterative learning process.

[1]We also compared our performance with sentiment sensitive thesaurus (SST) proposed by (Bollegala et al., 2013) and our algorithm outperformed on our protocol. However, we did not include comparative results because of difference in experimental protocol as SST is tailored for using multiple source domains and our protocol uses single source domain.

[2]Our implementation of SCL is used in this paper.

Table 3: Comparing the performance of individual classifiers and the ensemble for training on Books domain and test across different domains. C_s and C_t are applied on the test domain data before performing the iterating learning process.

SD → TD	C_s	C_t	Ensemble
B → D	63.1	34.8	72.1
B → E	64.5	39.1	75.8
B → K	68.4	42.3	76.2

Table 4: List some examples of domain specific discriminative features learned by the proposed algorithm on the Amazon review dataset.

Domain	Domain specific features
Books	*pictures_illustrations, more_detail, to_read*
DvDs	*Definite_buy, delivery_prompt*
Kitchen	*invaluable_resource, rust, delicious*
Electronics	*Bargain, Energy_saving, actually_use*

This further validates our assertion that the target specific features are more discriminative than the shared features in classifying target domain instances, which are efficiently captured by the proposed algorithm. Key observations and analysis from the experiments on different datasets is summarized below.

4.2.1 Results on the Amazon Review dataset

To study the effects of different components of the proposed algorithm, comprehensive experiments are performed on the Amazon review dataset[3].

***1) Effect of learning target specific features*:** Results in Figure 3 show that iteratively learning target specific feature representation (slow transfer as opposed to one-shot transfer) yields better performance across different cross-domain classification tasks as compared to SCL, SFA (Pan et al., 2010)[4] and the baseline. Unlike SCL and SFA, the proposed approach uses shared and target specific feature representations for the cross-domain classification task. Table 4 illustrates some examples of the target specific discriminative features learned by the proposed algorithm that leads to enhanced performance. At 95% confidence, parametric t-test suggests that the proposed algorithm and SCL are significantly (statistically) different.

***2) Effect of similarity on performance*:** It is observed that existing domain adaptation techniques enhance the accuracy for cross-domain classification, though, negative transfer exists in camou-

[3]Due to space restrictions, we show this analysis only on one dataset; however similar conclusions were drawn from other datasets as well.

[4]We directly compared our results with the performance reported in (Pan et al., 2010).

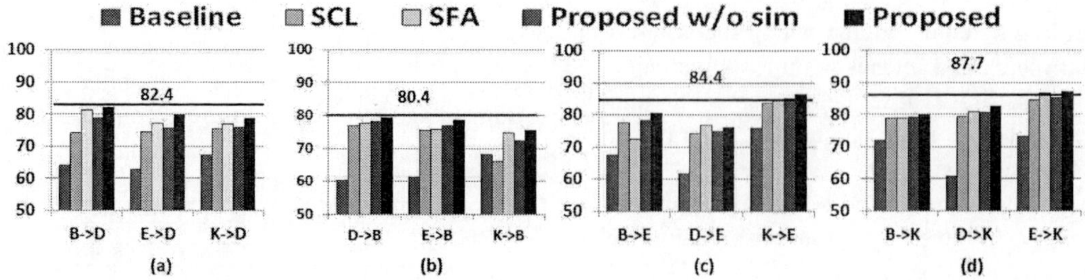

Figure 3: Comparing the performance of the proposed approach with existing techniques for cross-domain classification on Amazon review dataset.

flage. Results in Figure 3(b) (for the case K $\rightarrow$ B) describes an evident scenario for negative transfer where the adaptation performance with SCL descends lower than the baseline. However, the proposed algorithm still sustains the performance by transferring knowledge proportionate to similarity between the two domains. To further analyze the effect of similarity, we segregated the 12 cross-domain classification cases into two categories based on similarity between two the participating domains i.e. 1) > 0.5 and 2) < 0.5. Table 5 shows that for 6 out of 12 cases that fall in the first category, the average accuracy gain is 10.8% as compared to the baseline. While for the remaining 6 cases that fall in the second category, the average accuracy gain is 15.4% as compared to the baseline. This strongly elucidates that the proposed similarity-based iterative algorithm not only adapts well when the domain similarity is high but also yields gain in the accuracy when the domains are largely dissimilar. Figure 4 also shows how weight for the target domain classifier w_t varies with the number of iterations. It further strengthens our assertion that if domains are similar, algorithm can readily adapt and converges in a few iterations. On the other hand for dissimilar domains, slow iterative transfer, as opposed to one-shot transfer, can achieve similar performance; however, it may take more iterations to converge.While the effect of similarity on domain adaptation performance is evident, this work opens possibilities for further investigations.

3) Effect of varying threshold θ_1 ***&*** θ_2**:** Figure 5(a) explains the effect of varying θ_1 on the final classification accuracy. If θ_1 is low, C_t may get trained on incorrectly predicted pseudo labeled instances; whereas, if θ_1 is high, C_t may be deficient of instances to learn a good decision boundary. On the other hand, θ_2 influences the number of iterations required by the algorithm to reach the stopping criteria. If this threshold is low, the algorithm converges aggressively (in a few iterations) and does not benefit from the iterative nature of learning the target specific features. Whereas a high threshold tends to make the algorithm conservative. It hampers the accuracy because of the unavailability of sufficient instances to update the classifier after each iteration which also leads to large number of iterations to converge (may not even converge).

Table 5: Effect of similarity on accuracy gain for cross-domain classification on the Amazon review dataset.

Category	SD $\rightarrow$ TD	Sim	Gain	Avg. (SD)
> 0.5	E $\rightarrow$ K	0.78	13.1	10.8 (4.9)
	K $\rightarrow$ E	0.78	10.6	
	B $\rightarrow$ K	0.54	8.0	
	K $\rightarrow$ B	0.54	2.9	
	B $\rightarrow$ E	0.52	13.1	
	E $\rightarrow$ B	0.52	17.2	
< 0.5	K $\rightarrow$ D	0.34	8.9	15.4 (4.4)
	D $\rightarrow$ K	0.34	21.6	
	E $\rightarrow$ D	0.33	14.5	
	D $\rightarrow$ E	0.33	14.5	
	B $\rightarrow$ D	0.29	14.1	
	D $\rightarrow$ B	0.29	19.1	

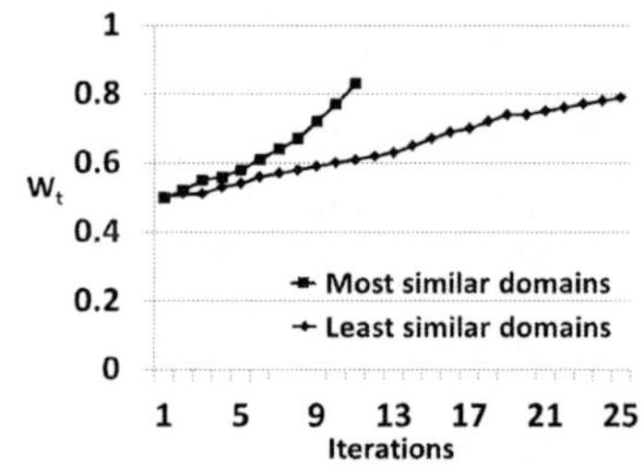

Figure 4: Illustrates how the weight (w_t) for target domain classifiers varies for the most and least similar domains with number of iterations.

θ_1 and θ_2 are set empirically on a held-out set, with values ranging from zero to distance of farthest classified instance from the SVM hyperplane (Hsu et al., 2003). The *knee-shaped* curve on the graphs in Figure 5 shows that there exists

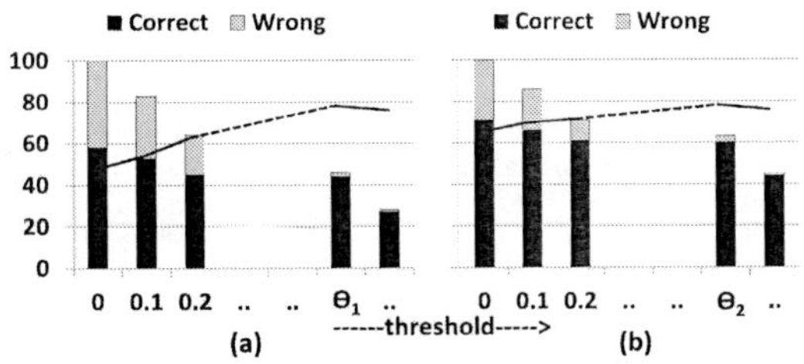

Figure 5: Bar plot shows % of data that crosses confidence threshold, lower and upper part of the bar represents % correctly and wrongly predicted pseudo labels. The black line shows how the final classification accuracy is effected with threshold.

an optimal value for θ_1 and θ_2 which yields the best accuracy. We observed that the best accuracy is obtained when the thresholds are set to the distance between the hyper plane and the farthest support vector in each class.

***4) Effect of using different shared representations in ensemble*:** To study the generalization ability of the proposed algorithm to different shared representations, experiments are performed using three different shared representations on the Amazon review dataset. Apart from using the SCL representation, the accuracy is compared with the proposed algorithm using two other representations, 1) common features between the two domains ("common") and 2) multi-view principal component analysis based representation ("MVPCA") (Ji et al., 2011) as they are previously used for cross-domain sentiment classification on the same dataset. Table 6 shows that the proposed algorithm yields significant gains in cross-domain classification accuracy with all three representations and is not restricted to any specific representation. The final accuracy depends on the initial classifier trained on the shared representation; therefore, if a shared representation sufficiently captures the characteristics of both source and target domains, the proposed algorithm can be built on any such representation for enhanced cross-domain classification accuracy.

4.2.2 Results on 20 Newsgroups data

Results in Figure 6 compares the accuracy of proposed algorithm with existing approaches on the 20 Newsgroups dataset. Since different domain are crafted out from the sub-categories of the same dataset, domains are exceedingly similar and therefore, the baseline accuracy is relatively better

Table 6: Comparing the accuracy of proposed algorithm built on different shared representations.

SD → TD	Common	MVPCA	SCL
B → D	66.8	76.4	**78.2**
B → E	69.0	79.2	**80.6**
B → K	71.4	79.2	**79.8**
D → B	64.5	78.4	**79.3**
D → E	62.8	**76.4**	76.2
D → K	64.3	80.9	**82.4**
E → B	68.9	77.8	**78.5**
E → D	65.7	77.0	**77.3**
E → K	75.1	85.4	**86.2**
K → B	**71.3**	71.0	71.1
K → D	70.4	75.0	**76.1**
K → E	76.7	85.7	**86.4**

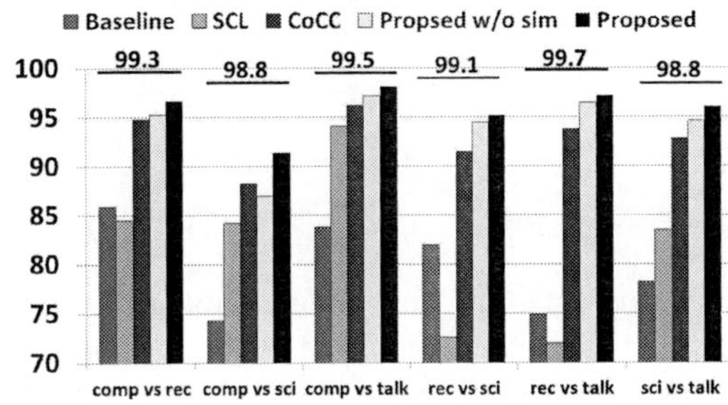

Figure 6: Results comparing the accuracy of proposed approach with existing techniques for cross domain categorization on 20 Newsgroups dataset.

than that on the other two datasets. The proposed algorithm still yields an improvement of at least 10.8% over the baseline accuracy. As compared to other existing domain adaptation approaches like SCL(Blitzer et al., 2007) and CoCC (Dai et al., 2007), the proposed algorithm outperforms by at least 4% and 1.9% respectively. This also validates our assertion that generally domain adaptation techniques accomplishes well when the participating domains are largely similar; however, the similarity aggregation and the iterative learning offer the proposed algorithm an edge over one-shot adaptation algorithms.

4.2.3 Results on real world data

Results in Figure 7 exhibit challenges associated with real world dataset. The baseline accuracy for cross-domain classification task is severely affected for this dataset. SCL based domain adaptation does not yields generous improvements as selecting the pivot features and computing the co-occurrence statistics with noisy short text is arduous and inept. On the other hand, the proposed algorithm iteratively learns discriminative target specific features from such perplexing data and translates it to an improvement of at least 6.4% and 3.5% over the baseline and the SCL respec-

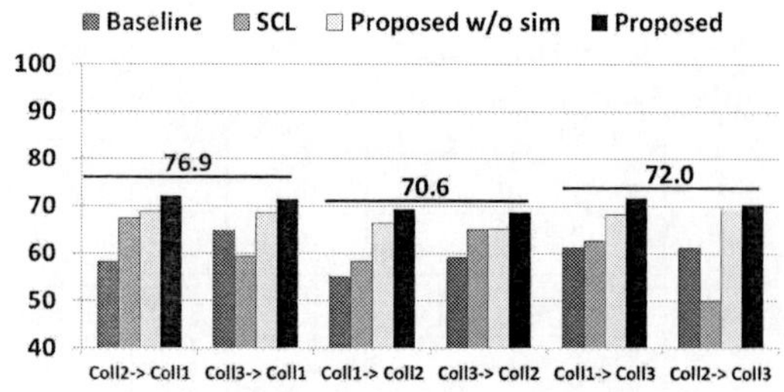

Figure 7: Results comparing the accuracy of the proposed approach with existing techniques for cross domain categorization on the real world dataset.

tively.

5 Conclusion

The paper presents an iterative similarity-aware domain adaptation algorithm that progressively learns domain specific features from the unlabeled test domain data starting with a shared feature representation. In each iteration, the proposed algorithm assigns pseudo labels to the unlabeled data which are then used to update the constituent classifiers and their weights in the ensemble. Updating the target specific classifier in each iteration helps better learn the domain specific features and thus, results in enhanced cross-domain classification accuracy. Similarity between the two domains is aggregated while updating weights of the constituent classifiers which facilitates gradual shift of knowledge from the source to the target domain. Finally, experimental results for cross-domain classification on different datasets show the efficacy of the proposed algorithm as compared to other existing approaches.

References

A. Aue and M. Gamon. 2005. Customizing sentiment classifiers to new domains: A case study. *Technical report, Microsoft Research.*

J. Blitzer, R. McDonald, and F. Pereira. 2006. Domain adaptation with structural correspondence learning. In *Proceedings of Conference on Empirical Methods in Natural Language Processing*, pages 120–128.

J. Blitzer, M. Dredze, and F. Pereira. 2007. Biographies, bollywood, boomboxes and blenders: Domain adaptation for sentiment classification. In *Proceedings of Association for Computational Linguistics*, pages 187–205.

D. Bollegala, D. Weir, and J. Carroll. 2011. Using multiple sources to construct a sentiment sensitive thesaurus for cross-domain sentiment classification. In *Proceedings of Association for Computational Linguistics: Human Language Technologies*, pages 132–141.

D. Bollegala, D. Weir, and J. Carroll. 2013. Cross-domain sentiment classification using a sentiment sensitive thesaurus. *IEEE Transactions on Knowledge and Data Engineering*, 25(8):1719–1731.

M. Chen, K. Q Weinberger, and J. Blitzer. 2011. Co-training for domain adaptation. In *Proceedings of Advances in Neural Information Processing Systems*, pages 2456–2464.

Si-Chi Chin. 2013. Knowledge transfer: what, how, and why.

W Dai, G-R Xue, Q Yang, and Y Yu. 2007. Co-clustering based classification for out-of-domain documents. In *Proceedings of International Conference on Knowledge Discovery and Data Mining*, pages 210–219.

Hal Daumé III. 2009. Frustratingly easy domain adaptation. *arXiv preprint arXiv:0907.1815.*

I. S. Dhillon, S. Mallela, and D. S Modha. 2003. Information-theoretic co-clustering. In *Proceedings of International Conference on Knowledge Discovery and Data Mining*, pages 89–98.

A. Garcia-Fernandez, O. Ferret, and M. Dinarelli. 2014. Evaluation of different strategies for domain adaptation in opinion mining. In *Proceedings of the International Conference on Language Resources and Evaluation*, pages 26–31.

C-W. Hsu, C.-C. Chang, and C.-J. Lin. 2003. A practical guide to support vector classification. Technical report, Department of Computer Science, National Taiwan University.

Y.-S. Ji, J.-J. Chen, G. Niu, L. Shang, and X.-Y. Dai. 2011. Transfer learning via multi-view principal component analysis. *Journal of Computer Science and Technology*, 26(1):81–98.

J. Jiang and C. Zhai. 2007. Instance weighting for domain adaptation in NLP. In *Proceedings of Association for Computational Linguistics*, volume 7, pages 264–271.

K Lang. 1995. Newsweeder: Learning to filter netnews. In *Proceedings of International Conference on Machine Learning*.

X. Liao, Y. Xue, and L. Carin. 2005. Logistic regression with an auxiliary data source. In *Proceedings of International Conference on Machine Learning*, pages 505–512.

C. Luo, Y. Ji, X. Dai, and J. Chen. 2012. Active learning with transfer learning. In *Proceedings of Association for Computational Linguistics Student Research Workshop*, pages 13–18. Association for Computational Linguistics.

S. J. Pan and Q. Yang. 2010a. A survey on transfer learning. *IEEE Transactions on Knowledge and Data Engineering*, 22(10):1345–1359.

Sinno Jialin Pan and Qiang Yang. 2010b. A survey on transfer learning. *Knowledge and Data Engineering, IEEE Transactions on*, 22(10):1345–1359.

Sinno Jialin Pan, James T Kwok, and Qiang Yang. 2008. Transfer learning via dimensionality reduction. In *AAAI*, volume 8, pages 677–682.

S. J. Pan, X. Ni, J-T Sun, Q. Yang, and Z. Chen. 2010. Cross-domain sentiment classification via spectral feature alignment. In *Proceedings International Conference on World Wide Web*, pages 751–760. ACM.

S. J. Pan, I. W. Tsang, J. T. Kwok, and Q. Yang. 2011. Domain adaptation via transfer component analysis. *IEEE Transactions on Neural Networks*, 22(2):199–210.

M. T. Rosenstein, Z. Marx, L. P. Kaelbling, and T. G. Dietterich. 2005. To transfer or not to transfer. In *Proceedings of Advances in Neural Information Processing Systems Workshop, Inductive Transfer: 10 Years Later*.

A. Saha, P. Rai, H. Daumé, S. Venkatasubramanian, and S. L. DuVall. 2011. Active supervised domain adaptation. In *Proceedings of European Conference on Machine Learning and Knowledge Discovery in Databases*, pages 97–112.

R. Xia, C. Zong, X. Hu, and E. Cambria. 2013. Feature ensemble plus sample selection: domain adaptation for sentiment classification. *IEEE Intelligent Systems*, 28(3):10–18.

P. Zhao and S. C. H. Hoi. 2010. OTL: A Framework of Online Transfer Learning. In *Proceeding of International Conference on Machine Learning*.

Analyzing Optimization for Statistical Machine Translation: MERT Learns Verbosity, PRO Learns Length

Francisco Guzmán **Preslav Nakov** and **Stephan Vogel**
ALT Research Group
Qatar Computing Research Institute, HBKU
{fguzman,pnakov,svogel}@qf.org.qa

Abstract

We study the impact of source length and verbosity of the tuning dataset on the performance of parameter optimizers such as MERT and PRO for statistical machine translation. In particular, we test whether the verbosity of the resulting translations can be modified by varying the length or the verbosity of the tuning sentences. We find that MERT learns the tuning set verbosity very well, while PRO is sensitive to both the verbosity and the length of the source sentences in the tuning set; yet, overall PRO learns best from high-verbosity tuning datasets.

Given these dependencies, and potentially some other such as amount of reordering, number of unknown words, syntactic complexity, and evaluation measure, to mention just a few, we argue for the need of controlled evaluation scenarios, so that the selection of tuning set and optimization strategy does not overshadow scientific advances in modeling or decoding. In the mean time, until we develop such controlled scenarios, we recommend using PRO with a large verbosity tuning set, which, in our experiments, yields highest BLEU across datasets and language pairs.

1 Introduction

Statistical machine translation (SMT) systems nowadays are complex and consist of many components such as a translation model, a reordering model, a language model, etc., each of which could have several sub-components. All components and their elements work together to score full and partial hypotheses proposed by the SMT system's search algorithms.

Thus, putting them together requires assigning them relative weights, e.g., how much weight we should give to the translation model vs. the language model vs. the reordering table. These relative weights are typically learned discriminatively in a log-linear framework, and their values are optimized to maximize some automatic metric, typically BLEU, on a tuning dataset.

Given this setup, it is clear that the choice of a tuning set and its characteristics, can have significant impact on the SMT system's performance: if the experimental framework (training data, tuning set, and test set) is highly consistent, i.e., there is close similarity in terms of genre, domain and verbosity,[1] then translation quality can be improved by careful selection of tuning sentences that exhibit high degree of similarity to the test set (Zheng et al., 2010; Li et al., 2010).

In our recent work (Nakov et al., 2012), we have studied the relationship between optimizers such as MERT, PRO and MIRA, and we have pointed out that PRO tends to generate relatively shorter translations, which could lead to lower BLEU scores on testing. Our solution there was to fix the objective function being optimized: PRO uses sentence-level smoothed BLEU+1, as opposed to the standard dataset-level BLEU.

Here we are interested in a related but different question: the relationship between properties of the tuning dataset and the optimizer's performance. More specifically, we study how the *verbosity*, i.e., the average target/source sentence length ratio, learned by optimizers such as MERT and PRO depends on the nature of the tuning dataset. This could potentially allow us to manipulate the *verbosity* of the translation hypotheses generated at test time by changing some characteristics of the tuning dataset.

[1] Verbosity also depends on the translator; it is often a stylistic choice. and not necessarily related to fluency or adequacy. This aspect is beyond the scope of the present work.

Proceedings of the 19th Conference on Computational Language Learning, pages 62–72,
Beijing, China, July 30-31, 2015.

2 Related Work

Tuning the parameters of a log-linear model for statistical machine translation is an active area of research. The standard approach is to use minimum error rate training, or MERT, (Och, 2003), which optimizes BLEU directly.

Recently, there has been a surge in new optimization techniques for SMT. Two parameter optimizers that have recently become popular include the margin-infused relaxed algorithm or MIRA (Watanabe et al., 2007; Chiang et al., 2008; Chiang et al., 2009), which is an on-line sentence-level perceptron-like passive-aggressive optimizer, and pairwise ranking optimization or PRO (Hopkins and May, 2011), which operates in batch mode and sees tuning as ranking.

A number of improved versions thereof have been proposed in the literature including a batch version of MIRA (Cherry and Foster, 2012), with local updates (Liu et al., 2012), a linear regression version of PRO (Bazrafshan et al., 2012), and a non-sampling version of PRO (Dreyer and Dong, 2015); another example is Rampeon (Gimpel and Smith, 2012). We refer the interested reader to three recent overviews on parameter optimization for SMT: (McAllester and Keshet, 2011; Cherry and Foster, 2012; Gimpel and Smith, 2012).

Still, MERT remains the de-facto standard in the statistical machine translation community. Its stability has been of concern, and is widely studied. Suggestions to improve it include using regularization (Cer et al., 2008), random restarts (Moore and Quirk, 2008), multiple replications (Clark et al., 2011), and parameter aggregation (Cettolo et al., 2011).

With the emergence of new optimization techniques there have been also studies that compare stability between MIRA–MERT (Chiang et al., 2008; Chiang et al., 2009; Cherry and Foster, 2012), PRO–MERT (Hopkins and May, 2011), MIRA–PRO–MERT (Cherry and Foster, 2012; Gimpel and Smith, 2012; Nakov et al., 2012). Pathological verbosity was reported when using MERT on recall-oriented metrics such as METEOR (Lavie and Denkowski, 2009; Denkowski and Lavie, 2011), as well as large variance with MIRA (Simianer et al., 2012). However, we are not aware of any previous studies of the impact of sentence length and dataset verbosity across optimizers.

3 Method

For the following analysis, we need to define the following four quantities:

- *source-side length*: the number of words in the source sentence;
- *length ratio*: the ratio of the number of words in the output hypothesis to those in the reference;[2]
- *verbosity*: the ratio of the number of words in the reference to those in the source;[3]
- *hypothesis verbosity*: the ratio of the number of words in the hypothesis to those in the source.

Naturally, the *verbosity* varies across different tuning/testing datasets, e.g., because of style, translator choice, etc. Interestingly, verbosity can also differ across sentences with different source lengths drawn from *the same* dataset. This is illustrated in Figure 1, which plots the average sample source length vs. the average verbosity for 100 samples, each containing 500 randomly selected sentence pairs, drawn from the concatenation of the MT04, MT05, MT06, MT09 datasets for Arabic-English and of newstest2008-2011 for Spanish-English.[4]

We can see that for Arabic-English, the English translations are longer than the Arabic source sentences, i.e., the *verbosity* is greater than one. This relationship is accentuated by length: *verbosity* increases with sentence length: see the slightly positive slope of the regression line. Note that the increasing verbosity can be observed in single-reference sets (we used the first reference), and to a lesser extent in multiple-reference sets (five references for MT04 and MT05, and four for MT06 and MT09). For Spanish-English, the story is different: here the English sentences tend to be shorter than the Spanish ones, and the *verbosity* decreases as the sentence length increases. Overall, in all three cases, the *verbosity* appears to be length-dependent.

[2]For multi-reference sets, we use the length of the reference that is closest to the length of the hypothesis. This is the *best match length* from the original paper on BLEU (Papineni et al., 2002); it is default in the NIST scoring tool v13a, which we use in our experiments.

[3]When dealing with multi-reference sets, we use the average reference length.

[4]The datasets we experiment with are described in more detail in Section 4 below.

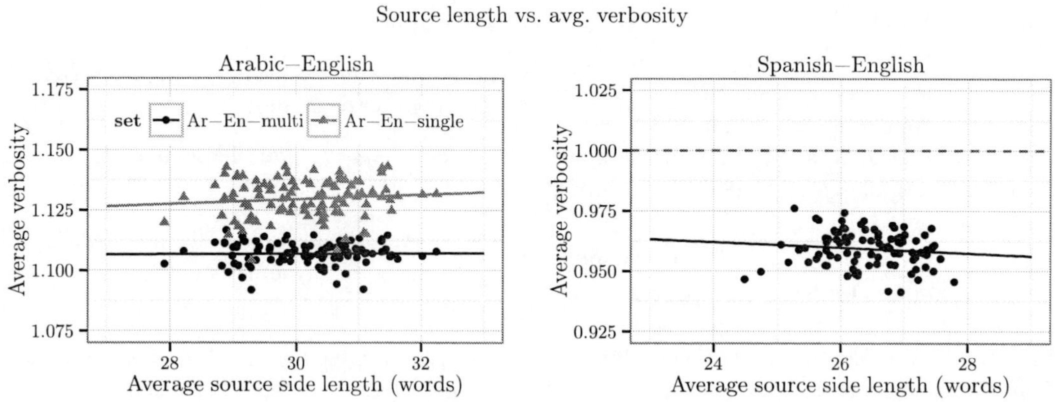

Figure 1: Average source sentence length (x axis) vs. average verbosity (y axis) for 100 random samples, each with 500 sentence pairs extracted from NIST (Left: Arabic-English, multi- and single-reference) and from WMT (Right: Spanish-English, single-reference) data.

The main research question we are interested in, and which we will explore in this paper, is whether the SMT parameter optimizers are able to learn the *verbosity* from the tuning set. We are also interested in the question of how the *hypothesis verbosity* learned by optimizers such as MERT and PRO depends on the nature of the tuning dataset, i.e., its *verbosity*. Understanding this could potentially allow us to manipulate the *hypothesis verbosity* of the translations generated at test time simply by changing the characteristics of the tuning dataset in a systematic and controlled way. While controlling the verbosity of a tuning set might be an appealing idea, this is unrealistic in practice, given that the verbosity of a test set is always unknown. However, the results in Figure 1 suggest that it is possible to manipulate *verbosity* by controlling the average source sentence length of the dataset (and the *source-side* length is always known for any test set). Thus, in our study, we use the source-side sentence length as a data selection criterion; still, we also report results for selection based on verbosity.

In order to shed some light on our initial question (whether the SMT parameter optimizers are able to learn the *verbosity* from the tuning dataset), we contrast the *verbosity* that two different optimizers, MERT and PRO, learn as a function of the average length of the sentences in the tuning dataset.[5]

[5] In this work, we consider both optimizers, MERT and PRO, as *black-boxes*. For a detailed analysis of how their inner workings can affect optimization, see our earlier work (Nakov et al., 2012).

4 Experiments and Evaluation

We experimented with single-reference and multi-reference tuning and testing datasets for two language pairs: Spanish-English and Arabic-English. For Spanish-English, we used the single-reference datasets newstest2008, newstest2009, newstest2010, and newstest2011 from the WMT 2012, Workshop on Machine Translation Evaluation.[6] For Arabic-English, we used the multi-reference datasets MT04, MT05, MT06, and MT09 from the NIST 2012 OpenMT Evaluation;[7] we further experimented with single-reference versions of the MT0x datasets, using the first reference only.

In addition to the above datasets, we constructed tuning sets of different source-side sentence lengths: *short*, *middle* and *long*. Given an original tuning dataset, we selected 50% of its sentence pairs: *shortest* 50%, *middle* 50%, or *longest* 50%. This yielded tuning datasets with the same number of sentence pairs but with different number of words, e.g., for our Arabic-English datasets, *longest* has about twice as many English words as *middle*, and about four times as many words as *shortest*. Constructing tuning datasets with the same number of sentences instead of the same number of tokens is intentional as we wanted to ensure that in each of the conditions, the SMT parameter optimizers learn on the same number of training examples.

[6] `www.statmt.org/wmt12/`

[7] `www.nist.gov/itl/iad/mig/openmt12.cfm`

4.1 Experimental Setup

We experimented with the phrase-based SMT model (Koehn et al., 2003) as implemented in Moses (Koehn et al., 2007). For Arabic-English, we trained on all data that was allowed for use in the NIST 2012 except for the UN corpus. For Spanish-English, we used all WMT12 data, again except for the UN data.

We tokenized and truecased the English and the Spanish side of all bi-texts and also the monolingual data for language modeling using the standard tokenizer of Moses. We segmented the words on the Arabic side using the MADA ATB segmentation scheme (Roth et al., 2008). We built our phrase tables using the Moses pipeline with max-phrase-length 7 and Kneser-Ney smoothing. We also built a lexicalized reordering model (Koehn et al., 2005): *msd-bidirectional-fe*. We used a 5-gram language model trained on GigaWord v.5 with Kneser-Ney smoothing using KenLM (Heafield, 2011).

On tuning and testing, we dropped the unknown words for Arabic-English, and we used monotone-at-punctuation decoding for Spanish-English. We tuned using MERT and PRO. We used the standard implementation of MERT from the Moses toolkit, and a fixed version of PRO, as we recommended in (Nakov et al., 2013), which solves instability issues when tuning on the *long* sentences; we will discuss our PRO fix and the reasons it is needed in Section 5 below. In order to ensure convergence, we allowed both MERT and PRO to run for up to 25 iterations (default: 16); we further used 1000-best lists (default: 100).

In our experiments below, we perform three reruns of parameter optimization, tuning on each of the twelve tuning datasets; in the figures, we plot the results of the three reruns, while in the tables, we report BLEU averaged over the three reruns, as suggested by Clark et al. (2011).

4.2 Learning Verbosity

We performed parameter optimization using MERT and PRO on each dataset, and we used the resulting parameters to translate the same dataset. The purpose of this experiment was to study the ability of the optimizers to learn the *verbosity* of the tuning sets. Getting the *hypothesis verbosity* right means that it is highly correlated with the tuning set *verbosity* , which in turn is determined by the dataset source length.

The results are shown in Figure 2. In each graph, there are 36 points (many of them very close and overlapping) since we performed three reruns with our twelve tuning datasets (three length-based subsets for each of the four original tuning datasets). There are several observations that we can make:

(1) MERT is fairly stable with respect to the length of the input tuning sentences. Note how the MERT regression lines imitate those in Figure 1. In fact, the correlation between the *verbosity* and the *hypothesis verbosity* for MERT is r=0.980. PRO, on the other hand, has harder time learning the tuning set verbosity, and the correlation with the *hypothesis verbosity* is only r=0.44. Interestingly, its *length ratio* is more sensitive to the input length (r=0.67): on *short* sentences, it learns to output translations that are slightly shorter than the reference, while on *long* sentences, it yields increasingly longer translations. The dependence of PRO on source length can be explained by the sentence-level smoothing in BLEU+1 and the broken balance between BLEU's precision component and BP (Nakov et al., 2012). The problem is bigger for short sentences since there +1 is added to smaller counts; this results in preference for shorter translations.

(2) Looking at the results for Arabic-English, we observe that having multiple references makes both MERT and PRO appear more stable, allowing them to generate hypotheses that are less spread, and closer to 1. This can be attributed to the *best match reference length*, which naturally dampens the effect of verbosity during optimization by selecting the reference that is closest to the respective hypothesis.

Overall, we can conclude that MERT learns the tuning set's *verbosity* more accurately than PRO. PRO learns *verbosity* that is more dependent on the *source side length* of the sentences in the tuning dataset.

4.3 Performance on the Test Dataset

Next, we study the performance of MERT and PRO when testing on datasets that are different from the one used for tuning. First, we test the robustness of the parameters obtained for specific tuning datasets when testing on various test datasets. Second, we test whether selecting a tuning dataset based on the length of the testing dataset (i.e., *closest*) is a good strategy.

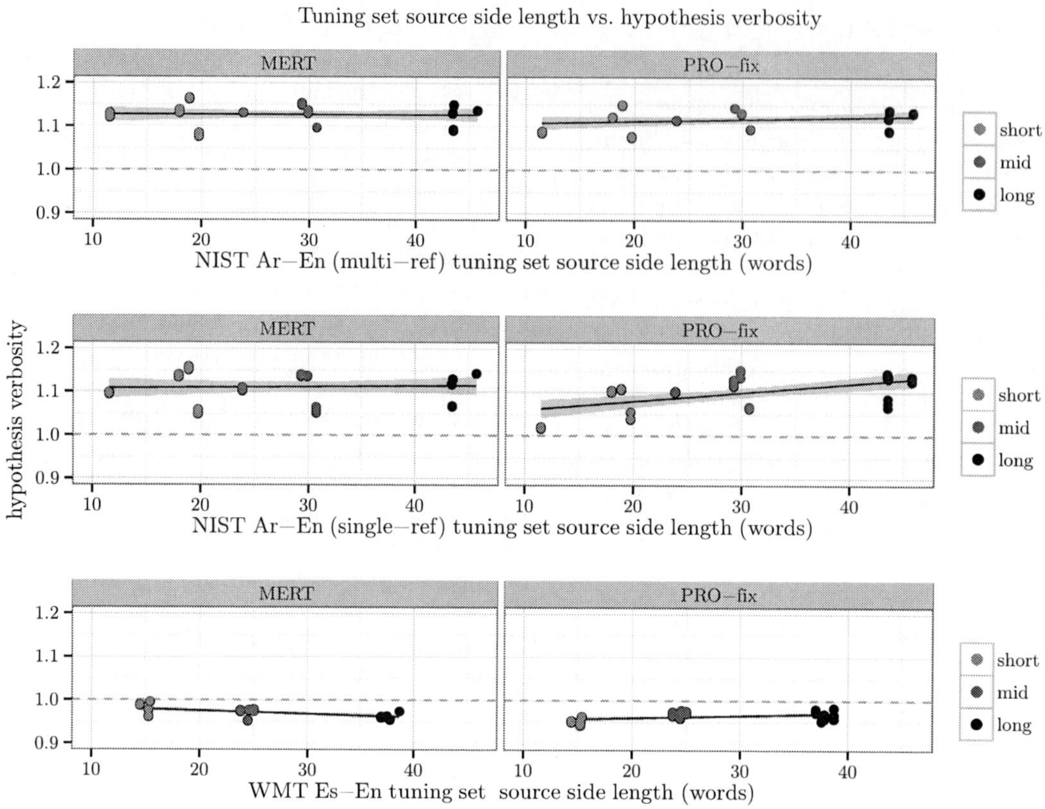

Figure 2: *Source-side length* vs. *hypothesis verbosity* for the tuning dataset. There are 36 points per language pair: four tuning sets, each split into three datasets (*short*, *middle*, and *long*) times three reruns.

For this purpose, we perform a grid comparison of tuning and testing on all our datasets: we tune on each *short/middle/long* dataset, and we test on the remaining *short/middle/long* datasets.

The results are shown in Table 1, where each cell is an average over 36 BLEU scores: four tuning sets times three test sets times three reruns. For example, 49.63 in row 1 (tune: short), column 2 (test: middle), corresponds to the average over three reruns of (i) tune on MT04-short and test on MT05-middle, MT06-middle, and MT09-middle, (ii) tune on MT05-short and test on MT04-middle, MT06-middle, and MT09-middle, (iii) tune on MT06-short and test on MT04-middle, MT05-middle, and MT09-middle, and (iv) tune on MT09-short and test on MT04-middle, MT05-middle, and MT06-middle. We further include two statistics: (1) the range of values (max-min), measuring test BLEU variance depending on the tuning set, and (2) the *loss* in BLEU when tuning on *closest* instead of on the best-performing dataset.

There are several interesting observations:

(1) PRO and MERT behave quite differently with respect to the input tuning set. For MERT, tuning on a specific length condition yields the best results when testing on a similar condition, i.e., *zero-loss*. This is a satisfactory result since it confirms the common wisdom that tuning datasets should be as similar as possible to test-time input in terms of *source side length*. In contrast, PRO behaves better when tuning on mid-length tuning sets. However, the average *loss* incurred by applying the *closest* strategy with PRO is rather small, and in practice, choosing a tuning set based on test set's average length is a good strategy.

(2) MERT has higher variance than PRO and fluctuates more depending on the input tuning set. PRO on the contrary, tends to perform more consistently, regardless of the length of the tuning set.

(3) MERT yields the best BLEU across datasets and language pairs. Thus, when several tuning sets are available, we recommend choosing the one closest in length to the test set and using MERT.

	test									
	Arabic-English (multi-ref)			**Arabic-English (1-ref)**			**WMT Spanish-English**			
tuning	**short**	**mid**	**long**	**short**	**mid**	**long**	**short**	**mid**	**long**	avg
MERT										
short	**47.26***	50.71	50.82	**26.69***	28.14	27.49	**25.17***	25.94	27.64	
mid	46.53	**51.11***	51.31	26.22	**28.39***	27.96	24.96	**26.27***	27.97	
long	46.23	50.84	**51.74***	25.80	28.20	**28.27***	24.57	26.08	**28.29***	
max-min	1.04	0.40	0.91	0.89	0.25	0.78	0.59	0.34	0.65	0.65
loss if using *closest*	0.00	0.00	0.00	0.00	0.00	0.00	0.00	0.00	0.00	0.00
PRO-fix										
short	**46.74**	50.57	50.97	25.95	27.66	27.28	24.66	**25.83**	**27.89**	
mid	46.59	**50.83**	**51.41**	**25.98**	**28.23**	**28.19**	**24.67**	25.81	27.64	
long	46.08	50.56	51.18	25.87	28.11	28.05	24.58	25.77	27.81	
max-min	0.66	0.27	0.44	0.11	0.58	0.92	0.09	0.06	0.25	0.38
loss if using *closest*	0.00	0.00	0.23	0.02	0.00	0.15	0.01	0.00	0.08	0.06

Table 1: Average test BLEU when tuning on each *short/mid/long* dataset, and testing on the remaining *short/mid/long* datasets. Each cell represents the average over 36 scores (see the text). The best score for either MERT or PRO is bold; the best overall score is marked with a *.

4.3.1 Performance vs. Length and Verbosity

The above results give rise to some interesting questions: What if we do not know the source-side length of the test set? What if we can choose a tuning set based on its verbosity? Would it then be better to choose based on length or based on verbosity?

To answer these questions, we analyzed the average results according to two orthogonal views: one based on the tuning set length (using the above 50% length-based subsets of tuning: *short*, *mid*, *long*), and another one based on the tuning set verbosity (using new 50% subsets verbosity-based subsets of tuning: *low-verb*, *mid-verb*, *high-verb*). This time, we translated the full test datasets (e.g., MT06, MT09); the results are shown in Table 2. We can make the following observations:

(1) The best results for PRO are better than the best results for MERT, in all conditions.

(2) Length-based tuning subsets: With a single reference, PRO performs best when tuning on short sentences, but with multiple references, it works best with mid-length sentences. MERT, on the other hand, prefers tuning on long sentences for all testing datasets.

(3) Verbosity-based tuning subsets: PRO yields best results when the tuning sets have high verbosity; in fact, the best verbosity-based results in the table are obtained with this setting. With multiple references, MERT performs best when tuning on high-verbosity datasets; however, with a single reference, it prefers mid-verbosity.

Based on the above results, we recommend that, whenever we have no access to the input side of the testing dataset beforehand, we should tune on datasets with high verbosity.

4.4 Test vs. Tuning Verbosity and Source Length

In the previous subsection, we have seen that MERT and PRO perform differently in terms of BLEU, depending on the characteristics of the tuning dataset. Here, we study a different aspect: i.e. how they behave with respect to *verbosity* and *source side length.*

We have seen that MERT and PRO perform differently in terms of BLEU depending on the characteristics of the tuning dataset. Below we study how other characteristics of the output of PRO and MERT are affected by tuning set *verbosity* and *source side length.*

4.4.1 MERT – Sensitive to Verbosity

Figure 3 shows a scatter plot of tuning *verbosity* vs. test *hypothesis verbosity* when using MERT to tune under different conditions, and testing on each of the unseen full datasets. We test on full datasets to avoid the *verbosity* bias that might occur for specific conditions (see Section 3).

We can see strong positive correlation between the tuning set *verbosity* and the *hypothesis verbosity* on the test datasets. The average correlation for Arabic-English is r=0.95 with multiple references and r=0.98 with a single reference; for Spanish-English, it is r=0.97.

	test					
	Arabic-English (multi-ref)		**Arabic-English (1-ref)**		**WMT Spanish-English**	
tuning	**MERT**	**PRO-fix**	**MERT**	**PRO-fix**	**MERT**	**PRO-fix**
length						
short	48.71	49.12	26.74	**27.35**	26.79	**27.07**
mid	49.27	**49.59**	26.97	27.23	26.99	26.88
long	**49.35**	49.20	**27.23**	27.28	**27.02**	26.84
verbosity						
low-verb	47.90	47.60	25.89	25.88	26.70	26.61
mid-verb	49.16	49.52	**27.69**	27.95	**27.09**	26.81
high-verb	**50.28**	**50.79***	27.36	**28.03***	27.01	**27.38***

Table 2: Average test BLEU scores when tuning on different length- and verbosity-based datasets, and testing on the remaining *full* datasets. Each cell represents the average over 36 scores. The best score for either MERT or PRO is bold; the best overall score is marked with a *.

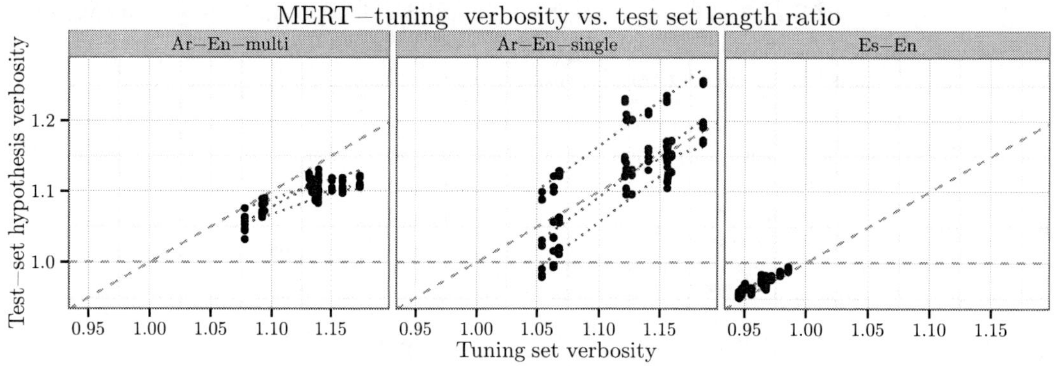

Figure 3: Tuning set *verbosity* vs. test *hypothesis verbosity* when using MERT. Each point represents the result for an unseen testing dataset, given a specific tuning condition. The linear regressions show the tendencies for each of the test datasets (note that they all overlap for Es-En and look like a single line).

These are very strong positive correlations and they show that MERT tends to learn SMT parameters that yield translations preserving the *verbosity*, e.g., lower *verbosity* on the tuning dataset will yield test-time translations that are less verbose, while higher *verbosity* on the tuning dataset will yield test-time translations that are more verbose. In other words, MERT learns to generate a fixed number of words per input word. This can be explained by the fact that MERT optimizes BLEU score directly, and thus learns to output the "right" *verbosity* on the tuning dataset (in contrast, PRO optimizes sentence-level BLEU+1, which is an approximation to BLEU, but it is not the actual BLEU). This explains why MERT performs best when the tuning conditions and the testing conditions are in sync. Yet, this makes it dependent on a parameter that we do not necessarily control or have access to beforehand: the length of the test *references*.

4.4.2 PRO – Sensitive to Source Length

Figure 4 shows the tuning set average *source-side length* vs. the testing hypothesis/reference *length ratio* when using PRO to tune on *short*, *middle*, and *long* and testing on each of the unseen full datasets, as in the previous subsection. We can see that there is positive correlation between the tuning set average *source side length* and the testing hypothesis/reference *length ratio*. For Spanish-English, it is quite strong (r=0.64), and for Arabic-English, it is more clearly expressed with one (r=0.42) than with multiple references (r=0.34). The correlation is significant ($p < 0.001$) when we take into account the contribution of the tuning set *verbosity* in the model. This suggests that for PRO, both *source length* and *verbosity* influence the hypotheses lengths, i.e., PRO learns the tuning set's *verbosity*, much like MERT; yet, the contribution of the length of the source sentences from the tuning dataset is not negligible.

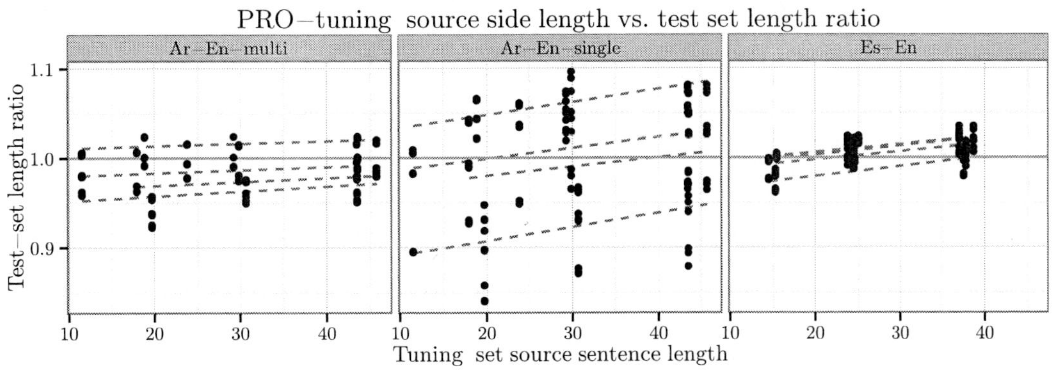

Figure 4: Tuning set average *source length* vs. test hypothesis/reference *length ratio* for PRO. Each point represents the result for an unseen testing dataset, given a specific tuning condition. The linear regressions shows the tendencies across each of the testing datasets.

Finally, note the "stratification" effect for the Arabic-English single-reference data. We attribute it to the differences across test datasets. These differences are attenuated with multiple references due to the *closest-match reference length*.

5 Discussion

We have observed that high-verbosity tuning sets yield better results with PRO. We have further seen that we can manipulate verbosity by adjusting the average length of the tuning dataset. This leads to the natural question: can this yield better BLEU? It turns out that the answer is "yes". Below, we present an example that makes this evident.

First, recall that for Arabic-English longer tuning datasets have higher verbosity. Moreover, our previous findings suggest that for PRO, higher-verbosity tuning datasets will perform better in this situation. Therefore, we should expect that longer tuning datasets could yield better BLEU. Table 3 presents the results for PRO with Arabic-English when tuning on MT06, or subsets thereof, and testing on MT09. The table shows the results for both multi- and single-reference experiments; naturally, manipulating the tuning set has stronger effect with a single reference. Lines 1-3 show that as the average length of the tuning dataset increases, so does the length ratio, which means better brevity penalty for BLEU and thus higher BLEU score. Line 4 shows that selecting a random-50% subset (included here to show the effect of using mixed-length sentences) yields results that are very close to those for *middle*.

Comparing line 3 to lines 4 and 5, we can see that tuning on *long* yields longer translations and also higher BLEU, compared to tuning on the full dataset or on *random*.

Next, lines 6 and 7 show the results when applying our smoothing fix for sentence-level BLEU+1 (Nakov et al., 2012), which prevents translations from becoming too short; we can see that *long* yields very comparable results. Yet, manipulating the tuning dataset might be preferable since it allows (*i*) faster tuning, by using part of the tuning dataset, (*ii*) flexibility in the selection of the desired verbosity, and (*iii*) applicability to other MT evaluation measures. Point (*ii*) is illustrated on Figure 5, which shows that there is direct positive correlation between verbosity, length ratio, and BLEU; note that the tuning set size does not matter much: in fact, better results are obtained when using less tuning data.

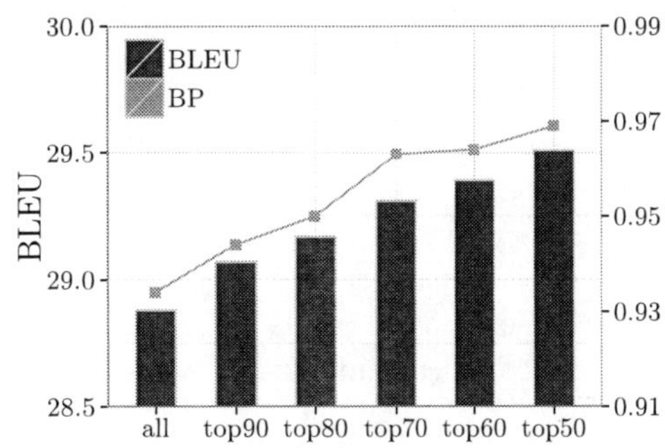

Figure 5: PRO, Arabic-English, 1-ref: tune on $N\%$ longest sentences from MT06, test on MT09.

	Tuning	multi-ref BLEU	multi-ref len. ratio	1-ref BLEU	1-ref len. ratio
1	tune-short	46.38	0.961	27.44	0.894
2	tune-mid	47.44	0.977	29.11	0.950
3	tune-long	**47.47**	0.980	**29.51**	0.969
4	tune-random	47.43	0.978	28.96	0.941
5	*tune-full*	*47.18*	*0.972*	*28.88*	*0.934*
6	tune-full, BP-smooth=1	**47.52**	0.984	**29.43**	0.962
7	tune-full, BP-smooth=1, grounded	**47.61**	0.991	**29.68**	0.979

Table 3: PRO, Arabic-English: tuning on MT06, or subsets thereof, and testing on MT09. Statistically significant improvements over *tune-full* are in bold: using the sign test (Collins et al., 2005), $p < 0.05$.

6 Conclusion and Future Work

Machine translation has, and continues to, benefit immensely from automatic evaluation measures. However, we frequently observe delicate dependencies between the evaluation metric, the system optimization strategy, and the pairing of tuning and test datasets. This leaves us with the situation that *getting lucky* in the selection of tuning datasets and optimization strategy overshadows scientific advances in modeling or decoding. Understanding these dependencies in detail puts us in a better position to construct tuning sets that match the test datasets in such a way that improvements in models, training, and decoding algorithms can be measured more reliably.

To this end, we have studied the impact that source-side length and verbosity of tuning sets have on the performance of the translation system when tuning the system with different optimizers such as MERT and PRO. We observed that MERT learns the verbosity of the tuning dataset very well, but this can be a disadvantage because we do not know the verbosity of unseen test sentences. In contrast, PRO is affected by both the verbosity and the source-side length of the tuning dataset.

There may be other characteristics of test datasets, e.g., amount of reordering, number of unknown words, complexity of the sentences in terms of syntactic structure, etc. that could have similar effects of creating good or bad luck when deciding how to tune an SMT system. Until we have such controlled evaluation scenarios, our short-term recommendations are as follows:

- Know your tuning datasets: Different language pairs and translation directions may have different *source-side length – verbosity* dependencies.
- When optimizing with PRO: select or construct a high-verbosity dataset as this could potentially compensate for PROs tendency to yield too short translations. Note that for Arabic-English, higher verbosity means longer tuning sentences, while for Spanish-English, it means shorter ones; translation direction might matter too.
- When optimizing with MERT: If you know beforehand the test set, select the *closest* tuning set. Otherwise, tune on longer sentences.

We plan to extend this study in a number of directions. First, we would like to include other parameter optimizers such as Rampeon (Gimpel and Smith, 2012) and MIRA. Second, we want to experiment with other metrics, such as TER (Snover et al., 2006), which typically yields short translations, and METEOR (Lavie and Denkowski, 2009), which yields too long translations. Third, we would like to explore other SMT models such as hierarchical (Chiang, 2005) and syntax-based (Galley et al., 2004; Quirk et al., 2005), and other decoders such as cdec (Dyer et al., 2010), Joshua (Li et al., 2009), and Jane (Vilar et al., 2010).

A long-term objective would be to design a metric that measures the closeness between tuning and test datasets, which includes the different characteristics, such as length distribution, verbosity distribution, syntactic complexity, etc., to guarantee a more stable evaluation situations, but which would also allow to systematically test the robustness of translation systems, when deviating from the matching conditions.

Acknowledgments

We would like to thank the anonymous reviewers for their constructive comments, which have helped us to improve the paper.

References

Marzieh Bazrafshan, Tagyoung Chung, and Daniel Gildea. 2012. Tuning as linear regression. In *Proceedings of the 2012 Annual Conference of the North American Chapter of the Association for Computational Linguistics: Human Language Technologies*, NAACL-HLT '12, pages 543–547, Montréal, Canada.

Daniel Cer, Daniel Jurafsky, and Christopher D Manning. 2008. Regularization and search for minimum error rate training. In *Proceedings of the Third Workshop on Statistical Machine Translation*, WMT '08, pages 26–34, Columbus, Ohio, USA.

Mauro Cettolo, Nicola Bertoldi, and Marcello Federico. 2011. Methods for smoothing the optimizer instability in SMT. In *Proceedings of the Thirteenth Machine Translation Summit*, MT Summit XIII, pages 32–39, Xiamen, China.

Colin Cherry and George Foster. 2012. Batch tuning strategies for statistical machine translation. In *Proceedings of the 2012 Annual Conference of the North American Chapter of the Association for Computational Linguistics: Human Language Technologies*, NAACL-HLT '12, pages 427–436, Montréal, Canada.

David Chiang, Yuval Marton, and Philip Resnik. 2008. Online large-margin training of syntactic and structural translation features. In *Proceedings of the 2008 Conference on Empirical Methods in Natural Language Processing*, EMNLP '08, pages 224–233, Honolulu, Hawaii, USA.

David Chiang, Kevin Knight, and Wei Wang. 2009. 11,001 new features for statistical machine translation. In *Proceedings of the 2009 Annual Conference of the North American Chapter of the Association for Computational Linguistics: Human Language Technologies*, NAACL-HLT '09, pages 218–226, Boulder, Colorado, USA.

David Chiang. 2005. A hierarchical phrase-based model for statistical machine translation. In *Proceedings of the 43rd Annual Meeting of the Association for Computational Linguistics*, ACL '05, pages 263–270, Ann Arbor, Michigan, USA.

Jonathan H. Clark, Chris Dyer, Alon Lavie, and Noah A. Smith. 2011. Better hypothesis testing for statistical machine translation: Controlling for optimizer instability. In *Proceedings of the 49th Annual Meeting of the Association for Computational Linguistics: Human Language Technologies*, ACL-HLT '11, pages 176–181, Portland, Oregon, USA.

Michael Collins, Philipp Koehn, and Ivona Kučerová. 2005. Clause restructuring for statistical machine translation. In *Proceedings of the 43rd Annual Meeting on Association for Computational Linguistics*, ACL '05, pages 531–540, Ann Arbor, Michigan.

Michael Denkowski and Alon Lavie. 2011. Meteor-tuned phrase-based SMT: CMU French-English and Haitian-English systems for WMT 2011. Technical report, Technical Report CMU-LTI-11-011, Language Technologies Institute, Carnegie Mellon University.

Markus Dreyer and Yuanzhe Dong. 2015. APRO: All-pairs ranking optimization for MT tuning. In *Proceedings of the 2015 Conference of the North American Chapter of the Association for Computational Linguistics: Human Language Technologies*, NAACL-HLT '15, pages 1018–1023, Denver, Colorado, USA.

Chris Dyer, Adam Lopez, Juri Ganitkevitch, Jonathan Weese, Ferhan Ture, Phil Blunsom, Hendra Setiawan, Vladimir Eidelman, and Philip Resnik. 2010. cdec: A decoder, alignment, and learning framework for finite-state and context-free translation models. In *Proceedings of the ACL 2010 System Demonstrations*, ACL '10, pages 7–12, Uppsala, Sweden.

Michel Galley, Mark Hopkins, Kevin Knight, and Daniel Marcu. 2004. What's in a translation rule? In *Proceedings of the 2004 Annual Conference of the North American Chapter of the Association for Computational Linguistics: Human Language Technologies*, NAACL-HLT '04, pages 273–280, Boston, Massachusetts, USA.

Kevin Gimpel and Noah A. Smith. 2012. Structured ramp loss minimization for machine translation. In *Proceedings of the 2012 Annual Conference of the North American Chapter of the Association for Computational Linguistics: Human Language Technologies*, NAACL-HLT '12, pages 221–231, Montréal, Canada.

Kenneth Heafield. 2011. KenLM: Faster and smaller language model queries. In *Proceedings of the Sixth Workshop on Statistical Machine Translation*, WMT '11, Edinburgh, United Kingdom.

Mark Hopkins and Jonathan May. 2011. Tuning as ranking. In *Proceedings of the 2011 Conference on Empirical Methods in Natural Language Processing*, EMNLP '11, pages 1352–1362, Edinburgh, Scotland, United Kingdom.

Philipp Koehn, Franz Josef Och, and Daniel Marcu. 2003. Statistical phrase-based translation. In *Proceedings of the 2003 Conference of the North American Chapter of the Association for Computational Linguistics on Human Language Technology (Volume 1)*, HLT-NAACL '03, pages 48–54, Edmonton, Canada.

Philipp Koehn, Amittai Axelrod, Alexandra Birch Mayne, Chris Callison-Burch, Miles Osborne, and David Talbot. 2005. Edinburgh system description for the 2005 IWSLT speech translation evaluation. In *Proceedings of the International Workshop on Spoken Language Translation*, IWSLT '05, Pittsburgh, Pennsylvania, USA.

Philipp Koehn, Hieu Hoang, Alexandra Birch, Chris Callison-Burch, Marcello Federico, Nicola Bertoldi, Brooke Cowan, Wade Shen, Christine Moran, Richard Zens, Chris Dyer, Ondrej Bojar, Alexandra Constantin, and Evan Herbst. 2007. Moses: Open source toolkit for statistical machine translation. In *Proceedings of the 45th Annual Meeting of the Association for Computational Linguistics (Demonstration session).*, ACL '07, pages 177–180, Prague, Czech Republic.

Alon Lavie and Michael J. Denkowski. 2009. The METEOR metric for automatic evaluation of machine translation. *Machine Translation*, 23:105–115.

Zhifei Li, Chris Callison-Burch, Chris Dyer, Sanjeev Khudanpur, Lane Schwartz, Wren Thornton, Jonathan Weese, and Omar Zaidan. 2009. Joshua: An open source toolkit for parsing-based machine translation. In *Proceedings of the Fourth Workshop on Statistical Machine Translation*, WMT '09, pages 135–139, Athens, Greece.

Mu Li, Yinggong Zhao, Dongdong Zhang, and Ming Zhou. 2010. Adaptive development data selection for log-linear model in statistical machine translation. In *Proceedings of the 23rd International Conference on Computational Linguistics*, COLING '10, pages 662–670, Beijing, China.

Lemao Liu, Hailong Cao, Taro Watanabe, Tiejun Zhao, Mo Yu, and Conghui Zhu. 2012. Locally training the log-linear model for SMT. In *Proceedings of the 2012 Joint Conference on Empirical Methods in Natural Language Processing and Computational Natural Language Learning*, EMNLP-CoNLL '12, pages 402–411, Jeju Island, Korea.

David McAllester and Joseph Keshet. 2011. Generalization bounds and consistency for latent structural probit and ramp loss. In J. Shawe-Taylor, R.S. Zemel, P. Bartlett, F.C.N. Pereira, and K.Q. Weinberger, editors, *Advances in Neural Information Processing Systems 24*, NIPS '11, pages 2205–2212, Granada, Spain.

Robert C Moore and Chris Quirk. 2008. Random restarts in minimum error rate training for statistical machine translation. In *Proceedings of the 22nd International Conference on Computational Linguistics-Volume 1*, COLING '08, pages 585–592, Manchester, United Kingdom.

Preslav Nakov, Francisco Guzmán, and Stephan Vogel. 2012. Optimizing for sentence-level BLEU+1 yields short translations. In *Proceedings of the 24th International Conference on Computational Linguistics*, COLING '12, pages 1979–1994, Mumbai, India.

Preslav Nakov, Francisco Guzmán, and Stephan Vogel. 2013. A tale about PRO and monsters. In *Proceedings of the 51st Annual Meeting of the Association for Computational Linguistics (Volume 2: Short Papers)*, ACL '13, pages 12–17, Sofia, Bulgaria.

Franz Josef Och. 2003. Minimum error rate training in statistical machine translation. In *Proceedings of the 41st Annual Meeting of the Association for Computational Linguistics*, ACL '03, pages 160–167, Sapporo, Japan.

Kishore Papineni, Salim Roukos, Todd Ward, and Wei-Jing Zhu. 2002. BLEU: a method for automatic evaluation of machine translation. In *Proceedings of the 40th Annual Meeting of the Association for Computational Linguistics*, ACL '02, pages 311–318, Philadelphia, Pennsylvania, USA.

Chris Quirk, Arul Menezes, and Colin Cherry. 2005. Dependency treelet translation: Syntactically informed phrasal smt. In *Proceedings of the 43rd Annual Meeting on Association for Computational Linguistics*, ACL '05, pages 271–279, Ann Arbor, Michigan, USA.

Ryan Roth, Owen Rambow, Nizar Habash, Mona Diab, and Cynthia Rudin. 2008. Arabic morphological tagging, diacritization, and lemmatization using lexeme models and feature ranking. In *Proceedings of the 46th Annual Meeting of the Association for Computational Linguistics: Human Language Technologies*, ACL '08, pages 117–120, Columbus, Ohio, USA.

Patrick Simianer, Stefan Riezler, and Chris Dyer. 2012. Joint feature selection in distributed stochastic learning for large-scale discriminative training in SMT. In *Proceedings of the 50th Annual Meeting of the Association for Computational Linguistics: Long Papers - Volume 1*, ACL '12, pages 11–21, Jeju Island, Korea.

Matthew Snover, Bonnie Dorr, Richard Schwartz, Linnea Micciulla, and John Makhoul. 2006. A study of translation edit rate with targeted human annotation. In *Proceedings of the 7th Biennial Conference of the Association for Machine Translation in the Americas*, AMTA '06, pages 223–231, Cambridge, Massachusetts, USA.

David Vilar, Daniel Stein, Matthias Huck, and Hermann Ney. 2010. Jane: Open source hierarchical translation, extended with reordering and lexicon models. In *Proceedings of the 5th Workshop on Statistical Machine Translation and MetricsMATR*, WMT '10, pages 262–270, Uppsala, Sweden.

Taro Watanabe, Jun Suzuki, Hajime Tsukada, and Hideki Isozaki. 2007. Online large-margin training for statistical machine translation. In *Proceedings of the 2007 Joint Conference on Empirical Methods in Natural Language Processing and Computational Natural Language Learning*, EMNLP-CoNLL '07, pages 764–773, Prague, Czech Republic.

Zhongguang Zheng, Zhongjun He, Yao Meng, and Hao Yu. 2010. Domain adaptation for statistical machine translation in development corpus selection. In *Proceedings of the 4th International Universal Communication Symposium*, IUCS '10, pages 2–7, Beijing, China.

Annotation Projection-based Representation Learning for Cross-lingual Dependency Parsing

Min Xiao and **Yuhong Guo**
Department of Computer and Information Sciences
Temple University, Philadelphia, PA 19122, USA
{minxiao,yuhong}@temple.edu

Abstract

Cross-lingual dependency parsing aims to train a dependency parser for an annotation-scarce target language by exploiting annotated training data from an annotation-rich source language, which is of great importance in the field of natural language processing. In this paper, we propose to address cross-lingual dependency parsing by inducing latent cross-lingual data representations via matrix completion and annotation projections on a large amount of unlabeled parallel sentences. To evaluate the proposed learning technique, we conduct experiments on a set of cross-lingual dependency parsing tasks with nine different languages. The experimental results demonstrate the efficacy of the proposed learning method for cross-lingual dependency parsing.

1 Introduction

The natural language processing (NLP) community has witnessed an enormous development of multilingual resources, which draws increasing attention to developing cross-lingual NLP adaptation systems. Cross-lingual dependency parsing aims to train a dependency parser for a target language where labeled data is rare or unavailable by exploiting the abundant annotated data from a source language. Cross-lingual dependency parsing can effectively reduce the expensive manual annotation effort in individual languages and has been increasingly studied in the multilingual community. Previous works have demonstrated the success of cross-lingual dependency parsing for a variety of languages (Durrett et al., 2012; McDonald et al., 2013; Täckström et al., 2013; Søgaard and Wulff, 2012).

One fundamental issue of cross-lingual dependency parsing lies in how to effectively transfer the *annotation* information from the source language domain to the target language domain. Due to the language divergence over the word-level representations and the sentence structures, simply training a monolingual dependency parser on the labeled source language data without adaptation learning will fail to produce a dependency parser that works in the target language domain. To tackle this problem, a variety of works in the literature have designed better algorithms to exploit the annotated resources in the source languages, including the cross-lingual annotation projection methods (Hwa et al., 2005; Smith and Eisner, 2009; Zhao et al., 2009), the cross-lingual direct transfer with linguistic constraints methods (Ganchev et al., 2009; Naseem et al., 2010; Naseem et al., 2012), and the cross-lingual representation learning methods (Durrett et al., 2012; Täckström et al., 2012; Zhang et al., 2012).

In this work, we propose a novel representation learning method to address cross-lingual dependency parsing, which exploits annotation projections on a large amount of unlabeled parallel sentences to induce latent cross-lingual features via matrix completion. It combines the advantages of the cross-lingual annotation projection methods, which project labeled information into the target language domain, and the cross-lingual representation learning methods, which learn latent interlingual features. Specifically, we first train a dependency parser on the labeled source language data and use it to infer labels for the unlabeled source language sentences of the parallel resources. We then project the annotations from the source language to the target language via the word alignments on the parallel sentences. Afterwards, we define a set of interlingual features and construct a word-*feature* matrix by associating each word with these language-independent features. We then use the original labeled source language data and the predicted (or projected) la-

Proceedings of the 19th Conference on Computational Language Learning, pages 73–82,
Beijing, China, July 30-31, 2015. ©2015 Association for Computational Linguistics

beled information on the parallel sentences to fill in the observed entries of the word-feature matrix, while matrix completion is performed to fill the remaining missing entries. The completed word-feature matrix provides a set of consistent cross-lingual representation features for the words in both languages. We use these features as augmenting features to train a dependency parsing system on the labeled data in the source language and perform prediction on the test sentences in the target language. To evaluate the proposed learning method, we conduct experiments on eight cross-lingual dependency parsing tasks with nine different languages. The experimental results demonstrate the superior performance of the proposed cross-lingual transfer learning method, comparing to other approaches.

2 Related Work

A variety of cross-lingual dependency parsing methods have been developed in the literature. We provide a brief review over the related works in this section.

Much work developed in the literature is based on annotation projection (Hwa et al., 2005; Liu et al., 2013; Smith and Eisner, 2009; Zhao et al., 2009). Basically, they exploit parallel sentences and first project the annotations of the source language sentences to the corresponding target language sentences via the word level alignments. Then, they train a dependency parser in the target language by using the target language sentences with projected annotations. The performance of annotation projection-based methods can be affected by the quality of word-level alignments and the specific projection schema. Therefore, Hwa et al. (2005) proposed to heuristically correct or modify the projected annotations in order to increase the projection performance while Smith and Eisner (2009) used a more robust projection method, quasi-synchronous grammar projection, to address cross-lingual dependency parsing. Moreover, Liu et al. (2013) proposed to project the discrete dependency arcs instead of the treebank as the training set. These works however assume that the parallel sentences are already available, or can be obtained by using free machine translation tools. Instead, Zhao et al. (2009) considered the cost of machine translation and used a bilingual lexicon to obtain a translated treebank with projected annotations from the source language.

A number of works are developed based on representation learning (Durrett et al., 2012; Täckström et al., 2012; Zhang et al., 2012; Xiao and Guo, 2014). In general, these methods first automatically learn some language-independent features and then train a dependency parser in this interlingual feature space with labeled data in the source language and apply it on the data in the target language. Durrett et al. (2012) used a bilingual lexicon, which can be manually constructed or induced on parallel sentences, to learn language-independent projection features for cross-lingual dependency parsing. Täckström et al. (2012) used unlabeled parallel sentences to induce cross-lingual word clusterings and used these word clusterings as interlingual features. Both (Durrett et al., 2012) and (Täckström et al., 2012) assumed that the twelve universal part-of-speech (POS) tags (Petrov et al., 2012) are available and used them as the basic interlingual features. Moreover, Zhang et al. (2012) proposed to automatically map language-specific POS tags to universal POS tags to address cross-lingual dependency parsing, instead of using the manually defined mapping rules. Recently, Xiao and Guo (2014) used a set of bilingual word pairs as pivots to learn interlingual distributed word representations via deep neural networks as augmenting features for cross-lingual dependency parsing.

Some other works are proposed based on multilingual linguistic constraints (Ganchev et al., 2009; Gillenwater et al., 2010; Naseem et al., 2010; Naseem et al., 2012). Basically, they first construct a set of linguistic constrains and then train a dependency parsing system by incorporating the linguistic constraints via posterior regularization. The constraints are expected to bridge the language differences. Ganchev et al. (2009) automatically learned the constraints by using parallel data while some other works manually constructed them by using the universal dependency rules (Naseem et al., 2010) or the typological features (Naseem et al., 2012).

3 Proposed Approach

In this section, we present a novel representation learning method for cross-lingual dependency parsing, which combines annotation projection and matrix completion-based feature representation learning together to produce effective interlingual features.

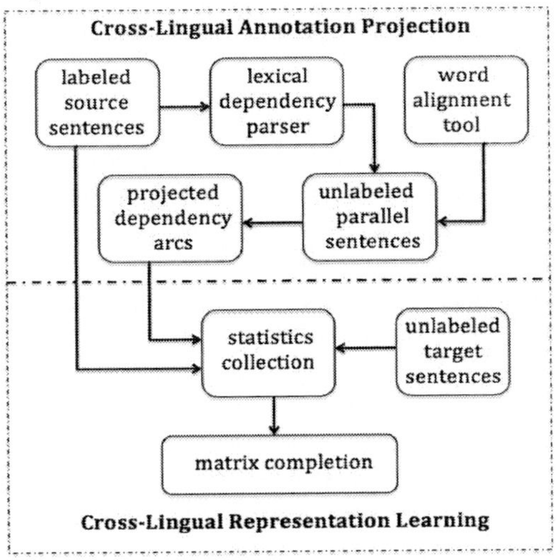

Figure 1: The architecture of the proposed cross-lingual representation learning framework, which consists of two steps, cross-lingual annotation projection and cross-lingual representation learning.

We consider the following cross-lingual dependency parsing setting. We have a large amount of labeled sentences in the source language and a set of unlabeled sentences in the target language. In addition, we also have a large set of auxiliary unlabeled parallel sentences across the two languages. We aim to learn interlingual feature representations such that a dependency parser trained in the source language sentences can be applied in the target language domain. The framework for the proposed cross-lingual representation learning system is given in Figure 1. The system has two steps: cross-lingual annotation projection and cross-lingual representation learning. We present each of the two steps below.

3.1 Cross-Lingual Annotation Projection

In the first step, we employ a large amount of unlabeled parallel sentences to transfer dependency relations from the source language to the target language. We first train a lexicalized dependency parser with the labeled training data in the source language. Then we use this parser to produce parse trees on the source language sentences of the auxiliary parallel data. Simultaneously, we perform word-level alignments on the unlabeled parallel sentences using existing alignment tools. Finally, we project the predicted dependency relations of the source language sentences to their parallel counterparts in the target language via the word-level alignments. Instead of projecting the whole dependency trees, which requires more sophisticated algorithms, we simply project each dependency arc on the source sentences to the target language side.

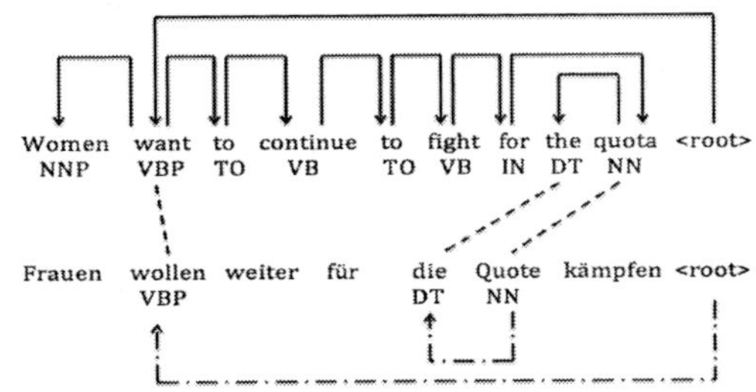

Figure 2: An example of cross-lingual annotation projection, where a partial word-level alignment is shown to demonstrate two cases of annotation projection.

We now use a specific example in Figure 2 to illustrate the projection step. This example contains an English sentence and its parallel sentence in German. The English sentence is fully labeled with each dependency relation indicated by a solid directed arc. The dashed lines between the English sentence and the German sentence show the alignments between them. For each dependency arc instance, we consider the following properties: the parent word, the child word, the parent POS, the child POS, the dependency direction, and the dependency distances. The projection of the dependency relations from the source language to the target language is conducted based on the word-level alignment. There are two different scenarios. The first scenario is that the two source language words involved in the dependency relation are aligned to two different words in the corresponding target sentence. For example, the English words "the" and "quota" are aligned to German words "die" and "Quote" separately. We then copy this dependency relation into the target language side. The second scenario is that a source language word is aligned to a word in the target language sentence and has a dependency relation with the "<root>" word. For example, the English word "want" is aligned to "wollen" and it has a dependency arc with "<root>". We then project the dependency relation from the English side to the German side as well. Moreover, we also directly project the POS tags of the source language

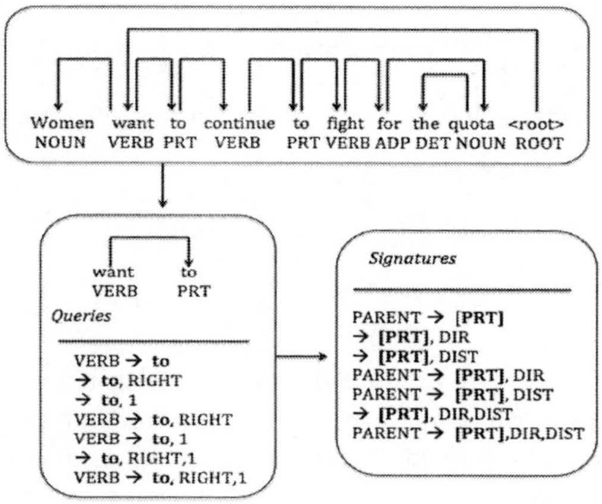

Figure 3: Example of how to collect queries for each specific dependency relation and how to obtain the abstract signatures (adapted from (Durrett et al., 2012)).

words onto the target language words. Since the word order for each aligned word pair in parallel sentences can be different, we recalculate the dependency direction and the dependency distance for the projected dependency arc instance. Note the example in Figure 2 only shows a partial word-level alignment to demonstrate the two cases of the annotation projection. The word alignment tool can align more words than shown in the example.

3.2 Cross-Lingual Representation Learning

After cross-lingual annotation projection, we have a set of projected dependency arc instances in the target language. However, the sentences in the target language are not fully labeled. Dependency relation related features are not readily available for all the words in the target language domain. Hence, in this step, we first generate a set of interlingual features and then automatically fill the missing feature values for the target language words with matrix completion based on the projected feature values.

3.2.1 Generating Interlingual Features

We use the signature method in (Durrett et al., 2012) to construct a set of interlingual *features* for the words in the source and target language domains . The signatures proposed in (Durrett et al., 2012) for dependency parsing are universal across different languages, and have numerical values that are computed in specific dependency relations. Here we illustrate the signature generation process by using an example in Figure 3, which is adapted from (Durrett et al., 2012). Note for each dependency relation between a parent (also known as the head) word and a child (also known as the dependent) word, we can collect a number of queries based on the dependency properties. For example, given the dependency arc between "want" and "to" in the English sentence in Figure 3, and assuming we consider the child word "to", we produce queries by considering a non-empty subset of the dependency properties (the parent POS, the dependency direction, the dependency distance), which provides us 7 queries: "VERB→to", "→to, RIGHT", "→to, 1", "VERB →to, RIGHT", "VERB→to, 1", "→to, RIGHT, 1", "VERB→to, RIGHT, 1", where VERB is the parent POS tag, RIGHT is the dependency direction and 1 is the dependency distance. Then we can abstract the specific queries to generate the signatures by replacing the considered word ("to") with its POS tag ("PRT"), and replacing the parent POS tag with "PARENT", the specific dependency distance with "DIST" and the dependency direction with "DIR". This produces the following 7 signatures: "PARENT→[PRT]", "→[PRT], DIR", "→[PRT], DIST", "PARENT→[PRT], DIST", "PARENT→[PRT], DIST", "→[PRT], DIR, DIST", and "PARENT→[PRT], DIR, DIST", where the brackets indicate the POS tags are for the considered word. Similarly, we can perform the same abstraction process for the parent word "want" and get another 7 signatures (see Table 1). Since each signature contains one POS tag and there are 13 different POS types (12 universal POS tags and 1 special type for the "<root>" word), we can get a total of $7 \times 2 \times 13 = 182$ signatures. These signatures are independent of specific languages, though their numerical values should be computed in a specific dependency relation for each considered target word.

A set of interlingual *features* can then be generated from these abstractive signatures by considering different instantiations of their items. For a given target word with an observed POS tag, it has 14 signatures (see Table 1). For each signature, we consider all possible instantiations of its other items given the fixed target word. For example, for the target word "to", its signature "→[PRT], DIR" can be instantiated into 2 features: "→ LEFT" and "→ RIGHT". Similarly, its signature "→[PRT],

Signatures	# Features
[PRT] → DIR	2
[PRT] → DIST	5
[PRT] → CHILD	13
[PRT] → DIR, DIST	10
[PRT] → CHILD, DIR	26
[PRT] → CHILD, DIST	65
[PRT] → CHILD, DIR, DIST	130
→ [PRT], DIR	2
→ [PRT], DIST	5
PARENT → [PRT]	13
→ [PRT], DIR, DIST	10
PARENT → [PRT], DIR	26
PARENT → [PRT], DIST	65
PARENT → [PRT], DIR, DIST	130
Total	502

Table 1: The number of induced "features" of each signature for a given word.

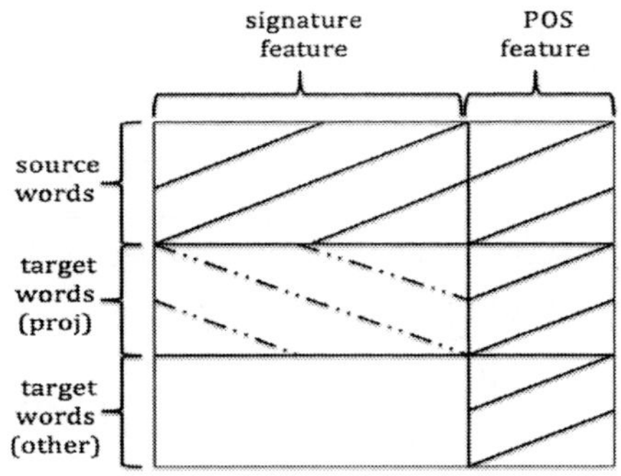

Figure 4: The word-feature matrix. There are three parts of words: the source language words, target language words from the projected dependency arc instances, and additional target language words. The signature features are the 502 interlingual features and the POS features are the 13 universal POS tags. Solid lines indicate observed entries, dashed lines indicate partially observed entries, while empty indicates missing entries.

DIST" can be instantiated into 5 features since DIST has 5 different values ({1, 2, 3–5, 6–10, 11+}), and its signature "[PRT]→CHILD" can be instantiated into 13 features since CHILD denotes the child word's POS tags and can have 13 different values. Hence as shown in Table 1, we can get 502 features from the 14 signatures.

3.2.2 Learning Feature Values with Matrix Completion

The signature-based 502 interlingual features together with the 13 universal POS tag features can be used as *language independent features* for all the words in the vocabulary constructed across the source and target language domains. In particular, we can form a *word-feature* matrix with the constructed vocabulary and the total 515 language independent features. For each word that appeared in the dependency relation arcs, we can use the number of appearances of its interlingual features as the corresponding feature values. However, the sentences in the target language are not fully labeled. Some words in the target language domain may not be observed in the projected dependency arc instances, and we cannot compute their feature values for the 502 interlingual features, though the 13 universal POS tag features are available for all words. Moreover, since we only have a limited number of projected dependency arc instances in the target language, even for some target words that appeared in the projected arc instances of the parallel data, we may only observe a subset of features among the total 502 interlingual features, with the rest features missing. Hence the constructed *word-feature* matrix is only partially observed, as shown in Figure 4. Furthermore, there could also be some noise in the observed feature values as some word features may not have received sufficient observations.

To solve the missing feature problem and simultaneously perform data denoising, we exploit a feature correlation assumption: the 502 constructed interlingual features and the 13 universal POS tags are not mutually independent; they usually contain a lot statistical correlation information. For example, for a word "want" with POS tag "VERB", its feature value for "VERB → **want**, RIGHT" is likely to be very small such as zero, while its feature value for "**want**→ NOUN, LEFT" is likely to be large. Moreover, the existence of any one of the two interlingual features in this example can also indicate the non-existence of the other feature. The existence of feature correlations establishes the low-rank property of the word-feature matrix. We hence propose to fill the missing feature values and reduce the noise in the word-feature matrix by performing matrix completion. Low-rank matrix completion has been successfully used in many applications to fill missing entries of partially observed low-rank matrices and perform matrix denoising (Cabral et al., 2011; Xiao and Guo, 2013) by exploiting the feature correlations and underlying low-dimensional representations. Following the same principle, we expect to automatically discover the missing feature values in our word-feature matrix and perform denoising through low-rank matrix completion.

Let $M^0 \in \mathbb{R}^{n \times k}$ denote the partially observed word-feature matrix in Figure 4, where n is the number of words and k is the dimensionality of the feature set, which is 515 in this study. Let Ω denote the set of indices for the observed entries. Hence for each observed entry $(i, j) \in \Omega$, M^0_{ij} contains the frequency collected for the j-th feature of the i-th word. We then formulate matrix completion as the following optimization problem to recover a full matrix M from the partially observed matrix M^0:

$$\min_{M \geq 0} \gamma \|M\|_* + \alpha \|M\|_{1,1} + \sum_{(i,j)\in\Omega} (M_{ij} - M^0_{ij})^2 \quad (1)$$

where the trace norm $\|M\|_*$ enforces the low-rank property of the matrix, and $\|M\|_{1,1}$ denotes the entrywise L1 norm. Since many words usually only have observed values for a small subset of the 502 interlingual features due to the simple fact that they are only associated with very few POS tags, a fully observed word-feature matrix is typically sparse and contains many zero entries. Hence we use the L1 norm regularizer to encode the sparsity of the matrix M. The nonnegativity constraint $M \geq 0$ encodes the fact that our frequency based feature values in the word-feature matrix are all nonnegative. The minimization problem in Eq (1) can be solved using a standard projected gradient descent algorithm (Xiao and Guo, 2013).

3.3 Cross-Lingual Dependency Parsing

After matrix completion, we can get a set of interlingual features for all the words in the word-feature matrix. We then use the interlingual features for each word as augmenting features and train a delexicalized dependency parser on the labeled sentences in the source language. The parser is then applied to perform prediction on the test sentences in the target language, which are also delexicalized and augmented with the interlingual features.

4 Experiments

4.1 Datasets

We used the multilingual dependency parsing dataset from the CoNLL-X shared tasks (Buchholz and Marsi, 2006; Nivre et al., 2007) and experimented with nine different languages: *Danish (Da), Dutch (Nl), English (En), German (De), Greek (El), Italian (It), Portuguese (Pt), Spanish (Es)* and *Swedish (Sv)*. For each language, the original dataset contains a training set and a test set. We constructed eight cross-lingual dependency parsing tasks, by using English as the label-rich source language and using each of the other eight languages as the label-poor target language. For example, the task *En2Da* means that we used English sentences as the source language data and Danish sentences as the target language data. For each task, we used the original training set in English as the labeled source language data, and used the original training set in the target language as unlabeled training data and the original test set in the target language as test sentences. Each sentence from the dataset is labeled with gold standard POS tags. We manually mapped these language-specific POS tags to 12 universal POS tags: NOUN (nouns), NUM (numerals), PRON (pronouns), ADJ (adjectives), ADP (prepositions or postpositions), ADV (adverbs), CONJ (conjunctions), DET (determiners), PRT (particles), PUNC (punctuation marks), VERB (verbs) and X (for others).

We used the unlabeled parallel sentences from the *European parliament proceedings parallel corpus* (Koehn, 2005), which contains parallel sentences between multiple languages, as auxiliary unlabeled parallel sentences in our experiments. For the representation learning over each cross-lingual dependency parsing task, we used all the parallel sentences for the given language pair from this corpus. The number of parallel sentences for the eight language pairs ranges from $1,235,976$ to $1,997,775$, and the number of tokens involved in these sentences in each language ranges from $31,929,703$ to $50,602,994$.

4.2 Representation Learning

For the proposed representation learning, we first trained a lexicalized dependency parser on the labeled source language data using the MSTParser tool (proj with the first order set) (McDonald et al., 2005) and used it to predict the parsing annotations of the source language sentences in the unlabeled parallel dataset. The sentences of the parallel data only contain sequences of words, without additional POS tag information. We then used an existing POS tagging tool (Collobert et al., 2011) to infer POS tags for them. Next we produced word-level alignments on the unlabeled parallel

Basic	Conj with dist	Conj with dir	Conj with dist and dir
upos_h	dist, upos_h	dir, upos_h	dist, dir, upos_h
upos_d	dist, upos_d	dir, upos_d	dist, dir, upos_d
upos_h, upos_d,	dist, upos_h, upos_d	dir, upos_h, upos_d	dist, dir, upos_h, upos_d

Table 2: Feature templates for training a basic delexicalized dependency parser. *upos* stands for the universal POS tag, *h* stands for the head word, *d* stands for the dependent word, *dist* stands for the dependency distance, which has five values $\{1, 2, 3-5, 6-10, 11+\}$, and *dir* stands for the dependency direction, which has two values {left, right}.

Tasks		Wikitionary				Parallel Data				
	Delex	Proj1	∇	DNN	∇	Proj2	∇	RLAP	∇	X-lingual
En2Da	36.5	41.3	4.8	42.6	6.1	42.9	6.4	43.6	7.1	38.7
En2De	46.2	49.2	3.0	49.5	3.3	49.7	3.5	50.5	4.3	50.7
En2El	61.5	62.4	0.9	63.0	1.5	63.5	2.0	64.3	2.8	63.0
En2Es	52.1	54.5	2.4	55.7	3.6	56.2	4.1	56.3	4.2	62.9
En2It	56.4	57.7	1.3	59.1	2.7	59.2	2.8	60.4	4.0	68.8
En2Nl	62.0	64.4	2.4	65.1	3.1	64.9	2.9	66.1	4.1	54.3
En2Pt	68.7	71.5	2.8	72.4	3.7	71.9	3.2	72.8	4.1	71.0
En2Sv	57.8	61.0	3.2	61.9	4.1	62.9	5.1	63.7	5.9	56.9
Average	55.2	57.8	2.6	58.7	3.5	58.9	3.8	59.7	4.6	58.3

Table 3: Comparison results in terms of unlabeled attachment score (UAS) for the eight cross-lingual dependency parsing tasks (English is used as the source language). The evaluation results are on *all the test sentences*. The *Delex* method uses no auxiliary resource, *Proj1* and *DNN* use Wikitionary as auxiliary resource, *Proj2, RLAP*, and *X-lingual* use parallel sentences as auxiliary resources. ∇ denotes the improvements of each method over the baseline *Delex* method. The bottom row contains the average results over the eight tasks.

sentences by using the Berkeley alignment tool (Liang et al., 2006). With the word alignments, we then projected the predicted dependency relations from the source language sentences of the parallel data to the target language side, which produces a set of dependency arc instances in the target language. Finally, we constructed the partially observed word-feature matrix from these labeled data and conducted matrix completion to recover the whole matrix. For matrix completion, we used the first task *En2Da* to perform parameter selection based on the test performance. We selected γ from $\{0.1, 1, 10\}$ and selected α from $\{10^3, 10^4, 10^5\}$. The selected values $\gamma = 1$ and $\alpha = 10^{-4}$ were then used for all the experiments.

4.3 Experimental Results

4.3.1 Test Results on All the Test Sentences

We first compared the proposed representation learning with annotation projection method, *RLAP*, to the following methods in our experiments: *Delex, Proj1, Proj2, DNN* and *X-lingual.* The *Delex* method is a baseline method, which replaces the language-specific word sequence with the universal POS tag sequence and then trains a delexicalized dependency parser. We listed the feature templates used in this baseline delexicalized dependency parser in Table 2. The *Proj1* and *Proj2* methods are from (Durrett et al., 2012). Durrett et al. (2012) proposed to use bilingual lexicon to learn cross-lingual features and provided two ways to construct the bilingual lexicon, one is based on Wikitionary and the other is based on unlabeled parallel sentences with observed word-level alignments. We used these two ways separately to construct the bilingual lexicon between the languages for learning cross-lingual features, which are then used as augmenting features for training delexicalized dependency parsers. We denote the Wikitionary-based method as *Proj1* and the parallel-sentence-based method as *Proj2*. The *DNN* method, developed in (Xiao and Guo,

Tasks	Delex	Proj2	∇	RLAP	∇	USR	PGI	PR	MLC
En2Da	46.7	54.6	7.9	55.7	9.0	51.9	41.6	44.0	-
En2De	62.0	63.0	1.0	64.0	2.0	-	-	39.6	62.8
En2El	60.9	61.9	1.0	63.2	2.3	-	-	-	61.4
En2Es	55.2	58.3	3.1	59.6	4.4	67.2	58.4	62.4	57.3
En2It	55.5	56.9	1.4	58.3	2.8	-	-	-	56.2
En2Nl	60.3	62.5	2.2	63.7	3.4	-	45.1	37.9	62.0
En2Pt	80.2	84.5	4.3	85.7	5.5	71.5	63.0	47.8	83.8
En2Sv	73.4	76.0	2.6	76.4	3.0	63.3	58.3	42.2	74.9
Average	61.8	64.7	2.9	65.8	4.1	-	-	-	-

Table 4: Comparison results on the short test sentences with length of 10 or less in terms of unlabeled attachment score (UAS). ∇ denotes the improvements of each method over the baseline *Delex* method.

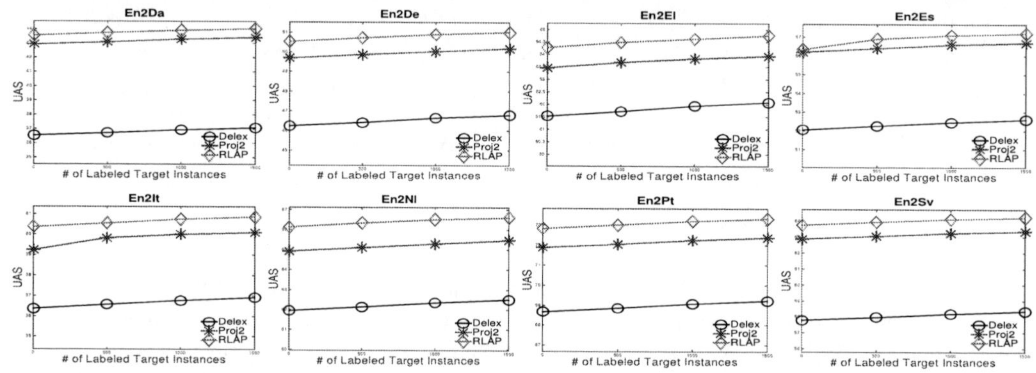

Figure 5: Unlabeled attachment score (UAS) on the whole test sentences in the target language by varying the number of labeled training sentences in the target language.

2014), uses Wikitionary to construct bilingual word pairs and then uses a deep neural network to learn interlingual word embeddings as augmenting features for training delexicalized dependency parsers. The *X-lingual* method uses unlabeled parallel sentences to induce cross-lingual word clusters as augmenting features for delexicalized dependency parser (Täckström et al., 2012). For *X-lingual*, we cited its results reported in its original paper. For other methods, we used the MSTParser (McDonald et al., 2005) as the underlying dependency parsing tool. To train the MSTParser, we set the number of maximum iterations for the perceptron training as 10 and set the number of best-k dependency tree candidates as 1.

We evaluated the empirical performance of each comparison method on all the test sentences. The comparison results on the eight cross-lingual dependency parsing tasks in terms of unlabeled attachment score (UAS) are reported in Table 3. We can see that the baseline method, *Delex*, performs poorly across the eight tasks. This is not surprising since the sequence of universal POS tags are not discriminative enough for the dependency parsing task. Note even for two sentences with the exact same sequence of POS tags, they may have different dependency trees. By using auxiliary bilingual word pairs via Wikitionary, the two cross-lingual representation learning methods, *Proj1* and *DNN*, outperform *Delex* across all the eight tasks. Between these two methods, *DNN* consistently outperforms *Proj1*, which suggests the interlingual word embeddings induced by deep neural networks are very effective. By using unlabeled parallel sentences as an auxiliary resource, the two methods, *Proj2* and *RLAP*, consistently outperform the baseline *Delex* method, while *X-lingual* outperforms *Delex* on six tasks. Moreover, *Proj2* outperforms its variant *Proj1* across all the eight tasks and achieves comparable performance with the deep neural network based method *DNN*. This suggests that unlabeled parallel sentences form a stronger auxiliary resource than the free Wikitionary. Our proposed approach, *RLAP*, which has the capacity of exploiting the unlabeled parallel sentences, consistently outperforms the four comparison methods, *Delex, Proj1, DNN* and *Proj2*, across all the eight tasks. It also outperforms the *X-lingual* method on five tasks. The average UAS over all the eight tasks for the *RLAP* method is 1.4 higher than the *X-lingual* method. All these results demonstrated the effectiveness of the proposed representation learning method for cross-lingual dependency parsing.

4.3.2 Test Results on Short Test Sentences

We also conducted empirical evaluations on short test sentences (with length of 10 or less). We compared *Delex, Proj2* and *RLAP* with four other methods, *USR, PGI, PR* and *MLC*. The *USR* method is a cross-lingual direct transfer method which uses universal dependency rules to construct linguistic constraints (Naseem et al., 2010). The *PGI* method is a phylogenetic grammar induction model (Berg-Kirkpatrick and Klein, 2010). The *PR* method is a posterior regularization approach (Gillenwater et al., 2010). The *MLC* method is the multilingual linguistic constraints-based method which uses typological features for cross-lingual dependency parsing (Naseem et al., 2012). Here we used this method in our setting with only one source domain. Moreover, since we do not have typological features for Danish, we did not conduct experiment on the first task with *MLC*. For the methods of *USR, PGI* and *PR*, we cited their results reported in their original papers. All the cited results are also produced on the short sentences of the CoNLL-X shard task dataset. We cited them as references on measuring the progress of cross-lingual dependency parsing on each given target language.

The comparison results are reported in Table 4. We can see that the results on the short test sentences are in general better than on the whole test set (in Table 3) for the same method across most tasks. This suggests that it is easier to infer the dependency tree for a short sentence than for a long sentence. Nevertheless, *Proj2* consistently outperforms *Delex* and *RLAP* consistently outperforms *Proj2* across all the tasks. Moreover, *RLAP* achieves the highest test scores in seven out of the eight cross-lingual tasks among all the comparison systems. This again demonstrated the efficacy of the proposed approach for cross-lingual dependency parsing.

4.4 Impact of Labeled Training Data in Target Language

We have also conducted experiments for the learning scenarios where a small set of labeled training sentences from the target language is available. Specifically, we conducted experiments with a few different numbers of additional labeled training sentences from the target language, {500, 1000, 1500}, using three methods, *RLAP, Delex* and *Proj2*. The comparison results on all the test sentences are reported in Figure 5. We can see that the performance of all three methods increases very slow but in a similar trend with more additional labeled training instances from the target language. However, both *Proj2* and *RLAP* outperform *Delex* with large margins across all experiments. Moreover, the proposed method, *RLAP*, produces the best results across all the eight tasks. The results again verified the efficacy of the proposed method, demonstrated that filling the missing feature values with matrix completion is indeed useful.

5 Conclusion

In this paper, we proposed a novel representation learning method with annotation projection to address cross-lingual dependency parsing. The proposed approach exploits unlabeled parallel sentences and combines cross-lingual annotation projection and matrix completion-based interlingual feature learning together to automatically induce a set of language-independent numerical features. We used these interlingual features as augmenting features to train a delexicalized dependency parser on the labeled sentences in the source language and tested it in the target language domain. Our experimental results on eight cross-lingual dependency parsing tasks showed the proposed representation learning method outperforms a number of comparison methods.

Acknowledgments

This research was supported in part by NSF grant IIS-1065397.

References

T. Berg-Kirkpatrick and D. Klein. 2010. Phylogenetic grammar induction. In *Proc. of the Annual Meeting of the Association for Comput. Linguistics (ACL)*.

S. Buchholz and E. Marsi. 2006. CoNLL-X shared task on multilingual dependency parsing. In *Proc. of the Conference on Computational Natural Language Learning (CoNLL)*.

R. Cabral, F. Torre, J. Costeira, and A. Bernardino. 2011. Matrix completion for multi-label image classification. In *Advances in Neural Information Processing Systems (NIPS)*.

R. Collobert, J. Weston, L. Bottou, M. Karlen, K. Kavukcuoglu, and P. Kuksa. 2011. Natural language processing (almost) from scratch. *J. of Machine Learning Research (JMLR)*, 12:2493–2537.

G. Durrett, A. Pauls, and D. Klein. 2012. Syntactic transfer using a bilingual lexicon. In *Proc. of the Joint Conference on Empirical Methods in Natural Language Processing and Computational Natural Language Learning (EMNLP-CoNLL)*.

K. Ganchev, J. Gillenwater, and B. Taskar. 2009. Dependency grammar induction via bitext projection constraints. In *Proc. of the Joint Conference of the Annual Meeting of the ACL and the International Joint Conference on Natural Language Processing of the AFNLP (ACL-IJCNLP)*.

J. Gillenwater, K. Ganchev, J. Graça, F. Pereira, and B. Taskar. 2010. Sparsity in dependency grammar induction. In *Proc. of the Annual Meeting of the Association for Computational Linguistics (ACL)*.

R. Hwa, P. Resnik, A. Weinberg, C. Cabezas, and O. Kolak. 2005. Bootstrapping parsers via syntactic projection across parallel texts. *Natural Language Engineering*, 11:11–311.

P. Koehn. 2005. Europarl: A Parallel Corpus for Statistical Machine Translation. In *Proc. of the Machine Translation Summit*.

P. Liang, B. Taskar, and D. Klein. 2006. Alignment by agreement. In *Proc. of the Conference on Human Language Technology Conference of the North American Chapter of the Association of Computational Linguistics (NAACL)*.

K. Liu, Y. Lü, W. Jiang, and Q. Liu. 2013. Bilingually-guided monolingual dependency parsing grammar induction. In *Proc. of the Conference on Annual Meeting of the Association for Computational Linguistics (ACL)*.

R. McDonald, K. Crammer, and F. Pereira. 2005. Online large-margin training of dependency parsers. In *Proc. of the Annual Meeting on Association for Computational Linguistics (ACL)*.

R. McDonald, J. Nivre, Y. Quirmbach-Brundage, Y. Goldberg, D. Das, K. Ganchev, K. Hall, S. Petrov, H. Zhang, O. Tëkström, C. Bedini, N. Castelló, and J. Lee. 2013. Universal dependency annotation for multilingual parsing. In *Proc. of the Annual Meeting on Association for Comput. Linguistics (ACL)*.

T. Naseem, H. Chen, R. Barzilay, and M. Johnson. 2010. Using universal linguistic knowledge to guide grammar induction. In *Proc. of the Conference on Empirical Methods in Natural Language Processing (EMNLP)*.

T. Naseem, R. Barzilay, and A. Globerson. 2012. Selective sharing for multilingual dependency parsing. In *Proc. of the Annual Meeting of the Association for Computational Linguistics (ACL)*.

J. Nivre, J. Hall, S. Kübler, R. McDonald, J. Nilsson, S. Riedel, and D. Yuret. 2007. The CoNLL 2007 shared task on dependency parsing. In *Proc. of the Joint Conference on Empirical Methods in Natural Language Processing and Computational Natural Language Learning (EMNLP-CoNLL)*.

S. Petrov, D. Das, and R. McDonald. 2012. A universal part-of-speech tagset. In *Proc. of the International Conference on Language Resources and Evaluation (LREC)*.

D. Smith and J. Eisner. 2009. Parser adaptation and projection with quasi-synchronous grammar features. In *Proc. of the Conf. on Empirical Methods in Natural Language Processing (EMNLP)*.

A. Søgaard and J. Wulff. 2012. An empirical study of non-lexical extensions to delexicalized transfer. In *Proc. of the Conference on Computational linguistics (COLING)*.

O. Täckström, R. McDonald, and J. Uszkoreit. 2012. Cross-lingual word clusters for direct transfer of linguistic structure. In *Proc. of the Conference of the North American Chapter of the Association for Computational Linguistics: Human Language Technologies (NAACL)*.

O. Täckström, R. McDonald, and J. Nivre. 2013. Target language adaptation of discriminative transfer parsers. In *Proc. of the Conf. of the North American Chapter of the Association for Comput. Linguistics: Human Language Technologies (NAACL)*.

M. Xiao and Y. Guo. 2013. A novel two-step method for cross language representation learning. In *Advances in Neural Inform. Process. Systems (NIPS)*.

M. Xiao and Y. Guo. 2014. Distributed word representation learning for cross-lingual dependency parsing. In *Proceedings of the Conference on Computational Natural Language Learning (CoNLL)*.

Y. Zhang, R. Reichart, R. Barzilay, and A. Globerson. 2012. Learning to map into a universal pos tagset. In *Proc. of the Joint Conf. on Empirical Methods in Natural Language Processing and Comput. Natural Language Learning (EMNLP-CoNLL)*.

H. Zhao, Y. Song, C. Kit, and G. Zhou. 2009. Cross language dependency parsing using a bilingual lexicon. In *Proc. of the Joint Conf. of ACL and AFNLP (ACL-IJCNLP)*.

Big Data Small Data, In Domain Out-of Domain, Known Word Unknown Word: The Impact of Word Representations on Sequence Labelling Tasks

Lizhen Qu[1,2], **Gabriela Ferraro**[1,2], **Liyuan Zhou**[1], **Weiwei Hou**[1],
Nathan Schneider[3] and **Timothy Baldwin**[1,4]

[1] NICTA, Australia
[2] The Australian National University
[3] University of Edinburgh
[4] The University of Melbourne

{lizhen.qu,gabriela.ferraro,liyuan.zho,weiwei.hou}@nicta.com.au
nschneid@cs.cmu.edu
tb@ldwin.net

Abstract

Word embeddings — distributed word representations that can be learned from unlabelled data — have been shown to have high utility in many natural language processing applications. In this paper, we perform an extrinsic evaluation of four popular word embedding methods in the context of four sequence labelling tasks: part-of-speech tagging, syntactic chunking, named entity recognition, and multiword expression identification. A particular focus of the paper is analysing the effects of task-based updating of word representations. We show that when using word embeddings as features, as few as several hundred training instances are sufficient to achieve competitive results, and that word embeddings lead to improvements over out-of-vocabulary words and also out of domain. Perhaps more surprisingly, our results indicate there is little difference between the different word embedding methods, and that simple Brown clusters are often competitive with word embeddings across all tasks we consider.

1 Introduction

Recently, distributed word representations have grown to become a mainstay of natural language processing (NLP), and have been shown to have empirical utility in a myriad of tasks (Collobert and Weston, 2008; Turian et al., 2010; Baroni et al., 2014; Andreas and Klein, 2014). The underlying idea behind distributed word representations is simple: to map each word w in vocabulary V onto a continuous-valued vector of dimensionality $d \ll |V|$. Words that are similar (e.g., with respect to syntax or lexical semantics) will ideally be mapped to similar regions of the vector space, implicitly supporting both generalisation across in-vocabulary (IV) items, and countering the effects of data sparsity for low-frequency and out-of-vocabulary (OOV) items.

Without some means of automatically deriving the vector representations without reliance on labelled data, however, word embeddings would have little practical utility. Fortunately, it has been shown that they can be "pre-trained" from unlabelled text data using various algorithms to model the distributional hypothesis (i.e., that words which occur in similar contexts tend to be semantically similar). Pre-training methods have been refined considerably in recent years, and scaled up to increasingly large corpora.

As with other machine learning methods, it is well known that the quality of the pre-trained word embeddings depends heavily on factors including parameter optimisation, the size of the training data, and the fit with the target application. For example, Turian et al. (2010) showed that the optimal dimensionality for word embeddings is task-specific. One factor which has received relatively little attention in NLP is the effect of "updating" the pre-trained word embeddings as part of the task-specific training, based on self-taught learning (Raina et al., 2007). Updating leads to word representations that are task-specific, but often at the cost of over-fitting low-frequency and OOV words.

In this paper, we perform an extensive evaluation of four recently proposed word embedding approaches under fixed experimental conditions, applied to four sequence labelling tasks: part-of-speech (POS) tagging, full-text chunking, named entity recognition (NER), and multiword expres-

Proceedings of the 19th Conference on Computational Language Learning, pages 83–93,
Beijing, China, July 30-31, 2015.

sion (MWE) identification.[1] We build on previous empirical studies (Collobert et al., 2011; Turian et al., 2010; Pennington et al., 2014) in considering a broader range of word embedding approaches and evaluating them over more sequence labelling tasks. In addition, we explore the following research questions:

RQ1: are word embeddings better than baseline approaches of one-hot unigram[2] features and Brown clusters?

RQ2: do word embeddings require less training data (i.e., generalise better) than one-hot unigram features? If so, to what degree can word embeddings reduce the amount of labelled data?

RQ3: what is the impact of updating word embeddings in sequence labelling tasks, both empirically over the target task and geometrically over the vectors?

RQ4: what is the impact of these word embeddings (with and without updating) on both OOV items (relative to the training data) and out-of-domain data?

RQ5: overall, are some word embeddings better than others in a sequence labelling context?

2 Word Representations

2.1 Types of Word Representations

Turian et al. (2010) identifies three varieties of word representations: *distributional*, *cluster-based*, and *distributed*.

Distributional representation methods map each word w to a context word vector $\mathbf{C}_w$, which is constructed directly from co-occurrence counts between w and its context words. The learning methods either store the co-occurrence counts between two words w and i directly in C_{wi} (Sahlgren, 2006; Turney and Pantel, 2010; Honkela, 1997) or project the concurrence counts between words into a lower dimensional space (Řehůřek and Sojka, 2010; Lund and Burgess, 1996), using dimensionality reduction techniques such as SVD (Dumais et al., 1988) or LDA (Blei et al., 2003).

Cluster-based representation methods build clusters of words by applying either soft or hard clustering algorithms (Lin and Wu, 2009; Li and McCallum, 2005). Some of them also rely on a co-occurrence matrix of words (Pereira et al., 1993). The Brown clustering algorithm (Brown et al., 1992) is the best-known method in this category.

Distributed representation methods usually map words into dense, low-dimensional, continuous-valued vectors, with $\mathbf{x} \in \mathbb{R}^d$, where d is referred to as the word dimension.

2.2 Selected Word Representations

Over a range of sequence labelling tasks, we evaluate four methods for inducing word representations: Brown clustering (Brown et al., 1992) ("BROWN"), the continuous bag-of-words model ("CBOW") (Mikolov et al., 2013a), the continuous skip-gram model ("SKIP-GRAM") (Mikolov et al., 2013b), and Global vectors ("GLOVE") (Pennington et al., 2014). All have been shown to be at or near state-of-the-art in recent empirical studies (Turian et al., 2010; Pennington et al., 2014).[3] The training of these word representations is unsupervised: the common underlying idea is to predict the occurrence of words in the neighbouring context. Their training objectives share the same form, which is a sum of local training factors $J(w, \text{ctx}(w))$,

$$L = \sum_{w \in T} J(w, \text{ctx}(w))$$

where T is the set of tokens in a given corpus, and $\text{ctx}(w)$ denotes the local context of word w. The local context of a word is conventionally its preceding m words, or alternatively the m words surrounding it. Local training factors are designed to capture the relationship between w and its local contexts of use, either by predicting w based on its local context, or using w to predict the context words. Other than BROWN, which utilises a cluster-based representation, all the other methods employ a distributed representation.

The starting point for CBOW and SKIP-GRAM is to employ softmax to predict word occurrence:

$$J(w, \text{ctx}(w)) = -\log\left(\frac{\exp(\mathbf{v}_w^{\mathrm{T}}\mathbf{v}_{\text{ctx}(w)})}{\sum_{j \in V}\exp(\mathbf{v}_j^{\mathrm{T}}\mathbf{v}_{\text{ctx}(w)})}\right)$$

[1] MWEs are lexicalized combinations of two or more simplex words that are exceptional enough to be considered as single units in the lexicon (Baldwin and Kim, 2010; Schneider et al., 2014a), e.g., *pick up* or *part of speech*.

[2] Word vectors with one-hot representation are binary vectors with a single dimension per word in the vocabulary (i.e., $d = |V|$), with the single dimension corresponding to the target word set to 1 and all other dimensions set to 0.

[3] The word embedding approach proposed in Collobert et al. (2011) is not considered because it was found to be inferior to our four target word embedding approaches in previous work.

where $\mathbf{v}_{\text{ctx}(w)}$ denotes the distributed representation of the local context of word w, and V is the vocabulary of a given corpus. CBOW derives $\mathbf{v}_{\text{ctx}(w)}$ based on averaging over the context words. That is, it estimates the probability of each w given its local context. In contrast, SKIP-GRAM applies softmax to each context word of a given occurrence of word w. In this case, $\mathbf{v}_{\text{ctx}(w)}$ corresponds to the representation of one of its context words. This model can be characterised as predicting context words based on w. In practice, softmax is too expensive to compute over large corpora, and thus Mikolov et al. (2013b) use hierarchical softmax and negative sampling to scale up the training.

GLOVE assumes the dot product of two word embeddings should be similar to the logarithm of the co-occurrence count X_{ij} of the two words. As such, the local factor $J(w, \text{ctx}(w))$ becomes:

$$g(X_{ij})(\mathbf{v}_i^{\mathrm{T}}\mathbf{v}_j + b_i + b_j - \log(X_{ij}))^2$$

where b_i and b_j are the bias terms of words i and j, respectively, and $g(X_{ij})$ is a weighting function based on the co-occurrence count. This weighting function controls the degree of agreement between the parametric function $\mathbf{v}_i^{\mathrm{T}}\mathbf{v}_j + b_i + b_j$ and $\log(X_{ij})$. Frequently co-occurring word pairs will have larger weight than infrequent pairs, up to a threshold.

BROWN partitions words into a finite set of word classes V. The conditional probability of seeing the next word is defined to be:

$$p(w_k|w_{k-m}^{k-1}) = p(w_k|h_k)p(h_k|h_{k-m}^{k-1})$$

where h_k denotes the word class of the word w_k, w_{k-m}^{k-1} are the previous m words, and h_{k-m}^{k-1} are their respective word classes. Then $J(w, \text{ctx}(w)) = -\log p(w_k|w_{k-m}^{k-1})$. Since there is no tractable method to find an optimal partition of word classes, the method uses only a bigram class model, and utilises hierarchical clustering as an approximation method to find a sufficiently good partition of words.

2.3 Building Word Representations

To ensure the comparison of different word representations is fair, we train BROWN, CBOW, SKIP-GRAM, and GLOVE on a fixed corpus, comprised of freely available corpora, as detailed in Table 1. The joint corpus was preprocessed with

Data set	Size	Words
UMBC (Han et al., 2013)	48.1GB	3G
One Billion (Chelba et al., 2013)	4.1GB	1G
English Wikipedia	49.6GB	3G

Table 1: Corpora used to pre-train the word embeddings

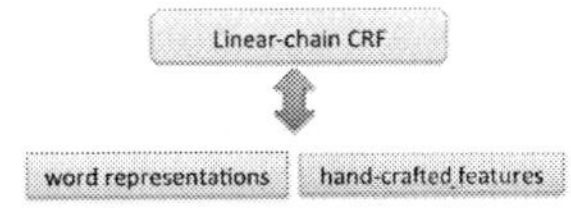

Figure 1: Linear-chain graph transformer

the Stanford CoreNLP sentence splitter and tokeniser. All consecutive digit substrings were replaced by NUM*f*, where *f* is the length of the digit substring (e.g., *10.20* is replaced by *NUM2.NUM2*.

The dimensionality of the word embeddings and the size of the context window are the key hyperparameters when learning distributed representations. We use all combinations of the following values to train word embeddings on the combined corpus:

- **Embedding dim.** $d \in \{25, 50, 100, 200\}$
- **Context window size** $m \in \{1, 5, 10\}$

BROWN requires only the number of clusters as a hyperparameter. Here, we perform clustering with $b \in \{250, 500, 1000, 2000, 4000\}$ clusters.

3 Sequence Labelling Tasks

We evaluate the different word representations over four sequence labelling tasks: POS tagging (POS tagging), full-text chunking (Chunking), NER (NER), and MWE identification (MWE). For each task, we fed features into a first-order linear-chain graph transformer (Collobert et al., 2011) made up of two layers: the upper layer is identical to a linear-chain CRF (Lafferty et al., 2001), and the lower layer consists of word representation and hand-crafted features. If we treat word representations as fixed, the graph transformer is a simple linear-chain CRF. On the other hand, if we can treat the word representations as model parameters, the model is equivalent to a neural network with word embeddings as the input layer, as shown in Figure 1. We trained all models using AdaGrad (Duchi et al., 2011).

As in Turian et al. (2010), at each word position, we construct word representation features from the words in a context window of size two to either side of the target word, based on the pre-trained representation of each word type. For BROWN, the features are the prefix features extracted from word clusters in the same way as Turian et al. (2010). As a baseline (and to test **RQ1**), we include a one-hot representation (which is equivalent to a linear-chain CRF with only lexical context features).

Our hand-crafted features for POS tagging, Chunking and MWE, are those used by Collobert et al. (2011), Turian et al. (2010) and Schneider et al. (2014b), respectively. For NER, we use the same feature space as Turian et al. (2010), except for the previous two predictions, because we want to evaluate all word representations with the same type of model — a first-order graph transformer.

In training the distributed word representations, we consider two settings: (1) the word representations are fixed during sequence model training; and (2) the graph transformer updated the token-level word representations during training.

As outlined in Table 2, for each sequence labelling task, we experiment over the de facto corpus, based on pre-existing training–dev–test splits where available:[4]

POS tagging: the Wall Street Journal portion of the Penn Treebank (Marcus et al. (1993): "WSJ") with Penn POS tags

Chunking: the Wall Street Journal portion of the Penn Treebank ("WSJ"), converted into IOB-style full-text chunks using the CoNLL conversion scripts for training and dev, and the WSJ-derived CoNLL-2000 full text chunking test data for testing (Tjong Kim Sang and Buchholz, 2000)

NER: the English portion of the CoNLL-2003 English Named Entity Recognition data set, for which the source data was taken from Reuters newswire articles (Tjong Kim Sang and De Meulder (2003): "Reuters")

MWE: the MWE dataset of Schneider et al. (2014b), over a portion of text from the English Web Treebank[5] ("EWT")

For all tasks other than MWE,[6] we additionally have an out-of-domain test set, in order to evaluate the out-of-domain robustness of the different word representations, with and without updating. These datasets are as follows:

POS tagging: the English Web Treebank with Penn POS tags ("EWT")

Chunking: the Brown Corpus portion of the Penn Treebank ("Brown"), converted into IOB-style full-text chunks using the CoNLL conversion scripts

NER: the MUC-7 named entity recognition corpus[7] ("MUC7")

For reproducibility, we tuned the hyperparameters with random search over the development data for each task (Bergstra and Bengio, 2012). In this, we randomly sampled 50 distinct hyperparameter sets with the same random seed for the non-updating models (i.e., the models that don't update the word representation), and sampled 100 distinct hyperparameter sets for the updating models (i.e., the models that do). For each set of hyperparameters and task, we train a model over its training set and choose the best one based on its performance on development data (Turian et al., 2010). We also tune the word representation hyperparameters — namely, the word vector size d and context window size m (distributed representations), and in the case of Brown, the number of clusters.

For the updating models, we found that the results over the test data were always inferior to those that do not update the word representations, due to the higher number of hyperparameters and small sample size (i.e., 100). Since the two-layer model of the graph transformer contains a distinct set of hyperparameters for each layer, we reuse the best-performing hyperparameter settings from the non-updating models, and only tune the hyperparameters of AdaGrad for the word representation layer. This method requires only 32 additional runs and achieves consistently better results than 100 random draws.

In order to test the impact of the volume of training data on the different models (**RQ2**), we split the training set into 10 partitions based on a base-2 log scale (i.e., the second smallest partition will be twice the size of the smallest partition), and created 10 successively larger training sets by merging these partitions from the smallest one to the largest one, and used each of these to train a model. From these, we construct learning

[4]For the MWE dataset, no such split pre-existed, so we constructed our own.

[5]https://catalog.ldc.upenn.edu/LDC2012T13

[6]Unfortunately, there is no second domain which has been hand-tagged with MWEs using the method of Schneider et al. (2014b) to use as an out-of-domain test corpus.

[7]https://catalog.ldc.upenn.edu/LDC2001T02

	Training	Development	*In-domain* Test	*Out-of-domain* Test
POS tagging	WSJ Sec. 0-18	WSJ Sec. 19–21	WSJ Sec. 22–24	EWT
Chunking	WSJ	WSJ (1K sentences)	WSJ (CoNLL-00 test)	Brown
NER	Reuters (CoNLL-03 train)	Reuters (CoNLL-03 dev)	Reuters (CoNLL-03 test)	MUC7
MWE	EWT (500 docs)	EWT (100 docs)	EWT (123 docs)	—

Table 2: Training, development and test (in- and out-of-domain) data for each sequence labelling task.

curves over each task.

For ease of comparison with previous results, we evaluate both in- and out-of-domain using chunk/entity/expression-level F1-measure ("F1") for all tasks except POS tagging, for which we use token-level accuracy ("ACC"). To test performance over OOV (unknown) tokens — i.e., the words that do not occur in the training set — we use token-level accuracy for all tasks (e.g., for Chunking, we evaluate whether the full IOB tag is correct or not), because chunks/NEs/MWEs can consist of a mixture of in-vocabulary and OOV tokens, which makes the use of chunk-based evaluation measures inappropriate.

4 Experimental Results and Discussion

We structure our evaluation by stepping through each of our five research questions (**RQ1–5**) from the start of the paper. In this, we make reference to: (1) the best-performing method both in- and out-of-domain vs. the state-of-the-art (Table 3); (2) a heat map for each task indicating the convergence rate for each word representation, with and without updating (Figure 2); (3) OOV accuracy both in-domain and out-of-domain for each task (Figure 3); and (4) visualisation of the impact of updating on word embeddings, based on t-SNE (Figure 4).

RQ1: Are the selected word embeddings better than one-hot unigram features and Brown clusters? As shown in Table 3, the best-performing method for every task except in-domain Chunking is a word embedding method, although the precise method varies greatly. Figure 2, on the other hand, tells a more subtle story: the difference between UNIGRAM and the other word representations is relatively modest, esp. as the amount of training data increases. Additionally, the difference between BROWN and the word embedding methods is modest across all tasks. So, the overall answer would appear to be: yes, word embeddings are better than unigrams when there is little training data, but they are not markedly better than Brown clusters.

RQ2: Do word embedding features require less training data? Figure 2 shows that for POS tagging and NER, with only several hundred training instances, word embedding features achieve superior results to UNIGRAM. For example, when trained with 561 instances, the POS tagging model using SKIP-GRAM+UP embeddings is 5.3% above UNIGRAM; and when trained with 932 instances, the NER model using SKIP-GRAM is 11.7% above UNIGRAM. Similar improvements are also found for other types of word embeddings and BROWN, when the training set is small. However, all word representations perform similarly for Chunking regardless of training data size. For MWE, BROWN performs slightly better than the other methods when trained with approximately 25% of the training instances. Therefore, we conjecture that the POS tagging and NER tasks benefit more from distributional similarity than Chunking and MWE.

RQ3: Does task-specific updating improve all word embeddings across all tasks? Based on Figure 2, updating of word representations can equally correct poorly-learned word representations, and harm pre-trained representations, due to overfitting. For example, GLOVE performs substantially worse than SKIP-GRAM for both POS tagging and NER without updating, but *with* updating, the relative empirical gap between the best performing method becomes smaller. In contrast, SKIP-GRAM performs worse over the test data with updating, despite the results on the development set improving by 1%.

To further investigate the effects of updating, we sampled 60 words and plotted the changes in their word embeddings under updating, using 2-d vector fields generated using matplotlib and t-SNE (van der Maaten and Hinton, 2008). Half of the words were chosen manually to include known word clusters such as days of the week and names of countries; the other half were selected randomly. Additional plots with 100 randomly-sampled words and the top-100 most frequent words, for all the methods and all the tasks, can be found in the supplementary material and at

Task	Benchmark	*In-domain* Test set	*Out-of-domain* Test set
POS tagging (ACC)	**0.972** (Toutanova et al., 2003)	0.959 (SKIP-GRAM+UP)	0.910 (SKIP-GRAM)
Chunking (F1)	**0.942** (Sha and Pereira, 2003)	0.938 (BROWN$_{b=2000}$)	0.676 (GLOVE)
NER (F1)	**0.893** (Ando and Zhang, 2005)	0.868 (SKIP-GRAM)	0.736 (SKIP-GRAM)
MWE (F1)	0.625 (Schneider et al., 2014a)	**0.654** (CBOW+UP)	—

Table 3: State-of-the-art results vs. our best results for in-domain and out-of-domain test sets.

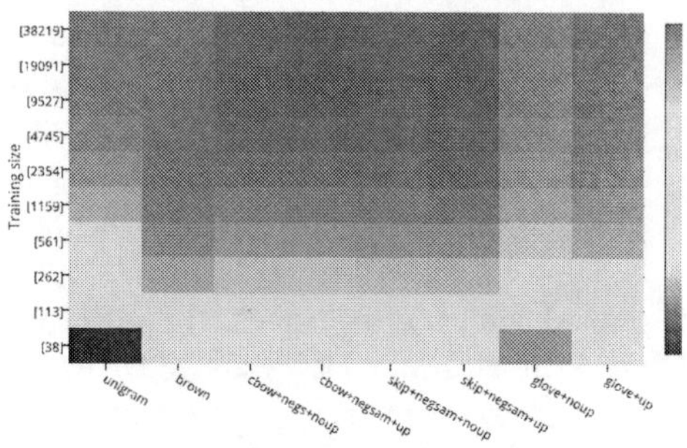

(a) POS tagging (ACC)

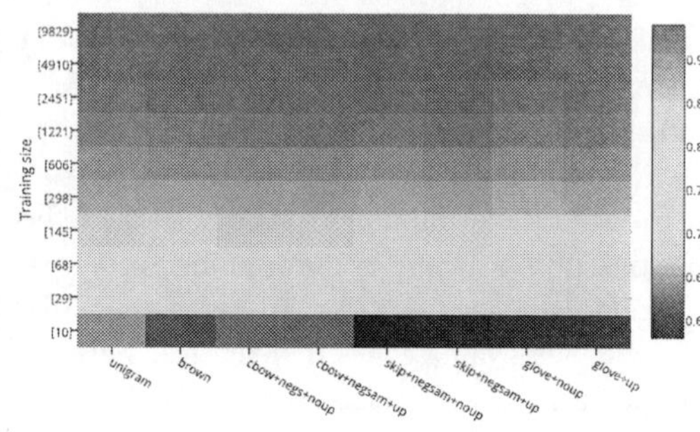

(b) Chunking (F1)

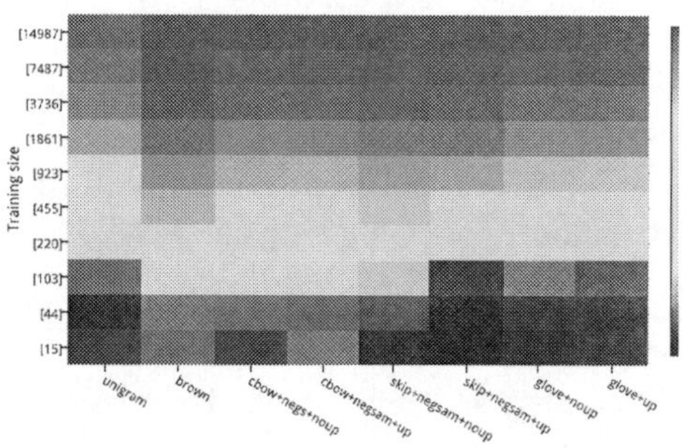

(c) NER (F1)

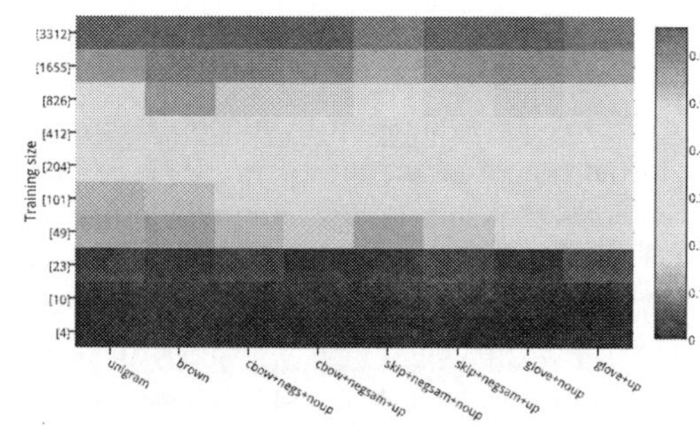

(d) MWE (F1)

Figure 2: Results for each type of word representation over POS tagging, Chunking, NER and MWE, optionally with updating ("+UP"). The y-axis indicates the training data sizes (on a log scale). Green = high performance, and red = low performance, based on a linear scale of the best- to worst-result for each task.

https://goo.gl/Y8bk2w. In each plot, a single arrow signifies one word, pointing from the position of the original word embedding to the updated representation.

In Figure 4, we show vector fields plots for Chunking and NER using SKIP-GRAM embeddings. For Chunking, most of the vectors were changed with similar magnitude, but in very different directions, including within the clusters of days of the week and country names. In contrast, for NER, there was more homogeneous change in word vectors belonging to the same cluster. This greater consistency is further evidence that semantic homogeneity appears to be more beneficial for NER than Chunking.

RQ4: What is the impact of word embeddings cross-domain and for OOV words? As shown in Table 3, results predictably drop when we evaluate out of domain. The difference is most pronounced for Chunking, where there is an absolute drop in F1 of around 30% for all methods, indicating that word embeddings and unigram features provide similar information for Chunking.

Another interesting observation is that updating often hurts out-of-domain performance because the distribution between domains is different. This suggests that, if the objective is to optimise performance across domains, it is best not to perform

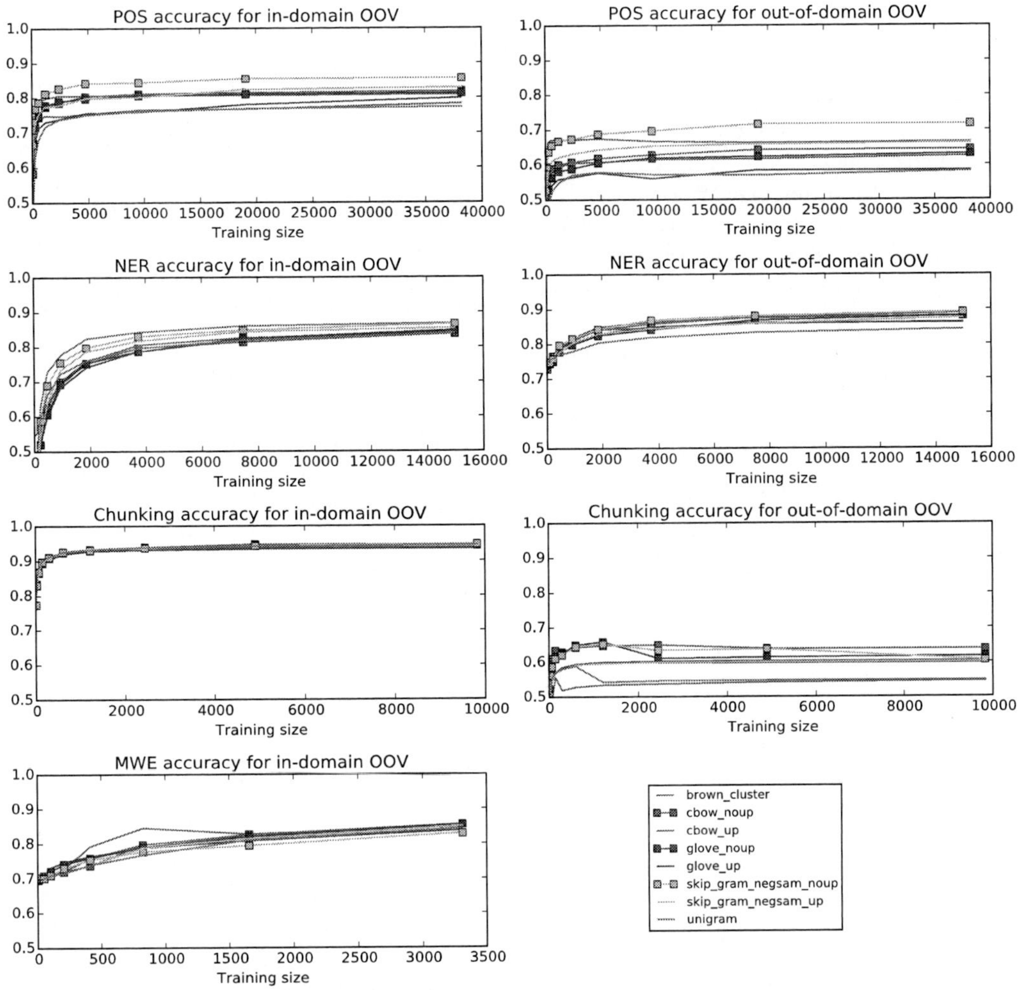

Figure 3: ACC over out-of-vocabulary (OOV) words for *in-domain* and *out-of-domain* test sets.

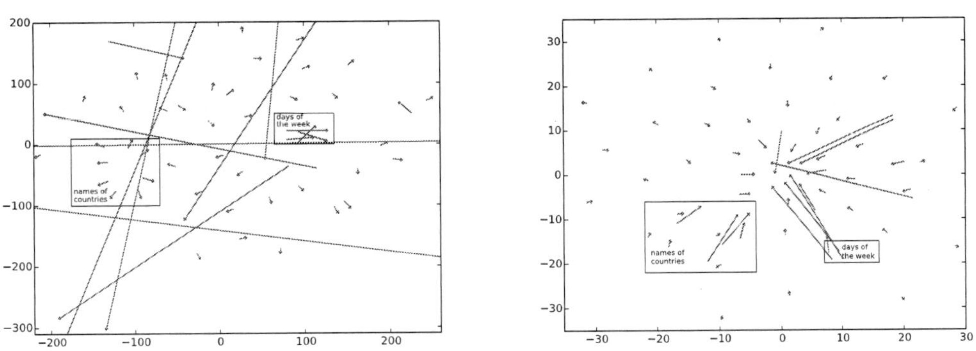

(a) Chunking (b) NER

Figure 4: A t-SNE plot of the impact of updating on SKIP-GRAM

updating.

We also analyze performance on OOV words both in-domain and out-of-domain in Figure 3. As expected, word embeddings and BROWN excel in out-of-domain OOV performance. Consistent with our overall observations about cross-domain generalisation, the OOV results are better when updating is not performed.

RQ5 Overall, are some word embeddings better than others? Comparing the different word embedding techniques over our four sequence labelling tasks, for the different evaluations (overall, out-of-domain and OOV), there is no clear winner among the word embeddings — for POS tagging, SKIP-GRAM appears to have a slight advantage, but this does not generalise to other tasks.

While the aim of this paper was not to achieve the state of the art over the respective tasks, it is important to concede that our best (in-domain) results for NER, POS tagging and Chunking are slightly worse than the state of the art (Table 3). The 2.7% difference between our NER system and the best performing system is due to the fact that we use a first-order instead of a second-order CRF (Ando and Zhang, 2005), and for the other tasks, there are similarly differences in the learner and the complexity of the features used. Another difference is that we tuned the hyperparameters with random search, to enable replication using the same random seed. In contrast, the hyperparameters for the state-of-the-art methods are tuned more extensively by experts, making them more difficult to reproduce.

5 Related Work

Collobert et al. (2011) proposed a unified neural network framework that learns word embeddings and applied it to POS tagging, Chunking, NER and semantic role labelling. When they combined word embeddings with hand-crafted features (e.g., word suffixes for POS tagging; gazetteers for NER) and applied other tricks like cascading and classifier combination, they achieved state-of-the-art performance. Similarly, Turian et al. (2010) evaluated three different word representations on NER and Chunking, and concluded that unsupervised word representations improved NER and Chunking. They also found that combining different word representations can further improve performance. Guo et al. (2014) also explored different ways of using word embeddings for NER. Owoputi et al. (2013) and Schneider et al. (2014a) found that BROWN clustering enhances Twitter POS tagging and MWE, respectively. Compared to previous work, we consider *more* word representations including the most recent work and evaluate them on *more* sequence labelling tasks, wherein the models are trained with training sets of varying size.

Bansal et al. (2014) reported that direct use of word embeddings in dependency parsing did not show improvement. They achieved an improvement only when they performed hierarchical clustering of the word embeddings, and used features extracted from the cluster hierarchy. In a similar vein, Andreas and Klein (2014) explored the use of word embeddings for constituency parsing and concluded that the information contained in word embeddings might duplicate the one acquired by a syntactic parser, unless the training set is extremely small. Other syntactic parsing studies that reported improvements by using word embeddings include Koo et al. (2008), Koo et al. (2010), Haffari et al. (2011), Tratz and Hovy (2011) and Chen and Manning (2014).

Word embeddings have also been applied to other (non-sequential NLP) tasks like grammar induction (Spitkovsky et al., 2011), and semantic tasks such as semantic relatedness, synonymy detection, concept categorisation, selectional preference learning and analogy (Baroni et al., 2014; Levy and Goldberg, 2014; Levy et al., 2015).

Huang and Yates (2009) demonstrated that using distributional word representations methods (like TF-IDF and LSA) as features, improves the labelling of OOV, when test for POS tagging and Chunking. In our study, we evaluate the labelling performance of OOV words for updated vs. non-updated word embedding representations, relative to the training set and with out-of-domain data.

6 Conclusions

We have performed an extensive extrinsic evaluation of four word embedding methods under fixed experimental conditions, and evaluated their applicability to four sequence labelling tasks: POS tagging, Chunking, NER and MWE identification. We found that word embedding features reliably outperformed unigram features, especially with limited training data, but that there was relatively little difference over Brown clusters, and no one embedding method was consistently superior across the different tasks and settings. Word embeddings and Brown clusters were also found to improve out-of-domain performance and for OOV words. We expected a performance gap between the fixed and task-updated embeddings, but the observed difference was marginal. Indeed, we found that updating can result in overfitting. We also carried out preliminary analysis of the impact of updating on the vectors, a direction which we intend to pursue further.

7 Acknowledgments

NICTA is funded by the Australian Government as represented by the Department of Broadband, Communications and the Digital Economy and the Australian Research Council through the ICT Centre of Excellence program.

References

Rie Kubota Ando and Tong Zhang. 2005. A framework for learning predictive structures from multiple tasks and unlabeled data. *Journal of Machine Learning Research*, 6:1817–1853.

Jacob Andreas and Dan Klein. 2014. How much do word embeddings encode about syntax? In *Proceedings of the 52nd Annual Meeting of the Association for Computational Linguistics (Volume 2: Short Papers)*, pages 822–827, Baltimore, USA.

Timothy Baldwin and Su Nam Kim. 2010. Multiword expressions. In Nitin Indurkhya and Fred J. Damerau, editors, *Handbook of Natural Language Processing*. CRC Press, Boca Raton, USA, 2nd edition.

Mohit Bansal, Kevin Gimpel, and Karen Livescu. 2014. Tailoring continuous word representations for dependency parsing. In *Proceedings of the 52nd Annual Meeting of the Association for Computational Linguistics (Volume 2: Short Papers)*, pages 809–815, Baltimore, USA.

Marco Baroni, Georgiana Dinu, and Germán Kruszewski. 2014. Don't count, predict! a systematic comparison of context-counting vs. context-predicting semantic vectors. In *Proceedings of the 52nd Annual Meeting of the Association for Computational Linguistics (Volume 1: Long Papers)*, pages 238–247, Baltimore, USA.

James Bergstra and Yoshua Bengio. 2012. Random search for hyper-parameter optimization. *Journal of Machine Learning Research*, 13(1):281–305.

David M Blei, Andrew Y Ng, and Michael I Jordan. 2003. Latent dirichlet allocation. *Journal of Machine Learning Research*, 3:993–1022.

Peter F. Brown, Peter V. deSouza, Robert L. Mercer, Vincent J. Della Pietra, and Jenifer C. Lai. 1992. Class-based n-gram models of natural language. *Computational Linguistics*, 18:467–479.

Ciprian Chelba, Tomas Mikolov, Mike Schuster, Qi Ge, Thorsten Brants, Phillipp Koehn, and Tony Robinson. 2013. One billion word benchmark for measuring progress in statistical language modeling. Technical report, Google.

Danqi Chen and Christopher D Manning. 2014. A fast and accurate dependency parser using neural networks. In *Proceedings of the 2014 Conference on Empirical Methods in Natural Language Processing (EMNLP 2014)*, pages 740–750, Doha, Qatar.

Ronan Collobert and Jason Weston. 2008. A unified architecture for natural language processing: Deep neural networks with multitask learning. In *Proceedings of the 25th International Conference on Machine Learning*, pages 160–167, Helsinki, Finland.

Ronan Collobert, Jason Weston, Léon Bottou, Michael Karlen, Koray Kavukcuoglu, and Pavel Kuksa. 2011. Natural language processing (almost) from scratch. *Journal of Machine Learning Research*, 12:2493–2537.

John Duchi, Elad Hazan, and Yoram Singer. 2011. Adaptive subgradient methods for online learning and stochastic optimization. *Journal of Machine Learning Research*, 12:2121–2159.

Susan T Dumais, George W Furnas, Thomas K Landauer, Scott Deerwester, and Richard Harshman. 1988. Using latent semantic analysis to improve access to textual information. In *Proceedings of the SIGCHI conference on Human Factors in Computing Systems*, pages 281–285.

Jiang Guo, Wanxiang Che, Haifeng Wang, and Ting Liu. 2014. Revisiting embedding features for simple semi-supervised learning. In *Proceedings of the 2014 Conference on Empirical Methods in Natural Language Processing (EMNLP 2014)*, pages 110–120, Doha, Qatar.

Gholamreza Haffari, Marzieh Razavi, and Anoop Sarkar. 2011. An ensemble model that combines syntactic and semantic clustering for discriminative dependency parsing. In *ACL 2011 (Short Papers)*, pages 710–714, Portland, USA.

Lushan Han, Abhay L. Kashyap, Tim Finin, James Mayfield, and Johnathan Weese. 2013. UMBC EBIQUITY CORE: Semantic textual similarity systems. In *Proceedings of the Second Joint Conference on Lexical and Computational Semantics*, pages 44–52, Atlanta, USA.

Timo Honkela. 1997. Self-organizing maps of words for natural language processing applications. In *Proceedings of the International ICSC Symposium on Soft Computing*, pages 401–407, Nimes, France.

Fei Huang and Alexander Yates. 2009. Distributional representations for handling sparsity in supervised sequence-labeling. In *Proceedings of the Joint Conference of the 47th Annual Meeting of the ACL and the 4th International Joint Conference on Natural Language Processing of the AFNLP: Volume 1 - Volume 1*, pages 495–503, Suntec, Singapore.

Terry Koo, Xavier Carreras, and Michael Collins. 2008. Simple semi-supervised dependency parsing. In *Proceedings of ACL-08: HLT*, pages 595–603, Columbus, USA.

Terry Koo, Alexander M. Rush, Michael Collins, Tommi Jaakkola, and David Sontag. 2010. Dual decomposition for parsing with non-projective head automata. In *Proceedings of the 2010 Conference on Empirical Methods in Natural Language Processing (EMNLP 2010)*, pages 1288–1298, Cambridge, USA.

John Lafferty, Andrew McCallum, and Fernando Pereira. 2001. Conditional random fields: Probabilistic models for segmenting and labeling sequence data. In *Proceedings of the 18th International Conference on Machine Learning*, pages 282–289, Williamstown, USA.

Omer Levy and Yoav Goldberg. 2014. Neural word embedding as implicit matrix factorization. In Z. Ghahramani, M. Welling, C. Cortes, N.D. Lawrence, and K.Q. Weinberger, editors, *Advances in Neural Information Processing Systems 27*, pages 2177–2185. Curran Associates, Inc.

Omer Levy, Yoav Goldberg, and Ido Dagan. 2015. Improving distributional similarity with lessons learned from word embeddings. *Transactions of the Association for Computational Linguistics*, 3(1):211–225.

Wei Li and Andrew McCallum. 2005. Semi-supervised sequence modeling with syntactic topic models. In *Proceedings of the National Conference on Artificial Intelligence*, Pittsburgh, USA.

Dekang Lin and Xiaoyun Wu. 2009. Phrase clustering for discriminative learning. In *Proceedings of the Joint Conference of the 47th Annual Meeting of the ACL and the 4th International Joint Conference on Natural Language Processing of the AFNLP*, pages 1030–1038, Suntec, Singapore.

Kevin Lund and Curt Burgess. 1996. Producing high-dimensional semantic spaces from lexical co-occurrence. *Behavior Research Methods, Instruments, & Computers*, 28(2):203–208.

Mitchell P. Marcus, Beatrice Santorini, and Mary Ann Marcinkiewicz. 1993. Building a large annotated corpus of English: the Penn treebank. *Computational Linguistics*, 19(2):313–330.

Tomas Mikolov, Kai Chen, Greg Corrado, and Jeffrey Dean. 2013a. Efficient estimation of word representations in vector space. *CoRR*, abs/1301.3781.

Tomas Mikolov, Ilya Sutskever, Kai Chen, Greg S Corrado, and Jeff Dean. 2013b. Distributed representations of words and phrases and their compositionality. In *Advances in Neural Information Processing Systems 26*, pages 3111–3119. Curran Associates, Inc.

Olutobi Owoputi, Brendan O'Connor, Chris Dyer, Kevin Gimpel, Nathan Schneider, and Noah A Smith. 2013. Improved part-of-speech tagging for online conversational text with word clusters. In *Proceedings of the 2013 Conference of the North American Chapter of the Association for Computational Linguistics: Human Language Technologies (NAACL HLT 2013)*, pages 380–390, Atlanta, USA.

Jeffrey Pennington, Richard Socher, and Christopher D. Manning. 2014. GloVe: Global vectors for word representation. In *Proceedings of the 2014 Conference on Empirical Methods in Natural Language Processing (EMNLP 2014)*, pages 1532–1543, Doha, Qatar.

Fernando Pereira, Naftali Tishby, and Lillian Lee. 1993. Distributional clustering of English words. In *Proceedings of the 31st Annual Meeting of the Association for Computational Linguistics*, pages 183–190, Columbus, USA.

Rajat Raina, Alexis Battle, Honglak Lee, Benjamin Packer, and Andrew Y Ng. 2007. Self-taught learning: transfer learning from unlabeled data. In *Proceedings of the 24th International Conference on Machine Learning*, pages 759–766, Corvallis, USA.

Radim Řehůřek and Petr Sojka. 2010. Software framework for topic modelling with large corpora. In *Proceedings of the LREC 2010 Workshop on New Challenges for NLP Frameworks*, pages 51–55, Valetta, Malta.

Magnus Sahlgren. 2006. *The Word-Space Model: Using distributional analysis to represent syntagmatic and paradigmatic relations between words in high-dimensional vector spaces*. Ph.D. thesis, Institutionen för lingvistik.

Nathan Schneider, Emily Danchik, Chris Dyer, and Noah A. Smith. 2014a. Discriminative lexical semantic segmentation with gaps: Running the MWE gamut. *Transactions of the Association of Computational Linguistics*, 2(1):193–206.

Nathan Schneider, Spencer Onuffer, Nora Kazour, Emily Danchik, Michael T. Mordowanec, Henrietta Conrad, and Noah A. Smith. 2014b. Comprehensive annotation of multiword expressions in a social web corpus. In *Proceedings of the Ninth International Conference on Language Resources and Evaluation*, pages 455–461, Reykjavík, Iceland.

Fei Sha and Fernando Pereira. 2003. Shallow parsing with conditional random fields. In *Proceedings of the 2003 Conference of the North American Chapter of the Association for Computational Linguistics on Human Language Technology - Volume 1*, pages 134–141, Edmonton, Canada.

Valentin I. Spitkovsky, Hiyan Alshawi, Angel X. Chang, and Daniel Jurafsky. 2011. Unsupervised dependency parsing without gold part-of-speech tags. In *Proceedings of the Conference on Empirical Methods in Natural Language Processing*, pages 1281–1290, Edinburgh, UK.

Erik F. Tjong Kim Sang and Sabine Buchholz. 2000. Introduction to the CoNLL-2000 shared task: Chunking. In *Proceedings of the 4th Conference on Computational Natural Language Learning (CoNLL-2000)*, pages 127–132, Lisbon, Portugal.

Erik F. Tjong Kim Sang and Fien De Meulder. 2003. Introduction to the CoNLL-2003 shared task: Language-independent named entity recognition. In *Proceedings of the 7th Conference on Natural Language Learning (CoNLL-2003)*, pages 142–147, Edmonton, Canada.

Kristina Toutanova, Dan Klein, Christopher D. Manning, and Yoram Singer. 2003. Feature-rich part-of-speech tagging with a cyclic dependency network. In *Proceedings of the 2003 Conference of the North American Chapter of the Association for Computational Linguistics on Human Language Technology - Volume 1*, pages 173–180, Edmonton, Canada.

Stephen Tratz and Eduard Hovy. 2011. A fast, accurate, non-projective, semantically-enriched parser. In *Proceedings of the Conference on Empirical Methods in Natural Language Processing*, pages 1257–1268, Edinburgh, UK.

Joseph Turian, Lev Ratinov, and Yoshua Bengio. 2010. Word representations: a simple and general method for semi-supervised learning. In *Proceedings of the 48th Annual Meeting of the Association for Computational Linguistics*, pages 384–394, Uppsala, Sweden.

Peter D. Turney and Patrick Pantel. 2010. From frequency to meaning: Vector space models of semantics. *Journal of Artificial Intelligence Research*, 37(1):141–188.

Laurens J.P. van der Maaten and Geoffrey Hinton. 2008. Visualizing high-dimensional data using t-sne. *Journal of Machine Learning Research*, 9:2579–2605.

Contrastive Analysis with Predictive Power: Typology Driven Estimation of Grammatical Error Distributions in ESL

Yevgeni Berzak
CSAIL MIT
berzak@mit.edu

Roi Reichart
Technion IIT
roiri@ie.technion.ac.il

Boris Katz
CSAIL MIT
boris@mit.edu

Abstract

This work examines the impact of cross-linguistic transfer on grammatical errors in English as Second Language (ESL) texts. Using a computational framework that formalizes the theory of Contrastive Analysis (CA), we demonstrate that *language specific error distributions* in ESL writing can be predicted from the typological properties of the native language and their relation to the typology of English. Our typology driven model enables to obtain accurate estimates of such distributions without access to any ESL data for the target languages. Furthermore, we present a strategy for adjusting our method to low-resource languages that lack typological documentation using a bootstrapping approach which approximates native language typology from ESL texts. Finally, we show that our framework is instrumental for linguistic inquiry seeking to identify first language factors that contribute to a wide range of difficulties in second language acquisition.

1 Introduction

The study of cross-linguistic transfer, whereby properties of a native language influence performance in a foreign language, has a long tradition in Linguistics and Second Language Acquisition (SLA). Much of the linguistic work on this topic was carried out within the framework of Contrastive Analysis (CA), a theoretical approach that aims to explain difficulties in second language learning in terms of the relations between structures in the native and foreign languages.

The basic hypothesis of CA was formulated by Lado (1957), who suggested that "we can predict and describe the patterns that will cause difficulty in learning, and those that will not cause difficulty, by comparing systematically the language and culture to be learned with the native language and culture of the student". In particular, Lado postulated that divergences between the native and foreign languages will negatively affect learning and lead to increased error rates in the foreign language. This and subsequent hypotheses were soon met with criticism, targeting their lack of ability to provide reliable predictions, leading to an ongoing debate on the extent to which foreign language errors can be explained and predicted by examining native language structure.

Differently from the SLA tradition, which emphasizes manual analysis of error case studies (Odlin, 1989), we address the heart of this controversy from a computational data-driven perspective, focusing on the issue of predictive power. We provide a formalization of the CA framework, and demonstrate that the relative frequency of grammatical errors in ESL can be reliably predicted from the typological properties of the native language and their relation to the typology of English using a regression model.

Tested on 14 languages in a leave-one-out fashion, our model achieves a Mean Average Error (MAE) reduction of 21.8% in predicting the language specific relative frequency of the 20 most common ESL structural error types, as compared to the relative frequency of each of the error types in the training data, yielding improvements across all the languages and the large majority of the error types. Our regression model also outperforms a stronger, nearest neighbor based baseline, that projects the error distribution of a target language from its typologically closest language.

While our method presupposes the existence of typological annotations for the test languages, we also demonstrate its viability in low-resource scenarios for which such annotations are not available. To address this setup, we present a bootstrap-

Proceedings of the 19th Conference on Computational Language Learning, pages 94–102,
Beijing, China, July 30-31, 2015.

ping framework in which the typological features required for prediction of grammatical errors are approximated from automatically extracted ESL morpho-syntactic features using the method of (Berzak et al., 2014). Despite the noise introduced in this process, our bootstrapping strategy achieves an error reduction of 13.9% compared to the average frequency baseline.

Finally, the utilization of typological features as predictors, enables to shed light on linguistic factors that could give rise to different error types in ESL. For example, in accordance with common linguistic knowledge, feature analysis of the model suggests that the main contributor to increased rates of determiner omission in ESL is the lack of determiners in the native language. A more complex case of missing pronouns is intriguingly tied by the model to native language subject pronoun marking on verbs.

To summarize, the main contribution of this work is a CA inspired computational framework for learning language specific grammatical error distributions in ESL. Our approach is both predictive and explanatory. It enables us to obtain improved estimates for language specific error distributions without access to ESL error annotations for the target language. Coupling grammatical errors with typological information also provides meaningful explanations to some of the linguistic factors that drive the observed error rates.

The paper is structured as follows. Section 2 surveys related linguistic and computational work on cross-linguistic transfer. Section 3 describes the ESL corpus and the typological data used in this study. In section 4 we motivate our native language oriented approach by providing a variance analysis for ESL errors across native languages. Section 5 presents the regression model for prediction of ESL error distributions. The bootstrapping framework which utilizes automatically inferred typological features is described in section 6. Finally, we present the conclusion and directions for future work in section 7.

2 Related Work

Cross linguistic-transfer was extensively studied in SLA, Linguistics and Psychology (Odlin, 1989; Gass and Selinker, 1992; Jarvis and Pavlenko, 2007). Within this area of research, our work is most closely related to the Contrastive Analysis (CA) framework. Rooted in the comparative linguistics tradition, CA was first suggested by Fries (1945) and formalized by Lado (1957). In essence, CA examines foreign language performance, with a particular focus on learner difficulties, in light of a structural comparison between the native and the foreign languages. From its inception, CA was criticized for the lack of a solid predictive theory (Wardhaugh, 1970; Whitman and Jackson, 1972), leading to an ongoing scientific debate on the relevance of comparison based approaches. Important to our study is that the type of evidence used in this debate typically relies on small scale manual case study analysis. Our work seeks to reexamine the issue of predictive power of CA based methods using a computational, data-driven approach.

Computational work touching on cross-linguistic transfer was mainly conducted in relation to the Native Language Identification (NLI) task, in which the goal is to determine the native language of the author of an ESL text. Much of this work focuses on experimentation with different feature sets (Tetreault et al., 2013), including features derived from the CA framework (Wong and Dras, 2009). A related line of inquiry which is closer to our work deals with the identification of ESL syntactic patterns that are specific to speakers of different native languages (Swanson and Charniak, 2013; Swanson and Charniak, 2014). Our approach differs from this research direction by focusing on grammatical errors, and emphasizing prediction of language specific patterns rather than their identification.

Previous work on grammatical error correction that examined determiner and preposition errors (Rozovskaya and Roth, 2011; Rozovskaya and Roth, 2014) incorporated native language specific priors in models that are otherwise trained on standard English text. Our work extends the native language tailored treatment of grammatical errors to a much larger set of error types. More importantly, this approach is limited by the availability of manual error annotations for the target language in order to obtain the required error counts. Our framework enables to bypass this annotation bottleneck by predicting language specific priors from typological information.

The current investigation is most closely related to studies that demonstrate that ESL signal can be used to infer pairwise similarities between native languages (Nagata and Whittaker, 2013; Berzak et al., 2014) and in particular, tie the similarities to the typological characteristics of these languages (Berzak et al., 2014). Our work inverts the direction of this analysis by starting with typological features, and utilizing them to predict error patterns in ESL. We also show that the two approaches can be combined in a bootstrapping strategy by first inferring typological properties from automatically extracted morpho-syntactic ESL features, and in turn, using these properties for prediction of language specific error distributions in ESL.

3 Data

3.1 ESL Corpus

We obtain ESL essays from the Cambridge First Certificate in English (FCE) learner corpus (Yannakoudakis et al., 2011), a publicly available subset of the Cambridge Learner Corpus (CLC)[1]. The corpus contains upper-intermediate level essays by native speakers of 16 languages[2]. Discarding Swedish and Dutch, which have only 16 documents combined, we take into consideration the remaining following 14 languages, with the corresponding number of documents in parenthesis: Catalan (64), Chinese (66), French (146), German (69), Greek (74), Italian (76), Japanese (82), Korean (86), Polish (76), Portuguese (68), Russian (83), Spanish (200), Thai (63) and Turkish (75). The resulting dataset contains 1228 documents with an average of 379 words per document.

The FCE corpus has an elaborate error annotation scheme (Nicholls, 2003) and high quality of error annotations, making it particularly suitable for our investigation. The annotation scheme encompasses 75 different error types, covering a wide range of grammatical errors on different levels of granularity. As the typological features used in this work refer mainly to *structural* properties, we filter out spelling errors, punctuation errors and open class semantic errors, remaining with a list of grammatical errors that are typically related to language structure. We focus on the 20 most frequent error types[3] in this list, which are presented and exemplified in table 1. In addition to concentrating on the most important structural ESL errors, this cutoff prevents us from being affected by data sparsity issues associated with less frequent errors.

3.2 Typological Database

We use the World Atlas of Language Structures (WALS; Dryer and Haspelmath, 2013), a repository of typological features of the world's languages, as our source of linguistic knowledge about the native languages of the ESL corpus authors. The features in WALS are divided into 11 categories: Phonology, Morphology, Nominal Categories, Nominal Syntax, Verbal Categories, Word Order, Simple Clauses, Complex Sentences, Lexicon, Sign Languages and Other. Table 2 presents examples of WALS features belonging to different categories. The features can be associated with different variable types, including binary, categorical and ordinal, making their encoding a challenging task. Our strategy for addressing this issue is feature binarization (see section 5.3).

An important challenge introduced by the WALS database is incomplete documentation. Previous studies (Daumé III, 2009; Georgi et al., 2010) have estimated that only 14% of all the language-feature combinations in the database have documented values. While this issue is most acute for low-resource languages, even the well studied languages in our ESL dataset are lacking a significant portion of the feature values, inevitably hindering the effectiveness of our approach.

We perform several preprocessing steps in order to select the features that will be used in this study. First, as our focus is on structural features that can be expressed in written form, we discard all the features associated with the categories Phonology, Lexicon[4], Sign Languages and Other. We further discard 24 features which either have a documented value for only one language, or have the same value in all the languages. The resulting feature-set contains 119 features, with an average of 2.9 values per feature, and 92.6 documented features per language.

4 Variance Analysis of Grammatical Errors in ESL

To motivate a native language based treatment of grammatical error distributions in ESL, we begin

[1] `http://www.cambridge.org/gb/elt/catalogue/subject/custom/item3646603`

[2] We plan to extend our analysis to additional proficiency levels and languages when error annotated data for these learner profiles will be publicly available.

[3] Filtered errors that would have otherwise appeared in the top 20 list, with their respective rank in brackets: Spelling (1), Replace Punctuation (2), Replace Verb (3), Missing Punctuation (7), Replace (8), Replace Noun (9) Unnecessary Punctuation (13), Replace Adjective (18), Replace Adverb (20).

[4] The discarded Lexicon features refer to properties such as the number of words in the language that denote colors, and identity of word pairs such as "hand" and "arm".

Rank	Code	Name	Example	Count	KW	MW
1	TV	Verb Tense	I hope I **give** *have given* you enough details	3324	**	34
2	RT	Replace Preposition	**on** *in* July	3311	**	31
3	MD	Missing Determiner	I went for *the* interview	2967	**	57
4	FV	Wrong Verb Form	had time to **played** *play*	1789	**	21
5	W	Word Order	**Probably** our homes will *probably* be	1534	**	34
6	MT	Missing Preposition	explain *to* you	1435	**	22
7	UD	Unnecessary Determiner	a course at **the** Cornell University	1321		
8	UT	Unnecessary Preposition	we need it **on** each minute	1079		
9	MA	Missing Pronoun	because *it* is the best conference	984	**	33
10	AGV	Verb Agreement	the teachers **was** *were* very experienced	916	**	21
11	FN	Wrong Form Noun	because of my **study** *studies*	884	**	24
12	RA	Replace Pronoun	she just met Sally, **which** *who*	847	**	17
13	AGN	Noun Agreement	two **month** *months* ago	816	**	24
14	RD	Replace Determiner	of **a** *the* last few years	676	**	35
15	DJ	Wrongly Derived Adjective	The mother was **pride** *proud*	608	*	8
16	DN	Wrongly Derived Noun	**working place** *workplace*	536		
17	DY	Wrongly Derived Adverb	**Especial** *Especially*	414	**	14
18	UA	Unnecessary Pronoun	feel **ourselves** comfortable	391	*	9
19	MC	Missing Conjunction	reading, *and* playing piano at home	346	*	11
20	RC	Replace Conjunction	not just the car, **and** *but* also the train	226		

Table 1: The 20 most frequent error types in the FCE corpus that are related to language structure. In the Example column, words marked in italics are corrections for the words marked in bold. The Count column lists the overall count of each error type in the corpus. The KW column depicts the result of the Kruskal-Wallis test whose null hypothesis is that the relative error frequencies for different native languages are drawn from the same distribution. Error types for which this hypothesis is rejected with $p < 0.01$ are denoted with '*'. Error types with $p < 0.001$ are marked with '**'. The MW column denotes the number of language pairs (out of the total 91 pairs) which pass the post-hoc Mann-Whitney test with $p < 0.01$.

ID	Category	Name	Values
23A	Morphology	Locus of Marking in the Clause	No case marking, Core cases only, Core and non-core, No syncretism
67A	Verbal Categories	The Future Tense	Inflectional future, No inflectional future.
30A	Nominal Categories	Number of Genders	None, Two, Three, Four, Five or more.
87A	Word Order	Order of Adjective and Noun	AN, NA, No dominant order, Only internally headed relative clauses.

Table 2: Examples of WALS features.

by examining whether there is a statistically significant difference in ESL error rates based on the native language of the learners. This analysis provides empirical justification for our approach, and to the best of our knowledge was not conducted in previous studies.

To this end, we perform a Kruskal-Wallis (KW) test (Kruskal and Wallis, 1952) for each error type[5]. We treat the relative error frequency per word in each document as a sample[6] (i.e. the relative frequencies of all the error types in a document sum to 1). The samples are associated with 14 groups, according to the native language of the document's author. For each error type, the null hypothesis of the test is that error fraction samples of all the native languages are drawn from the same underlying distribution. In other words, rejection of the null hypothesis implies a significant difference between the relative error frequencies of at least one language pair.

As shown in table 1, we can reject the null hypothesis for 16 of the 20 grammatical error types with $p < 0.01$, where Unnecessary Determiner, Unnecessary Preposition, Wrongly Derived Noun, and Replace Conjunction are the error types that do not exhibit dependence on the native language.

[5]We chose the non-parametric KW rank-based test over ANOVA, as according to the Shapiro-Wilk (1965) and Levene (1960) tests, the assumptions of normality and homogeneity of variance do not hold for our data. In practice, the ANOVA test yields similar results to those of the KW test.

[6]We also performed the KW test on the absolute error frequencies (i.e. raw counts) per word, obtaining similar results to the ones reported here on the relative frequencies per word.

Furthermore, the null hypothesis can be rejected for 13 error types with $p < 0.001$. These results suggest that the relative error rates of the majority of the common structural grammatical errors in our corpus indeed differ between native speakers of different languages.

We further extend our analysis by performing pairwise post-hoc Mann-Whitney (MW) tests (Mann and Whitney, 1947) in order to determine the number of language pairs that significantly differ with respect to their native speakers' error fractions in ESL. Table 1 presents the number of language pairs that pass this test with $p < 0.01$ for each error type. This inspection suggests Missing Determiner as the error type with the strongest dependence on the author's native language, followed by Replace Determiner, Verb Tense, Word Order, Missing Pronoun and Replace Preposition.

5 Predicting Language Specific Error Distributions in ESL

5.1 Task Definition

Given a language $l \in L$, our task is to predict for this language the relative error frequency $y_{l,e}$ of each error type $e \in E$, where L is the set of all native languages, E is the set of grammatical errors, and $\sum_e y_{l,e} = 1$.

5.2 Model

In order to predict the error distribution of a native language, we train regression models on individual error types:

$$\hat{y}'_{l,e} = \theta_{l,e} \cdot f(t_l, t_{eng}) \quad (1)$$

In this equation $\hat{y}'_{l,e}$ is the predicted relative frequency of an error of type e for ESL documents authored by native speakers of language l, and $f(t_l, t_{eng})$ is a feature vector derived from the typological features of the native language t_l and the typological features of English t_{eng}.

The model parameters $\theta_{l,e}$ are obtained using Ordinary Least Squares (OLS) on the training data D, which consists of typological feature vectors paired with relative error frequencies of the remaining 13 languages:

$$D = \{(f(t_{l'}, t_{eng}), y_{e,l'}) | l' \in L, l' \neq l\} \quad (2)$$

To guarantee that the individual relative error frequency estimates sum to 1 for each language, we renormalize them to obtain the final predictions:

$$\hat{y}_{l,e} = \frac{\hat{y}'_{l,e}}{\sum_e \hat{y}'_{l,e}} \quad (3)$$

5.3 Features

Our feature set can be divided into two subsets. The first subset, used in a version of our model called *Reg*, contains the typological features of the native language. In a second version of our model, called *RegCA*, we also utilize additional features that explicitly encode differences between the typological features of the native language, and the and the typological features of English.

5.3.1 Typological Features

In the *Reg* model, we use the typological features of the native language that are documented in WALS. As mentioned in section 3.2, WALS features belong to different variable types, and are hence challenging to encode. We address this issue by binarizing all the features. Given k possible values v_k for a given WALS feature t_i, we generate k binary typological features of the form:

$$f_{i,k}(t_l, t_{eng}) = \begin{cases} 1 & \text{if } t_{l,i} = v_k \\ 0 & \text{otherwise} \end{cases} \quad (4)$$

When a WALS feature of a given language does not have a documented value, all k entries of the feature for that language are assigned the value of 0. This process transforms the original 119 WALS features into 340 binary features.

5.3.2 Divergences from English

In the spirit of CA, in the model *RegCA*, we also utilize features that explicitly encode differences between the typological features of the native language and those of English. These features are also binary, and take the value 1 when the value of a WALS feature in the native language is different from the corresponding value in English:

$$f_i(t_l, t_{eng}) = \begin{cases} 1 & \text{if } t_{l,i} \neq t_{eng,i} \\ 0 & \text{otherwise} \end{cases} \quad (5)$$

We encode 104 such features, in accordance with the typological features of English available in WALS. The features are activated only when a typological feature of English has a corresponding documented feature in the native language. The addition of these divergence features brings the total number of features in our feature set to 444.

5.4 Results

We evaluate the model predictions using two metrics. The first metric, Absolute Error, measures the distance between the predicted and the true relative frequency of each grammatical error type[7]:

$$\text{Absolute Error} = |\hat{y}_{l,e} - y_{l,e}| \qquad (6)$$

When averaged across different predictions we refer to this metric as Mean Absolute Error (MAE).

The second evaluation score is the Kullback-Leibler divergence D_{KL}, a standard measure for evaluating the difference between two distributions. This metric is used to evaluate the predicted grammatical error distribution of a native language:

$$D_{KL}(y_l||\hat{y}_l) = \sum_e y_{l,e} \ln \frac{y_{l,e}}{\hat{y}_{l,e}} \qquad (7)$$

	Base	NN	Reg	RegCA
MAE	1.28	1.11	1.02	**1.0**
Error Reduction	-	13.3	20.4	**21.8**
#Languages	-	9/14	12/14	**14/14**
#Mistakes	-	11/20	**15/20**	14/20
AVG D_{KL}	0.052	0.046	0.033	**0.032**
#Languages	-	10/14	**14/14**	**14/14**

Table 3: Results for prediction of relative error frequencies using the *MAE* metric across languages and error types, and the D_{KL} metric averaged across languages. *#Languages* and *#Mistakes* denote the number of languages and grammatical error types on which a model outperforms *Base*.

Table 3 summarizes the grammatical error prediction results[8]. The baseline model *Base* sets the relative frequencies of the grammatical errors of a test language to the respective relative error frequencies in the training data. We also consider a stronger, language specific model called *Nearest Neighbor (NN)*, which projects the error distribution of a target language from the typologically closest language in the training set, according to the cosine similarity measure. This baseline provides a performance improvement for the majority of the languages and error types, with an average error reduction of 13.3% on the *MAE* metric compared to *Base*, and improving from 0.052 to 0.046 on the KL divergence metric, thus emphasizing the general advantage of a native language adapted approach to ESL error prediction.

Our regression model introduces further substantial performance improvements. The *Reg* model, which uses the typological features of the native language for predicting ESL relative error frequencies, achieves 20.4% *MAE* reduction over the *Base* model. The *RegCA* version of the regression model, which also incorporates differences between the typological features of the native language and English, surpasses the *Reg* model, reaching an average error reduction of 21.8% from the *Base* model, with improvements across all the languages and the majority of the error types. Strong performance improvements are also obtained on the KL divergence measure, where the *RegCA* model scores 0.032, compared to the baseline score of 0.052.

To illustrate the outcome of our approach, consider the example in table 4, which compares the top 10 predicted errors for Japanese using the *Base* and *RegCA* models. In this example, *RegCA* correctly places Missing Determiner as the most common error in Japanese, with a significantly higher relative frequency than in the training data. Similarly, it provides an accurate prediction for the Missing Preposition error, whose frequency and rank are underestimated by the *Base* model. Furthermore, *RegCA* correctly predicts the frequency of Replace Preposition and Word Order to be lower than the average in the training data.

5.5 Feature Analysis

An important advantage of our typology-based approach are the clear semantics of the features, which facilitate the interpretation of the model. Inspection of the model parameters allows us to gain insight into the typological features that are potentially involved in causing different types of ESL errors. Although such inspection is unlikely to provide a comprehensive coverage of all the relevant causes for the observed learner difficulties, it can serve as a valuable starting point for exploratory linguistic analysis and formulation of a cross-linguistic transfer theory.

Table 5 lists the most salient typological features, as determined by the feature weights aver-

[7] For clarity of presentation, all the reported results on this metric are multiplied by 100.

[8] As described in section 5.2, we report the performance of regression models trained and evaluated on relative error frequencies obtained by normalizing the rates of the different error types. We also experimented with training and evaluating the models on absolute error counts per word, obtaining results that are similar to those reported here.

Rank	Base	Frac.	RegCA	Frac.	True	Frac.
1	**Replace Preposition**	**0.14**	**Missing Determiner**	**0.18**	**Missing Determiner**	**0.20**
2	Tense Verb	0.14	Tense Verb	0.12	Tense Verb	0.12
3	**Missing Determiner**	**0.12**	**Replace Preposition**	**0.12**	**Replace Preposition**	**0.10**
4	Wrong Verb Form	0.07	**Missing Preposition**	**0.08**	**Missing Preposition**	**0.08**
5	**Word Order**	**0.06**	Unnecessary Determiner	0.06	Unnecessary Preposition	0.06
6	**Missing Preposition**	**0.06**	Wrong Verb Form	0.05	Unnecessary Determiner	0.05
7	Unnecessary Determiner	0.06	Unnecessary Preposition	0.05	Replace Determiner	0.05
8	Unnecessary Preposition	0.04	Wrong Noun Form	0.05	Wrong Verb Form	0.05
9	Missing Pronoun	0.04	**Word Order**	**0.05**	**Word Order**	**0.04**
10	Wrong Noun Form	0.04	Verb Agreement	0.04	Wrong Noun Form	0.06

Table 4: Comparison between the fractions and ranks of the top 10 predicted error types by the *Base* and *RegCA* models for Japanese. As opposed to the *Base* method, the *RegCA* model correctly predicts Missing Determiner to be the most frequent error committed by native speakers of Japanese. It also correctly predicts Missing Preposition to be more frequent and Replace Preposition and Word Order to be less frequent than in the training data.

aged across the models of different languages, for the error types Missing Determiner and Missing Pronoun. In the case of determiners, the model identifies the lack of definite and indefinite articles in the native language as the strongest factors related to increased rates of determiner omission. Conversely, features that imply the presence of an article system in the native language, such as 'Indefinite word same as one' and 'Definite word distinct from demonstrative' are indicative of reduced error rates of this type.

A particularly intriguing example concerns the Missing Pronoun error. The most predictive typological factor for increased pronoun omissions is pronominal subject marking on the verb in the native language. Differently from the case of determiners, it is not the lack of the relevant structure in the native language, but rather its different encoding that seems to drive erroneous pronoun omission. Decreased error rates of this type correlate most strongly with obligatory pronouns in subject position, as well as a verbal person marking system similar to the one in English.

Missing Determiner	
37A Definite Articles: Different from English	.057
38A Indefinite Articles: No definite or indefinite article	.055
37A Definite Articles: No definite or indefinite article	.055
49A Number of Cases: 6-7 case	.052
100A Alignment of Verbal Person Marking: Accusative	-.073
38A Indefinite Article: Indefinite word same as 'one'	-.050
52A Comitatives and Instrumentals: Identity	-.044
37A Definite Articles: Definite word distinct from demonstrative	-.036
Missing Pronoun	
101A Expression of Pronominal Subjects: Subject affixes on verb	.015
71A The Prohibitive: Different from English	.012
38A Indefinite Articles: Indefinite word same as 'one'	.011
71A The Prohibitive: Special imperative + normal negative	.010
104A Order of Person Markers on the Verb: A & P do not or do not both occur on the verb	-.016
102A Verbal Person Marking: Only the A argument	-.013
101A Expression of Pronominal Subjects: Obligatory pronouns in subject position	-.011
71A The Prohibitive: Normal imperative + normal negative	-.010

Table 5: The most predictive typological features of the *RegCA* model for the errors Missing Determiner and Missing Pronoun. The right column depicts the feature weight averaged across all the languages. Missing determiners are related to the absence of a determiner system in the native language. Missing pronouns are correlated with subject pronoun marking on the verb.

6 Bootstrapping with ESL-based Typology

Thus far, we presupposed the availability of substantial typological information for our target languages in order to predict their ESL error distributions. However, the existing typological documentation for the majority of the world's languages is scarce, limiting the applicability of this approach for low-resource languages.

We address this challenge for scenarios in which an unannotated collection of ESL texts authored by native speakers of the target language is available. Given such data, we propose a bootstrapping strategy which uses the method proposed in (Berzak et al., 2014) in order to approximate the typology of the native language from morpho-syntactic features in ESL. The inferred typological features serve, in turn, as a proxy for the true typology of that language in order to predict its speakers' ESL grammatical error rates with our regression model.

To put this framework into effect, we use the FCE corpus to train a log-linear model for native language classification using morpho-syntactic features obtained from the output of the Stanford Parser (de Marneffe et al., 2006):

$$p(l|x;\theta) = \frac{\exp(\theta \cdot f(x,l))}{\sum_{l' \in L} \exp(\theta \cdot f(x,l'))} \quad (8)$$

where l is the native language, x is the observed English document and θ are the model parameters. We then derive pairwise similarities between languages by averaging the uncertainty of the model with respect to each language pair:

$$S'_{ESL_{l,l'}} = \begin{cases} \frac{1}{|D_l|} \sum\limits_{(x,l) \in D_l} p(l'|x;\theta) & \text{if } l' \neq l \\ 1 & \text{otherwise} \end{cases} \quad (9)$$

In this equation, x is an ESL document, θ are the parameters of the native language classification model and D_l is a set of documents whose native language is l. For each pair of languages l and l' the matrix S'_{ESL} contains an entry $S'_{ESL_{l,l'}}$ which represents the average probability of confusing l for l', and an entry $S'_{ESL_{l',l}}$, which captures the opposite confusion. A similarity estimate for a language pair is then obtained by averaging these two scores:

$$S_{ESL_{l,l'}} = S_{ESL_{l',l}} = \frac{1}{2}(S'_{ESL_{l,l'}} + S'_{ESL_{l',l}}) \quad (10)$$

As shown in (Berzak et al., 2014), given the similarity matrix S_{ESL}, one can obtain an approximation for the typology of a native language by projecting the typological features from its most similar languages. Here, we use the typology of the closest language, an approach that yields 70.7% accuracy in predicting the typological features of our set of languages.

In the bootstrapping setup, we train the regression models on the true typology of the languages in the training set, and use the approximate typology of the test language to predict the relative error rates of its speakers in ESL.

6.1 Results

Table 6 summarizes the error prediction results using approximate typological features for the test languages. As can be seen, our approach continues to provide substantial performance gains despite the inaccuracy of the typological information used for the test languages. The best performing method, *RegCA* reduces the *MAE* of *Base* by 13.9%, with performance improvements for most of the languages and error types. Performance gains are also obtained on the D_{KL} metric, whereby *RegCA* scores 0.041, compared to the *Base* score of 0.052, improving on 11 out of our 14 languages.

	Base	**NN**	**Reg**	**RegCA**
MAE	1.28	1.12	1.13	**1.10**
Error Reduction	-	12.6	11.6	**13.9**
#Languages	-	**11/14**	**11/14**	**11/14**
#Mistakes	-	10/20	10/20	**11/20**
AVG D_{KL}	0.052	0.048	0.043	**0.041**
#Languages	-	10/14	**11/14**	**11/14**

Table 6: Results for prediction of relative error frequencies using the bootstrapping approach. In this setup, the true typology of the test language is substituted with approximate typology derived from morpho-syntactic ESL features.

7 Conclusion and Future Work

We present a computational framework for predicting native language specific grammatical error distributions in ESL, based on the typological properties of the native language and their compatibility with the typology of English. Our regression model achieves substantial performance improvements as compared to a language oblivious baseline, as well as a language dependent nearest neighbor baseline. Furthermore, we address scenarios in which the typology of the native language is not available, by bootstrapping typological features from ESL texts. Finally, inspection of the model parameters allows us to identify native language properties which play a pivotal role in generating different types of grammatical errors.

In addition to the theoretical contribution, the outcome of our work has a strong potential to be beneficial in practical setups. In particular, it can be utilized for developing educational curricula that focus on the areas of difficulty that are characteristic of different native languages. Furthermore, the derived error frequencies can be integrated as native language specific priors in systems for automatic error correction. In both application areas, previous work relied on the existence of error tagged ESL data for the languages of interest. Our approach paves the way for addressing these challenges even in the absence of such data.

Acknowledgments

This material is based upon work supported by the Center for Brains, Minds, and Machines (CBMM), funded by NSF STC award CCF-1231216.

References

Yevgeni Berzak, Roi Reichart, and Boris Katz. 2014. Reconstructing native language typology from foreign language usage. In *Proceedings of the Eighteenth Conference on Computational Natural Language Learning*, pages 21–29. Association for Computational Linguistics, June.

Hal Daumé III. 2009. Non-parametric Bayesian areal linguistics. In *Proceedings of human language technologies: The 2009 annual conference of the north american chapter of the association for computational linguistics*, pages 593–601. Association for Computational Linguistics.

Marie-Catherine de Marneffe, Bill MacCartney, Christopher D Manning, et al. 2006. Generating typed dependency parses from phrase structure parses. In *Proceedings of LREC*, volume 6, pages 449–454.

Charles C Fries. 1945. Teaching and learning english as a foreign language.

Susan M Gass and Larry Selinker. 1992. *Language Transfer in Language Learning: Revised edition*, volume 5. John Benjamins Publishing.

Ryan Georgi, Fei Xia, and William Lewis. 2010. Comparing language similarity across genetic and typologically-based groupings. In *Proceedings of the 23rd International Conference on Computational Linguistics*, pages 385–393. Association for Computational Linguistics.

Scott Jarvis and Aneta Pavlenko. 2007. *Crosslinguistic influence in language and cognition*. Routledge.

William H Kruskal and W Allen Wallis. 1952. Use of ranks in one-criterion variance analysis. *Journal of the American statistical Association*, 47(260):583–621.

Robert Lado. 1957. Linguistics across cultures: Applied linguistics for language teachers.

Howard Levene. 1960. Robust tests for equality of variances. *Contributions to probability and statistics: Essays in honor of Harold Hotelling*, 2:278–292.

Henry B Mann and Donald R Whitney. 1947. On a test of whether one of two random variables is stochastically larger than the other. *The annals of mathematical statistics*, pages 50–60.

Ryo Nagata and Edward Whittaker. 2013. Reconstructing an indo-european family tree from non-native english texts. In *Proceedings of the 51st Annual Meeting of the Association for Computational Linguistics*, pages 1137–1147, Sofia, Bulgaria. Association for Computational Linguistics.

Diane Nicholls. 2003. The cambridge learner corpus: Error coding and analysis for lexicography and elt. In *Proceedings of the Corpus Linguistics 2003 conference*, pages 572–581.

Terence Odlin. 1989. *Language transfer: Cross-linguistic influence in language learning*. Cambridge University Press.

Alla Rozovskaya and Dan Roth. 2011. Algorithm selection and model adaptation for esl correction tasks. In *Proceedings of the 49th Annual Meeting of the Association for Computational Linguistics: Human Language Technologies-Volume 1*, pages 924–933. Association for Computational Linguistics.

Alla Rozovskaya and Dan Roth. 2014. Building a state-of-the-art grammatical error correction system. *Transactions of the Association for Computational Linguistics*, 2(10):419–434.

Samuel Sanford Shapiro and Martin B Wilk. 1965. An analysis of variance test for normality (complete samples). *Biometrika*, pages 591–611.

Ben Swanson and Eugene Charniak. 2013. Extracting the native language signal for second language acquisition. In *HLT-NAACL*, pages 85–94.

Ben Swanson and Eugene Charniak. 2014. Data driven language transfer hypotheses. *EACL 2014*, page 169.

Joel Tetreault, Daniel Blanchard, and Aoife Cahill. 2013. A report on the first native language identification shared task. In *Proceedings of the Eighth Workshop on Innovative Use of NLP for Building Educational Applications*, pages 48–57. Citeseer.

Ronald Wardhaugh. 1970. The contrastive analysis hypothesis. *TESOL quarterly*, pages 123–130.

Randal L Whitman and Kenneth L Jackson. 1972. The unpredictability of contrastive analysis. *Language learning*, 22(1):29–41.

Sze-Meng Jojo Wong and Mark Dras. 2009. Contrastive analysis and native language identification. In *Proceedings of the Australasian Language Technology Association Workshop*, pages 53–61. Citeseer.

Helen Yannakoudakis, Ted Briscoe, and Ben Medlock. 2011. A new dataset and method for automatically grading ESOL texts. In *ACL*, pages 180–189.

Cross-lingual syntactic variation over age and gender

Anders Johannsen, Dirk Hovy, and Anders Søgaard
Center for Language Technology
University of Copenhagen, Denmark
Njalsgade 140
{ajohannsen,dirk.hovy,soegaard}@hum.ku.dk

Abstract

Most computational sociolinguistics studies have focused on *phonological* and *lexical* variation. We present the first large-scale study of *syntactic* variation among demographic groups (age and gender) across several languages. We harvest data from online user-review sites and parse it with universal dependencies. We show that several age and gender-specific variations hold across languages, for example that women are more likely to use VP conjunctions.

1 Introduction

Language varies between demographic groups. To detect this variation, sociolinguistic studies require *both* a representative corpus of text *and* meta-information about the speakers. Traditionally, this data was collected from a combination of interview transcriptions and questionnaires. Both methods are time-consuming, so population sizes have been small, sometimes including less than five subjects (Rickford and Price, 2013). While these resources enable detailed qualitative analyses, small sample sizes may lead to false research findings (Button et al., 2013). Sociolinguistic studies, in other words, often lack statistical power to establish relationships between language use and socio-economic variables.

Obtaining large enough data sets becomes even more challenging the more complex the target variables are. So while syntactic variation has been identified as an important factor of variation (Cheshire, 2005), it was not approached, due to its high complexity. This paper addresses the issue systematically on a large scale. In contrast to previous work in both sociolinguistics and NLP, we consider syntactic variation across groups at the level of *treelets*, as defined by dependency structures, and make use of a large corpus that includes demographic information on both age and gender.

The impact of such findings goes beyond sociolinguistic insights: knowledge about systematic differences among demographic groups can help us build better and fairer NLP tools. Volkova et al. (2013), Hovy and Søgaard (2015), Jørgensen et al. (2015), and Hovy (2015) have shown the impact of demographic factors on NLP performance. Recently, the company Textio introduced a tool to help phrase job advertisements in a gender-neutral way.[1] While their tool addresses lexical variation, our results indicate that linguistic differences extend to the syntactic level.

Previous work on demographic variation in both sociolinguistics and NLP has begun to rely on corpora from social media, most prominently Twitter. Twitter offers a sufficiently large data source with broad coverage (albeit limited to users with access to social media). Indeed, results show that this resource reflects the *phonological* and *morpho-lexical* variation of spoken language (Eisenstein, 2013b; Eisenstein, 2013a; Doyle, 2014).

However, Twitter is not well-suited for the study of *syntactic* variation for two reasons. First, the limited length of the posts compels the users to adopt a terse style that leaves out many grammatical markers. As a consequence, performance of syntactic parsers is prohibitive for linguistic analysis in this domain. Second, Twitter provides little meta-information about the users, except for regional origin and time of posting. Existing work has thus been restricted to these demographic variables. One line of research has focused on predictive models for age and gender (Alowibdi et al., 2013; Ciot et al., 2013) to add meta-data on Twitter, but again, error rates are too high for use in sociolinguistic hypothesis testing.

We use a new source of data, namely the user

[1] http://recode.net/2015/04/20/textio-spell-checks-for-gender-bias/

Proceedings of the 19th Conference on Computational Language Learning, pages 103–112,
Beijing, China, July 30-31, 2015. ©2015 Association for Computational Linguistics

review site Trustpilot. The meta-information on Trustpilot is both more prevalent and more reliable, and textual data is not restricted in length (see Table 2). We use state-of-the-art dependency parsers trained on universal treebanks (McDonald et al., 2013) to obtain comparable syntactic analyses across several different languages and demographics.

Contributions We present the first study of morpho-syntactic variation with respect to demographic variables across several languages at a large scale. We collect syntactic features within demographic groups and analyze them to retrieve the most significant differences. For the analysis we use a method that preserves statistical power, even when the number of possible syntactic features is very large. Our results show that demographic differences extend *beyond* lexical choice.

2 Data collection

The TRUSTPILOT CORPUS consists of user reviews from the Trustpilot website. On Trustpilot, users can review company websites and leave a one to five star rating, as well as a written review. The data is available for 24 countries, using 13 different languages (Danish, Dutch, English, Finnish, French, German, Italian, Norwegian, Polish, Portuguese, Russian, Spanish, Swedish). In our study, we are limited by the availability of comparable syntactically annotated corpora (McDonald et al., 2013) for five languages used in eleven countries, i.e., English (Australia, Canada, UK, and US), French (Belgium and France), German (Switzerland and Germany), Italian, Spanish, and Swedish. We treat the different variants of these languages separately in the experiments below.[2]

Many users opt to provide a public profile. There are no mandatory fields, other than name, but many also supply their birth year, gender, and location. We crawl the publicly available information on the web site for users and reviews, with different fields. Table 1 contains a list of the fields that are available for each type of entity. For more information on the data as a source for demographic information, see Hovy et al. (2015).

We enhance the data set for our analysis by adding gender information based on first names. In order to add missing gender information, we

Users	Name, ID, profile text, location (city and country), gender, year of birth
Reviews	Title, text, rating (1–5), User ID, Company ID, Date and time of review

Table 1: Meta-information in TRUSTPILOT data

measure the distribution over genders for each name. If a name occurs with sufficient frequency and is found predominantly in one gender, we propagate this gender to all occurrences of the name that lack gender information. In our experiments, we used a gender-purity factor of 0.95 (name occurs with one gender 95% of the time) and a minimum frequency of 3 (name appears at least 3 times in the data). Since names are language-specific (*Angel* is male in Spanish, but female in English), we run this step separately on each language. On average, this measure doubled the amount of gender information for a language.

Note that the domain (reviews) potentially introduces a bias, but since our analysis is largely at the syntactic level, we expect the effect to be limited. While there is certainly a domain effect at the lexical level, we assume that the syntactic findings generalize better to other domains.

	Users	Age	Gender	Place	All
UK	1,424k	7%	62%	5%	4%
France	741k	3%	53%	2%	1%
Denmark	671k	23%	87%	17%	16%
US	648k	8%	59%	7%	4%
Netherlands	592k	9%	39%	7%	5%
Germany	329k	8%	47%	6%	4%
Sweden	170k	5%	64%	4%	3%
Italy	132k	10%	61%	8%	6%
Spain	56k	6%	37%	5%	3%
Norway	51k	5%	50%	4%	3%
Belgium	36k	13%	42%	11%	8%
Australia	31k	8%	36%	7%	5%
Finland	16k	6%	36%	5%	3%
Austria	15k	10%	43%	7%	5%
Switzerland	14k	8%	41%	7%	4%
Canada	12k	10%	19%	9%	4%
Ireland	12k	8%	30%	7%	4%

Table 2: No. of users per variable per country (after augmentations), for countries with $10k+$ users.

3 Methodology

For each language, we train a state-of-the-art dependency parser (Martins et al., 2013) on a

[2]While this might miss some dialectal idiosyncrasies, it is based on standard NLP practice, e.g., when using WSJ-trained parsers in translation of (British) Europarl.

treebank annotated with the Stanford dependency labels (McDonald et al., 2013) and universal POS tag set (Petrov et al., 2011). This gives us syntactic analyses across all languages that describe the same syntactic phenomena the same way. Figure 1 shows two corpus sentences annotated with this harmonized representation.

The style of the reviews is much more canonical than social web data, say Twitter. Expected parse performance can be estimated from the SANCL 2012 shared task on dependency parsing of web data (Petrov and McDonald, 2012). The best result on the review domain there was 83.86 LAS and 88.31 UAS, close to the average over all web domains (83.45 LAS and 87.62 UAS).

From the parses, we extract all subtrees of up to three tokens (*treelets*). We do not distinguish between right- and left-branching relations: the representation is basically a "bag of relations". The purpose of this is to increase comparability across languages with different word orderings (Naseem et al., 2012). A one-token treelet is simply the POS tag of the token, e.g. NOUN or VERB. A two-token treelet is a typed relation between head and dependent, e.g. VERB $\xrightarrow{\text{NSUBJ}}$ NOUN. Treelets of three tokens have two possible structures. Either the head directly dominates two tokens, or the tokens are linked together in a chain, as shown below:

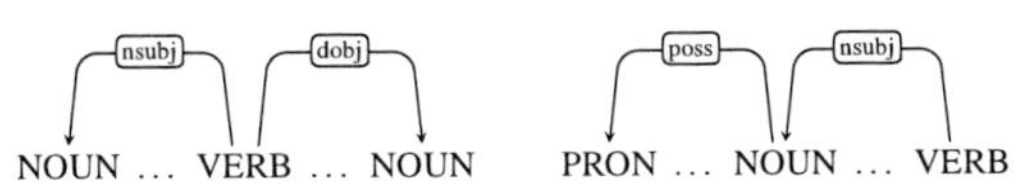

3.1 Treelet reduction

We extract between 500,000 to a million distinct treelets for each language. In principle, we could directly check for significant differences in the demographic groups and use Bonferroni correction to control the family-wise error (i.e., the probability of obtaining a false positive). However, given the large number of treelets, the correction for multiple comparisons would underpower our analyses and potentially cause us to miss many significant differences. We therefore reduce the number of treelets by two methods.

First, we set the minimum number of occurrences of a feature in each language to 50. We apply this heuristic both to ensure statistical power and to focus our analyses on prevalent rather than rare syntactic phenomena.

Second, we perform feature selection using L_1 randomized logistic regression models, with age or gender as target variable, and the treelets as input features. However, direct feature selection with L_1 regularized models (Ng, 2004) is problematic when variables are highly correlated (as in our treelets, where e.g. three-token structures can subsume smaller ones). As a result, small and inessential variations in the dataset can determine which of the variables are selected to represent the group, so we end up with random within-group feature selection.

We therefore use *stability selection* (Meinshausen and Bühlmann, 2010). Stability selection mitigates the correlation problem by fitting the logistic regression model hundreds of times with perturbed data (75% subsampling and feature-wise regularization scaling). Features that receive non-zero weights across many runs can be assumed to be highly indicative. Stability selection thus gives *all* features a chance to be selected. It controls the false positive rate, which is less conservative than family-wise error. We use the default parameters of a publicly available stability selection implementation[3], run it on the whole data set, and discard features selected less than 50% of the time.

With the reduced feature set, we check for usage differences in demographic groups (age and gender) using a χ^2 test. We distinguish two age groups: speakers that are younger than 35, and speakers older than 45. These thresholds were chosen to balance the size of both groups. At this stage we set the desired p-value at 0.02 and apply Bonferroni correction, effectively dividing the p-value threshold by the number of remaining treelets.[4]

Note, finally, that the average number of words written by a reviewer differs between the demographic groups (younger users tend to write more than older ones, women more than men). To counteract this effect, the expected counts in our null hypothesis use the proportion of *words* written by people in a group, rather than the proportion of *people* in the group (which would skew the results towards the groups with longer reviews).

[3] `http://scikit-learn.org/`

[4] Choosing a p-value is somewhat arbitrary. Effectively, our p-value cutoff is several orders of magnitude lower than 0.02, due to the Bonferroni correction.

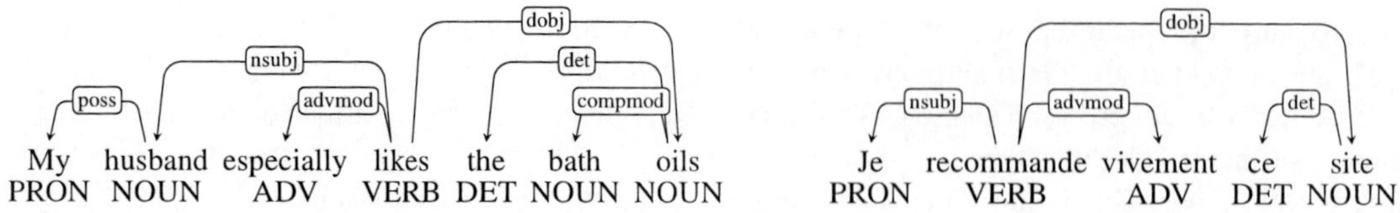

Figure 1: Universal dependency relations for an English and a French sentence, both with adverbial modifiers.

Signif. in # lang.	Rank	Feature	Effect High	Effect By	Subsumes
11	1	NUM	M	32 %	
	2	PRON	F	11 %	
	3	NOUN	M	6 %	
10	4	VERB $\xrightarrow{\text{ACOMP}}$ ADJ	F	22 %	5
	5	VERB	F	6 %	
9	6	ADJ $\xleftarrow{\text{ACOMP}}$ VERB $\xrightarrow{\text{CONJ}}$ VERB	F	36 %	4, 5, 14
	7	VERB $\xrightarrow{\text{ACOMP}}$ ADJ $\xrightarrow{\text{ADVMOD}}$ ADV	F	35 %	4, 5
	8	NOUN $\xrightarrow{\text{COMPMOD}}$ NOUN	M	22 %	3
	9	VERB $\xrightarrow{\text{NSUBJ}}$ PRON	F	14 %	2, 5
8	10	VERB $\xrightarrow{\text{CONJ}}$ VERB $\xrightarrow{\text{ACOMP}}$ ADJ	F	40 %	4, 5, 14
	11	VERB $\xrightarrow{\text{ACOMP}}$ ADJ $\xrightarrow{\text{CONJ}}$ ADJ	F	36 %	4, 5
	12	ADJ $\xleftarrow{\text{ACOMP}}$ VERB $\xrightarrow{\text{CC}}$ CONJ	F	28 %	4, 5
	13	CONJ $\xleftarrow{\text{CC}}$ VERB $\xrightarrow{\text{CONJ}}$ VERB	F	16 %	5, 14
	14	VERB $\xrightarrow{\text{CONJ}}$ VERB	F	14 %	5
	15	ADP $\xleftarrow{\text{ADPMOD}}$ VERB $\xrightarrow{\text{NSUBJ}}$ NOUN	M	14 %	3, 5
	16	NOUN $\xrightarrow{\text{ADPMOD}}$ ADP $\xrightarrow{\text{ADPOBJ}}$ NOUN	M	13 %	3, 17
	17	NOUN $\xrightarrow{\text{ADPMOD}}$ ADP	M	13 %	3
	18	VERB $\xrightarrow{\text{AUX}}$ VERB	F	10 %	5
7	19	ADP $\xrightarrow{\text{ADPOBJ}}$ NUM	M	43 %	1
	20	ADJ $\xleftarrow{\text{ACOMP}}$ VERB $\xrightarrow{\text{NSUBJ}}$ PRON	F	41 %	2, 4, 5, 9

Table 3: **Gender comparison**: Significant syntactic features across languages. Features ordered by number of languages in which they are significant. Right-hand side shows the gender for which the feature is indicative, by which margin, and whether it subsumes other features (indexed by rank)

4 Results

We are interested in robust syntactic variation across languages; that is, patterns that hold across most or all of the languages considered here. We therefore score each of the identified treelets by the number of languages with a significant difference in occurrence between the groups of the given demographic variable. Again, we use a rather conservative non-parametric hypothesis test, with Bonferroni correction.

Tables 3 and 4 show the results for age and gender, respectively. The first column shows the number of languages in which the treelet (third column) is significant. The fourth and fifth column indicate for which age or gender subgroup the feature is indicative, and how much larger the rate of occurrence is there in percent. The indices in the last column represent containment relationships, i.e., when a treelet is strictly contained in another treelet (indexed by the rank given in the second column).

In the case of gender, three atomic treelets (parts of speech) correlate significantly across *all* 11 languages. Two treelets correlate significantly across 10 languages. For age, five treelets correlate significantly across 10 languages.

In sum, men seem to use numerals and nouns more than women across languages, whereas women use pronouns and verbs more often. Men use nominal compounds more often than women in nine out of eleven languages. Women, on the other hand, use VP coordinations more in eight out of eleven languages.

For age, some of the more striking patterns

involve prepositional phrases, which see higher use in the older age group. In atomic treelets, noun use is slightly higher in the older group, while pronouns are more often used by younger reviewers.

Our results address a central question in variational linguistics, namely whether syntax plays a role in language variation among groups. While this has been long suspected, it was never empirically researched due to the perceived complexity. Our findings are the first to corroborate the hypotheses that language variation goes beyond the lexical level.

	FR	DE	IT	ES	SE	UK	US
FR	**592**	42%	73%	88%	46%	47%	38%
DE		**365**	46%	56%	45%	52%	43%
IT			**138**	50%	32%	72%	65%
ES				**78**	28%	79%	73%
SE					**182**	49%	45%
UK						**1056**	88%
US							**630**

	FR	DE	UK	US
FR	**108**	57%	53%	35%
DE		**237**	46%	27%
UK			**370**	56%
US				**173**

Table 5: **Gender (top) and age (bottom)**: Pairwise overlap in significant features. Languages with 50 or less significant features were left out. Diagonal gives the number of features per language.

We also present the pairwise overlap in significant treelets between (a subset of the) languages. See Table 5. Their diagonal values give the number of significant treelets for that language. Percentages in the pairwise comparisons are normalized by the smallest of the pair. For instance, the 49 % overlap between Sweden (SE) and United Kingdom (UK) in Table 5 means that 49 % of the 182 SE treelets were also significant in UK.

We observe that English variants (UK and US) share many features. The Romance languages also share many features with each other, but Italian and Spanish also share many features with English. In Section 5, we analyze our results in more depth.

5 Analysis of syntactic variation

Due to space constraints, we restrict our analysis to a few select treelets with good coverage and interpretable results.

5.1 Gender differences

The top features for gender differences are mostly atomic (pre-terminals), indicating that we observe the same effect as mentioned previously in the literature (Schler et al., 2006), namely that certain parts-of-speech are prevalent in one gender.

[1], [2], [3] For all languages, the use of numerals and nouns is significantly correlated with men, while pronouns and verbs are more indicative of women. When looking at the types of pronouns used by men and women, we see very similar distributions, but men tend to use impersonal pronouns (*it*, *what*) more than women do. Nouns and numbers are associated with the alleged "information emphasis" of male language use (Schler et al., 2006). Numbers typically indicate prices or model numbers, while nouns are usually company names.

The robustness of POS features could to some extent be explained by the different company categories reviewed by each gender: in COMPUTER & ACCESSORIES and CAR LIGHTS the reviews are predominately by men, while the reviews in the PETS and CLOTHES & FASHION categories are mainly posted by women. Using numerals and nouns is more likely when talking about computers and car lights than when talking about pets and clothing, for example.

[4] In English, this treelet is instantiated by examples such as:

(1) is/was/are great/quick/easy and is/was/arrived

In German, the corresponding examples would be:

(2) bin/war zufrieden und werde/würde wieder bestellen (am/was satisfied and will/would order again)

[8] This feature mainly encompasses noun compounds, incl., company names. Again, this feature is indicative of male language use. This may be a side-effect of male use of nouns, but note that the effect is much larger with noun compounds.

Signif. in # lang.	Rank	Feature	Effect High	Effect By	Subsumes
8	$\boxed{1}$	NOUN	>45	5 %	
7	$\boxed{2}$	ADP $\xrightarrow{\text{ADPOBJ}}$ NOUN $\xrightarrow{\text{ADPMOD}}$ ADP	>45	20 %	$\boxed{1}$, $\boxed{5}$, $\boxed{9}$
	$\boxed{3}$	NOUN $\xrightarrow{\text{ADPMOD}}$ ADP $\xrightarrow{\text{ADPOBJ}}$ NOUN	>45	14 %	$\boxed{1}$, $\boxed{5}$, $\boxed{9}$
	$\boxed{4}$	VERB $\xrightarrow{\text{ADVMOD}}$ ADV	<35	12 %	
	$\boxed{5}$	ADP $\xrightarrow{\text{ADPOBJ}}$ NOUN	>45	8 %	$\boxed{1}$
6	$\boxed{6}$	ADV $\xleftarrow{\text{ADVMOD}}$ VERB $\xrightarrow{\text{CONJ}}$ VERB	<35	34 %	$\boxed{4}$, $\boxed{19}$
	$\boxed{7}$	VERB $\xleftarrow{\text{ADVCL}}$ VERB $\xrightarrow{\text{ADVMOD}}$ ADV	<35	27 %	$\boxed{4}$, $\boxed{20}$
	$\boxed{8}$	VERB $\xrightarrow{\text{CC}}$ CONJ	<35	15 %	
	$\boxed{9}$	NOUN $\xrightarrow{\text{ADPMOD}}$ ADP	>45	12 %	$\boxed{1}$
	$\boxed{10}$	PRON	<35	10 %	
5	$\boxed{11}$	ADP $\xleftarrow{\text{ADPMOD}}$ NOUN $\xrightarrow{\text{COMPMOD}}$ NOUN	>45	40 %	$\boxed{1}$, $\boxed{9}$, $\boxed{18}$
	$\boxed{12}$	VERB $\xrightarrow{\text{CONJ}}$ VERB $\xrightarrow{\text{NSUBJ}}$ PRON	<35	32 %	$\boxed{10}$, $\boxed{19}$
	$\boxed{13}$	ADV $\xleftarrow{\text{ADVMOD}}$ VERB $\xrightarrow{\text{CC}}$ CONJ	<35	25 %	$\boxed{4}$, $\boxed{8}$
	$\boxed{14}$	ADP $\xrightarrow{\text{ADPOBJ}}$ NOUN $\xrightarrow{\text{COMPMOD}}$ NOUN	>45	23 %	$\boxed{1}$, $\boxed{5}$, $\boxed{18}$
	$\boxed{15}$	CONJ $\xleftarrow{\text{CC}}$ VERB $\xrightarrow{\text{NSUBJ}}$ PRON	<35	21 %	$\boxed{8}$, $\boxed{10}$
	$\boxed{16}$	CONJ $\xleftarrow{\text{CC}}$ VERB $\xrightarrow{\text{CONJ}}$ VERB	<35	20 %	$\boxed{8}$, $\boxed{19}$
	$\boxed{17}$	ADV $\xleftarrow{\text{ADVMOD}}$ VERB $\xrightarrow{\text{NSUBJ}}$ PRON	<35	19 %	$\boxed{4}$, $\boxed{10}$
	$\boxed{18}$	NOUN $\xrightarrow{\text{COMPMOD}}$ NOUN	>45	17 %	$\boxed{1}$
	$\boxed{19}$	VERB $\xrightarrow{\text{CONJ}}$ VERB	<35	16 %	
	$\boxed{20}$	VERB $\xrightarrow{\text{ADVCL}}$ VERB	<35	11 %	

Table 4: **Age group comparison**: Significant syntactic features across languages. Layout as in Table 3

5.2 Age differences

For age, features vary a lot more than for gender, i.e., there is less support for each than there was for the gender features. A few patterns still stand out.

$\boxed{2}$ This pattern, which is mostly used by the $>$ 45 age group, is often realized in English to express temporal relations, such as

(1) (with)in a couple/days/hours of
(2) in time for

In German, it is mostly used to express comparisons

(1) im Vergleich/Gegensatz zu (compared/in contrast to)
(2) auf Suche nach (in search of)
(3) in Höhe/im Wert von (valued at)

$\boxed{3}$ This pattern, which is indicative of the $>$ 45 age group, is mostly realized in English to express a range of prepositional phrases, some of them overlapping with the previous pattern:

(1) value for money
(2) couple of days
(3) range of products

German also shows prepositional phrases, yet no overlap with $\boxed{2}$

(1) Qualität zu Preisen (quality for price)
(2) Auswahl an Weinen/Hotels (selection of wines/hotels)

In French, this mostly talks about delivery

(1) délai(s) de livraison (delivery)
(2) rapidité de livraison (speed of delivery)

And in Spanish, the main contenders are complex (and slightly more formal) expressions

(1) gastos de envío (shipping)
(2) atención al cliente (customer service)

$\boxed{4}$ This pattern is mostly used by the younger group, and realized to express positive recommendations in all languages:

(1) use again/definitely
(2) recommend highly/definitely

German:

(1) empfehle nur/sehr (just recommend)
(2) bestelle wieder/dort/schon (order again/there/already)

French:

(1) recommande vivement (vividly recommend)
(2) emballé/passé/fait bien (packaged/delivered/made well)

$\boxed{5}$ This pattern is again predominant in the older group, and mostly used in English to complement the prepositional phrases in $\boxed{3}$

(1) at price
(2) with service

In German, it is mostly used to express comparisons

(1) in Ordnung (alright)
(2) am Tag (on the day)

6 Semantic variation within syntactic categories

Given that a number of the indicative features are single treelets (POS tags), we wondered whether there are certain semantic categories that fill these slots. Since we work across several languages, we are looking for semantically equivalent classes. We collect the most significant adjectives and adverbs for each gender for each language and map the words to all of their possible lexical groups in BabelNet (Navigli and Ponzetto, 2010). This creates lexical equivalence classes. Table 6 shows the results. We purposefully exclude nouns and verbs here, as there is too much variation to detect any patterns.

The number of languages that share lexical items from the same BabelNet class is typically smaller than the number of languages that share a treelet. Nevertheless, we observe certain patterns.

The results for gender are presented in Table 6. For adverbs, the division seems to be about intensity: men use more *downtoners* (*approximately*; *almost*; *still*), while women use more *intensifiers* (*actually*; *really*; *truly*; *quite*; *lots*). This finding is new, in that it directly contradicts the perceived wisdom of female language as being more restrained and hedging.

In their use of adjectives, on the other hand, men highlight "factual" properties of the subject, such as price (*inexpensive*) and quality (*cheap*; *best*; *professional*), whereas women use more qualitative adjectives that express the speaker's opinion about the subject (*fantastic*; *amazing*; *pretty*) or their own state (*happy*), although we also find the "factual" assessment *simple*.

Table 7 shows the results for age. There are not many adjectives that group together, and they do not show a clear pattern. Most of the adverbs are indicative of the younger group, although there is overlap with the older group (this is due to different sets of words mapping to the same class). We did not find any evidence for pervasive age effects across languages.

Langs.	BABELNET class	Highest
	Adverbs	
5	just about; approximately	M
	actually; indeed	F
	real; really; very	F
	really; truly; genuinely	F
	quite	F
4	almost; nearly; virtually	M
	still	M
	however; still; nevertheless	M
	soon; presently; shortly	F
	a good deal; lots; very much	F
	Adjectives	
6	fantastic; wondrous; wonderful	F
5	inexpensive; cheap; economic	M
	amazing; awesome; marvelous	F
	tinny; bum; cheap	M
4	happy	F
	best (quality)	M
	professional	M
	pretty	F
	easy; convenient; simple	F
	okay; o.k.; all right	M

Table 6: **Gender**: equivalence classes in BabelNet

7 Related Work

Sociolinguistic studies investigate the relation between a speaker's linguistic choices and socio-economic variables. This includes regional origin (Schmidt and Herrgen, 2001; Nerbonne, 2003; Wieling et al., 2011), age (Barke, 2000; Barbieri, 2008; Rickford and Price, 2013), gender (Holmes, 1997; Rickford and Price, 2013), social class (Labov, 1964; Milroy and Milroy, 1992; Macaulay, 2001; Macaulay, 2002), and ethnicity (Carter, 2013; Rickford and Price, 2013). We focus on age and gender in this work.

Corpus-based studies of variation have largely been conducted either by testing for the presence or absence of a set of pre-defined words (Pennebaker et al., 2001; Pennebaker et al., 2003), or by analysis of the unigram distribution (Barbieri, 2008). This approach restricts the findings to the phenomena defined in the hypothesis, in this case the word list used. In contrast, our approach works beyond the lexical level, is data-driven and thus unconstrained by prior hypotheses.

Eisenstein et al. (2011) use multi-output

Langs.	BABELNET class	Highest
	Adverbs	
5	actually; really; in fact	<35
	truly; genuinely; really	<35
4	however; nevertheless	<35
	however	<35
3	merely; simply; just	<35
	reasonably; moderately; fairly	<35
	very	>45
	in truth; really	<35
	very; really; real	>45
	very; really; real	<35
	Adjectives	
3	easy; convenient; simple	<35
	quick; speedy	>45
	costly; pricy; expensive	<35
	simple	<35
	excellent; first-class	>45
2	spacious; wide	<35
	expensive	<35
	simple (unornamented)	<35
	new	>45
	best	<35

Table 7: **Age**: Lexical equivalences in BabelNet

regression to predict demographic attributes from term frequencies, and vice versa. Using sparsity-inducing priors, they identify key lexical variations between linguistic communities. While they mention syntactic variation as possible future work, their method has not yet been applied to syntactically parsed data. Our method is simpler than theirs, yet goes beyond words. We learn demographic attributes from raw counts of syntactic treelets rather than term frequencies, and test for group differences between the most predictive treelets and the demographic variables. We also use a sparsity-inducing regularizer.

Kendall et al. (2011) study dative alternations on a 250k-words corpus of transcribed spoken Afro-American Vernacular English. They use logistic regression to correlate syntactic features and dialect, similar to Eisenstein et al. (2011), but their study differs from ours in using manually annotated data, studying only one dialect and demographic variable, and using much less data.

Stewart (2014) uses POS tags to study morpho-syntactic features of Afro-American Vernacular English on Twitter, such as copula deletion, habitual *be*, null genitive marking, etc. Our study is different from his in using full syntactic analyses, studying variation across age and gender rather than ethnicity, and in studying syntactic variation across several languages.

8 Conclusion

Syntax has been identified as an important factor in language variation among groups, but not addressed. Previous work has been limited by data size or availability of demographic meta-data. Existing studies on variation have thus mostly focused on lexical and phonological variation.

In contrast, we study the effect of age and gender on syntactic variation across several languages. We use a large-scale data source (international user-review websites) and parse the data, using the same formalisms to maximize comparability. We find several highly significant age- and gender-specific syntactic patterns.

As NLP applications for social media become more widespread, we need to address their performance issues. Our findings suggest that including extra-linguistic factors (which become more and more available) could help improve performance of these systems. This requires a discussion of approaches to corpora construction and the development of new models.

Acknowledgements

We would like to thank the anonymous reviewers for their comments that helped improve the paper. This research is funded by the ERC Starting Grant LOWLANDS No. 313695.

References

Jalal S Alowibdi, Ugo A Buy, and Philip Yu. 2013. Empirical evaluation of profile characteristics for gender classification on twitter. In *Machine Learning and Applications (ICMLA), 2013 12th International Conference on*, volume 1, pages 365–369. IEEE.

Federica Barbieri. 2008. Patterns of age-based linguistic variation in American English. *Journal of sociolinguistics*, 12(1):58–88.

Andrew J Barke. 2000. The Effect of Age on the Style of Discourse among Japanese Women. In *Proceedings of the 14th Pacific Asia Conference on Language, Information and Computation*, pages 23–34.

Katherine Button, John Ioannidis, Claire Mokrysz, Brian Nosek, Jonathan Flint, Emma Robinson, and

Marcus Munafo. 2013. Power failure: why small sample size undermines the reliability of neuroscience. *Nature Reviews Neuroscience*, 14:365–376.

Phillip M Carter. 2013. Shared spaces, shared structures: Latino social formation and african american english in the us south. *Journal of Sociolinguistics*, 17(1):66–92.

Jenny Cheshire. 2005. Syntactic variation and beyond: Gender and social class variation in the use of discourse-new markers1. *Journal of Sociolinguistics*, 9(4):479–508.

Morgane Ciot, Morgan Sonderegger, and Derek Ruths. 2013. Gender inference of twitter users in non-english contexts. In *Proceedings of the 2013 Conference on Empirical Methods in Natural Language Processing, Seattle, Wash*, pages 18–21.

Gabriel Doyle. 2014. Mapping dialectal variation by querying social media. In *EACL*.

Jacob Eisenstein, Noah Smith, and Eric Xing. 2011. Discovering sociolinguistic associations with structured sparsity. In *Proceedings of ACL*.

Jacob Eisenstein. 2013a. Phonological factors in social media writing. In *Workshop on Language Analysis in Social Media, NAACL*.

Jacob Eisenstein. 2013b. What to do about bad language on the internet. In *Proceedings of NAACL*.

Janet Holmes. 1997. Women, language and identity. *Journal of Sociolinguistics*, 1(2):195–223.

Dirk Hovy and Anders Søgaard. 2015. Tagging performance correlates with author age. In *Proceedings of ACL*.

Dirk Hovy, Anders Johannsen, and Anders Søgaard. 2015. User review-sites as a source for large-scale sociolinguistic studies. In *Proceedings of WWW*.

Dirk Hovy. 2015. Demographic factors improve classification performance. In *Proceedings of ACL*.

Anna Jørgensen, Dirk Hovy, and Anders Søgaard. 2015. Challenges of studying and processing dialects in social media. In *Workshop on Noisy User-generated Text (W-NUT)*.

Tyler Kendall, Joan Bresnan, and Gerard van Herk. 2011. The dative alternation in african american english. *Corpus Linguistics and Linguistic Theory*, 7(2):229–244.

William Labov. 1964. *The social stratification of English in New York City*. Ph.D. thesis, Columbia university.

Ronald Macaulay. 2001. You're like 'why not?' the quotative expressions of glasgow adolescents. *Journal of Sociolinguistics*, 5(1):3–21.

Ronald Macaulay. 2002. Extremely interesting, very interesting, or only quite interesting? adverbs and social class. *Journal of Sociolinguistics*, 6(3):398–417.

André FT Martins, Miguel Almeida, and Noah A Smith. 2013. Turning on the turbo: Fast third-order non-projective turbo parsers. In *ACL (2)*, pages 617–622.

Ryan McDonald, Joakim Nivre, Yvonne Quirmbach-Brundage, Yoav Goldberg, Dipanjan Das, Kuzman Ganchev, Keith Hall, Slav Petrov, Hao Zhang, Oscar Täckström, Claudia Bedini, Núria Bertomeu Castelló, and Jungmee Lee. 2013. Universal dependency annotation for multilingual parsing. In *ACL*.

Nicolai Meinshausen and Peter Bühlmann. 2010. Stability selection. *Journal of the Royal Statistical Society: Series B (Statistical Methodology)*, 72(4):417–473.

Lesley Milroy and James Milroy. 1992. Social network and social class: Toward an integrated sociolinguistic model. *Language in society*, 21(01):1–26.

Tahira Naseem, Regina Barzilay, and Amir Globerson. 2012. Selective sharing for multilingual dependency parsing. In *Proceedings of the 50th Annual Meeting of the Association for Computational Linguistics: Long Papers-Volume 1*, pages 629–637. Association for Computational Linguistics.

Roberto Navigli and Simone Paolo Ponzetto. 2010. Babelnet: Building a very large multilingual semantic network. In *Proceedings of the 48th annual meeting of the association for computational linguistics*, pages 216–225. Association for Computational Linguistics.

John Nerbonne. 2003. Linguistic variation and computation. In *Proceedings of EACL*, pages 3–10. Association for Computational Linguistics.

Andrew Y Ng. 2004. Feature selection, l 1 vs. l 2 regularization, and rotational invariance. In *Proceedings of the twenty-first international conference on Machine learning*, page 78. ACM.

James W Pennebaker, Martha E Francis, and Roger J Booth. 2001. Linguistic inquiry and word count: Liwc 2001. *Mahway: Lawrence Erlbaum Associates*, 71:2001.

James W Pennebaker, Matthias R Mehl, and Kate G Niederhoffer. 2003. Psychological aspects of natural language use: Our words, our selves. *Annual review of psychology*, 54(1):547–577.

Slav Petrov and Ryan McDonald. 2012. Overview of the 2012 shared task on parsing the web. In *Notes of the First Workshop on Syntactic Analysis of Non-Canonical Language (SANCL)*, volume 59. Citeseer.

Slav Petrov, Dipanjan Das, and Ryan McDonald. 2011. A universal part-of-speech tagset. CoRR abs/1104.2086.

John Rickford and Mackenzie Price. 2013. Girlz ii women: Age-grading, language change and stylistic variation. *Journal of Sociolinguistics*, 17(2):143–179.

Jonathan Schler, Moshe Koppel, Shlomo Argamon, and James W Pennebaker. 2006. Effects of age and gender on blogging. In *AAAI Spring Symposium: Computational Approaches to Analyzing Weblogs*, volume 6, pages 199–205.

Jürgen Erich Schmidt and Joachim Herrgen. 2001. Digitaler Wenker-Atlas (DiWA). Bearbeitet von Alfred Lameli, Tanja Giessler, Roland Kehrein, Alexandra Lenz, Karl-Heinz Müller, Jost Nickel, Christoph Purschke und Stefan Rabanus. Erste vollständige Ausgabe von Georg Wenkers "Sprachatlas des Deutschen Reichs".

Ian Stewart. 2014. Now we stronger than ever: African-american syntax in twitter. *EACL 2014*, page 31.

Svitlana Volkova, Theresa Wilson, and David Yarowsky. 2013. Exploring demographic language variations to improve multilingual sentiment analysis in social media. In *Proceedings of EMNLP*, pages 1815–1827.

Martijn Wieling, John Nerbonne, and R Harald Baayen. 2011. Quantitative social dialectology: Explaining linguistic variation geographically and socially. *PloS one*, 6(9):e23613.

Cross-lingual Transfer for Unsupervised Dependency Parsing Without Parallel Data

Long Duong,[12] **Trevor Cohn,**[1] **Steven Bird,**[1] and **Paul Cook**[3]
[1]Department of Computing and Information Systems, University of Melbourne
[2]National ICT Australia, Victoria Research Laboratory
[3]Faculty of Computer Science, University of New Brunswick
lduong@student.unimelb.edu.au {t.cohn,sbird}@unimelb.edu.au paul.cook@unb.ca

Abstract

Cross-lingual transfer has been shown to produce good results for dependency parsing of resource-poor languages. Although this avoids the need for a target language treebank, most approaches have still used large parallel corpora. However, parallel data is scarce for low-resource languages, and we report a new method that does not need parallel data. Our method learns syntactic word embeddings that generalise over the syntactic contexts of a bilingual vocabulary, and incorporates these into a neural network parser. We show empirical improvements over a baseline delexicalised parser on both the CoNLL and Universal Dependency Treebank datasets. We analyse the importance of the source languages, and show that combining multiple source-languages leads to a substantial improvement.

1 Introduction

Dependency parsing is a crucial component of many natural language processing (NLP) systems for tasks such as relation extraction (Bunescu and Mooney, 2005), statistical machine translation (Xu et al., 2009), text classification (Özgür and Güngör, 2010), and question answering (Cui et al., 2005). Supervised approaches to dependency parsing have been very successful for many resource-rich languages, where relatively large treebanks are available (McDonald et al., 2005a). However, for many languages, annotated treebanks are not available, and are very costly to create (Böhmová et al., 2001). This motivates the development of unsupervised approaches that can make use of unannotated, monolingual data. However, purely unsupervised approaches have relatively low accuracy (Klein and Manning, 2004; Gelling et al., 2012).

Most recent work on unsupervised dependency parsing for low-resource languages has used the idea of delexicalized parsing and cross-lingual transfer (Zeman et al., 2008; Søgaard, 2011; McDonald et al., 2011; Ma and Xia, 2014). In this setting, a delexicalized parser is trained on a resource-rich *source* language, and is then applied directly to a resource-poor *target* language. The only requirement here is that the source and target languages are POS tagged must use the same tagset. This assumption is pertinent for resource-poor languages since it is relatively quick to manually POS tag the data. Moreover, there are many reports of high accuracy POS tagging for resource-poor languages (Duong et al., 2014; Garrette et al., 2013; Duong et al., 2013b). The cross-lingual delexicalized approach has been shown to significantly outperform unsupervised approaches (McDonald et al., 2011; Ma and Xia, 2014).

Parallel data can be used to boost the performance of a cross-lingual parser (McDonald et al., 2011; Ma and Xia, 2014). However, parallel data may be hard to acquire for truly resource-poor languages.[1] Accordingly, we propose a method to improve the performance of a cross-lingual delexicalized parser using only monolingual data.

Our approach is based on augmenting the delexicalized parser using syntactic word embeddings. Words from both source and target language are mapped to a shared low-dimensional space based on their syntactic context, without recourse to parallel data. While prior work has struggled to efficiently incorporate word embedding information into the parsing model (Bansal et al., 2014; Andreas and Klein, 2014; Chen et al., 2014), we present a method for doing so using a neural net-

[1]Note that most research in this area (as do we) evaluates on simulated low-resource languages, through selective use of data in high-resource languages. Consequently parallel data is plentiful, however this is often not the case in the real setting, e.g., for Tagalog, where only scant parallel data exists (e.g., dictionaries, Wikipedia and the Bible).

Proceedings of the 19th Conference on Computational Language Learning, pages 113–122,
Beijing, China, July 30-31, 2015. ©2015 Association for Computational Linguistics

work parser. We train our parser using a two stage process: first learning cross-lingual syntactic word embeddings, then learning the other parameters of the parsing model using a source language treebank. When applied to the target language, we show consistent gains across all studied languages.

This work is a stepping stone towards the more ambitious goal of a universal parser that can efficiently parse many languages with little modification. This aspiration is supported by the recent release of the Universal Dependency Treebank (Nivre et al., 2015) which has consensus dependency relation types and POS annotation for many languages.

When multiple source languages are available, we can attempt to boost performance by choosing the best source language, or combining information from several source languages. To the best of our knowledge, no prior work has proposed a means for selecting the best source language given a target language. To address this, we introduce two metrics which outperform the baseline of always picking English as the source language. We also propose a method for combining all available source languages which leads to substantial improvement.

The rest of this paper is organized as follows: Section 2 reviews prior work on unsupervised cross-lingual dependency parsing. Section 3 presents the methods for improving the delexicalized parser using syntactic word embeddings. Section 4 describes experiments on the CoNLL dataset and Universal Dependency Treebank. Section 5 presents methods for selecting the best source language given a target language.

2 Unsupervised Cross-lingual Dependency Parsing

There are two main approaches for building dependency parsers for resource-poor languages without using target-language treebanks: delexicalized parsing and projection (Hwa et al., 2005; Ma and Xia, 2014; Täckström et al., 2013; McDonald et al., 2011).

The delexicalized approach was proposed by Zeman et al. (2008). They built a delexicalized parser from a treebank in a resource-rich source language. This parser can be trained using any standard supervised approach, but without including any lexical features, then applied directly to parse sentences from the resource-poor language. Delexicalized parsing relies on the fact that parts-of-speech are highly informative of dependency relations. For example, an English lexicalized discriminative arc-factored dependency parser achieved 84.1% accuracy, whereas a delexicalized version achieved 78.9% (McDonald et al., 2005b; Täckström et al., 2013). Zeman et al. (2008) build a parser for Swedish using Danish, two closely-related languages. Søgaard (2011) adapt this method for less similar languages by choosing sentences from the source language that are similar to the target language. Täckström et al. (2012) additionally use cross-lingual word clustering as a feature for their delexicalized parser. Also related is the work by Naseem et al. (2012) and Täckström et al. (2013) who incorporated linguistic features from the World Atlas of Language Structures (WALS; Dryer and Haspelmath (2013)) for joint modelling of multi-lingual syntax.

In contrast, projection approaches use parallel data to project source language dependency relations to the target language (Hwa et al., 2005). Given a source-language parse tree along with word alignments, they generate the target-language parse tree by projection. However, their approach relies on many heuristics which would be difficult to adapt to other languages. McDonald et al. (2011) exploit both delexicalized parsing and parallel data, using an English delexicalized parser as the seed parser for the target languages, and updating it according to word alignments. The model encourages the target-language parse tree to look similar to the source-language parse tree with respect to the head-modifier relation. Ma and Xia (2014) use parallel data to transfer source language parser constraints to the target side via word alignments. For the null alignment, they used a delexicalized parser instead of the source language lexicalized parser.

In summary, existing work generally starts with a delexicalized parser, and uses parallel data typological information to improve it. In contrast, we want to improve the delexicalized parser, but without using parallel data or any explicit linguistic resources.

3 Improving Delexicalized Parsing

We propose a novel method to improve the performance of a delexicalized cross-lingual parser without recourse to parallel data. Our method uses no additional resources and is designed to complement other methods. The approach is based on syntactic word embeddings where a word is represented as a low-dimensional vector in syntactic space. The idea is simple: we want to relexicalize the delexicalized parser using word embeddings, where source and target language lexical items are represented in the same space.

Word embeddings typically capture both syntactic and semantic information. However, we hypothesize (and later show empirically) that for dependency parsing, word embeddings need to better reflect syntax. In the next subsection, we review some cross-lingual word embedding methods and propose our syntactic word embeddings. Section 4 empirically compares these word embeddings when incorporated into a dependency parser.

3.1 Cross-lingual word embeddings

We review methods that can represent words in both source and target languages in a low-dimensional space. There are many benefits of using a low-dimensional space. Instead of the traditional "one-hot" representation with the number of dimensions equal to vocabulary size, words are represented using much fewer dimensions. This confers the benefit of generalising over the vocabulary to alleviate issues of data sparsity, through learning representations encoding lexical relations such as synonymy.

Several approaches have sought to learn cross-lingual word embeddings from parallel data (Hermann and Blunsom, 2014a; Hermann and Blunsom, 2014b; Xiao and Guo, 2014; Zou et al., 2013; Täckström et al., 2012). Hermann and Blunsom (2014a) induced a cross-lingual word representation based on the idea that representations for parallel sentences should be close together. They constructed a sentence level representation as a bag-of-words summing over word-level representations, and then optimized a hinge loss function to match a latent representation of both sides of a parallel sentence pair. While this might seem well suited to our needs as a word representation in cross-lingual parsing, it may lead to overly semantic embeddings, which are important for translation, but less useful for parsing. For example, "*economic*" and "*economical*" will have a similar representation despite having different syntactic features.

Also related is (Täckström et al., 2012) who build cross-lingual word representations using a variant of the Brown clusterer (Brown et al., 1992) applied to parallel data. Bansal et al. (2014) and Turian et al. (2010) showed that for monolingual dependency parsing, the simple Brown clustering based algorithm outperformed many word embedding techniques. In this paper we compare our approach to forming cross-lingual word embeddings with those of both Hermann and Blunsom (2014a) and Täckström et al. (2012).

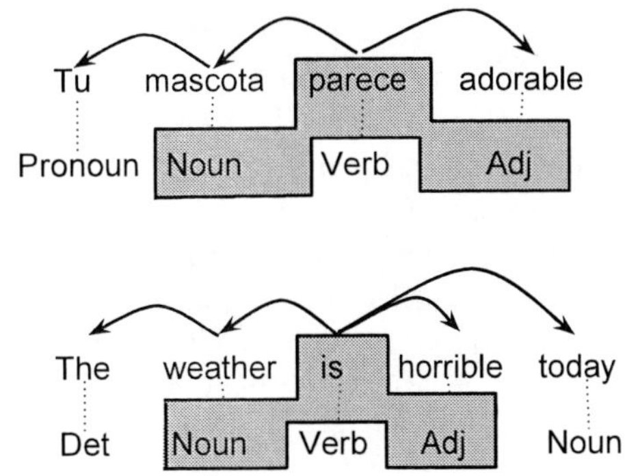

Figure 1: Examples of the syntactic word embeddings for Spanish and English. In each case, the highlighted tags are predicted by the highlighted word. The Spanish sentence means "*your pet looks lovely*".

3.2 Syntactic Word Embedding

We now propose a novel approach for learning cross-lingual word embeddings that is more heavily skewed towards syntax. Word embedding methods typically exploit word co-occurrences, building on traditional techniques for distributional similarity, e.g., the co-occurrences of words in a context window about a central word. Bansal et al. (2014) suggested that for dependency parsing, word embeddings be trained over dependency relations, instead of adjacent tokens, such that embeddings capture head and modifier relations. They showed that this strategy performed much better than surface embeddings for monolingual dependency parsing. However, their method is not applicable to our low resource setting, as it requires a parse tree for training. Instead we consider a simpler representation, namely part-of-speech contexts. This requires only POS tagging, rather than full parsing, while providing syntactic information linking words to their POS context, which we expect to be informative for characterising dependency relations.

Algorithm 1 Syntactic word embedding

1: Match the source and target tagsets to the Universal Tagset.
2: Extract word n-gram sequences for both the source and target language.
3: For each n-gram, keep the middle word, and replace the other words by their POS.
4: Train a skip-gram word embedding model on the resulting list of word and POS sequences from both the source and target language

We assume the same POS tagset is used for both the source and target language,[2] and learn word embeddings for each word type in both languages into the same syntactic space of nearby POS contexts. In particular, we develop a predictive model of the tags to the left and right of a word, as illustrated in Figure 1 and outlined in Algorithm 1. Figure 1 illustrates two training contexts extracted from our English source and Spanish target language, where the highlighted fragments reflect the tags being predicted around each focus word. Note that for this example, the POS contexts for the English and Spanish verbs are identical, and therefore the model would learn similar word embeddings for these terms, and bias the parser to generate similar dependency structures for both terms.

There are several motivations for our approach: (1) POS tags are too coarse-grained for accurate parsing, but with access to local context they can be made more informative; (2) leaving out the middle tag avoids duplication because this is already known to the parser; (3) dependency edges are often local, as shown in Figure 1, i.e., there are dependency relations between most words and their immediate neighbours. Consequently, training our embeddings to predict adjacent tags is likely to learn similar information to training over dependency edges.[3] Bansal et al. (2014) studied the effect of word embeddings on dependency parsing, and found that larger embedding windows captured more semantic information, while smaller windows better reflected syntax. Therefore we choose a small ± 1 word window in our experiments. We also experimented with bigger windows ($\pm 2, \pm 3$) but observed performance degradation in these cases, supporting the argument above.

[2]Later we consider multiple source languages, but for now assume a single source language.

[3]For the 16 languages in the CoNLL-X and CoNLL-07 datasets we observed that approx. 50% of dependency relations span a distance of one word and 20% span two words. Thus our POS context of a ± 1 word window captures the majority of dependency relations.

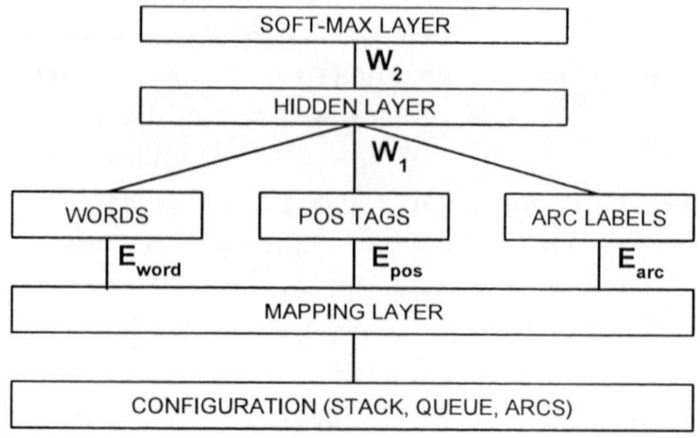

Figure 2: Neural Network Parser Architecture from Chen and Manning (2014)

Step 4 of Algorithm 1 finds the word embeddings as a side-effect of training a neural language model. We use the skip-gram model (Mikolov et al., 2013), trained to predict context tags for each word. The model is formulated as a simple bilinear logistic classifier

$$P(t_c|w) = \frac{\exp(\mathbf{u}_{t_c}^\top \mathbf{v}_w)}{\sum_{z=1}^{T} \exp(\mathbf{u}_z^\top \mathbf{v}_w)} \tag{1}$$

where t_c is the context tag around the current word w, $\mathbf{U} \in \mathbb{R}^{T \times D}$ is the tag embedding matrix, $\mathbf{V} \in \mathbb{R}^{V \times D}$ is the word embedding matrix, with T the number of tags, V is the total number of word types over both languages and D the capacity of the embeddings. Given a training set of word and POS contexts, $(t_i^L, w_i, t_i^R)_{i=1}^N$,[4] we maximize the log-likelihood $\sum_{i=1}^N \log P(t_i^L|w_i) + \log P(t_i^R|w_i)$ with respect to $\mathbf{U}$ and $\mathbf{V}$ using stochastic gradient descent. The learned $\mathbf{V}$ matrix of word embeddings is later used in parser training (the source word embeddings) and inference (the target word embeddings).

3.3 Parsing Algorithm

In this Section, we show how to incorporate the syntactic word embeddings into a parsing model. Our parsing model is built based on the work of Chen and Manning (2014). They built a transition-based dependency parser using a neural-network. The neural network classifier will decide which transition is applied for each configuration.

[4]Note that w here can be a word type in either the source or target language, such that both embeddings will be learned for all word types in both languages.

The architecture of the parser is illustrated in Figure 2, where each layer is fully connected to the layer above.

For each configuration, the selected list of words, POS tags and labels from the Stack, Queue and Arcs are extracted. Each word, POS or label is mapped to a low-dimension vector representation (embedding) through the Mapping Layer. This layer simply concatenates the embeddings which are then fed into a two-layer neural network classifier to predict the next parsing action. The set of parameters for the neural network classifier is $E_{word}, E_{pos}, E_{labels}$ for the mapping layer, W_1 for the hidden layer and W_2 for the soft-max output layer. We incorporate the syntactic word embeddings into the neural network model by setting E_{word} to the syntactic word embeddings, which remain fixed during training so as to retain the cross-lingual mapping.[5]

3.4 Model Summary

To apply the parser to a resource-poor target language, we start by building syntactic word embeddings between source and target languages as shown in algorithm 1. Next we incorporate syntactic word embeddings using the algorithm proposed in Section 3.3. The third step is to substitute source- with target-language syntactic word embeddings. Finally, we parse the target language using this substituted model. In this way, the model will recognize lexical items for the target language.

4 Experiments

We test our method of incorporating syntactic word embeddings into a neural network parser, for both the existing CoNLL dataset (Buchholz and Marsi, 2006; Nivre et al., 2007) and the newly-released Universal Dependency Treebank (Nivre et al., 2015). We employed the Unlabeled Attachment Score (UAS) without punctuation for comparison with prior work on the CoNLL dataset. Where possible we also report Labeled Attachment Score (LAS) without punctuation. We use English as the source language for this experiment.

[5]This is a consequence of only training the parser on the source language. If we were to update embeddings during parser training this would mean they no longer align with the target language embeddings.

4.1 Experiments on CoNLL Data

In this section we report experiments involving the CoNLL-X and CoNLL-07 datasets. Running on this dataset makes our model comparable with prior work. For languages included in both datasets, we use the newer one only. Crucially, for the delexicalized parser we map language-specific tags to the universal tagset (Petrov et al., 2012). The syntactic word embeddings are trained using POS information from the CoNLL data.

There are two baselines for our experiment. The first one is the unsupervised dependency parser of Klein and Manning (2004), the second one is the delexicalized parser of Täckström et al. (2012). We also compare our syntactic word embedding with the cross-lingual word embeddings of Hermann and Blunsom (2014a). These word embeddings are induced by running each language pair using Europarl (Koehn, 2005). We incorporated Hermann and Blunsom (2014a)'s cross-lingual word embeddings into the parsing model in the same way as for the syntactic word embeddings. Table 1 shows the UAS for 8 languages for several models. The first observation is that the direct transfer delexicalized parser outperformed the unsupervised approach. This is consistent with many prior studies. Our implementation of the direct transfer model performed on par with Täckström et al. (2012) on average. Table 1 also shows that using HB embeddings improve the performance over the Direct Transfer model. Our model using syntactic word embedding consistently out-performed the Direct Transfer model and HB embedding across all 8 languages. On average, it is 1.5% and 1.3% better. [6] The improvement varies across languages compared with HB embedding, and falls in the range of 0.3 to 2.6%. This confirms our initial hypothesis that we need word embeddings that capture syntactic instead of semantic information.

It is not strictly fair to compare our method with prior approaches to unsupervised dependency parsing, since they have different resource requirement, i.e. parallel data or typological resources. Compared with the baseline of the direct transfer model, our approach delivered a 1.5% mean performance gain, whereas Täckström et al. (2012) and McDonald et al. (2011) report approximately 3% gain, Ma and Xia (2014) and Naseem et al. (2012) report an approximately 6% gain. As we

[6]All performance comparisons in this paper are absolute.

	da	de	el	es	it	nl	pt	sv	Avg
Unsupervised	33.4	18.0	39.9	28.5	43.1	38.5	20.1	44.0	33.2
Täckström et al. (2012) DT	36.7	48.9	59.5	60.2	64.4	52.8	66.8	55.4	55.6
Our Direct Transfer	44.1	44.9	63.3	52.2	57.7	59.7	67.5	55.4	55.6
Our Model + HB embedding	45.0	44.5	63.8	52.2	56.7	59.8	68.7	55.6	55.8
Our Model + Syntactic embedding	45.9	45.9	64.1	52.9	59.1	61.1	69.5	58.1	57.1

Table 1: Comparative results on the CoNLL corpora showing UAS for several parsers: unsupervised induction Klein and Manning (2004), Direct Transfer (DT) delexicalized parser of Täckström et al. (2012), our implementation of Direct Transfer and our neural network parsing model using cross-lingual embeddings Hermann and Blunsom (2014a) (HB) and our proposed syntactic embeddings.

	cs	de	en	es	fi	fr	ga	hu	it	sv
Train	1173.3	269.6	204.6	382.4	162.7	354.7	16.7	20.8	194.1	66.6
Dev	159.3	12.4	25.1	41.7	9.2	38.9	3.2	3.0	10.5	9.8
Test	173.9	16.6	25.1	8.5	9.1	7.1	3.8	2.7	10.2	20.4
Total	1506.5	298.6	254.8	432.6	181	400.7	23.7	26.5	214.8	96.8

Table 2: Number of tokens ($\times$ 1000) for each language in the Universal Dependency Treebank.

have stated above, our approach is complementary to the approaches used in these other systems. For example, we could incorporate the cross-lingual word clustering feature (Täckström et al., 2012) or WALS features (Naseem et al., 2012) into our model, or use our improved delexicalized parser as the reference model for Ma and Xia (2014), which we expect would lead to better results yet.

4.2 Experiments with Universal Dependency Treebank

We also experimented with the Universal Dependency Treebank V1.0, which has many desirable properties for our system, e.g. dependency types and coarse POS are the same across languages. This removes the need for mapping the source and target language tagsets to a common tagset, as was done for the CoNLL data. Secondly, instead of only reporting UAS we can report LAS, which is impossible on CoNLL dataset where the dependency edge labels differed among languages.

Table 2 shows the size in thousands of tokens for each language in the treebank. The first thing to observe is that some languages have abundant amount of data such as Czech (cs), French (fr) and Spanish (es). However, there are languages with modest size i.e. Hungarian (hu) and Irish (ga).

We ran our model with and without syntactic word embeddings for all languages with English as the source language. The results are shown in Table 3. The first observation is that our model using syntactic word embeddings out-performed direct transfer for all the languages on both UAS and LAS. We observed an average improvement of 3.6% (UAS) and 3.1% (LAS). This consistent improvement shows the robustness of our method of incorporating syntactic word embedding to the model. The second observation is that the gap between UAS and LAS is as big as 13% on average for both models. This reflects the increase difficulty of labelling the edges, with unlabelled edge prediction involving only a 3-way classification[7] while labelled edge prediction involves an 81-way classification.[8] Narrowing the gap between UAS and LAS for resource-poor languages is an important research area for future work.

5 Different Source Languages

In the previous sections, we used English as the source language. However, English might not be the best choice. For the delexicalized parser, it is crucial that the source and target languages have similar syntactic structures. Therefore a different choice of source language might substantially change the performance, as observed in prior studies (Täckström et al., 2013; Duong et al., 2013a; McDonald et al., 2011).

[7]Since there are only 3 transitions: SHIFT, LEFT-ARC, RIGHT-ARC.

[8]Since the Universal Dependency Treebank has 40 universal relations, each relation is attached to LEFT-ARC or RIGHT-ARC. The number 81 comes from 1 (SHIFT) + 40 (LEFT-ARC) + 40 (RIGHT-ARC).

	cs	de	es	fi	fr	ga	hu	it	sv	UAS	LAS
Direct Transfer	47.2	57.9	64.7	44.9	64.8	49.1	47.8	64.9	55.5	55.2	42.7
Our Model + Syntactic embedding	50.2	60.9	67.9	51.4	66.0	51.6	52.3	69.2	59.6	58.8	45.8

Table 3: Results comparing a direct transfer parser and our model with syntactic word embeddings. Evaluating UAS over the Universal Dependency Treebank. (We observed a similar pattern for LAS.) The rightmost UAS and LAS columns shows the average scores for the respective metric across 9 languages.

		Target Language											
		cs	de	en	es	fi	fr	ga	hu	it	sv	UAS	LAS
Source Language	cs	76.8	**65.9**	60.8	70.0	**53.7**	66.8	**59.0**	55.2	70.7	56.8	62.1	38.7
	de	60.0	78.2	61.7	63.1	52.4	60.6	49.8	**56.7**	64.0	59.5	58.6	45.5
	en	50.2	60.9	81.0	67.9	51.4	66.0	51.6	52.3	69.2	**59.6**	58.8	45.8
	es	**60.5**	58.5	60.4	80.9	45.7	**73.3**	53.8	46.9	**77.4**	55.3	59.1	46.2
	fi	49.0	41.8	44.5	33.6	71.5	35.2	24.4	44.6	31.7	43.1	38.7	25.5
	fr	54.2	55.7	**63.2**	**74.8**	43.6	79.2	54.7	44.3	76.2	54.8	57.9	46.3
	ga	32.8	35.3	39.8	56.3	23.5	52.6	72.3	26.0	58.3	32.6	39.7	26.7
	hu	42.3	53.4	45.4	43.8	53.3	42.1	29.2	72.1	41.2	42.5	43.7	22.7
	it	57.6	53.4	53.2	72.1	42.7	71.4	54.7	42.2	85.9	54.2	55.7	45.0
	sv	49.1	59.2	54.9	59.8	47.9	55.7	48.5	52.7	62.2	78.4	54.4	41.2

Table 4: UAS for each language pair in the Universal Dependency Treebank using our best model. The UAS/LAS column show the average UAS/LAS for all target languages, excluding the source language. The best UAS for each target language is shown in bold.

In this section we assume that we have multiple source languages. To see how the performance changes when using a different source language, we run our best model (i.e., using syntactic embeddings) for each language pair in the Universal Dependency Treebank. Table 4 shows the UAS for each language pair, and the average across all target languages for each source language. We also considered LAS, but observed similar trends, and therefore only report the average LAS for each source language. Observe that English is rarely the best source language; Czech and French give a higher average UAS and LAS, respectively. Interestingly, while Czech gives high UAS on average, it performs relatively poorly in terms of LAS.

One might expect that the relative performance from using different source languages is affected by the source corpus size, which varies greatly. We tested this question by limiting the source corpora 66K sentences (and excluded the very small *ga* and *hu* datasets), which resulted in a slight reduction in scores but overall a near identical pattern of results to the use of the full sized source corpora reported in Table 4. Only in one instance did the best source language change (for target *fi* with source *de* not *cs*), and the average rankings by UAS and LAS remained unchanged.

The ten languages considered belong to five families: *Romance* (French, Spanish, Italian), *Germanic* (German, English, Swedish), *Slavic* (Czech), *Uralic* (Hungarian, Finnish), and *Celtic* (Irish). At first glance it seems that language pairs in the same family tend to perform well. For example, the best source language for both French and Italian is Spanish, while the best source language for Spanish is French. However, this doesn't hold true for many target languages. For example, the best source language for both Finnish and German is Czech. It appears that the best choice of an appropriate source language is not predictable from language family information.

We therefore propose two methods to predict the best source language for a given target language. In devising these methods we assume that for a given resource-poor target language we do not have access to any parsed data, as this is expensive to construct. The first method is based on the Jensen-Shannon divergence between the distributions of POS n-grams ($1 < n < 6$) in a pair of languages. The second method converts each language into a vector of binary features based on word-order information from WALS, the World

	cs	de	en	es	fi	fr	ga	hu	it	sv	UAS	LAS
English	50.2	60.9	—	67.9	51.4	66.0	51.6	52.3	69.2	59.6	58.8	45.8
WALS	50.2	59.2	44.5	72.1	51.4	73.3	53.8	44.6	77.4	59.6	60.2	47.1
POS	49.1	58.5	53.2	74.8	53.7	73.3	53.8	56.7	76.2	56.8	61.4	47.7
Oracle	60.5	65.9	63.2	74.8	53.7	73.3	59.0	56.7	77.4	59.6	64.5	50.8
Combined	61.1	67.5	64.4	75.1	54.2	72.8	58.7	57.9	76.7	60.5	64.9	52.0

Table 5: UAS for target languages where the source language is selected in different ways. English uses English as the source language. WALS and POS choose the best source language using the WALS or POS ngrams based methods, respectively. Oracle always uses the best source language. Combined is the model that combines information from all available sources language. The UAS/LAS columns show the UAS/LAS average performance across 9 languages (English is excluded).

Atlas of Language Structures (Dryer and Haspelmath, 2013). These features include the relative order of adjective and noun, etc, and we compute the cosine similarity between the vectors for a pair of languages.

As an alternative to selecting a single source language, we further propose a method to combine information from all available source languages to build a parser for a target language. To do so we first train the syntactic word embeddings on all the languages. After this step, lexical items from all source languages and the target language will be in the same space. We train our parser with syntactic word embeddings on the combined corpus of all source languages. This parser is then applied to the target language directly. The intuition here is that training on multiple source languages limits over-fitting to the source language, and learns the "universal" structure of languages.

Table 5 shows the performance of each target language with the source language given by the model (in the case of models that select a single source language). Always choosing English as the source language performs worst. Using WALS features out-performs English on 7 out of 9 languages. Using POS ngrams out-performs the WALS feature model on average for both UAS and LAS, although the improvement is small. The combined model, which combines information from all available source languages, out-performs choosing a single source language. Moreover, this model performs even better than the oracle model, which always chooses the single best source language, especially for LAS. Compared with the baseline of always choosing English, our combined model gives an improvement about 6% for both UAS and LAS.

6 Conclusions

Most prior work on cross-lingual transfer dependency parsing has relied on large parallel corpora. However, parallel data is scarce for resource-poor languages. In the first part of this paper we investigated building a dependency parser for a resource-poor language without parallel data. We improved the performance of a delexicalized parser using syntactic word embeddings using a neural network parser. We showed that syntactic word embeddings are better at capturing syntactic information, and particularly suitable for dependency parsing. In contrast to the state-of-the-art for unsupervised cross-lingual dependency parsing, our method does not rely on parallel data. Although the state-of-the-art achieves bigger gains over the baseline than our method, our approach could be more-widely applied to resource-poor languages because of its lower resource requirements. Moreover, we have described how our method could be used to complement previous approaches.

The second part of this paper studied ways of improving performance when multiple source languages are available. We proposed two methods to select a single source language that both lead to improvements over always choosing English as the source language. We then showed that we can further improve performance by combining information from all the source languages. In summary, without any parallel data, we managed to improve the direct transfer delexicalized parser by about 10% for both UAS and LAS on average, for 9 languages in the Universal Dependency Treebank.

In this paper we focused only on word embeddings, however, in future work we could also build the POS embeddings and the arc-label embeddings across languages. This could help our system to move more freely across languages, facilitating not only the development of NLP for resource-poor languages, but also cross-language comparisons.

Acknowledgments

This work was supported by the University of Melbourne and National ICT Australia (NICTA). Dr Cohn is the recipient of an Australian Research Council Future Fellowship (project number FT130101105).

References

Jacob Andreas and Dan Klein. 2014. How much do word embeddings encode about syntax? In *Proceedings of the 52nd Annual Meeting of the Association for Computational Linguistics (Volume 2: Short Papers)*, pages 822–827, Baltimore, Maryland.

Mohit Bansal, Kevin Gimpel, and Karen Livescu. 2014. Tailoring continuous word representations for dependency parsing. In *Proceedings of the 52nd Annual Meeting of the Association for Computational Linguistics (Volume 2: Short Papers)*, pages 809–815.

Alena Böhmová, Jan Hajič, Eva Hajičová, and Barbora Hladká. 2001. The Prague Dependency Treebank: A Three-Level Annotation Scenario. In Anne Abeillé, editor, *Treebanks: Building and Using Syntactically Annotated Corpora*, pages 103–127.

Peter F. Brown, Peter V. deSouza, Robert L. Mercer, Vincent J. Della Pietra, and Jenifer C. Lai. 1992. Class-based n-gram models of natural language. *Computational Linguistics*, 18:467–479.

Sabine Buchholz and Erwin Marsi. 2006. CoNLL-X shared task on multilingual dependency parsing. In *Proceedings of the Tenth Conference on Computational Natural Language Learning*.

Razvan C. Bunescu and Raymond J. Mooney. 2005. A shortest path dependency kernel for relation extraction. In *Proceedings of the Conference on Human Language Technology and Empirical Methods in Natural Language Processing*, HLT '05, pages 724–731.

Danqi Chen and Christopher Manning. 2014. A fast and accurate dependency parser using neural networks. In *Proceedings of the 2014 Conference on Empirical Methods in Natural Language Processing (EMNLP)*, pages 740–750, Doha, Qatar.

Wenliang Chen, Yue Zhang, and Min Zhang. 2014. Feature embedding for dependency parsing. In *Proceedings of COLING 2014, the 25th International Conference on Computational Linguistics: Technical Papers*, pages 816–826, Dublin, Ireland.

Hang Cui, Renxu Sun, Keya Li, Min-Yen Kan, and Tat-Seng Chua. 2005. Question answering passage retrieval using dependency relations. In *Proceedings of the 28th Annual International ACM SIGIR Conference on Research and Development in Information Retrieval*, SIGIR '05, pages 400–407, New York, NY, USA.

Matthew S. Dryer and Martin Haspelmath, editors. 2013. *WALS Online*. Leipzig.

Long Duong, Paul Cook, Steven Bird, and Pavel Pecina. 2013a. Increasing the quality and quantity of source language data for Unsupervised Cross-Lingual POS tagging. In *Proceedings of the Sixth International Joint Conference on Natural Language Processing*, pages 1243–1249, Nagoya, Japan.

Long Duong, Paul Cook, Steven Bird, and Pavel Pecina. 2013b. Simpler unsupervised POS tagging with bilingual projections. In *Proceedings of the 51st Annual Meeting of the Association for Computational Linguistics (Volume 2: Short Papers)*, pages 634–639, Sofia, Bulgaria.

Long Duong, Trevor Cohn, Karin Verspoor, Steven Bird, and Paul Cook. 2014. What can we get from 1000 tokens? a case study of multilingual pos tagging for resource-poor languages. In *Proceedings of the 2014 Conference on Empirical Methods in Natural Language Processing (EMNLP)*, pages 886–897, Doha, Qatar.

Dan Garrette, Jason Mielens, and Jason Baldridge. 2013. Real-world semi-supervised learning of pos-taggers for low-resource languages. In *Proceedings of the 51st Annual Meeting of the Association for Computational Linguistics (ACL-2013)*, pages 583–592, Sofia, Bulgaria.

Douwe Gelling, Trevor Cohn, Phil Blunsom, and Joo Graa. 2012. The pascal challenge on grammar induction.

Karl Moritz Hermann and Phil Blunsom. 2014a. Multilingual Distributed Representations without Word Alignment. In *Proceedings of ICLR*.

Karl Moritz Hermann and Phil Blunsom. 2014b. Multilingual models for compositional distributed semantics. *CoRR*, abs/1404.4641.

Rebecca Hwa, Philip Resnik, Amy Weinberg, Clara Cabezas, and Okan Kolak. 2005. Bootstrapping parsers via syntactic projection across parallel texts. *Natural Language Engineering*, 11:311–325.

Dan Klein and Christopher Manning. 2004. Corpus-based induction of syntactic structure: Models of dependency and constituency. In *Proceedings of the 42nd Annual Meeting on Association for Computational Linguistics*, ACL '04.

Philipp Koehn. 2005. Europarl: A Parallel Corpus for Statistical Machine Translation. In *Proceedings of the Tenth Machine Translation Summit (MT Summit X)*, pages 79–86, Phuket, Thailand.

Xuezhe Ma and Fei Xia. 2014. Unsupervised dependency parsing with transferring distribution via parallel guidance and entropy regularization. In *Proceedings of the 52nd Annual Meeting of the Association for Computational Linguistics (Volume 1: Long Papers)*, pages 1337–1348.

Ryan McDonald, Koby Crammer, and Fernando Pereira. 2005a. Online large-margin training of dependency parsers. In *Proceedings of the 43rd Annual Meeting on Association for Computational Linguistics*, ACL '05, pages 91–98.

Ryan McDonald, Fernando Pereira, Kiril Ribarov, and Jan Hajič. 2005b. Non-projective dependency parsing using spanning tree algorithms. In *Proceedings of the Conference on Human Language Technology and Empirical Methods in Natural Language Processing*, HLT '05, pages 523–530.

Ryan McDonald, Slav Petrov, and Keith Hall. 2011. Multi-source transfer of delexicalized dependency parsers. In *Proceedings of the Conference on Empirical Methods in Natural Language Processing*, EMNLP '11, pages 62–72.

Tomas Mikolov, Ilya Sutskever, Kai Chen, Greg S. Corrado, and Jeff Dean. 2013. Distributed representations of words and phrases and their compositionality. In C.j.c. Burges, L. Bottou, M. Welling, Z. Ghahramani, and K.q. Weinberger, editors, *Advances in Neural Information Processing Systems 26*, pages 3111–3119.

Tahira Naseem, Regina Barzilay, and Amir Globerson. 2012. Selective sharing for multilingual dependency parsing. In *Proceedings of the 50th Annual Meeting of the Association for Computational Linguistics: Long Papers - Volume 1*, ACL '12, pages 629–637.

Joakim Nivre, Johan Hall, Sandra Kübler, Ryan McDonald, Jens Nilsson, Sebastian Riedel, and Deniz Yuret. 2007. The CoNLL 2007 shared task on dependency parsing. In *Proceedings of the CoNLL Shared Task Session of EMNLP-CoNLL 2007*, pages 915–932, Prague, Czech Republic.

Joakim Nivre, Cristina Bosco, Jinho Choi, Marie-Catherine de Marneffe, Timothy Dozat, Richárd Farkas, Jennifer Foster, Filip Ginter, Yoav Goldberg, Jan Hajič, Jenna Kanerva, Veronika Laippala, Alessandro Lenci, Teresa Lynn, Christopher Manning, Ryan McDonald, Anna Missilä, Simonetta Montemagni, Slav Petrov, Sampo Pyysalo, Natalia Silveira, Maria Simi, Aaron Smith, Reut Tsarfaty, Veronika Vincze, and Daniel Zeman. 2015. Universal dependencies 1.0.

Levent Özgür and Tunga Güngör. 2010. Text classification with the support of pruned dependency patterns. *Pattern Recognition Letter*, 31:1598–1607.

Slav Petrov, Dipanjan Das, and Ryan McDonald. 2012. A universal part-of-speech tagset. In *Proceedings of the Eight International Conference on Language Resources and Evaluation (LREC'12)*, Istanbul, Turkey.

Anders Søgaard. 2011. Data point selection for cross-language adaptation of dependency parsers. In *Proceedings of the 49th Annual Meeting of the Association for Computational Linguistics: Human Language Technologies: Short Papers - Volume 2*, HLT '11, pages 682–686.

Oscar Täckström, Ryan McDonald, and Jakob Uszkoreit. 2012. Cross-lingual word clusters for direct transfer of linguistic structure. In *Proceedings of the 2012 Conference of the North American Chapter of the Association for Computational Linguistics: Human Language Technologies*, NAACL HLT '12, pages 477–487.

Oscar Täckström, Ryan McDonald, and Joakim Nivre. 2013. Target language adaptation of discriminative transfer parsers. In *Proceedings of the 2013 Conference of the North American Chapter of the Association for Computational Linguistics: Human Language Technologies*, pages 1061–1071, Atlanta, Georgia.

Joseph Turian, Lev-Arie Ratinov, and Yoshua Bengio. 2010. Word representations: A simple and general method for semi-supervised learning. In *Proceedings of the 48th Annual Meeting of the Association for Computational Linguistics*, pages 384–394, Uppsala, Sweden.

Min Xiao and Yuhong Guo, 2014. *Proceedings of the Eighteenth Conference on Computational Natural Language Learning*, chapter Distributed Word Representation Learning for Cross-Lingual Dependency Parsing, pages 119–129.

Peng Xu, Jaeho Kang, Michael Ringgaard, and Franz Och. 2009. Using a dependency parser to improve smt for subject-object-verb languages. In *Proceedings of Human Language Technologies: The 2009 Annual Conference of the North American Chapter of the Association for Computational Linguistics*, pages 245–253, Boulder, Colorado.

Daniel Zeman, Univerzita Karlova, and Philip Resnik. 2008. Cross-language parser adaptation between related languages. In *In IJCNLP-08 Workshop on NLP for Less Privileged Languages*, pages 35–42.

Will Y. Zou, Richard Socher, Daniel Cer, and Christopher D. Manning. 2013. Bilingual word embeddings for phrase-based machine translation. In *Proceedings of the 2013 Conference on Empirical Methods in Natural Language Processing*, pages 1393–1398, Seattle, Washington, USA.

Detecting Semantically Equivalent Questions in Online User Forums

Dasha Bogdanova*, **Cícero dos Santos†**, **Luciano Barbosa†** and **Bianca Zadrozny†**
*ADAPT centre, School of Computing, Dublin City University, Dublin, Ireland
dbogdanova@computing.dcu.ie
†IBM Research, 138/146 Av. Pasteur, Rio de Janeiro, Brazil
{cicerons,lucianoa,biancaz}@br.ibm.com

Abstract

Two questions asking the same thing could be too different in terms of vocabulary and syntactic structure, which makes identifying their semantic equivalence challenging. This study aims to detect semantically equivalent questions in online user forums. We perform an extensive number of experiments using data from two different Stack Exchange forums. We compare standard machine learning methods such as Support Vector Machines (SVM) with a convolutional neural network (CNN). The proposed CNN generates distributed vector representations for pairs of questions and scores them using a similarity metric. We evaluate in-domain word embeddings versus the ones trained with Wikipedia, estimate the impact of the training set size, and evaluate some aspects of domain adaptation. Our experimental results show that the convolutional neural network with in-domain word embeddings achieves high performance even with limited training data.

1 Introduction

Question-answering (Q&A) community sites, such as Yahoo! Answers,[1] Quora[2] and Stack Exchange,[3] have gained a lot of attention in the recent years. Most Q&A community sites advise users to search the forum for an answer before posting a new question. However, this is not always an easy task because different users could formulate the same question in completely different ways. Some user forums, such as those of the Stack Exchange online community, have a duplication policy. Exact duplicates, such as copy-and-paste questions, and nearly exact duplicates are usually quickly detected, closed and removed from the forum. Nevertheless, some duplicate questions are kept. The main reason for that is that *there are many ways to ask the same question, and a user might not be able to find the answer if they are asking it a different way.*[4]

In this study we define two questions as semantically equivalent if they can be adequately answered by the exact same answer. Table 1 presents an example of a pair of such questions from Ask Ubuntu forum. Detecting semantically equivalent questions is a very difficult task due to two main factors: (1) the same question can be rephrased in many different ways; and (2) two questions could be asking different things but look for the same solution. Therefore, traditional similarity measures based on word overlap such as shingling and Jaccard coefficient (Broder, 1997) and its variations (Wu et al., 2011) are not able to capture many cases of semantic equivalence.

In this paper, we propose a convolutional neural network architecture to detect semantically equivalent questions. The proposed CNN first transforms words into word embeddings (Mikolov et al., 2013), using a large collection of unlabeled data, and then applies a convolutional network to build distributed vector representations for pairs of questions. Finally, it scores the questions using a similarity metric. Pairs of questions with similarity above a threshold, defined based on a held-out set, are considered duplicates. CNN is trained using positive and negative pairs of semantically equivalent questions. During training, CNN is *induced* to produce similar vector representations for questions that are semantically equivalent.

We perform an extensive number of experiments using data from two different Stack Exchange forums. We compare CNN performance with a traditional classification algorithm (Support

[1] https://answers.yahoo.com/
[2] http://www.quora.com
[3] http://stackexchange.com/
[4] http://stackoverflow.com/help/duplicates

Proceedings of the 19th Conference on Computational Language Learning, pages 123–131,
Beijing, China, July 30-31, 2015. ©2015 Association for Computational Linguistics

Title: I can't download anything and I can't watch videos	Title: How can I install Windows software or games?
Body: Two days ago I tried to download skype and it says an error occurred it says *end of central directory signature not found Either this file is not a zipfile, or it constitutes one disk of a multi-part archive. In the latter case the central directory and zipfile comment will be found on the last disk(s) of this archive. zipinfo: cannot find zipfile directory in one of /home/maria/Downloads/SkypeSetup-aoc-jd.exe* or */home/maria/Downloads/SkypeSetup-aoc-jd.exe.zip, and cannot find /home/maria/Downloads/SkypeSetup-aoc-jd.exe.ZIP* pe... this happens whenever I try to download anything like games and also i can't watch videoss it's looking for plug ins but it doesn't find them i hate this [sic!]	**Body:** Can *.exe* and *.msi* files (Windows software) be installed in Ubuntu? [sic!]
Link: `http://askubuntu.com/questions/364350`	`http://askubuntu.com/questions/988`
Possible Answer (Shortened version): .exe files are not binary-compatible with Ubuntu. There are, however, compatibility layers for Linux, such as Wine, that are capable of running .exe.	

Table 1: An example of semantically equivalent questions from Ask Ubuntu community.

Vector Machines (Cortes and Vapnik, 1995)) and a duplicate detection approach (shingling (Broder, 1997)). The results show CNN outperforms the baselines by a large margin.

We also investigate the impact of different word embeddings by analyzing the performance of the network with: (1) word embeddings pre-trained on in-domain data and all of the English Wikipedia; (2) word vectors of different dimensionalities; (3) training sets of different sizes; and (4) out-of-domain training data and in-domain word embeddings. The numbers show that: (1) word embeddings pre-trained on domain-specific data achieve very high performance; (2) bigger word embeddings obtain higher accuracy; (3) in-domain word embeddings provide better performance independent of the training set size; and (4) in-domain word embeddings achieve relatively high accuracy even using out-of-domain training data.

2 Task

This work focuses on the task of predicting semantically equivalent questions in online user forums. Following the duplication policy of the Stack Exchange online community,[5] we define semantically equivalent questions as follows:

Definition 1. *Two questions are semantically equivalent if they can be adequately answered by the exact same answer.*

Since our definition of semantically equivalent questions corresponds to the rules of the Stack Exchange duplication policy, we assume that all questions of this community that were marked as duplicates are semantically equivalent. An example of such questions is given in Table 1. These questions vary significantly in vocabulary, style, length and content quality. However, both questions require the exact same answer.

The exact task that we approach in this study consists in, given two problem definitions, predicting if they are semantically equivalent. By *problem definition* we mean the concatenation of the title and the body of a question. Throughout this paper we use the term *question* as a synonym of problem definition.

3 Related Work

The development of CNN architectures for tasks that involve sentence-level and document-level processing is currently an area of intensive research in natural language processing and information retrieval, with many recent encouraging results.

Kim (2014) proposes a simple CNN for sentence classification built on top of `word2vec` (2013). A multichannel variant which combines static word vectors from `word2vec` and word vectors which are fine-tuned via backpropagation is also proposed. Experiments with different variants are performed on a number of benchmarks for sentence classification, showing that the simple CNN performs remarkably well, with state-of-the-art results in many of the benchmarks, highlighting the importance of using unsupervised pre-training of word vectors for this task.

Hu et al.(2014) propose a CNN architecture for hierarchical sentence modeling and, based on that, two architectures for sentence matching.

[5] http://blog.stackoverflow.com/2010/11/dr-strangedupe-or-how-i-learned-to-stop-worrying-and-love-duplication/; http://meta.stackexchange.com/questions/32311/do-not-delete-good-duplicates

They train the latter networks using a ranking-based loss function on three sentence matching tasks of different nature: sentence completion, response matching and paraphrase identification. The proposed architectures outperform previous work for sentence completion and response matching, while the results are slightly worse than the state-of-the-art in paraphrase identification.

Yih et al.(2014) focus on the task of answering single-relation factual questions, using a novel semantic similarity model based on a CNN architecture. Using this architecture, they train two models: one for linking a question to an entity in the DB and the other mapping a relation pattern to a relation in the DB. Both models are then combined for inferring the entity that is the answer. This approach leads to a higher precision on Q&A data from the WikiAnswers corpus than the existing rules-based approach for this task.

Dos Santos & Gatti (2014) developed a CNN architecture for sentiment analysis of short texts that jointly uses character-level, word-level and sentence-level information, achieving state-of-the-art results on well known sentiment analysis benchmarks.

For the specific task of semantically equivalent questions detection that we address in this paper, we are not aware of any previous work using CNNs. Muthmann and Petrova (2014) approach the task of identifying topical near-duplicate relations between questions from social media as a classification task. They use a simple lexico-syntactical feature set and different classifiers are evaluated, with logistic regression reported as the best performing one. However, it is not possible to directly compare our results to theirs because their experimental methodology is not clearly described in the paper.

There are several tasks related to identifying semantically equivalent questions. These tasks include near-duplicate detection, paraphrase identification and textual semantic similarity estimation. In what follows, we outline the differences between these tasks and the one addressed in this work.

Duplicate and Near-Duplicate Detection aims to detect exact copies or almost exact copies of the same document in corpora. Duplicate detection is an important component of systems for Web crawling and Web search, where it is important to identify redundant data in large corpora. Common techniques to detect duplicate documents include shingling (Broder, 1997; Alonso et al., 2013) and fingerprinting (Manku et al., 2007). State-of-the-art work also focuses on the efficiency issues of the task (Wu et al., 2011). It is worth noting that even though all duplicate and near-duplicate questions are also semantically equivalent, the reverse is not true. Semantically equivalent questions could have small or no word overlap (see Table 1 for an example), and thus, are not duplicates.

Paraphrase Identification is the task of examining two sentences and determining whether they have the same meaning (Socher et al., 2011). If two questions are paraphrases, they are also semantically equivalent. However, many semantically equivalent questions are not paraphrases. The questions shown in Table 1 significantly differ in the details they provide, and thus, could not be considered as having the same meaning. State-of-the-art approaches to paraphrase identification include using Machine Translation evaluation metrics (Madnani et al., 2012) and Deep Learning techniques (Socher et al., 2011).

Textual Semantic Similarity is the task of measuring the degree of semantic similarity between two texts, usually on a graded scale from 0 to 5, with 5 being the most similar (Agirre et al., 2013) and meaning that the texts are paraphrases. All semantically equivalent questions are somewhat semantically similar, but semantic equivalence of questions defined here does not correspond to the highest value of the textual semantic similarity for the same reasons these questions are not always paraphrases.

4 Neural Network Architecture

In this section, we present our neural-network strategy for detecting semantically equivalent questions.

4.1 Feed Forward Processing

As detailed in Figure 1, the input for the network is tokenized text strings of the two questions. In the first step, the CNN transforms words into real-valued feature vectors, also known as word embeddings or word representations. Next, a convolutional layer is used to construct two distributed vector representations r_{q_1} and r_{q_2}, one for each input question. Finally, the CNN computes a similarity score between r_{q_1} and r_{q_2}. Pairs of questions with similarity above a threshold, defined based on

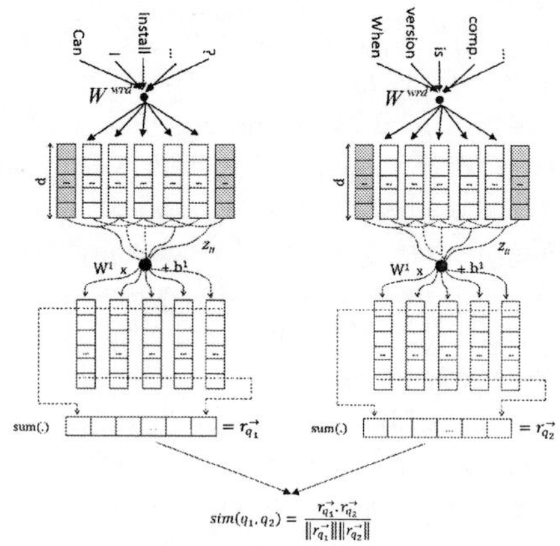

Figure 1: Convolutional neural network for semantically equivalent questions detection.

a heldout set, are considered duplicates.

4.2 Word Representations

The first layer of the network transforms words into representations that capture syntactic and semantic information about the words. Given a question consisting of N words $q = \{w_1, w_2, ..., w_N\}$, every word w_n is converted into a real-valued vector r^{w_n}. Therefore, for each question, the input to the next NN layer is a sequence of real-valued vectors $q^{emb} = \{r^{w_1}, r^{w_2}, ..., r^{w_N}\}$

Word representations are encoded by column vectors in an embedding matrix $W^0 \in \mathbb{R}^{d \times |V|}$, where V is a fixed-sized vocabulary. Each column $W_i^0 \in \mathbb{R}^d$ corresponds to the word embedding of the i-th word in the vocabulary. We transform a word w into its word embedding r^w by using the matrix-vector product:

$$r^w = W^0 v^w \tag{1}$$

where v^w is a vector of size $|V|$ which has value 1 at index w and zero in all other positions. The matrix W^0 is a parameter to be learned, and the size of the word embedding d is a hyper-parameter to be chosen by the user.

4.3 Question Representation and Scoring

The next step in the CNN consists in creating distributed vectors from word embeddings representations of the input questions. To perfom this task, the CNN must deal with two main challenges: different questions can have different sizes; and important information can appear at any position in the question. The convolutional approach (Waibel et al., 1989) is a natural choice to tackle these challenges. In recent work, convolutional approaches have been used to solve similar problems when creating representations for text segments of different sizes (dos Santos and Gatti, 2014) and character-level representations of words of different sizes (dos Santos and Zadrozny, 2014). Here, we use a convolutional layer to compute the question-wide distributed vector representations r_{q_1} and r_{q_2}. For each question, the convolutional layer first produces local features around each word in the question. Then, it combines these local features using a sum operation to create a fixed-sized feature vector (representation) for the question.

Given a question q_1, the convolutional layer applies a matrix-vector operation to each window of size k of successive windows in $q_1^{emb} = \{r^{w_1}, r^{w_2}, ..., r^{w_N}\}$. Let us define the vector $z_n \in \mathbb{R}^{dk}$ as the concatenation of a sequence of k word embeddings, centralized in the n-th word:[6]

$$z_n = \left(r^{w_{n-(k-1)/2}}, ..., r^{w_{n+(k-1)/2}}\right)^T$$

The convolutional layer computes the j-th element of the vector $r_{q_1} \in \mathbb{R}^{cl_u}$ as follows:

$$[r_{q_1}]_j = f\left(\sum_{1<n<N} \left[f\left(W^1 z_n + b^1\right)\right]_j\right) \tag{2}$$

where $W^1 \in \mathbb{R}^{cl_u \times dk}$ is the weight matrix of the convolutional layer and f is the hyperbolic tangent function. The same matrix is used to extract local features around each word window of the given question. The *global* fixed-sized feature vector for the question is obtained by using the sum over all word windows.[7] Matrix W^1 and vector b^1 are parameters to be learned. The number of convolutional units cl_u (which corresponds to the size of the question representation), and the size of the word context window k are hyper-parameters to be chosen by the user.

Given r_{q_1} and r_{q_2}, the representations for the input pair of questions (q_1, q_2), the last layer of the CNN computes a similarity score between q_1 and q_2. In our experiments we use the cosine similarity $s(q_1, q_2) = \frac{\vec{r_{q_1}} \cdot \vec{r_{q_2}}}{\|\vec{r_{q_1}}\| \|\vec{r_{q_2}}\|}$.

[6] Words with indices outside of the sentence boundaries use a common *padding embedding*.

[7] Using max operation instead of sum produces very similar results.

4.4 Training Procedure

Our network is trained by minimizing the mean-squared error over the training set D. Given a question pair (q_1, q_2), the network with parameter set θ computes a similarity score $s_\theta(q_1, q_2)$. Let $y_{(q_1,q_2)}$ be the correct *label* of the pair, where its possible values are 1 (equivalent questions) or 0 (not equivalent questions). We use stochastic gradient descent (SGD) to minimize the mean-squared error with respect to θ:

$$\theta \mapsto \sum_{(x,y)\in D} \frac{1}{2}(y - s_\theta(x))^2 \tag{3}$$

where $x = (q_1, q_2)$ corresponds to a question pair in the training set D and y represents its respective label $y_{(q_1,q_2)}$.

We use the backpropagation algorithm to compute gradients of the network. In our experiments, we implement the CNN architecture and the backpropagation algorithm using Theano (Bergstra et al., 2010).

5 Experimental Setup

5.1 Data

In our experiments we use data from the Ask Ubuntu Community Questions and Answers (Q&A) site.[8] Ask Ubuntu is a community for Ubuntu users and developers, and it is part of the Stack Exchange[9] Q&A communities. The users of these communities can ask and answer questions, and vote up and down both questions and answers. Users with high reputation become moderators and can label a new question as a duplicate to an existing question.[10] Usually it takes five votes from different moderators to close a question or to mark it as a duplicate.

We use the Ask Ubuntu data dump provided in May 2014. We extract all question pairs linked as duplicates. The data dump we use contains 15277 such pairs. For our experiments, we randomly select a training set of 24K pairs, a test set of 6K and a validation set of 1K, making sure there are no overlaps between the sets. Half of each set contains pairs of semantically equivalent questions (positive pairs) and half are pairs of questions that are not semantically equivalent. The latter pairs are randomly generated from the corpus. The data was tokenized with NLTK (Bird et al., 2009), and all links were replaced by a unique string.

For the experiments on a different domain (see Section 6.4) we use the Meta Stack Exchange[11] data dump provided in September 2014. Meta Stack Exchange (Meta) is used to discuss the Stack Exchange community itself. People ask questions about the rules, features and possible bugs. The data dump we use contains 67746 questions, where 19456 are marked as duplicates. For the experiments on this data set, we select random balanced disjoint sets of 20K pairs for training, 1K for validation and 4K for testing. We prepare the data in exactly the same manner as the Ask Ubuntu data.

5.2 Baselines

We explore three main baselines: a method based on the Jaccard coefficient which was reported to provide high accuracy for the task of duplicate detection (Wu et al., 2011), a Support Vector Machines (SVM) classifier (Cortes and Vapnik, 1995) and the combination of the two.

For the first baseline, documents are first represented as sets of shingles of lengths from one to four, and then the Jaccard coefficient for a pair of documents is calculated as follows:

$$J(S(d_1), S(d_2)) = \frac{S(d_1) \cap S(d_2)}{S(d_1) \cup S(d_2)},$$

where $S(d_i)$ is the set of shingles generated from the ith document. High values of the Jaccard coefficient denote high similarity between the documents. If the value exceeds a threshold T, the documents are considered semantically equivalent. In this case, the training data is used to select the optimal threshold T.

For the SVM baseline, we represent documents with n-grams of length up to four. For each pair of questions and each n-gram we generate three features: (1) if the n-gram is present in the first question; (2) if the n-gram is present in the second question; (3) the overall normalized count of the n-gram in the two questions. We use the RBF kernel and perform grid search to optimize the values of C and γ parameters. We use a frequency threshold[12] to reduce the number of features. The

[8] http://askubuntu.com/

[9] http://stackexchange.com

[10] More information about Stack Exchange communities could be found here: http://stackexchange.com/tour

[11] meta.stackexchange.com

[12] Several values (2, 5, 35 and 100) were tried with cross-validation, the threshold with value 5 was selected

implementation provided by LibSVM (Chang and Lin, 2011) is used.

In order to combine the two baselines, for a pair of questions we calculate the values of the Jaccard coefficient with shingles size up to four, and then add these values as additional features used by the SVM classifier.

5.3 Word Embeddings

The word embeddings used in our experiments are initialized by means of unsupervised pre-training. We perform pre-training using the skip-gram NN architecture (Mikolov et al., 2013) available in the word2vec[13] tool. Two different corpora are used to train word embeddings for most of the experiments: the English Wikipedia and the Ask Ubuntu community data. The experiments presented in Section 6.4 also use word embeddings trained on the Meta Stack Exchange community data.

In the experiments with the English Wikipedia word embeddings, we use the embeddings previously produced by dos Santos & Gatti (2014). They have used the December 2013 snapshot of the English Wikipedia corpus to obtain word embeddings with word2vec.

In the experiments with Ask Ubuntu and Meta Stack Exchange word embeddings, we use the Stack Exchange data dump provided in May 2014 to train word2vec. Three main steps are used to process all questions and answers from these Stack Exchange dumps: (1) tokenization of the text using the NLTK tokenizer; (2) image removal, URL replacement and prefixing/removal of the code if necessary (see Section 6.1 for more information); (3) lowercasing of all tokens. The resulting corpora contains about 121 million and 19 million tokens for Ask Ubuntu and Meta Stack Exchange, respectively.

6 Experimental Results

6.1 Comparison with Baselines

Ask Ubuntu community gives users an opportunity to format parts of their posts as code by using *code* tags (an example is in italic in Table 1). It includes not only programming code, but commands, paths to directories, names of packages, error messages and links. Around 30% of all posts in the data dump contain *code* tags. Since the rules for code formatting are not well defined, it was not clear if a learning algorithm would benefit from including it or not. Therefore, for each algorithm we tested three different approaches to handling code: keeping it as text; removing it; and prefixing it with a special tag. The latter is done in order to distinguish between the same term used within text or within code or a command (e.g., a *for* as a preposition and a *for* in a for loop). When creating the word embeddings, the same approach to the code as for the training data was followed.

[13] http://code.google.com/p/word2vec/

System	Valid. Acc.	Test Acc.
SVM + shingles	85.5	82.4
CNN + Askubuntu	93.4	92.9

Table 3: CNN and SVM accuracy on the validation and the test set using the full training set.

The 1K example validation set is used to tune the hyper-parameters of the algorithms. In order to speed up computations, we perform our initial experiments using a 4K examples balanced subset of the training set. The best validation accuracies are reported in Table 2.

We test the shingling-based approach with different shingle sizes. As Table 2 indicates, the accuracy decreases with the increase of the shingle size. The fact that much better accuracy is achieved when comparing questions based on simple word overlap (shingle size 1), suggests that semantically equivalent questions are not duplicates but rather have topical similarity. The SVM baseline performs well only when combined with the shingling approach by using the values of the Jaccard coefficient for shingle size up to four as additional features. A possible reason for this is that n-gram representations do not capture enough information about semantic equivalence. The CNN with word embeddings outperforms the baselines by a significant margin.

The results presented in Table 2 indicate that the algorithms do not benefit from including the code. This is probably because the code tags are not always used appropriately and some code examples include long error messages, which make the user generated data even more noisy. Therefore, in the following experiments the code is removed.

The validation accuracy and the test accuracy using the full 24K training set is presented in Table 3. The SVM with four additional shingling features is found best among the baselines (see Table 2) and is used as a baseline in this experiment. Again, the CNN with word embeddings outperforms the best baseline by a significant margin.

Algorithm	Features	Code	Best validation acc.	Optimal hyper-parameters
SVM-RBF	binary + freq.	kept	66.2	C=8.0, γ ≈3.05e-05
SVM-RBF	binary + freq.	removed	66.53	C=2.0, γ ≈1.2e-04
SVM-RBF	binary + freq.	prefixed	66.53	C=8.0, γ ≈3.05e-05
Shingling (size 1)	-	kept	72.35	-
Shingling (size 1)	-	removed	72.65	-
Shingling (size 1)	-	prefixed	70.94	-
Shingling (size 2)	-	kept	69.24	-
Shingling (size 2)	-	removed	66.83	-
Shingling (size 2)	-	prefixed	67.74	-
Shingling (size 3)	-	kept	65.23	-
Shingling (size 3)	-	removed	62.93	-
Shingling (size 3)	-	prefixed	64.43	-
SVM-RBF	binary + freq. + shingles	kept	74.0	C=32.0, γ ≈3.05e-05
SVM-RBF	binary + freq. + shingles	removed	**77.4**	C=32.0, γ ≈3.05e-05
SVM-RBF	binary + freq. + shingles	prefixed	73.6	C=32.0, γ ≈3.05e-05
CNN	Askubuntu word vectors	kept	91.3	
CNN	Askubuntu word vectors	removed	**92.4**	d=200, k=3, cl_u=300, λ=0.005
CNN	Askubuntu word vectors	prefixed	91.4	

Table 2: Validation Accuracy and best parameters for the baselines and the Convolutional Neural Network.

6.2 Impact of Domain-Specific Word Embeddings

We perform two experiments to evaluate the impact of the word embeddings on the CNN accuracy. In the first experiment, we gradually increase the dimensionality of word embeddings from 50 to 400. The results are presented in Figure 2. The vertical axis corresponds to validation accuracy and the horizontal axis represents the training time in epochs. As has been shown in (Mikolov et al., 2013), word embeddings of higher dimensionality trained on a large enough data set capture semantic information better than those of smaller dimensionality. The experimental results presented in Figure 2 correspond to these findings: we can see improvements in the neural network performance when increasing the word embeddings dimensionality from 50 to 100 and from 100 to 200. However, the Ask Ubuntu data set containing approximately 121M tokens is not big enough for an improvement when increasing the dimensionality from 200 to 400.

In the second experiment, we evaluate the impact of in-domain word embeddings on the network's performance. We obtain word embeddings trained on two different corpora: Ask Ubuntu community data and English Wikipedia (see Section 5.3). Both word embeddings have 200 dimensions. The results presented in Table 4 show that training on in-domain data is more beneficial for the network, even though the corpus used to create word embeddings is much smaller.

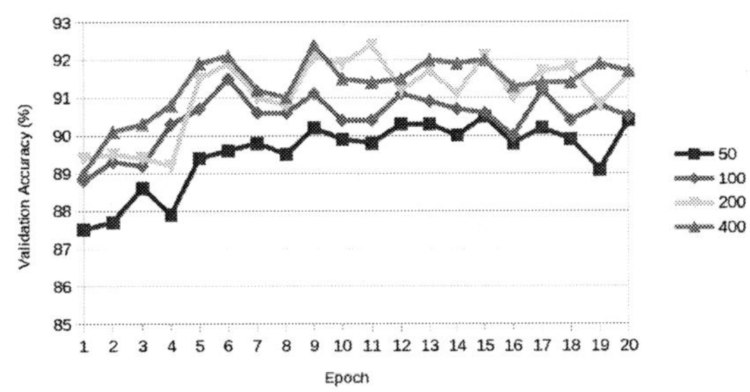

Figure 2: CNN accuracy depending on the size of word embeddings

Word Embeddings	Num.tokens	Valid.Acc.
Wikipedia	≈1.6B	85.5
AskUbuntu	≈121M	92.4

Table 4: Validation Accuracy of the CNN with word embeddings pre-trained on different corpora.

6.3 Impact of Training Set Size

In order to measure the impact of the training set size, we perform experiments using subsets of the training data, starting from 100 question pairs and gradually increasing the size to the full 24K training set.[14] Figure 3 compares the learning curves for the SVM baseline (with parameters and features described in Section 6.1) and for the CNN with word embeddings trained on Ask Ubuntu and English Wikipedia. The vertical axis corresponds to the validation accuracy, and the horizontal axis represents the training set size. As Figure 3 indicates, increasing the size of the training set pro-

[14] We use sets of 100, 1000, 4000, 12000 and 24000 question pairs.

vides improvements. Nonetheless, the difference in accuracy when training with the full 24K training set and 4K subset is about 9% for SVM and only about 1% for the CNN. This difference is small for both word embeddings pre-trained on Ask Ubuntu and Wikipedia but, the in-domain word embeddings provide better performance independently of the training set size.

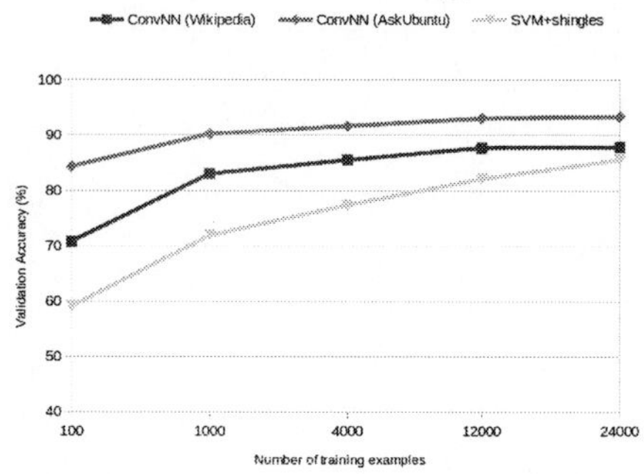

Figure 3: Validation accuracy for the baseline and the CNN depending on the size of training set.

6.4 Domain Adaptation

Muthmann and Petrova (2014) report that the Meta Stack Exchange Community[15] is one of the hardest for finding semantically equivalent questions.

We perform the same experiments described in previous sections using the Meta data set. In Table 5, we can see that the CNN accuracy on Meta test data (92.68%) is similar to the one for Ask Ubuntu community on test data (92.4%) (see Table 3).

Also, in Table 5, we show results of a domain adaptation experiment in which we do not use training data from the Meta forum. In this case, the CNN is trained using Ask Ubuntu data only. The numbers show that even in this case using in-domain word embeddings helps to achieve relatively high accuracy: 83.35% on the test set.

7 Error Analysis

As we have expected, the CNN with in-domain word vectors outperforms the vocabulary-based baselines in identifying semantically equivalent questions that are too different in terms of vocabulary. The CNN is also better at distinguishing questions with similar vocabulary but different meanings. For example, the question pair, (q_1) *How can I install Ubuntu without removing Windows?* and (q_2) *How do I upgrade from x86 to x64 without losing settings?*[16] is erroneously classified as a positive pair by the SVM, while the CNN classifies it correctly as a negative pair.

[15] http://meta.stackexchange.com/

Train.Data	Size	Word Vect.	Val.Acc.	Test.Acc.
META	4K	META	91.1	89.97
META	4K	Wikipedia	86.9	86.27
META	20K	META	**92.8**	**92.68**
META	20K	Wikipedia	90.6	90.52
AskUbuntu	24K	META	83.9	83.35
AskUbuntu	24K	AskUbuntu	76.8	80.0

Table 5: Convolutional Neural Network Accuracy tested on Meta Stack Exchange community data.

There are some cases where both CNN and SVM fail to identify semantic equivalence. Some of these cases include questions where essential information is presented as an image, e.g., a screenshot, which was removed during preprocessing.[17]

8 Conclusions and Future Work

In this paper, we propose a method for identifying semantically equivalent questions based on a convolutional neural network. We experimentally show that the proposed CNN achieves very high accuracy especially when the word embeddings are pre-trained on in-domain data. The performance of an SVM-based approach to this task was shown to depend highly on the size of the training data. In contrast, the CNN with in-domain word embeddings provides very high performance even with limited training data. Furthermore, experiments on a different domain have demonstrated that the neural network achieves high accuracy independently of the domain.

The next step in our research is building a system for retrieval of semantically equivalent questions. In particular, given a corpus and a question, the task is to find all questions that are semantically equivalent to the given one in the corpus. We believe that a CNN architecture similar to the one proposed in this paper might be a good fit to tackle this problem.

Acknowledgments

The work of Dasha Bogdanova is supported by Science Foundation Ireland through the CNGL

[16] Due to space constraints we only report the titles of the questions

[17] For instance, http://askubuntu.com/questions/450843

Programme (Grant 12/CE/I2267) in the ADAPT Centre (www.adaptcentre.ie) at Dublin City University. Her contributions were made during an internship at IBM Research.

References

Eneko Agirre, Daniel Cer, Mona Diab, Aitor Gonzalez-Agirre, and Weiwei Guo. 2013. *sem 2013 shared task: Semantic textual similarity. In *Second Joint Conference on Lexical and Computational Semantics (*SEM), Volume 1*, pages 32–43, Atlanta, Georgia, USA, June.

Omar Alonso, Dennis Fetterly, and Mark Manasse. 2013. Duplicate news story detection revisited. In Rafael E. Banchs, Fabrizio Silvestri, Tie-Yan Liu, Min Zhang, Sheng Gao, and Jun Lang, editors, *Information Retrieval Technology*, volume 8281 of *Lecture Notes in Computer Science*, pages 203–214. Springer Berlin Heidelberg.

James Bergstra, Olivier Breuleux, Frédéric Bastien, Pascal Lamblin, Razvan Pascanu, Guillaume Desjardins, Joseph Turian, David Warde-Farley, and Yoshua Bengio. 2010. Theano: a CPU and GPU math expression compiler. In *Proceedings of the Python for Scientific Computing Conference (SciPy)*.

Steven Bird, Ewan Klein, and Edward Loper. 2009. Natural Language Processing with Python: Analyzing Text with the Natural Language Toolkit.

A. Broder. 1997. On the resemblance and containment of documents. In *Proceedings of the Compression and Complexity of Sequences 1997*, SEQUENCES'97, Washington, DC, USA. IEEE Computer Society.

Chih-Chung Chang and Chih-Jen Lin. 2011. LIBSVM: A library for support vector machines. *ACM Transactions on Intelligent Systems and Technology*, 2:27:1–27:27. Software available at `http://www.csie.ntu.edu.tw/~cjlin/libsvm`.

Corinna Cortes and Vladimir Vapnik. 1995. Support-vector networks. *Machine Learning, Volume 20(3)*, pages 273–297.

Cícero Nogueira dos Santos and Maíra Gatti. 2014. Deep convolutional neural networks for sentiment analysis of short texts. In *Proceedings of the 25th International Conference on Computational Linguistics (COLING)*, Dublin, Ireland.

Cícero Nogueira dos Santos and Bianca Zadrozny. 2014. Learning character-level representations for part-of-speech tagging. In *Proceedings of the 31st International Conference on Machine Learning (ICML), JMLR: W&CP volume 32*, Beijing, China.

Baotian Hu, Zhengdong Lu, Hang Li, and Qingcai Chen. 2014. Convolutional neural network architectures for matching natural language sentences. In *Advances in Neural Information Processing Systems 27: Annual Conference on Neural Information Processing Systems 2014*, pages 2042–2050, Montreal, Quebec, Canada.

Yoon Kim. 2014. Convolutional neural networks for sentence classification. In *Proceedings of the 2014 Conference on Empirical Methods for Natural Language Processing*, pages 1746–1751, Doha, Qatar.

Nitin Madnani, Joel Tetreault, and Martin Chodorow. 2012. Re-examining machine translation metrics for paraphrase identification. In *Proceedings of the 2012 Conference of the North American Chapter of the Association for Computational Linguistics: Human Language Technologies*, pages 182–190, Montréal, Canada.

Gurmeet Singh Manku, Arvind Jain, and Anish Das Sarma. 2007. Detecting near-duplicates for web crawling. In *Proceedings of the 16th International Conference on World Wide Web*, WWW '07, pages 141–150, New York, NY, USA.

Tomas Mikolov, Kai Chen, Greg Corrado, and Jeffrey Dean. 2013. Efficient estimation of word representations in vector space. In *Proceedings of International Conference on Learning Representations*, ICLR 2013, Scottsdale, AZ, USA.

Klemens Muthmann and Alina Petrova. 2014. An Automatic Approach for Identifying Topical Near-Duplicate Relations between Questions from Social Media Q/A . In *Proceedings of Web-scale Classification: Classifying Big Data from the Web WSCBD 2014*.

Richard Socher, Eric H. Huang, Jeffrey Pennington, Andrew Y. Ng, and Christopher D. Manning. 2011. Dynamic pooling and unfolding recursive autoencoders for paraphrase detection. In John Shawe-Taylor, Richard S. Zemel, Peter L. Bartlett, Fernando C. N. Pereira, and Kilian Q. Weinberger, editors, *Advances in Neural Information Processing Systems 24*, pages 801–809.

Alexander Waibel, Toshiyuki Hanazawa, Geoffrey Hinton, Kiyohiro Shikano, and Kevin J. Lang. 1989. Phoneme recognition using time-delay neural networks. *IEEE Transactions on Acoustics, Speech and Signal Processing*, Volume 37(3), pages 328–339.

Yan Wu, Qi Zhang, and Xuanjing Huang. 2011. Efficient near-duplicate detection for q&a forum. In *Proceedings of 5th International Joint Conference on Natural Language Processing*, pages 1001–1009, Chiang Mai, Thailand.

Wen-tau Yih, Xiaodong He, and Christopher Meek. 2014. Semantic parsing for single-relation question answering. In *Proceedings of the 52nd Annual Meeting of the Association for Computational Linguistics (Volume 2: Short Papers)*, pages 643–648.

Entity Linking Korean Text: An Unsupervised Learning Approach using Semantic Relations

Youngsik Kim
KAIST / Korea, The Republic of
twilight@kaist.ac.kr

Key-Sun Choi
KAIST / Korea, The Republic of
kschoi@kaist.edu

Abstract

Although entity linking is a widely researched topic, the same cannot be said for entity linking geared for languages other than English. Several limitations including syntactic features and the relative lack of resources prevent typical approaches to entity linking to be used as effectively for other languages in general. We describe an entity linking system that leverage semantic relations between entities within an existing knowledge base to learn and perform entity linking using a minimal environment consisting of a part-of-speech tagger. We measure the performance of our system against Korean Wikipedia abstract snippets, using the Korean DBpedia knowledge base for training. Based on these results, we argue both the feasibility of our system and the possibility of extending to other domains and languages in general.

1 Introduction

A crucial step in creating the Web of Data is the process of extracting structured data, or RDF (Adida et al., 2012) from unstructured text. This step enables machines to read and understand unstructured Web pages that consist the majority of the Web. Three tasks play a part in extracting RDF from unstructured text: Named entity recognition(NER), where strings representing named entities are extracted from the given text; entity linking(EL), where each named entity recognized from NER is mapped to a appropriate resource from a knowledge base; and relation extraction(Usbeck et al., 2014). Although entity linking is an extensively researched field, most research done is aimed primarily for the English language. Research about entity linking for languages other than English have also been performed (Jakob et al., 2013), but most state-of-art entity linking systems are not fully language independent.

The reason for this is two-fold. Firstly, most entity linking systems depend on an existing system to perform named entity recognition beforehand. For instance, the system proposed by Usbeck (2014) uses FOX (Speck et al., 2014) to perform named entity recognition as the starting point. The problem with this approach is that an existing named entity recognition system is required, and thus the performance of entity linking is bound by the performance of the named entity recognition system. Named entity recognition systems for English achieve high performance even by utilizing a simple dictionary-based approach augmented by part-of-speech annotations, but this approach does not work in all languages in general. CJK[1] languages in particular are difficult to perform named entity recognition on because language traits such as capitalization and strict token separation by white-space do not exist. Other approaches to named entity recognition such as statistical models or projection models respectively require a large amount of annotated training data and an extensive parallel corpus to work, but the cost of creating these resources is also non-trivial. Some approaches to entity linking utilizing supervised and semi-supervised learning also suffer from the lack of manually annotated training data for some languages. Currently, there is no proper golden standard dataset for entity linking for the Korean language.

In this paper, we present an entity linking system for Korean that overcomes these obstacles with an unsupervised learning approach utilizing semantic relations between entities obtained from a given knowledge base. Our system uses these semantic relations as hints to learn feature values

[1] Chinese, Japanese, Korean

Proceedings of the 19th Conference on Computational Language Learning, pages 132–141,
Beijing, China, July 30-31, 2015.

for both named entity recognition and entity linking. In Section 3, we describe the requirements of our system, and present the architecture of both the training and actual entity linking processes. In Section 4, we compare the performance of our system against both a rule-based baseline and the current state-of-art system based on Kim's (2014) research.

2 Related Work

The current state-of-art entity linking system for Korean handles both named entity recognition and entity linking as two separate steps (Kim et al., 2014). This system uses hyperlinks within the Korean Wikipedia and a small amount of text manually annotated with entity information as training data. It employs a SVM model trained with character-based features to perform named entity recognition, and uses the TF*ICF (Mendes et al., 2011) and LDA metrics to disambiguate between entity resources during entity linking. Kim (2014) reports an F1-score of 75.66% for a simplified task in which only surface forms and entities which appear as at least one hyperlink within the Korean Wikipedia are recognized as potential entity candidates.

Our system utilizes relations between entities, which can be said to be a graph-based approach to entity linking. There have been recent research about entity linking that exploit the graph structure of both the named entities within text and RDF knowledge bases. Han (2011) uses a graph-based collective method which can model and exploit the global interdependence between different entity linking decisions. Alhelbawy (2014) uses graph ranking combined with clique partitioning. Moro (2014) introduces Babelfy, a unified graph-based approach to entity linking and word sense disambiguation based on a loose identification of candidate meanings coupled with a densest subgraph heuristic which selects high-coherence semantic interpretations. Usbeck (2014) combines the Hypertext-Induced Topic Search (HITS) algorithm with label expansion strategies and string similarity measures.

There also has been research about named entity recognition for Korean. Kim (2012) proposes a method to automatically label multilingual data with named entity tags, combining Wikipedia meta-data with information obtained through English-foreign language parallel Wikipedia sentences. We do not use this approach in our system because our scope of entities is wider than the named entity scope defined in the MUC-7 annotation guidelines, which is the scope of Kim's research.

3 The System

Due to the limitations of performing entity linking for the Korean language described in Section 1, our system is designed with some requirements in mind. The requirements are:

- The system should be able to be trained and ran within a minimal environment, which we define as an existing RDF knowledge base containing semantic relations between entities, and a part-of-speech tagger. In this paper, we use the 2014 Korean DBpedia RDF knowledge base and the ETRI Korean part-of-speech tagger.
- The system should be able to perform entity linking without using external information not derived from the knowledge base.

We define the task of our system as follows: Given a list of entity uniform resource identifiers(URI) derived from the knowledge base, annotate any given text with the appropriate entity URIs and their positions within the text.

3.1 Preprocessing

The preprocessing step of our system consists of querying the knowledge base to build a dictionary of entity URIs and their respective surface forms. As we are using the Korean DBpedia as our knowledge base, we define all resources with a URI starting with the namespace 'http://ko.dbpedia.org/resource/' and which are not mapped to disambiguation nor redirection Wikipedia pages as valid entities. For each entity, we define all literal strings connected via the property 'rdfs:label' to the entity and all entities that disambiguate or redirect to the entity as possible surface forms.

The dictionary that results from preprocessing contains 303,779 distinct entity URIs and 569,908 entity URI-surface form pairs.

3.2 Training

After the preprocessing step, our system performs training by adjusting feature values based on data from a large amount of unannotated text documents. As the given text is not annotated with entity data, we use the following assumption to help distinguish potential entities within the text:

Assumption. Entity candidates which have a high degree of semantic relations with nearby entity candidates are likely actual entities. We define an 'entity candidate' of a document as a substring-entity URI pair in which the substring appears at a specific position within the document and the pair exists in the dictionary created during preprocessing, and a 'semantic relation' between two entity candidates c_1, c_2 ($RelPred(c_1, c_2)$) as an undirected relation consisting of all predicates in the knowledge base that connect the entity URIs of the entity candidates.

The basis for this assumption is that some mentions of 'popular'(having a high degree within the knowledge base RDF graph) entity URIs will be accompanied with related terms, and that the knowledge base will have RDF triples connecting the entity to the other entity URIs representing the related terms. Thus we assume that by selecting all entity candidates with a high degree of semantic relations, these candidates display features more representative of actual entities than the remaining entity candidates do.

For each document in the training set, we first perform part-of-speech tagging to split the text into individual morphemes. Because the concatenation of the morphemes of a Korean word is not always identical to the word itself, we transform the morphemes into 'atomic' sub-strings which represent minimal building blocks for entity candidates and can have multiple POS tags.

After part-of-speech tagging is complete, we then gather a set of entity candidates from the document. We first find all non-overlapping substrings within the document that correspond to entity surface forms. It is possible for these sub-strings to overlap with each other([[Chicago] Bulls]); and because the average length of entity surface forms in Korean is very short(between 2 to 3 characters), we opt to reduce the problem size of the training process by choosing only the substring with the longest length when multiple substrings overlap with each other.

As to further reduce the number of entity candidates we consider for training, we only use the entity candidate with the most 'popular' entity URI

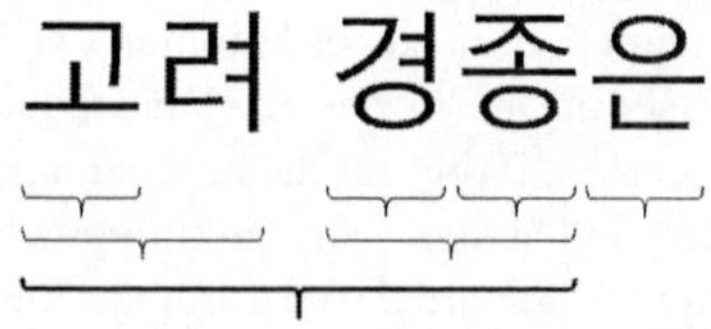

Figure 1: All possible entity candidates within the text fragment 'Gyeongjong of Goryeo is' (Kim et al., 2014)

per group of candidates that share the same substring within the document. We define the 'popularity' of an entity URI in terms of the RDF triples in the knowledge base that has the URI as the *object*. More formally, we define $UriPop(c)$ for an entity candidate c with the entity URI c_u with the equations below. A larger $UriPop$ value means a more 'popular' entity URI, and $Pred$ is meant to prevent overly frequent predicates in the knowledge base from dominating $UriPop$.

$$UriPop(c) = log(\sum_{p \in KBpredicates} Pred(p) \times |\{s | (s, p, c_u) \in KB\}|) \quad (1)$$

$$Pred(p) = 1 - \frac{|\{(s, o) | (s, p, o) \in KB\}|}{|\{(s, p, o) \in KB\}|} \quad (2)$$

At this stage of the training process, we have a set of non-overlapping entity candidates. We now classify these candidates into two classes: e_T(entity) and e_F(non-entity) according to our previous assumption. We measure the degree of semantic relations of an entity candidate c, $SemRel(c)$, with the following equation where N_c is the set of entity candidates which are within 20 words from the target candidate in the document:

$$SemRel(c) = \frac{\sum_{c' \in N_c} \sum_{p \in RelPred(c,c')} Pred(p)}{|N_c|} \quad (3)$$

Since we do not have enough evidence at this point to distinguish entities from non-entities, we use semantic relations from all nearby entity candidates to calculate $SemRel$. We order the entity candidates into a list in decreasing order of $SemRel$, and classify entity candidates from the start of the list into e_T until either 1) $\frac{e_T}{\text{document word \#}} > l_w$ or 2) $SemRel(c) < l_s$ are satisfied, where both l_w and l_s are constants that continuously get adjusted during the training process. The remaining entity candidates all get classified into e_F.

We now update the current feature values based on the entity candidates in e_T and e_F. For each feature f, we first define two sub-classes $e_{fT} = \{e|e \text{ has } f \wedge e \in e_T\}$ and $e_{fF} = \{e|e \text{ has } f \wedge e \in e_F\}$. We then update the feature value of f from $\frac{\alpha}{\beta}$ to $\frac{\alpha+|e_{fT}|}{\beta+|e_{fT}|+|e_{fF}|}$, which represents the probability of an entity candidate having feature f to be classified into e_T(is an entity). The full list of features we used is shown below:

f_1: **String length** The length (in characters) of the sub-string of the candidate.

f_2: **POS tag** The POS tag(s) of the sub-string of the candidate. If multiple POS tags exist, we take the average of the f_2 values for each tag as the representive f_2 value.

f_3: **Head POS tag** The first POS tag of the sub-string of the candidate.

f_4: **Tail POS tag** The last POS tag of the sub-string of the candidate.

f_5: **Previous POS tag** The POS tag of the sub-string right before the candidate. If the candidate is preceded by white-space, we use the special tag 'BLANK'.

f_6: **Next POS tag** The POS tag of the sub-string right after the candidate. If the candidate is followed by white-space, we use the special tag 'BLANK'.

f_7: **UriPop** The *UriPop* score of the entity URI of the candidate. Since *UriPop* has a continuous range, we keep separate features for *UriPop* score intervals of 0.2.

Given these features, we define $IndScore(c)$ of an entity candidate c, which represents the overall probability c would be classified in e_T independently of its surrounding context, as the average of the feature values for c.

We also define $WeightedSemRel(c)$ as the amount of evidence via semantic relations c has of being classified in e_T. We define this score in terms of semantic relations relative to the *UriPop* score of c in order to positively consider entity candidates which have more semantic relations than their entity URIs would normally have.

Finally, we define $EntityScore(c)$ representing the overall evidence for c to be in e_T. The respective equations for these scores are shown below.

$$WeightedSemRel(c) = \frac{\sum_{c' \in N_c} \sum_{p \in RelPred(c,c')} Pred(p) \times UriPop(c')}{UriPop(c)} \quad (4)$$

$$EntityScore(c) = IndScore(c) + WeightedSemRel(c) \quad (5)$$

As we want to assign stronger evidence for semantic relations with entity candidates that are likely actual entities (as opposed to relations with non-entities), we define *WeightedSemRel* to be have a recursive relation with *EntityScore*.

We end the training process for a single document by computing the *EntityScore* for each entity candidate in e_T and e_F, and adding these scores respectively into the lists of scores $dist_T$ and $dist_F$. As the *EntityScore* for the same entity candidate will change as training proceeds, we only maintain the 10,000 most recent scores for both lists.

3.3 Entity Linking

Since the actual entity linking process is also about selecting entity candidates from the given document, the process itself is similar to the training process. We list the differences of the entity linking process compared to training below.

When we choose the initial entity candidates, we do not remove candidates with overlapping sub-strings. Although we do limit the number of candidates that map to the same sub-string, we choose the top 3 candidates based on *UriPop* instead of just 1.

We compute the *EntityScore* for each entity candidate without performing candidate classification nor feature value updates. Although the value of $EntityScore(c)$ is intended to be proportional to the possibility the candidate c is actually an entity, we need a way to define a threshold constant to determine which candidates to actually classify as entities. Thus, we then normalize any given $EntityScore(c)$ score of an entity candidate c into a confidence score $Conf(c)$, which represents the relative probability of c being a member of e_T against being a member of e_F. This is computed by comparing the score against the lists $dist_T$ and $dist_F$, as shown in the following equations:

$$ConfT(c) = \frac{|\{x|x \in dist_T \wedge x < EntityScore(c)\}|}{|dist_T|} \quad (6)$$

$$ConfF(c) = \frac{|\{x|x \in dist_F \wedge x > EntityScore(c)\}|}{|dist_F|} \quad (7)$$

$$Conf(c) = \frac{ConfT(c)}{ConfT(c) + ConfF(c)} \quad (8)$$

$Conf$ is a normalized score which satisfies $0 \leq Conf(c) \leq 1$ for any entity candidate c. This gives us the flexibility to define a threshold $0 \leq \gamma \leq 1$ so that only entity candidates satisfying $Conf(c) \geq \gamma$ are classified as entities.

Algorithm 1 The entity selection algorithm

```
E ← []
for all c ∈ C do
  if Conf(c) ≥ γ then
    unsetE ← []
    valid = true
    for all e ∈ E do
      if sub-string of c contains e then
        unsetE ← unsetE + e
      else if sub-string of c overlaps with e
      then
        valid = false
      end if
    end for
    if valid is true then
      E ← E + c
      for all e ∈ unsetE do
        E ← E − e
      end for
    end if
  end if
end for
return E
```

Algorithm 1 shows the entity selection process, where C is initialized as a list of all entity candidates ordered by decreasing score of $Conf$. We only select entity candidates which have a confidence score of at least γ. When the sub-strings of multiple entity candidates overlap with each other, we prioritize the candidate with the highest confidence with the exception of candidates that contain(one is completely covered by the other, without the two being identical) other candidates in which we choose the candidate that contains the other candidates.

4 Experiments

4.1 Entity Linking for Korean

4.1.1 The Dataset

Although the dataset used by Kim (2014) exists, we do not use this dataset because it is for a simplified version of the entity linking problem as discussed in Section 2. We instead have created a new dataset intended to serve as answer data for the entity linking for Korean task, based on guidelines that were derived from the TAC KBP 2014[2] guidelines. The guidelines used to annotate text for our dataset are shown below:

- All entities must be tagged with an entity URI that exists in the 2014 Korean DBpedia knowledge base.
- All entities must be tagged with an entity URI which is correct to appear within the context of the entity.
- All entity URIs must identify a single thing, not a group of things.
- Verbs and adjectives that have an equivalent noun that is identified by an entity URI should not be tagged as entities.
- Only words that directly identify the entity should be tagged.
- If several possible entities are contained within each other, the entity that contains all other entities should be tagged.
- If several consecutive words each can be represented by the same entity URI, these words must be tagged as a single entity, as opposed to tagging each separate word.
- Indirect mentions of entity URIs (ex: pronouns) should not be tagged even if coresolution can be performed in order to identify the entity URI the mention stands for.

Our dataset consists of 60 Korean Wikipedia abstract documents annotated by 3 different annotators.

[2] http://nlp.cs.rpi.edu/kbp/2014/elquery.pdf

4.1.2 Evaluation

We evaluate our system against the work of Kim (2014) in terms of precision, recall, and F1-score metrics. As Kim's (2014) system(which we will refer to as KEL2014) was originally trained with the Korean Wikipedia, it required only slight adjustments to properly operate for our dataset.

We first train our system using 4,000 documents randomly gathered from the Korean Wikipedia. We then evaluate our system with our dataset, while adjusting the confidence threshold γ from 0.01 to 0.99 in increments of 0.01. We compare our results with those of the best-performing settings of KEL2014.

4.1.3 Results

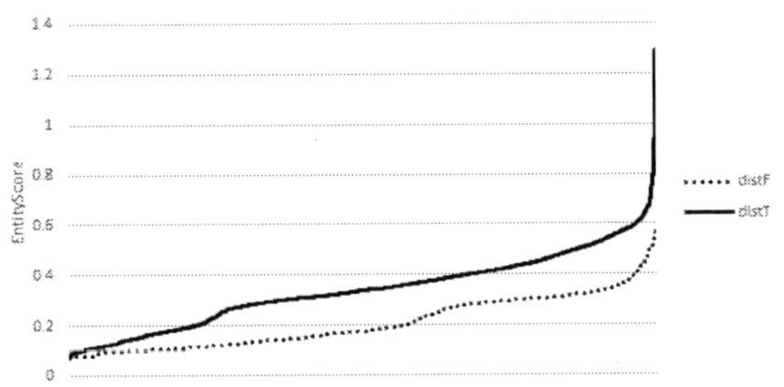

Figure 2: The distribution of $dist_T$ and $dist_F$ after training with 4,000 documents

The results of the training process is shown in Figure 2. We can see that the *EntityScore* values of entity candidates classified in e_T are generally higher than those in e_F. This can be seen as evidence to our claim that the features of entities with a high degree of semantic relations can be used to distinguish entities from non-entities in general.

We show additional evidence to this claim with Table 1, which lists the feature values for the feature f_1(sub-string length) after the training process is complete. We observe that this feature gives relatively little weight to entity candidates with a substring of length 1, which is consistent with our initial observation that most of these candidates are not entities.

Figure 3 shows the performance of our system compared to the performance of KEL2014 against our dataset. As we increase the confidence threshold, the recall decreases and the precision increases. The maximum F1-score of our system using our dataset, 0.630, was obtained with the confidence threshold $\gamma = 0.79$. This is an improvement over KEL2014 which scored an F1-score of 0.598. Although the performance difference itself is small, this shows that our system trained with unannotated text documents performs better than KEL2014, which is trained with both partially annotated documents (Wikipedia articles) and a small number of documents completely annotated with entity data. This also shows that KEL2014 does not perform as well outside the scope of the simplified version of entity linking it was designed for.

Length	e_T	$e_T + e_F$	Value
1	37629	312543	0.120
2	41355	168672	0.245
3	20164	41098	0.490
4	12542	19619	0.637
5	13953	19722	0.704
6	5299	7503	0.698
7	3223	4187	0.753
8	2686	4282	0.616
9	2346	3034	0.751
10	922	1099	0.774
11	917	1011	0.830
12	477	546	0.750
13	249	276	0.687
14	218	274	0.615
15	155	170	0.618
16	109	116	0.567
17	99	118	0.523
18	48	52	0.434
19	49	55	0.433
20	34	40	0.384

Table 1: Feature values of the feature f_1 after training with 4,000 documents

Our system currently is implemented as a simple RESTful service where both training and actual entity linking are initiated via POST requests. Our system can be deployed to a server at its initial state or at a pre-trained state.

4.2 Alternative Methods and Deviations

4.2.1 Using Feature Subsets

In order to test the effectiveness of each feature we use in training, we compare the results obtained in Section 4.1.3 against the performance of our system trained with smaller subsets of the features shown in Section 3.2. Using the same training data as in Section 4.1.2, we evaluate the performance of our system using two different subsets of features as shown below:

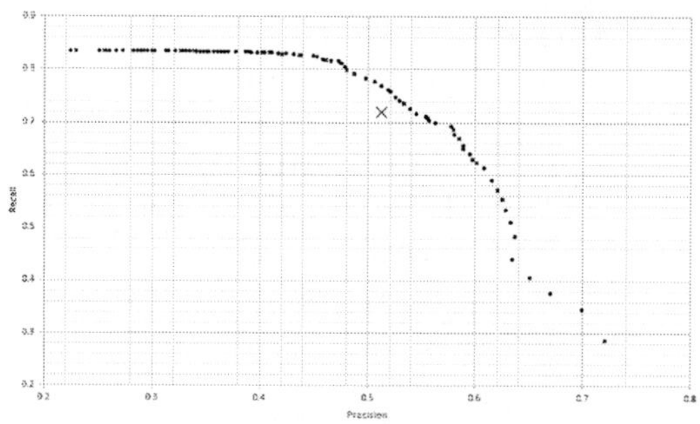

Figure 3: The performance of our system against KEL2014. The dots represent the results of our system, and the cross represents the results of KEL2014.

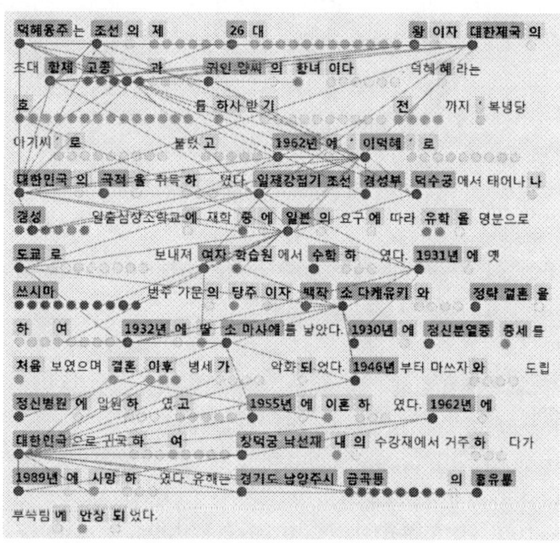

Figure 4: A temporary web interface for our system showing entity linking results for a sample text snippet

Dev1 All features except POS-related ones: f_1, f_7.

Dev2 All POS-related features only: f_2, f_3, f_4, f_5, f_6.

Figures 5 and 6 shows the performance of our system using the feature subsets Dev1 and Dev2. For the feature subset Dev1, our system displays a maximum F1-score of 0.433 with $\gamma = 0.99$; for the features subset Dev2, our system performs best with $\gamma = 0.98$ for an F1-score of 0.568.

As expected, both deviations perform worse than our system trained with the full set of features. We observe that the performance of Dev1 is significantly worse than that of Dev2. This suggests that POS-based features are more important

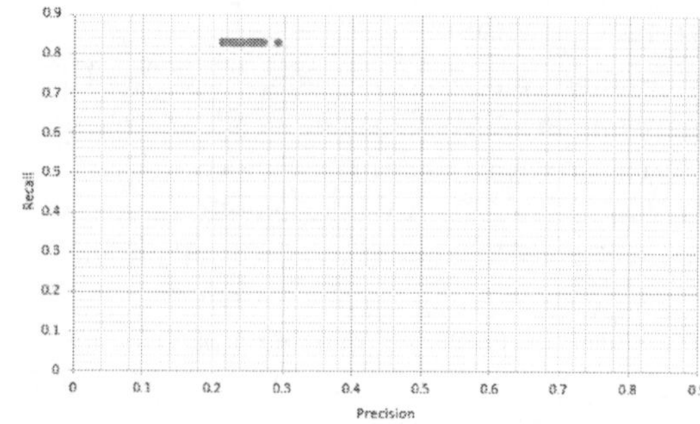

Figure 5: The performance of our system using the feature subset Dev1.

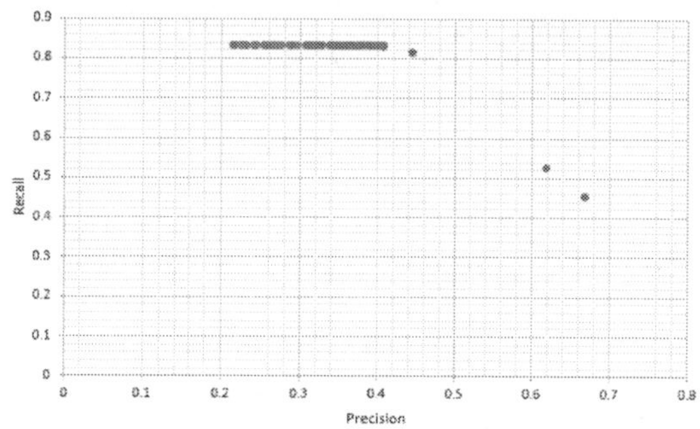

Figure 6: The performance of our system using the feature subset Dev2.

in distinguishing entities from non-entities than the other features.

4.2.2 Using SVM Models

Kim (2014) effectively utilized trained SVM models to detect entities within text. Based on Kim's experiments, we investigate whether SVM can be also used to raise performance of our system.

Although we now need to base entity predictions with a trained SVM model instead of the confidence metric $Conf$, the training process described in Section 3.2 is mostly unaltered because it the classification of entity candidate into e_T and e_F results in the training data required to train a SVM binary classification model. The differences in the training process are shown below:

- After we process each document, a list of features is produced for each entity candidate classified as e_T or e_F. Instead of appending the $EntityScore$ values of these entity candidates to $dist_T$ and $dist_F$, we append the feature lists of each entity candidate themselves into two lists of lists, $list_T$ and $list_F$. These lists still contain only the data of the newest

10,000 entity candidates.

- After the entire training set is processed, we use the list of feature lists in $list_T$ and $list_F$ to train the SVM model. As the original features are not all numbers, we transform each list of features into 7-dimensional vectors by replacing each feature key into the feature value of the respective feature.

We use the same training data as in Section 4.1.2, and train a SVM model with a 3-degree polynomial kernel. We choose this kernel according to Kim's (2014) work, where Kim compares the performance of SVM for the task of entity linking for Korean using multiple kernels.

Our system, using a trained SVM model results in a F1-score of 0.569, which is about 0.07 lower than the best performance of our system using the confidence model. One possible reason our system performed worse using SVM classification is that the training data that we feed to the classifier is not correctly classified, but rather based on the semantic relations assumption in Section 3.2. As this assumption does not cover any characteristics of non-entities, the effectiveness of SVM decreases as many entity candidates which are actual entities get classified as e_F due to them not having enough semantic relations.

4.3 Application on Other Languages

As our system does not explicitly exploit any characteristics of the Korean language, it theoretically is a language-independent entity linking system. We investigate this point using Japanese as a sample language, and MeCab[3] as the part-of-speech tagger.

As no proper dataset for the entity linking for Korean task exists, we have created a new dataset in order to measure the performance of our system. As we believe many other languages will also lack a proper dataset, we must devise an alternative method to measure the performance of our system for other languages in general.

We use Wikipedia documents and the links annotated within them as the dataset to use for measuring performance of our system for languages other than Korean. Although the manually annotated links within Wikipedia documents do represent actual entities and their surface forms, we cannot completely rely on these links as answer data because of the following reasons:

- The majority of entities within a Wikipedia document are not actually tagged as links. This includes self-references (entities that appear within the document describing that entity), frequently appearing entities that were tagged as links for their first few occurrences but were not tagged afterwards, and entities that were not considered important enough to tag as links by the annotators. Due to the existence of so many untagged entities, we effectively cannot use precision as a performance measure.

- Some links represent entities that are outside the scope of our research. This includes links that point to non-existent Wikipedia pages ('red links'), and links that require co-resolution to resolve.

Due to these problems, we only use the recall metric to measure the approximate performance of our system when using Wikipedia documents as answer data. We compare the performance of our system for Korean and Japanese by first training our system with 3,000 Wikipedia docuem-nts, and measuring the recall of our system for 100 Wikipedia documents for both respective languages while adjusting the confidence threshold γ from 0.01 to 0.99 in increments of 0.01.

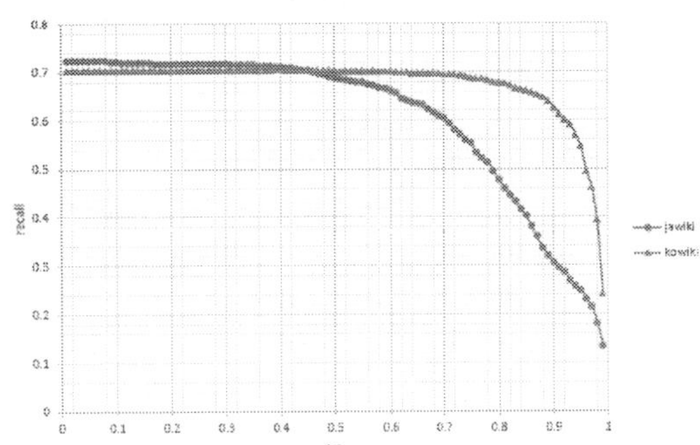

Figure 7: The recall of our system against Korean and Japanese Wikipedia documents

Figure 7 shows the recall of our system against Korean and Japanese Wikipedia documents. For the confidence threshold optimized via the experiments performed in Section 4.1 (γ = 0.79), our system shows a large difference of recall between

[3]http://taku910.github.io/mecab/

Korean and Japanese. Although this does not accurately represent the actual performance of our system, we leave the task of improving our system to display consistent performance across multiple languages as future work.

5 Future Work

As our system currently only uses labels of entity URIs to determine surface forms of entities, it can not detect entities with irregular surface forms. For instance, the entity 'Steve Jobs' has the labels 'Steve Jobs' and 'Jobs' within the Korean DBpedia knowledge base, but does not have the label 'Steve'. This results in the inability of our system to detect certain entities within our dataset, regardless of training. We plan to improve our system to handle derivative surface forms such as 'Steve' for 'Steve Jobs', without relying on external dictionaries if possible.

Kim (2014) shows that a SVM classifier using character-based features trained with Wikipedia articles achieves better named entity recognition performance than a rule-based classifier using part-of-speech tags. Although our system uses trained features based on part-of-speech tags rather than a rule-based method, we may be able to remove even the part-of-speech tagger from the requirements of our system by substituting these features with the character-based features suggested in Kim's (2014) work.

Finally, future work must be performed about replacing the part-of-speech tagger currently used in our system with a chunking algorithm that does not utilize supervised training. Our system currently utilizes the list of morphemes and their respective POS tags that are produced from the part-of-speech tagger. Since our system does not require this information to be completely accurate, a dictionary-based approach to chunking might be applicable as well.

6 Conclusion

In this paper, we present an entity linking system for Korean that utilizes several features trained with plain text documents. By taking an unsupervised learning approach, our system is able to perform entity linking with a minimal environment consisting of an RDF knowledge base and a part-of-speech tagger. We compare the performance of our system against the state-of-art system KEL2014, and show that our system outperforms KEL2014 in terms of F1-score. We also briefly describe variations to our system training process, such as using feature subsets and utilizing SVM models instead of our confidence metric.

Many languages including Korean are not as rich in resources as the English language, and the lack of resources might prohibit the state-of-art systems for entity linking for English from performing as well in other languages. By utilizing a minimal amount of resources, our system may provide a firm starting point for research about entity linking for these languages.

7 Acknowledgements

This work was supported by Institute for Information & communications Technology Promotion(IITP) grant funded by the Korea government(MSIP) (No. R0101-15-0054, WiseKB: Big data based self-evolving knowledge base and reasoning platform)

References

B. Adida, I. Herman, M. Sporny, and M. Birbeck. RDFa 1.1 Primer. Technical report, World Wide Web Consortium, http://www.w3.org/TR/2012/NOTE-rdfa-primer- 20120607/, June 2012.

Usbeck, R., Ngomo, A. C. N., Rder, M., Gerber, D., Coelho, S. A., Auer, S., and Both, A. (2014). AGDISTIS-graph-based disambiguation of named entities using linked data. In The Semantic WebISWC 2014 (pp. 457-471). Springer International Publishing.

Daiber, J., Jakob, M., Hokamp, C., and Mendes, P. N. (2013, September). Improving efficiency and accuracy in multilingual entity extraction. In Proceedings of the 9th International Conference on Semantic Systems (pp. 121-124). ACM.

Speck, R., and Ngomo, A. C. N. (2014). Ensemble learning for named entity recognition. In The Semantic WebISWC 2014 (pp. 519-534). Springer International Publishing.

Y. Kim, Y. Hamn, J. Kim, D. Hwang, and K.-S. Choi, A Non-morphological Approach for DBpedia URI Spotting within Korean Text, Proc. of HCLT 2014, Chuncheon, 2014.

P. N. Mendes, M. Jakob, A. Garca-Silve, and C. Bizer, "DBpedia spotlight: shedding light on the web of documents," Proc. of i-SEMANTICS 2011 (7th Int. Conf. on Semantic Systems, 2011.

Han, X., Sun, L., and Zhao, J. (2011, July). Collective entity linking in web text: a graph-based method. In Proceedings of the 34th international ACM SIGIR conference on Research and development in Information Retrieval (pp. 765-774). ACM.

Alhelbawy, Ayman, and Robert Gaizauskas. "Collective Named Entity Disambiguation using Graph Ranking and Clique Partitioning Approaches."

Moro, Andrea, Alessandro Raganato, and Roberto Navigli. "Entity linking meets word sense disambiguation: a unified approach." Transactions of the Association for Computational Linguistics 2 (2014): 231-244.

Kim, S., Toutanova, K., and Yu, H. (2012, July). Multilingual named entity recognition using parallel data and metadata from wikipedia. In Proceedings of the 50th Annual Meeting of the Association for Computational Linguistics: Long Papers-Volume 1 (pp. 694-702). Association for Computational Linguistics.

Incremental Recurrent Neural Network Dependency Parser with Search-based Discriminative Training

Majid Yazdani
Computer Science Department
University of Geneva
majid.yazdani@unige.ch

James Henderson
Xerox Research Center Europe
james.henderson@xrce.xerox.com

Abstract

We propose a discriminatively trained recurrent neural network (RNN) that predicts the actions for a fast and accurate shift-reduce dependency parser. The RNN uses its output-dependent model structure to compute hidden vectors that encode the preceding partial parse, and uses them to estimate probabilities of parser actions. Unlike a similar previous generative model (Henderson and Titov, 2010), the RNN is trained discriminatively to optimize a fast beam search. This beam search prunes after each shift action, so we add a *correctness probability* to each shift action and train this score to discriminate between correct and incorrect sequences of parser actions. We also speed up parsing time by caching computations for frequent feature combinations, including during training, giving us both faster training and a form of backoff smoothing. The resulting parser is over 35 times faster than its generative counterpart with nearly the same accuracy, producing state-of-art dependency parsing results while requiring minimal feature engineering.

1 Introduction and Motivation

There has been significant interest recently in machine learning and natural language processing community in models that learn hidden multi-layer representations to solve various tasks. Neural networks have been popular in this area as a powerful and yet efficient models. For example, feed forward neural networks were used in language modeling (Bengio et al., 2003; Collobert and Weston, 2008), and recurrent neural networks (RNNs) have yielded state-of-art results in language modeling (Mikolov et al., 2010), language generation (Sutskever et al., 2011) and language understanding (Yao et al., 2013).

1.1 Neural Network Parsing

Neural networks have also been popular in parsing. These models can be divided into those whose design are motivated mostly by inducing useful vector representations (e.g. (Socher et al., 2011; Socher et al., 2013; Collobert, 2011)), and those whose design are motivated mostly by efficient inference and decoding (e.g. (Henderson, 2003; Henderson and Titov, 2010; Henderson et al., 2013; Chen and Manning, 2014)).

The first group of neural network parsers are all deep models, such as RNNs, which gives them the power to induce vector representations for complex linguistic structures without extensive feature engineering. However, decoding in these models can only be done accurately if they are used to re rank the best parse trees of another parser (Socher et al., 2013).

The second group of parsers use a shift-reduce parsing architecture so that they can use search based decoding algorithms with effective pruning strategies. The more accurate parsers also use a RNN architecture (see Section 6), and use generative models to allow beam search. These models are accurate but are relatively slow, and accuracy degrades when you choose decoding settings to optimize speed. Because they are generative, they need to predict the words as the parse proceeds through the sentence, which requires normalization over all the vocabulary of words. Also, the beam search must maintain many candidates in the beam in order to check how well each one predicts future words. Recently (Chen and Manning, 2014) propose a discriminative neural network shift-reduce parser, which is very fast but less accurate (see Section 6). However, this parser uses a feed-forward neural network with a large set of hand-coded features, making it of limited inter-

Proceedings of the 19th Conference on Computational Language Learning, pages 142–152,
Beijing, China, July 30-31, 2015.

est for inducing vector representations of complex linguistic structures.

1.2 Incremental Recurrent Neural Network Architecture

In both approaches to neural network parsing, RNN models have the advantage that they need minimal feature engineering and therefore they can be used with little effort for a variety of languages and applications. As with other deep neural network architectures, RNNs induce complex features automatically by passing induced (hidden) features as input to other induced features in a recursive structure. This is a particular advantage for domain adaptation, multi-task learning, transfer learning, and semi-supervised learning, where hand-crafted feature engineering is often particularly difficult. The information that is transferred from one task to another is embedded in the induced feature vectors in a shared latent space, which is input to another hidden layer for the target model (Henderson et al., 2013; Raina et al., 2007; Collobert et al., 2011; Glorot et al., 2011). This transferred information has proven to be particularly useful when it comes from very large datasets, such as web-scale text corpora, but learning and inference on such datasets is only practical with efficient algorithms.

In this work, we propose a fast discriminative RNN model of shift-reduce dependency parsing. We choose a left-to-right shift-reduce dependency parsing architecture to benefit from efficient decoding. It also easily supports incremental interpretation in dialogue systems, or incremental language modeling for speech recognition. We choose a RNN architecture to benefit from the automatic induction of informative vector representations of complex linguistic structures and the resulting reduction in the required feature engineering. This hidden vector representation is trained to encode the partial parse tree that has been built by the preceding parse, and is used to predict the next parser action conditioned on this history.

As our RNN architecture, we use the neural network approximation of ISBNs (Henderson and Titov, 2010), which we refer to as an Incremental Neural Network (INN). INNs are a kind of RNN where the model structure is built incrementally as a function of the values of previous output variables. In our case, the hidden vector used to make the current parser decision is connected to the hidden vector from previous decisions based on the partial parse structure that has been built by the previous decisions. So any information about the unbounded parse history can potentially be passed to the current decision through a chain of hidden vectors that reflects locality in the parse tree, and not just locality in the derivation sequence (Henderson, 2003; Titov and Henderson, 2007b). As in all deep neural network architectures, this chaining of nonlinear vector computations gives the model a very powerful mechanism to induce complex features from combinations of features in the history, which is difficult to replicate with hand-coded features.

1.3 Search-based Discriminative Training

We propose a discriminative model because it allows us to use lookahead instead of word prediction. As mentioned above, generative word prediction is costly, both to compute and because it requires larger beams to be effective. With lookahead, it is possible to condition on words that are farther ahead in the string, and thereby avoid hypothesizing parses that are incompatible with those future words. This allows the parser to prune much more aggressively without losing accuracy. Discriminative learning further improves this aggressive pruning, because it can optimize for the discrete choice of whether to prune or not (Huang et al., 2012; Zhang and Clark, 2011).

Our proposed model primarily differs from previous discriminative models of shift-reduce dependency parsing in the nature of the discriminative choices that are made and the way these decisions are modeled and learned. Rather than learning to make pruning decisions at each parse action, we learn to choose between sequences of actions that occur in between two shift actions. This way of grouping action sequences into chunks associated with each word has been used previously for efficient pruning strategies in generative parsing (Henderson, 2003), and for synchronizing syntactic parsing and semantic role labeling in a joint model (Henderson et al., 2013). We show empirically that making discriminative parsing decisions at the scale of these chunks also provides a good balance between grouping decisions so that more context can be used to make accurate parsing decisions and dividing decisions so that the space of alternatives for each decision can be considered quickly (see Figure 4 below).

In line with this pruning strategy, we define a score called the *correctness probability* for every shift action. This score is trained discriminatively to indicate whether the entire parse prefix is correct or not. This gives us a score function that is trained to optimize the pruning decisions during search (c.f. (Daumé III and Marcu, 2005)). By combining the scores for all the shift actions in each candidate parse, we can also discriminate between multiple parses in a beam of parses, thereby giving us the option of using beam search to improve accuracy in cases where bounded lookahead does not provide enough information to make a deterministic decision. The *correctness probability* is estimated by only looking at the hidden vector at its shift action, which encourages the hidden units to encode any information about the parse history that is relevant to deciding whether this is a good or bad parse, including long distance features.

1.4 Feature Decomposition and Caching

Another popular method of previous neural network models that we use and extend in this paper is the decomposition of input feature parameters using vector-matrix multiplication (Bengio et al., 2003; Collobert et al., 2011; Collobert and Weston, 2008). As the previous work shows, this decomposition overcomes the features sparsity common in NLP tasks and also enables us to use unlabeled data effectively. For example, the parameter vector for the feature *word-on-top-of-stack* is decomposed into the multiplication of a parameter vector representing the word and a parameter matrix representing *top-of-stack*. But sparsity is not always a problem, since the frequency of such features follows a power law distribution, so there are some very frequent feature combinations. Previous work has noticed that the vector-matrix multiplication of these frequent feature combinations takes most of the computation time during testing, so they cache these computations (Bengio et al., 2003; Devlin et al., 2014; Chen and Manning, 2014).

We note that these computations also take most of the computation time during training, and that the abundance of data for these feature combinations removes the statistical motivation for decomposing them. We propose to treat the cached vectors for high frequency feature combinations as parameters in their own right, using them both during training and during testing.

In summary, this paper makes several contributions to neural network parsing by considering different scales in the parse sequence and in the parametrization. We propose a discriminative recurrent neural network model of dependency parsing that is trained to optimize an efficient form of beam search that prunes based on the sub-sequences of parser actions between two shifts, rather than pruning after each parser action. We cache high frequency parameter computations during both testing and training, and train the cached vectors as separate parameters. As shown in section 6, these improvements significantly reduce both training and testing times while preserving accuracy.

2 History Based Neural Network Parsing

In this section we briefly specify the action sequences that we model and the neural network architecture that we use to model them.

2.1 The Parsing Model

In shift-reduce dependency parsing, at each step of the parse, the configuration of the parser consists of a stack S of words, the queue Q of words and the partial labeled dependency trees constructed by the previous history of parser actions. The parser starts with an empty stack S and all the input words in the queue Q, and terminates when it reaches a configuration with an empty queue Q. We use an arc-eager algorithm, which has 4 actions that all manipulate the word s on top of the stack S and the word q on the front of the queue Q: The decision *Left-Arc*$_r$ adds a dependency arc from q to s labeled r. Word s is then popped from the stack. The decision *Right-Arc*$_r$ adds an arc from s to q labeled r. The decision *Reduce* pops s from the stack. The decision *Shift* shifts q from the queue to the stack. For more details we refer the reader to (Nivre et al., 2004). In this paper we chose the exact definition of the parse actions that are used in (Titov and Henderson, 2007b).

At each step of the parse, the parser needs to choose between the set of possible next actions. To train a classifier to choose the best actions, previous work has proposed memory-based classifiers (Nivre et al., 2004), SVMs (Nivre et al., 2006), structured perceptron (Huang et al., 2012; Zhang and Clark, 2011), two-layer neural networks (Chen and Manning, 2014), and Incremental Sigmoid Belief Networks (ISBN) (Titov and

Henderson, 2007b), amongst other approaches.

We take a history based approach to model these sequences of parser actions, which decomposes the conditional probability of the parse using the chain rule:

$$P(T|S) = P(D^1 \cdots D^m|S) = \prod_t P(D^t|D^1 \cdots D^{t-1}, S)$$

where T is the parse tree, $D^1 \cdots D^m$ is its equivalent sequence of shift-reduce parser actions and S is the input sentence. The probability of *Left-Arc*$_r$ and *Right-Arc*$_r$ include both the probability of the attachment decision and the chosen label r. But unlike in (Titov and Henderson, 2007b), the probability of *Shift* does not include a probability predicting the next word, since all the words S are included in the conditioning.

2.2 Estimating Action Probabilities

To estimate each $P(D^t|D^1 \cdots D^{t-1}, S)$, we need to handle the unbounded nature of both $D^1 \cdots D^{t-1}$ and S. We can divide S into the words that have already been shifted, which are handled as part of our encoding of $D^1 \cdots D^{t-1}$, and the words on the queue. To condition on the words in the queue, we use a bounded lookahead:

$$P(T|S) \approx \prod_t P(D^t|D^1 \cdots D^{t-1}, w^t_{a_1} \cdots w^t_{a_k})$$

where $w^t_{a_1} \cdots w^t_{a_k}$ is the first k words on the front of the queue at time t. At every *Shift* action the lookahead changes, moving one word onto the stack and adding a new word from the input.

To estimate the probability of a decision at time t conditioned on the history of actions $D^1 \cdots D^{t-1}$, we overcome the problem of conditioning on an unbounded amount of information by using a neural network to induce hidden representations of the parse history sequence. The relevant information about the whole parse history at time t is encoded in its hidden representation, denoted by the vector h^t of size d.

$$\prod_t P(D^t|D^1 \cdots D^{t-1}, w^t_{a_1} \cdots w^t_{a_k}) = \prod_t P(D^t|h^t)$$

The hidden representation at time t is induced from hidden representations of the relevant previous states, plus pre-defined features $\mathcal{F}$ computed from the previous decision and the current queue and stack:

$$h^t = \sigma(\sum_{c \in \mathcal{C}} h^{t_c} W^c_{HH} + \sum_{f \in \mathcal{F}} W_{IH}(f,:))$$

In which $\mathcal{C}$ is the set of link types for the previous relevant hidden representations, h^{t_c} is the hidden representation of time $t_c<t$ that is relevant to h^t by the relation c, W^c_{HH} is the hidden to hidden transition weights for the link type c, and W_{IH} is the weights from features $\mathcal{F}$ to hidden representations. σ is the sigmoid function and $W(i,:)$ shows row i of matrix W. $\mathcal{F}$ and $\mathcal{C}$ are the only hand-coded parts of the model.

The decomposition of features has attracted a lot of attention in NLP tasks, because it overcomes feature sparsity. There is transfer learning from the same word (or POS tag, Dependency label, etc.) in different positions or to similar words. Also unsupervised training of word embeddings can be used effectively within decomposed features. The use of unsupervised word embeddings in various natural language processing tasks has received much attention (Bengio et al., 2003; Collobert and Weston, 2008; Collobert, 2011). Word embeddings are real-valued feature vectors that are induced from large corpora of unlabeled text data. Using word embeddings with a large dictionary improves domain adaptation, and in the case of a small training set can improve the performance of the model.

Given these advantages, we use feature decompositions to define the input-to-hidden weights W_{IH}.

$$W_{IH}(f,:) = W_{emb.}(val(f),:)W^f_{HH}$$

Every row in $W_{emb.}$ is an embedding for a feature value, which may be a word, lemma, pos tag, or dependency relation. $val(f)$ is the index of the value for feature type f, for example the particular word that is at the front of the queue. Matrix W^f_{HH} is the transition matrix from the feature value embeddings to the hidden vector, for the given feature type f. For simplicity, we assume here that the size of the embeddings and the size of the hidden representations of the INN are the same.

In this way, the parameters of the embedding matrix $W_{emb.}$ is shared among various feature input link types f, which can improve the model in the case of sparse features. It also allows the use of word embeddings that are available on the web to improve coverage of sparse features, but we leave this investigation to future work since it is orthogonal to the contributions of this paper.

Finally, the probability of each decision is normalized across other alternative decisions, and only conditioned on the hidden representation (softmax layer):

$$P(D^t{=}d|h^t) = \frac{e^{h^t W_{HO}(:,d)}}{\sum_{d'} e^{h^t W_{HO}(:,d')}}$$

where W_{HO} is the weight matrix from hidden representations to the outputs.

3 Discrimination of Partial Parses

Unlike in a generative model, the above formulas for computing the probability of a tree make independence assumptions in that words to the right of $w^t_{a_k}$ are assumed to be independent of D^t. And even for words in the lookahead it can be difficult to learn dependencies with the unstructured lookahead string. The generative model first constructs a structure and then uses word prediction to test how well that matches the next word. If a discriminative model uses normalized estimates for decisions, then once a wrong decision is made there is no way for the estimates to express that this decision has lead to a structure that is incompatible with the current or future lookahead string (see (Lafferty et al., 2001) for more discussion). More generally, any discriminative model that is trained to predict individual actions has this problem. In this section we discuss how to overcome this issue.

3.1 Discriminating Correct Parse Chunks

Due to this problem, discriminative parsers typically make irrevocable choices for each individual action in the parse. We propose a method for training a discriminative parser which addresses this problem in two ways. First, we train the model to discriminate between larger sub-sequences of actions, namely the actions between two *Shift* actions, which we call *chunks*. This allows the parser to delay choosing between actions that occur early in a chunk until all the structure associated with that chunk has been built. Second, the model's score can be used to discriminate between two parses long after they have diverged, making it appropriate for a beam search.

We employ a search strategy where we prune at each shift action, but in between shift actions we consider all possible sequences of actions, similarly to the generative parser in (Henderson, 2003). The INN model is discriminatively trained to choose between these chunks of sequences of actions.

The most straightforward way to model these chunk decisions would be to use unnormalized scores for the decisions in a chunk and sum these scores to make the decision, as would be done for a structured perceptron or conditional random field. Preliminary experiments applying this approach to our INN parser did not work as well as having local normalization of action decisions. We hypothesize that the main reason for this result is that updating on entire chunks does not provide a sufficiently focused training signal. With a locally normalized action score, such as softmax, increasing the score of the correct chunk has the effect of decreasing the score of all the incorrect actions at each individual action decision. This update is an approximation to a discriminative update on all incorrect parses that continue from an incorrect decision (Henderson, 2004). Another possible reason is that local normalization prevents one action's score from dominating the score of the whole parse, as can happen with high frequency decisions. In general, this problem can not be solved just by using norm regularization on weights.

The places in a parse where the generative update and the discriminative update differ substantially are at word predictions, where the generative model considers that all words are possible but a discriminative model already knows what word comes next and so does not need to predict anything. We discriminatively train the INN to choose between chunks of actions by adding a new score at these places in the parse. After each shift action, we introduce a *correctness probability* that is trained to discriminate between cases where the chunk of actions since the previous shift is correct and those where this chunk is incorrect. Thus, the search strategy chooses between all possible sequences of actions between two shifts using a combination of the normalized scores for each action and the *correctness probability*.

In addition to discriminative training at the chunk level, the *correctness probability* allows us to search using a beam of parses. If a correct decision can not be disambiguated, because of the independence assumptions with words beyond the lookahead or because of the difficulty of inferring from an unstructured lookahead, the *correctness*

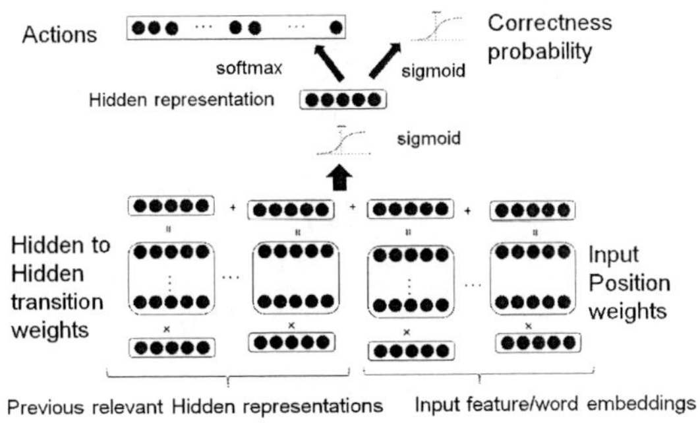

Figure 1: INN computations for one decision

probability score will drop whenever the mistake becomes evident. This means that we can not only compare two partial parses that differ in the most recent chunk, but we can also compare two partial parses that differ in earlier chunks. This allows us to use beam search decoding. Instead of deterministically choosing a single partial parse at each shift action, we can maintain a small beam of alternatives and choose between them based on how compatible they are with future lookahead strings by comparing their respective correctness probabilities for those future shifts.

We combine this *correctness probability* with the action probabilities by simply multiplying:

$$P(T|S) \approx \prod_t P(D^t|h^t)P(Correct|h^t)$$

where we train $P(Correct|h^t)$ to be the *correctness probability* for the cases where D^t is a shift action, and define $P(Correct|h^t) = 1$ otherwise. For the shift actions, $P(Correct|h^t)$ is defined using the sigmoid function:

$$P(Correct|h^t) = \sigma(h^t W_{Cor})$$

In this way, the hidden representations are trained not only to choose the right action, but also to encode correctness of the partial parses. Figure 1 shows the model schematically.

3.2 Training the Parameters

We want to train the *correctness probabilities* to discriminate correct parses from incorrect parses. The correct parses can be extracted from the training treebank by converting each dependency tree into its equivalent sequence of arc-eager shift-reduce parser actions (Nivre et al., 2004; Titov and Henderson, 2007b). These sequences of actions provide us with positive examples. For discriminative training, we also need incorrect parses to act as the negative examples. In particular, we want negative examples that will allow us to optimize the pruning decisions made by the parser.

To optimize the pruning decisions made by the parsing model, we use the parsing model itself to generate the negative examples (Collins and Roark, 2004). Using the current parameters of the model, we apply our search-based decoding strategy to find our current approximation to the highest scoring complete parse, which is the output of our current parsing model. If this parse differs from the correct one, then we train the parameters of all the *correctness probabilities* in each parse so as to increase the score of the correct parse and decrease the score of the incorrect output parse. By repeatedly decreasing the score of the incorrect best parse as the model parameters are learned, training will efficiently decreases the score of all incorrect parses.

As discussed above, we train the scores of individual parser actions to optimize the locally-normalized conditional probability of the correct action. Putting this together with the above training of the *correctness probabilities* $P(Correct|h^t)$, we get the following objective function:

$$argmax_{\phi} \sum_{T \in T_{pos}} \sum_{t \in T} logP(d^t|h^t) + logP(Correct|h^t) - \sum_{T \in T^{\phi}_{neg}} \sum_{t \in T} logP(Correct|h^t)$$

where ϕ is the set of all parameters of the model (namely W_{HH}, $W_{emb.}$, W_{HO}, and W_{Cor}), T_{pos} is the set of correct parses, and T^{ϕ}_{neg} is the set of incorrect parses which the model ϕ scores higher than their corresponding correct parses. The derivative of this objective function is the error signal that the neural network learns to minimize. This error signal is illustrated schematically in Figure 2.

We optimize the above objective using stochastic gradient descent. For each parameter update, a positive tree is chosen randomly and a negative tree is built using the above strategy. The resulting error signals are backpropagated through the INN to compute the derivatives for gradient descent.

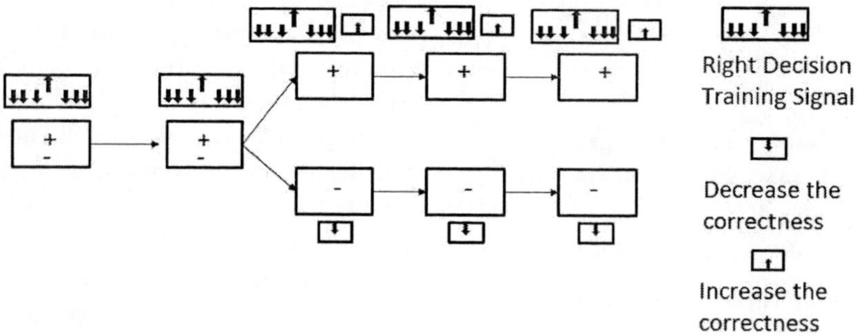

Figure 2: Positive and negative derivation branches and their training signals

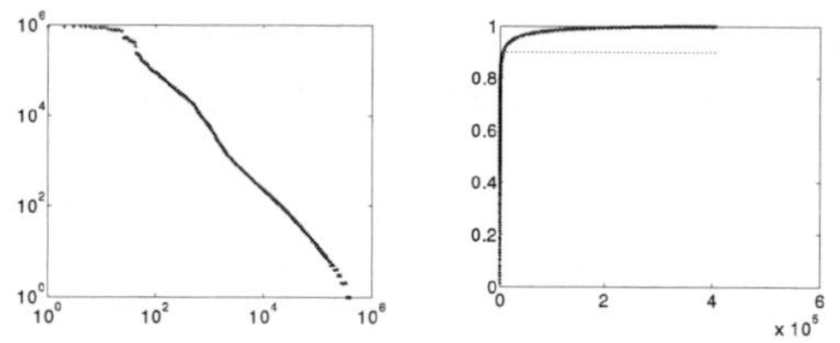

(a) Log-Log frequency by rank of features

(b) Cumulative fraction of features ranked by frequency

Figure 3: Feature frequency distributions

4 Caching Frequent Features

Decomposing the parametrization of input features using vector-matrix multiplication, as was described in section 2, overcomes the features sparsity common in NLP tasks and also makes it possible to use unlabeled data effectively. But it adds a huge amount of computation to both the training and decoding, since for every input feature a vector-matrix multiplication is needed. This problem is even more severe in our algorithm because at every training iteration we search for the best incorrect parse.

The frequency of features follows a power law distribution; there are a few very frequent features, and a long tail of infrequent features. Previous work has noticed that the vector-matrix multiplication of the frequent features takes most of the computation time during testing, so they cache these computations (Bengio et al., 2003; Devlin et al., 2014; Chen and Manning, 2014). For example in the Figure 3(b), only 2100 features are responsible of 90% of the computations among ∼400k features, so cashing these computations can have a huge impact on speed. We note that these computations also take most of the computation time during training. First, this computation is the dominant part of the forward and backward error computations. Second, at every iteration we need to decode to find the highest scoring incorrect parse.

We propose to treat the cached vectors for high frequency features as parameters in their own right, using them both during training and during testing. This speeds up training because it is no longer necessary to do the high-frequency vector-matrix multiplications, neither to do the forward error computations nor to do the backpropagation through the vector-matrix multiplications. Also, the cached vectors used in decoding do not need to be recomputed every time the parameters change, since the vectors are updated directly by the parameter updates.

Another possible motivation for treating the cached vectors as parameters is that it results in a kind of backoff smoothing; high frequency features are given specific parameters, and for low frequency features we back off to the decomposed model. Results from smoothing methods for symbolic statistical models indicate that it is better to smooth low frequency features with other low frequency features, and treat high frequency features individually. In this paper we do not systematically investigate this potential advantage, leaving this for future work.

In our experiments we cache features that make up to 90% of the feature frequencies. This gives us about a 20 times speed up during training and about a 7 times speed up during testing, while performance is preserved.

5 Parsing Complexity

If the length of the latent vectors is d, for a sentence of length L, and beam B, the decoding com-

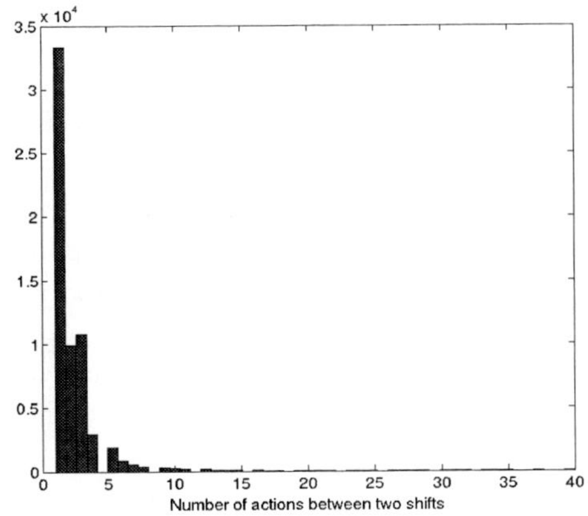

Figure 4: Histogram of number of candidate actions between shifts

plexity is $O(L \times M \times B \times (|\mathcal{F}| + |\mathcal{C}|) \times d^2)$.[1] If we choose the best partial parse tree at every shift, then $B = 1$. M is the total number of actions in the candidate chunks that are generated between two shifts, so $L \times M$ is the total number of candidate actions in a parse. For shift-reduce dependency parsing, the total number of *chosen* actions is necessarily linear in L, but because we are applying best-first search in between shifts, M is not necessarily independent of L. To investigate the impact of M on the speed of the parser, we empirically measure the number of candidate actions generated by the parser between 33368 different shifts. The resulting distribution is plotted in Figure 4. We observe that it forms a power law distribution. Most of the time the number of actions is very small (2 or 3), with the maximum number being 40, and the average being 2.25. We conclude from this that the value of M is not a major factor in the parser's speed.

Remember that $|\mathcal{F}|$ is the number of input feature types. Caching 90% of the input feature computations allows us to reasonably neglect this term. Because $|\mathcal{C}|$ is the number of hidden-to-hidden connection types, we cannot apply caching to reduce this term. However, $|\mathcal{C}|$ is much smaller than $|\mathcal{F}|$ (here $|\mathcal{C}|$=3). This is why caching input feature computations has such a large impact on parser speed.

[1]For this analysis, we assume that the output computation is negligable compared to the hidden representation computation, because the output computation grows with d while the hidden computation grows with d^2.

6 Experimental Results

We used syntactic dependencies from the English section of the CoNLL 2009 shared task dataset (Hajič et al., 2009). Standard splits of training, development and test sets were used. We compare our model to the generative INN model (Titov and Henderson, 2007b), MALT parser, MST parser, and the feed-forward neural network parser of (Chen and Manning, 2014) ("C&M"). All these models and our own models are trained only on the CoNLL 2009 syntactic data; they use no external word embeddings or other unsupervised training on additional data. This is one reason for choosing these models for comparison. In addition, the generative model ("Generative INN, large beam" in Table 1) was compared extensively to state-of-art parsers on various languages and tasks in previous work (Titov and Henderson, 2007b; Titov and Henderson, 2007a; Henderson et al., 2008). Therefore, here our objective is not repeating an extensive comparison to the available parsers.

Table 1 shows the labeled and unlabeled accuracy of attachments for these models. The MALT and MST parser scores come from (Surdeanu and Manning, 2010), which compared different parsing models using CoNLL 2008 shared task dataset, which is the same as CoNLL 2009 for English syntactic parsing. The results for the generative INN with a large beam were taken from (Henderson and Titov, 2010), which uses an architecture with 80 hidden units. We replicate this setting for the other generative INN results and our discriminative INN results. The parser of (Chen and Manning, 2014) was run with their architecture of 200 hidden units with dropout training ("C&M"). All parsing speeds were computed using the latest downloadable versions of the parsers, on a single 3.4GHz CPU.

Our model with beam 1 (i.e. deterministic choices of chunks) ("DINN, beam 1") produces state-of-the-art results while it is over 35 times faster than the generative model with beam size 10. Moreover, we are able to achieve higher accuracies using larger beams ("DINN, beam 10"). The discriminative training of the *correctness probabilities* to optimize search is crucial to these levels of accuracy, as indicated by the relatively poor performance of our model when this training is removed ("Discriminative INN, no search training"). Previous deterministic shift-reduce parsers ("$MALT_{AE}$" and "C&M") are around twice as fast

Model	LAA	UAA	wrd/sec
$MALT_{AE}$	85.96	88.64	7549
C&M	86.49	89.17	9589
MST	87.07	89.95	290
MALT-MST	87.45	90.22	NA
Generative INN,			
beam 1	77.83	81.49	1122
beam 10	87.67	90.61	107
large beam	88.65	91.44	NA
Discriminative INN,			
no search training	85.28	88.98	4012
DINN, beam 1	87.26	90.13	4035
DINN, beam 10	88.14	90.75	433

Table 1: Labelled and unlabelled attachment accuracies and speeds on the test set.

Model	German		Spanish		Czech	
	LAA	UAA	LAA	UAA	LAA	UAA
C&M	82.5	86.1	81.5	85.4	58.6	70.6
MALT	80.7	83.1	82.4	86.6	67.3	77.4
MST	84.1	87.6	82.7	87.3	73.4	81.7
DINN	86.0	89.6	85.4	88.3	77.5	85.2

Table 2: Labelled and unlabelled attachment accuracies on the test set of CoNLL 2009.

as our beam 1 model, but at the cost of significant reductions in accuracy.

To evaluate our RNN model's ability to induce informative features automatically, we trained our deterministic model, MALT, MST and C&M on three diverse languages from CoNLL 2009, using the same features as used in the above experiments on English (model "DINN, beam 1"). We did no language-specific feature engineering for any of these parsers. Table 2 shows that our RNN model generalizes substantially better than all these models to new languages, demonstrating the power of this model's feature induction.

7 Conclusion

We propose an efficient and accurate recurrent neural network dependency parser that uses neural network hidden representations to encode arbitrarily large partial parses for predicting the next parser action. This parser uses a search strategy that prunes to a deterministic choice at each shift action, so we add a *correctness probability* to each shift operation, and train this score to discriminate between correct and incorrect sequences of parser actions. All other probability estimates are trained to optimize the conditional probability of the parse given the sentence. We also speed up both parsing and training times by only decomposing infrequent features, giving us both a form of backoff smoothing and twenty times faster training.

The discriminative training for this pruning strategy allows high accuracy to be preserved while greatly speeding up parsing time. The recurrent neural network architecture provides powerful automatic feature induction, resulting in high accuracy on diverse languages without tuning.

Acknowledgments

The research leading to this work was funded by the EC FP7 programme FP7/2011-14 under grant agreement no. 287615 (PARLANCE).

References

Yoshua Bengio, Réjean Ducharme, Pascal Vincent, and Christian Janvin. 2003. A neural probabilistic language model. *J. Mach. Learn. Res.*, 3:1137–1155, March.

Danqi Chen and Christopher Manning. 2014. A fast and accurate dependency parser using neural networks. In *Proceedings of the 2014 Conference on Empirical Methods in Natural Language Processing (EMNLP)*, pages 740–750. Association for Computational Linguistics, October.

Michael Collins and Brian Roark. 2004. Incremental parsing with the perceptron algorithm. In *Proceedings of the 42nd Annual Meeting on Association for Computational Linguistics*, ACL '04. Association for Computational Linguistics.

Ronan Collobert and Jason Weston. 2008. A unified architecture for natural language processing: Deep neural networks with multitask learning. In *Proceedings of the 25th International Conference on Machine Learning*, ICML '08, pages 160–167. ACM.

Ronan Collobert, Jason Weston, Léon Bottou, Michael Karlen, Koray Kavukcuoglu, and Pavel Kuksa. 2011. Natural language processing (almost) from scratch. *J. Mach. Learn. Res.*, 12:2493–2537, November.

Ronan Collobert. 2011. Deep learning for efficient discriminative parsing. In *Proceedings of the Fourteenth International Conference on Artificial Intelligence and Statistics (AISTATS-11)*, volume 15, pages 224–232. Journal of Machine Learning Research - Workshop and Conference Proceedings.

Hal Daumé III and Daniel Marcu. 2005. Learning as search optimization: Approximate large margin methods for structured prediction. In *Proceedings* of the 22nd International Conference on Machine Learning, pages 169–176.

Jacob Devlin, Rabih Zbib, Zhongqiang Huang, Thomas Lamar, Richard Schwartz, and John Makhoul. 2014. Fast and robust neural network joint models for statistical machine translation. In *Proceedings of the 52nd Annual Meeting of the Association for Computational Linguistics (Volume 1: Long Papers)*. Association for Computational Linguistics.

Xavier Glorot, Antoine Bordes, and Yoshua Bengio. 2011. Domain adaptation for large-scale sentiment classification: A deep learning approach. In *Proceedings of the 28th International Conference on Machine Learning (ICML-11)*, ICML '11, pages 513–520. ACM, June.

Jan Hajič, Massimiliano Ciaramita, Richard Johansson, Daisuke Kawahara, Maria Antònia Martí, Lluís Màrquez, Adam Meyers, Joakim Nivre, Sebastian Padó, Jan Štěpánek, Pavel Straňák, Mihai Surdeanu, Nianwen Xue, and Yi Zhang. 2009. The conll-2009 shared task: Syntactic and semantic dependencies in multiple languages. In *Proceedings of the Thirteenth Conference on Computational Natural Language Learning: Shared Task*, CoNLL '09, pages 1–18. Association for Computational Linguistics.

James Henderson and Ivan Titov. 2010. Incremental sigmoid belief networks for grammar learning. *J. Mach. Learn. Res.*, 11:3541–3570, December.

James Henderson, Paola Merlo, Gabriele Musillo, and Ivan Titov. 2008. A latent variable model of synchronous parsing for syntactic and semantic dependencies. In *Proceedings of the Twelfth Conference on Computational Natural Language Learning*, CoNLL '08, pages 178–182. Association for Computational Linguistics.

James Henderson, Paola Merlo, Ivan Titov, and Gabriele Musillo. 2013. Multilingual joint parsing of syntactic and semantic dependencies with a latent variable model. *Comput. Linguist.*, 39(4):949–998, December.

James Henderson. 2003. Inducing history representations for broad coverage statistical parsing. In *Proceedings of the 2003 Conference of the North American Chapter of the Association for Computational Linguistics on Human Language Technology - Volume 1*, NAACL '03, pages 24–31. Association for Computational Linguistics.

James Henderson. 2004. Discriminative training of a neural network statistical parser. In *Proceedings of the 42nd Meeting of the Association for Computational Linguistics (ACL'04), Main Volume*, pages 95–102, July.

Liang Huang, Suphan Fayong, and Yang Guo. 2012. Structured perceptron with inexact search. In *Proceedings of the 2012 Conference of the North American Chapter of the Association for Computational Linguistics: Human Language Technologies*, pages 142–151. Association for Computational Linguistics, June.

John D. Lafferty, Andrew McCallum, and Fernando C. N. Pereira. 2001. Conditional random fields: Probabilistic models for segmenting and labeling sequence data. In *Proceedings of the Eighteenth International Conference on Machine Learning*, ICML '01, pages 282–289. Morgan Kaufmann Publishers Inc.

Tomáš Mikolov, Martin Karafiát, Lukáš Burget, Jan Černocký, and Sanjeev Khudanpur. 2010. Recurrent neural network based language model. In *Proceedings of the 11th Annual Conference of the International Speech Communication Association (INTERSPEECH 2010)*, volume 2010, pages 1045–1048. International Speech Communication Association.

Joakim Nivre, Johan Hall, and Jens Nilsson. 2004. Memory-based dependency parsing. In Hwee Tou Ng and Ellen Riloff, editors, *HLT-NAACL 2004 Workshop: Eighth Conference on Computational Natural Language Learning (CoNLL-2004)*, pages 49–56. Association for Computational Linguistics, May 6 - May 7.

Joakim Nivre, Johan Hall, Jens Nilsson, Gülşen Eryiğit, and Svetoslav Marinov. 2006. Labeled pseudo-projective dependency parsing with support vector machines. In *Proceedings of the Tenth Conference on Computational Natural Language Learning*, CoNLL-X '06, pages 221–225. Association for Computational Linguistics.

Rajat Raina, Alexis Battle, Honglak Lee, Benjamin Packer, and Andrew Y. Ng. 2007. Self-taught learning: Transfer learning from unlabeled data. In *Proceedings of the 24th International Conference on Machine Learning*, ICML '07, pages 759–766. ACM.

Richard Socher, Cliff Chiung-Yu Lin, Andrew Ng, and Chris Manning. 2011. Parsing natural scenes and natural language with recursive neural networks. In *Proceedings of the 28th International Conference on Machine Learning (ICML-11)*, ICML '11, pages 129–136. ACM.

Richard Socher, John Bauer, Christopher D. Manning, and Ng Andrew Y. 2013. Parsing with compositional vector grammars. In *Proceedings of the 51st Annual Meeting of the Association for Computational Linguistics (Volume 1: Long Papers)*, pages 455–465. Association for Computational Linguistics, August.

Mihai Surdeanu and Christopher D. Manning. 2010. Ensemble models for dependency parsing: Cheap and good? In *Human Language Technologies: The 2010 Annual Conference of the North American Chapter of the Association for Computational Linguistics*, HLT '10, pages 649–652. Association for Computational Linguistics.

Ilya Sutskever, James Martens, and Geoffrey Hinton. 2011. Generating text with recurrent neural networks. In *Proceedings of the 28th International Conference on Machine Learning (ICML-11)*, ICML '11, pages 1017–1024. ACM, June.

Ivan Titov and James Henderson. 2007a. Fast and robust multilingual dependency parsing with a generative latent variable model. In *Proceedings of the CoNLL Shared Task Session of EMNLP-CoNLL 2007*, pages 947–951. Association for Computational Linguistics, June.

Ivan Titov and James Henderson. 2007b. A latent variable model for generative dependency parsing. In *Proceedings of the 10th International Conference on Parsing Technologies*, IWPT '07, pages 144–155. Association for Computational Linguistics.

Kaisheng Yao, Geoffrey Zweig, Mei-Yuh Hwang, Yangyang Shi, and Dong Yu. 2013. Recurrent neural networks for language understanding. In *INTERSPEECH*, pages 2524–2528.

Yue Zhang and Stephen Clark. 2011. Syntactic processing using the generalized perceptron and beam search. *Comput. Linguist.*, 37(1):105–151, March.

Instance Selection Improves Cross-Lingual Model Training for Fine-Grained Sentiment Analysis

Roman Klinger[*‡]
[*]Institute for Natural Language Processing
University of Stuttgart
70569 Stuttgart, Germany

Philipp Cimiano[‡]
[‡]Semantic Computing Group, CIT-EC
Bielefeld University
33615 Bielefeld, Germany

roman.klinger@ims.uni-stuttgart.de
cimiano@cit-ec.uni-bielefeld.de

Abstract

Scarcity of annotated corpora for many languages is a bottleneck for training fine-grained sentiment analysis models that can tag aspects and subjective phrases. We propose to exploit statistical machine translation to alleviate the need for training data by projecting annotated data in a source language to a target language such that a supervised fine-grained sentiment analysis system can be trained. To avoid a negative influence of poor-quality translations, we propose a filtering approach based on machine translation quality estimation measures to select only high-quality sentence pairs for projection. We evaluate on the language pair German/English on a corpus of product reviews annotated for both languages and compare to in-target-language training. Projection without any filtering leads to 23 % F_1 in the task of detecting aspect phrases, compared to 41 % F_1 for in-target-language training. Our approach obtains up to 47 % F_1. Further, we show that the detection of subjective phrases is competitive to in-target-language training without filtering.

1 Introduction

An important task in fine-grained sentiment analysis and opinion mining is the extraction of mentioned aspects, evaluative subjective phrases and the relation between them. For instance, in the sentence

> "I really like the display but the battery seems weak to me."

the task is to detect evaluative (subjective) phrases (in this example "really like" and "seems weak") and aspects ("display" and "battery") as well as their relation (that "really like" refers to "display" and "seems weak" refers to "battery").

Annotating data for learning a model to extract such detailed information is a tedious and time-consuming task. Therefore, given the scarcity of such annotated corpora in most languages, it is interesting to generate models which can be applied on languages without manually created training data. In this paper, we perform annotation projection, which is one of the two main categories for cross-language model induction (next to direct model transfer (Agić et al., 2014)).

Figure 1 shows an example of a sentence together with its automatically derived translation (source language on top, target language on bottom) and the alignment between both. Such an alignment can be used to project annotations across languages, *e. g.*, from a source to target language, to produce data to train a system for the target language. As shown in the example, translation errors as well as alignment errors can occur. When using a projection-based approach, the performance of a system on the target language crucially depends on the quality of the translation and the alignment. In this paper we address two questions:

- What is the performance on the task when training data for the source language is projected into a target language, compared to an approach where training data for the target language is available?
- Can the performance be increased by selecting only high-quality translations and alignments?

Towards answering these questions, we present the following contributions:

Proceedings of the 19th Conference on Computational Language Learning, pages 153–163,
Beijing, China, July 30-31, 2015.

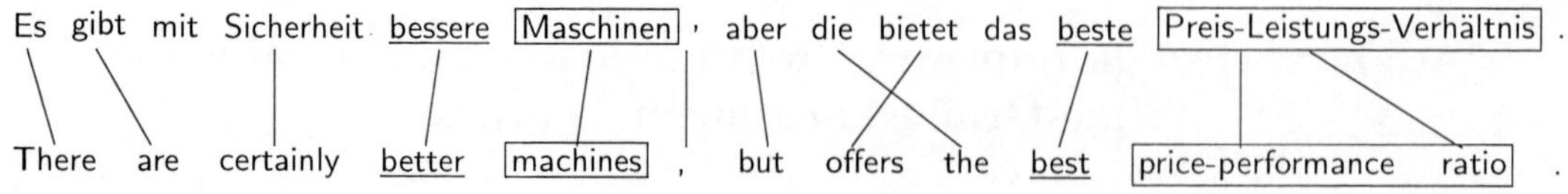

Figure 1: Example for the projection of an annotation from the source language to the target language. The translation has been generated with the Google translate API (https://cloud.google.com/translate/). The alignment is induced with FastAlign (Dyer et al., 2013).

- We propose to use a supervised approach to induce a fine-grained sentiment analysis model to predict aspect and subjective phrases on some target language, given training data in some source language. This approach relies on automatic translation of source training data and projection of annotations to the target language data.

- We present an instance selection method that only selects sentences with a certain translation quality. For this, we incorporate different measures of translation and alignment confidence. We show that such an instance selection method leads to increased performance compared to a system without instance selection for the prediction of aspects. Remarkably, for the prediction of aspects the performance is comparable to an upper baseline using manually annotated target language data for training (we refer to the latter setting as *in-target-language training*).

- In contrast, for the prediction of subjective phrases, we show that, while a competitive result compared to target language training can be observed when training with the projected training data, there is no beneficial effect of the filtering.

In the following, we describe our methodology in detail, including the description of the machine translation, annotation projection, and quality estimation methods (Section 2), and present the evaluation on manually annotated data (Section 3). Related work is discussed in Section 4. We conclude with Section 5 and mention promising future steps.

2 Methods

2.1 Supervised Model for Aspect and Subjective Phrase Detection

We use a supervised model induced from training data to detect aspect phrases, subjective (evaluative) phrases and their relations. The structure follows the proposed pipeline approach by Klinger and Cimiano (2013).[1] However, in contrast to their work, we focus on the detection of phrases only, and exploit the detection of relations only during inference, such that the detection of relations has an effect on the detection of phrases, but is not evaluated directly.

The phrase detection follows the idea of semi-Markov conditional random fields (Sarawagi and Cohen, 2004; Yang and Cardie, 2012) and models phrases as spans over tokens as variables. Factor templates for spans of type *aspect* and *subjective* take into account token strings, prefixes, suffixes, the inclusion of digits, and part-of-speech tags, both as full string and as bigrams, for the spans and their vicinity. In addition, the length of the span is modeled by cumulative binning. The relation template indicates how close an aspect is to a subjective phrase based on token distance and on the length of the shortest path in the dependency tree. The edge names of the shortest path are also included as features. It is further checked if no other noun than the aspect is close to the subjective phrase.

Inference during training and testing is done via Markov Chain Monte Carlo (MCMC). In each sampling step (with options of adding a span, removing a span, adding an aspect as target to a subjective phrase), the respective factors lead to an associated model score. The model parameters are adapted based on sample rank (Wick et al., 2011) using an objective function which computes the fraction of correctly predicted tokens in a span. For details on the model configuration and its implementation in FACTORIE (McCallum et al., 2009), we refer to the description in the original paper (Klinger and Cimiano, 2013). The objective function to evaluate a span $\mathbf{r}$ during training is

$$f(\mathbf{r}) = \max_{\mathbf{g} \in \mathbf{s}} \frac{|\mathbf{r} \cap \mathbf{g}|}{|\mathbf{g}|} - \alpha \cdot |\mathbf{r} \backslash \mathbf{g}|,$$

[1] https://bitbucket.org/rklinger/jfsa

where $\mathbf{g}$ is the set of all gold spans, and $|\mathbf{r} \cap \mathbf{g}|$ is the number of tokens shared by gold and predicted span and $|\mathbf{r} \backslash \mathbf{g}|$ the number of predicted tokens which are not part of the gold span. The parameter α is set to 0.1 as in the original paper.[2]. The objective for the predictions in a whole sentence s containing spans is $f(\mathbf{s}) = \sum_{\mathbf{r} \in s} f(\mathbf{r})$.

This model does not take into account language-specific features and can therefore be trained for different languages. In the following, we explain our procedure for inducing a model for a target language for which no annotations are available.

2.2 Statistical Machine Translation and Annotation Projection

Annotating textual corpora with fine-grained sentiment information is a time-consuming and therefore costly process. In order to adapt a model to a new domain and to a new language, corresponding training data is needed. In order to circumvent the need for additional training data when addressing a new language, we project training data automatically from a source to a target language. As input to our approach we require a corpus annotated for some source language and a translation from the source to a target language. As the availability of a parallel training corpus cannot be assumed in general, we use statistical machine translation (SMT) methods, relying on phrase-based translation models that use large amounts of parallel data for training (Koehn, 2010).

While using an open-source system such as Moses[3] would have been an option, we note that the quality would be limited by whether the system can be trained on a representative corpus. A standard dataset that SMT systems are trained on is EuroParl (Koehn, 2005). EuroParl covers 21 languages and contains 1.920.209 sentences for the pair German/English. The corpus includes only 4 sentences with the term "toaster", 12 with "knives" (mostly in the context of violence), 6 with "dishwasher" (in the context of regulations) and 0 with "trash can". The terms "camera" and "display" are more frequent, with 208 and 1186 mentions, respectively, but they never occur together.[4] The corpus is thus not representative for product reviews as we consider in this paper.

[2]Note that the learning is independent from the actual value for all $0 < \alpha < (\max_{g \in \text{Corpus}} |g|)^{-1}$.

[3]www.statmt.org/moses/

[4]These example domains are taken from the USAGE corpus (Klinger and Cimiano, 2014), which is used in Section 3.

Thus, we opt for using a closed translation system that is trained on larger amounts of data, that is Google Translate, through the available API[5]. The alignment is then computed as a post processing step relying on FastAlign (Dyer et al., 2013), a reparametrization of IBM Model 2 with a reduced set of parameters. It is trained in an unsupervised fashion via expectation maximization.

Projecting the annotations from the source to the target language works as follows: given an annotated sentence in the source language $s_1, \ldots, s_n$ and some translation of this sentence $t_1, \ldots, t_m$ into the target language, we induce an inductive mapping $a : [1 \ldots n] \rightarrow [1 \ldots m]$ using FastAlign. For a source language phrase $s_{i,j} = s_i, \ldots, s_j$ we refer by $a(s_{i,j})$ to the set of tokens that some token in $s_{i,j}$ has been aligned to, that is: $a(s_{i,j}) = \cup_{i \le k \le j} \{a(k)\}$. Note that the tokens in $a(s_{i,j})$ are not necessarily consecutive, therefore the annotation in the target language is defined as the minimal sequence including all tokens $t_k \in a(s_{i,j})$, *i. e.*, the most left and most right tokens define the span of the target annotation.

This procedure leads to the same number of span annotations in source and target language with the only exception that we exclude projected annotations for which $|n - m| > 10$.

2.3 Quality Estimation-based Instance Filtering

The performance of an approach relying on projection of training data from a source to a target language and using this automatically projected data to train a supervised model crucially depends on the quality of the translations and alignments. In order to reduce the impact of spurious translations, we filter out low-quality sentence pairs. To estimate this quality, we take three measures into consideration (following approaches described by Shah and Specia (2014), in addition to a manual assessment of the translation quality as an upper baseline):

1. The probability of the sentence in the source language given a language model build on unannotated text in the source language (measuring if the language to be translated is typical, referred to as *Source LM*).

2. The probability of the machine translated sentence given a language model built on unanno-

[5]https://cloud.google.com/translate/

	# reviews	
	en	de
coffee machine	75	108
cutlery	49	72
microwave	100	100
toaster	100	4
trash can	100	99
vacuum cleaner	51	140
washing machine	49	88
dish washer	98	0

Table 1: Frequencies of the corpus used in our experiments (Klinger and Cimiano, 2014).

tated text in the target language (measuring if the translation is typical, referred to as *Target LM*).

3. The likelihood that the alignment is correct, directly computed on the basis of the alignment probability (referred to as *Alignment*): $p(\mathbf{e} \mid \mathbf{f}) = \prod_{i=1^m} p(e_i \mid \mathbf{f}, m, n)$, where $\mathbf{e}$ and $\mathbf{f}$ are source and target sentences and m and n denote the sentence lengths (Dyer et al., 2013, Eq. 1f.).

For building the language models, we employ the toolkit SRILM (Stolcke, 2002; Stolcke et al., 2011). The likelihood for the alignment as well as the language model probability are normalized by the number of tokens in the sentence.

3 Experiments

3.1 Corpus and Setting

The proposed approach is evaluated on the language pair German/English in both directions (projecting German annotations into an automatically generated English corpus and testing on English annotations and vice versa). As a resource, we use the recently published USAGE corpus (Klinger and Cimiano, 2014), which consists of 622 English and 611 German product reviews from http://www.amazon.com/ and http://www.amazon.de/, respectively. The reviews are on coffee machines, cutlery sets, microwaves, toasters, trash cans, vacuum cleaners, washing machines, and dish washers. Frequencies of entries in the corpus are summarized in Table 1. Each review has been annotated by two annotators. We take into account the data generated by the first annotator in this work to avoid the design of an aggregation procedure. The corpus is unbalanced between the product classes. The average numbers of annotated aspects in each review in the German corpus (10.4) is smaller than in English (13.7). The average number of subjective phrases is more similar with 8.6 and 8.3, respectively. The total number of aspects is 8545 for English and 6340 in German, the number of subjective phrases is 5321 and 5086, respectively.

The experiments are performed in a leave-one-domain-out setting, *e. g.*, testing on coffee machine reviews is based on a model trained on all other products except coffee machines. This holds for the cross-language and the in-target-language training results and leads therefore to comparable settings. We use exact match precision, recall and F_1-measure for evaluation. However, it should be noted that partial matching scores are also commonly applied in fine-grained sentiment analysis due to the fact that boundaries of annotations can differ substantially between annotators. For simplicity, we limit ourselves to the more strict evaluation measure.

The language models are trained on 7,413,774 German and 9,650,633 English sentences sampled from Amazon product reviews concerning the product categories in the USAGE corpus. The FastAlign model is trained on the EuroParl corpus and the automatically translated USAGE corpus in both directions (German translated to English and English translated to German).

3.2 Results

We evaluate and compare the impact of the three automatic quality estimation methods and compare them to a manual sentence-based judgement for the language projection from German to English (testing on English). The manual judgement was performed by assigning values ranging from 0 (not understandable), over 1 and 2 (slightly understandable) to 8 (some flaws in translation), 9 (minor flaws in translation) to 10 (perfect translation).[6]

Figure 2 shows the results for all four methods (including manual quality assessment) from German to English for the product category of coffee machines compared to in-target-language training results. The x-axis corresponds to different values for the filtering threshold. Thus, when increasing the threshold, the number of sentences used for training decreases. For all quality estimation meth-

[6]This annotated data is available at http://www.romanklinger.de/translation-quality-review-corpus

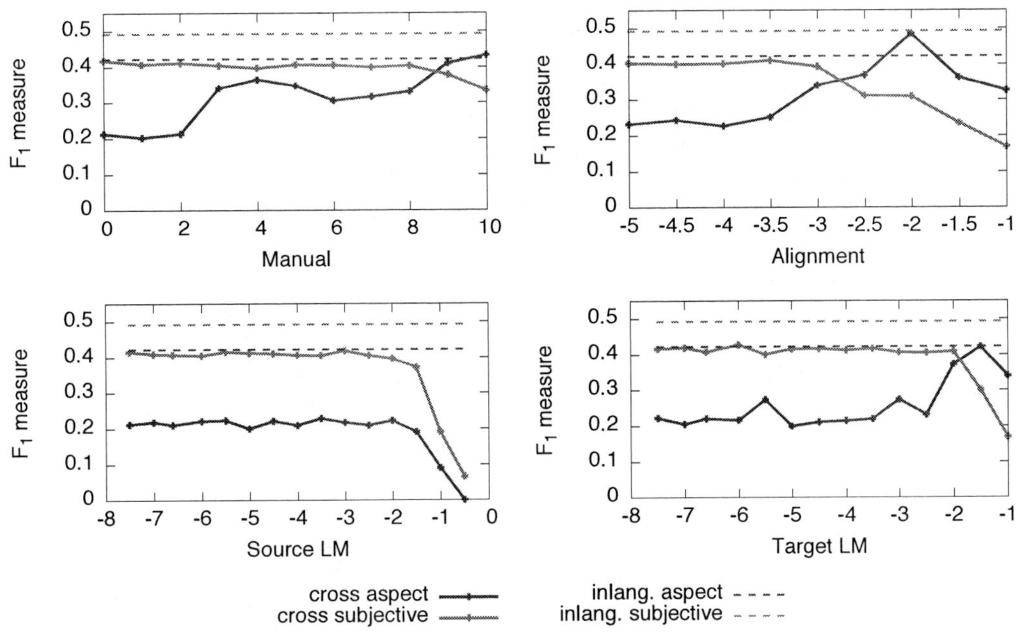

Figure 2: Complete results for the reviews for coffee machines for the projection direction German to English.

ods except for the language model for the source language, the performance on the target language increases significantly for the prediction of aspect phrases. The English in-target-language training performance represents an upper baseline, resulting from training the system on manually annotated data for the target language ($F_1 = 0.42$). Without any instance filtering, relying on all automatically produced translations to induce projected annotations for the target language, an F_1 measure of 0.21 is reached. With filtering based on the manually assigned translation quality estimation, a result of $F_1 = 0.43$ is reached. Using the alignment as quality score for filtering, the best result obtained is $F_1 = 0.48$. However, results start decreasing from this threshold value on, which is likely due to the fact that the positive effect of instance filtering is outweighed by the performance drop due to training with a smaller dataset. The filtering based on the target language model leads to $F_1 = 0.42$, while the source language model cannot filter the training instances such that the performance increases over the initial value.

Surprisingly, instance filtering has no impact on the detection of subjective phrases. Without any filtering, for the prediction of subjective phrases we get an F_1 of 0.42, which is close to the performance of in-target-language training of $F_1 = 0.49$. For the case of phrase detection, the difference between training with all data (21%) and in-target-language training (42%) is considerably higher. Decreasing the size of the training set by filtering only decreases the F_1 measure.

Figure 3 shows the macro-average results summarizing the different domains in precision, recall and F_1 measure. The thresholds for the filtering have been fixed to the best result of the product coffee machine for all products. The manual quality estimation as well as the alignment and target language model lead to comparable (or superior) results compared to target language training for aspect detection. This holds for nearly all product domains, only for trash cans and cutlery the performance achieved by filtering is slightly lower for the direction German-to-English. The initial performance for the whole data set is on average higher for the projection direction English to German; therefore the values for the source language model are comparably higher than for the other projection direction.

For the aspect detection, all filtering methods except using the source language model lead to an improvement over the baseline (without filtering) that is significant according to a Welch t-test ($\alpha =$

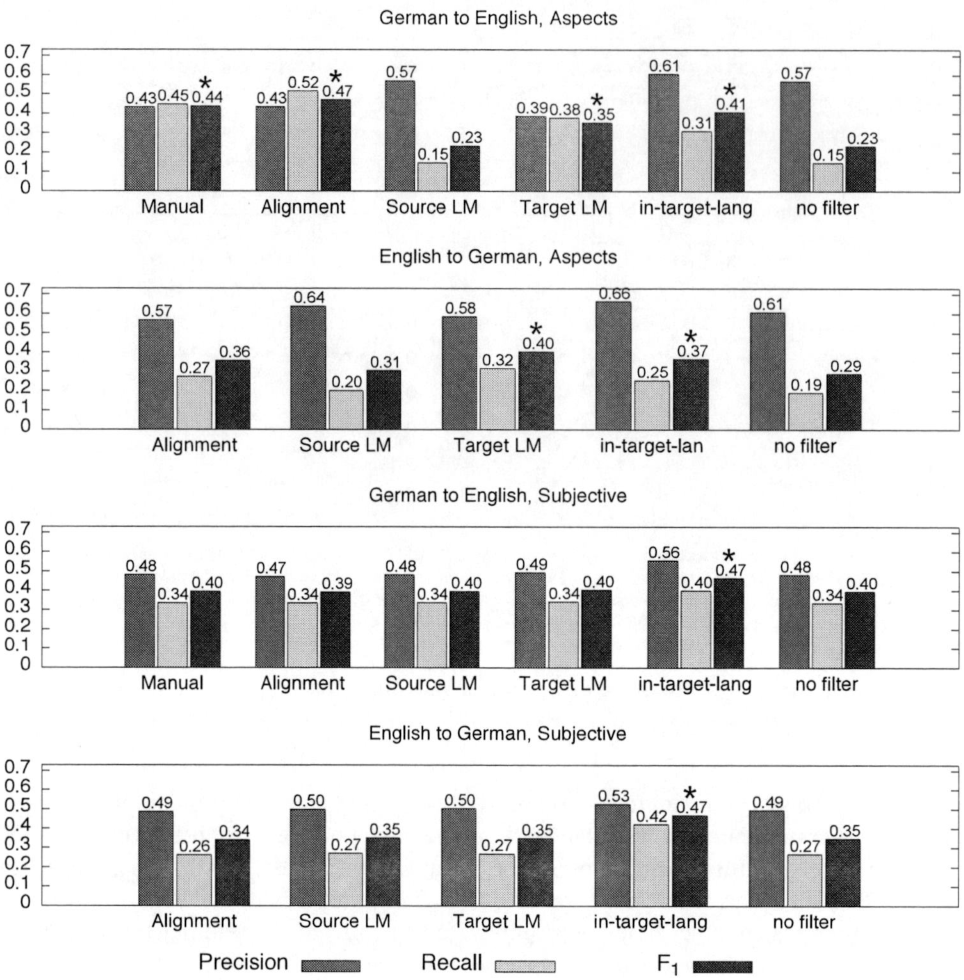

Figure 3: Macro-average results of cross-language training over the different domains showing precision, recall and F_1 measure. Significant differences of the F_1 results to the no-filter-baseline are marked with a star (Welch t-test comparing the different separate domain results, $p < 0.05$).

0.05). For English to German, in-target-language training and the target language model filtering provide improved results over the baseline that are significant. For subjective phrase detection, the in-language training is significantly better than the baseline.

It is notable that in all experiments the model's performance without filtering is mainly limited in recall, which drops the performance in F_1. Instance filtering therefore has mainly an effect on the recall.

3.3 Discussion

Our results show that an approach based on automatic training data projection across languages is feasible and provides competitive results compared to training on manually annotated target language data. We have in particular quantified the loss of performance of such an automatic approach compared to using a system trained on manually annotated data in the target language. We have shown that the performance of aspect detection of a system using all available projected training data yields a drop of $\approx 50\,\%$ in F_1-measure compared to a model trained using manually annotated data in the target language. The instance filtering approaches in which only the sentences with highest quality are selected to project training data to the target language using a threshold has a significant positive impact on the performance of a model trained on automatically projected training data when predicting aspect phrases on the target language, increasing results from 23 % to 47 % on average. Our approach relying on instance filtering comes close to results produced by a system trained on manually annotated data for the target language on the task of predicting aspect phrases.

In contrast to these results for the aspect phrase recognition, the impact of filtering training instances is negligible for the detection of subjective phrases. The highest performance is achieved with the full set of training instances. Therefore, it may be concluded that for aspect name detection, high quality training is crucial. For subjective phrase detection, a greater training set is crucial. In contrast to aspect recognition, the drop in subjective phrase recognition performance is comparatively low when training on all instances.

Filtering translations by manually provided translation scores (as an upper baseline for the filtering) yields comparable results to using the alignment and the language model on the target language. Using the language model on the source language for filtering does not lead to any improvement. Predicting the quality of translation relying on the probability of the source sentence via a source language model therefore seems not to be a viable approach on the task in question. Using the target language model as a filter leads to the most consistent results and is therefore to be preferred over the source language model and the alignment score.

Including more presumably noisy instances by using a smaller filtering threshold leads to a decreased recall throughout all methods in aspect detection and to a lesser extent for subjective phrase detection. The precision is affected to a smaller degree. This can as well be observed in the number of predictions the models based on different thresholds generate: While the number of true positive aspects for the coffee machine subdomain is 1100, only 221 are predicted with a threshold of the manual quality assignment of 0. However, a treshold of 9 leads to 560 predictions and a threshold of 10 to 1291. This effect can be observed for subjective phrases as well. It increases from 465 to 827 while the gold number is 676. These observations hold for all filtering methods analogously.

4 Related Work

In-target-language training approaches for fine-grained sentiment analysis include those targeting the extraction of phrases or modelling it as text classification (Choi et al., 2010; Johansson and Moschitti, 2011; Yang and Cardie, 2012; Hu and Liu, 2004; Li et al., 2010; Popescu and Etzioni, 2005; Jakob and Gurevych, 2010b). Such models are typically trained or optimized on manually annotated data (Klinger and Cimiano, 2013; Yang and Cardie, 2012; Jakob and Gurevych, 2010a; Zhang et al., 2011). The necessary data, at least containing fine-grained annotations for aspects and subjective phrases instead of only an overall polarity score, are mainly available for the English language to a sufficient extent. Popular corpora used for training are for instance the J.D. Power and Associates Sentiment Corpora (Kessler et al., 2010) or the MPQA corpora (Wilson and Wiebe, 2005).

Non-English resources are scarce. Examples are a YouTube corpus consisting of English and Italian comments (Uryupina et al., 2014), a not publicly available German Amazon review corpus of 270 sentences (Boland et al., 2013), in addition to the USAGE corpus (Klinger and Cimiano, 2014) we have used in this work, consisting of German and English reviews. The (non-fine-grained annotated) Spanish TASS corpus consists of Twitter messages (Saralegi and Vicente, 2012). The "Multilingual Subjectivity Analysis Gold Standard Data Set" focuses on subjectivity in the news domain (Balahur and Steinberger, 2009). A Chinese corpus annotated at the aspect and subjective phrase level is described by Zhao et al. (2014).

There has not been too much work on approaches to transfer a model either directly or via annotation projection in the area of sentiment analysis. One example is based on sentence level annotations which are automatically translated to yield a resource in another language. This approach has been proven to work well across several languages (Banea et al., 2010; Mihalcea et al., 2007; Balahur and Turchi, 2014). Recent work approached multilingual opinion mining on the above-mentioned multi-lingual Youtube corpus with tree kernels predicting the polarity of a comment and whether it concerns the product or the video in which the product is featured. (Severyn et al., 2015). Brooke et al. (2009) compare dictionary and classification transfer from English to Spanish in a similar classification setting.

While cross-lingual annotation projection has been investigated in the context of polarity computation, we are only aware of two approaches exploiting cross-lingual annotation projection on the task of identifying aspects specifically with an evaluation on manually annotated data in more than one language. The CLOpinionMiner (Zhou et al., 2015) uses an English data set which is transfered to Chinese. Models are further improved by co-training. Xu et al. (2013) perform self-training based on a projected corpus from English to Chinese to detect opinion holders. Due to the lack of existing manually annotated resources, to our knowledge no cross-language projection approach for fine-grained annotation at the level of aspect and subjective phrases has been proposed before.

The projection of annotated data sets has been investigated in a variety of applications. Early work includes an approach to the projection of part-of-speech tags and noun phrases (Yarowsky et al., 2001; Yarowsky and Ngai, 2001) and parsing information (Hwa et al., 2005) on a parallel corpus. Especially in syntactic and semantic parsing, heuristics to remove or correct spuriously projected annotations have been developed (Padó and Lapata, 2009; Agić et al., 2014). It is typical for these approaches to be applied on existing parallel corpora (one counter example is the work by Basili et al. (2009) who perform postprocessing of machine translated resources to improve the annotation for training semantic role labeling models). In cases in which no such parallel resources are available containing pertinent annotations, models can be transfered after training. Early work includes a cross-lingual parser adaption (Zeman and Resnik, 2008). A recent example is the projection of a metaphor detection model using a bilingual dictionary (Tsvetkov et al., 2014). A combination of model transfer and annotation projection for dependency parsing has been proposed by Kozhevnikov and Titov (2014).

To improve quality of the overall corpus of projected annotations, the selection of data points for dependency parsing has been studied (Søgaard, 2011). Similarly, Axelrod et al. (2011) improve the average quality of machine translation systems by selection of promising training examples and show that such a selection approach has a positive impact. Related to the latter, a generic instance weighting scheme has been proposed for domain adaptation (Jiang and Zhai, 2007).

Other work has attempted to exploit information available in multiple languages to induce a model for a language for which sufficient training data is not available. For instance, universal tag sets take advantage of annotations that are aligned across languages (Snyder et al., 2008). Delexicalization allows for applying a model to other languages (McDonald et al., 2011).

Focusing on cross-lingual sentiment analysis, joint training of classification models on multiple languages shows an improvement over separated models. Balahur and Turchi (2014) analyzed the impact of using different machine translation approaches in such settings. Differences in sentiment expressions have been analyzed between English and Dutch (Bal et al., 2011). Co-training with non-annotated corpora has been shown to yield good results for Chinese (Wan, 2009). Ghorbel (2012) analyzed the impact of automatic translation on sentiment analysis.

Finally, SentiWordNet has been used for multilingual sentiment analysis (Denecke, 2008). Building dictionaries for languages with scarce resources can be supported by bootstrapping approaches (Banea et al., 2008).

Estimating the quality of machine translation can be understood as a ranking problem and thus be modeled as regression or classification. An important research focus is on investigating the impact of different features on predicting translation quality. For instance, sentence length, the output probability, number of unknown words of a target language as well as parsing-based features have been used (Avramidis et al., 2011). The alignment context can also be taken into account (Bach et al., 2011). An overview on confidence measures for machine translation is for instance provided by Ueffing et al. (2003). The impact of different features has been analyzed by Shah et al. (2013). A complete system and framework for quality estimation (including a list of possible features) is QuEst (Specia et al., 2013).

For an overview of other cross-lingual applications and methods, we refer to Bikel and Zitouni (2012).

5 Conclusion and Future Work

We have presented an approach that alleviates the need of training data for a target language when adapting a fine-grained sentiment analysis system to a new language. Our approach relies on training data available for a source language and on automatic machine translation, in particular statistical methods, to project training data to the target language, thus creating a training corpus on which a supervised sentiment analysis approach can be trained on. We have in particular shown that our results are competitive to training with manually annotated data in the target language, both for the prediction of aspect phrases as well as subjective phrases. We have further shown that performance for aspect detection can be almost doubled by estimating the quality of translations and selecting only the translations with highest quality for training. Such an effect cannot be observed in the prediction of subjective phrases, which nevertheless delivers results comparable to training using target language data using all automatically projected training data. Predicting translation quality by both the alignment probability and the target language model probability have been shown to deliver good results, while an approach exploiting source language model probability does not perform well.

Our hypothesis for the failure of translation filtering for the prediction of subjective phrases is that translation quality for subjective phrases is generally higher as their coverage in standard parallel corpora is reasonable and they are often domain-independent. A further possible explanation is that subjective phrases have a more complex structure (for instance, their average length is 2.38 tokens in English and 2.57 tokens in German, while the aspect length is 1.6 and 1.3, respectively). Therefore, translation as well as filtering might be more challenging. These hypotheses should be verified and investigated further in future work.

Further work should also be devoted to the investigation of other quality estimation procedures, in particular combinations of those investigated in this paper. Preliminary experiments have shown that the correlation between the filters incorporated in this paper is low. Thus, their combination could indeed have an additional impact. Similarly, the projection quality can be affected by the translation itself and by the alignment. These two aspects should be analyzed separately.

In addition, instead of Boolean filtering (using an instance or not), weighting the impact of the instance in the learning procedure might be beneficial as lower-quality instances can still be taken into account, although with a lower impact proportional to their corresponding score or probability.

In addition to the presented approach of projecting annotations, a comparison to directly transferring a trained model across languages would allow for a deeper understanding of the processes involved. Finally, it is an important and promising step to apply the presented methods on other languages.

Acknowledgments

We thank Nils Reiter, John McCrae, and Matthias Hartung for fruitful discussions. Thanks to Lucia Specia for her comments on quality estimation methods in our work. We thank Chris Dyer for his help with FastAlign. Thanks to the anonymous reviewers for their comments. This research was partially supported by the "It's OWL" project ("Intelligent Technical Systems Ostwestfalen-Lippe", http://www.its-owl.de/), a leading-edge cluster of the German Ministry of Education and Research and by the Cluster of Excellence Cognitive Interaction Technology 'CITEC' (EXC 277) at Bielefeld University, which is funded by the German Research Foundation (DFG).

References

Željko Agić, Jörg Tiedemann, Danijela Merkler, Simon Krek, Kaja Dobrovoljc, and Sara Moze. 2014. Cross-lingual dependency parsing of related languages with rich morphosyntactic tagsets. In *Workshop on Language Technology for Closely Related Languages and Language Variants, EMNLP.*

Eleftherios Avramidis, Maja Popović, David Vilar, and Aljoscha Burchardt. 2011. Evaluate with confidence estimation: Machine ranking of translation outputs using grammatical features. In *Workshop on Statistical Machine Translation, ACL.*

Amittai Axelrod, Xiaodong He, and Jianfeng Gao. 2011. Domain adaptation via pseudo in-domain data selection. In *EMNLP.*

Nguyen Bach, Fei Huang, and Yaser Al-Onaizan. 2011. Goodness: A method for measuring machine translation confidence. In *ACL-HLT.*

Daniella Bal, Malissa Bal, Arthur van Bunningen, Alexander Hogenboom, Frederik Hogenboom, and Flavius Frasincar. 2011. Sentiment analysis with a multilingual pipeline. In *Web Information System Engineering WISE 2011.*

Alexandra Balahur and Ralf Steinberger. 2009. Rethinking sentiment analysis in the news: from theory to practice and back. In *Proceeding of Workshop on Opinion Mining and Sentiment Analysis (WOMSA).*

Alexandra Balahur and Marco Turchi. 2014. Comparative experiments using supervised learning and machine translation for multilingual sentiment analysis. *Computer Speech & Language*, 28(1).

Carmen Banea, Rada Mihalcea, and Janyce Wiebe. 2008. A bootstrapping method for building subjectivity lexicons for languages with scarce resources. In *LREC*.

Carmen Banea, Rada Mihalcea, and Janyce Wiebe. 2010. Multilingual subjectivity: Are more languages better? In *COLING*.

Roberto Basili, Diego De Cao, Danilo Croce, Bonaventura Coppola, and Alessandro Moschitti. 2009. Cross-language frame semantics transfer in bilingual corpora. In *CICLING*, volume 5449 of *Lecture Notes in Computer Science*. Springer Berlin Heidelberg.

Daniel Bikel and Imed Zitouni, editors. 2012. *Multilingual Natural Language Processing Applications: From Theory to Practice*. IBM Press, 1st edition.

Katarina Boland, Andias Wira-Alam, and Reinhard Messerschmidt. 2013. Creating an annotated corpus for sentiment analysis of german product reviews. Technical Report 2013/05, GESIS Institute.

Julian Brooke, Milan Tofiloski, and Maite Taboada. 2009. Cross-linguistic sentiment analysis: From english to spanish. In *RANLP*, Borovets, Bulgaria, September. Association for Computational Linguistics.

Yoonjung Choi, Seongchan Kim, and Sung-Hyon Myaeng. 2010. Detecting Opinions and their Opinion Targets in NTCIR-8. In *NTCIR8*.

Kerstin Denecke. 2008. Using sentiwordnet for multilingual sentiment analysis. In *ICDEW*.

Chris Dyer, Victor Chahuneau, and Noah A. Smith. 2013. A simple, fast, and effective reparameterization of ibm model 2. In *NAACL*.

Hatem Ghorbel. 2012. Experiments in cross-lingual sentiment analysis in discussion forums. In Karl Aberer, Andreas Flache, Wander Jager, Ling Liu, Jie Tang, and Christophe Guret, editors, *Social Informatics*, volume 7710 of *Lecture Notes in Computer Science*. Springer Berlin Heidelberg.

Minqing Hu and Bing Liu. 2004. Mining and summarizing customer reviews. In *ACM SIGKDD*.

Rebecca Hwa, Philip Resnik, Amy Weinberg, Clara Cabezas, and Okan Kolak. 2005. Bootstrapping parsers via syntactic projection across parallel texts. *Nat. Lang. Eng.*, 11(3), September.

Niklas Jakob and Iryna Gurevych. 2010a. Extracting opinion targets in a single- and cross-domain setting with conditional random fields. In *EMNLP*.

Niklas Jakob and Iryna Gurevych. 2010b. Using anaphora resolution to improve opinion target identification in movie reviews. In *ACL*.

Jing Jiang and ChengXiang Zhai. 2007. Instance weighting for domain adaptation in nlp. In *ACL*.

Richard Johansson and Alessandro Moschitti. 2011. Extracting opinion expressions and their polarities: exploration of pipelines and joint models. In *ACL-HLT*.

Jason S. Kessler, Miriam Eckert, Lyndsie Clark, and Nicolas Nicolov. 2010. The 2010 ICWSM JDPA Sentment Corpus for the Automotive Domain. In *Proc. od the 4th International AAAI Conference on Weblogs and Social Media Data Workshop Challenge (ICWSM-DWC 2010)*.

Roman Klinger and Philipp Cimiano. 2013. Bi-directional inter-dependencies of subjective expressions and targets and their value for a joint model. In *ACL*.

Roman Klinger and Philipp Cimiano. 2014. The usage review corpus for fine grained multi lingual opinion analysis. In *LREC*.

Philipp Koehn. 2005. Europarl: A Parallel Corpus for Statistical Machine Translation. In *Conference Proceedings: the tenth Machine Translation Summit*. AAMT.

Philipp Koehn. 2010. *Statistical Machine Translation*. Cambridge University Press, New York, NY, USA, 1st edition.

Mikhail Kozhevnikov and Ivan Titov. 2014. Cross-lingual model transfer using feature representation projection. In *ACL*.

Fangtao Li, Minlie Huang, and Xiaoyan Zhu. 2010. Sentiment analysis with global topics and local dependency. In *AAAI*.

Andrew McCallum, Karl Schultz, and Sameer Singh. 2009. FACTORIE: Probabilistic programming via imperatively defined factor graphs. In *NIPS*.

Ryan McDonald, Slav Petrov, and Keith Hall. 2011. Multi-source transfer of delexicalized dependency parsers. In *EMNLP*.

Rada Mihalcea, Carmen Banea, and Janyce Wiebe. 2007. Learning multilingual subjective language via cross-lingual projections. In *ACL*.

Sebastian Padó and Mirella Lapata. 2009. Cross-lingual annotation projection for semantic roles. *Journal of Artificial Intelligence Research (JAIR)*, 36.

Ana-Maria Popescu and Oren Etzioni. 2005. Extracting product features and opinions from reviews. In *HLT-EMNLP*.

Xabier Saralegi and Iñaki San Vicente. 2012. Tass: Detecting sentiments in spanish tweets. In *Workshop on Sentiment Analisis at SEPLN (TASS)*. SEPLN, 09/2012.

Sunita Sarawagi and William W. Cohen. 2004. Semi-markov conditional random fields for information extraction. In *NIPS*.

Aliaksei Severyn, , Alessandro Moschitti, Olga Uryupina, Barbara Plank, and Katja Filippova. 2015. Multi-lingual opinion mining on youtube. *Information Processing and Management.* in press.

Kashif Shah and Lucia Specia. 2014. Quality estimation for translation selection. In *Conference of the European Association for Machine Translation*, EAMT, Dubrovnik, Croatia.

Kashif Shah, Trevor Cohn, and Lucia Specia. 2013. An investigation on the effectiveness of features for translation quality estimation. In *Machine Translation Summit XIV*.

Benjamin Snyder, Tahira Naseem, Jacob Eisenstein, and Regina Barzilay. 2008. Unsupervised multilingual learning for POS tagging. In *EMNLP*.

Anders Søgaard. 2011. Data point selection for cross-language adaptation of dependency parsers. In *ACL-HLT*.

Lucia Specia, Kashif Shah, Jose G.C. de Souza, and Trevor Cohn. 2013. Quest - a translation quality estimation framework. In *ACL*.

Andreas Stolcke, Jing Zheng, Wen Wang, and Victor Abrash. 2011. SRILM at sixteen: Update and outlook. In *Proceedings IEEE Automatic Speech Recognition and Understanding Workshop*.

Andreas Stolcke. 2002. Srilm-an extensible language modeling toolkit. In *Proceedings International Conference on Spoken Language Processing*.

Yulia Tsvetkov, Leonid Boytsov, Anatole Gershman, Eric Nyberg, and Chris Dyer. 2014. Metaphor detection with cross-lingual model transfer. In *ACL*.

Nicola Ueffing, Klaus Macherey, and Hermann Ney. 2003. Confidence measures for statistical machine translation. In *In Proc. MT Summit IX*.

Olga Uryupina, Barbara Plank, Aliaksei Severyn, Agata Rotondi, and Alessandro Moschitti. 2014. Sentube: A corpus for sentiment analysis on youtube social media. In *LREC*.

Xiaojun Wan. 2009. Co-training for cross-lingual sentiment classification. In Keh-Yih Su, Jian Su, and Janyce Wiebe, editors, *ACL/IJCNLP*.

M. Wick, K. Rohanimanesh, K. Bellare, A. Culotta, and A. McCallum. 2011. SampleRank: Training factor graphs with atomic gradients. In *ICML*.

Theresa Wilson and Janyce Wiebe. 2005. Annotating attributions and private states. In *CorpusAnno, ACL*.

Ruifeng Xu, Lin Gui, Jun Xu, Qin Lu, and Kam-Fai Wong. 2013. Cross lingual opinion holder extraction based on multi-kernel svms and transfer learning. *World Wide Web Journal*.

Bishan Yang and Claire Cardie. 2012. Extracting opinion expressions with semi-markov conditional random fields. In *EMNLP-CoNLL*.

David Yarowsky and Grace Ngai. 2001. Inducing multilingual pos taggers and np bracketers via robust projection across aligned corpora. In *NAACL*.

David Yarowsky, Grace Ngai, and Richard Wicentowski. 2001. Inducing multilingual text analysis tools via robust projection across aligned corpora. In *HLT*.

Daniel Zeman and Philip Resnik. 2008. Cross-language parser adaptation between related languages. In *IJCNLP-08 Workshop on NLP for Less Privileged Languages*.

Qi Zhang, Yuanbin Wu, Yan Wu, and Xuanjing Huang. 2011. Opinion mining with sentiment graph. In *Proceedings of the 2011 IEEE/WIC/ACM International Conferences on Web Intelligence and Intelligent Agent Technology - Volume 01*.

Y. Zhao, B. Qin, and T. Liu. 2014. Creating a fine-grained corpus for chinese sentiment analysis. *Intelligent Systems, IEEE*, PP(99).

Xinjie Zhou, Xiaojun Wan, and Jianguo Xiao. 2015. Clopinionminer: Opinion target extraction in a cross-language scenario. *IEEE/ACM Transactions on Audio, Speech & Language Processing*, 23(4).

Labeled Morphological Segmentation with Semi-Markov Models

Ryan Cotterell[1,2] **Thomas Müller**[2]
Department of Computer Science[1]
Johns Hopkins University, USA
ryan.cotterell@jhu.edu

Alexander Fraser[2] **Hinrich Schütze**[2]
Center for Information and Language Processing[2]
University of Munich, Germany
muellets@cis.lmu.de

Abstract

We present labeled morphological segmentation—an alternative view of morphological processing that unifies several tasks. We introduce a new hierarchy of morphotactic tagsets and CHIPMUNK, a discriminative morphological segmentation system that, contrary to previous work, explicitly models morphotactics. We show improved performance on three tasks for all six languages: (i) morphological segmentation, (ii) stemming and (iii) morphological tag classification. For morphological segmentation our method shows absolute improvements of 2-6 points F_1 over a strong baseline.

1 Introduction

Morphological processing is often an overlooked problem since many well-studied languages (e.g., Chinese and English) are morphologically impoverished. But for languages with complex morphology (e.g., Finnish and Turkish) morphological processing is essential. A specific form of morphological processing, morphological segmentation, has shown its utility for machine translation (Dyer et al., 2008), sentiment analysis (Abdul-Mageed et al., 2014), bilingual word alignment (Eyigöz et al., 2013), speech processing (Creutz et al., 2007b) and keyword spotting (Narasimhan et al., 2014), inter alia. We advance the state-of-the-art in supervised morphological segmentation by describing a high-performance, data-driven tool for handling complex morphology, even in low-resource settings.

In this work, we make the distinction between *unlabeled morphological segmentation* (*UMS*) (often just called "morphological segmentation") and *labeled morphological segmentation* (LMS). The labels in our supervised discriminative model for LMS capture the distinctions between different types of morphemes and directly model the morphotactics. We further create a hierarchical universal tagset for labeling morphemes, with different levels appropriate for different tasks. Our hierarchical tagset was designed by creating a standard representation from heterogeneous resources for six languages. This allows us to use a *single unified framework* to obtain strong performance on three common morphological tasks that have typically been viewed as *separate problems* and addressed using *different methods*. We give an overview of the tasks addressed in this paper in Figure 1. The figure shows the expected output for the Turkish word *gençleşmelerin* 'of rejuvenatings'. In particular, it shows the full labeled morphological segmentation, from which three representations can be directly derived: the unlabeled morphological segmentation, the stem/root [1] and the structured morphological tag containing POS and inflectional features.

We model these tasks with CHIPMUNK, a semi-Markov conditional random field (semi-CRF) (Sarawagi and Cohen, 2004), a model that is well-suited for morphology. We provide a robust evaluation and analysis on six languages and CHIPMUNK yields strong results on all three tasks, including state-of-the-art accuracy on morphological segmentation.

Section 2 presents our LMS framework and the morphotactic tagsets we use, i.e., the labels of the sequence prediction task CHIPMUNK solves. Section 3 introduces our semi-CRF model. Section 4 presents our novel features. Section 5 compares CHIPMUNK to previous work. Section 6 presents experiments on the three complementary tasks of segmentation (UMS), stemming, and morpholog-

[1]Terminological notes: We use *root* to refer to a morpheme with concrete meaning, *stem* to refer to the concatenation of all roots and derivational affixes, *root detection* to refer to stripping both derivational *and* inflectional affixes, and *stemming* to refer to stripping only inflectional affixes.

Proceedings of the 19th Conference on Computational Language Learning, pages 164–174,
Beijing, China, July 30-31, 2015.

gençleşmelerin					
UMS	genç	leş	me	ler	in
Gloss	young	-ate	-ion	-s	GENITIVE MARKER
LMS	genç ROOT:ADJECTIVAL	leş SUFFIX:DERIV:VERB	me SUFFIX:DERIV:NOUN	ler SUFFIX:INFL:NOUN:PLURAL	in SUFFIX:INFL:NOUN:GENITIVE
Root	genç	**Stem**	gençleşme	**Morphological Tag**	PLURAL:GENITIVE

Figure 1: Examples of the tasks addressed for the Turkish word *gençleşmelerin* 'of rejuvenatings': Traditional unlabeled segmentation (UMS), Labeled morphological segmentation (LMS), stemming / root detection and (inflectional) morphological tag classification. The morphotactic annotations produced by LMS allow us to solve these tasks using a single model.

ical tag classification. Section 7 briefly discusses finite-state morphology. Section 8 concludes.

The datasets created in this work, additional description of our novel tagsets and CHIPMUNK can be found at `http://cistern.cis.lmu.de/chipmunk`.

2 Labeled Segmentation and Tagset

We define the framework of *labeled morphological segmentation* (LMS), an enhancement of morphological segmentation that—in addition to identifying the boundaries of segments—*assigns a fine-grained morphotactic tag to each segment*. LMS leads to both better modeling of segmentation and subsumes several other tasks, e.g., stemming.

Most previous approaches to morphological segmentation are either unlabeled or use a small, coarse-grained set such as prefix, root, suffix. In contrast, our labels are fine-grained. This finer granularity has two advantages. (i) The labels are needed for many tasks, for instance in sentiment analysis detecting morphologically encoded negation, as in Turkish, is crucial. In other words, for many applications UMS is insufficient. (ii) The LMS framework allows us to learn a probabilistic model of morphotactics. Working with LMS results in higher UMS accuracy. So even in applications that only need segments and no labels, LMS is beneficial. Note that the concatenation of labels *across* segments yields a bundle of morphological attributes similar to those found in the CoNLL datasets often used to train morphological taggers (Buchholz and Marsi, 2006)—thus LMS helps to unify UMS and morphological tagging. We believe that LMS is a needed extension of current work in morphological segmentation. Our framework concisely allows the model to capture interdependencies among various morphemes and model relations between entire morpheme classes—a neglected aspect of the problem.

We first create a hierarchical tagset with increasing granularity, which we created by analyzing the heterogeneous resources for the six languages we work on. The optimal level of granularity is task and language dependent: the level is a trade-off between simplicity and expressivity. We illustrate our tagset with the decomposition of the German word *Enteisungen* 'defrostings' (Figure 2).

The level 0 tagset involves a single tag indicating a segment. It ignores morphotactics completely and is similar to previous work. The level 1 tagset crudely approximates morphotactics: it consists of the tags {PREFIX, ROOT, SUFFIX}. This scheme has been successfully used by unsupervised segmenters, e.g., MORFESSOR CAT-MAP (Creutz et al., 2007a). It allows the model to learn simple morphotactics, for instance that a prefix cannot be followed by a suffix. This makes a decomposition like *reed* → *re+ed* unlikely. We also add an additional UNKNOWN tag for morphemes that do not fit into this scheme. The level 2 tagset splits affixes into DERIVATIONAL and INFLECTIONAL, effectively increasing the maximal tagset size from 4 to 6. These tags can encode that many languages allow for transitions from derivational to inflectional endings, but rarely the opposite. This makes the incorrect decomposition of German *Offenheit* 'openness' into *Off*, inflectional *en* and derivational *heit* unlikely[2]. This tagset is also useful for building statistical stemmers. The level 3 tagset adds POS, i.e., whether a root is VERBAL, NOMINAL or ADJECTIVAL, and the POS of the word that an affix derives. The level 4 tagset includes the inflectional feature a suffix adds, e.g., CASE or NUMBER. This is helpful for certain agglutinative languages, in which,

[2]Like *en* in English *open*, *en* in German *Offen* is part of the root.

5	PREFIX:DERIV:VERB	ROOT:NOUN	SUFFIX:DERIV:NOUN	SUFFIX:INFL:NOUN:PLURAL
4	PREFIX:DERIV:VERB	ROOT:NOUN	SUFFIX:DERIV:NOUN	SUFFIX:INFL:NOUN:NUMBER
3	PREFIX:DERIV:VERB	ROOT:NOUN	SUFFIX:DERIV:NOUN	SUFFIX:INFL:NOUN
2	PREFIX:DERIV	ROOT	SUFFIX:DERIV	SUFFIX:INFL
1	PREFIX	ROOT	SUFFIX	SUFFIX
0	SEGMENT	SEGMENT	SEGMENT	SEGMENT
German	Ent	eis	ung	en
English	de	frost	ing	s

Figure 2: Example of the different morphotactic tagset granularities for German *Enteisungen* 'defrostings'.

level:	0	1	2	3	4
English	1	4	5	13	16
Finnish	1	4	6	14	17
German	1	4	6	13	17
Indonesian	1	4	4	8	8
Turkish	1	3	4	10	20
Zulu	1	4	6	14	17

Table 1: Morphotactic tagset size at each level of granularity.

e.g., CASE must follow NUMBER. The level 5 tagset adds the actual value of the inflectional feature, e.g., PLURAL, and corresponds to the annotation in the datasets. In preliminary experiments we found that the level 5 tagset is too rich and does not yield consistent improvements, we thus do not explore it. Table 1 shows tagset sizes for the six languages.[3]

3 Model

CHIPMUNK is a supervised model implemented using the well-understood semi-Markov conditional random field (semi-CRF) (Sarawagi and Cohen, 2004) that naturally fits the task of LMS. Semi-CRFs generalize linear-chain CRFs and model segmentation jointly with sequence labeling. Just as linear-chain CRFs are discriminative adaptations of *hidden Markov models* (Lafferty et al., 2001), semi-CRFs are an analogous adaptation of *hidden semi-Markov models* (Murphy, 2002). Semi-CRFs allow us to elegantly integrate new features that look at complete segments, this is not possible with CRFs, making semi-CRFs a natural choice for morphology.

A semi-CRF represents $\boldsymbol{w}$ (a word) as a sequence of segments $\boldsymbol{s} = \langle s_1, \ldots, s_n \rangle$, each of which is assigned a label ℓ_i. The concatenation of all segments equals $\boldsymbol{w}$. We seek a log-linear distribution $p_{\boldsymbol{\theta}}(\boldsymbol{s}, \boldsymbol{\ell} \mid \boldsymbol{w})$ over all possible segmentations and label sequences for $\boldsymbol{w}$, where $\boldsymbol{\theta}$ is the parameter vector. Note that we recover the standard CRF if we restrict the segment length to 1. Formally, we define $p_{\boldsymbol{\theta}}$ as

$$p_{\boldsymbol{\theta}}(\boldsymbol{s}, \boldsymbol{\ell} \mid \boldsymbol{w}) \stackrel{\text{def}}{=} \frac{1}{Z_{\boldsymbol{\theta}}(\boldsymbol{w})} \prod_i e^{\boldsymbol{\theta}^T \boldsymbol{f}(s_i, \ell_i, \ell_{i-1}, i)}, \quad (1)$$

where $\boldsymbol{f}$ is the feature function and $Z_{\boldsymbol{\theta}}(\boldsymbol{w})$ is the partition function. To keep the notation uncluttered, we will write $\boldsymbol{f}$ without all its arguments in the future. We use a generalization of the forward-backward algorithm for efficient gradient computation (Sarawagi and Cohen, 2004). Inspection of the semi-Markov forward recursion,

$$\boldsymbol{\alpha}(t, l) = \sum_i \sum_{\ell'} e^{\boldsymbol{\theta}^T \boldsymbol{f}} \cdot \boldsymbol{\alpha}(t - i, \ell'), \quad (2)$$

shows that algorithm runs in $\mathcal{O}(n^2 \cdot L^2)$ time where n is the length of the word $\boldsymbol{w}$ and L is the number of labels (size of the tagset).

We employ the maximum-likelihood criterion to estimate the parameters with L-BFGS (Liu and Nocedal, 1989), a gradient-based optimization algorithm. As in all exponential family models, the gradient of the log-likelihood takes the form of the difference between the observed and expected features counts (Wainwright and Jordan, 2008) and can be computed efficiently with the semi-Markov extension of the forward-backward algorithm. We use L_2 regularization with a regularization coefficient tuned during cross-validation.

We note that semi-Markov models have the potential to obviate typical errors made by standard Markovian sequence models with an IOB labeling scheme over characters. For instance, consider the incorrect segmentation of the English verb *sees* into *se+es*. These are reasonable split positions as many English stems end in *se* (e.g., consider *abuse-s*). Semi-CRFs have a major advantage here as they can have *segmental* features that allow them to learn *se* is not a good morph.

[3] As converting segmentation datasets to tagsets is not always straightforward, we include tags that lack some features, e.g., some level 4 German tags lack POS because our German data does not specify it.

	# Affixes	Random Examples
English	394	-ard -taxy -odon -en -otic -fold
Finnish	120	-tä -llä -ja -t -nen -hön -jä -ton
German	112	-nomie -lichenes -ell -en -yl -iv
Indonesian	5	-kau -an -nya -ku -mu
Turkish	263	-ten -suz -mek -den -t -ünüz
Zulu	72	i- u- za- tsh- mi- obu- olu-

Table 2: Sizes of the various affix gazetteers.

English	119,839
Finnish	6,690,417
German	364,564
Indonesian	35,269
Turkish	80,261
Zulu	73,525

Table 3: Number of words covered by the respective ASPELL dictionary

4 Features

We introduce several novel features for LMS. We exploit existing resources, e.g., spell checkers and Wiktionary, to create straightforward and effective features and we incorporate ideas from related areas: named-entity recognition (NER) and morphological tagging.

Affix Features and Gazetteers. In contrast to syntax and semantics, the morphology of a language is often simple to document and a list of the most common morphs can be found in any good grammar book. Wiktionary, for example, contains affix lists for all the six languages used in our experiments.[4] Providing a supervised learner with such a list is a great boon, just as gazetteer features aid NER (Smith and Osborne, 2006)—perhaps even more so since suffixes and prefixes are generally *closed-class*; hence these lists are likely to be comprehensive. These features are binary and fire if a given substring occurs in the gazetteer list. In this paper, we simply use suffix lists from English Wiktionary, except for Zulu, for which we use a prefix list, see Table 2.

We also include a feature that fires on the conjunction of tags and substrings observed in the training data. In the level 5 tagset this allows us to link all allomorphs of a given morpheme. In the lower level tagsets, this links related morphemes. Virpioja et al. (2010) explored this idea for unsupervised segmentation. Linking allomorphs together under a single tag helps combat sparsity in modeling the morphotactics.

Stem Features. A major problem in statistical segmentation is the reluctance to posit morphs not observed in training; this particularly affects roots, which are *open-class*. This makes it nearly impossible to correctly segment compounds that contain unseen roots, e.g., to correctly segment *homework* you need to know that *home* and *work* are independent English words. We solve this problem by incorporating spell-check features: binary features that fire if a segment is valid for a given spell checker. Spell-check features function effectively as a proxy for a "root detector". We use the open-source ASPELL dictionaries as they are freely available in 91 languages. Table 3 shows the coverage of these dictionaries.

Integrating the Features. Our model uses the features discussed in this section and additionally the simple n-gram context features of Ruokolainen et al. (2013). The n-gram features look at variable length substrings of the word on both the right and left side of each potential boundary. We create conjunctive features from the cross-product between the morphotactic tagset (Section 2) and the features.

5 Related Work

Van den Bosch and Daelemans (1999) and Marsi et al. (2005) present memory-based approaches to discriminative learning of morphological segmentation. This is the previous work most similar to our work. They address the problem of LMS. We distinguish our work from theirs in that we define a cross-lingual schema for defining a hierarchical tagset for LMS. Morever, we tackle the problem with a feature-rich log-linear model, allowing us to easily incorporate disparate sources of knowledge into a single framework, as we show in our extensive evaluation.

UMS has been mainly addressed by unsupervised algorithms. LINGUISTICA (Goldsmith, 2001) and MORFESSOR (Creutz and Lagus, 2002) are built around an idea of optimally encoding the data, in the sense of minimal description length (MDL). MORFESSOR CAT-MAP (Creutz et al., 2007a) formulates the model as sequence prediction based on HMMs over a morph dictionary and MAP estimation. The model also attempts to induce basic morphotactic categories (PREFIX, ROOT, SUFFIX). Kohonen et al. (2010a,b) and Grönroos et al. (2014) present variations of MORFESSOR for semi-supervised learning. Poon et

[4] A good example of such a resource is en.wiktionary.org/wiki/Category:Turkish_suffixes.

al. (2009) introduces a Bayesian state-space model with corpus-wide priors. The model resembles a semi-CRF, but dynamic programming is no longer possible due to the priors. They employ the three-state tagset of Creutz and Lagus (2004) (row 1 in Figure 2) for Arabic and Hebrew UMS. Their gradient and objective computation is based on an enumeration of a heuristically chosen subset of the exponentially many segmentations. This limits its applicability to language with complex *concatenative* morphology, e.g., Turkish and Finnish.

Ruokolainen et al. (2013) present an averaged perceptron (Collins, 2002), a discriminative structured prediction method, for UMS. The model outperforms the semi-supervised model of Poon et al. (2009) on Arabic and Hebrew morpheme segmentation as well as the semi-supervised model of Kohonen et al. (2010a) on English, Finnish and Turkish.

Finally, Ruokolainen et al. (2014) get further consistent improvements by using features extracted from large corpora, based on the letter successor variety (LSV) model (Harris, 1995) and on unsupervised segmentation models such as Morfessor CatMAP (Creutz et al., 2007a). The idea behind LSV is that for example *talking* should be split into *talk* and *ing*, because *talk* can also be followed by different letters then *i* such as *e* (talked) and *s* (talks).

Chinese word segmentation (CWS) is related to UMS. Andrew (2006) successfully apply semi-CRFs to CWS. The problem of joint CWS and POS tagging (Ng and Low, 2004; Zhang and Clark, 2008) is related to LMS. To our knowledge, joint CWS and POS tagging has not been addressed by a simple single semi-CRF, possibly because POS tagsets typically used in Chinese treebanks are much bigger than our morphotactic tagsets and the morphological poverty of Chinese makes higher-order models necessary and the direct application of semi-CRFs infeasible.

6 Experiments

We experimented on six languages from diverse language families. The segmentation data for English, Finnish and Turkish was taken from MorphoChallenge 2010 (Kurimo et al., 2010).[5] Despite typically being used for UMS tasks, the MorphoChallenge datasets do contain morpheme level labels. The German data was extracted from the CELEX2 collection (Baayen et al., 1993). The Zulu data was taken from the Ukwabelana corpus (Spiegler et al., 2010). Finally, the Indonesian portion was created applying the rule-based analyzer MORPHIND (Larasati et al., 2011) to the Indonesian portion of an Indonesian-English bilingual corpus.[6]

	Un. Data	Train+Tune+Dev			Test
		Train	Tune	Dev	
English	878k	800	100	100	694
Finnish	2,928k	800	100	100	835
German	2,338k	800	100	100	751
Indonesian	88k	800	100	100	2500
Turkish	617k	800	100	100	763
Zulu	123k	800	100	100	9040

Table 4: Dataset sizes (number of types).

We did not have access to the MorphoChallenge test set and thus used the original development set as our final evaluation set (Test). We developed CHIPMUNK using 10-fold cross-validation on the 1000 word training set and split every fold into training (Train), tuning (Tune) and development sets (Dev).[7] For German, Indonesian and Zulu we randomly selected 1000 word forms as training set and used the rest as evaluation set. For our final evaluation we trained CHIPMUNK on the concatenation of Train, Tune and Dev (the original 1000 word training set), using the optimal parameters from the cross-evaluation and tested on Test.

One of our baselines also uses unlabeled training data. MorphoChallenge provides word lists for English, Finnish, German and Turkish. We use the unannotated part of Ukwabelana for Zulu; and for Indonesian, data from Wikipedia and the corpus of Krisnawati and Schulz (2013).

Table 4 shows the important statistics of our datasets.

In all evaluations, we use variants of the standard MorphoChallenge evaluation approach. Importantly, for word types with multiple correct segmentations, this involves finding the maximum score by comparing our hypothesized segmentation with each correct segmentation, as is standardly done in MorphoChallenge.

[5] http://research.ics.aalto.fi/events/morphochallenge2010/

[6] https://github.com/desmond86/Indonesian-English-Bilingual-Corpus

[7] We used both Tune and Dev in order to both optimize hyperparameters on held-out data (Tune) and perform qualitative error analysis on separate held-out data (Dev).

	English	Finnish	Indonesian	German	Turkish	Zulu
CRF-MORPH	83.23	81.98	93.09	84.94	88.32	88.48
CRF-MORPH +LSV	84.45	84.35	93.50	86.90	89.98	89.06
First-order CRF	84.66	85.05	93.31	85.47	90.03	88.99
Higher-order CRF	84.66	84.78	93.88	85.40	90.65	88.85
CHIPMUNK	84.40	84.40	93.76	85.53	89.72	87.80
CHIPMUNK +Morph	83.27	84.71	93.17	84.84	90.48	90.03
CHIPMUNK +Affix	83.81	86.02	93.51	85.81	89.72	89.64
CHIPMUNK +Dict	86.10	86.11	95.39	87.76	90.45	88.66
CHIPMUNK +Dict,+Affix,+Morph	**86.31**	**88.38**	**95.41**	**87.85**	**91.36**	**90.16**

Table 5: Test F_1 for UMS. Features: LSV = letter successor variety, Affix = affix, Dict = dictionary, Morph = optimal (on Tune) morphotactic tagset.

6.1 UMS Experiments

We first evaluate CHIPMUNK on UMS, by predicting LMS and then discarding the labels. Our primary baseline is the state-of-the-art supervised system CRF-MORPH of Ruokolainen et al. (2013). We ran the version of the system that the authors published on their website.[8] We optimized the model's two hyperparameters on Tune: the number of epochs and the maximal length of n-gram character features. The system also supports Harris's letter successor variety (LSV) features (Section 5), extracted from large unannotated corpora, our second baseline. For completeness, we also compare CHIPMUNK with a first-order CRF and a higher-order CRF (Müller et al., 2013), both used the same n-gram features as CRF-MORPH, but without the LSV features.[9] We evaluate all models using the traditional macro F_1 of the segmentation boundaries.

Discussion. The UMS results on held-out data are displayed in Table 5. Our most complex model beats the best baseline by between 1 (German) and 3 (Finnish) points F1 on all six languages. We additionally provide extensive ablation studies to highlight the contribution of our novel features. We find that the properties of each specific language highly influences which features are most effective. For the agglutinative languages, i.e, Finnish, Turkish and Zulu, the affix based features (+Affix) and the morphotactic tagset (+Morph) yield consistent improvements over the semi-CRF models with a single state. Improvements for the affix features range from 0.2 for Turkish to 2.14 for Zulu. The morphological tagset yields improvements of 0.77 for Finnish, 1.89 for Turkish and 2.10 for Zulu. We optimized tagset granularity on Tune and found that levels 4 and level 2 yielded the best results for the three agglutinative and the three other languages, respectively.

The dictionary features (+Dict) help universally, but their effects are particularly salient in languages with productive compounding, i.e., English, Finnish and German, where we see improvements of > 1.7.

In comparison with previous work (Ruokolainen et al., 2013) we find that our most complex model yields consistent improvements over CRF-MORPH +LSV for all languages: The improvements range from > 1 for German over > 1.5 for Zulu, English, and Indonesian to > 2 for Turkish and > 4 for Finnish.

To illustrate the effect of modeling morphotactics through the larger morphotactic tagset on performance, we provide a detailed analysis of Turkish. See Table 6. We consider three different feature sets and increase the size of the morphotactic tagsets depicted in Figure 2. The results evince the general trend that improved morphotactic modeling benefits segmentation. Additionally, we observe that the improvements are complementary to those from the other features.

As discussed earlier, a key problem in UMS, especially in low-resource settings, is the detection of novel roots and affixes. Since many of our features were designed to combat this problem specifically, we investigated this aspect independently. Table 7 shows the number of novel roots and affixes found by our best model and the baseline. In all languages, CHIPMUNK correctly identifies between 5% (English) and 22% (Finnish) more novel roots than the baseline. We do not see major im-

[8] http://users.ics.tkk.fi/tpruokol/software/crfs_morph.zip

[9] Model order, maximal character n-gram length and regularization coefficients were optimized on Tune.

		+Affix	+Dict,+Affix
Level 0	90.11	90.13	91.66
Level 1	90.73	90.68	92.80
Level 2	89.80	90.46	92.04
Level 3	91.03	90.83	92.31
Level 4	91.80	92.19	**93.21**

Table 6: Example of the effect of larger tagsets (Figure 2) on Turkish segmentation measured on our development set. As Turkish is an agglutinative language with hundreds of affixes, the efficacy of our approach is expected to be particularly salient here. Recall we optimized for the best tagset granularity for our experiments on Tune.

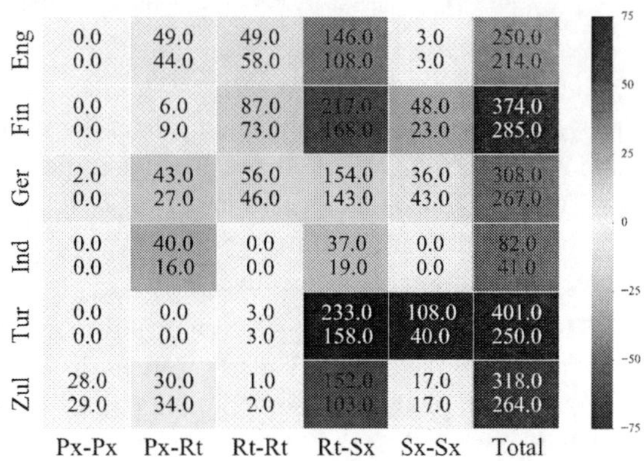

Figure 3: This figure represents a comparative analysis of undersegmentation. Each column (labels at the bottom) shows how often CRF-MORPH +LSV (top number in heatmap) and CHIPMUNK (bottom number in heatmap) select a segment that is two separate segments in the gold standard. E.g., Rt-Sx indicates how a root and a suffix were treated as a single segment. The color depends on the difference of the two counts.

provements for affixes, but this is of less interest as there are far fewer novel affixes.

We further explore how CHIPMUNK and the baseline perform on different boundary types by looking at missing boundaries between different morphotactic types; this error type is also known as *undersegmentation*. Figure 3 shows a heatmap that overviews errors broken down by morphotactic tag. We see that most errors are caused between root and suffixes across all languages. This is related to the problem of finding new roots, as a new root is often mistaken as a root-affix composition.

6.2 Root Detection and Stemming

Root detection[1] and stemming[1] are two important NLP problems that are closely related to morphological segmentation and used in applications such as MT, information retrieval, parsing and information extraction. Here we explore the utility of CHIPMUNK as a statistical stemmer and root detector.

	CRF-MORPH		CHIPMUNK	
	Roots	Affixes	Roots	Affixes
English	614	6	644	12
Finnish	502	10	613	11
German	360	6	414	9
Indonesian	593	0	639	0
Turkish	435	22	514	19
Zulu	146	10	160	11

Table 7: Dev number of unseen root and affix types correctly identified by CRF-MORPH +LSV and CHIPMUNK +Affix,+Dict,+Morph.

Stemming is closely related to the task of *lemmatization*, which involves the additional step of normalizing to the canonical form.[10] Consider the German particle verb participle *auf-ge-schrieb-en* 'written down'. The participle is built by applying an alternation to the verbal root *schreib* 'write' adding the participial circumfix *ge-en* and finally adding the verb particle *auf.* In our segmentation-based definition, we would consider *schrieb* 'write' as its root and *auf-schrieb* as its stem. In order to additionally to restore the lemma, we would also have to reverse the stem alternation that replaced *ei* with *ie* and add the infinitival ending *en* yielding the infinitive *auf-schreib-en.*

Our baseline MORFETTE (Chrupala et al., 2008) is a statistical transducer that first extracts edit paths between input and output and then uses a perceptron classifier to decide which edit path to apply. In short, MORFETTE treats the task as a string-to-string transduction problem, whereas we view it as a labeled segmentation problem.[11] Note, that MORFETTE would in principle be able to handle stem alternations, although these usually lead to an increase in the number of edit paths. We use level 2 tagsets for all experiments—the smallest tagsets complex enough for stemming—and extract the relevant segments.

Discussion. Our results are shown in Table 8. We see consistent improvements across all tasks. For the fusional languages (English, German and Indonesian) we see modest gains in performance on both root detection and stemming. However, for the agglutinative languages (Finnish, Turkish and Zulu) we see absolute gains as high as 50%

[10] Thus in our experiments there are *no* stem alternations. The output is equivalent to that of the Porter stemmer (Porter, 1980).

[11] Note that MORFETTE is a pipeline that first tags and *then* lemmatizes. We only make use of this second part of MORFETTE for which it is a strong string-to-string transduction baseline.

		English	Finnish	German	Indonesian	Turkish	Zulu
Root Detection	MORFETTE	62.82	39.28	43.81	86.00	26.08	30.76
	CHIPMUNK	**70.31**	**69.85**	**67.37**	**90.00**	**75.62**	**62.23**
Stemming	MORFETTE	91.35	51.74	79.49	86.00	28.57	58.12
	CHIPMUNK	**94.24**	**79.23**	**85.75**	**89.36**	**85.06**	**67.64**

Table 8: Test Accuracies for root detection and stemming.

		Finnish	Turkish
F1	MaxEnt	75.61	69.92
	MaxEnt +Split	74.02	76.61
	CHIPMUNK +All	**80.34**	**85.07**
Acc.	MaxEnt	60.96	37.88
	MaxEnt +Split	59.04	44.30
	CHIPMUNK +All	**65.00**	**56.06**

Table 9: Test F-Scores / accuracies for morphological tag classification.

	Morpheme Tags	Full Word Tags
Finnish	43	172
Turkish	50	636

Table 10: Number of full word and morpheme tags in the datasets.

(Turkish) in accuracy. This significant improvement is due to the complexity of the tasks in these languages—their productive morphology increases sparsity and makes the unstructured string-to-string transduction approach suboptimal. We view this as solid evidence that labeled segmentation has utility in many components of the NLP pipeline.

6.3 Morphological Tag Classification

The joint modeling of segmentation and morphotactic tags allows us to use CHIPMUNK for a crude form of morphological analysis: the task of *morphological tag classification* , which we define as *annotation of a word with its most likely inflectional features.*[12] To be concrete, our task is to predict the inflectional features of word type based only on its character sequence and not its sentential context. To this end, we take Finnish and Turkish as two examples of languages that should suit our approach particularly well as both have highly complex inflectional morphologies. We use our most fine-grained tagset and replace all non-inflectional tags with a simple segment tag. The tagset sizes are listed in Table 10.

We use the same experimental setup as in Section 6.2 and compare CHIPMUNK to a maximum entropy classifier (MaxEnt), whose features are character n-grams of up to a maximal length of k. [13] The maximum entropy classifier is L_1-regularized and its regularization coefficient as well as the value for k are optimized on Tune. As a second, stronger baseline we use a MaxEnt classifier that splits tags into their constituents and concatenates the features with every constituent as well as the complete tag (MaxEnt +Split). Both of the baselines in Table 9 are 0th-order versions of the state-of-the-art CRF-based morphological tagger MARMOT (Müller et al., 2013) (since our model is type-based), making this a strong baseline. We report full analysis accuracy and macro F_1 on the set of individual inflectional features.

Discussion. The results in Table 9 show that our proposed method outperforms both baselines on both performance metrics. We see gains of over 6% in accuracy in both languages. This is evidence that our proposed approach could be successfully integrated into a morphological tagger to give a stronger character-based signal.

7 Comparison to Finite-State Morphology

A morphological finite-state analyzer is customarily a hand-crafted tool that generates all the possible morphological readings with their associated features. We believe that, for many applications, high quality finite-state morphological analysis is superior to our techniques. Finite-state morphological analyzers output a small set of linguistically valid analyses of a type, typically with only limited overgeneration. However, there are two significant problems. The first is that significant effort is required to develop the transducers modeling the "grammar" of the morphology and

[12] We recognize that this task is best performed with sentential context (token-based). Integration with a POS tagger, however, is beyond the scope of this paper.

[13] Prefixes and suffixes are explicitly marked.

there is significant effort in creating and updating the lexicon. The second is, it is difficult to use finite-state morphology to guess analyses involving roots not covered in the lexicon.[14] In fact, this is usually solved by viewing it as a different problem, *morphological guessing*, where linguistic knowledge similar to the features we have presented is used to try to guess POS and morphological analysis for types with no analysis.

In contrast, our training procedure learns a probabilistic transducer, which is a soft version of the type of hand-engineered grammar that is used in finite-state analyzers. The 1-best labeled morphological segmentation our model produces offers a simple and clean representation which will be of great use in many downstream applications. Furthermore our model unifies analysis and guessing into a single simple framework. Nevertheless, finite-state morphologies are still extremely useful, high-precision tools. A primary goal of future work will be to use CHIPMUNK to attempt to induce higher-quality morphological processing systems.

8 Conclusion and Future Work

We have presented *labeled morphological segmentation* (LMS) in this paper, a new approach to morphological processing. LMS unifies three tasks that were solved before by different methods—unlabeled morphological segmentation, stemming, and morphological tag classification. LMS annotation itself has great potential for use in downstream NLP applications. Our hierarchy of labeled morphological segmentation tagsets can be used to map the heterogeneous data in six languages we work with to universal representations of different granularities. We plan future creation of gold standard segmentations in more languages using our annotation scheme.

We further presented CHIPMUNK a semi-CRF-based model for LMS that allows for the integration of various linguistic features and consistently out-performs previously presented approaches to *unlabeled morphological segmentation*. An important extension of CHIPMUNK is embedding it in a context-sensitive POS tagger. Current state-of-the-art models only employ character level n-gram features to model word-internals (Müller et al., 2013). We have demonstrated that our structured approach outperforms this baseline. We leave this natural extension to future work.

The datasets used in this work, additional description of our novel tagsets and CHIPMUNK can be found at `http://cistern.cis.lmu.de/chipmunk`.

[14]While one can in theory put in wildcard root states, this does not work in practice due to overgeneration.

Acknowledgments

We would like to thank Jason Eisner, Helmut Schmid, Özlem Çetinoğlu and the anonymous reviewers for their comments. This material is based upon work supported by a Fulbright fellowship awarded to the first author by the German-American Fulbright Commission and the National Science Foundation under Grant No. 1423276. The second author is a recipient of the Google Europe Fellowship in Natural Language Processing, and this research is supported by this Google Fellowship. The fourth author was partially supported by Deutsche Forschungsgemeinschaft (grant SCHU 2246/10-1). This project has received funding from the European Union's Horizon 2020 research and innovation programme under grant agreement No 644402 (HimL) and the DFG grant *Models of Morphosyntax for Statistical Machine Translation*.

References

Muhammad Abdul-Mageed, Mona T. Diab, and Sandra Kübler. 2014. SAMAR: Subjectivity and sentiment analysis for Arabic social media. *Computer Speech & Language*.

Galen Andrew. 2006. A hybrid Markov/semi-Markov conditional random field for sequence segmentation. In *Proceedings of EMNLP*.

R Harald Baayen, Richard Piepenbrock, and Leon Gulikers. 1993. The CELEX lexical database on CD-ROM. Technical report, Linguistic Data Consortium.

Sabine Buchholz and Erwin Marsi. 2006. CoNLL-X shared task on multilingual dependency parsing. In *Proceedings of CoNLL*.

Grzegorz Chrupala, Georgiana Dinu, and Josef van Genabith. 2008. Learning morphology with morfette. In *Proceedings of LREC*.

Michael Collins. 2002. Discriminative training methods for hidden Markov models: Theory and experiments with perceptron algorithms. In *Proceedings of EMNLP*.

Mathias Creutz and Krista Lagus. 2002. Unsupervised discovery of morphemes. In *Proceedings of SIGMORPHON*.

Mathias Creutz and Krista Lagus. 2004. Induction of a simple morphology for highly-inflecting languages. In *Proceedings of SIGMORPHON*.

Mathias Creutz, Teemu Hirsimäki, Mikko Kurimo, Antti Puurula, Janne Pylkkönen, Vesa Siivola, Matti Varjokallio, Ebru Arisoy, Murat Saraclar, and Andreas Stolcke. 2007a. Analysis of morph-based speech recognition and the modeling of out-of-vocabulary words across languages. In *Proceedings of HLT-NAACL*.

Mathias Creutz, Teemu Hirsimäki, Mikko Kurimo, Antti Puurula, Janne Pylkkönen, Vesa Siivola, Matti Varjokallio, Ebru Arisoy, Murat Saraclar, and Andreas Stolcke. 2007b. Morph-based speech recognition and modeling of out-of-vocabulary words across languages. *TSLP*.

Christopher Dyer, Smaranda Muresan, and Philip Resnik. 2008. Generalizing word lattice translation. In *Proceedings of ACL*.

Elif Eyigöz, Daniel Gildea, and Kemal Oflazer. 2013. Simultaneous word-morpheme alignment for statistical machine translation. In *Proceedings of HLT-NAACL*.

John Goldsmith. 2001. Unsupervised learning of the morphology of a natural language. *Computational Linguistics*.

Stig-Arne Grönroos, Sami Virpioja, Peter Smit, and Mikko Kurimo. 2014. Morfessor FlatCat: An HMM-based method for unsupervised and semi-supervised learning of morphology. In *Proceedings of COLING*.

Zellig Harris. 1995. From phoneme to morpheme. *Language*.

Oskar Kohonen, Sami Virpioja, and Krista Lagus. 2010a. Semi-supervised learning of concatenative morphology. In *Proceedings of SIGMORPHON*.

Oskar Kohonen, Sami Virpioja, Laura Leppänen, and Krista Lagus. 2010b. Semi-supervised extensions to Morfessor baseline. In *Proceedings of the Morpho Challenge Workshop*.

Lucia D. Krisnawati and Klaus U. Schulz. 2013. Plagiarism detection for Indonesian texts. In *Proceedings of iiWAS*.

Mikko Kurimo, Sami Virpioja, Ville Turunen, and Krista Lagus. 2010. Morpho challenge competition 2005–2010: Evaluations and results. In *Proceedings of SIGMORPHON*.

John Lafferty, Andrew McCallum, and Fernando Pereira. 2001. Conditional random fields: Probabilistic models for segmenting and labeling sequence data. In *Proceedings of ICML*.

Septina Dian Larasati, Vladislav Kuboň, and Daniel Zeman. 2011. Indonesian morphology tool (morphind): Towards an Indonesian corpus. In *Systems and Frameworks for Computational Morphology*. Springer.

Dong C Liu and Jorge Nocedal. 1989. On the limited memory BFGS method for large scale optimization. *Mathematical Programming*.

Erwin Marsi, Antal van den Bosch, and Abdelhadi Soudi. 2005. Memory-based morphological analysis generation and part-of-speech tagging of Arabic. In *Proceedings of ACL Workshop: Computational Approaches to Semitic Languages*.

Kevin P Murphy. 2002. Hidden semi-Markov models (hsmms). Technical report, Massachusetts Institute of Technology.

Thomas Müller, Helmut Schmid, and Hinrich Schütze. 2013. Efficient higher-order CRFs for morphological tagging. In *Proceedings of EMNLP*.

Karthik Narasimhan, Damianos Karakos, Richard Schwartz, Stavros Tsakalidis, and Regina Barzilay. 2014. Morphological segmentation for keyword spotting. In *Proceedings of EMNLP*.

Hwee Tou Ng and Jin Kiat Low. 2004. Chinese part-of-speech tagging: One-at-a-time or all-at-once? word-based or character-based? In *Proceedings of EMNLP*.

Hoifung Poon, Colin Cherry, and Kristina Toutanova. 2009. Unsupervised morphological segmentation with log-linear models. In *Proceedings of NAACL*.

Martin F Porter. 1980. An algorithm for suffix stripping. *Program*.

Teemu Ruokolainen, Oskar Kohonen, Sami Virpioja, and Mikko Kurimo. 2013. Supervised morphological segmentation in a low-resource learning setting using conditional random fields. In *Proceedings of CoNLL*.

Teemu Ruokolainen, Oskar Kohonen, Sami Virpioja, and Mikko Kurimo. 2014. Painless semi-supervised morphological segmentation using conditional random fields. *Proceedings of EACL*.

Sunita Sarawagi and William W Cohen. 2004. Semi-Markov conditional random fields for information extraction. In *Proceedings of NIPS*.

Andrew Smith and Miles Osborne. 2006. Using gazetteers in discriminative information extraction. In *Proceedings of CoNLL*.

Sebastian Spiegler, Andrew Van Der Spuy, and Peter A Flach. 2010. Ukwabelana: An open-source morphological Zulu corpus. In *Proceedings of COLING*.

Antal Van den Bosch and Walter Daelemans. 1999. Memory-based morphological analysis. In *Proceedings of ACL*. Association for Computational Linguistics.

Sami Virpioja, Oskar Kohonen, and Krista Lagus. 2010. Unsupervised morpheme analysis with Allomorfessor. In *Multilingual Information Access Evaluation*. Springer.

Martin J Wainwright and Michael I Jordan. 2008. Graphical models, exponential families, and variational inference. *Foundations and Trends in Machine Learning*.

Yue Zhang and Stephen Clark. 2008. Joint word segmentation and POS tagging using a single perceptron. In *Proceedings of ACL*.

Learning to Exploit Structured Resources for Lexical Inference

Vered Shwartz† **Omer Levy**† **Ido Dagan**† **Jacob Goldberger**§
† Computer Science Department, Bar-Ilan University
§ Faculty of Engineering, Bar-Ilan University
vered1986@gmail.com {omerlevy,dagan}@cs.biu.ac.il
jacob.goldberger@biu.ac.il

Abstract

Massive knowledge resources, such as Wikidata, can provide valuable information for lexical inference, especially for proper-names. Prior resource-based approaches typically select the subset of each resource's relations which are relevant for a particular given task. The selection process is done manually, limiting these approaches to smaller resources such as WordNet, which lacks coverage of proper-names and recent terminology. This paper presents a supervised framework for automatically selecting an optimized subset of resource relations for a given target inference task. Our approach enables the use of large-scale knowledge resources, thus providing a rich source of high-precision inferences over proper-names.[1]

1 Introduction

Recognizing lexical inference is an important component in semantic tasks. Various lexical-semantic relations, such as synonomy, class-membership, part-of, and causality may be used to infer the meaning of one word from another, in order to address lexical variability. For instance, a question answering system asked "which artist's net worth is $450 million?" might retrieve the candidates *Beyoncé Knowles* and *Lloyd Blankfein*, who are both worth $450 million. To correctly answer the question, the application needs to know that Beyoncé is an artist, and that Lloyd Blankfein is not.

Corpus-based methods are often employed to recognize lexical inferences, based on either co-occurrence patterns (Hearst, 1992; Turney, 2006) or distributional representations (Weeds and Weir, 2003; Kotlerman et al., 2010). While earlier methods were mostly unsupervised, recent trends introduced supervised methods for the task (Baroni et al., 2012; Turney and Mohammad, 2015; Roller et al., 2014). In these settings, a targeted lexical inference relation is implicitly defined by a training set of term-pairs, which are annotated as positive or negative examples of this relation. Several such datasets have been created, each representing a somewhat different flavor of lexical inference.

While corpus-based methods usually enjoy high recall, their precision is often limited, hindering their applicability. An alternative common practice is to mine high-precision lexical inferences from structured resources, particularly WordNet (Fellbaum, 1998). Nevertheless, WordNet is an ontology of the English language, which, by definition, does not cover many proper-names ($Beyoncé \rightarrow artist$) and recent terminology ($Facebook \rightarrow social\ network$). A potential solution may lie in rich and up-to-date structured knowledge resources such as Wikidata (Vrandečić, 2012), DBPedia (Auer et al., 2007), and Yago (Suchanek et al., 2007). In this paper, we investigate how these resources can be exploited for lexical inference over proper-names.

We begin by examining whether the common usage of WordNet for lexical inference can be extended to larger resources. Typically, a subset of WordNet relations is manually selected (e.g. all synonyms and hypernyms). By nature, each application captures a different aspect of lexical inference, and thus defines different relations as *indicative* of its particular flavor of lexical infer-

[1]Our code and data are available at:
https://github.com/vered1986/LinKeR

Proceedings of the 19th Conference on Computational Language Learning, pages 175–184,
Beijing, China, July 30-31, 2015.

Resource Relation	Example
position_held	David Petraeus → Director of CIA
performer	Sheldon Cooper → Jim Parsons
operating_system	iPhone → iOS

Table 1: Examples of Wikidata relations that are indicative of lexical inference.

Resource	#Entities	#Properties	Version
DBPedia	4,500,000	1,367	July 2014
Wikidata	6,000,000	1,200	July 2014
Yago	10,000,000	70	December 2014
WordNet	150,000	13	3.0

Table 2: Structured resources explored in this work.

ence. For instance, the *hypernym* relation is indicative of the *is_a* flavor of lexical inference (e.g. *musician* → *artist*), but does not indicate causality.

Since WordNet has a relatively simple schema, manually finding such an optimal subset is feasible. However, structured knowledge resources' schemas contain thousands of relations, dozens of which may be indicative. Many of these are not trivial to identify by hand, as shown in Table 1. A manual effort to construct a distinct subset for each task is thus quite challenging, and an automated method is required.

We present a principled supervised framework, which automates the selection process of resource relations, and optimizes this subset for a given target inference relation. This automation allows us to leverage large-scale resources, and extract many high-precision inferences over proper-names, which are absent from WordNet. Finally, we show that our framework complements state-of-the-art corpus-based methods. Combining the two approaches can particularly benefit real-world tasks in which proper-names are prominent.

2 Background

2.1 Common Use of WordNet for Inference

WordNet (Fellbaum, 1998) is widely used for identifying lexical inference. It is usually used in an unsupervised setting where the relations relevant for each specific inference task are manually selected a priori.

One approach looks for chains of these predefined relations (Harabagiu and Moldovan, 1998), e.g. *dog* → *mammal* using a chain of hypernyms: *dog* → *canine* → *carnivore* → *placental mammal* → *mammal*. Another approach is via WordNet Similarity (Pedersen et al., 2004), which takes two synsets and returns a numeric value that represents their similarity based on WordNet's hierarchical hypernymy structure.

While there is a broad consensus that synonyms entail each other (*elevator* ↔ *lift*) and hyponyms entail their hypernyms (*cat* → *animal*), other relations, such as meronymy, are not agreed upon, and may vary depending on task and context (e.g. *living in London* → *living in England*, but *leaving London* ↛ *leaving England*). Overall, there is no principled way to select the subset of relevant relations, and a suitable subset is usually tailored to each dataset and task. This work addresses this issue by automatically learning the subset of relations relevant to the task.

2.2 Structured Knowledge Resources

While WordNet is quite extensive, it is handcrafted by expert lexicographers, and thus cannot compete in terms of scale with community-built knowledge bases such as Wikidata (Vrandečić, 2012), which connect millions of entities through a rich variety of structured relations (properties).

Using these resources for various NLP tasks has become exceedingly popular (Wu and Weld, 2010; Rahman and Ng, 2011; Unger et al., 2012; Berant et al., 2013). Little attention, however, was given to leveraging them for identifying lexical inference; the exception being Shnarch et al. (2009), who used structured data from Wikipedia for this purpose.

In this paper, we experimented with such resources, in addition to WordNet. *DBPedia* (Auer et al., 2007) contains structured information from Wikipedia: info boxes, redirections, disambiguation links, etc. *Wikidata* (Vrandečić, 2012) contains facts edited by humans to support Wikipedia and other Wikimedia projects. *Yago* (Suchanek et al., 2007) is a semantic knowledge base derived from Wikipedia, WordNet, and GeoNames.[2]

Table 2 compares the scale of the resources we used. The massive scale of the more recent resources and their rich schemas can potentially increase the coverage of current WordNet-based approaches, yet make it difficult to manually select an optimized subset of relations for a task. Our method automatically learns such a subset, and provides lexical inferences on entities that are absent from WordNet, particularly proper-names.

[2]We also considered Freebase, but it required significantly larger computational resources to work in our framework, which, at the time of writing, exceeded our capacity. §4.1 discusses complexity.

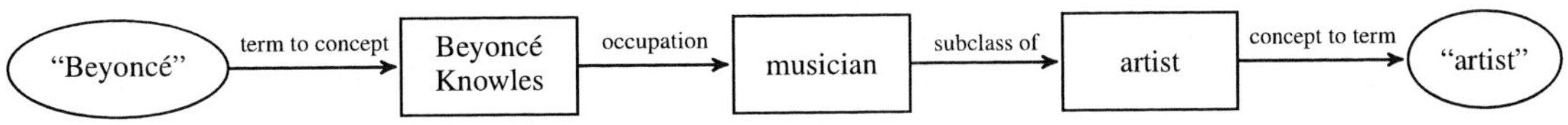

Figure 1: An excerpt of a resource graph (Wikidata) connecting "Beyoncé" to "artist". Resource graphs contain two types of nodes: terms (ellipses) and concepts (rectangles).

3 Task Definition and Representation

We wish to leverage the information in structured resources to identify whether a certain lexical-inference relation $\mathcal{R}$ holds between a pair of terms. Formally, we wish to classify whether a term-pair (x, y) satisfies the relation $\mathcal{R}$. $\mathcal{R}$ is implicitly defined by a training set of (x, y) pairs, annotated as positive or negative examples. We are also given a set of structured resources, which we will utilize to classify (x, y).

Each resource can be naturally viewed as a directed graph G (Figure 1). There are two types of nodes in G: *term* (lemma) nodes and *concept* (synset) nodes. The edges in G are each labeled with a property (*edge type*), defining a wide range of semantic relations between concepts (e.g. occupation, subclass_of). In addition, terms are mapped to the concepts they represent via term-concept edge types.

When using multiple resources, G is a disconnected graph composed of a subgraph per resource, without edges connecting nodes from different resources. One may consider connecting multiple resource graphs at the term nodes. However, this may cause sense-shifts, i.e. connect two distinct concepts (in different resources) through the same term. For example, the concept $January\ 1^{st}$ in Wikidata is connected to the concept $fruit$ in WordNet through the polysemous term $date$. The alternative, aligning resources in the concept space, is not trivial. Some partial mappings exist (e.g. Yago-WordNet), which can be explored in future work.

4 Algorithmic Framework

We present an algorithmic framework for learning whether a term-pair (x, y) satisfies a relation $\mathcal{R}$, given an annotated set of term-pairs and a resource graph G. We first represent (x, y) as the set of paths connecting x and y in G (§4.1). We then classify each such path as indicative or not of $\mathcal{R}$, and decide accordingly whether $x\mathcal{R}y$ (§4.2).

4.1 Representing Term-Pairs as Path-Sets

We represent each (x, y) pair as the set of *paths* that link x and y within each resource. We retain only the shortest paths (all paths $x \rightsquigarrow y$ of minimal length) as they yielded better performance.

Resource graphs are densely connected, and thus have a huge branching factor b. We thus limited the maximum path length to $\ell = 8$ and employed bidirectional search (Russell and Norvig, 2009, Ch.3) to find the shortest paths. This algorithm runs two simultaneous instances of breadth-first search (BFS), one from x and another from y, halting when they meet in the middle. It is much more efficient, having a complexity of $O(b^{\ell/2}) = O(b^4)$ instead of BFS's $O(b^\ell) = O(b^8)$.

To further reduce complexity, we split the search to two phases: we first find all nodes along the shortest paths between x and y, and then reconstruct the actual paths. Searching for relevant nodes ignores edge types, inducing a simpler resource graph, which can be represented as a sparse adjacency matrix and manipulated efficiently with matrix operations (elaborated in appendix A). Once the search space is limited to relevant nodes alone, path-finding becomes trivial.

4.2 Classification Framework

We consider edge types that typically connect between concepts in $\mathcal{R}$ to be "indicative"; for example, the $occupation$ edge type is indicative of the is_a relation, as in "Beyoncé is_a musician". Our framework's goal is to learn which edge types are indicative of a given relation $\mathcal{R}$, and use that information to classify new (x, y) term-pairs.

Figure 2 presents the dependencies between edge types, paths, and term-pairs. As discussed in the previous section, we represent each term-pair as a set of paths. In turn, we represent each path as a "bag of edges", a vector with an entry for each edge type.[3] To model the edges' "indicativeness", we assign a parameter to each edge type, and learn these parameters from the term-pair level supervision provided by the training data.

In this work, we are not only interested in optimizing accuracy or F_1, but in exploring the entire recall-precision trade-off. Therefore, we optimize

[3] We add special markers to the first and last edges within each path. This allows the algorithm to learn that applying term-to-concept and concept-to-term edge types in the middle of a path causes sense-shifts.

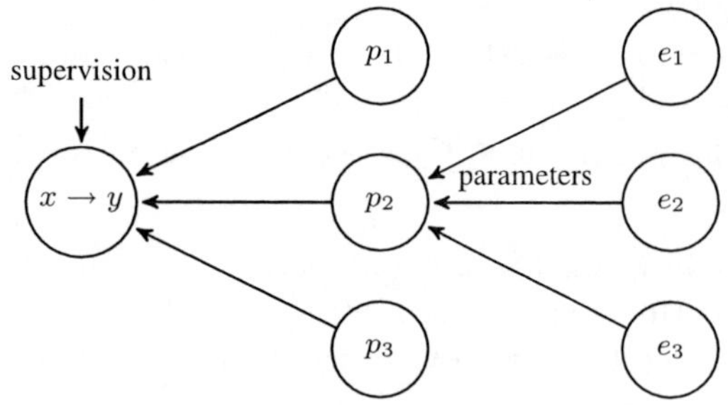

Figure 2: The dependencies between term-pairs ($x \to y$), paths (p_j), and edge types (e_i).

the F_β objective, where β^2 balances the recall-precision trade-off.[4] In particular, we expect structured resources to facilitate high-precision inferences, and are thus more interested in lower values of β^2, which emphasize precision over recall.

4.2.1 Weighted Edge Model

A typical neural network approach is to assign a *weight* w_i to each edge type e_i, where more indicative edge types should have higher values of w_i. The indicativeness of a path ($\hat{p}$) is modeled using logistic regression: $\hat{p} \triangleq \sigma(\vec{w} \cdot \vec{\phi})$, where $\vec{\phi}$ is the path's "bag of edges" representation, i.e. a feature vector of each edge type's frequency in the path.

The probability of a term-pair being positive can be determined using either the sum of all path scores or the score of its most indicative path (max-pooling). We trained both variants with back-propagation (Rumelhart et al., 1986) and gradient ascent. In particular, we optimized F_β using a variant of Jansche's (2005) derivation of F_β-optimized logistic regression (see suplementary material[5] for full derivation).

This model can theoretically quantify how indicative each edge type is of $\mathcal{R}$. Specifically, it can differentiate weakly indicative edges (e.g. meronyms) from those that contradict $\mathcal{R}$ (e.g. antonyms). However, on our datasets, this model yielded sub-optimal results (see §6.1), and therefore serves as a baseline to the binary model presented in the following section.

4.2.2 Binary Edge Model

Preliminary experiments suggested that in most datasets, each edge type is either indicative or non-indicative of the target relation $\mathcal{R}$. We therefore developed a binary model, which defines a global set of edge types that are indicative of $\mathcal{R}$: a *whitelist*.

Classification We represent each path p as a binary "bag of edges" ϕ, i.e. the set of edge types that were applied in p. Given a term-pair (x, y) represented as a path-set $paths(x, y)$, and a whitelist w, the model classifies (x, y) as positive if:

$$\exists \phi \in paths(x, y) : \phi \subseteq w \tag{1}$$

In other words:

1. A *path* is classified as indicative if all its edge types are whitelisted.
2. A *term-pair* is classified as positive if at least one of its paths is indicative.[6]

The first design choice essentially assumes that $\mathcal{R}$ is a transitive relation. This is usually the case in most inference relations (e.g. hypernymy, causality). In addition, notice that the second modeling assumption is unidirectional; in some cases $x\mathcal{R}y$, yet an indicative path between them does not exist. This can happen, for example, if the relation between them is not covered by the resource, e.g. causality in WordNet.

Training Learning the optimal whitelist over a training set can be cast as a subset selection problem: given a set of possible edge types $E = \{e_1, ..., e_n\}$ and a utility function $u : 2^E \to \mathbb{R}$, find the subset (whitelist) $w \subseteq E$ that maximizes the utility, i.e. $w^* = \arg\max_w u(w)$. In our case, the utility u is the F_β score over the training set.

Structured knowledge resources contain hundreds of different edge types, making E very large, and an exhaustive search over its powerset infeasible. The standard approach to this class of subset selection problems is to apply local search algorithms, which find an approximation of the optimal subset. We tried several local search algorithms, and found that genetic search (Russell and Norvig, 2009, Ch.4) performed well. In general, genetic search is claimed to be a preferred strategy for subset selection (Yang and Honavar, 1998).

In our application of genetic search, each individual (candidate solution) is a whitelist, represented by a bit vector with a bit for each edge type. We defined the fitness function of a whitelist w according to the F_β score of w over the training set.

[4] $F_\beta = \frac{(1+\beta^2) \cdot precision \cdot recall}{\beta^2 \cdot precision + recall}$

[5] http://u.cs.biu.ac.il/%7enlp/wp-content/uploads/LinKeR-sup.pdf

[6] As a corollary, if $x\not\mathcal{R}y$, then every path between them is non-indicative.

Dataset	#Instances	#Positive	#Negative
kotlerman2010	2,940	880	2,060
turney2014	1,692	920	772
levy2014	12,602	945	11,657
proper2015	1,500	750	750

Table 3: Datasets evaluated in this work.

We also applied L_2 regularization to reduce the fitness of large whitelists.

The binary edge model works well in practice, successfully replicating the common practice of manually selected relations from WordNet (see §6.1). In addition, the model outputs a human-interpretable set of indicative edges.

Although the weighted model's hypothesis space subsumes the binary model's, the binary model performed better on our datasets. We conjecture that this stems from the limited amount of training instances, which prevents a more general model from converging into an optimal solution.

5 Datasets

We used 3 existing common-noun datasets and one new proper-name dataset. Each dataset consists of annotated (x, y) term-pairs, where both x and y are noun phrases. Since each dataset was created in a slightly different manner, the underlying semantic relation $\mathcal{R}$ varies as well.

5.1 Existing Datasets

`kotlerman2010` (Kotlerman et al., 2010) is a manually annotated lexical entailment dataset of distributionally similar nouns. `turney2014` (Turney and Mohammad, 2015) is based on a crowdsourced dataset of semantic relations, from which we removed non-nouns and lemmatized plurals. `levy2014` (Levy et al., 2014) was generated from manually annotated entailment graphs of subject-verb-object tuples. Table 3 provides metadata on each dataset.

Two additional datasets were created using WordNet (Baroni and Lenci, 2011; Baroni et al., 2012), whose definition of $\mathcal{R}$ can be trivially captured by a resource-based approach using WordNet. Hence, they are omitted from our evaluation.

5.2 A New Proper-Name Dataset

An important linguistic component that is missing from these lexical-inference datasets is proper-names. We conjecture that much of the added value in utilizing structured resources is the ability to cover terms such as celebrities (Lady Gaga) and recent terminology (social networks) that do not appear in WordNet. We thus created a new dataset of (x, y) pairs in which x is a proper-name, y is a common noun, and $\mathcal{R}$ is the is_a relation. For instance, $(Lady\ Gaga, singer)$ is true, but $(Lady\ Gaga, film)$ is false.

To construct the dataset, we sampled 70 articles in 9 different topics from a corpus of recent events (online magazines). As candidate (x, y) pairs, we extracted 24,000 pairs of noun phrases x and y that belonged to the same paragraph in the original text, selecting those in which x is a proper-name. These pairs were manually annotated by graduate students, who were instructed to use their world knowledge and the original text for disambiguation (e.g. $England \rightarrow team$ in the context of football). The agreement on a subset of 4,500 pairs was $\kappa = 0.954$.

After annotation, we had roughly 800 positive and 23,000 negative pairs. To balance the dataset, we sampled negative examples according to the frequency of y in positive pairs, creating "harder" negative examples, such as $(Sherlock, lady)$ and $(Kylie\ Minogue, vice\ president)$.

6 Results

We first validate our framework by checking whether it can automatically replicate the common manual usage of WordNet. We then evaluate it on the proper-name dataset using additional resources. Finally, we compare our method to state-of-the-art distributional methods.

Experimental Setup While F_1 is a standard measure of performance, it captures only one point on the recall-precision curve. Instead, we present the entire curve, while expecting the contribution of structured resources to be in the high-precision region. To create these curves, we optimized our method and the baselines using F_β with 40 values of $\beta^2 \in (0, 2)$.

We randomly split each dataset into 70% train, 25% test and 5% validation.[7] We applied L_2 regularization to our method and the baselines, tuning the regularization parameter on the validation set.

6.1 Performance on WordNet

We examine whether our algorithm can replicate the common use of WordNet (§2.1), by manually constructing 4 whitelists based on the literature

[7] Since our methods do not use lexical features, we did not use lexical splits as in (Levy et al., 2015).

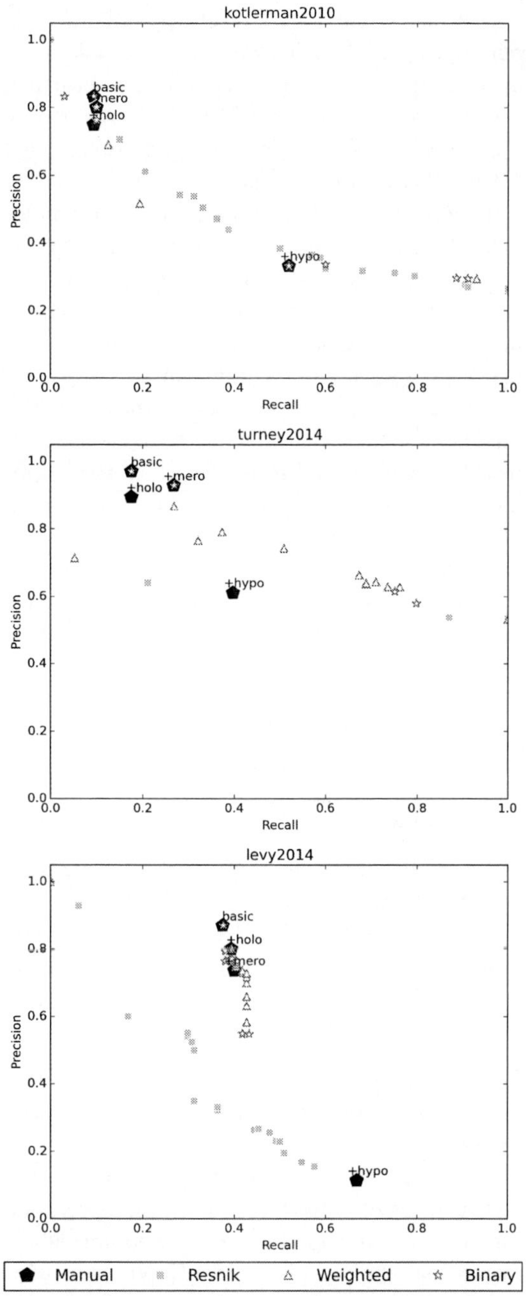

Figure 3: Recall-precision curve of each dataset with WordNet as the only resource. Each point in the graph stands for the performance on a certain value of β. Notice that in some of the graphs, different β values yield the same performance, causing less points to be displayed.

(see Table 4), and evaluating their performance using the classification methods in §4.2. In addition, we compare our method to Resnik's (1995) WordNet similarity, which scores each pair of terms based on their lowest common hypernym. This score was used as a single feature in F_β-optimized logistic regression to create a classifier.

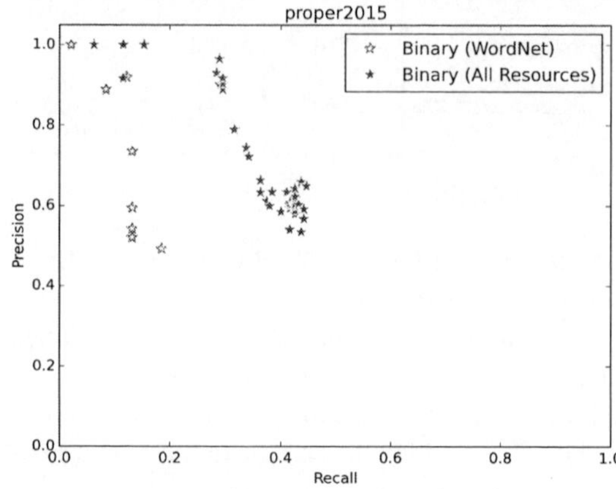

Figure 4: Recall-precision curve for `proper2015`.

Name	Edge Types
basic	{synonym, hypernym, instance_hypernym}
+holo	basic ∪ {holonym}
+mero	basic ∪ {meronym}
+hypo	basic ∪ {hyponym}

Table 4: The manual whitelists commonly used in WordNet.

Figure 3 compares our algorithm to WordNet's baselines, showing that our binary model always replicates the best-performing manually-constructed whitelists, for certain values of β^2. Synonyms and hypernyms are often selected, and additional edges are added to match the semantic flavor of each particular dataset. In `turney2014`, for example, where meronyms are common, our binary model learns that they are indicative by including meronymy in its whitelist. In `levy2014`, however, where meronyms are less indicative, the model does not select them.

We also observe that, in most cases, our algorithm outperforms Resnik's similarity. In addition, the weighted model does not perform as well as the binary model, as discussed in §4.2. We therefore focus our presentation on the binary model.

6.2 Lexical Inference over Proper-Names

We evaluated our model on the new proper-name dataset `proper2015` described in §5.2. This time, we incorporated all the resources described in §2.2 (including WordNet) into our framework, and compared the performance to that of using WordNet alone. Indeed, our algorithm is able to exploit the information in the additional resources and greatly increase performance, particularly recall, on this dataset (Figure 4).[8]

[8] We also evaluated our algorithm on the common-nouns datasets with all resources, but apparently, adding resources did not significantly improve performance.

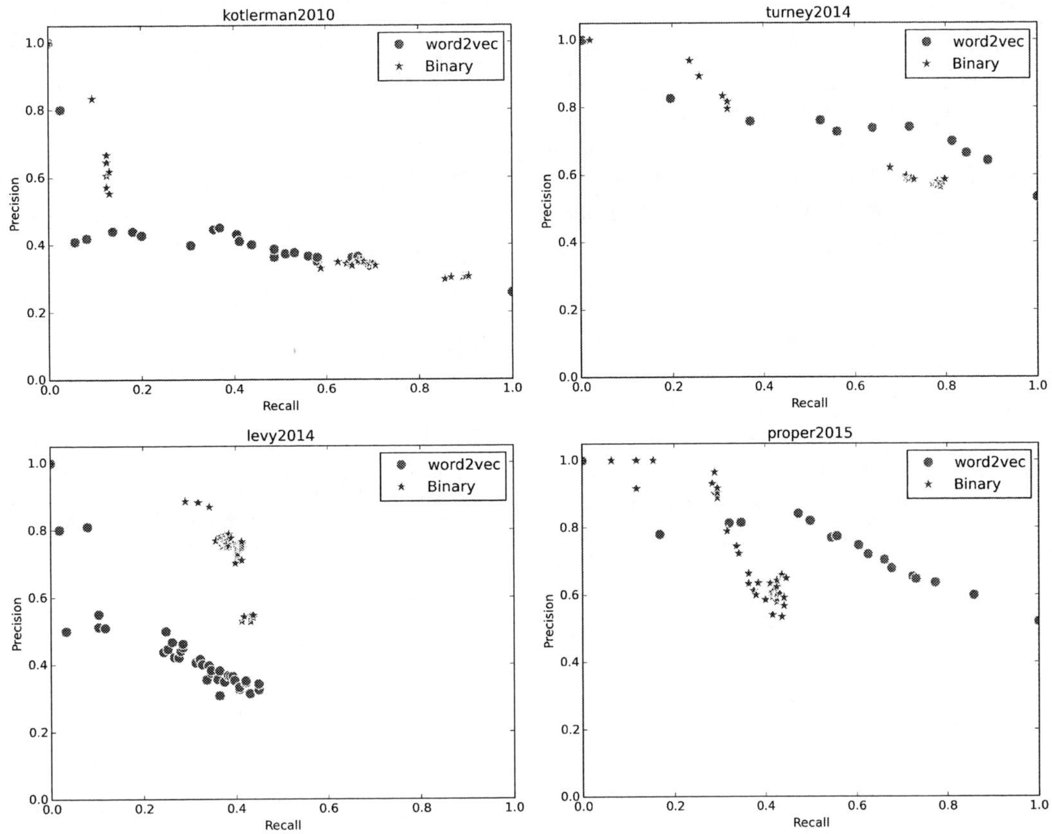

Figure 5: Recall-precision curve of each dataset using: (1) Supervised word2vec (2) Our binary model.

The binary model yields 97% precision at 29% recall, at the top of the "precision cliff". The whitelist learnt at this point contains 44 edge types, mainly from Wikidata and Yago. Even though the is_a relation implicitly defined in `proper2015` is described using many different edge types, our binary model still manages to learn which of the over 2,500 edge types are indicative. Table 5 shows some of the learnt edge types (see the supplementary material for the complete list).

The performance boost in `proper2015` demonstrates that community-built resources have much added value when considering proper-names. As expected, many proper-names do not appear in WordNet (*Doctor Who*). That said, even when both terms appear in WordNet, they often lack important properties covered by other resources (*Louisa May Alcott* is a *woman*).

Edge Type	Example
occupation	Daniel Radcliffe → actor
sex_or_gender	Louisa May Alcott → woman
instance_of	Doctor Who → series
acted_in	Michael Keaton → Beetlejuice
genre	Touch → drama
position_played_on_team	Jason Collins → center

Table 5: An excerpt of the whitelist learnt for `proper2015` by the binary model with accompanying true-positives that do not have an indicative path in WordNet.

6.3 Comparison to Corpus-based Methods

Lexical inference has been thoroughly explored in distributional semantics, with recent supervised methods (Baroni et al., 2012; Turney and Mohammad, 2015) showing promising results. While these methods leverage huge corpora to increase coverage, they often introduce noise that affects their precision. Structured resources, on the other hand, are precision-oriented. We therefore expect our approach to complement distributional methods in high-precision scenarios.

To represent term-pairs with distributional features, we downloaded the pre-trained `word2vec` embeddings.[9] These vectors were trained over a huge corpus (100 billion words) using a state-of-the-art embedding algorithm (Mikolov et al., 2013). Since each vector represents a single term (either x or y), we used 3 state-of-the-art meth-

[9] `http://code.google.com/p/word2vec/`

ods to construct a feature vector for each term-pair: concatenation $\vec{x} \oplus \vec{y}$ (Baroni et al., 2012), difference $\vec{y} - \vec{x}$ (Roller et al., 2014; Fu et al., 2014; Weeds et al., 2014), and similarity $\vec{x} \cdot \vec{y}$. We then used F_β-optimized logistic regression to train a classifier. Figure 5 compares our methods to concatenation, which was the best-performing corpus-based method.[10]

In `turney2014` and `proper2015`, the embeddings retain over 80% precision while boasting higher recall than our method's. In `turney2014`, it is often a result of the more associative relations prominent in the dataset ($football \rightarrow playbook$), which seldom are expressed in structured resources. In `proper2015`, the difference in recall seems to be from missing terminology ($Twitter \rightarrow social\ network$). However, the corpus-based method's precision does not exceed the low 80's, while our binary algorithm yields 93% @ 27% precision-at-recall on `turney2014` and 97% @ 29% on `proper2015`.

In `levy2014`, there is an overwhelming advantage to our resource-based method over the corpus-based method. This dataset contains healthcare terms and might require a domain-specific corpus to train the embeddings. Having said that, many of its examples are of an ontological nature (drug x treats disease y), which may be more suited to our resource-based approach, regardless of domain.

7 Error Analysis

Since resource-based methods are precision-oriented, we analyzed our binary model by selecting the setting with the highest attainable recall that maintains high precision. This point is often at the top of a "precision cliff" in Figures 3 and 4. These settings are presented in Table 6.

The high-precision settings we chose resulted in few false positives, most of which are caused by annotation errors or resource errors. Naturally, regions of higher recall and lower precision will yield more false positives and less false negatives. We thus focus the rest of our discussion on false negatives (Table 7).

While structured resources cover most terms,

Dataset	β	Whitelist	Prec.	Rec.
`kotlerman2010`	0.05	basic	83%	9%
`turney2014`	0.05	+mero	93%	27%
`levy2014`	10^{-5}	basic	87%	37%
`proper2015`	0.3	44 edge types from all resources (see supplementary material)	97%	29%

Table 6: The error analysis setting of each dataset.

Error Type	kotlerman 2010	levy 2014	turney 2014	proper 2015
Not Covered	2%	12%	4%	13%
No Indicative Paths	35%	48%	73%	75%
Whitelist Error	6%	3%	5%	8%
Resource Error	15%	11%	7%	0%
Annotation Error	40%	23%	7%	1%
Other	2%	3%	4%	3%

Table 7: Analysis of false negatives in each dataset. We observed the following errors: (1) One of the terms is out-of-vocabulary (2) All paths are not indicative (3) An indicative path exists, but discarded by the whitelist (4) The resource describes an inaccurate relation between the terms (5) The term-pair was incorrectly annotated as positive.

the majority of false negatives stem from the lack of indicative paths between them. Many important relations are not explicitly covered by the resources, such as noun-quality ($saint \rightarrow holiness$), which are abundant in `turney2014`, or causality ($germ \rightarrow infection$), which appear in `levy2014`. These examples are occasionally captured by other (more specific) relations, and tend to be domain-specific.

In `kotlerman2010`, we found that many false negatives are caused by annotation errors in this dataset. Pairs are often annotated as positive based on associative similarity (e.g. $transport \rightarrow environment$, $financing \rightarrow management$), making it difficult to even manually construct a coherent whitelist for this dataset. This may explain the poor performance of our method and other baselines on this dataset.

8 Conclusion and Future Work

In this paper, we presented a supervised framework for utilizing structured resources to recognize lexical inference. We demonstrated that our framework replicates the common practice of WordNet and can increase the coverage of proper-names by exploiting larger structured resources. Compared to the prior practice of manually identifying useful relations in structured resources, our contribution offers a principled learning approach for automating and optimizing this common need.

While our method enjoys high-precision, its recall is limited by the resources' coverage. In future work, combining our method with high-recall

[10]Note that the corpus-based method benefits from lexical memorization (Levy et al., 2015), overfitting for the lexical terms in the training set, while our resource-based method does not. This means that Figure 5 paints a relatively optimistic picture of the embeddings' actual performance.

corpus-based methods may have synergistic results. Another direction for increasing recall is to use cross-resource mappings to allow cross-resource paths (connected at the concept-level).

Finally, our method can be extended to become context-sensitive, that is, deciding whether the lexical inference holds in a given context. This may be done by applying a resource-based WSD approach similar to (Brody et al., 2006; Agirre et al., 2014), detecting the concept node that matches the term's sense in the given context.

Acknowledgments

This work was supported by an Intel ICRI-CI grant, the Google Research Award Program and the German Research Foundation via the German-Israeli Project Cooperation (DIP, grant DA 1600/1-1).

References

Eneko Agirre, Oier Lopez de Lacalle, and Aitor Soroa. 2014. Random walks for knowledge-based word sense disambiguation. *Computational Linguistics*, 40(1):57–84.

Sören Auer, Christian Bizer, Georgi Kobilarov, Jens Lehmann, Richard Cyganiak, and Zachary Ives. 2007. *Dbpedia: A nucleus for a web of open data*. Springer.

Marco Baroni and Alessandro Lenci. 2011. How we blessed distributional semantic evaluation. In *Proceedings of the GEMS 2011 Workshop on GEometrical Models of Natural Language Semantics*, pages 1–10, Edinburgh, UK, July. Association for Computational Linguistics.

Marco Baroni, Raffaella Bernardi, Ngoc-Quynh Do, and Chung-chieh Shan. 2012. Entailment above the word level in distributional semantics. In *Proceedings of the 13th Conference of the European Chapter of the Association for Computational Linguistics*, pages 23–32, Avignon, France, April. Association for Computational Linguistics.

Jonathan Berant, Andrew Chou, Roy Frostig, and Percy Liang. 2013. Semantic parsing on Freebase from question-answer pairs. In *Proceedings of the 2013 Conference on Empirical Methods in Natural Language Processing*, pages 1533–1544, Seattle, Washington, USA, October. Association for Computational Linguistics.

Samuel Brody, Roberto Navigli, and Mirella Lapata. 2006. Ensemble methods for unsupervised wsd. In *Proceedings of the 21st International Conference on Computational Linguistics and the 44th annual meeting of the Association for Computational Linguistics*, pages 97–104. Association for Computational Linguistics.

Christiane Fellbaum. 1998. *WordNet*. Wiley Online Library.

Ruiji Fu, Jiang Guo, Bing Qin, Wanxiang Che, Haifeng Wang, and Ting Liu. 2014. Learning semantic hierarchies via word embeddings. In *Proceedings of the 52nd Annual Meeting of the Association for Computational Linguistics (Volume 1: Long Papers)*, pages 1199–1209, Baltimore, Maryland, June. Association for Computational Linguistics.

Sanda Harabagiu and Dan Moldovan. 1998. Knowledge processing on an extended wordNet. *WordNet: An electronic lexical database*, 305:381–405.

Marti A Hearst. 1992. Automatic acquisition of hyponyms from large text corpora. In *COLING 1992 Volume 2: The 15th International Conference on Computational Linguistics*, pages 529–545, Nantes, France.

Martin Jansche. 2005. Maximum expected f-measure training of logistic regression models. In *Proceedings of Human Language Technology Conference and Conference on Empirical Methods in Natural Language Processing*, pages 692–699, Vancouver, British Columbia, Canada, October. Association for Computational Linguistics.

Lili Kotlerman, Ido Dagan, Idan Szpektor, and Maayan Zhitomirsky-Geffet. 2010. Directional distributional similarity for lexical inference. *Natural Language Engineering*, 16(04):359–389.

Omer Levy, Ido Dagan, and Jacob Goldberger. 2014. Focused entailment graphs for open ie propositions. In *Proceedings of the Eighteenth Conference on Computational Natural Language Learning*, pages 87–97, Ann Arbor, Michigan, June. Association for Computational Linguistics.

Omer Levy, Steffen Remus, Chris Biemann, and Ido Dagan. 2015. Do supervised distributional methods really learn lexical inference relations? In *Proceedings of the 2015 Conference of the North American Chapter of the Association for Computational Linguistics: Human Language Technologies*, pages 970–976, Denver, Colorado, May–June. Association for Computational Linguistics.

Tomas Mikolov, Ilya Sutskever, Kai Chen, Gregory S Corrado, and Jeffrey Dean. 2013. Distributed representations of words and phrases and their compositionality. In *Advances in Neural Information Processing Systems*, pages 3111–3119.

Ted Pedersen, Siddharth Patwardhan, and Jason Michelizzi. 2004. Wordnet::similarity - measuring the relatedness of concepts. In Daniel Marcu Susan Dumais and Salim Roukos, editors, *HLT-NAACL 2004: Demonstration Papers*, pages 38–41, Boston, Massachusetts, USA, May 2 - May 7. Association for Computational Linguistics.

Altaf Rahman and Vincent Ng. 2011. Coreference resolution with world knowledge. In *Proceedings of the 49th Annual Meeting of the Association for Computational Linguistics: Human Language Technologies*, pages 814–824, Portland, Oregon, USA, June. Association for Computational Linguistics.

Philip Resnik. 1995. Using information content to evaluate semantic similarity in a taxonomy. In *Proceedings of the 14th international joint conference on Artificial intelligence - Volume 1*, IJCAI'95, pages 448–453. Morgan Kaufmann Publishers Inc.

Stephen Roller, Katrin Erk, and Gemma Boleda. 2014. Inclusive yet selective: Supervised distributional hypernymy detection. In *Proceedings of COLING 2014, the 25th International Conference on Computational Linguistics: Technical Papers*, pages 1025–1036, Dublin, Ireland, August. Dublin City University and Association for Computational Linguistics.

D E Rumelhart, G E Hinton, and R J Williams. 1986. Learning representations by back-propagating errors. *Nature*, pages 533–536.

Stuart Russell and Peter Norvig. 2009. *Artificial Intelligence: A Modern Approach*. Prentice Hall.

Eyal Shnarch, Libby Barak, and Ido Dagan. 2009. Extracting lexical reference rules from wikipedia. In *Proceedings of the Joint Conference of the 47th Annual Meeting of the ACL and the 4th International Joint Conference on Natural Language Processing of the AFNLP*, pages 450–458, Suntec, Singapore, August. Association for Computational Linguistics.

Fabian M Suchanek, Gjergji Kasneci, and Gerhard Weikum. 2007. Yago: a core of semantic knowledge. In *Proceedings of the 16th international conference on World Wide Web*, pages 697–706. ACM.

Peter D Turney and Saif M Mohammad. 2015. Experiments with three approaches to recognizing lexical entailment. *Natural Language Engineering*, 21(03):437–476.

Peter D Turney. 2006. Similarity of semantic relations. *Computational Linguistics*, 32(3):379–416.

Christina Unger, Lorenz Bühmann, Jens Lehmann, Axel-Cyrille Ngonga Ngomo, Daniel Gerber, and Philipp Cimiano. 2012. Template-based question answering over rdf data. In *Proceedings of the 21st international conference on World Wide Web*, pages 639–648. ACM.

Denny Vrandečić. 2012. Wikidata: A new platform for collaborative data collection. In *Proceedings of the 21st international conference companion on World Wide Web*, pages 1063–1064. ACM.

Julie Weeds and David Weir. 2003. A general framework for distributional similarity. In Michael Collins and Mark Steedman, editors, *Proceedings of the 2003 Conference on Empirical Methods in Natural Language Processing*, pages 81–88.

Julie Weeds, Daoud Clarke, Jeremy Reffin, David Weir, and Bill Keller. 2014. Learning to distinguish hypernyms and co-hyponyms. In *Proceedings of COLING 2014, the 25th International Conference on Computational Linguistics: Technical Papers*, pages 2249–2259, Dublin, Ireland, August. Dublin City University and Association for Computational Linguistics.

Fei Wu and Daniel S. Weld. 2010. Open information extraction using wikipedia. In *Proceedings of the 48th Annual Meeting of the Association for Computational Linguistics*, pages 118–127, Uppsala, Sweden, July. Association for Computational Linguistics.

Jihoon Yang and Vasant Honavar. 1998. Feature subset selection using a genetic algorithm. In *Feature extraction, construction and selection*, pages 117–136. Springer.

Appendix A Efficient Path-Finding

We split the search to two phases: we first find all nodes along the shortest paths between x and y, and then reconstruct the actual paths. The first phase ignores edge types, inducing a simpler resource graph, which we represent as a sparse adjacency matrix and manipulate efficiently with matrix operations (Algorithm 1). Once the search space is limited to relevant nodes only, the second phase becomes trivial.

Algorithm 1 Find Relevant Nodes

1: **function** NODESINPATH($\vec{n}_x, \vec{n}_y, len$)
2:    **if** $len == 1$ **then**
3:       **return** $\vec{n}_x \cup \vec{n}_y$
4:    **for** $0 < k \leq len$ **do**
5:       **if** k is odd **then**
6:          $\vec{n}_x = \vec{n}_x \cdot A$
7:       **else**
8:          $\vec{n}_y = \vec{n}_y \cdot A^T$
9:       **if** $\vec{n}_x \cdot \vec{n}_y > 0$ **then**
10:          $\vec{n}_{xy} = \vec{n}_x \cap \vec{n}_y$
11:          $\vec{n}_{forward} = nodesInPath(\vec{n}_x, \vec{n}_{xy}, \lceil \frac{k}{2} \rceil)$
12:          $\vec{n}_{backward} = nodesInPath(\vec{n}_{xy}, \vec{n}_y, \lfloor \frac{k}{2} \rfloor)$
13:          **return** $\vec{n}_{forward} \cup \vec{n}_{backward}$
14:    **return** $\vec{0}$

The algorithm finds all nodes in the paths between x and y subject to the maximum length (len). A is the resource adjacency matrix and $\vec{n}_x, \vec{n}_y$ are one-hot vectors of x, y.
At each iteration, we either make a forward (line 6) or a backward (8) step. If the forward and backward search meet (9), we recursively call the algorithm for each side (11-12), and merge their results (13). The stop conditions are $len = 0$, returning an empty set when no path was found, and $len = 1$, merging both sides when they are connected by single edges.

Linking Entities Across Images and Text

Rebecka Weegar
DSV
Stockholm University

Kalle Åström
Dept. of Mathematics
Lund University

Pierre Nugues
Dept. of Computer Science
Lund University

rebeckaw@dsv.su.se, kalle@maths.lth.se, Pierre.Nugues@cs.lth.se

Abstract

This paper describes a set of methods to link entities across images and text. As a corpus, we used a data set of images, where each image is commented by a short caption and where the regions in the images are manually segmented and labeled with a category. We extracted the entity mentions from the captions and we computed a semantic similarity between the mentions and the region labels. We also measured the statistical associations between these mentions and the labels and we combined them with the semantic similarity to produce mappings in the form of pairs consisting of a region label and a caption entity. In a second step, we used the syntactic relationships between the mentions and the spatial relationships between the regions to rerank the lists of candidate mappings. To evaluate our methods, we annotated a test set of 200 images, where we manually linked the image regions to their corresponding mentions in the captions. Eventually, we could match objects in pictures to their correct mentions for nearly 89 percent of the segments, when such a matching exists.

1 Introduction

Linking an object in an image to a mention of that object in an accompanying text is a challenging task, which we can imagine useful in a number of settings. It could, for instance, improve image retrieval by complementing the geometric relationships extracted from the images with textual descriptions from the text. A successful mapping would also make it possible to translate knowledge and information across image and text.

In this paper, we describe methods to link mentions of entities in captions to labeled image segments and we investigate how the syntactic structure of a caption can be used to better understand the contents of an image. We do not address the closely related task of object recognition in the images. This latter task can be seen as a complement to entity linking across text and images. See Russakovsky et al. (2015) for a description of progress and results to date in object detection and classification in images.

2 An Example

Figure 1 shows an example of an image from the Segmented and Annotated IAPR TC-12 data set (Escalantea et al., 2010). It has four regions labeled *cloud*, *grass*, *hill*, and *river*, and the caption:

> a flat landscape with a dry meadow in the foreground, a lagoon behind it and many clouds in the sky

containing mentions of five entities that we identify with the words *meadow*, *landscape*, *lagoon*, *cloud*, and *sky*. A correct association of the mentions in the caption to the image regions would

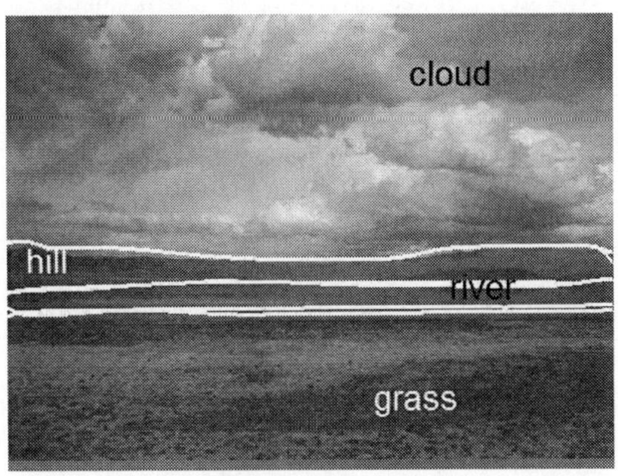

Figure 1: Image from the Segmented and Annotated IAPR TC-12 data set with the caption: *a flat landscape with a dry meadow in the foreground, a lagoon behind it and many clouds in the sky*

Proceedings of the 19th Conference on Computational Language Learning, pages 185–193,
Beijing, China, July 30-31, 2015.

map *clouds* to the region labeled *cloud*, *meadow* to *grass*, and *lagoon* to *river*.

This image, together with its caption, illustrates a couple of issues: The objects or regions labelled or visible in an image are not always mentioned in the caption, and for most of the images in the data set, more entities are mentioned in the captions than there are regions in the images. In addition, for a same entity, the words used to mention it are usually different from the words used as labels (the categories), as in the case of *grass* and *meadow*.

3 Previous Work

Related work includes the automatic generation of image captions that describes relevant objects in an image and their relationships. Kulkarni et al. (2011) assign each detected image object a visual attribute and a spatial relationship to the other objects in the image. The spatial relationships are translated into selected prepositions in the resulting captions. Elliott and Keller (2013) used manually segmented and labeled images and introduced *visual dependency representations* (VDRs) that describe spatial relationships between the image objects. The captions are generated using templates. Both Kulkarni et al. (2011) and Elliott and Keller (2013) used the BLEU-score and human evaluators to assess grammatically the generated captions and on how well they describe the image.

Although much work has been done to link complete images to a whole text, there are only a few papers on the association of elements inside a text and an image. Naim et al. (2014) analyzed parallel sets of videos and written texts, where the videos show laboratory experiments. Written instructions are used to describe how to conduct these experiments. The paper describes models for matching objects detected in the video with mentions of those objects in the instructions. The authors mainly focus on objects that get touched by a hand in the video. For manually annotated videos, Naim et al. (2014) could match objects to nouns nearly 50% of the time.

Karpathy et al. (2014) proposed a system for retrieving related images and sentences. They used neural networks and they show that the results are improved if image objects and sentence fragments are included in the model. Sentence fragments are extracted from dependency graphs, where each edge in the graphs corresponds to a fragment.

4 Entity Pairs

4.1 Data Set

We used the *Segmented and Annotated IAPR TC-12 Benchmark* data set (Escalantea et al., 2010) that consists of about 20,000 photographs with a wide variety of themes. Each image has a short caption that describes its content, most often consisting of one to three sentences separated by semicolons. The images are manually segmented into regions with, on average, about 5 segments in each image.

Each region is labelled with one out of 275 predefined image labels. The labels are arranged in a hierarchy, where all the nodes are available as labels and where `object` is the top node. The labels `humans`, `animals`, `man-made`, `landscape/nature`, `food`, and `other` form the next level.

4.2 Entities and Mentions

An image caption describes a set of entities, the caption entities CE, where each entity CE_i is referred to by a set of mentions M. To detect them, we applied the Stanford CoreNLP pipeline (Toutanova et al., 2003) that consists of a part-of-speech tagger, lemmatizer, named entity recognizer (Finkel et al., 2005), dependency parser, and coreference solver. We considered each noun in a caption as an entity candidate. If an entity CE_i had only one mention M_j, we identified it by the head noun of its mention. We represented the entities mentioned more than once by the head noun of their most representative mention. We applied the entity extraction to all the captions in the data set, and we found 3,742 different nouns or noun compounds to represent the entities.

In addition to the caption entities, each image has a set of labeled segments (or regions) corresponding to the image entities, IE. The Cartesian product of these two sets results in pairs P generating all the possible mappings of caption entities to image labels. We considered a pair (IE_i, CE_j) a correct mapping, if the image label IE_i and the caption entity CE_j referred to the same entity. We represented a pair by the region label and the identifier of the caption entity, *i.e.* the head noun of the entity mention. In Fig. 1, the correct pairs are (grass, meadow), (river, lagoon), and (cloud, clouds).

4.3 Building a Test Set

As the Segmented and Annotated IAPR TC-12 data set does not provide information on links between the image regions and the mentions, we annotated a set of 200 randomly selected images from the data set to evaluate the automatic linking accuracy. We assigned the image regions to entities in the captions and we excluded these images from the training set. The annotation does not always produce a 1:1 mapping of caption entities to regions. In many cases, objects are grouped or divided into parts differently in the captions and in the segmentation. We created a set of guidelines to handle these mappings in a consistent way. Table 1 shows the sizes of the different image sets and the fraction of image regions that have a corresponding entity mention in the caption.

Set	Files	Regions	Mappings	%
Data set	19,176	–	–	–
Train. set	18,976	–	–	–
Test set	200	928	730	78.7

Table 1: The sizes of the different image sets.

5 Ranking Entity Pairs

To identify the links between the regions of an image and the entity identifiers in its caption, we first generated all the possible pairs. We then ranked these pairs using a semantic distance derived from WordNet (Miller, 1995), statistical association metrics, and finally, a combination of both techniques.

5.1 Semantic Distance

The image labels are generic English words that are semantically similar to those used in the captions. In Fig. 1, *cloud* and *clouds* are used both as label and in the caption, but the region labeled *grass* is described as a *meadow* and the region labeled *river*, as a *lagoon*. We used the WordNet Similarity for Java library, (WS4J), (Shima, 2014) to compute the semantic similarity of the region labels and the entity identifiers. WS4J comes with a number of metrics that approximate similarity as distances between WordNet synsets: PATH, WUP (Wu and Palmer, 1994), RES, (Resnik, 1995), JCN (Jiang and Conrath, 1997), HSO (Hirst and St-Onge, 1998), LIN (Lin, 1998), LCH (Leacock and Chodorow, 1998), and LESK (Banerjee and Banerjee, 2002).

We manually lemmatized and simplified the image labels and the entity mentions so that they are compatible with WordNet entries. It resulted in a smaller set of labels: 250 instead of the 275 original labels. We also simplified the named entities from the captions. When a person or location was not present in WordNet, we used its named entity type as identifier. In some cases, it was not possible to find an entity identifier in WordNet, mostly due to misspellings in the caption, like *buldings*, or *buidling*, or because of POS-tagging errors. We chose to identify these entities with the word *entity*. The normalization reduced the 3,742 entity identifiers to 2,216 unique ones.

Finally, we computed a 250×2216 matrix containing the similarity scores for each (image label, entity identifier) pair for each of the WS4J semantic similarity metrics.

5.2 Statistical Associations

We used three functions to reflect the statistical association between an image label and an entity identifier:

- Co-occurrence counts, i.e. the frequencies of the region labels and entity identifiers that occur together in the pictures of the training set;
- Pointwise mutual information (PMI) (Fano, 1961) that compares the joint probability of the occurrence of a (image label, entity identifier) pair to the independent probability of the region label and the caption entity occurring by themselves; and finally
- The simplified Student's t-score as described in Church and Mercer (1993).

As with the semantic similarity scores, we used matrices to hold the scores for all the (image label, entity identifier) pairs for the three association metrics.

5.3 The Mapping Algorithm

To associate the region labels of an image to the entities in its caption, we mapped the label L_i to the caption entity E_j that had the highest score with respect to L_i. We did this for the three association scores and the eight semantic metrics. Note that a region label is not systematically paired with the same caption entity, since each caption contains different sets of entities.

Background and *foreground* are two of the most frequent words in the captions and they were frequently assigned to image regions. Since they rarely represent entities, but merely tell *where* the entities are located, we included them in a list of stop words, as well as *middle*, *left*, *right*, and *front* that we removed from the identifiers.

We applied the linking algorithm to the annotated set. We formed the Cartesian product of the image labels and the entity identifiers and, for each image region, we ranked the caption entities using the individual scoring functions. This results in an ordered list of entity candidates for each region. Table 2 shows the average ranks of the correct candidate for each of the scoring functions and the total number of correct candidates at different ranks.

6 Reranking

The algorithm in Sect. 5.3 determines the relationship holding between a pair of entities, where one element in the pair comes from the image and the other from the caption. The entities on each side are considered in isolation. We extended their description with relationships inside the image and the caption. Weegar et al. (2014) showed that pairs of entities in a text that were linked by the prepositions *on*, *at*, *with*, or *in*, often corresponded to pairs of segments that were close to each other. We further investigated the idea that spatial relationships in the image relate to syntactical relationships in the captions and we implemented it in the form of a reranker.

For each label-identifier pair, we included the relationship between the image segment in the pair and the closest segment in the image. As in Weegar et al. (2014), we defined the closeness as the Euclidean distance between the gravity centers of the bounding boxes of the segments. We also added the relationship between the caption entity in the label-identifier pair and the entity mentions which were the closest in the caption. We parsed the captions and we measured the distance as the number of edges between the two entities in the dependency graph.

6.1 Spatial Features

The Segmented and Annotated IAPR TC-12 data set comes with annotations for three different types of spatial relationships holding between the segment pairs in each image: Topological, horizontal, and vertical (Hernández-Gracidas and Sucar, 2007). The possible values are *adjacent* or *disjoint* for the topological category, *beside* or *horizontally aligned* for the horizontal one, and finally *above*, *below*, or *vertically aligned* for the vertical one.

6.2 Syntactic Features

The syntactic features are all based on the structure of the sentences' dependency graphs. We followed the graph from the caption-entity in the pair to extract its closest ancestors and descendants. We only considered children to the right of the candidate. We also included all the prepositions between the entity and these ancestor and descendant.

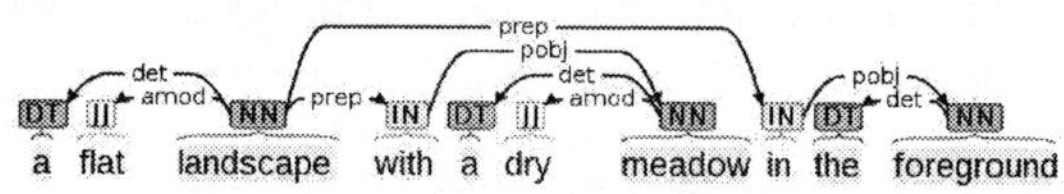

Figure 2: Dependency graph of the sentence *a flat landscape with a dry meadow in the foreground*

Figure 2 shows the dependency graph of the sentence *a flat landscape with a dry meadow in the foreground.* The descendants of the *landscape* entity are *meadow* and *foreground* linked respectively by the prepositions *with* and *in*. Its ancestor is the *root* node and the distance between *landscape* and *meadow* is 2. The syntactic features we extract for the entities in this sentence arranged in the order ancestor, distance to ancestor, preposition, descendant, distance to descendant, and preposition are for *landscape*, (root, 1, null, meadow, 2, with) and (root, 1, null, foreground, 2, in), for *meadow*, (landscape, 2, with, null, –, null), and for *foreground*, (landscape, 2, in, null, –, null). We discard *foreground* as it is part of the stop words.

6.3 Pairing Features

The single features consist of the label, entity identifier, and score of the pair. To take interaction into account, we also paired features characterizing properties across image and text. The list of these features is (Table 3):

1. The label of the image region and the identifier of the caption entity. In Fig 2, we create `grass_meadow` from *(grass, meadow)*.

2. The label of the closest image segment to the ancestor of the caption entity. The closest

Scoring function	Average rank	Rank = 1	Rank ≤ 2	Rank ≤ 3	Rank ≤ 4
co-occurrence	1.58	338	525	609	667
PMI	1.61	340	527	624	673
t-scores	1.59	337	540	623	669
PATH	1.19	559	604	643	668
HSO	1.18	**574**	**637**	**666**	**691**
JCN	1.22	535	580	626	653
LCH	1.19	559	604	643	668
LESK	1.19	560	609	646	670
LIN	1.19	542	581	623	652
RES	**1.17**	559	611	638	665
WUP	1.21	546	599	640	663

Table 2: Average rank of the correct candidate obtained by each scoring function on the 200 annotated images of the test set, and number of correct candidates that are ranked first, first or second, etc. The ceiling is 730

`Label`: Simplified segment label	`Entity`: Identifier for the caption entity	`Label_Entity`: Label and entity features combined
`Score`: Score given by the current scoring function	`Anc_ClosestSeg`: Closest segment label with the ancestor of the caption entity	`Desc_ClosestSeg`: Closest segment label with the descendant of the caption entity
`AncDist`: Distance between the ancestor and the caption entity, and distance between segments	`DescDist`: Distance between the descendant and the caption entity, and distance between the segments	`TopoRel_DescPreps`: Topological relationship between segments and the prepositions linking the caption entity with its descendant
`TopoRel_AncPreps`: Topological relationship between the segments and the prepositions linking the caption entity with its ancestor	`XRel_DescPreps`: Horizontal relationship between segments and the prepositions linking the caption entity with its descendant	`XRel_AncPreps`: Horizontal relationship between segments and the prepositions linking the caption entity with its ancestor
`YRel_DescPreps`: Vertical relationship between segments and the prepositions linking the caption entity with its descendant	`YRel_AncPreps`: Vertical relationship between segments and the prepositions linking the caption entity with its ancestor	`SegmentDist`: Distance (in pixels) between the gravity center of the bounding boxes framing the two closest segments

Table 3: The reranking features using the current segment and its closest segment in the image

segment of the *grass* segment is *river* and the ancestor of *meadow* is *landscape*. This gives the paired feature `meadow_landscape`. The labels of the segments closest to the current segment and the descendant of *meadow* are also paired.

3. The distance between the segment pairs in the image divided into seven intervals with the distance between the caption entities. We measured the distance in pixels since all the images have the same pixel dimensions.

4. The spatial relationships of the closest segments with the prepositions found between their corresponding caption entities. The segments *grass* and *river* in the image are *adjacent* and *horizontally aligned* and *grass* is located *below* the segment labeled *river*. Each of the spatial features is paired with the prepositions for both the ancestor and the descendant.

We trained the reranking models from the pairs of labeled segments and caption entities, where the correct mappings formed the positive examples and the rest, the negative ones. In Fig. 1, the mapping *(grass, meadow)* is marked as correct for the region labeled *grass*, while the mappings *(grass, lagoon)* and *(grass, cloud)* are marked as incorrect. We used the manually annotated images (200 images, Table 1) as training data, a leave-one-out cross-validation, and L2-regularized logistic regression from LIBLINEAR (Fan et al., 2008). We applied a cutoff of 3 for the list of candidates in the reranking and we multiplied the original score of the label-identifier pairs with the reranking probability.

6.4 Reranking Example

Table 4, upper part, shows the two top candidates obtained from the co-occurrence scores for the

Label	Entity 1	Score	Entity 2	Score
cloud	sky	2207	cloud	1096
grass	sky	1489	meadow	887
hill	sky	861	cloud	327
river	sky	655	cloud	250
cloud	cloud	769	sky	422
grass	meadow	699	landscape	176
hill	landscape	113	cloud	28
river	cloud	37	meadow	10

Table 4: An example of an assignment before (upper part) and after (lower part) reranking. The caption entities are ranked according to the number of co-occurrences with the label. We obtain the new score for a label-identifier pair by multiplying the original score by the output of the reranker for this pair

Feature	*(grass, meadow)*	*(grass, sky)*
Label	grass	grass
Entity	meadow	sky
Label_Entity	grass_meadow	grass_sky
Score	881	1,477
Anc_ClosestSeg	landscape_river	cloud_river
Desc_ClosestSeg	lagoon_river	null_river
AncDist	2_a	2_a
DescDist	1_a	100_a
TopoRel_DescPrep	adj_null	adj_null
TopoRel_AncPrep	adj_with	adj_in
XRel_DescPrep	horiz_null	horiz_null
XRel_AncPrep	horiz_with	horiz_in
YRel_DescPrep	below_null	below_null
YRel_AncPrep	below_with	below_in
SegmentDist	24	24
Classification	correct	incorrect

Table 5: Feature vectors for the pairs *(grass, meadow)* and *(grass, sky)*. The ancestor distance 2_a means that there are two edges in the dependency graph between the words *meadow* and *landscape*, and *a* represents the smallest of the distance intervals, meaning that the two segments *grass* and *river* are less than 50 pixels apart

four regions in Fig. 1. The column *Entity 1* shows that the scoring function maps the caption entity *sky* to all of the regions. We created a reranker's feature vector for each of the 8 label-identifier pairs. Table 5 shows two of them corresponding to the pairs *(grass, sky)* and *(grass, meadow)*. The pair *(grass, meadow)* is a correct mapping, but it has a lower co-occurrence score than the incorrect pair *(grass, sky)*.

In the cross-validation evaluation, we applied the classifier to these vectors and we obtained the reranking scores of 0.0244 for *(grass, sky)* and 0.79 for *(grass, meadow)* resulting in the respective final scores of 36 and 699. Table 4, lower part, shows the new rankings, where the highest scores correspond to the associations: *(cloud, cloud)*, *(grass, meadow)*, *(hill, landscape)*, and *(river, cloud)*, which are all correct except the last one.

7 Results

7.1 Individual Scoring Functions

We evaluated the three scoring functions: Co-occurrence, mutual information, and t-score, and the semantic similarity functions. Each labeled segment in the annotated set was assigned the caption-entity that gave the highest scoring label-identifier pair.

To confront the lack of annotated data we also investigated a self-training method. We used the statistical associations we derived from the training set and we applied the mapping procedure in Sect. 5.3 to this set. We repeated this procedure with the three statistical scoring functions. We counted all the mappings we obtained between the region labels and the caption identifiers and we used these counts to create three new scoring functions denoted with a $\sum$ sign.

Table 6 shows the performance comparison between the different functions. The second column shows how many correct mappings were found by each function. The fourth column shows the improved score when the stop words were removed. The removal of the stop words as entity candidates improved the co-occurrence and t-score scoring functions considerably, but provided only marginal improvement for the scoring functions based on semantic similarity and pointwise mutual information. The percentage of correct mappings is based on the 730 regions that have a matching caption entity in the annotated test set.

The semantic similarity functions – PATH, HSO, JCN, LCH, LESK, LIN, RES and WUP – outperform the statistical one and the self-trained versions of the statistical scoring functions yield better results than the original ones.

We applied an ensemble voting procedure with the individual scoring functions, where each function was given a number of votes to place on its preferred label-identifier pair. We counted the votes and the entity that received the majority of the votes was selected as the mapping for the current label. Table 7 shows the results, where

Function	With stop words # correct	%	Without stop words # correct	%
co-oc.	208	28.5	338	46.3
PMI	339	46.4	340	46.6
t-score	241	33.0	337	46.1
∑ co-oc.	226	30.0	387	53.0
∑ PMI	457	62.6	458	62.7
∑ t-score	247	33.8	397	54.4
PATH	552	75.6	559	76.6
HSO	**562**	**77.0**	**574**	**78.6**
JCN	527	72.2	535	73.3
LCH	552	75.6	559	76.6
LESK	549	75.2	560	76.7
LIN	532	72.9	542	74.2
RES	539	73.8	559	76.6
WUP	540	74.0	546	74.8

Table 6: Comparison of the individual scoring functions. This test is performed on the annotated set of 200 images, with 730 possible correct mappings

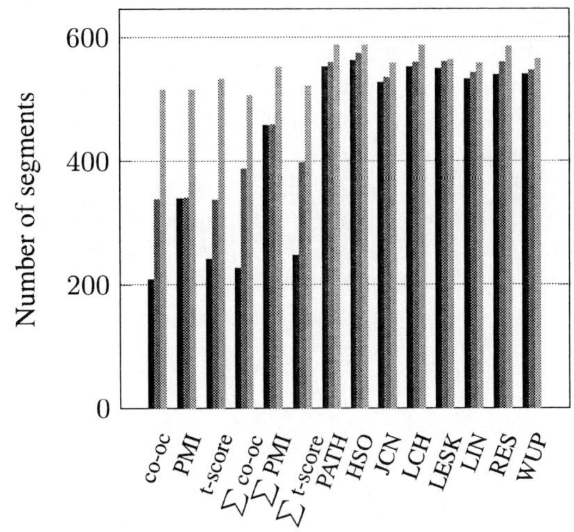

Figure 3: A comparison of the number of correctly assigned labels when using the different scoring functions. The leftmost bars show the results of the original functions, the middle bars show the performance when the stop words are removed, and the rightmost ones show the performance of the reranked functions

we reached a maximum 79.45% correct mappings when all the functions were used together with one vote each.

Scoring function	Number of votes		
co-oc.	1	0	1
PMI	1	0	1
t-score	1	0	1
∑ co-oc.	1	0	1
∑ PMI	1	0	1
∑ t-score	1	0	1
PATH	0	1	1
HSO	0	1	1
JCN	0	1	1
LCH	0	1	1
LESK	0	1	1
LIN	0	1	1
RES	0	1	1
WUP	0	1	1
number correct	382	569	580
percent correct	52	78	**79**

Table 7: Results of ensemble voting on the annotated set

7.2 Reranking

We reranked all the scoring functions using the methods described in Sect. 6. We used the three label-identifier pairs with the highest score for each segment and function to build the model and we also reranked the top three label-identifier pairs for each of the assignments. Table 8 shows the results we obtained with the reranker compared to the original scoring functions. The reranking procedure improves the performance of all the scoring functions, especially the statistical ones, where the maximal improvement reaches 58%.

Function	correct	correct rerank.	% Improv.
co-oc.	338	515	52.4
PMI	340	515	51.5
t-score	337	532	**57.9**
∑ co-oc.	387	506	30.7
∑ PMI	458	**552**	20.5
∑ t-score	397	521	31.2
PATH	559	**587**	5.0
HSO	574	**587**	2.3
JCN	535	558	4.3
LCH	559	586	4.8
LESK	560	563	0.5
LIN	542	558	3.0
RES	559	585	4.7
WUP	546	565	3.5

Table 8: The performance of the reranked scoring functions compared to the original scoring functions

Figure 3 shows the comparison between the original scoring functions, the scoring functions without stop words, and the reranked versions. There is a total of 928 segments, where 730 have a matching entity in the caption.

We applied an ensemble voting with the reranked functions (Table 9). Reranking yields a significant improvement for the statistical scoring functions. When they get one vote each in the ensemble voting, the results increase from 52% correct mappings to 75%. When used in an ensemble with the semantic similarity scoring functions, the results improve further.

Scoring function	Number of votes		
Reranked co-oc.	1	0	1
Reranked PMI	1	0	1
Reranked t-score	1	0	1
Reranked $\sum$ co-oc.	1	0	1
Reranked $\sum$ PMI	1	0	1
Reranked $\sum$ t-score	1	0	1
Reranked PATH	0	1	1
Reranked HSO	0	1	1
Reranked JCN	0	1	1
Reranked LCH	0	1	1
Reranked LESK	0	1	1
Reranked LIN	0	1	1
Reranked RES	0	1	1
Reranked WUP	0	1	1
number correct	546	594	633
percent correct	75	81	**87**

Table 9: Results of ensemble voting with reranked assignments segments

We also evaluated ensemble voting with different numbers of votes for the different functions. We tested all the permutations of integer weights in the interval {0,3} on the development set. Table 10 shows the best result for both the original assignments and the reranked assignments on the test set. The reranked assignments gave the best results, 88.76% correct mappings, and this is also the best result we have been able to reach.

	Number of votes	
Scoring function	Original	Reranked
co-oc.	0	0
PMI	2	3
t-score	0	0
$\sum$ co-oc.	0	1
$\sum$ PMI	2	1
$\sum$ t-score	0	1
PATH	1	1
HSO	2	3
JCN	0	0
LCH	0	0
LESK	1	0
LIN	2	0
RES	0	0
WUP	0	0
number correct	298	316
percent correct	83.71	**88.76**

Table 10: Results of weighted ensemble voting.

8 Conclusion and Future Work

The extraction of relations across text and image is a new area for research. We showed in this paper that we could use semantic and statistical functions to link the entities in an image to mentions of the same entities in captions describing this image. We also showed that using the syntactic structure of the caption and the spatial structure of the image improves linking accuracy. Eventually, we managed to map correctly nearly 89% of the image segments in our data set, counting only segments that have a matching entity in the caption.

The semantic similarity functions form the most accurate mapping tool, when using functions in isolation. The statistical functions improve significantly their results when they are used in an ensemble. This shows that it is preferable to use multiple scoring functions, as their different properties contribute to the final score.

Including the syntactic structures of the captions and pairing them with the spatial structures of the images is also useful when mapping entities to segments. By training a model on such features and using this model to rerank the assignments, the ordering of entities in the assignments is improved with a better precision for all the scoring functions.

Although we used images manually annotated with segments and labels, we believe the methods we described here can be applied on automatically segmented and labeled images. Using image recognition would then certainly introduce incorrectly classified image regions and thus probably decrease the linking scores.

Acknowledgments

This research was supported by Vetenskapsrådet under grant 621-2010-4800, and the *Det digitaliserade samhället* and eSSENCE programs.

References

Satanjeev Banerjee and Satanjeev Banerjee. 2002. An adapted Lesk algorithm for word sense disambiguation using Wordnet. In *Proceedings of the Third International Conference on Intelligent Text Processing and Computational Linguistics*, pages 136–145.

Kenneth Church and Robert Mercer. 1993. Introduction to the special issue on computational linguistics using large corpora. *Computational Linguistics*, 19(1):1–24.

Desmond Elliott and Frank Keller. 2013. Image description using visual dependency representations. In *Proceedings of the 2013 Conference on Empirical Methods in Natural Language Processing*, pages 1292–1302, Seattle, Washington, USA, October. Association for Computational Linguistics.

Hugo Jair Escalantea, Carlos A. Hernándeza, Jesus A. Gonzaleza, A. López-Lópeza, Manuel Montesa, Eduardo F. Moralesa, L. Enrique Sucara, Luis Villaseñora, and Michael Grubinger. 2010. The segmented and annotated IAPR TC-12 benchmark. *Computer Vision and Image Understanding*, 114:419–428.

Rong-En Fan, Kai-Wei Chang, Cho-Jui Hsieh, Xiang-Rui Wang, and Chih-Jen Lin. 2008. LIBLINEAR: A library for large linear classification. *Journal of Machine Learning Research*, 9:1871–1874.

Robert Fano. 1961. *Transmission of Information: A Statistical Theory of Communications.* MIT Press, Cambridge, MA.

Jenny Rose Finkel, Trond Grenager, and Christopher Manning. 2005. Incorporating non-local information into information extraction systems by gibbs sampling. In *Proceedings of the 43rd Annual Meeting of the ACL*, pages 363–370, Ann Arbor.

Carlos Arturo Hernández-Gracidas and Luis Enrique Sucar. 2007. Markov random fields and spatial information to improve automatic image annotation. In Domingo Mery and Luis Rueda, editors, *PSIVT*, volume 4872 of *Lecture Notes in Computer Science*, pages 879–892. Springer.

Graeme Hirst and David St-Onge. 1998. Lexical chains as representations of context for the detection and correction of malapropisms. In Christiane Fellbaum, editor, *WordNet: An Electronic Lexical Database*. MIT Press, Cambridge, MA.

Jay J. Jiang and David W. Conrath. 1997. Semantic similarity based on corpus statistics and lexical taxonomy. *CoRR*, cmp-lg/9709008.

Andrej Karpathy, Armand Joulin, and Li Fei-Fei. 2014. Deep fragment embeddings for bidirectional image sentence mapping. *CoRR*, abs/1406.5679.

Girish Kulkarni, Visruth Premraj, Sagnik Dhar, Siming Li, Yejin Choi, Alexander C Berg, and Tamara L Berg. 2011. Baby talk: Understanding and generating image descriptions. In *Proceedings of the 24th CVPR*.

Claudia Leacock and Martin Chodorow. 1998. Combining local context and wordnet similarity for word sense identification. In Christiane Fellbaum, editor, *WordNet: An Electronic Lexical Database*. MIT press, Cambridge, MA.

Dekang Lin. 1998. An information-theoretic definition of similarity. In *Proceedings of the 15th International Conference on Machine Learning*, pages 296–304. Morgan Kaufmann.

George A. Miller. 1995. WordNet: A lexical database for English. *Communications of the ACM*, 38(11):39–41, November.

Iftekhar Naim, Young Chol Song, Qiguang Liu, Henry Kautz, Jiebo Luo, and Daniel Gildea. 2014. Unsupervised alignment of natural language instructions with video segments. In *Proceedings of the National Conference on Artificial Intelligence (AAAI-14)*.

Philip Resnik. 1995. Using information content to evaluate semantic similarity in a taxonomy. In *Proceedings of the 14th International Joint Conference on Artificial Intelligence*, pages 448–453.

Olga Russakovsky, Jia Deng, Hao Su, Jonathan Krause, Sanjeev Satheesh, Sean Ma, Zhiheng Huang, Andrej Karpathy, Aditya Khosla, Michael Bernstein, Alexander C. Berg, and Li Fei-Fei. 2015. ImageNet Large Scale Visual Recognition Challenge. *International Journal of Computer Vision (IJCV)*.

Hideki Shima. 2014. WordNet Similarity for Java, February.

Kristina Toutanova, Dan Klein, Christopher D. Manning, and Yoram Singer. 2003. Feature-rich part-of-speech tagging with a cyclic dependency network. In *Proceedings of the 2003 Conference of the HLT-NAACL*, pages 252–259, Edmonton.

Rebecka Weegar, Linus Hammarlund, Agnes Tegen, Magnus Oskarsson, Kalle Åström, and Pierre Nugues. 2014. Visual entity linking: A preliminary study. In *Proceedings of the AAAI 2014 Workshop on Cognitive Computing for Augmented Human Intelligence*, pages 46–49, Québec, July 27.

Zhibiao Wu and Martha Palmer. 1994. Verbs semantics and lexical selection. In *Proceedings of the 32nd Annual Meeting of the Association for Computational Linguistics*, ACL '94, pages 133–138, Stroudsburg, PA, USA. Association for Computational Linguistics.

Making the Most of Crowdsourced Document Annotations: Confused Supervised LDA

Paul Felt
Dept. of Computer Science
Brigham Young University
paul.lewis.felt@gmail.com

Eric K. Ringger
Dept. of Computer Science
Brigham Young University
ringger@cs.byu.edu

Jordan Boyd-Graber
Dept. of Computer Science
University of Colorado Boulder
Jordan.Boyd.Graber@colorado.edu

Kevin Seppi
Dept. of Computer Science
Brigham Young University
kseppi@byu.edu

Abstract

Corpus labeling projects frequently use low-cost workers from microtask marketplaces; however, these workers are often inexperienced or have misaligned incentives. Crowdsourcing models must be robust to the resulting systematic and non-systematic inaccuracies. We introduce a novel crowdsourcing model that adapts the discrete supervised topic model sLDA to handle multiple corrupt, usually conflicting (hence "confused") supervision signals. Our model achieves significant gains over previous work in the accuracy of deduced ground truth.

1 Modeling Annotators and Abilities

Supervised machine learning requires labeled training corpora, historically produced by laborious and costly annotation projects. Microtask markets such as Amazon's Mechanical Turk and Crowdflower have turned crowd labor into a commodity that can be purchased with relatively little overhead. However, crowdsourced judgments can suffer from high error rates. A common solution to this problem is to obtain multiple redundant human judgments, or annotations,[1] relying on the observation that, in aggregate, non-experts often rival or exceed experts by averaging over individual error patterns (Surowiecki, 2005; Snow et al., 2008; Jurgens, 2013).

A *crowdsourcing model* harnesses the wisdom of the crowd and infers labels based on the evidence of the available annotations, imperfect though they be. A common baseline crowdsourcing method aggregates annotations by *majority vote*, but this approach ignores important information. For example, some annotators are more reliable than others and their judgments ought to be upweighted accordingly. State-of-the-art crowdsourcing methods account for annotator expertise, often through a probabilistic formalism. Compounding the challenge, assessing unobserved annotator expertise is tangled with estimating ground truth from imperfect annotations; thus, joint inference of these interrelated quantities is necessary. State-of-the-art models also take the data into account, because data features can help ratify or veto human annotators.

We introduce a model that improves on state of the art crowdsourcing algorithms by modeling not only the annotations but also the features of the data (e.g., words in a document). Section 2 identifies modeling deficiencies affecting previous work and proposes a solution based on topic modeling; Section 2.4 presents inference for the new model. Experiments that contrast the proposed model with select previous work on several text classification datasets are presented in Section 3. In Section 4 we highlight additional related work.

2 Latent Representations that Reflect Labels and Confusion

Most crowdsourcing models extend the item-response model of Dawid and Skene (1979). The Bayesian version of this model, referred to here as ITEMRESP, is depicted in Figure 1. In the generative story for this model, a confusion matrix γ_j is drawn for each human annotator j. Each row γ_{jc} of the confusion matrix γ_j is drawn from

[1] In this paper, we call human judgments *annotations* to distinguish them from gold standard class *labels*.

Proceedings of the 19th Conference on Computational Language Learning, pages 194–203,
Beijing, China, July 30-31, 2015.

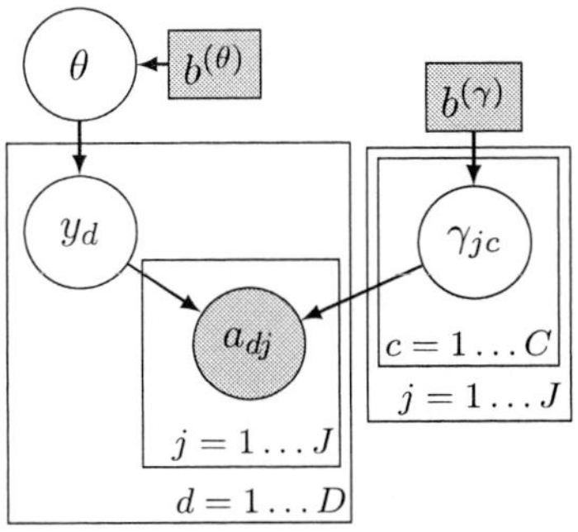

Figure 1: **ITEMRESP** as a plate diagram. Round nodes are random variables. Rectangular nodes are free parameters. Shaded nodes are observed. D, J, C are the number of documents, annotators, and classes, respectively.

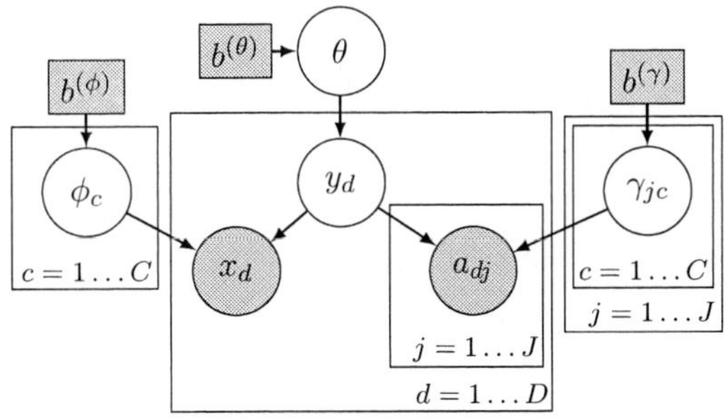

Figure 2: **MOMRESP** as a plate diagram. $|x_d| = V$, the size of the vocabulary. Documents with similar feature vectors x tend to share a common label y. Reduces to mixture-of-multinomials clustering when no annotations a are observed.

a symmetric Dirichlet distribution $Dir(b_{jc}^{(\gamma)})$ and encodes a categorical probability distribution over label classes that annotator j is apt to choose when presented with a document whose true label is c. Then for each document d an unobserved document label y_d is drawn. Annotations are generated as annotator j corrupts the true label y_d according to the categorical distribution $Cat(\gamma_{jy_d})$.

2.1 Leveraging Data

Some extensions to ITEMRESP model the features of the data (e.g., words in a document). Many data-aware crowdsourcing models condition the labels on the data (Jin and Ghahramani, 2002; Raykar et al., 2010; Liu et al., 2012; Yan et al., 2014), possibly because discriminative classifiers dominate supervised machine learning. Others model the data generatively (Bragg et al., 2013; Lam and Stork, 2005; Felt et al., 2014; Simpson and Roberts, 2015). Felt et al. (2015) argue that generative models are better suited than conditional models to crowdsourcing scenarios because generative models often learn faster than their conditional counterparts (Ng and Jordan, 2001)—especially early in the learning curve. This advantage is amplified by the annotation noise typical of crowdsourcing scenarios.

Extensions to ITEMRESP that model document features generatively tend to share a common high-level architecture. After the document class label y_d is drawn for each document d, features are drawn from class-conditional distributions. Felt et al. (2015) identify the MOMRESP model, reproduced in Figure 2, as a strong representative of generative crowdsourcing models. In MOMRESP, the feature vector x_d for document d is drawn from the multinomial distribution with parameter vector ϕ_{y_d}. This class-conditional multinomial model of the data inherits many of the strengths and weaknesses of the naïve Bayes model that it resembles. Strengths include easy inference and a strong inductive bias which helps the model be robust to annotation noise and scarcity. Weaknesses include overly strict conditional independence assumptions among features, leading to overconfidence in the document model and thereby causing the model to overweight feature evidence and underweight annotation evidence. This imbalance can result in degraded performance in the presence of high quality or many annotations.

2.2 Confused Supervised LDA (CSLDA)

We solve the problem of imbalanced feature and annotation evidence observed in MOMRESP by replacing the class-conditional structure of previous generative crowdsourcing models with a richer generative story where documents are drawn first and class labels y_d are obtained afterwards via a log-linear mapping. This move towards conditioning classes on documents content is sensible because in many situations document content is authored first, whereas label structure is not imposed until afterwards. It is plausible to assume that there will exist some mapping from a latent document structure to the desired document label distinctions. Moreover, by jointly modeling topics and the mapping to labels, we can learn the latent document representations that best explain how best to predict and correct annotator errors.

Term	Definition
N_d	Size of document d
N_{dt}	$\sum_n \mathbb{1}(z_{dn} = t)$
N_t	$\sum_{d,n} \mathbb{1}(z_{dn} = t)$
$N_{jcc'}$	$\sum_d a_{djc'} \mathbb{1}(y_d = c)$
N_{jc}	$\langle N_{jc1} \cdots N_{jcC} \rangle$
N_{vt}	$\sum_{dn} \mathbb{1}(w_{dn} = v \wedge z_{dn} = t)$
N_t	$\sum_{dn} \mathbb{1}(z_{dn} = t)$
$\hat{N}$	Count excludes variable being sampled
$\bar{z}_d$	Vector where $\bar{z}_{dt} = \frac{1}{N_d} \sum_n \mathbb{1}(z_{dn} = t)$
$\hat{\bar{z}}_d$	Excludes the z_{dn} being sampled

Table 1: Definition of counts and select notation. $\mathbb{1}(\cdot)$ is the indicator function.

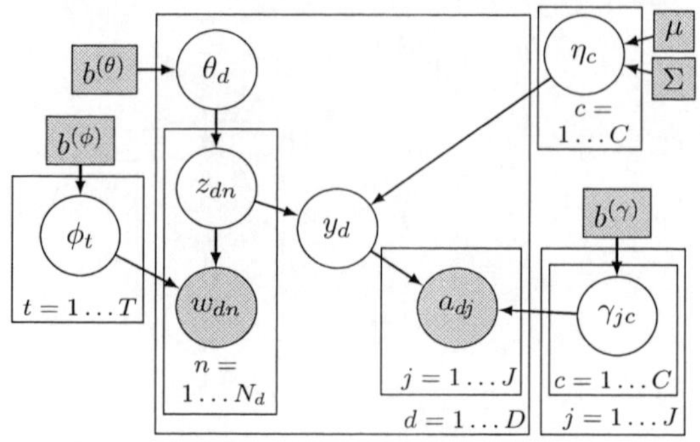

Figure 3: **CSLDA** as a plate diagram. D, J, C, T are the number of documents, annotators, classes, and topics, respectively. N_d is the size of document d. $|\phi_t| = V$, the size of the vocabulary. η_c is a vector of regression parameters. Reduces to LDA when no annotations a are observed.

We call our model **confused supervised LDA** (**CSLDA**, Figure 3), based on supervised topic modeling. Latent Dirichlet Allocation (Blei et al., 2003, LDA) models text documents as admixtures of word distributions, or topics. Although pre-calculated LDA topics as features can inform a crowdsourcing model (Levenberg et al., 2014), supervised LDA (sLDA) provides a principled way of incorporating document class labels and topics into a single model, allowing topic variables and response variables to co-inform one another in joint inference. For example, when sLDA is given movie reviews labeled with sentiment, inferred topics cluster around sentiment-heavy words (Mcauliffe and Blei, 2007), which may be quite different from the topics inferred by unsupervised LDA. One way to view CSLDA is as a discrete sLDA in settings with noisy supervision from multiple, imprecise annotators.

The generative story for CSLDA is:

1. Draw per-topic word distributions ϕ_t from $Dir(b^{(\theta)})$.
2. Draw per-class regression parameters η_c from $Gauss(\mu, \Sigma)$.
3. Draw per-annotator confusion matrices γ_j with row γ_{jc} drawn from $Dir(b^{(\gamma)}_{jc})$.
4. For each document d,
   (a) Draw topic vector θ_d from $Dir(b^{(\theta)})$.
   (b) For each token position n, draw topic z_{dn} from $Cat(\theta_d)$ and word w_{dn} from $Cat(\phi_{z_{dn}})$.
   (c) Draw class label y_d with probability proportional to $\exp[\eta_{y_d}^\intercal \bar{z}_d]$.
   (d) For each annotator j draw annotation vector a_{dj} from $\gamma_{j y_d}$.

2.3 Stochastic EM

We use stochastic expectation maximization (EM) for posterior inference in CSLDA, alternating between sampling values for topics z and document class labels y (the E-step) and optimizing values of regression parameters η (the M-step). To sample z and y efficiently, we derive the full conditional distributions of z and y in a collapsed model where θ, ϕ, and γ have been analytically integrated out. Omitting multiplicative constants, the collapsed model joint probability is

$$p(z, w, y, a|\eta) = p(z)p(w|z)p(y|z,\eta)p(a|y) \quad (1)$$
$$\propto M(a) \cdot \left(\prod_d B(N_d + b^{(\theta)}) \right) \cdot \left(\prod_t B(N_t + b_t^{(\phi)}) \right)$$
$$\cdot \left(\prod_d \frac{\exp(\eta_{y_d}^\intercal \bar{z}_d)}{\sum_c \exp(\eta_c^\intercal \bar{z}_d)} \right) \cdot \left(\prod_j \prod_c B(N_{jc} + b_{jc}^{(\gamma)}) \right)$$

where $B(\cdot)$ is the Beta function (multivariate as necessary), counts N and related symbols are defined in Table 1, and $M(a) = \prod_{d,j} M(a_{dj})$ where $M(a_{dj})$ is the multinomial coefficient.

Simplifying Equation 1 yields full conditionals for each word z_{dn},

$$p(z_{dn} = t | \hat{z}, w, y, a, \eta) \propto \left(\hat{N}_{dt} + b_t^{(\theta)} \right) \quad (2)$$
$$\cdot \frac{\hat{N}_{w_{dn} t} + b_{w_{dn}}^{(\phi)}}{\hat{N}_t + |b^{(\phi)}|_1} \cdot \frac{\exp(\frac{\eta_{y_d t}}{N_d})}{\sum_c \exp(\frac{\eta_{ct}}{N_d} + \eta_c^\intercal \hat{\bar{z}}_d)},$$

and similarly for document label y_d:

$$p(y_d = c|z, w, y, a, \eta) \propto \frac{\exp(\eta_c^\mathsf{T} \bar{z}_d)}{\sum_{c'} \exp(\eta_{c'}^\mathsf{T} \bar{z}_d)} \cdot \prod_j \frac{\prod_{c'} \left(\hat{N}_{jcc'} + b^{(\gamma)}\right)^{\overline{a_{djc'}}}}{\left(\sum_{c'} \hat{N}_{jcc'} + b^{(\gamma)}_{jcc'}\right)^{\overline{\sum_{c'} a_{djc'}}}}, \quad (3)$$

where $x^{\overline{k}} \triangleq x(x+1)\cdots(x+k-1)$ is the rising factorial. In Equation 2 the first and third terms are independent of word n and can be cached at the document level for efficiency.

For the M-step, we train the regression parameters η (containing one vector per class) by optimizing the same objective function as for training a logistic regression classifier, assuming that class y is given:

$$p(y = c|z, \eta) = \prod_d \frac{\exp(\eta_c^\mathsf{T} \bar{z}_d)}{\sum_{c'} \exp(\eta_{c'}^\mathsf{T} \bar{z}_d)}. \quad (4)$$

We optimize the objective (Equation 4) using L-BFGS and a regularizing Gaussian prior with $\mu = 0, \sigma^2 = 1$.

While EM is sensitive to initialization, CSLDA is straightforward to initialize. Majority vote is used to set initial y values $\tilde{y}$. Corresponding initial values for z and η are obtained by clamping y to $\tilde{y}$ and running stochastic EM on z and η.

2.4 Hyperparameter Optimization

Ideally, we would test CSLDA performance under all of the many algorithms available for inference in such a model. Although that is not feasible, Asuncion et al. (2009) demonstrate that hyperaparameter optimization in LDA topic models helps to bring the performance of alternative inference algorithms into approximate agreement. Accordingly, in Section 2.4 we implement hyperparameter optimization for CSLDA to make our results as general as possible.

Before moving on, however, we take a moment to validate that the observation of Asuncion et al. generalizes from LDA to the ITEMRESP model, which, together with LDA, comprises CSLDA. Figure 4 demonstrates that three ITEMRESP inference algorithms, Gibbs sampling (Gibbs), mean-field variational inference (Var), and the iterated conditional modes algorithm (ICM) (Besag, 1986), are brought into better agreement after optimizing their hyperparameters via grid search. That

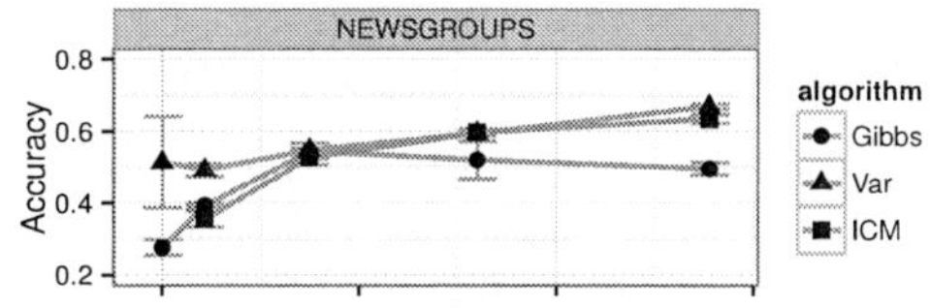

(a) Hyperparameters fixed

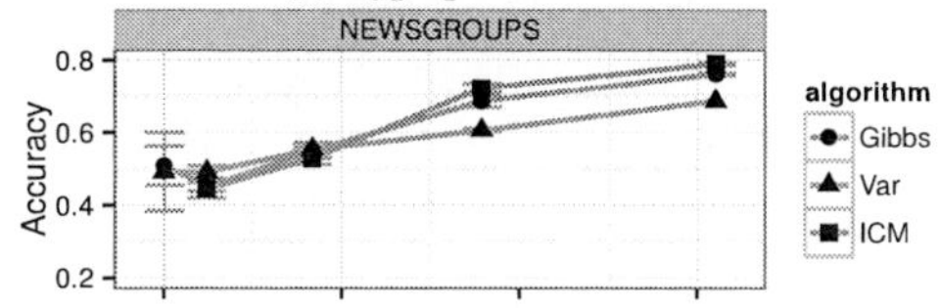

(b) Hyperparameters optimized via grid search on validation data

Figure 4: Differences among the inferred label accuracy learning curves of three ITEMRESP inference algorithms are reduced when hyperparameters are optimized.

is, the algorithms in Figure 4b are in better agreement, particularly near the extremes, than the algorithms in Figure 4a. This difference is subtle, but it holds to an equal and greater extent in other simulation conditions we tested (experiment details are similar to those reported in Section 3).

Fixed-point Hyperparameter Updates

Although a grid search is effective, it is not practical for a model with many hyperparameters such as CSLDA. For efficiency, therefore, we use the fixed-point updates of Minka (2000). Our updates differ slightly from Minka's since we tie hyperparameters, allowing them to be learned more quickly from less data. In our implementation the matrices of hyperparameters $b^{(\phi)}$ and $b^{(\theta)}$ over the Dirichlet-multinomial distributions are completely tied such that $b_{tv}^{(\phi)} = b^{(\phi)} \forall t, v$ and $b_t^{(\theta)} = b^{(\theta)} \forall t$. This leads to

$$b^{(\phi)} \leftarrow b^{(\phi)} \cdot \frac{\sum_{t,v}[\Psi(N_{tv} + b^{(\phi)})] - TV\Psi(b^{(\phi)})}{V[\Psi(N_t + Vb^{(\phi)}) - \Psi(Vb^{(\phi)})]} \quad (5)$$

and

$$b^{(\theta)} \leftarrow b^{(\theta)} \cdot \frac{\sum_{d,t}[\Psi(N_{dt} + b^{(\theta)})] - NT\Psi(b^{(\theta)})}{T[\Psi(N_d + Tb^{(\theta)}) - \Psi(Tb^{(\theta)})]}. \quad (6)$$

The updates for $b^{(\gamma)}$ are slightly more involved since we choose to tie the diagonal entries $b_d^{(\gamma)}$ and separately the off-diagonal entries $b_o^{(\gamma)}$, updating each separately:

$$b_d^{(\gamma)} \leftarrow b_d^{(\gamma)} \cdot \frac{\sum_{j,c}[\Psi(N_{jcc} + b_d^{(\gamma)})] - JC\Psi(b_d^{(\gamma)})}{Z(b^{(\gamma)})} \quad (7)$$

and $b_o^{(\gamma)} \leftarrow$

$$b_o^{(\gamma)} \cdot \frac{\sum_{j,c,c' \neq c} [\Psi(N_{jcc'}+b_o^{(\gamma)})] - JC(C-1)\Psi(b_o^{(\gamma)})]}{(C-1)Z(b^{(\gamma)})} \tag{8}$$

where

$$Z(b^{(\gamma)}) = \sum_{j,c} [\Psi(N_{jc} + b_d^{(\gamma)} + (C-1)b_o^{(\gamma)})] \\ - JC\Psi(b_d^{(\gamma)} + (C-1)b_o^{(\gamma)}).$$

As in the work of Asuncion et al. (2009), we add an algorithmic gamma prior ($b^{(\cdot)} \sim G(\alpha, \beta)$) for smoothing by adding $\frac{\alpha-1}{b^{(\cdot)}}$ to the numerator and β to the denominator of Equations 5-8. Note that these algorithmic gamma "priors" should not be understood as first-class members of the CSLDA model (Figure 3). Rather, they are regularization terms that keep our hyperparameter search algorithm from straying towards problematic values such as 0 or ∞.

3 Experiments

For all experiments we set CSLDA's number of topics T to 1.5 times the number of classes in each dataset. We found that model performance was reasonably robust to this parameter. Only when T drops below the number of label classes does performance suffer. As per Section 2.3, z and η values are initialized with 500 rounds of stochastic EM, after which the full model is updated with 1000 additional rounds. Predictions are generated by aggregating samples from the last 100 rounds (the mode of the approximate marginal posterior).

We compare CSLDA with (1) a majority vote baseline, (2) the ITEMRESP model, and representatives of the two main classes of data-aware crowdsourcing models, namely (3) data-generative and (4) data-conditional. MOMRESP represents a typical data-generative model (Bragg et al., 2013; Felt et al., 2014; Lam and Stork, 2005; Simpson and Roberts, 2015). Data-conditional approaches typically model data features conditionally using a log-linear model (Jin and Ghahramani, 2002; Raykar et al., 2010; Liu et al., 2012; Yan et al., 2014). For the purposes of this paper, we refer to this model as LOGRESP. For ITEMRESP, MOMRESP, and LOGRESP we use the variational inference methods presented by Felt et al. (2015). Unlike that paper, in this work we have augmented inference with the in-line hyperparameter updates described in Section 2.4.

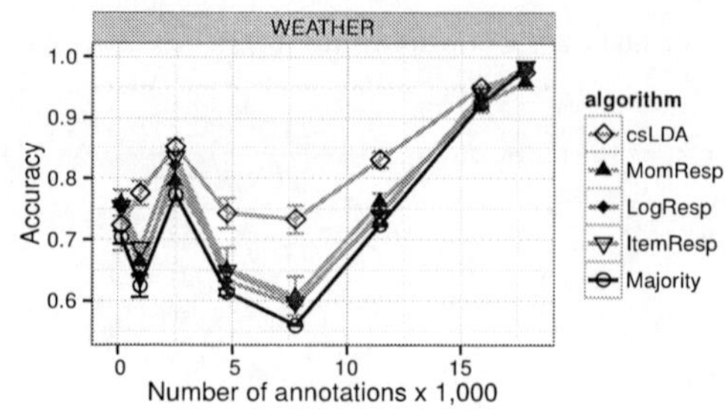

Figure 5: Inferred label accuracy of models on sentiment-annotated weather tweets.

3.1 Human-generated Annotations

To gauge the effectiveness of data-aware crowdsourcing models, we use the sentiment-annotated tweet dataset distributed by CrowdFlower as a part of its "data for everyone" initiative.[2] In the "Weather Sentiment" task, 20 annotators judged the sentiment of 1000 tweets as either positive, negative, neutral, or unrelated to the weather. In the secondary "Weather Sentiment Evaluated" task, 10 additional annotators judged the correctness of each consensus label. We construct a gold standard from the consensus labels that were judged to be correct by 9 of the 10 annotators in the secondary task.

Figure 5 plots learning curves of the accuracy of model-inferred labels as annotations are added (ordered by timestamp). All methods, including majority vote, converge to roughly the same accuracy when all 20,000 annotations are added. When fewer annotations are available, statistical models beat majority vote, and CSLDA is considerably more accurate than other approaches. Learning curves are bumpy because annotation order is not random and because inferred label accuracy is calculated only over documents with at least one annotation. Learning curves collectively increase when average annotation depth (the number of annotations per item) increases and decrease when new documents are annotated and average annotation depth decreases. CSLDA stands out by being more robust to these changes than other algorithms, and also by maintaining a higher level of accuracy across the board. This is important because high accuracy using fewer annotations translates to decreased annotations costs.

[2] http://www.crowdflower.com/data-for-everyone

	D	C	V	$\frac{1}{N}\sum_d N_d$
20 News	16,995	20	22,851	111
WebKB	3,543	4	5,781	131
Reuters8	6,523	8	6,776	53
Reuters52	7,735	52	5,579	58
CADE12	34,801	12	41,628	110
Enron	3,854	32	14,069	431

Table 2: Dataset statistics. D is number of documents, C is number of classes, V is number of features, and $\frac{1}{N}\sum_d N_d$ is average document size. Values are calculated after setting aside 15% as validation data and doing feature selection.

3.2 Synthetic Annotations

Datasets including both annotations and gold standard labels are in short supply. Although plenty of text categorization datasets have been annotated, common practice reflects that initial noisy annotations be discarded and only consensus labels be published. Consequently, we follow previous work in achieving broad validation by constructing synthetic annotators that corrupt known gold standard labels. We base our experimental setup on the annotations gathered by Felt et al. (2015),[3] who paid CrowdFlower annotators to relabel 1000 documents from the well-known 20 Newsgroups classification dataset. In that experiment, 136 annotators contributed, each instance was labeled an average of 6.9 times, and annotator accuracies were distributed approximately according to a $Beta(3.6, 5.1)$ distribution. Accordingly we construct 100 synthetic annotators, each parametrized by an accuracy drawn from $Beta(3.6, 5.1)$ and with errors drawn from a symmetric Dirichlet $Dir(1)$. Datasets are annotated by selecting an instance (at random without replacement) and then selecting K annotators (at random without replacement) to annotate it before moving on. We choose $K = 7$ to mirror the empirical average in the CrowdFlower annotation set.

We evaluate on six text classification datasets, summarized in Table 2. The 20 Newsgroups, WebKB, Cade12, Reuters8, and Reuters52 datasets are described in more detail by Cardoso-Cachopo (2007). The LDC-labeled Enron emails dataset is described by Berry et al. (2001). Each dataset is

[3]The dataset is available via git at `git://nlp.cs.byu.edu/plfl/crowdflower-newsgroups.git`

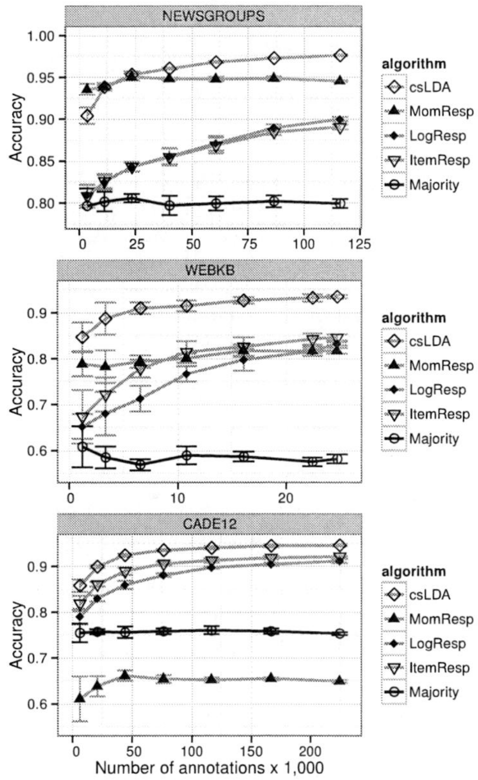

Figure 6: Inferred label accuracy of models on synthetic annotations. The first instance is annotated 7 times, then the second, and so on.

preprocessed via Porter stemming and by removal of the stopwords from MALLET's stopword list (McCallum, 2002). Features occurring fewer than 5 times in the corpus are discarded. In the case of MomResp, features are fractionally scaled so that each document is the same length, in keeping with previous work in multinomial document models (Nigam et al., 2006).

Figure 6 plots learning curves on three representative datasets (Enron resembles Cade12, and the Reuters datasets resemble WebKB). csLDA consistently outperforms LogResp, ItemResp, and majority vote. The generative models (csLDA and MomResp) tend to excel in low-annotation portions of the learning curve, partially because generative models tend to converge quickly and partially because generative models naturally learn from unlabeled documents (i.e., semi-supervision). However, MomResp tends to quickly reach a performance plateau after which additional annotations do little good. The performance of MomResp is also highly dataset de-

95% Accuracy	CSLDA	MOMRESP	LOGRESP	ITEMRESP	Majority
20 News	**85 (5.0x)**	150 (8.8x)	152 (8.9x)	168 (9.9x)	233 (13.7x)
WebKB	**31 (8.8x)**	-	46 (13.0x)	46 (13.0x)	-
Reuters8	**25 (3.8x)**	-	73 (11.2x)	62 (9.5x)	-
Reuters52	**33 (4.3x)**	73 (9.4x)	67.5 (8.7x)	60 (7.8x)	87 (11.2x)
CADE12	**250 (7.2x)**	-	295 (8.5x)	290 (8.3x)	570 (16.4x)
Enron	**31 (8.0x)**	-	40 (10.4x)	38 (9.9x)	47 (12.2x)

Table 3: The number of annotations $\times 1000$ at which the algorithm reaches 95% inferred label accuracy on the indicated dataset (average annotations per instance are in parenthesis). All instances are annotated once, then twice, and so on. Empty entries ('-') do not reach 95% even with 20 annotations per instance.

pendent: it is good on 20 Newsgroups, mediocre on WebKB, and poor on CADE12. By contrast, CSLDA is relatively stable across datasets.

To understand the different behavior of the two generative models, recall that MOMRESP is identical to ITEMRESP save for its multinomial data model. Indeed, the equations governing inference of label y in MOMRESP simply sum together terms from an ITEMRESP model and terms from a mixture of multinomials clustering model (and for reasons explained in Section 2.1, the multinomial data model terms tend to dominate). Therefore when MOMRESP diverges from ITEMRESP it is because MOMRESP is attracted toward a y assignment that satisfies the multinomial data model, grouping similar documents together. This can both help and hurt. When data clusters and label classes are misaligned, MOMRESP falters (as in the case of the Cade12 dataset). In contrast, CSLDA's flexible mapping from topics to labels is less sensitive: topics can diverge from label classes so long as there exists some linear transformation from the topics to the labels.

Many corpus annotation projects are not complete until the corpus achieves some target level of quality. We repeat the experiment reported in Figure 6, but rather than simulating seven annotations for each instance before moving on, we simulate one annotation for each instance, then two, and so on until each instance in the dataset is annotated 20 times. Table 3 reports the minimal number of annotations before an algorithm's inferred labels reach an accuracy of 95%, a lofty goal that can require significant amounts of annotation when using poor quality annotations. CSLDA achieves 95% accuracy with fewer annotations, corresponding to reduced annotation cost.

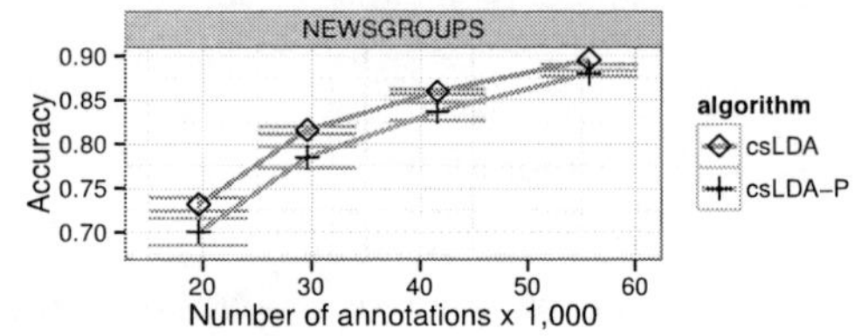

Figure 7: Joint inference for CSLDA vs pipeline inference (CSLDA-P).

3.3 Joint vs Pipeline Inference

To isolate the effectiveness of joint inference in CSLDA, we compare against the pipeline alternative where topics are inferred first and then held constant during inference (Levenberg et al., 2014). Joint inference yields modest but consistent benefits over a pipeline approach. Figure 7 highlights a portion of the learning curve on the Newsgroups dataset (based on the experiments summarized in Table 3). This trend holds across all of the datasets that we examined.

3.4 Error Analysis

Class-conditional models like MOMRESP include a feature that data-conditional models like CSLDA lack: an explicit prior over class prevalence. Figure 8a shows that CSLDA performs poorly on the CrowdFlower-annotated Newsgroups documents described at the beginning of Section 3 (not the synthetic annotations). Error analysis uncovers that CSLDA lumps related classes together in this dataset. This is because annotators could specify up to 3 simultaneous labels for each annotation, so that similar labels (e.g., "talk.politics.misc" and "talk.politics.mideast") are usually chosen in blocks. Suppose each member of a set of documents with similar topical content is annotated

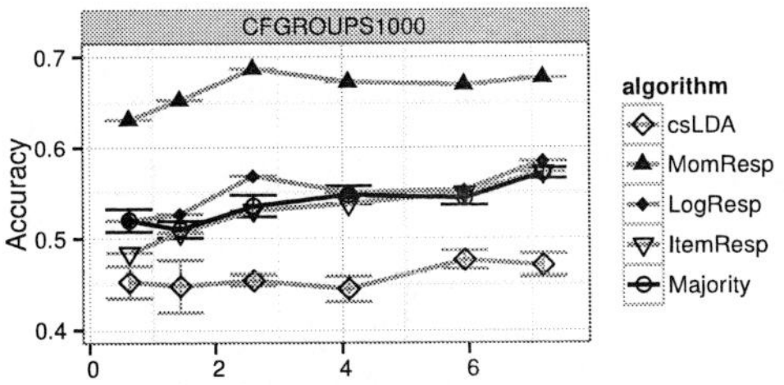

(a) Original data

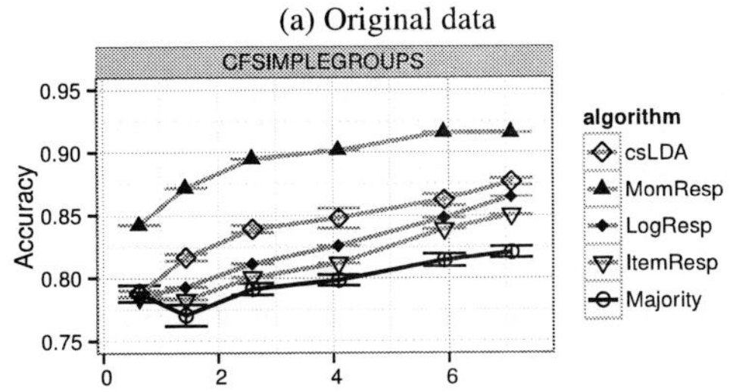

(b) After combining frequently co-annotated label classes

Figure 8: An illustrative failure case. CSLDA, lacking a class label prior, prefers to combine label classes that are highly co-annotated.

with both label A and B. In this scenario it is apparent that CSLDA will achieve its best fit by inferring all documents to have the same label either A or B. By contrast, MOMRESP's uniform prior distribution over θ leads it to prefer solutions with a balance of A and B.

The hypothesis that class combination explains CSLDA's performance is supported by Figure 8b, which shows that CSLDA recovers after combining the classes that were most frequently co-annotated. We greedily combine label class pairs to maximize Krippendorf's α until only 10 labels were left: "alt.atheism," religion, and politics classes were combined; also, "sci.electronics" and the computing classes. The remaining eight classes were unaltered. However, one could also argue that the original behavior of CSLDA is in some ways desirable. That is, if two classes of documents are mostly the same both topically and in terms of annotator decisions, perhaps those classes ought to be collapsed. We are not overly concerned that MOMRESP beats CSLDA in Figure 8, since this result is consistent with early relative performance in simulation.

4 Additional Related Work

This section reviews related work not already discussed. A growing body of work extends the item-response model to account for variables such as item difficulty (Whitehill et al., 2009; Passonneau and Carpenter, 2013; Zhou et al., 2012), annotator trustworthiness (Hovy et al., 2013), correlation among various combinations of these variables (Zhou et al., 2014), and change in annotator behavior over time (Simpson and Roberts, 2015).

Welinder et al. (2010) carefully model the process of annotating objects in images, including variables for item difficulty, item class, and class-conditional perception noise. In follow-up work, Liu et al. (2012) demonstrate that similar levels of performance can be achieved with the simple item-response model by using variational inference rather than EM. Alternative inference algorithms have been proposed for crowdsourcing models (Dalvi et al., 2013; Ghosh et al., 2011; Karger et al., 2013; Zhang et al., 2014). Some crowdsourcing work regards labeled data not as an end in itself, but rather as a means to train classifiers (Lin et al., 2014). The fact-finding literature assigns trust scores to assertions made by untrusted sources (Pasternack and Roth, 2010).

5 Conclusion and Future Work

We describe CSLDA, a generative, data-aware crowdsourcing model that addresses important modeling deficiencies identified in previous work. In particular, CSLDA handles data in which the natural document clusters are at odds with the intended document labels. It also transitions smoothly from situations in which few annotations are available to those in which many annotations are available. Because of the flexible mapping in CSLDA to class labels, many structural variants are possible in future work. For example, this mapping could depend not just on inferred topical content but also directly on data features (c.f. Nguyen et al. (2013)) or learned embedded feature representations.

The large number of parameters in the learned confusion matrices of crowdsourcing models present difficulty at scale. This could be addressed by modeling structure both inside of the annotators and classes. Redundant annotations give unique insights into both inter-annotator and inter-class relationships and could be used to induce annotator or label class hierarchies with parsimonious representations. Simpson et al. (2013) identify annotator clusters using community detection algorithms but do not address annotator hierarchy or scalable confusion representations.

Acknowledgments This work was supported by the collaborative NSF Grant IIS-1409739 (BYU) and IIS-1409287 (UMD). Boyd-Graber is also supported by NSF grants IIS-1320538 and NCSE-1422492. Any opinions, findings, conclusions, or recommendations expressed here are those of the authors and do not necessarily reflect the view of the sponsor.

References

Arthur Asuncion, Max Welling, Padhraic Smyth, and Yee Whye Teh. 2009. On smoothing and inference for topic models. In *Proceedings of Uncertainty in Artificial Intelligence*.

Michael W. Berry, Murray Browne, and Ben Signer. 2001. Topic annotated Enron email data set. *Linguistic Data Consortium*.

Julian Besag. 1986. On the statistical analysis of dirty pictures. *Journal of the Royal Statistical Society*, 48(3):259–302.

David M. Blei, Andrew Y. Ng, and Michael I. Jordan. 2003. Latent Dirichlet allocation. *Journal of Machine Learning Research*, 3:993–1022.

Jonathan Bragg, Mausam, and Daniel S. Weld. 2013. Crowdsourcing multi-label classification for taxonomy creation. In *First AAAI Conference on Human Computation and Crowdsourcing*.

Ana Margarida de Jesus Cardoso-Cachopo. 2007. *Improving Methods for Single-label Text Categorization*. Ph.D. thesis, Universidade Tecnica de Lisboa.

Nilesh Dalvi, Anirban Dasgupta, Ravi Kumar, and Vibhor Rastogi. 2013. Aggregating crowdsourced binary ratings. In *Proceedings of World Wide Web Conference*.

Alexander P. Dawid and Allan M. Skene. 1979. Maximum likelihood estimation of observer error-rates using the EM algorithm. *Applied Statistics*, pages 20–28.

Paul Felt, Robbie Haertel, Eric Ringger, and Kevin Seppi. 2014. MomResp: A Bayesian model for multi-annotator document labeling. In *International Language Resources and Evaluation*.

Paul Felt, Eric Ringger, Kevin Seppi, and Robbie Haertel. 2015. Early gains matter: A case for preferring generative over discriminative crowdsourcing models. In *Conference of the North American Chapter of the Association for Computational Linguistics*.

Arpita Ghosh, Satyen Kale, and Preston McAfee. 2011. Who moderates the moderators?: crowdsourcing abuse detection in user-generated content. In *Proceedings of the 12th ACM conference on Electronic commerce*.

Dirk Hovy, Taylor Berg-Kirkpatrick, Ashish Vaswani, and Eduard H. Hovy. 2013. Learning whom to trust with MACE. In *Conference of the North American Chapter of the Association for Computational Linguistics*.

Rong Jin and Zoubin Ghahramani. 2002. Learning with multiple labels. In *Proceedings of Advances in Neural Information Processing Systems*, pages 897–904.

David Jurgens. 2013. Embracing ambiguity: A comparison of annotation methodologies for crowdsourcing word sense labels. In *Proceedings of NAACL-HLT*, pages 556–562.

David R. Karger, Sewoong Oh, and Devavrat Shah. 2013. Efficient crowdsourcing for multi-class labeling. In *ACM SIGMETRICS Performance Evaluation Review*, volume 41, pages 81–92. ACM.

Chuck P. Lam and David G. Stork. 2005. Toward optimal labeling strategy under multiple unreliable labelers. In *AAAI Spring Symposium: Knowledge Collection from Volunteer Contributors*.

Abby Levenberg, Stephen Pulman, Karo Moilanen, Edwin Simpson, and Stephen Roberts. 2014. Predicting economic indicators from web text using sentiment composition. *International Journal of Computer and Communication Engineering*, 3(2):109–115.

Christopher H. Lin, Mausam, and Daniel S. Weld. 2014. To re (label), or not to re (label). In *Second AAAI Conference on Human Computation and Crowdsourcing*.

Qiang Liu, Jian Peng, and Alex T. Ihler. 2012. Variational inference for crowdsourcing. In *Proceedings of Advances in Neural Information Processing Systems*.

Jon D. Mcauliffe and David Blei. 2007. Supervised topic models. In *Proceedings of Advances in Neural Information Processing Systems*.

Andrew McCallum. 2002. Mallet: A machine learning for language toolkit. http://mallet.cs.umass.edu.

Thomas Minka. 2000. Estimating a Dirichlet distribution.

Andrew Y. Ng and Michael I. Jordan. 2001. On discriminative vs. generative classifiers: A comparison of logistic regression and Naive Bayes. *Proceedings of Advances in Neural Information Processing Systems*.

Viet-An Nguyen, Jordan L. Boyd-Graber, and Philip Resnik. 2013. Lexical and hierarchical topic regression. In *Proceedings of Advances in Neural Information Processing Systems*.

Kamal Nigam, Andrew McCallum, and Tom Mitchell. 2006. Semi-supervised text classification using EM. *Semi-Supervised Learning*, pages 33–56.

Rebecca J. Passonneau and Bob Carpenter. 2013. The benefits of a model of annotation. In *Proceedings of the 7th Linguistic Annotation Workshop and Interoperability with Discourse*, pages 187–195.

Jeff Pasternack and Dan Roth. 2010. Knowing what to believe (when you already know something). In *Proceedings of International Conference on Computational Linguistics*.

Vikas C. Raykar, Shipeng Yu, Linda H. Zhao, Gerardo Hermosillo Valadez, Charles Florin, Luca Bogoni, and Linda Moy. 2010. Learning from crowds. *Journal of Machine Learning Research*, 11:1297–1322.

Edwin Simpson and Stephen Roberts. 2015. Bayesian methods for intelligent task assignment in crowdsourcing systems. In *Decision Making: Uncertainty, Imperfection, Deliberation and Scalability*, pages 1–32. Springer.

E. Simpson, S. Roberts, I. Psorakis, and A. Smith. 2013. Dynamic bayesian combination of multiple imperfect classifiers. In *Decision Making and Imperfection*, pages 1–35. Springer.

Rion Snow, Brendan O'Connor, Daniel Jurafsky, and Andrew Y. Ng. 2008. Cheap and fast—but is it good?: Evaluating non-expert annotations for natural language tasks. In *Proceedings of EMNLP*. ACL.

James Surowiecki. 2005. *The Wisdom of Crowds*. Random House LLC.

Peter Welinder, Steve Branson, Pietro Perona, and Serge J. Belongie. 2010. The multidimensional wisdom of crowds. In *NIPS*, pages 2424–2432.

Jacob Whitehill, Ting-fan Wu, Jacob Bergsma, Javier R Movellan, and Paul L. Ruvolo. 2009. Whose vote should count more: Optimal integration of labels from labelers of unknown expertise. *NIPS*, 22:2035–2043.

Yan Yan, Rómer Rosales, Glenn Fung, Ramanathan Subramanian, and Jennifer Dy. 2014. Learning from multiple annotators with varying expertise. *Machine Learning*, 95(3):291–327.

Yuchen Zhang, Xi Chen, Dengyong Zhou, and Michael I. Jordan. 2014. Spectral methods meet em: A provably optimal algorithm for crowdsourcing. In *Advances in Neural Information Processing Systems 27*, pages 1260–1268. Curran Associates, Inc.

Dengyong Zhou, Sumit Basu, Yi Mao, and John C. Platt. 2012. Learning from the wisdom of crowds by minimax entropy. In *NIPS*, volume 25, pages 2204–2212.

Dengyong Zhou, Qiang Liu, John Platt, and Christopher Meek. 2014. Aggregating ordinal labels from crowds by minimax conditional entropy. In *Proceedings of the International Conference of Machine Learning*.

Multichannel Variable-Size Convolution for Sentence Classification

Wenpeng Yin and **Hinrich Schütze**
Center for Information and Language Processing
University of Munich, Germany
wenpeng@cis.uni-muenchen.de

Abstract

We propose *MVCNN*, a convolution neural network (CNN) architecture for sentence classification. It (i) combines diverse versions of pretrained word embeddings and (ii) extracts features of multigranular phrases with variable-size convolution filters. We also show that *pretraining* MVCNN is critical for good performance. MVCNN achieves state-of-the-art performance on four tasks: on small-scale binary, small-scale multi-class and large-scale Twitter sentiment prediction and on subjectivity classification.

1 Introduction

Different sentence classification tasks are crucial for many Natural Language Processing (NLP) applications. Natural language sentences have complicated structures, both sequential and hierarchical, that are essential for understanding them. In addition, how to decode and compose the features of component units, including single words and variable-size phrases, is central to the sentence classification problem.

In recent years, deep learning models have achieved remarkable results in computer vision (Krizhevsky et al., 2012), speech recognition (Graves et al., 2013) and NLP (Collobert and Weston, 2008). A problem largely specific to NLP is how to detect features of linguistic units, how to conduct composition over variable-size sequences and how to use them for NLP tasks (Collobert et al., 2011; Kalchbrenner et al., 2014; Kim, 2014). Socher et al. (2011a) proposed recursive neural networks to form phrases based on parsing trees. This approach depends on the availability of a well performing parser; for many languages and domains, especially noisy domains, reliable parsing is difficult. Hence, convolution neural networks (CNN) are getting increasing attention, for they are able to model long-range dependencies in sentences via hierarchical structures (Dos Santos and Gatti, 2014; Kim, 2014; Denil et al., 2014). Current CNN systems usually implement a convolution layer with fixed-size filters (i.e., feature detectors), in which the concrete filter size is a hyper-parameter. They essentially split a sentence into multiple sub-sentences by a sliding window, then determine the sentence label by using the dominant label across all sub-sentences. The underlying assumption is that the sub-sentence with that granularity is potentially good enough to represent the whole sentence. However, it is hard to find the granularity of a "good sub-sentence" that works well across sentences. This motivates us to implement *variable-size filters* in a convolution layer in order to extract features of *multigranular phrases*.

Breakthroughs of deep learning in NLP are also based on learning distributed word representations – also called "word embeddings" – by neural language models (Bengio et al., 2003; Mnih and Hinton, 2009; Mikolov et al., 2010; Mikolov, 2012; Mikolov et al., 2013a). Word embeddings are derived by projecting words from a sparse, 1-of-V encoding (V: vocabulary size) onto a lower dimensional and dense vector space via hidden layers and can be interpreted as feature extractors that encode semantic and syntactic features of words.

Many papers study the comparative performance of different versions of word embeddings, usually learned by different neural network (NN) architectures. For example, Chen et al. (2013) compared HLBL (Mnih and Hinton, 2009), SENNA (Collobert and Weston, 2008), Turian (Turian et al., 2010) and Huang (Huang et al., 2012), showing great variance in quality and characteristics of the semantics captured by the tested embedding versions. Hill et al. (2014) showed that embeddings learned by neural machine translation models outperform three repre-

Proceedings of the 19th Conference on Computational Language Learning, pages 204–214,
Beijing, China, July 30-31, 2015. ©2015 Association for Computational Linguistics

sentative monolingual embedding versions: skip-gram (Mikolov et al., 2013b), GloVe (Pennington et al., 2014) and C&W (Collobert et al., 2011) in some cases. These prior studies motivate us to explore combining multiple versions of word embeddings, treating each of them as a distinct description of words. Our expectation is that the combination of these embedding versions, trained by different NNs on different corpora, should contain more information than each version individually. We want to leverage this diversity of different embedding versions to extract higher quality sentence features and thereby improve sentence classification performance.

The letters "M" and "V" in the name "MVCNN" of our architecture denote the multichannel and variable-size convolution filters, respectively. "Multichannel" employs language from computer vision where a color image has red, green and blue channels. Here, a channel is a description by an embedding version.

For many sentence classification tasks, only relatively small training sets are available. MVCNN has a large number of parameters, so that overfitting is a danger when they are trained on small training sets. We address this problem by *pretraining* MVCNN on unlabeled data. These pretrained weights can then be fine-tuned for the specific classification task.

In sum, we attribute the success of MVCNN to: (i) designing variable-size convolution filters to extract variable-range features of sentences and (ii) exploring the combination of multiple public embedding versions to initialize words in sentences. We also employ two "tricks" to further enhance system performance: mutual learning and pretraining.

In remaining parts, Section 2 presents related work. Section 3 gives details of our classification model. Section 4 introduces two tricks that enhance system performance: mutual-learning and pretraining. Section 5 reports experimental results. Section 6 concludes this work.

2 Related Work

Much prior work has exploited deep neural networks to model sentences.

Blacoe and Lapata (2012) represented a sentence by element-wise addition, multiplication, or recursive autoencoder over embeddings of component single words. Yin and Schütze (2014) extended this approach by composing on words and phrases instead of only single words.

Collobert and Weston (2008) and Yu et al. (2014) used one layer of convolution over phrases detected by a sliding window on a target sentence, then used max- or average-pooling to form a sentence representation.

Kalchbrenner et al. (2014) stacked multiple layers of *one-dimensional* convolution by dynamic k-max pooling to model sentences. We also adopt dynamic k-max pooling while our convolution layer has variable-size filters.

Kim (2014) also studied multichannel representation and variable-size filters. Differently, their multichannel relies on a single version of pretrained embeddings (i.e., pretrained Word2Vec embeddings) with two copies: one is kept stable and the other one is fine-tuned by backpropagation. We develop this insight by incorporating diverse embedding versions. Additionally, their idea of variable-size filters is further developed.

Le and Mikolov (2014) initialized the representation of a sentence as a parameter vector, treating it as a global feature and combining this vector with the representations of context words to do word prediction. Finally, this fine-tuned vector is used as representation of this sentence. Apparently, this method can only produce generic sentence representations which encode no task-specific features.

Our work is also inspired by studies that compared the performance of different word embedding versions or investigated the combination of them. For example, Turian et al. (2010) compared Brown clusters, C&W embeddings and HLBL embeddings in NER and chunking tasks. They found that Brown clusters and word embeddings both can improve the accuracy of supervised NLP systems; and demonstrated empirically that *combining different word representations is beneficial.* Luo et al. (2014) adapted CBOW (Mikolov et al., 2013a) to train word embeddings on different datasets: free text documents from Wikipedia, search click-through data and user query data, showing that *combining them gets stronger results than using individual word embeddings* in web search ranking and word similarity task. However, these two papers either learned word representations on the same corpus (Turian et al., 2010) or enhanced the embedding quality by extending training corpora, not learning algorithms (Luo et al., 2014). In our work, there is no limit to the type of embedding versions we can use and they leverage not only the diversity of corpora, but also the different principles of learning algorithms.

3 Model Description

We now describe the architecture of our model *MVCNN*, illustrated in Figure 1.

Multichannel Input. The input of MVCNN includes *multichannel feature maps* of a considered sentence, each is a matrix initialized by a different embedding version. Let s be sentence length, d dimension of word embeddings and c the total number of different embedding versions (i.e., channels). Hence, the whole initialized input is a three-dimensional array of size $c \times d \times s$. Figure 1 depicts a sentence with $s = 12$ words. Each word is initialized by $c = 5$ embeddings, each coming from a different channel. In implementation, sentences in a mini-batch will be padded to the same length, and unknown words for corresponding channel are randomly initialized or can acquire good initialization from the *mutual-learning* phase described in next section.

Multichannel initialization brings two advantages: 1) a frequent word can have c representations in the beginning (instead of only one), which means it has more available information to leverage; 2) a rare word missed in some embedding versions can be "made up" by others (we call it "partially known word"). Therefore, this kind of initialization is able to make use of information about partially known words, without having to employ full random initialization or removal of unknown words. The vocabulary of the binary sentiment prediction task described in experimental part contains 5232 words unknown in HLBL embeddings, 4273 in Huang embeddings, 3299 in GloVe embeddings, 4136 in SENNA embeddings and 2257 in Word2Vec embeddings. But only 1824 words find no embedding from any channel! Hence, multichannel initialization can considerably reduce the number of unknown words.

Convolution Layer (Conv). For convenience, we first introduce how this work uses a convolution layer on one input feature map to generate one higher-level feature map. Given a sentence of length s: $w_1, w_2, \ldots, w_s$; $\mathbf{w}_i \in \mathbb{R}^d$ denotes the embedding of word w_i; a convolution layer uses sliding *filters* to extract local features of that sentence. The filter width l is a parameter. We first concatenate the initialized embeddings of l consecutive words ($\mathbf{w}_{i-l+1}, \ldots, \mathbf{w}_i$) as $\mathbf{c}_i \in \mathbb{R}^{ld}$ ($1 \leq i < s + l$), then generate the feature value of this phrase as $\mathbf{p}_i$ (the whole vector $\mathbf{p} \in \mathbb{R}^{s+l-1}$ contains all the local features) using a tanh activation function and a linear projection vector $\mathbf{v} \in \mathbb{R}^{ld}$ as:

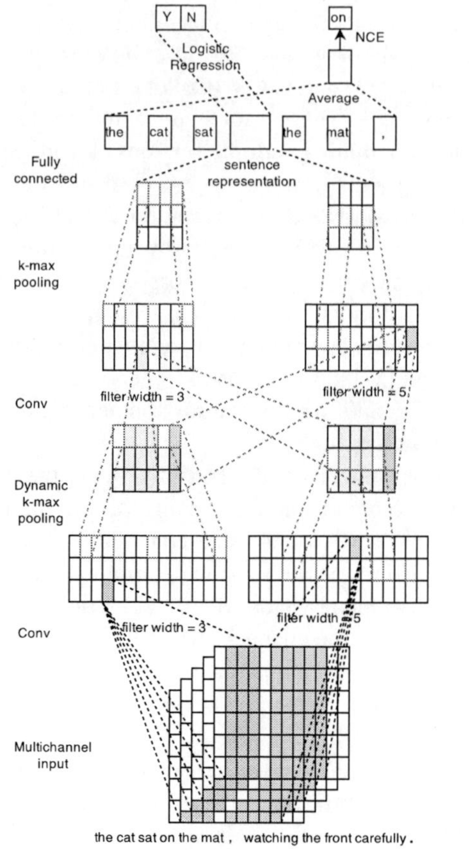

Figure 1: MVCNN: supervised classification and pretraining.

$$\mathbf{p}_i = \tanh(\mathbf{v}^{\mathrm{T}}\mathbf{c}_i + b) \tag{1}$$

More generally, convolution operation can deal with multiple input feature maps and can be stacked to yield feature maps of increasing layers. In each layer, there are usually multiple filters of the same size, but with different weights (Kalchbrenner et al., 2014). We refer to a filter with a specific set of weights as a *kernel*. The goal is often to train a model in which different kernels detect different kinds of features of a local region. However, this traditional way can not detect the features of regions of different granularity. Hence we keep the property of multi-kernel while extending it to variable-size in the same layer.

As in CNN for object recognition, to increase the *number* of kernels of a certain layer, multiple feature maps may be computed in parallel at the same layer. Further, to increase the *size diversity* of kernels in the same layer, more feature maps containing various-range dependency features can be learned. We denote a feature map of the ith layer by $\mathbf{F}_i$, and assume totally n feature maps exist in layer $i-1$: $\mathbf{F}_{i-1}^1, \ldots, \mathbf{F}_{i-1}^n$. Considering a specific filter size l in layer i, each feature map $\mathbf{F}_{i,l}^j$ is computed by convolving a distinct set of filters of size l, arranged in a matrix $\mathbf{V}_{i,l}^{j,k}$, with each feature map $\mathbf{F}_{i-1}^k$ and summing the results:

$$\mathbf{F}_{i,l}^j = \sum_{k=1}^{n} \mathbf{V}_{i,l}^{j,k} * \mathbf{F}_{i-1}^k \qquad (2)$$

where $*$ indicates the convolution operation and j is the index of a feature map in layer i. The weights in $\mathbf{V}$ form a rank 4 tensor.

Note that we use *wide convolution* in this work: it means word representations $\mathbf{w}_g$ for $g \leq 0$ or $g \geq s+1$ are actually zero embeddings. Wide convolution enables that each word can be detected by all filter weights in $\mathbf{V}$.

In Figure 1, the first convolution layer deals with an input with $n = 5$ feature maps.[1] Its filters have sizes 3 and 5 respectively (i.e., $l = 3, 5$), and each filter has $j = 3$ kernels. This means this convolution layer can detect three kinds of features of phrases with length 3 and 5, respectively.

DCNN in (Kalchbrenner et al., 2014) used one-dimensional convolution: each higher-order feature is produced from values of a single dimension in the lower-layer feature map. Even though that work proposed *folding* operation to model the dependencies between adjacent dimensions, this type of dependency modeling is still limited. Differently, convolution in present work is able to model dependency across dimensions as well as adjacent words, which obviates the need for a folding step. This change also means our model has substantially fewer parameters than the DCNN since the output of each convolution layer is smaller by a factor of d.

Dynamic k-max Pooling. Kalchbrenner et al. (2014) pool the k most active features compared with simple max (1-max) pooling (Collobert and Weston, 2008). This property enables it to connect multiple convolution layers to form a deep architecture to extract high-level abstract features. In this work, we directly use it to extract features for variable-size feature maps. For a given feature map in layer i, dynamic k-max pooling extracts k_i top values from each dimension and k_{top} top values in the top layer. We set

$$k_i = \max(k_{top}, \lceil \frac{L-i}{L} s \rceil) \qquad (3)$$

where $i \in \{1, 2, \ldots L\}$ is the order of convolution layer from bottom to top in Figure 1; L is the total numbers of convolution layers; k_{top} is a constant determined empirically, we set it to 4 as (Kalchbrenner et al., 2014).

As a result, the second convolution layer in Figure 1 has an input with two same-size feature maps, one results from filter size 3, one from filter size 5. The values in the two feature maps are for phrases with different granularity. The motivation of this convolution layer lies in that a feature reflected by a short phrase may be not trustworthy while the longer phrase containing the short one is trustworthy, or the long phrase has no trustworthy feature while its component short phrase is more reliable. This and even higher-order convolution layers therefore can *make a trade-off* between the features of different granularity.

Hidden Layer. On the top of the final k-max pooling, we stack a fully connected layer to learn sentence representation with given dimension (e.g., d).

Logistic Regression Layer. Finally, sentence representation is forwarded into logistic regression layer for classification.

In brief, our MVCNN model learns from (Kalchbrenner et al., 2014) to use dynamic k-max pooling to stack multiple convolution layers, and gets insight from (Kim, 2014) to investigate variable-size filters in a convolution layer. Compared to (Kalchbrenner et al., 2014), MVCNN has rich feature maps as input and as output of each convolution layer. Its convolution operation is not only more flexible to extract features of variable-range phrases, but also able to model dependency among all dimensions of representations. MVCNN extends the network in (Kim, 2014) by hierarchical convolution architecture and

[1] A reviewer expresses surprise at such a small number of maps. However, we will use four variable sizes (see below), so that the overall number of maps is 20. We use a small number of maps partly because training times for a network are on the order of days, so limiting the number of parameters is important.

further exploration of multichannel and variable-size feature detectors.

4 Model Enhancements

This part introduces two training tricks that enhance the performance of MVCNN in practice.

Mutual-Learning of Embedding Versions. One observation in using multiple embedding versions is that they have different vocabulary coverage. An unknown word in an embedding version may be a known word in another version. Thus, there exists a proportion of words that can only be partially initialized by certain versions of word embeddings, which means these words lack the description from other versions.

To alleviate this problem, we design a *mutual-learning* regime to predict representations of unknown words for each embedding version by learning projections between versions. As a result, all embedding versions have the same vocabulary. This processing ensures that more words in each embedding version receive a good representation, and is expected to give most words occurring in a classification dataset more comprehensive initialization (as opposed to just being randomly initialized).

Let c be the number of embedding versions in consideration, $V_1, V_2, \ldots, V_i, \ldots, V_c$ their vocabularies, $V^* = \cup_{i=1}^{c} V_i$ their union, and $V_i^- = V^* \backslash V_i$ $(i = 1, \ldots, c)$ the vocabulary of unknown words for embedding version i. Our goal is to learn embeddings for the words in V_i^- by knowledge from the other $c-1$ embedding versions.

We use the overlapping vocabulary between V_i and V_j, denoted as V_{ij}, as training set, formalizing a projection f_{ij} from space V_i to space V_j $(i \neq j; i, j \in \{1, 2, \ldots, c\})$ as follows:

$$\hat{\mathbf{w}}_j = \mathbf{M}_{ij}\mathbf{w}_i \tag{4}$$

where $\mathbf{M}_{ij} \in \mathbb{R}^{d \times d}$, $\mathbf{w}_i \in \mathbb{R}^d$ denotes the representation of word w in space V_i and $\hat{\mathbf{w}}_j$ is the projected (or learned) representation of word w in space V_j. Squared error between $\mathbf{w}_j$ and $\hat{\mathbf{w}}_j$ is the training loss to minimize. We use $\hat{\mathbf{w}}_j = f_{ij}(\mathbf{w}_i)$ to reformat Equation 4. Totally $c(c-1)/2$ projections f_{ij} are trained, each on the vocabulary intersection V_{ij}.

Let w be a word that is unknown in V_i, but is known in $V_1, V_2, \ldots, V_k$. To compute an embedding for w in V_i, we first compute the k projections $f_{1i}(\mathbf{w}_1)$, $f_{2i}(\mathbf{w}_2)$, ..., $f_{ki}(\mathbf{w}_k)$ from the source spaces $V_1, V_2, \ldots, V_k$ to the target space V_i. Then, the element-wise average of $f_{1i}(\mathbf{w}_1)$, $f_{2i}(\mathbf{w}_2)$, ..., $f_{ki}(\mathbf{w}_k)$ is treated as the representation of w in V_i. Our motivation is that – assuming there is a true representation of w in V_i (e.g., the one we would have obtained by training embeddings on a much larger corpus) and assuming the projections were learned well – we would expect all the projected vectors to be close to the true representation. Also, each source space contributes potentially complementary information. Hence averaging them is a balance of knowledge from all source spaces.

As discussed in Section 3, we found that for the binary sentiment classification dataset, many words were unknown in at least one embedding version. But of these words, a total of 5022 words did have coverage in another embedding version and so will benefit from mutual-learning. In the experiments, we will show that this is a very effective method to learn representations for unknown words that increases system performance if learned representations are used for initialization.

Pretraining. Sentence classification systems are usually implemented as supervised training regimes where training loss is between true label distribution and predicted label distribution. In this work, we use pretraining on the unlabeled data of each task and show that it can increase the performance of classification systems.

Figure 1 shows our pretraining setup. The "sentence representation" – the output of "Fully connected" hidden layer – is used to predict the component words ("on" in the figure) in the sentence (instead of predicting the sentence label Y/N as in supervised learning). Concretely, the sentence representation is averaged with representations of some surrounding words ("the", "cat", "sat", "the", "mat", "," in the figure) to predict the middle word ("on").

Given sentence representation $\mathbf{s} \in \mathbb{R}^d$ and initialized representations of $2t$ context words (t left words and t right words): $\mathbf{w}_{i-t}$, ..., $\mathbf{w}_{i-1}$, $\mathbf{w}_{i+1}$, ..., $\mathbf{w}_{i+t}$; $\mathbf{w}_i \in \mathbb{R}^d$, we average the total $2t+1$ vectors element-wise, depicted as "Average" operation in Figure 1. Then, this resulting vector is treated as a predicted representation of the middle word and is used to find the true middle word by means of noise-contrastive estimation (NCE) (Mnih and Teh, 2012). For each true example, 10 noise words are sampled.

Note that in pretraining, there are three places

where each word needs initialization. (i) Each word in the sentence is initialized in the "Multichannel input" layer to the whole network. (ii) Each context word is initialized as input to the average layer ("Average" in the figure). (iii) Each target word is initialized as the output of the "NCE" layer ("on" in the figure). In this work, we use multichannel initialization for case (i) and random initialization for cases (ii) and (iii). Only fine-tuned multichannel representations (case (i)) are kept for subsequent supervised training.

The rationale for this pretraining is similar to auto-encoder: for an object composed of smaller-granular elements, the representations of the whole object and its components can learn each other. The CNN architecture learns sentence features layer by layer, then those features are justified by all constituent words.

During pretraining, all the model parameters, including mutichannel input, convolution parameters and fully connected layer, will be updated until they are mature to extract the sentence features. Subsequently, the same sets of parameters will be fine-tuned for supervised classification tasks.

In sum, this pretraining is designed to produce good initial values for both model parameters and word embeddings. It is especially helpful for pretraining the embeddings of unknown words.

5 Experiments

We test the network on four classification tasks. We begin by specifying aspects of the implementation and the training of the network. We then report the results of the experiments.

5.1 Hyperparameters and Training

In each of the experiments, the top of the network is a logistic regression that predicts the probability distribution over classes given the input sentence. The network is trained to minimize cross-entropy of predicted and true distributions; the objective includes an L_2 regularization term over the parameters. The set of parameters comprises the word embeddings, all filter weights and the weights in fully connected layers. A dropout operation (Hinton et al., 2012) is put before the logistic regression layer. The network is trained by back-propagation in mini-batches and the gradient-based optimization is performed using the AdaGrad update rule (Duchi et al., 2011)

In all data sets, the initial learning rate is 0.01, dropout probability is 0.8, L_2 weight is $5 \cdot 10^{-3}$, batch size is 50. In each convolution layer, filter sizes are $\{3, 5, 7, 9\}$ and each filter has five kernels (independent of filter size).

5.2 Datasets and Experimental Setup

Standard Sentiment Treebank (Socher et al., 2013). This small-scale dataset includes two tasks predicting the sentiment of movie reviews. The output variable is binary in one experiment and can have five possible outcomes in the other: {negative, somewhat negative, neutral, somewhat positive, positive}. In the *binary* case, we use the given split of 6920 training, 872 development and 1821 test sentences. Likewise, in the *fine-grained* case, we use the standard 8544/1101/2210 split. Socher et al. (2013) used the Stanford Parser (Klein and Manning, 2003) to parse each sentence into subphrases. The subphrases were then labeled by human annotators in the same way as the sentences were labeled. Labeled phrases that occur as subparts of the training sentences are treated as independent training instances as in (Le and Mikolov, 2014; Kalchbrenner et al., 2014).

Sentiment140[2] (Go et al., 2009). This is a large-scale dataset of tweets about sentiment classification, where a tweet is automatically labeled as positive or negative depending on the emoticon that occurs in it. The training set consists of 1.6 million tweets with emoticon-based labels and the test set of about 400 hand-annotated tweets. We preprocess the tweets minimally as follows. 1) The equivalence class symbol "url" (resp. "username") replaces all URLs (resp. all words that start with the @ symbol, e.g., @thomasss). 2) A sequence of $k > 2$ repetitions of a letter c (e.g., "cooooooool") is replaced by two occurrences of c (e.g., "cool"). 3) All tokens are lowercased.

Subj. Subjectivity classification dataset[3] released by (Pang and Lee, 2004) has 5000 subjective sentences and 5000 objective sentences. We report the result of 10-fold cross validation as baseline systems did.

5.2.1 Pretrained Word Vectors

In this work, we use five embedding versions, as shown in Table 1, to initialize words. Four of them are directly downloaded from the Internet.

[2]http://help.sentiment140.com/for-students

[3]http://www.cs.cornell.edu/people/pabo/movie-review-data/

Set	Training Data	Vocab Size	Dimensionality	Source
HLBL	Reuters English newswire	246,122	50	download
Huang	Wikipedia (April 2010 snapshot)	100,232	50	download
Glove	Twitter	1,193,514	50	download
SENNA	Wikipedia	130,000	50	download
Word2Vec	English Gigawords	418,129	50	trained from scratch

Table 1: Description of five versions of word embedding.

	Binary	Fine-grained	Senti140	Subj
HLBL	5,232	5,562	344,632	8,621
Huang	4,273	4,523	327,067	6,382
Glove	3,299	3,485	257,376	5,237
SENNA	4,136	4,371	323,501	6,162
W2V	2257	2,409	288,257	4,217
Voc size	18,876	19,612	387,877	23,926
Full hit	12,030	12,357	30,010	13,742
Partial hit	5,022	5,312	121,383	6,580
No hit	1,824	1,943	236,484	3,604

Table 2: Statistics of five embedding versions for four tasks. The first block with five rows provides the number of unknown words of each task when using corresponding version to initialize. Voc size: vocabulary size. Full hit: embedding in all 5 versions. Partial hit: embedding in 1–4 versions, No hit: not present in any of the 5 versions.

(i) **HLBL.** Hierarchical log-bilinear model presented by Mnih and Hinton (2009) and released by Turian et al. (2010);[4] size: 246,122 word embeddings; training corpus: RCV1 corpus, one year of Reuters English newswire from August 1996 to August 1997. (ii) **Huang.**[5] Huang et al. (2012) incorporated global context to deal with challenges raised by words with multiple meanings; size: 100,232 word embeddings; training corpus: April 2010 snapshot of Wikipedia. (iii) **GloVe.**[6] Size: 1,193,514 word embeddings; training corpus: a Twitter corpus of 2B tweets with 27B tokens. (iv) **SENNA.**[7] Size: 130,000 word embeddings; training corpus: Wikipedia. Note that we use their 50-dimensional embeddings. (v) **Word2Vec.** It has no 50-dimensional embeddings available online. We use released code[8] to train *skip-gram* on English Gigaword Corpus (Parker et al., 2009) with setup: window size 5, negative sampling, sampling rate 10^{-3}, threads 12. It is worth emphasizing that above embeddings sets are derived on different corpora with different algorithms. This is the very property that we want to make use of to promote the system performance.

Table 2 shows the number of unknown words in each task when using corresponding embedding version to initialize (rows "HLBL", "Huang", "Glove", "SENNA", "W2V") and the number of words fully initialized by five embedding versions ("Full hit" row), the number of words partially initialized ("Partial hit" row) and the number of words that cannot be initialized by any of the embedding versions ("No hit" row).

About 30% of words in each task have partially initialized embeddings and our mutual-learning is able to initialize the missing embeddings through projections. Pretraining is expected to learn good representations for all words, but pretraining is especially important for words without initialization ("no hit"); a particularly clear example for this is the Senti140 task: 236,484 of 387,877 words or 61% are in the "no hit" category.

5.2.2 Results and Analysis

Table 3 compares results on test of MVCNN and its variants with other baselines in the four sentence classification tasks. Row 34, "MVCNN (overall)", shows performance of the best configuration of MVCNN, optimized on dev. This version uses five versions of word embeddings, four filter sizes (3, 5, 7, 9), both mutual-learning and pretraining, three convolution layers for Senti140 task and two convolution layers for the other tasks. Overall, our system gets the best results, beating all baselines.

The table contains five blocks from top to bottom. Each block investigates one specific configurational aspect of the system. All results in the five blocks are with respect to row 34, "MVCNN (overall)"; e.g., row 19 shows what happens when

[4]http://metaoptimize.com/projects/wordreprs/

[5]http://ai.stanford.edu/ ehhuang/

[6]http://nlp.stanford.edu/projects/glove/

[7]http://ml.nec-labs.com/senna/

[8]http://code.google.com/p/word2vec/

		Model	Binary	Fine-grained	Senti140	Subj
baselines	1	RAE (Socher et al., 2011b)	82.4	43.2	–	–
	2	MV-RNN (Socher et al., 2012)	82.9	44.4	–	–
	3	RNTN (Socher et al., 2013)	85.4	45.7	–	–
	4	DCNN (Kalchbrenner et al., 2014)	86.8	48.5	*87.4*	–
	5	Paragraph-Vec (Le and Mikolov, 2014)	87.7	*48.7*	–	–
	6	CNN-rand (Kim, 2014)	82.7	45.0	–	89.6
	7	CNN-static (Kim, 2014)	86.8	45.5	–	93.0
	8	CNN-non-static (Kim, 2014)	87.2	48.0	–	93.4
	9	CNN-multichannel (Kim, 2014)	*88.1*	47.4	–	93.2
	10	NBSVM (Wang and Manning, 2012)	–	–	–	93.2
	11	MNB (Wang and Manning, 2012)	–	–	–	*93.6*
	12	G-Dropout (Wang and Manning, 2013)	–	–	–	93.4
	13	F-Dropout (Wang and Manning, 2013)	–	–	–	*93.6*
	14	SVM (Go et al., 2009)	–	–	81.6	–
	15	BINB (Go et al., 2009)	–	–	82.7	–
	16	MAX-TDNN (Kalchbrenner et al., 2014)	–	–	78.8	–
	17	NBOW (Kalchbrenner et al., 2014)	–	–	80.9	–
	18	MAXENT (Go et al., 2009)	–	–	83.0	–
versions	19	MVCNN (-HLBL)	88.5	48.7	88.0	93.6
	20	MVCNN (-Huang)	89.2	49.2	88.1	93.7
	21	MVCNN (-Glove)	88.3	48.6	87.4	93.6
	22	MVCNN (-SENNA)	89.3	49.1	87.9	93.4
	23	MVCNN (-Word2Vec)	88.4	48.2	87.6	93.4
filters	24	MVCNN (-3)	89.1	49.2	88.0	93.6
	25	MVCNN (-5)	88.7	49.0	87.5	93.4
	26	MVCNN (-7)	87.8	48.9	87.5	93.1
	27	MVCNN (-9)	88.6	49.2	87.8	93.3
tricks	28	MVCNN (-mutual-learning)	88.2	49.2	87.8	93.5
	29	MVCNN (-pretraining)	87.6	48.9	87.6	93.2
layers	30	MVCNN (1)	89.0	49.3	86.8	93.8
	31	MVCNN (2)	89.4	49.6	87.6	93.9
	32	MVCNN (3)	88.6	48.6	88.2	93.1
	33	MVCNN (4)	87.9	48.2	88.0	92.4
	34	MVCNN (overall)	**89.4**	**49.6**	**88.2**	**93.9**

Table 3: Test set results of our CNN model against other methods. **RAE**: Recursive Autoencoders with pretrained word embeddings from Wikipedia (Socher et al., 2011b). **MV-RNN**: Matrix-Vector Recursive Neural Network with parse trees (Socher et al., 2012). **RNTN**: Recursive Neural Tensor Network with tensor-based feature function and parse trees (Socher et al., 2013). **DCNN, MAX-TDNN, NBOW**: Dynamic Convolution Neural Network with k-max pooling, Time-Delay Neural Networks with Max-pooling (Collobert and Weston, 2008), Neural Bag-of-Words Models (Kalchbrenner et al., 2014). **Paragraph-Vec**: Logistic regression on top of paragraph vectors (Le and Mikolov, 2014). **SVM, BINB, MAXENT**: Support Vector Machines, Naive Bayes with unigram features and bigram features, Maximum Entropy (Go et al., 2009). **NBSVM, MNB**: Naive Bayes SVM and Multinomial Naive Bayes with uni-bigrams from Wang and Manning (2012). **CNN-rand/static/multichannel/nonstatic**: CNN with word embeddings randomly initialized / initialized by pretrained vectors and kept static during training / initialized with two copies (each is a "channel") of pretrained embeddings / initialized with pretrained embeddings while fine-tuned during training (Kim, 2014). **G-Dropout, F-Dropout**: Gaussian Dropout and Fast Dropout from Wang and Manning (2013). Minus sign "-" in MVCNN (-Huang) etc. means "Huang" is not used. "**versions / filters / tricks / layers**" denote the MVCNN variants with different setups: discard certain embedding version / discard certain filter size / discard mutual-learning or pretraining / different numbers of convolution layer.

HLBL is removed from row 34, row 28 shows what happens when mutual learning is removed from row 34 etc.

The block "baselines" (1–18) lists some systems representative of previous work on the corresponding datasets, including the state-of-the-art systems (marked as italic). The block "versions" (19–23) shows the results of our system when one of the embedding versions was *not* used during training. We want to explore to what extend different embedding versions contribute to performance. The block "filters" (24–27) gives the results when individual filter width is discarded. It also tells us how much a filter with specific size influences. The block "tricks" (28–29) shows the system performance when no mutual-learning or no pretraining is used. The block "layers" (30–33) demonstrates how the system performs when it has different numbers of convolution layers.

From the "layers" block, we can see that our system performs best with two layers of convolution in Standard Sentiment Treebank and Subjectivity Classification tasks (row 31), but with three layers of convolution in Sentiment140 (row 32). This is probably due to Sentiment140 being a much larger dataset; in such a case deeper neural networks are beneficial.

The block "tricks" demonstrates the effect of mutual-learning and pretraining. Apparently, pretraining has a bigger impact on performance than mutual-learning. We speculate that it is because pretraining can influence more words and all learned word embeddings are tuned on the dataset after pretraining.

The block "filters" indicates the contribution of each filter size. The system benefits from filters of each size. Sizes 5 and 7 are most important for high performance, especially 7 (rows 25 and 26).

In the block "versions", we see that each embedding version is crucial for good performance: performance drops in every single case. Though it is not easy to compare fairly different embedding versions in NLP tasks, especially when those embeddings were trained on different corpora of different sizes using different algorithms, our results are potentially instructive for researchers making decision on which embeddings to use for their own tasks.

6 Conclusion

This work presented *MVCNN*, a novel CNN architecture for sentence classification. It combines multichannel initialization – diverse versions of pretrained word embeddings are used – and variable-size filters – features of multigranular phrases are extracted with variable-size convolution filters. We demonstrated that multichannel initialization and variable-size filters enhance system performance on sentiment classification and subjectivity classification tasks.

7 Future Work

As pointed out by the reviewers the success of the multichannel approach is likely due to a combination of several quite different effects.

First, there is the effect of the embedding learning algorithm. These algorithms differ in many aspects, including in sensitivity to word order (e.g., SENNA: yes, word2vec: no), in objective function and in their treatment of ambiguity (explicitly modeled only by Huang et al. (2012).

Second, there is the effect of the corpus. We would expect the size and genre of the corpus to have a big effect even though we did not analyze this effect in this paper.

Third, complementarity of word embeddings is likely to be more useful for some tasks than for others. Sentiment is a good application for complementary word embeddings because solving this task requires drawing on heterogeneous sources of information, including syntax, semantics and genre as well as the core polarity of a word. Other tasks like part of speech (POS) tagging may benefit less from heterogeneity since the benefit of embeddings in POS often comes down to making a correct choice between two alternatives – a single embedding version may be sufficient for this.

We plan to pursue these questions in future work.

Acknowledgments

Thanks to CIS members and anonymous reviewers for constructive comments. This work was supported by Baidu (through a Baidu scholarship awarded to Wenpeng Yin) and by Deutsche Forschungsgemeinschaft (grant DFG SCHU 2246/8-2, SPP 1335).

References

Yoshua Bengio, Réjean Ducharme, Pascal Vincent, and Christian Janvin. 2003. A neural probabilistic language model. *The Journal of Machine Learning Research*, 3:1137–1155.

William Blacoe and Mirella Lapata. 2012. A comparison of vector-based representations for semantic composition. In *Proceedings of the 2012 Joint Conference on Empirical Methods in Natural Language Processing and Computational Natural Language Learning*, pages 546–556. Association for Computational Linguistics.

Yanqing Chen, Bryan Perozzi, Rami Al-Rfou, and Steven Skiena. 2013. The expressive power of word embeddings. In *ICML Workshop on Deep Learning for Audio, Speech, and Language Processing*.

Ronan Collobert and Jason Weston. 2008. A unified architecture for natural language processing: Deep neural networks with multitask learning. In *Proceedings of the 25th international conference on Machine learning*, pages 160–167. ACM.

Ronan Collobert, Jason Weston, Léon Bottou, Michael Karlen, Koray Kavukcuoglu, and Pavel Kuksa. 2011. Natural language processing (almost) from scratch. *The Journal of Machine Learning Research*, 12:2493–2537.

Misha Denil, Alban Demiraj, Nal Kalchbrenner, Phil Blunsom, and Nando de Freitas. 2014. Modelling, visualising and summarising documents with a single convolutional neural network. *arXiv preprint arXiv:1406.3830*.

Cıcero Nogueira Dos Santos and Maıra Gatti. 2014. Deep convolutional neural networks for sentiment analysis of short texts. In *Proceedings of the 25th International Conference on Computational Linguistics*.

John Duchi, Elad Hazan, and Yoram Singer. 2011. Adaptive subgradient methods for online learning and stochastic optimization. *The Journal of Machine Learning Research*, 12:2121–2159.

Alec Go, Richa Bhayani, and Lei Huang. 2009. Twitter sentiment classification using distant supervision. *CS224N Project Report, Stanford*, pages 1–12.

Alex Graves, A-R Mohamed, and Geoffrey Hinton. 2013. Speech recognition with deep recurrent neural networks. In *Acoustics, Speech and Signal Processing, 2013 IEEE International Conference on*, pages 6645–6649. IEEE.

Felix Hill, KyungHyun Cho, Sebastien Jean, Coline Devin, and Yoshua Bengio. 2014. Not all neural embeddings are born equal. In *NIPS Workshop on Learning Semantics*.

Geoffrey E Hinton, Nitish Srivastava, Alex Krizhevsky, Ilya Sutskever, and Ruslan R Salakhutdinov. 2012. Improving neural networks by preventing co-adaptation of feature detectors. *arXiv preprint arXiv:1207.0580*.

Eric H Huang, Richard Socher, Christopher D Manning, and Andrew Y Ng. 2012. Improving word representations via global context and multiple word prototypes. In *Proceedings of the 50th Annual Meeting of the Association for Computational Linguistics: Long Papers-Volume 1*, pages 873–882. Association for Computational Linguistics.

Nal Kalchbrenner, Edward Grefenstette, and Phil Blunsom. 2014. A convolutional neural network for modelling sentences. In *Proceedings of the 52nd Annual Meeting of the Association for Computational Linguistics*. Association for Computational Linguistics.

Yoon Kim. 2014. Convolutional neural networks for sentence classification. In *Proceedings of the 2014 Conference on Empirical Methods in Natural Language Processing*, October.

Dan Klein and Christopher D Manning. 2003. Accurate unlexicalized parsing. In *Proceedings of the 41st Annual Meeting on Association for Computational Linguistics-Volume 1*, pages 423–430. Association for Computational Linguistics.

Alex Krizhevsky, Ilya Sutskever, and Geoffrey E Hinton. 2012. Imagenet classification with deep convolutional neural networks. In *Advances in neural information processing systems*, pages 1097–1105.

Quoc V Le and Tomas Mikolov. 2014. Distributed representations of sentences and documents. In *Proceedings of the 31st international conference on Machine learning*.

Yong Luo, Jian Tang, Jun Yan, Chao Xu, and Zheng Chen. 2014. Pre-trained multi-view word embedding using two-side neural network. In *Twenty-Eighth AAAI Conference on Artificial Intelligence*.

Tomas Mikolov, Martin Karafiát, Lukas Burget, Jan Cernockỳ, and Sanjeev Khudanpur. 2010. Recurrent neural network based language model. In *INTERSPEECH 2010, 11th Annual Conference of the International Speech Communication Association, Makuhari, Chiba, Japan, September 26-30, 2010*, pages 1045–1048.

Tomas Mikolov, Kai Chen, Greg Corrado, and Jeffrey Dean. 2013a. Efficient estimation of word representations in vector space. In *Proceedings of Workshop at ICLR*.

Tomas Mikolov, Ilya Sutskever, Kai Chen, Greg S Corrado, and Jeff Dean. 2013b. Distributed representations of words and phrases and their compositionality. In *Advances in Neural Information Processing Systems*, pages 3111–3119.

Tomas Mikolov. 2012. Statistical language models based on neural networks. *Presentation at Google, Mountain View, 2nd April*.

Andriy Mnih and Geoffrey E Hinton. 2009. A scalable hierarchical distributed language model. In *Advances in neural information processing systems*, pages 1081–1088.

Andriy Mnih and Yee Whye Teh. 2012. A fast and simple algorithm for training neural probabilistic language models. In *Proceedings of the 29th International Conference on Machine Learning*, pages 1751–1758.

Bo Pang and Lillian Lee. 2004. A sentimental education: Sentiment analysis using subjectivity summarization based on minimum cuts. In *Proceedings of the 42nd annual meeting on Association for Computational Linguistics*, page 271. Association for Computational Linguistics.

Robert Parker, Linguistic Data Consortium, et al. 2009. *English gigaword fourth edition*. Linguistic Data Consortium.

Jeffrey Pennington, Richard Socher, and Christopher D Manning. 2014. Glove: Global vectors for word representation. *Proceedings of the Empiricial Methods in Natural Language Processing*, 12.

Richard Socher, Eric H Huang, Jeffrey Pennin, Christopher D Manning, and Andrew Y Ng. 2011a. Dynamic pooling and unfolding recursive autoencoders for paraphrase detection. In *Advances in Neural Information Processing Systems*, pages 801–809.

Richard Socher, Jeffrey Pennington, Eric H Huang, Andrew Y Ng, and Christopher D Manning. 2011b. Semi-supervised recursive autoencoders for predicting sentiment distributions. In *Proceedings of the Conference on Empirical Methods in Natural Language Processing*, pages 151–161. Association for Computational Linguistics.

Richard Socher, Brody Huval, Christopher D Manning, and Andrew Y Ng. 2012. Semantic compositionality through recursive matrix-vector spaces. In *Proceedings of the 2012 Joint Conference on Empirical Methods in Natural Language Processing and Computational Natural Language Learning*, pages 1201–1211. Association for Computational Linguistics.

Richard Socher, Alex Perelygin, Jean Y Wu, Jason Chuang, Christopher D Manning, Andrew Y Ng, and Christopher Potts. 2013. Recursive deep models for semantic compositionality over a sentiment treebank. In *Proceedings of the conference on empirical methods in natural language processing*, volume 1631, page 1642. Citeseer.

Joseph Turian, Lev Ratinov, and Yoshua Bengio. 2010. Word representations: a simple and general method for semi-supervised learning. In *Proceedings of the 48th annual meeting of the association for computational linguistics*, pages 384–394. Association for Computational Linguistics.

Sida Wang and Christopher D Manning. 2012. Baselines and bigrams: Simple, good sentiment and topic classification. In *Proceedings of the 50th Annual Meeting of the Association for Computational Linguistics: Short Papers-Volume 2*, pages 90–94. Association for Computational Linguistics.

Sida Wang and Christopher Manning. 2013. Fast dropout training. In *Proceedings of the 30th International Conference on Machine Learning*, pages 118–126.

Wenpeng Yin and Hinrich Schütze. 2014. An exploration of embeddings for generalized phrases. *Proceedings of the 52nd annual meeting of the association for computational linguistics, student research workshop*, pages 41–47.

Lei Yu, Karl Moritz Hermann, Phil Blunsom, and Stephen Pulman. 2014. Deep learning for answer sentence selection. *NIPS deep learning workshop*.

Opinion Holder and Target Extraction based on the Induction of Verbal Categories

Michael Wiegand
Spoken Language Systems
Saarland University
D-66123 Saarbrücken, Germany
michael.wiegand@lsv.uni-saarland.de

Josef Ruppenhofer
Dept. of Information Science
and Language Technology
Hildesheim University
D-31141 Hildesheim, Germany
ruppenho@uni-hildesheim.de

Abstract

We present an approach for opinion role induction for verbal predicates. Our model rests on the assumption that opinion verbs can be divided into three different types where each type is associated with a characteristic mapping between semantic roles and opinion holders and targets. In several experiments, we demonstrate the relevance of those three categories for the task. We show that verbs can easily be categorized with semi-supervised graph-based clustering and some appropriate similarity metric. The seeds are obtained through linguistic diagnostics. We evaluate our approach against a new manually-compiled opinion role lexicon and perform in-context classification.

1 Introduction

While there has been much research in sentiment analysis on subjectivity detection and polarity classification, there has been less work on the extraction of opinion roles, i.e. entities that express an opinion (*opinion holders*), and entities or propositions at which sentiment is directed (*opinion targets*). Previous research relies on large amounts of labeled training data or leverages general semantic resources which are expensive to construct, e.g. FrameNet (Baker et al., 1998).

In this paper, we present an approach to induce opinion roles of verbal predicates. The input is a set of opinion verbs that can be found in a common sentiment lexicon. Our model rests on the assumption that those verbs can be divided into three different types. Each type has a characteristic mapping between semantic roles and opinion holders and targets. Thus, the problem of opinion role induction is reduced to automatically categorizing opinion verbs.

We frame the task of opinion role extraction as a triple $(pred, const, role)$ where $pred$ is a predicate evoking an opinion (we exclusively focus on opinion verbs), $const$ is some constituent bearing a semantic role assigned by $pred$, and $role$ is the opinion role that is assigned to $const$.

Our work assumes the knowledge of opinion words. We do not cover polarity classification. Many lexicons with that kind of information already exist. Our sole interest is the assignment of opinion holder and target given some opinion verb. There does not exist any publicly available lexical resource specially designed for this task.

For the induction of opinion verb types, we consider semi-supervised graph clustering with some appropriate similarity metric. We also propose an effective method for deriving seeds automatically by applying some linguistic diagnostics.

Our approach is evaluated in a supervised learning scenario on a set of sentences with annotated opinion holders and targets. We employ different kinds of features, including features derived from a semantic parser based on FrameNet. We also compare our proposed model based on the three opinion verb types against a new manually-compiled lexicon in which the semantic roles of opinion holders and targets for each individual verb have been explicitly enumerated.

We also evaluate our approach in the context of cross-domain opinion holder extraction. Thus we demonstrate the importance of our approach in the context of previous datasets and classifiers.

This is the first work that proposes to induce both opinion holders and targets evoked by opinion verbs with data-driven methods. Unlike previous work, we are able to categorize all verbs of a pre-specified set of opinion verbs. Our approach is a low-resource approach that is also applicable to languages other than English. We demonstrate this on German. A by-product of our study are new resources including a verb lexicon specifying

Proceedings of the 19th Conference on Computational Language Learning, pages 215–225,
Beijing, China, July 30-31, 2015.

semantic roles for holders and targets.

2 Lexicon-based Opinion Role Extraction

Opinion holder and target extraction is a hard task (Ruppenhofer et al., 2008). Conventional syntactic or semantic levels of representation do not capture sufficient information that allows a reliable prediction of opinion holders and targets. This is illustrated by (1) and (2) which show that, even with common semantic roles, i.e. *agent* and *patient*[1], assigned to the entities, one may not be able to discriminate between the opinion roles.

(1) Peter_{agent} **criticized** $\text{Mary}_{patient}$.
$(criticize, Peter, holder)$ & $(criticize, Mary, target)$

(2) Peter_{agent} **disappoints** $\text{Mary}_{patient}$.
$(disappoint, Peter, target)$ & $(disappoint, Mary, holder)$

We assume that it is lexical information that decides what semantic role an opinion holder or opinion target takes. As a consequence, we built a gold-standard lexicon for verbs that encodes such information. For example, it states that the target of *criticize* is its patient, while for *disappoint*, the target is its agent. This **fine-grained lexicon** also accounts for the fact that a constituent can have several roles given the same opinion verb. An extreme case is:

(3) $[\text{Peter}]_1$ **persuades** $[\text{Mary}]_2$ $[\text{to accept his invitation}]_3$.

The sentence conveys that:

- Peter wants Mary to do something. *($view_1$)*
- Mary is influenced by Peter. *($view_2$)*
- Peter has some attitude towards Mary accepting his invitation. *($view_3$)*
- Mary has some attitude towards accepting Peter's invitation. *($view_4$)*

This corresponds to the role assignments:

- $view_1$: $(persuade, [1], holder)$, $(persuade, [2], target)$
- $view_2$: $(persuade, [2], holder)$, $(persuade, [1], target)$
- $view_3$: $(persuade, [1], holder)$, $(persuade, [3], target)$
- $view_4$: $(persuade, [2], holder)$, $(persuade, [3], target)$

(in short: 2 opinion holders and 3 opinion targets).

Our lexicon also includes another dimension neglected in many previous works. Many opinion verbs predominantly express the sentiment of the speaker of the utterance (or some nested source) (4). This concept is also known as *expressive subjectivity* (Wiebe et al., 2005) or *speaker subjectivity* (Maks and Vossen, 2012). In such opinions, the opinion holder is not realized as a dependent of the opinion verb.

(4) At my work, $[\text{they}]_1$ are constantly **gossiping**.
$(gossip, \texttt{speaker}, holder)$ & $(gossip, [1], target)$

[1]By *agent* and *patient*, we mean constituents labeled as $A0$ and $A1$ in PropBank (Kingsbury and Palmer, 2002).

Our lexicon covers the 1175 verb lemmas contained in the Subjectivity Lexicon (Wilson et al., 2005). We annotated the semantic roles similar to the format of PropBank (Kingsbury and Palmer, 2002). The basis of the annotation were online dictionaries (e.g. *Macmillan Dictionary*) which provide both a verb definition and example sentences. We do not annotate implicature-related information about effects (Deng and Wiebe, 2014) but inherent sentiment *(the data release[2] includes more details regarding the annotation process and our notion of holders and targets).*

On a sample of 400 verbs, we measured an interannotation agreement of Cohen's $\kappa = 60.8$ for opinion holders, $\kappa = 62.3$ for opinion targets and $\kappa = 59.9$ for speaker views. This agreement is mostly substantial (Landis and Koch, 1977).

3 The Three Verb Categories

Rather than induce the opinion roles for individual verbs, we group verbs that share similar opinion role subcategorization. Thus, the main task for induction is to decide which type an opinion verb belongs to. Once the verb type has been established, the typical semantic roles for opinion holders and targets can be derived from that type. The verb categorization is motivated by the semantic roles of the three common views (Table 1) that an opinion holder can take. In our lexicon, all of the opinion holders were observed with either of these semantic roles. For facilitating induction, we assume that those types are disjoint (see also §3.4).

3.1 Verbs with Agent View (AG)

Verbs with an agent view, such as *criticize*, *love* and *believe*, convey the sentiment of its agent. Therefore, those verbs take the agent as opinion holder and the patient as opinion target. Table 1 also exemplifies semantic role labels as a suitable basis to align opinion holders and targets within a particular verb type. For example, targets of AG-verbs align to the patient, yet the patient can take the form of various phrase types (i.e. NPs, PPs or infinitive/complement phrases[3]).

[2]available at: `www.coli.uni-saarland.de/~miwieg/conll_2015_op_roles_data.tgz`

[3]Note that infinitive and complement clauses may represent a semantic role other than *patient* (e.g. the infinitive clause in (3)). As these types of clauses are fairly unambiguous, we marked them as targets even if they are no patients.

Type	Example	Holder	Target
AG	$[\text{They}]_{agent}$ **like** $[\text{the idea}]_{patient}$.	agent	pat.
	$[\text{The guests}]_{agent}$ **complained** $[\text{about noise}]_{patient}$.		
	$[\text{They}]_{agent}$ **argue** $[\text{that this plan is infeasible}]_{patient}$.		
PT	$[\text{The noise}]_{agent}$ **irritated** $[\text{the guests}]_{patient}$.	pat.	agent
	$[\text{That gift}]_{agent}$ **pleased** $[\text{her}]_{patient}$ very much.		
SP	$[\text{They}]_{agent}$ **cheated** $[\text{in the exam}]_{adjunct}$.	-N/A-	agent,
	$[\text{He}]_{agent}$ **besmirched** $[\text{the King's name}]_{patient}$.		(pat.)

Table 1: Verb types for opinion role extraction.

Type	Freq	Type	Freq
verbs with **AG**-view	868	verbs with **PT**-view	392
verbs with exclusive **AG**-view	371	verbs with exclusive **PT**-view	117
verbs with **AG**- and SP-view	352	verbs with **PT**- and AG-view	226
verbs with **AG**- and PT-view	226	verbs with **PT**- and SP-view	139
verbs with **SP**-view	537		
verbs with exclusive **SP**-view	134		
verbs with **SP**- and AG-view	352		
verbs with **SP**- and PT-view	139		

Table 2: Verb types in the fine-grained lexicon.

Agent (AG)		Patient (PT)		Speaker (SP)	
Freq	Percent	Freq	Percent	Freq	Percent
450	38.3	188	16.0	537	45.7

Table 3: Verb types in the coarse-grained lexicon.

3.2 Verbs with Patient View (PT)

Verbs with a patient view (*irritate*, *upset* and *disappoint*) are opposite to AG-verbs in that those verbs have the patient as opinion holder and the agent as opinion target.

3.3 Verbs with Speaker View (SP)

The third type we consider comprises all verbs whose perspective is that of the speaker. That is, these are verbs whose sentiment is primarily that of the speaker of the utterance rather than persons involved in the action to which is referred. Typical examples are *gossip*, *improve* or *cheat*.

While the agent is usually the target of the sentiment of the speaker, it depends on the specific verb whether its patient is also a target or not (in Table 1, only the patient of the second SP-verb, i.e. *besmirch*, is considered a target[4]). Since we aim at a precise induction approach, we will always (only) mark the agent of an induced SP-verb as a target.

3.4 Relation to Fine-Grained Lexicon

Table 2 provides statistics as to how clear-cut the three prototypical verb types are in the manually-compiled fine-grained lexicon. These numbers suggest that many verbs evoke several opinion views (e.g. a verb with an AG-view may also evoke a PT-view). While the fine-grained lexicon is fairly exhaustive in listing semantic roles for opinion holders and targets, it may also occasionally overgenerate. One major reason for this is that we do not annotate on the sense-level (word-sense disambiguation (Wiebe and Mihalcea, 2006) is still in its infancy) but on the lemma-level. Accordingly, we attribute all views to all senses, whereas actually certain views pertain only to specific senses. However, we found that usually one view is conveyed by most (if not all) senses of a word. For example, the lexicon lists both an AG-view and a PT-view for *appease*. This is correct for (5) but wrong for (6). The AG-view is derived from a definition *to give your opponents what they want.* (6) does not convey an agent's volitional action. Here, the verb just conveys *make someone feel less angry*. Similarly, the lexicon lists an SP-view and an AG-view for *degrade*, which is right for (7) but wrong for (8). The AG-view is derived from a lexicon definition *to treat someone in a way that makes them stop respecting themselves.* (8) does not convey an agent's volitional action. The verb just conveys *to make something worse*. That is, neither (6) nor (8) evoke an AG-view. We found that these variations regularly occur. We adopt the heuristic that verbs with an SP-view and AG- or PT-view preserve the SP-view across their uses (7)-(8). Verbs with both PT- and AG-view preserve their PT-view (5)-(6). Following these observations, we converted our fine-grained lexicon into a gold standard **coarse-grained lexicon** (only 3% of the verbs needed to be manually corrected after the automatic conversion) in which a verb is classified as AG, PT or SP according to its **dominant view**. The final class distribution of this lexicon is shown in Table 3. In §5.2, we show through an in-context evaluation that our coarse-grained representation preserves most of the information captured by the fine-grained representation.

(5) $[\text{Chamberlain}]_{agent}$ **appeased** $[\text{Hitler}]_{patient}$.
(6) $[\text{The orange juice}]_{agent}$ **appeased** $[\text{him}]_{patient}$ for a while.
(7) $[\text{Mary}]_{agent}$ **degrades** $[\text{Henrietta}]_{patient}$.
(8) $[\text{This technique}]_{agent}$ **degrades** $[\text{the local water supply}]_{patient}$.

4 Induction of Verb Categories

The task is to categorize each verb as a predominant AG-, PT-, or SP-verb. Our approach comprises two steps. In the first step, seeds for the different verb types are extracted (§4.1). In the sec-

[4] We consider the patient a target since the speaker has a positive (non-defeasible) sentiment towards that entity.

AG	argue, contend, speculate, fear, doubt, complain, consider, praise, recommend, view, acknowledge, hope
PT	interest, surprise, please, excite, disappoint, delight, impress, shock, trouble, embarrass, annoy, distress
SP	murder, plot, incite, blaspheme, bewitch, bungle, despoil, plagiarize, prevaricate, instigate, molest, conspire

Table 4: The top 12 extracted verb seeds.

ond step, a similarity metric (§4.2) is employed in order to propagate the verb type labels from the seeds to the remaining opinion verbs (§4.3). The *North American News Text Corpus* is used for seed extraction and computation of verb similarities.

Wiegand and Klakow (2012) proposed methods for extracting AG- and PT-verbs. We will re-use these methods for generating seeds. A major contribution of this paper is the introduction of the third dimension, i.e. SP-verbs, in the context of induction. We show that in combination with this third dimension, one can categorize all opinion verbs contained in a sentiment lexicon. Furthermore, given this three-way classification, we also obtain better results on the detection of AG-verbs and PT-verbs than by just detecting those verbs in isolation without graph clustering (this will be shown in Table 7 and discussed in §5.1).

A second major contribution of this work is that we show that these methods are also equally important for *opinion target extraction*. So far, the significance of AG- and PT-verbs has only been demonstrated for opinion holder extraction.

In this work, we exclusively focus on the set of 1175 opinion verbs from the Subjectivity Lexicon. However, this is owed solely to the effort required to generate larger sets of evaluation data. In principle, our induction approach is applicable to any set of opinion verbs of arbitrary (e.g. larger) size.

4.1 Pattern-based Seed Initialization

For AG-verbs, we rely on the findings of Wiegand and Klakow (2012) who suggest that verbs predictive for opinion holders can be induced with the help of *prototypical opinion holders*. These common nouns, e.g. *opponents* (9) or *critics* (10), act like opinion holders and, therefore, can be seen as a proxy. Verbs co-occurring with prototypical opinion holders do not represent the entire range of opinion verbs but coincide with AG-verbs.

(9) **Opponents** *claim* these arguments miss the point.
(10) **Critics** *argued* that the proposed limits were unconstitutional.

For PT-verbs, we make use of the *adjective heuristic* proposed by Wiegand and Klakow (2012). The authors make use of the observation that morphologically related adjectives exist for PT-verbs, unlike for AG- and SP-verbs. Therefore, in order to extract PT-verbs, one needs to check whether a verb in its past participle form, such as *upset* in (11), is identical to some predicate adjective (12).

(11) He had $upset_{verb}$ me.
(12) I am $upset_{adj}$.

We are not aware of any previously published approach effectively inducing SP-verbs. Noticing that many of those verbs contain some form of reproach, we came up with the patterns *accused of* X_{VBG} and *blamed for* X_{VBG} as in (13) and (14).

(13) He was **accused of** *falsifying* the documents.
(14) The UN was **blamed for** *misinterpreting* climate data.

Table 4 lists for each of the verb types the 12 seeds most frequently occurring with the respective patterns. We observed that the SP-verb seeds are exclusively negative polar expressions. That is why we also extracted seeds from an additional pattern *help to* X_{VB} producing prototypical *positive* SP-verbs, such as *stabilize*, *allay* or *heal*.

4.2 Similarity Metrics

4.2.1 Word Embeddings

Recent research in machine learning has focused on inducing vector representations of words. As an example of a competitive word embedding method, we induce vectors for our opinion verbs with *Word2Vec* (Mikolov et al., 2013). Baroni et al. (2014) showed that this method outperforms count vector representations on a variety of tasks. For the similarity between two verbs, we compute the cosine-similarity between their vectors.

4.2.2 WordNet::Similarity

We use *WordNet::Similarity* (Pedersen et al., 2004) as an alternative source for similarity metrics. The metrics are based on WordNet's graph structure (Miller et al., 1990). Various relations within WordNet have been shown to be effective for polarity classification (Esuli and Sebastiani, 2006; Rao and Ravichandran, 2009).

4.2.3 Coordination

Another method to measure similarity is obtained by leveraging coordination. Coordination is known to be a syntactic relation that also preserves great semantic coherence (Ziering et al., 2013), e.g. (15). It has been successfully applied not only to noun categorization (Riloff and Shepherd, 1997; Roark and Charniak, 1998) but also to different tasks in sentiment analysis, including polarity classification (Hatzivassiloglou and McKeown, 1997), the induction of patient polarity verbs (Goyal et al., 2010) and connotation learning (Kang et al., 2014). We use the dependency relation from Stanford parser (Klein and Manning, 2003) to detect coordination (16).

(15) They *criticize* **and** *hate* him.
(16) `conj(criticize,hate)`

As a similarity function, we simply take the absolute frequency of observing two words w_1 and w_2 in a conjunction, i.e. $sim(w_1, w_2) = freq(conj(w_1, w_2))$.

4.2.4 Dependency-based Similarity

The metric proposed by Lin (1998) exploits the rich set of dependency-relation labels in the context of distributional similarity. Moreover, it has been effectively used for the related task of extending frames of unknown predicates in semantic parsing (Das and Smith, 2011).

The metric is based on dependency triples (w, r, w') where w and w' are words and r is a dependency relation (e.g. `(argue-V, nsubj, critics-N)`). The metric is defined as: $sim(w_1, w_2) = \frac{\sum_{(r,w)\in T(w_1)\cap T(w_2)}(I(w_1,r,w)+I(w_2,r,w))}{\sum_{(r,w)\in T(w_1)} I(w_1,r,w)+\sum_{(r,w)\in T(w_2)} I(w_2,r,w)}$ where $I(w, r, w') = log\frac{\|w,r,w'\| \times \|*,r,*\|}{\|w,r,*\| \times \|*,r,w'\|}$ and $T(w)$ is defined as the set of pairs (r, w') such that $log\frac{\|w,r,w'\| \times \|*,r,*\|}{\|w,r,*\| \times \|*,r,w'\|} > 0$.

4.3 Propagation Methods

We use the k **nearest neighbour classifier (kNN)** (Cover and Hart, 1967) as a simple method for propagating labels from seeds to other instances. Alternatively, we consider verb categorization as a **clustering task on a graph** $G = (V, E, W)$ where V is the set of nodes (i.e. our opinion verbs), E is the set of edges connecting them with weights $W : E \rightarrow \mathbb{R}^+$. W can be directly derived from any of the similarity metrics (§4.2.1-§4.2.4). The aim is that all nodes $v \in V$ are assigned a label $l \in \{AG, PT, SP\}$. Initially, only the verb seeds are labeled. We then use the Adsorption label propagation algorithm from *junto* (Talukdar et al., 2008) in order propagate the labels from the seeds to the remaining verbs.

		Acc	Prec	Rec	F1
Baselines	**Majority Class**	45.7	14.2	33.3	20.9
	Only Seeds	8.9	87.0	9.8	17.6
Coordination	**kNN**	45.2	61.5	47.3	53.4
	graph	42.7	68.7	39.7	50.4
WordNet	**kNN**	52.8	51.5	50.7	51.1
	graph	51.1	51.9	51.5	51.5
Embedding	**kNN**	59.3	58.4	61.0	59.7
	graph	64.0	70.5	59.4	64.5
Dependency	**kNN**	65.7	63.8	65.4	64.5
	graph	**70.3**	**72.0**	**68.0**	**70.6**

Table 5: Eval. of similarity metrics and classifiers.

5 Experiments

5.1 Evaluation of the Induced Lexicon

Table 5 compares the performance of the different similarity metrics when incorporated in either kNN or graph clustering. The resulting categorizations are compared against the gold standard coarse-grained lexicon (§3.4). For kNN, we set $k = 3$ for which we obtained best performance in all our experiments.

As seeds, we took the top 40 AG-verbs, 30 PT-verbs and 50 SP-verbs produced by the respective initialization methods (§4.1). The seed proportions should vaguely correspond to the actual class distribution (Table 3). Large increases of the seed sets do not improve the quality (as shown below). 10 of the 50 SP-verbs are extracted from the positive SP-patterns, while the remaining verbs are extracted from the negative SP-patterns (§4.1).

As baselines, we include a classifier only employing the seeds and a majority class classifier always predicting an SP-verb. For word embeddings (§4.2.1) and WordNet::Similarity (§4.2.2), we only report the performance of the best metric/configuration, i.e. for embeddings, the continuous bag-of-words model with 500 dimensions and for WordNet::Similarity, the *Wu & Palmer* measure (Wu and Palmer, 1994).

Table 5 shows that the baselines can be outperformed by large margins. The performance of the different similarity metrics varies. The dependency-based metric performs notably better than the other metrics. Together with word embeddings, it is the only metric for which graph clustering produces a notable improvement over kNN.

Table 6 illustrates the quality of the similarity metrics for the present task. The table shows that the dependency-based similarity metric provides the most suitable output. The poor quality of coordination may come as a surprise. That

Coordin.	appear, believe, refuse, vow, want, offend, shock, help, exhilarate, challenge, support, distort
WordNet	appal, scandalize, anger, rage, sicken, temper, hate, fear, love, alarm, dread, tingle
Embedd.	anger, dismay, disgust, protest, alarm, enrage, shock, regret, concern, horrify, appal, sorrow
Depend.	anger, infuriate, alarm, shock, stun, enrage, incense, dismay, upset, appal, offend, disappoint

Table 6: The 12 most similar verbs to *outrage* (PT-verb) according to the different metrics (verbs other than PT-verbs are underlined).

AG-verbs		**PT-verbs**		**SP-verbs**	
no graph (Wiegand 2012)	graph	no graph (Wiegand 2012)	graph	no graph	graph
55.45	**69.12**	38.59	**67.66**	52.16	**72.03**

Table 7: F-scores of entire output of pattern-based extraction (§4.1) where no propagation is applied (*no graph*) vs. best proposed induction method from Table 5 (*graph*).

method suffers from data-sparsity. In our corpus, the frequency of verbs co-occurring with *outrage* in a conjunction is 5 or lower.[5] The table also shows that WordNet may not be appropriate for our present verb categorization task. However, it may be suitable for other subtasks in sentiment analysis, particularly polarity classification. If we consider the similar entries of *outrage* provided by that metric, we find that polarity is largely preserved (10 out of 12 verbs are negative). This observation is consistent with Esuli and Sebastiani (2006) and Rao and Ravichandran (2009).

In Table 5 we only used the top 40/30/50 verbs from the initialization methods as seeds. We can also compare the output of these methods (combined with propagation, i.e. graph clustering) with the *entire* verb lists produced by these pattern-based initialization methods where no propagation is applied. As far as AG- and PT-verbs are concerned, the entire lists of these initialization methods correspond to the original approach of Wiegand and Klakow (2012). Table 7 shows the result. The new graph-induction always outperforms the original induction method by a large margin.

In Table 8, we compare our automatically generated seeds using the patterns from §4.1 (*Pattern*) with seeds extracted from our gold standard (*Gold*). We rank those verbs by frequency. Size and verb type distribution are preserved. We also examine what impact doubling the size of seeds ($Gold|Pattern_{double}$) and halving them ($Gold|Pattern_{half}$) has on classification. Dependency-based similarity and graph clustering is used for all configurations. Only if we double the amount of seeds are the gold seeds notably better than the automatically generated seeds.

[5]We found that for frequently occurring opinion verbs, this similarity metric produces more reasonable output.

Pattern$_{half}$	**Pattern**	**Pattern**$_{double}$	**Gold**$_{half}$	**Gold**	**Gold**$_{double}$
68.71	70.59	66.50	66.21	70.31	73.77

Table 8: Comparison of automatic and gold seeds *(evaluation measure: macro-average F-score).*

		Coordin.		**WordNet**		**Embedd.**		**Depend.**	
	Major.	**kNN**	**graph**	**kNN**	**graph**	**kNN**	**graph**	**kNN**	**graph**
English	20.9	53.4	50.4	51.1	51.5	59.7	64.5	64.5	**70.6**
German	22.9	43.8	48.9	53.2	59.9	54.3	60.9	58.3	**63.1**

Table 9: Comparison of English and German data *(evaluation measure: macro-average F-score).*

Since our induction approach just requires a sentiment lexicon and aims at low-resource languages, we replicated the experiments for German, as shown in Table 9. We use the PolArt-sentiment lexicon (Klenner et al., 2009) (1416 entries). (As a gold standard, we manually annotated that lexicon according to our three verb types.) As an unlabeled corpus, we chose the *Huge German Corpus*[6]. As a parser, we used ParZu (Sennrich et al., 2009). Instead of WordNet, we used *GermaNet* (Hamp and Feldweg, 1997). The automatically generated seeds were manually translated from English to German. Table 9 shows that as on English data, dependency-based similarity combined with graph clustering performs best. The fact that we can successfully replicate our approach in another language supports the general applicability of our proposed categorization of verbs into three types for opinion role extraction.

5.2 In-Context Evaluation

We now evaluate our induced knowledge in the task of extracting opinion holders and targets from actual text. For this in-context evaluation, we sampled sentences from the North American News Corpus in which our opinion verbs occurred. We annotated all holders and targets of those verbs. (A constituent may have several roles for the same verb (§2).) The dataset contains about 1100 sentences. We need to rely on this dataset since it is the only corpus in which our opinion verbs are

[6]`www.ims.uni-stuttgart.de/forschung/ressourcen/korpora/hgc.html`

Features	Description
cand_lemma	head lemma of candidate (phrase)
cand_pos	part-of-speech tag of head of candidate phrase
cand_phrase	phrase label of candidate
cand_person	is candidate a person
verb_lemma	verb lemmatized
verb_pos	part of speech tag of verb
word	bag of words: all words within the sentence
pos	part-of-speech sequence between cand. and verb
distance	token distance between candidate and verb
const	path from constituency parse tree from cand. to verb
subcat	subcategorization frame of verb
$\text{srl}_{propbank}$/dep	semantic role/dependency path between cand. and verb (semantic roles based on PropBank)
brown	Brown-clusters of cand_word/verb_word/word
$\text{srl}_{framenet}$	frame element name assigned to candidate and the frame name (to which frame element belongs)
fine-grain_lex	is candidate holder/target/$\text{target}_{speaker}$ according to the fine-grained lexicon
coarse-grain_lex	is candidate holder/target/$\text{target}_{speaker}$ according to the coarse-grained lexicon
induc_{graph}	is candidate holder/target/$\text{target}_{speaker}$ according to the coarse-grained lexicon automatically induced with graph clustering (and induced seeds (§4.1))

Table 10: Feature set for in-context classification.

widely represented and both holders and targets are annotated.

We solve this task with supervised learning. As a classifier, we employ Support Vector Machines as implemented in SVM^{light} (Joachims, 1999). The task is to extract three different entities: opinion holders, opinion targets and opinion targets evoked by speaker views. All those entities are always put into the relation to a specific opinion verb in the sentence. The instance space thus consists of tuples $(verb, const)$, where $verb$ is the mention of an opinion verb and $const$ is any possible (syntactic) constituent in the respective sentence. The dataset contains 753 holders, 745 targets and 499 targets of a speaker view. Since a constituent may have several roles at the same time, we train three binary classifiers for either of the entity types. On a sample of 200 sentences, we measured an interannotation agreement of Cohen's $\kappa = 0.69$ for holders, $\kappa = 0.63$ for targets and also $\kappa = 0.63$ for targets of a speaker view.

Table 10 shows the features used in our supervised classifier. They have been previously found effective (Choi et al., 2005; Jakob and Gurevych, 2010; Wiegand and Klakow, 2012; Yang and Cardie, 2013). The ***standard features*** are the features from *cand_word* to *brown*. For semantic role labeling of PropBank-structures, we used *mate-tools* (Björkelund et al., 2009). For person detection, we employ named-entity tagging (Finkel et al., 2005) and WordNet (Miller et al., 1990).

Features	Holder	Target	$\text{Target}_{Speaker}$
standard	63.59	54.18	40.06
$+\text{srl}_{framenet}$	65.44^{*}	55.70^{*}	42.14
$+\text{induc}_{graph}$	$68.06^{*\circ}$	$59.61^{*\circ}$	$46.66^{*\circ}$
$+\text{srl}_{framenet}+\text{induc}_{graph}$	$69.70^{*\circ}$	$60.47^{*\circ}$	$47.33^{*\circ}$
+coarse-grain_lex	$68.56^{*\circ}$	$59.89^{*\circ}$	$54.31^{*\circ\dagger}$
$+\text{srl}_{framenet}$+coarse-grain_lex	$69.70^{*\circ}$	$60.68^{*\circ}$	$54.06^{*\circ\dagger}$
+fine-grain_lex	$69.83^{*\circ\dagger}$	$62.89^{*\circ\dagger}$	$\mathbf{56.71}^{*\circ\dagger}$
$+\text{srl}_{framenet}$+fine-grain_lex	$\mathbf{70.80}^{*\circ\dagger}$	$\mathbf{63.72}^{*\circ\dagger}$	$56.64^{*\circ\dagger}$

statistical significance testing (paired t-test, significance level $p < 0.05$) *: better than *standard*; $^{\circ}$: better than $+srl_{framenet}$; †: better than $+induc_{graph}$

Table 11: In-context evaluation (*eval.: F-score*).

For semantic role labeling of FrameNet-structures ($srl_{framenet}$), we used *Semafor* (Das et al., 2010) with the argument identification based on dual decomposition (Das et al., 2012). We run the configuration that also assigns frame structures to unknown predicates (Das and Smith, 2011). This is necessary as 45% of our opinion verbs are not contained in FrameNet (v1.5). FrameNet has been shown to enable a correct role assignment for AG- and PT-verbs (Bethard et al., 2004; Kim and Hovy, 2006). For instance, in (17) and (18), the opinion holder is assigned to the same frame element EXPERIENCER. However, the PropBank representation does not produce a correct alignment: In (17), the opinon holder is the agent of the opinion verb, while in (18), the opinion holder is the patient of the opinion verb.

(17) $\text{Peter}^{\text{EXPERIENCER}}_{agent}$ **dislikes** $\text{Mary}_{patient}$.
$(dislike, Peter, holder)$

(18) Peter_{agent} **disappoints** $\text{Mary}^{\text{EXPERIENCER}}_{patient}$.
$(disappoint, Mary, holder)$

With the feature ***fine-grain_lex***, we want to validate that our manually-compiled opinion role lexicon for verbs (§2), i.e. the lexicon that also allows multiple opinion roles for the same semantic roles, is effective for in-context evaluation. ***Coarse-grain_lex*** is derived from the fine-grained lexicon (§3.4). With this feature, we measure how much we lose by dropping the fine-grained representation. $\textbf{\textit{Induc}}_{graph}$ induces the verb types of the coarse representation automatically by employing the best induction method obtained in Table 5.

Table 11 compares the different features on 10-fold crossvalidation. The table shows that the features encoding opinion role information, including our induction approach, are more effective than $srl_{framenet}$. Even though the fine-grained lexicon produces the best results, we almost reach that performance with the coarse-grained lexicon. This is

		manual lexicons	
Features	**induc$_{graph}$**	**coarse-grain**	**fine-grain**
lexicon feature only (≈ *unsuperv.*)	52.38	55.81	60.68
lexicon with all other features	59.90*	61.71*	63.92°

statistical significance testing (paired t-test, significance level $p < 0.05$) *: better than *lexicon feature only*; $^\circ$: only significant on 2 out of 3 roles

Table 12: Lexical resources and the impact of other (not lexicon-based) features (*evaluation measure: macro-average F-score*).

	Distribution of Verb Types			
Corpus	**AG**	**PT**	**SP**	**# sentences**
MPQA *(training+test)*	77.5	7.7	14.8	15,753
FICTION *(test)*	67.5	15.1	17.3	614
VERB *(test)*	34.8	14.0	52.7	1,073

Table 13: Statistics on the different corpora used.

further evidence that our proposed three-way verb categorization, which is also the basis of our induction approach, is adequate.

Table 12 compares the performance of the different lexicons in isolation (this is comparable with an *unsupervised* classifier, as each lexicon feature has three values each predicting either of the opinion roles) and in combination with the standard (+srl$_{framenet}$) features. The table shows that all lexicon features are strong features on their own. The score of induction is lowest but this feature has been created without manual supervision. Moreover, the improvement by adding the other features is much larger for induction than for the manually-built fine-grained lexicon. This means that we can compensate some lexical knowledge missing in induction by standard features.

Since we could substantially outperform the features relying on FrameNet with our new lexical resources, we looked closer at the predicted frame structures. Beside obvious errors in automatic frame assignment, we also found that there are problems inherent in the frame design. Particularly, the notion of SP-verbs (§3.3) is not properly reflected. Many frames, such as SCRUTINY, typically devised for AG-verbs, such as *investigate* or *analyse*, also contain SP-verbs like *pry*. This observation is in line with Ruppenhofer and Rehbein (2012) who claim that extensions to FrameNet are necessary to properly represent opinions evoked by verbal predicates.

5.3 Comparison to Previous Cross-Domain Opinion Holder Extraction

We now compare our proposed induction approach with previous work on opinion holder extraction. We replicate several classifiers and compare them to our new approach. (Because of the limited space of this paper, we cannot also address cross-domain opinion target extraction.) We consider three different corpora as shown in Table 13. **MPQA** (Wiebe et al., 2005) is the standard corpus for fine-grained sentiment analysis. **FICTION**, introduced in Wiegand and Klakow (2012), is a collection of summaries of classic literary works. **VERB** is the new corpus used in the previous evaluation (§5.2). VERB and MPQA both originate from the news domain but VERB is sampled in such a way that mentions of *all* opinion verbs of the Subjectivity Lexicon are represented. The other corpora consist of contiguous sentences. They will have a bias towards only those opinion verbs frequently occurring in that particular domain. This also results in different distributions of verb types as shown in Table 13. For example, SP-verbs are rare in MPQA. However, there exist plenty of them (Table 3). Other domains may have much more frequent SP-verbs (just as FICTION has more PT-verbs than MPQA). A robust domain-independent classifier should therefore be able to cope equally well with all three verb types.

	in domain	*out of domain*	
Config	**MPQA**	**FICTION**	**VERB**
MultiRel	**72.54**$^{*\circ}$	53.02	44.80
CK	62.98	52.91	43.88
CK + induc$_{Wiegand\ 2012}$	65.15	57.33*	50.83*
CK + induc$_{graph}$	66.06*	**65.03**$^{*\circ}$	60.91$^{*\circ}$
CK + coarse-grain_lex	66.82*	64.13$^{*\circ}$	63.72$^{*\circ\dagger}$
CK + fine-grain_lex	66.16*	64.98$^{*\circ}$	**70.85**$^{*\circ\dagger\ddagger}$

statistical significance testing (permutation test, significance level $p < 0.05$) *: better than *CK*; $^\circ$: better than *CK + induc*$_{Wiegand\ 2012}$; †: better than *CK + induc*$_{graph}$; ‡: better than *CK + coarse-grain_lex*

Table 14: Evaluation on opinion holder extraction on various corpora (*evaluation measure: F-score*).

MPQA is also the largest corpus. Following Wiegand and Klakow (2012), this corpus is chosen as a training set.[7] Despite its size, however, almost every second opinion verb from our set of opinion verbs is not contained in that corpus.

In the evaluation, we only consider the opinion holders of our opinion verbs. (Other opinion holders, both in the gold standard and the predictions of the classifiers are ignored.) Recall that we take the knowledge of what is an opinion verb as given. Our graph-based induction can be arbitrarily extended by increasing the set of opinion verbs.

[7]The split-up of training and test set on the MPQA corpus follows the specification of Johansson and Moschitti (2013).

For classifiers, we consider convolution kernels ***CK*** from Wiegand and Klakow (2012) and the sequence labeler from Johansson and Moschitti (2013) ***MultiRel*** that incorporates relational features taking into account interactions between multiple opinion cues. It is currently the most sophisticated opinion holder extractor. *CK* can be combined with additional knowledge. We compare $induc_{graph}$ with $\boldsymbol{induc}_{Wiegand\ 2012}$, which employs the word lists induced for AG- and PT-verbs in the fashion of Wiegand and Klakow (2012), i.e. without graph clustering. As an upper bound for the induction methods, *coarse_grain_lex* and *fine_grain_lex* are used.[8] The combination of *CK* with this additional knowledge follows the best settings from Wiegand and Klakow (2012).[9]

Table 14 shows the results. *MultiRel* produces the best performance on MPQA but suffers similarly from a domain-mismatch as *CK* on FICTION and VERB. *MultiRel* and *CK* cannot handle many PT- and SP-verbs in those corpora, simply because many of them do not occur in MPQA. On MPQA, only the new induction approach and the lexicons significantly improve *CK*. The knowledge of opinion roles has a lower impact on MPQA. In that corpus, most opinion verbs take their opinion holder as an agent. Given the large size of MPQA, this information can be easily learned from the training data. The situation is different for FICTION and VERB where the knowledge from induction largely improves classification. In these corpora, opinion holders as agents are much less frequent than on MPQA. The new induction proposed in this paper also notably outperforms the induction from Wiegand and Klakow (2012).

Although the fine-grained lexicon is among the top performing systems, we only note large improvements on VERB. VERB has the highest proportion of PT- and SP-verbs (Table 13). Knowledge about role-assignment is most critical here.

6 Related Work

Most approaches for opinion role extraction employ supervised learning. The feature design is mainly inspired by semantic role labeling (Bethard et al., 2004; Li et al., 2012). Some work also employs information from existing semantic role labelers based on FrameNet (Kim and Hovy, 2006) or PropBank (Johansson and Moschitti, 2013; Wiegand and Klakow, 2012). Although those resources give extra information for opinion role extraction in comparison to syntactic or other surface features, we showed in this work that further task-specific knowledge, i.e. either opinion verb types or a manually-built opinion role lexicon, provide even more accurate information.

There has been a substantial amount of research on opinion target extraction. It focuses, however, on the extraction of topic-specific opinion terms (Jijkoun et al., 2010; Qiu et al., 2011) rather than the variability of semantic roles for opinion holders and targets. Mitchell et al. (2013) present a low-resource approach for target extraction but their aim is to process Twitter messages without using general *syntax* tools. In this work, we use such tools. Our notion of *low resources* is different in that we mean the absence of *semantic* resources helpful for our task (e.g. FrameNet).

7 Conclusion

We presented an approach for opinion role induction for verbal predicates. We assume that those predicates can be divided into three different verb types where each type is associated with a characteristic mapping between semantic roles and opinion holders and targets. In several experiments, we demonstrated the relevance of those three types. We showed that verbs can effectively be categorized with graph clustering given a suitable similarity metric. The seeds are automatically selected. Our proposed induction approach outperforms both a previous induction approach and features derived from semantic role labelers. We also pointed out the importance of the knowledge gained by induction in supervised cross-domain classification.

Acknowledgements

The authors would like to thank Stephanie Köser for annotating parts of the resources presented in this paper. For proof-reading the paper, the authors would also like to thank Ines Rehbein, Asad Sayeed and Marc Schulder. We also thank Ashutosh Modi for advising us on word embeddings. The authors were partially supported by the German Research Foundation (DFG) under grants RU 1873/2-1 and WI 4204/2-1.

---

[8] Wiegand and Klakow (2012) use a lexicon *Lex* which just comprises the notion of AG and PT verbs, so our manual lexicons are more accurate and harder to beat.

[9] For in-domain evaluation (i.e. MPQA) the trees (tree structures are the input to *CK*) are augmented with verb category information. For out-of-domain evaluation (i.e. FICTION and VERB), we add to the predictions of *CK* the prediction of a rule-based classifier using the opinion role assignment according to the respective lexicon or induction method.

References

Collin F. Baker, Charles J. Fillmore, and John B. Lowe. 1998. The Berkeley FrameNet Project. In *Proceedings of COLING/ACL.*

Marco Baroni, Georgiana Dinu, and Germán Kruszewski. 2014. Don't count, predict! A systematic comparison of context-counting vs. context-predicting semantic vectors. In *Proceedings of ACL.*

Steven Bethard, Hong Yu, Ashley Thornton, Vasileios Hatzivassiloglou, and Dan Jurafsky. 2004. Extracting Opinion Propositions and Opinion Holders using Syntactic and Lexical Cues. In *Computing Attitude and Affect in Text: Theory and Applications.* Springer-Verlag.

Anders Björkelund, Love Hafdell, and Pierre Nugues. 2009. Multilingual Semantic Role Labeling. In *Proceedings of the CoNLL – Shared Task.*

Yejin Choi, Claire Cardie, Ellen Riloff, and Siddharth Patwardhan. 2005. Identifying Sources of Opinions with Conditional Random Fields and Extraction Patterns. In *Proceedings of HLT/EMNLP.*

Thomas Cover and Peter Hart. 1967. Nearest neighbor pattern classification. *Information Theory*, 13(1):21–27.

Dipanjan Das and Noah A. Smith. 2011. Semi-Supervised Frame-Semantic Parsing for Unknown Predicates. In *Proceedings of ACL.*

Dipanjan Das, Nathan Schneider, Desai Chen, and Noah A. Smith. 2010. Probabilistic Frame-Semantic Parsing. In *Proceedings of HLT/NAACL.*

Dipanjan Das, André F.T. Martins, and Noah A. Smith. 2012. An Exact Dual Decomposition Algorithm for Shallow Semantic Parsing with Constraints. In *Proceedings of *SEM.*

Lingjia Deng and Janyce Wiebe. 2014. Sentiment Propagation via Implicature Constraints. In *Proceedings of EACL.*

Andrea Esuli and Fabrizio Sebastiani. 2006. SentiWordNet: A Publicly Available Lexical Resource for Opinion Mining. In *Proceedings of LREC.*

Jenny Rose Finkel, Trond Grenager, and Christopher Manning. 2005. Incorporating Non-local Information into Information Extraction Systems by Gibbs Sampling. In *Proceedings of ACL.*

Amit Goyal, Ellen Riloff, and Hal Daume III. 2010. Automatically Producing Plot Unit Representations for Narrative Text. In *Proceedings of EMNLP.*

Birgit Hamp and Helmut Feldweg. 1997. GermaNet - a Lexical-Semantic Net for German. In *Proceedings of ACL workshop Automatic Information Extraction and Building of Lexical Semantic Resources for NLP Applications.*

Vasileios Hatzivassiloglou and Kathleen R. McKeown. 1997. Predicting the Semantic Orientation of Adjectives. In *Proceedings of EACL.*

Niklas Jakob and Iryna Gurevych. 2010. Extracting Opinion Targets in a Single- and Cross-Domain Setting with Conditional Random Fields. In *Proceedings of EMNLP.*

Valentin Jijkoun, Maarten de Rijke, and Wouter Weerkamp. 2010. Generating Focused Topic-Specific Sentiment Lexicons. In *Proceedings of ACL.*

Thorsten Joachims. 1999. Making Large-Scale SVM Learning Practical. In B. Schölkopf, C. Burges, and A. Smola, editors, *Advances in Kernel Methods - Support Vector Learning*, pages 169–184. MIT Press.

Richard Johansson and Alessandro Moschitti. 2013. Relational Features in Fine-Grained Opinion Analysis. *Computational Linguistics*, 39(3):473–509.

Jun Seok Kang, Song Feng, Leman Akoglu, and Yejin Choi. 2014. ConnotationWordNet: Learning Connotation over the Word+Sense Network. In *Proceedings of ACL.*

Soo-Min Kim and Eduard Hovy. 2006. Extracting Opinions, Opinion Holders, and Topics Expressed in Online News Media Text. In *Proceedings of ACL Workshop on Sentiment and Subjectivity in Text.*

Paul Kingsbury and Martha Palmer. 2002. From TreeBank to PropBank. In *Proceedings of LREC.*

Dan Klein and Christopher D. Manning. 2003. Accurate Unlexicalized Parsing. In *Proceedings of ACL.*

Manfred Klenner, Angela Fahrni, and Stefanos Petrakis. 2009. PolArt: A Robust Tool for Sentiment Analysis. In *Proceedings of NoDaLiDa.*

J. Richard Landis and Gary G. Koch. 1977. The Measurement of Observer Agreement for Categorical Data. *Biometrics*, 33(1):159–174.

Shoushan Li, Rongyang Wang, and Guodong Zhou. 2012. Opinion Target Extraction via Shallow Semantic Parsing. In *Proceedings of AAAI.*

Dekang Lin. 1998. Automatic Retrieval and Clustering of Similar Words. In *Proceedings of ACL/COLING.*

Isa Maks and Piek Vossen. 2012. A lexicon model for deep sentiment analysis and opinion mining applications. *Decision Support Systems*, 53:680–688.

Tomas Mikolov, Kai Chen, Greg Corrado, and Jeffrey Dean. 2013. Efficient Estimation of Word Representations in Vector Space. In *Proceedings of Workshop at ICLR.*

George Miller, Richard Beckwith, Christine Fellbaum, Derek Gross, and Katherine Miller. 1990. Introduction to WordNet: An On-line Lexical Database. *International Journal of Lexicography*, 3:235–244.

Margaret Mitchell, Jacqueline Aguilar, Theresa Wilson, and Benjamin Van Durme. 2013. Open Domain Targeted Sentiment. In *Proceedings of EMNLP*.

Ted Pedersen, Siddharth Patwardhan, and Jason Michelizzi. 2004. WordNet::Similarity – Measuring the Relatedness of Concepts. In *Proceedings of HLT/NAACL*.

Guang Qiu, Bing Liu, Jiajun Bu, and Chun Chen. 2011. Opinion Word Expansion and Target Extraction through Double Propagation. *Computational Linguistics*, 37(1):9–27.

Delip Rao and Deepak Ravichandran. 2009. Semi-Supervised Polarity Lexicon Induction. In *Proceedings of EACL*.

Ellen Riloff and Jessica Shepherd. 1997. A Corpus-Based Approach for Building Semantic Lexicons. In *Proceedings of EMNLP*.

Brian Roark and Eugene Charniak. 1998. Noun-phrase co-occurrence statistics for semi-automatic semantic lexicon construction. In *Proceedings of COLING*.

Josef Ruppenhofer and Ines Rehbein. 2012. Semantic frames as an anchor representation for sentiment analysis. In *Proceedings of WASSA*.

Josef Ruppenhofer, Swapna Somasundaran, and Janyce Wiebe. 2008. Finding the Source and Targets of Subjective Expressions. In *Proceedings of LREC*.

Rico Sennrich, Gerold Schneider, Martin Volk, and Martin Warin. 2009. A New Hybrid Dependency Parser for German. In *Proceedings of GSCL*.

Partha Pratim Talukdar, Joseph Reisinger, Marius Pasca, Deepak Ravichandran, Rahul Bhagat, and Fernando Pereira. 2008. Weakly-Supervised Acquisition of Labeled Class Instances using Graph Random Walks. In *Proceedings of EMNLP*.

Janyce Wiebe and Rada Mihalcea. 2006. Word Sense and Subjectivity. In *Proceedings of COLING/ACL*.

Janyce Wiebe, Therea Wilson, and Claire Cardie. 2005. Annotating Expressions of Opinions and Emotions in Language. *Language Resources and Evaluation*, 39(2/3):164–210.

Michael Wiegand and Dietrich Klakow. 2012. Generalization Methods for In-Domain and Cross-Domain Opinion Holder Extraction. In *Proceedings of EACL*.

Thesesa Wilson, Janyce Wiebe, and Paul Hoffmann. 2005. Recognizing Contextual Polarity in Phrase-level Sentiment Analysis. In *Proceedings of HLT/EMNLP*.

Zhibiao Wu and Martha Palmer. 1994. Verb semantics and lexcial selection. In *Proceedings of ACL*.

Bishan Yang and Claire Cardie. 2013. Joint Inference for Fine-grained Opinion Extraction. In *Proceedings of ACL*.

Patrick Ziering, Lonneke van der Plas, and Hinrich Schuetze. 2013. Bootstrapping Semantic Lexicons for Technical Domains. In *Proceedings of IJCNLP*.

Quantity, Contrast, and Convention in Cross-Situated Language Comprehension

Ian Perera and **James F. Allen**
University of Rochester, Department of Computer Science, Rochester, NY 14627 USA
Institute for Human and Machine Cognition, Pensacola, FL 32502 USA
{iperera,jallen}@ihmc.us

Abstract

Typically, visually-grounded language learning systems only accept feature data about objects in the environment that are explicitly mentioned, whether through annotation labels or direct reference through natural language. We show that when objects are described ambiguously using natural language, a system can use a combination of the pragmatic principles of Contrast and Conventionality, and multiple-instance learning to learn from ambiguous examples in an online fashion. Applying child language learning strategies to visual learning enables more effective learning in real-time environments, which can lead to enhanced teaching interactions with robots or grounded systems in multi-object environments.

1 Introduction

As opposed to the serial nature of labeled data presented to a machine learning classifier, children and robots "in the wild" must learn object names and attributes like color, size, and shape while being surrounded by a number of stimuli and possible referents. When a child hears "the red ball", they must first identify the object mentioned, then use existing knowledge to identify that "red" and "ball" are distinct concepts, and over time, learn that objects called "red" share some similarity in color while objects called "ball" share some similarity in shape. Learning for them therefore requires both identification and establishing joint attention with the speaker before assigning a label to an object, while also applying other language learning strategies to narrow down the search space of possible referents, as illustrated by Quine's "gavagai" problem (1964).

Trying to learn attributes and objects without non-linguistic cues such as pointing and gaze might seem an insurmountable challenge. Yet a child experiences many such situations and can nevertheless learn grounded concepts over time. Fortunately, adult speakers tend to understand the limitation of these cues in certain situations and adjust their speech in accordance to Grice's Maxim of Quantity when referring to objects : be only as informative as necessary (Grice, 1975). We therefore treat the language describing a particular object in a scene as an expression of an iterative process, where the speaker is attempting to guide the listener towards the referent in a way that avoids both ambiguity and unnecessary verbosity.

Language learners additionally make use of the pragmatic assumptions of Conventionality, that speakers agree upon the meaning of a word, and Contrast, that different words have different meanings (Clark, 2009). The extension of these principles to grounded language learning yields the assumptions that the referents picked out by a referring expression will have some similarity (perceptual in our domain), and will be dissimilar compared to objects not included in the reference. Children will eventually generalize learned concepts or accept synonyms in a way that violates these principles (Baldwin, 1992), but these assumptions aid in the initial acquisition of concepts. In our system, we manifest these principles using distance metrics and thereby allow significant flexibility in the implementation of object and attribute representations while allowing a classifier to aid in reference resolution.

When faced with unresolvable ambiguity in determining the correct referent, past, ambiguous experiences can be called upon to resolve ambiguity in the current situation in a strategy called Cross-Situational Learning (XSL). There is some debate over whether people use XSL, as it requires considerable memory and computational

Proceedings of the 19th Conference on Computational Language Learning, pages 226–236,
Beijing, China, July 30-31, 2015.

load (Trueswell et al., 2013). However, other experiments show evidence for XSL in adults and children in certain situations (Smith and Yu, 2008; Smith et al., 2011). We believe these instances that show evidence of XSL certainly merit an implementation both for better understanding language learning and for advancing grounded language learning in the realm of robotics where such limitations do not exist. We show that by reasoning over multiple ambiguous learning instances and constraining possibilities with pragmatic inferences, a system can quickly learn attributes and names of objects without a single unambiguous training example.

Our overarching research goal is to learn compositional models of grounded attributes towards describing an object in a scene, rather than just identifying it. That is, we do not only learn to recognize instances of objects, but also learn attributes constrained to feature spaces that will be compatible with contextual modifiers such as *dark/light* in terms of color, or *small/large* in terms of size and object classification. Therefore, we approach the static, visual aspects of the symbol grounding problem with an eye towards ensuring that our grounded representations of attributes can be composed in the same way that their semantic analogues can. We continue our previous work (Perera and Allen, 2013) with two evaluations to demonstrate the effectiveness of applying the principles of Quantity, Contrast, and Conventionality, as well as incorporating quantifier constraints, negative information, and classification in the training step. Our first evaluation is reference resolution to determine how well the system identifies the correct objects to attend to, and our second is description generation to determine how well the system uses those training examples to understand attributes and object classes.

2 Related Work

Our algorithm for reference resolution and XSL fits into our previous work on a situated language learning system for grounding linguistic symbols in perception. The integration of language in a multi-modal task is a burgeoning area of research, with the grounded data being any of a range of possible situations, from objects on a table (Matuszek et al., 2012) to wetlab experiments (Naim et al., 2014). Our end goal of using natural language to learn from visual scenes is similar to work by Krishnamurthy and Kollar (2013) and Yu and Siskind (2013), and our emphasis on attributes is related to work by Farhadi et al. (2009). However, our focus is on learning from situations that a child would be exposed to, without using annotated data, and to test implementations of child language learning strategies in a computational system.

We use a tutor-directed approach to training our system where the speaker presents objects to the system and describes them, as in work by Skocaj et al. (2011). The focus of this work is in evaluating referring expressions as in work by Mohan et al. (2013), although without any dialogue for disambiguation. Kollar et al. (2013) also incorporate quantifier and pragmatic constraints on reference resolution in a setting similar to ours. In this work, we undertake a more detailed analysis of the effects of different pragmatic constraints on system performance.

The task of training a classifier from "bags" of instances with a label applying to only some of the instances contained within is referred to as Multiple-Instance Learning (MIL) (Dietterich, 1997), and is the machine-learning analogue of cross-situational learning. There is a wide range of methods used in MIL and a number of different assumptions that can be made to fit the task at hand (Foulds and Frank, 2010). Online MIL methods so far have been used for object tracking (Li et al., 2010), and Dindo and Zambuto (2010) apply MIL to grounded language learning, but we are not aware of any research that investigates the application of online MIL to studying cognitive models of incremental grounded language learning. In addition, we find that we must relax many assumptions used in MIL to handle natural language references, such as the 1-of-N assumption used by Dindo and Zambuto. The lack of appropriate algorithms for handling this task motivates our development of a novel algorithm for language learning situations.

3 Experimental Design

3.1 Learning Environment and Data Collection

Our environment in this experiment consists of a table with blocks of nine different shapes and two toy cars, with the objects spanning four colors. A person stands behind the table, places a randomly chosen group of objects in a designated demonstration area on the table as shown in Figure 1,

Figure 1: One of the training examples, described as "The two red blocks [left-most two blocks in this figure] are next to the other blocks."

and describes one or more of the objects directly while possibly mentioning some relation to the surrounding objects. The goal of this setup is to facilitate object descriptions that more closely approximate child-directed speech, compared to the language in captioned images. Audio is recorded and transcribed by hand with timestamps at the utterance level, but there are no other annotations beyond timestamps. We use these intervals to match the spoken descriptions to the video data, which is recorded using the Microsoft Kinect to obtain RGB + Depth information.

3.2 Training and Test Instances

All training instances involved multiple objects, with an average of 2.8 objects per demonstration. The subject could select any set of objects to describe (often with respect to the other objects). References to objects varied in detail, from "the cube" to "a tall yellow rectangle". Since a set of objects might have different shapes, the most common descriptor was "block". The majority (80%) of the quantifiers were definite or numeric, and 85% of the demonstrations referred to a single object. Test instances consisted solely of single objects presented one at a time. 20% of the objects used as test instances appeared in training because of the limited set of objects available, yet the objects were placed in slightly different orientations and at different locations, deforming the shape contour due to perspective.

3.3 Prior System Knowledge

We encode some existing linguistic and perceptual knowledge into the system to aid in learning from unconstrained object descriptions. The representative feature, defined as the system's feature space assigned to a property name (*e.g.*, color for "white", or shape for "round"), was prechosen for the task's vocabulary to reduce the number of factors affecting the evaluation of the system. In previous work, we showed that the accuracy of the system's automatic choice of representative features can reach 78% after about 50 demonstrations of objects presented one at a time (Perera and Allen, 2013). In addition, we developed an extension to a semantic parser that distinguishes between attributes and object names using syntactic constructions.

3.4 Language Processing

The transcribed utterances are passed through the TRIPS parser (Allen et al., 2008) for simultaneous lexicon learning and recognition of object descriptions. The parser outputs generalized quantifiers and numeric constraints (capturing singular/-plural instances, as well as specific numbers) in referring expressions, which are used for applying quantifier constraints to the possibilities of the referent object or group of objects. The parser's ability to distinguish between attributes and objects through syntax greatly increases learning performance, as demonstrated in our previous work (Perera and Allen, 2013). We extract the speech act (for detecting when an utterance is demonstrating a new object or adding additional information to a known object) and the referring expression from the TRIPS semantic output. Figure 2 shows the format of such a referring expression.

```
(MENTIONED :ID ONT::V11915
  :TERMS
    ((TERM ONT::V11915 :CLASS (:*
        ONT::REFERENTIAL-SEM W::BLOCK)
          :PROPERTIES ((:*
              ONT::MODIFIER W::YELLOW))
        :QUAN ONT::THE)))
```

Figure 2: Primary referring expression extraction from the semantic parse for "The yellow block is next to the others".

Although there may be many objects or groups of objects mentioned, we only store the properties of the reference that is the subject of the sentence. For example, in, "Some blue cars are next to the yellow ones", we will extract that there exists at least two blue cars. Because it is an indefinite reference, we cannot draw any further inference about whether the reference set includes all examples of blue cars.

3.5 Feature Extraction

To extract features, we first perform object segmentation using Kinect depth information, which provides a pixel-level contour around each of the objects in the scene. Then for each object, we record its dimensions and location, extract visual features corresponding to color, shape, size, color variance, and texture. No sophisticated tracking algorithm is needed as the objects are stationary on the table. Color is represented in LAB space for perceptual similarity to humans using Euclidean distance, shape is captured using scale- and rotation-invariant 25-dimensional Zernike moments (Khotanzad and Hong, 1990), and texture is captured using 13-dimensional Haralick features (Haralick et al., 1973).

3.6 Classification and Distance Measures

To determine the similarity of new properties and objects to the system's previous knowledge of such descriptors, we use a k-Nearest Neighbor classifier (k-NN) with Mahalanobis distance metric (Mahalanobis, 1936), distance weighting, and class weighting using the method described in Brown and Koplowitz (1979).

Our k-NN implementation allows negative examples so as to incorporate information that we infer about unmentioned objects. We do not train the system with any explicit negative information (*i.e.*, we have no training examples described as "This is not a red block.", but if the system is confident that an object is not red, it can mark a training example as such). A negative example contributes a weight to the voting equal and opposite to what its weight would have been if it were a positive example of that class.

The Mahalanobis distance provides a way to incorporate a k-nearest neighbor classifier into a probabilistic framework. Because the squared Mahalanobis distance is equal to the number of standard deviations from the mean of the data assuming a normal distribution (Rencher, 2003), we can convert the Mahalanobis distance to a probability measure to be used in probabilistic reasoning.

4 The Reference Lattice

To learn from underspecified training examples, we must resolve the referring expression and assign the properties and object name in the expression to the correct referents. To incorporate existing perceptual knowledge, semi-supervised methods, and pragmatic constraints in the reference resolution task, we use a probabilistic lattice structure that we call the *reference lattice*.

The reference lattice consists of nodes corresponding to possible partitions of the scene for each descriptor (either property or object name). There is one column of nodes for each descriptor, with the object name as the final column. Edges signify the set-intersection of the connected nodes along a path.

Paths through the lattice correspond to a successive application of these set-intersections, ultimately resulting in a set of objects corresponding to the hypothesized referent group. In this way, paths represent a series of steps in referring expression generation where the speaker provides salient attributes sequentially to eventually make the referent set clear.

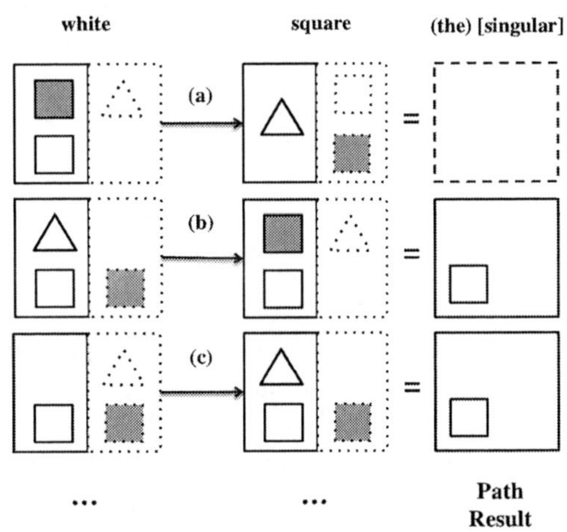

Figure 3: Three examples of paths in the reference lattice for the referring expression "the white square", when the visible objects are a grey square, white square, and a white triangle.

4.1 Lattice Generation

For each descriptor, we generate a node for every possible partition of the scene into positive and negative examples of that descriptor. For example, if the descriptor is "red", each node is a hypothesized split that attempts to put red objects in the positive set and non-red objects in the negative set. For each column there are $2^n - 1$ nodes, where n is the number of objects in the scene (the empty set is not included, as it would lead to an empty reference set). We then generate lattice edges between every pair of partitions in adjacent columns.

We can discard a large proportion of these edges, as many will correspond to the intersection of disjoint partitions and will therefore be empty. Finally, we generate all possible paths through the lattice, and, if using quantifier constraints, discard any paths with a final output referent set that does not agree with the number constraints on the mentioned referent group.

The structure of the lattice is shown in Figure 3. In this figure, partitions are represented by split boxes in the first two columns, with positive examples in solid lines and negative examples in dotted lines. Not shown are edges connecting each partition in one column with each partition in the next and the paths they create. The intersection of the partitions in path (a) lead to a null set, and the path is removed from the lattice. Path (b) is the ground truth path, as the individual partitions accurately describe the composition of the attributes. Path (c) contains an overspecified edge and achieves the correct referent set albeit using incorrect assumptions about the attributes. The result sets from both (b) and (c) agree with the quantifier constraint (definite singular).

4.2 Node Probabilities

We consider two probabilities for determining the probability of a partition: that which can be determined from distance data (considering distances between objects in the partition), and that which requires previous labeled data to hypothesize a class using the classifier (considering distances from each object to the mean of the data labeled with the descriptor).

The distance probability, our implementation of the principle of Contrast, is a prior that enforces minimum intraclass distance for the positive examples and maximum interclass distance across the partition. The motivation and implementation shares some similarities with the Diverse Density framework for multiple instance learning (Maron and Lozano-Pérez, 1998), although here it also acts as an unsupervised clustering for determining the best reference set. It is the product of the minimum probability that any two objects in the positive examples are in the same set multiplied by the complement of the maximum probability that any two objects across the partition are in the same class. Therefore, for partition N with positive examples $+$ and negative examples $-$:

$$P_{intra} = \min_{x,y \in +} P(x_c = y_c)$$

$$P_{inter} = \begin{cases} \max_{x\in +, y\in -} P(x_c = y_c) & \text{if } |-| > 0 \\ 1 & \text{if } |-| = 0 \end{cases}$$

$$P_{distance} = P_{intra} \times (1 - P_{inter})$$

The classifier probability is similar, except rather than comparing objects to other objects in the partition, the objects are compared to the mean of the column's descriptor C in the descriptor's representative feature. If the descriptor is a class name, we instead choose the Zernike shape feature, implementing the shape bias children show in word learning (Landau et al., 1998).

If there is insufficient labeled data to use, then the classifier probability is set to 1 for the entire column, meaning only the distance probabilities will affect the probabilities of the nodes. For a given descriptor C, the classifier probabilities are as follows:

$$P_{pos}(C) = \min_{x\in +} P(x_c = C)$$

$$P_{neg}(C) = \begin{cases} \max_{x\in -} P(x_c = C) & \text{if } |-| > 0 \\ 1 & \text{if } |-| = 0 \end{cases}$$

$$P_{classifier}(C) = P_{pos}(C) \times (1 - P_{neg}(C))$$

The final probability of a partition is the product of the distance probability and the classifier probability, and the node probabilities are normalized for each column.

4.3 Overspecification and Edge Probabilities

Edges have a constant transition probability equal to the overspecification probability if overspecified, or equal to the complement otherwise. We use these probabilities to incorporate the phenomenon of overspecification in our model, where, contrary to a strict interpretation of Grice's Maxim of Quantity, speakers will give more information than is needed to identify a referent (Koolen et al., 2011). An edge is considered overspecified if the hypothesis for the objects that satisfy the next descriptor does not add additional information, i.e., the set-intersection it corresponds to does not remove any possible objects from the referent set. Thus the model will prefer hypotheses for the next descriptor that narrow down the hypothesized set of referents.

4.4 Path Probabilities

The probability of each path is the product of probabilities of each of the partitions along its path and the edge (overspecification) probabilities. If there is a single path with a probability greater than all others by an amount ϵ, the labels of the partitions along that path are assigned to the positive examples while also being assigned as negative properties for the negative examples. We perform this updating step after each utterance to simulate incremental continuous language learning and to provide the most current knowledge available for resolving new ambiguous data.

If there are multiple best paths within ϵ of the highest probability path, then the learning example is considered ambiguous and saved in memory to resolve with information from future examples.

4.5 Multiple-Instance Learning

In many cases, especially in the system's first learning instances, there is not enough information to unambiguously learn from the demonstration. Without any unambiguous examples, our system would struggle to learn no matter how much data was available to it. An ambiguous training example yields more than one highest probability path. Our goal is to use new information from each new training demonstration to reevaluate these paths and determine a singular best path, which allows us to update our knowledge accordingly.

To do this, we independently consider columns for each unknown descriptors from unresolved demonstrations containing that descriptor and combine them to form super-partitions which are then evaluated using our distance probability function. For example, consider two instances described with "the red box". The first has a red and a blue box, while the second has a red and a green box. Individually they are ambiguous to a system that does not know what "red" means and therefore each demonstration would have two paths with equal probability. If we combine the partitions across the two demonstrations into four super-partitions, the highest probability will be generated when the two red boxes are in the positive set. This probability is stored in each of the constituent partitions as a *meta-probability*, which is otherwise 1 when multiple-instance learning is not required to resolve ambiguity. The meta-probability allows us to find the most probable path given previous instances.

5 System Pipeline

5.1 Training

To train the system on a video, we transcribe the video with sentence-level timestamps, and extract features from the demonstration video. The system takes as input the feature data aligned with utterances from the demonstration video. It then finds the most likely path through the reference lattice and adds all hypothesized positive examples for the descriptor as class examples for the classifier. If there is more than one likely path, it saves the lattice for later resolution using multiple-instance learning.

5.2 Description Generation

During testing, the system generates a description for an object in the test set by finding examples of properties and objects similar to it in previously seen objects. For properties, the system checks each feature space separately to find previous examples of objects similar in that feature space and adds each found property label to the k-NN voting set, weighted by the distance. If the majority label does not have the matching representative feature, the system skips this feature space for adding a property to the description. The object name is chosen using a distance generated from the sum of the distances (normalized and weighted through the Mahalanobis distance metric) to the most similar previous examples. More details about the description generation process can be found in our previous paper (Perera and Allen, 2013).

6 Evaluation

To evaluate our system, we use two metrics: our evaluation method used in previous work for rating the quality of generated descriptions (Perera and Allen, 2013), and a standard precision/recall measurement to determine the accuracy of reference resolution.

The description generated by the system is compared with a number of possible ground truth descriptions which are generated using precision and recall equivalence classes from our previous work. Precision is calculated according to which words in the description could be found in a ground truth description, while recall is calculated according to which words in the closest ground truth description were captured by the system's description. As an example, a system output of "red rectangle"

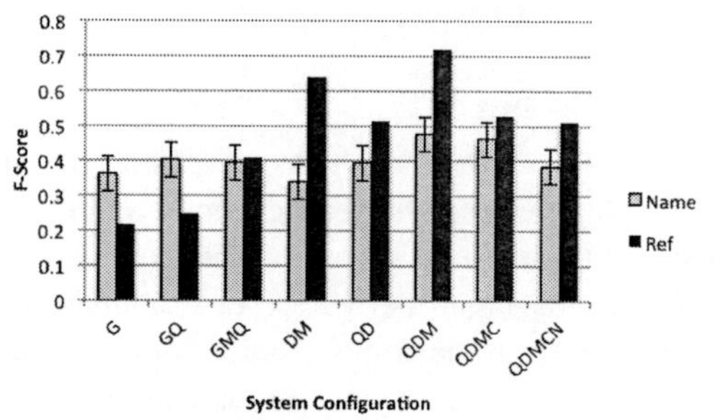

Figure 4: F-Score for Description Generation in grey and Reference Resolution in black for various configurations of the system run on 4 underspecificed videos. Error bars are one standard deviation.

when the ground truth description is "red square" or "red cube" would have a precision score of 1 (because both "red" and "rectangle" are accurate descriptors of the object) but a recall of .5 (because the square-ness was not captured by the system's description).

In the reference resolution evaluation, precision and recall are calculated on the training set according to the standard measures by comparing the referent set obtained by the system and the ground truth referent set (those objects actually referred to by the speaker). Training instances lacking feature data because of an error in recording were excluded from the F1-score for reference resolution.

Each underspecified demonstration video consisted of 15-20 demonstrations containing one or more focal objects referenced in the description and, in most cases, distractor objects that are not mentioned. We used the same test video from our previous work with objects removed that could not be described using terms used in the training set, leaving 15 objects.

We tested eight different system configurations. The baseline system simply guessed at a path through the lattice without any multiple-instance learning (G). We then added multiple instance learning (M), distance probabilities (D), classifier probabilities (C), quantifier constraints (Q), and negative information (N). We show the data for these different methods in Figure 4.

7 Results and Discussion

7.1 Learning Methods

Rather than comparing our language learning system to others on a common dataset, we choose to focus our analysis on how our implementations of pragmatic inference and child language learning strategies affected performance of reference resolution and description generation.

The relatively strong naming performance of G can be attributed to the fact that many demonstrations had similarities among the objects presented that could be learned from choosing any of the objects. However, reference resolution performance for G averaged a .34 F1-score compared with a .70 F1-score for our best performing configuration. Adding quantifier constraints (GQ) did not help, although quantifier constraints with multiple-instance learning (GMQ) led to a significant increase in reference resolution performance.

Multiple-instance learning provided a significant gain in reference resolution performance, and with quantifier constraints also yielded the highest naming performance (QDM and QDML). The relative lower performance by inclusion of classifier probabilities with this limited training data is due to errors in classification that compound in this online-learning framework. In multiple-instance cases where there are a number of previous examples to draw from, then the information provided by classifier probability is redundant and less accurate. However, as the approach scales and retaining previous instances is intractable, the classifier probabilities provide a more concise representation of knowledge to be used in future learning.

We found that negative information hurt performance in this framework (QDMCN vs. QDMC) for two reasons. First, the risk of introducing negative information is high compared to its possible reward. While it promises to remove some errors in classification, an accurate piece of negative information only removes one class from consideration when multiple other alternatives exist, while an inaccurate piece of negative information contributes to erroneous classification.

Second, situations where negative information might be inferred are induced by a natural language description which, by Grice's Maxims, will attempt to be as clear as possible given the listener's information. This means that, adhering to the Contrast principle, negative examples are likely already far from the positive examples for the class.

Figure 5 shows results from the averaging of random combinations of 4 underspecified videos, using our highest-scoring configuration QDM to

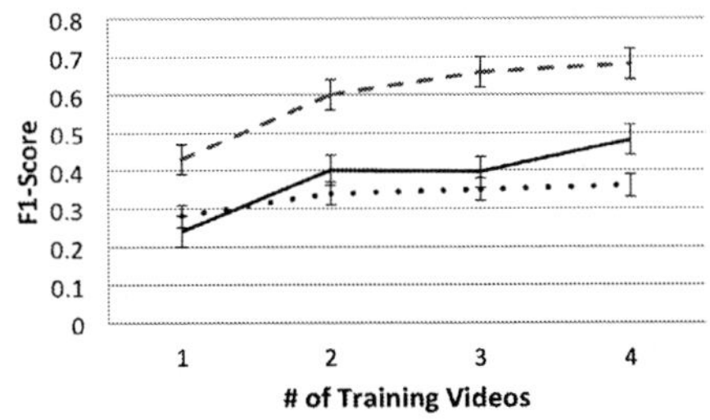

Figure 5: Description generation results from training according to the number of training videos with standard error bars. The solid line is the QDM's performance learning from underspecified videos. The dashed line is the system's performance learning from videos where objects are presented one at a time. The dotted line is the baseline (G). F1-score for reference resolution in the underspecified case was consistent across videos (mean .7, SD .01).

show the increase in performance as more training data is provided to the system. We compare our results on videos with multiple objects to the performance of the system with objects presented one at a time and with the baseline G. Because the training objects are slightly different, we present results on a subset of objects where at least a ground truth object name was present in the training data. Our results show that while the performance is lower in the ambiguous case, the general learning rate per video is comparable with the single-object case. In the 1-video case, guessing is equally as effective as our method due to the system being too tentative with assigning labels to objects without more information to minimize errors affecting learning in later demonstrations.

We did see an effect of the order in which videos were presented to the system on performance, suggesting that learning the correct concepts early on can have long-term ramifications for an online learning process. Possible ways to mitigate this effect include a memory model with forgetting or a more robust classifier. We leave such efforts to future work.

7.2 Running Time Performance

While the number of nodes and paths in the lattice is exponential in the number of objects in the scene, our system can still perform quickly enough to serve as a language learning agent suitable for real-time interaction. The pragmatic constraints on possible referent sets allow us to remove a large number of paths, which is especially important when there are many objects in the scene or when the referring expression contains a number of descriptors. In situations with more than 4-5 objects, we expect that other cues can establish joint attention with enough resolution to remove some objects from consideration.

Visual features can be extracted from video at 3 frames per second, which is acceptable for real-time interaction as only 5 frames are needed for training or testing. Not including the feature extraction (performed separately), the QUM configuration processed our 55 demonstrations in about 1 minute on a 2.3 GHz Intel Core i7.

7.3 Relation Between Evaluation Metrics

We compared our results from the description generation metric with the reference resolution metric to evaluate how the quality of reference resolution affected learning performance. The description generation F-score was more strongly positively correlated with the reference resolution precision than with the recall. We found a reference resolution F-score with $\beta = .7$ (as opposed to the standard $\beta = 1$) had the highest Pearson correlation with the F-score ($r = .63, p < .0001$), indicating that reference resolution precision is roughly 1.4 times more important than recall in predicting learning performance in this system.

This result provides evidence that the quality of the first data in a limited data learning algorithm can be critical in establishing long-term performance, especially in an online learning system, and suggests that our results could be improved by correcting hypotheses that once appeared reasonable to the system. It also suggests that F1-score may not be the most appropriate measure for performance of a component that is relied upon to give accurate data for further learning.

7.4 Overspecification

Accounting for overspecification in the model more closely approximates human speech at the expense of a strict interpretation of the Maxim of Quantity. It allows us to use graded pragmatic constraints that admit helpful heuristics for learning without treating them as a rule. In our training data, the speaker was typically over-descriptive, leading to a high optimal overspecification. Figure 6 shows the effect of different values for the overspecification probability on the performance of the

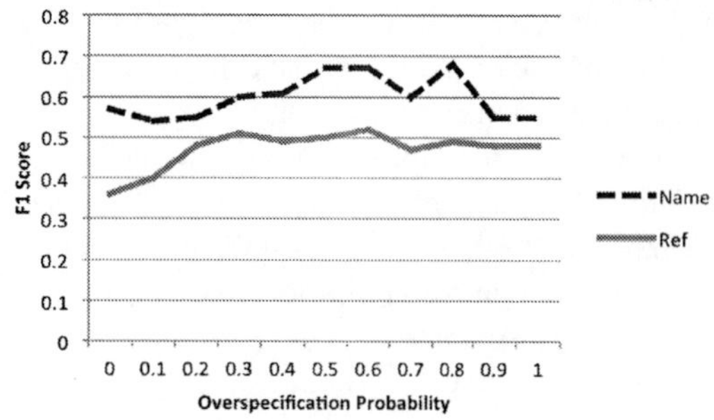

Figure 6: Effect of varying overspecification probability on the F1 score for both Description Generation (black dashed) and Reference Resolution (grey solid), calculated on a dataset with hand location information.

system. The strong dip in reference resolution performance at an overspecification probability of 0 shows the significant negative effect a strict interpretation of the Maxim of Quantity would have in this situation. The correct value for overspecification probability for a given situation depends on a number of factors such as scene complexity and descriptor type (Koolen et al., 2011), but we have not yet incorporated these factors into our overspecification probability in this work.

7.5 Comparison to Other Multi-Instance Learning Methods

Our multi-instance learning procedure can be classified as instance-level with witnesses, which means that we identify the positive examples that lead to the label of the "bag", or demonstration in this case. In addition, we relax the assumption that there is only a single positive instance corresponding to the label of the demonstration. This relaxation increases the complexity of cross-instance relationships, but allows for references to multiple objects simultaneously and therefore faster training than a sequential presentation would allow. In accounting for overspecification, we also must establish a dependence on the labels of the image via the edges of the lattice. This adds additional complexity, but our results show that accounting for overspecification can lead to increased performance.

8 Future Work

Work on this system is ongoing, with extensions planned for improving performance, generating more complete symbol grounding, and allowing more flexibility in both environment and language.

While the parser in our system can interpret phrases such as "the tall block", we do not have a way of resolving the non-intersective predicate "tall" in our current framework. Non-intersective predicates add complexity to the system because their reference point is not necessarily the other objects in the scene - it may be a reference to other objects in the same class (i.e., blocks).

Also, our set of features is rather rudimentary and could be improved, as we chose low-dimensional, continuous features in an attempt to facilitate a close connection between language and vision. The use of continuous features ensures that primitive concepts are grounded solely in perception and not higher-order conceptual models (Perera and Allen, 2014). Initial results using 3D shape features show a considerable performance increase on a kitchen dataset we are developing.

9 Conclusion

We have proposed a probabilistic framework for using pragmatic inference to learn from underspecified visual descriptions. We show that this system can use pragmatic assumptions attenuated by overspecification probability to learn attributes and object names from videos that include a number of distractors. We also analyzed various learning methods in an attempt to gain a deeper understanding of the theoretical and practical considerations of situated language learning, finding that Conventionality and Contrast learning strategies with quantifiers and overspecification probabilities yielded the best performing system. These results support the idea that an understanding of how humans learn and communicate can lead to better visually grounded language learning systems. We believe this work is an important step towards systems in which natural language not only stands in for manual annotation, but also enables new methods of training robots and other situated systems.

10 Acknowledgements

This work was funded by The Office of Naval Research (N000141210547), the Nuance Foundation, and DARPA Big Mechanism program under ARO contract W911NF-14-1-0391.

References

J. Allen, Mary Swift, and Will de Beaumont. 2008. Deep Semantic Analysis of Text. In *Symp. Semant. Syst. Text Process.*, volume 2008, pages 343–354, Morristown, NJ, USA. Association for Computational Linguistics.

D A Baldwin. 1992. Clarifying the role of shape in children's taxonomic assumption. *J. Exp. Child Psychol.*, 54(3):392–416.

T Brown and J Koplowitz. 1979. The Weighted Nearest Neighbor Rule for Class Dependent Sample Sizes. *IEEE Trans. Inf. Theory*, I(5):617–619.

Eve V. Clark. 2009. On the pragmatics of contrast. *J. Child Lang.*, 17(02):417, February.

T Dietterich. 1997. Solving the multiple instance problem with axis-parallel rectangles. *Artif. Intell.*, 89:31–71.

Haris Dindo and Daniele Zambuto. 2010. A probabilistic approach to learning a visually grounded language model through human-robot interaction. *IEEE/RSJ 2010 Int. Conf. Intell. Robot. Syst. IROS 2010 - Conf. Proc.*, pages 790–796.

A. Farhadi, I. Endres, D. Hoiem, and D. Forsyth. 2009. Describing objects by their attributes. *2009 IEEE Conf. Comput. Vis. Pattern Recognit.*, pages 1778–1785, June.

James Foulds and Eibe Frank. 2010. A review of multi-instance learning assumptions. *Knowl. Eng. Rev.*, 25:1.

HP Grice. 1975. Logic and conversation. In Peter Cole and Jerry L. Morgan, editors, *Syntax Semant.*, pages 41–58. Academic Press.

Robert M. Haralick, K. Shanmugam, and Its'hak Dinstein. 1973. Textural features for image classification. *IEEE Trans. Syst. Man, Cybern. SMC-3*.

A Khotanzad and Y H Hong. 1990. Invariant Image Recognition by Zernike Moments. *IEEE Trans. Pattern Anal. Mach. Intell.*, 12(5):489–497, May.

Thomas Kollar, Jayant Krishnamurthy, and Grant Strimel. 2013. Toward interactive grounded language acquisition. *Proc. Robot. Sci. Syst.*

Ruud Koolen, Albert Gatt, Martijn Goudbeek, and Emiel Krahmer. 2011. Factors causing overspecification in definite descriptions. *J. Pragmat.*, 43(13):3231–3250, October.

Jayant Krishnamurthy and Thomas Kollar. 2013. Jointly Learning to Parse and Perceive: Connecting Natural Language to the Physical World. *Trans. Assoc. Comput. Linguist.*, 1:193–206.

Barbara Landau, Linda Smith, and Susan Jones. 1998. Object Shape, Object Function, and Object Name. *J. Mem. Lang.*, 38(1):1–27, January.

Mu Li, James T. Kwok, and Bao Liang Lu. 2010. Online multiple instance learning with no regret. *Proc. IEEE Comput. Soc. Conf. Comput. Vis. Pattern Recognit.*, pages 1395–1401.

PC C Mahalanobis. 1936. On The Generalized Distance in Statistics. *Proc. Natl. Inst. Sci. India*, pages 49–55.

Oded Maron and Tomás Lozano-Pérez. 1998. A framework for multiple-instance learning. *Adv. Neural Inf. Process. Syst.*, 10:570 – 576.

Cynthia Matuszek, N FitzGerald, Luke Zettlemoyer, Liefeng Bo, and Dieter Fox. 2012. A Joint Model of Language and Perception for Grounded Attribute Learning. In *Proc. Int. Conf. Mach. Learn.*

Shiwali Mohan, John E Laird, and Laird Umich Edu. 2013. Towards an Indexical Model of Situated Language Comprehension for Real-World Cognitive Agents. 2013:153–170.

Iftekhar Naim, Young Chol Song, Qiguang Liu, Henry Kautz, Jiebo Luo, and Daniel Gildea. 2014. Unsupervised Alignment of Natural Language Instructions with Video Segments. In *AAAI*.

Ian Perera and JF Allen. 2013. SALL-E: Situated Agent for Language Learning. In *Twenty-Seventh AAAI Conf. Artif. Intell.*

Ian Perera and James F Allen. 2014. What is the Ground ? Continuous Maps for Grounding Perceptual Primitives. In P Bello, M. Guarini, M McShane, and Brian Scassellati, editors, *Proc. 36th Annu. Conf. Cogn. Sci. Soc.*, Austin, TX. Cognitive Science Society.

A C Rencher. 2003. *Methods of Multivariate Analysis*. Wiley Series in Probability and Statistics. Wiley.

Danijel Skocaj, Matej Kristan, Alen Vrecko, Marko Mahnic, Miroslav Janicek, Geert-Jan M. Kruijff, Marc Hanheide, Nick Hawes, Thomas Keller, Michael Zillich, and Kai Zhou. 2011. A system for interactive learning in dialogue with a tutor. In *2011 IEEE/RSJ Int. Conf. Intell. Robot. Syst.*, pages 3387–3394. IEEE, September.

Linda Smith and Chen Yu. 2008. Infants rapidly learn word-referent mappings via cross-situational statistics. *Cognition*, 106:1558–1568.

Kenny Smith, Andrew D M Smith, and Richard a. Blythe. 2011. Cross-situational learning: An experimental study of word-learning mechanisms. *Cogn. Sci.*, 35:480–498.

John C Trueswell, Tamara Nicol Medina, Alon Hafri, and Lila R Gleitman. 2013. Propose but verify: fast mapping meets cross-situational word learning. *Cogn. Psychol.*, 66(1):126–56, February.

W Van Orman Quine. 1964. *Word and Object*. MIT Press paperback series. MIT Press.

Haonan Yu and Jeffrey Mark Siskind. 2013. Grounded Language Learning from Video Described with Sentences. In *Proc. 51st Annu. Meet. Assoc. Comput. Linguist.*, pages 53–63.

Recovering Traceability Links in Requirements Documents

Zeheng Li Mingrui Chen LiGuo Huang
Department of Computer Science & Engineering
Southern Methodist University
Dallas, TX 75275-0122
{zehengl,mingruic,lghuang}@smu.edu

Vincent Ng
Human Language Technology Institute
University of Texas at Dallas
Richardson, TX 75083-0688
vince@hlt.utdallas.edu

Abstract

Software system development is guided by the evolution of requirements. In this paper, we address the task of *requirements traceability*, which is concerned with providing bi-directional traceability between various requirements, enabling users to find the origin of each requirement and track every change made to it. We propose a *knowledge-rich* approach to the task, where we extend a supervised baseline system with (1) additional training instances derived from human-provided annotator rationales; and (2) additional features derived from a hand-built ontology. Experiments demonstrate that our approach yields a relative error reduction of 11.1–19.7%.

1 Introduction

Software system development is guided by the evolution and refinement of requirements. Requirements specifications, which are mostly documented using natural language, are refined with additional design details and implementation information as the development life cycle progresses. A crucial task throughout the entire development life cycle is *requirements traceability*, which is concerned with linking requirements in which one is a *refinement* of the other.

Specifically, one is given a set of high-level (coarse-grained) requirements and a set of low-level (fine-grained) requirements, and the goal of requirements traceability is to find for each high-level requirement all the low-level requirements that refine it. Note that the resulting mapping between high- and low-level requirements is *many-to-many*, because a low-level requirement can potentially refine more than one high-level requirement. As an example, consider the three high-level requirements and two low-level requirements shown in Figure 1 about the well-known Pine email system. In this example, three traceability links should be established: (1) HR01 is refined by UC01 (because UC01 specifies the shortcut key for saving an entry in the address book); (2) HR02 is refined by UC01 (because UC01 specifies how to store contacts in the address book); and (3) HR03 is refined by UC02 (because both of them are concerned with the help system).

From a text mining perspective, requirements traceability is a very challenging task. First, there could be abundant information irrelevant to the establishment of a link in one or both of the requirements. For instance, all the information under the Description section in UC01 is irrelevant to the establishment of the link between UC01 and HR02. Worse still, as the goal is to induce a many-to-many mapping, information irrelevant to the establishment of one link could be relevant to the establishment of another link involving the same requirement. For instance, while the Description section is irrelevant when linking UC01 and HR02, it is crucial for linking UC01 and HR01. Above all, a link can exist between a pair of requirements (HR01 and UC01) even if they do not possess any overlapping or semantically similar content words.

Virtually all existing approaches to the requirements traceability task were developed in the software engineering (SE) research community. Related work on this task can be broadly divided into two categories. In *manual approaches*, requirements traceability links are recovered manually by developers. *Automated approaches*, on the other

Proceedings of the 19th Conference on Computational Language Learning, pages 237–246,
Beijing, China, July 30-31, 2015.

High-Level Requirements

HR01
The underlined character in each menu selection shall be a shortcut key. When control and the shortcut key are pressed, the menu selection should be loaded.

HR02
The system shall have an address book available to store contacts.

HR03
The system shall have a help system that offers tips and explanation for each screen and each item on the screens upon demand.

……

Low-Level Requirements

UC01	
Use case name:	store a contact's information
Summary:	the address book should store a contact's name, email, address and phone number
Description:	1. enter "pine" command in terminal 2. either enter "a" or use arrows to make "address book" line highlighted and enter "enter" 3. enter "@" 4. enter nickname, fullname, fcc, comment and addresses. may leave some fields blank 5. press ctrl+x to save the entry

UC02	
Use case name:	access help system
Summary:	user accesses help system
Description:	user presses help key

……

Figure 1: Samples of high- and low-level requirements.

hand, have relied on information retrieval (IR) techniques, which recover links based on computing the similarity between a given pair of requirements. Hence, such similarity-based approaches are unable to recover links between those pairs that do not contain overlapping or semantically similar words or phrases.

In light of this weakness, we recast requirements traceability as a supervised binary classification task, where we classify each pair of high- and low-level requirements as positive (having a link) or negative (not having a link). In particular, we propose a *knowledge-rich* approach to the task, where we extend a supervised baseline employing only word pairs and LDA-induced topics as features (see Section 4) with two types of human-supplied knowledge. First, we employ *annotator rationales*. In the context of requirements traceability, rationales are human-annotated words or phrases in a pair of high- and low-level requirements that motivated a human annotator to establish a link between the two. In other words, rationales contain the information relevant to the establishment of a link. Therefore, using them could allow a learner to focus on the relevant portions of a requirement. Motivated by Zaidan et al. (2007), we employ rationales to create additional training instances for the learner.

Second, we employ an ontology hand-built by a domain expert. A sample ontology built for the Pine domain is shown in Table 1. As we can see, the ontology contains a *verb clustering* and a *noun clustering*: the verbs are clustered by the function they perform, whereas a noun cluster corresponds to a (domain-specific) semantic type. We employ the ontology to derive additional features.

There are at least two reasons why the ontology-based features might be useful for identifying traceability links. First, since only those verbs and nouns that (1) appear in the training data and (2) are deemed relevant by the domain expert for link identification are included in the ontology, it provides guidance to the learner as to which words/phrases in the requirements it should focus on in the learning process.[1] Second, the verb and noun clusters provide a robust generalization of the words/phrases in the requirements. For instance, a word pair that is relevant for link identification may still be ignored by the learner due to its infrequency of occurrence. The features computed based on these clusters, on the other hand, will be more robust to the infrequency problem and could therefore provide better generalizations.

Our contributions are three-fold. First, the knowledge-rich approach we propose for requirements traceability significantly outperforms a supervised baseline on two traceability datasets, Pine and WorldVistA. Second, we increase the NLP community's awareness of this under-studied, challenging, yet important problem in SE, which could lead to fruitful inter-disciplinary collaboration. Third, to facilitate future research on this problem, we make our annotated resources, including the datasets, the rationales, and the ontolo-

[1]Note that both the rationales and the words/phrases in the ontology could help the learner by allowing it to focus on *relevant* materials in a given pair of requirements. Nevertheless, they are not identical: rationales are words/phrases that are relevant to the establishment of a particular traceability link, whereas the words/phrases in the ontology are relevant to link establishment in general in the given domain.

Category	Terms
Message	mail, message, email, e-mail, PDL, subjects
Contact	contact, addresses, multiple addresses
Folder	folder, folder list, tree structure
Location	address book, address field, entry, address
Platform	windows,unix,window system,unix system
Module	help system, spelling check, Pico, shell
Protocol	MIME,SMTP
Command	shortcut key, ctrl+c, ctrl+m, ctrl+p, ctrl+x

(a) Noun clustering

Category	Terms
System Operation	evoke, operate, set up, activate, log
Message Search	search, find
Contact Manipulation	add, store, capture
Message Manipulation	compose, delete, edit, save, print
Folder Manipulation	create, rename, delete, nest
Message Communication	reply, send, receive, forward, cc, bcc
User Input	input, type, enter, press, hit, choose
Visualization	display, list, show, prompt, highlight
Movement	move,navigate
Function	support, have, perform, allow, use

(b) Verb clustering

Table 1: Manual ontology for Pine.

gies, publicly available.[2]

2 Related Work

Related work on traceability link prediction can be broadly divided into two categories, manual approaches and automatic approaches.

Manual requirement tracing. Traditional manual requirements tracing is usually accomplished by system analysts with the help of requirement management tools, where analysts visually examine each pair of requirements documented in the requirement management tools to build the Requirement Traceability Matrix (RTM). Most existing requirement management tools (e.g., Rational DOORS[3], Rational RequisitePro[4], CASE[5]) support traceability analysis. Manual tracing is often based on observing the potential relevance between a pair of requirements belonging to different categories or at different levels of detail. The manual process is human-intensive and error-prone given a large set of requirements.

[2]See our website at http://lyle.smu.edu/~lghuang/research/Traceability/ for these annotated resources.

[3]http://www-03.ibm.com/software/products/en/ratidoor

[4]http://www.ibm.com/developerworks/downloads/r/rrp

[5]http://www.analysttool.com

Automated requirement tracing. Automated or semi-automated requirements traceability, on the other hand, generates traceability links automatically, and hence significantly increases efficiency. Pierce (1978) designed a tool that maintains a requirements database to aid automated requirements tracing. Jackson (1991) proposed a keyphrase-based approach for tracing a large number of requirements of a large Surface Ship Command System. More advanced approaches relying on information retrieval (IR) techniques, such as the *tf-idf*-based vector space model (Sundaram et al., 2005), Latent Semantic Indexing (Lormans and Van Deursen, 2006; De Lucia et al., 2007; De Lucia et al., 2009), probabilistic networks (Cleland-Huang et al., 2005), and Latent Dirichlet Allocation (Port et al., 2011), have been investigated, where traceability links were generated by calculating the textual similarity between requirements using similarity measures such as Dice, Jaccard, and Cosine coefficients (Dag et al., 2002). All these methods were developed based on either matching keywords or identifying similar words across a pair of requirements, and none of them have studied the feasibility of employing supervised learning to accomplish this task, unlike ours.

3 Datasets

For evaluation, we employ two publicly-available datasets annotated with traceability links. The first dataset, annotated by Sultanov and Hayes (2010), involves the Pine email system developed at the University of Washington. The second dataset, annotated by Cleland-Huang et al. (2010), involves WorldVistA, an electronic health information system developed by the USA Veterans Administration. Statistics on these datasets are shown in Table 2. For Pine, 2499 instances can be created by pairing the 49 high-level requirements with the 51 low-level use cases. For WorldVistA, 9193 instances can be created by pairing the 29 high-level requirements with the 317 low-level specifications. As expected, these datasets have skewed class distributions: only 10% (Pine) and 4.3% (WorldVistA) of the pairs are linked.

While these datasets have been annotated with traceability links, they are not annotated with annotator rationales. Consequently, we employed a software engineer specializing in requirements traceability to perform rationale annotation. We asked him to annotate rationales for a pair of re-

Datasets	Pine	WorldVistA
# of (high-level) requirements	49	29
# of (low-level) specifications	51	317
Avg. # of words per requirement	17	18
Avg. # of words per specification	148	26
Avg. # of links per requirement	5.1	13.6
Avg. # of links per specification	4.9	1.2
# of pairs that have links	250	394
# of pairs that do not have links	2249	8799

Table 2: Statistics on the datasets.

quirements only if he believed that there should be a traceability link between them. The reason is that in traceability prediction, the absence of a traceability link between two requirements is attributed to the *lack* of evidence that they should be linked, rather than the presence of evidence that they should not be linked. More specifically, we asked the annotator to identify as rationales all the words/phrases in a pair of requirements that motivated him to label the pair as positive. For instance, for the link between HR01 and UC01 in Figure 1, he identified two rationales from HR01 ("shortcut key" and "control and the shortcut key are pressed") and one from UC01 ("press ctrl+x").

4 Hand-Building the Ontologies

A traceability link prediction ontology is composed of a verb clustering and a noun clustering. We asked a software engineer with expertise in requirements traceability to hand build the ontology for each of the two datasets. Using his domain expertise, the engineer first identified the noun categories and verb categories that are relevant for traceability prediction. Then, by inspecting the training data, he manually populated each noun/verb category with words and phrases collected from the training data.

As will be discussed in Section 8, we evaluate our approach using five-fold cross validation. Since the nouns/verbs in the ontology were collected only from the training data, the software engineer built five ontologies for each dataset, one for each fold experiment. Hence, nouns/verbs that appear in only the test data in a fold experiment are *not* included in that experiment's ontology. In other words, our test data are truly held-out w.r.t. the construction of the ontology. Tables 1 and 3 show the complete lists of noun and verb categories identified for Pine and WorldVistA, respectively, as well as sample nouns and verbs that populate each category. Note that the five ontologies employ the *same* set of noun and verb categories, differing only w.r.t. the nouns and verbs that populate each category. As we can see, for Pine, eight groups of nouns and ten groups of verbs are defined, and for WorldVistA, 31 groups of nouns and 14 groups of verbs are defined. Each noun category represents a domain-specific semantic class, and each verb category corresponds to a function performed by the action underlying a verb.

Category	Terms
Signature	signature, co-signature, identity
Prescription	prescription, electronic prescription
Authorization	authorized users, administrator
Patient Info	patient data, health summary
General Info	information, data
Component	platform, interface, integration
Laboratory	lab test results, laboratory results
Customization	individual customization,customization
Discharge	discharge, discharge instruction
Records	progress note, final note, saved note
Details	specifications, order details
Medication	medications, drug
Side-effect	allergy, drug-drug interaction, reaction
Code	ICD-9, standards, management code
User	user class hierarchy, roles, user roles
Order	orderable file, order, medication order
List	problem list,problem/diagnosis list
Rules	business rules, C32, HITSP C32
Document	documents, level 2 CCD documents
Schedule	appointments, schedule, reminders
Warning	warning, notice warning
Encounter	encounter, encounter data
Hospitalization	hospitalization data,procedure data
Arrangement	templates, clinical templates, data entry
Immunization	immunization, immunization record
Protocol	protocol,HL7,HTTP,FTP,HL7-ASTM
System data	codified data,invalid data,data elements
Key	key, security key, computer key
Identity	social security number,account number
Audit	audit log, audit records, audit trail
Duty	assignment, task

(a) Noun clustering

Category	Terms
Interface actions	click, select, search, browse
Authentication	sign, co-sign, cosign, authenticate
Customization	fit, customize, individualize
Notification	check, alert
Security control	control, prevent, prohibit, protect
Data manipulation	capture,associate,document,create
Visualization	display, view, provide, generate
Recording	audit, log
Data retrieval	export, retrieve
Deletion	remove, delete
System operation 1	save, retain
System operation 2	abort, restrict, delay, lock
Search	find, query
Communication	forward, redirect

(b) Verb clustering

Table 3: Manual ontology for WorldVistA.

5 Baseline Systems

In this section, we describe three baseline systems for traceability prediction.

5.1 Unsupervised Baselines

The Tf-idf baseline. We employ *tf-idf* as our first unsupervised baseline. Each document is represented as a vector of unigrams. The value of each vector entry is its associated word's *tf-idf* value. Cosine similarity is used to compute the similarity between two documents. Any pair of requirements whose similarity exceeds a given threshold is labeled as positive.

The LDA baseline. We employ LDA (Blei et al., 2003) as our second unsupervised baseline. We train an LDA model on our data to produce n topics. For Pine, we set n to 10, 20, ..., 50. For WorldVistA, because of its larger size, we set n to 50, 60, ..., 100. We then represent each document as a vector of length n, with each entry set to the probability that the document belongs to one of the topics. Cosine similarity is used as the similarity measure. Any pair of requirements whose similarity exceeds a given threshold is labeled as positive.

5.2 Supervised Baseline

Each instance corresponds to a high-level requirement and a low-level requirement. Hence, we create instances by pairing each high-level requirement with each low-level requirement. The class value of an instance is positive if the two requirements involved should be linked; otherwise, it is negative. Each instance is represented using two types of features:

Word pairs. We create one binary feature for each word pair (w_i, w_j) collected from the training instances, where w_i and w_j are words appearing in a high-level requirement and a low-level requirement respectively. Its value is 1 if w_i and w_j appear in the high-level and low-level pair under consideration, respectively.

LDA-induced topic pairs. Motivated by previous work, we create features based on the topics induced by an LDA model for a requirement. Specifically, we first train an LDA model on our data to obtain n topics, where n is to be tuned jointly with C on the development (dev) set.[6] Then, we create one binary feature for each topic pair (t_i, t_j), where t_i and t_j are the topics corresponding to a high-level requirement and a low-level requirement, respectively. Its value is 1 if t_i and t_j are the most probable topics of the high-level and low-level pair under consideration, respectively.

We employ LIBSVM (Chang and Lin, 2011) to train a binary SVM classifier on the training set. We use a linear kernel, setting all learning parameters to their default values except for the C (regularization) parameter, which we tune jointly with n (the number of LDA-induced topics) to maximize F-score on the dev set.[7] Since we conduct five-fold cross validation, in all experiments that require a dev set, we use three folds for training, one fold for dev, and one fold for evaluation.

6 Exploiting Rationales

In this section, we describe our first extension to the baseline: exploiting rationales to generate additional training instances for the SVM learner.

6.1 Background

The idea of using annotator rationales to improve binary text classification was proposed by Zaidan et al. (2007). A rationale is a human-annotated text fragment that motivated an annotator to assign a particular label to a *training* document. In their work on classifying the sentiment expressed in movie reviews as positive or negative, Zaidan et al. generate additional *training* instances by removing rationales from documents. Since these pseudo-instances lack information that the annotators thought was important, an SVM learner should be less confident about the labels of these weaker instances, and should therefore place the hyperplane closer to them. A learner that successfully learns this difference in confidence assigns a higher importance to the pieces of text that are present only in the original instances. Thus the pseudo-instances help the learner both by indicating which parts of the documents are important and by increasing the number of training instances.

6.2 Application to Traceability Prediction

Unlike in sentiment analysis, where rationales can be identified for both positive and negative training reviews, in traceability prediction, rationales

[6] As in the LDA baseline, for Pine we set n to 10, 20, ..., 50, and for WorldVistA, we set n to 50, 60, ..., 100.

[7] C was selected from the set $\{1, 10, 100, 1000, 10000\}$.

can only be identified for the positive training instances (i.e., pairs with links). As noted before, the reason is that in traceability prediction, an instance is labeled as negative because of the *absence* of evidence that the two requirements involved should be linked, rather than the presence of evidence that they should not be linked.

Using these rationales, we can create *positive* pseudo-instances. Note, however, that we *cannot* employ Zaidan et al.'s method to create positive pseudo-instances. According to their method, we would (1) take a pair of linked requirements, (2) remove the rationales from both of them, (3) create a positive pseudo-instance from the remaining text fragments, and (4) add a constraint to the SVM learner forcing it to classify it less confidently than the original positive instance. Creating positive pseudo-instances in this way is problematic for our task. The reason is simple: as discussed previously, a negative instance in our task stems from the *absence* of evidence that the two requirements should be linked. In other words, after removing the rationales from a pair of linked requirements, the pseudo-instance created from the remaining text fragments should be labeled as negative.

Given this observation, we create a *positive* pseudo-instance from each pair of linked requirements by removing any text fragments from the pair that are *not* part of a rationale. In other words, we use *only* the rationales to create positive pseudo-instances. This has the effect of amplifying the information present in the rationales.

As mentioned above, while Zaidan et al.'s method cannot be used to create positive pseudo-instances, it can be used to create negative pseudo-instances. For each pair of linked requirements, we create three negative pseudo-instances. The first one is created by removing all and only the rationales from the high-level requirement in the pair. The second one is created by removing all and only the rationales from the low-level requirement in the pair. The third one is created by removing all the rationales from both requirements in the pair.

To better understand our annotator rationale framework, let us define it more formally. Recall that in a standard soft-margin SVM, the goal is to find $\mathbf{w}$ and ξ to minimize

$$\frac{1}{2}|\mathbf{w}|^2 + C\sum_i \xi_i$$

subject to

$$\forall i : c_i \mathbf{w} \cdot \mathbf{x}_i \geq 1 - \xi_i, \xi_i > 0$$

where $\mathbf{x}_i$ is a training example; $c_i \in \{-1, 1\}$ is the class label of $\mathbf{x}_i$; ξ_i is a slack variable that allows $\mathbf{x}_i$ to be misclassified if necessary; and $C > 0$ is the misclassification penalty (a.k.a. the regularization parameter).

To enable this standard soft-margin SVM to also learn from the positive pseudo-instances, we add the following constraints:

$$\forall i : \mathbf{w} \cdot \mathbf{v}_i \geq \mu(1 - \xi_i),$$

where $\mathbf{v}_i$ is the positive pseudo-instance created from positive example $\mathbf{x}_i$, $\xi_i \geq 0$ is the slack variable associated with $\mathbf{v}_i$, and μ is the margin size (which controls how confident the classifier is in classifying the pseudo-instances).

Similarly, to learn from the negative pseudo-instances, we add the following constraints:

$$\forall i, j : \mathbf{w} \cdot \mathbf{u}_{ij} \leq \mu(1 - \xi_{ij}),$$

where $\mathbf{u}_{ij}$ is the jth negative pseudo-instance created from positive example $\mathbf{x}_i$, $\xi_{ij} \geq 0$ is the slack variable associated with $\mathbf{u}_{ij}$, and μ is the margin size.

We let the learner decide how confidently it wants to classify these additional training instances based on the dev data. Specifically, we tune this *confidence* parameter μ jointly with the C value to maximize F-score on the dev set.[8]

7 Extension 2: Exploiting an Ontology

Next, we describe our second extension to the baseline: exploiting ontology-based features.

7.1 Ontology-Based Features

As mentioned before, we derive additional features for the SVM learner from the verb and noun clusters in the hand-built ontology. Specifically, we derive five types of features:

Verb pairs. We create one binary feature for each verb pair (v_i, v_j) collected from the training instances, where (1) v_i and v_j appear in a high-level requirement and a low-level requirement respectively, and (2) both verbs appear in the ontology. Its value is 1 if v_i and v_j appear in the high-level and low-level pair under consideration, respectively. Using these verb pairs as features may

[8] C was selected from the set {1, 10, 100, 100, 10000}, and μ was selected from the set {0.2, 0.3, 1, 3, 5}.

allow the learner to focus on verbs that are relevant to traceability prediction.

Verb group pairs. For each verb pair feature described above, we create one binary feature by replacing each verb in the pair with its cluster id in the ontology. Its value is 1 if the two verb groups in the pair appear in the high-level and low-level pair under consideration, respectively. These features may enable the resulting classifier to provide robust generalizations in cases where the learner chooses to ignore certain useful verb pairs owing to their infrequency of occurrence.

Noun pairs. We create one binary feature for each noun pair (n_i, n_j) collected from the training instances, where (1) n_i and n_j appear in a high-level requirement and a low-level requirement respectively, and (2) both nouns appear in the ontology. Its value is computed in the same manner as the verb pairs. These noun pairs may help the learner to focus on verbs that are relevant to traceability prediction.

Noun group pairs. For each noun pair feature described above, we create one binary feature by replacing each noun in the pair with its cluster id in the ontology. Its value is computed in the same manner as the verb group pairs. These features may enable the classifier to provide robust generalizations in cases where the learner chooses to ignore certain useful noun pairs owing to their infrequency of occurrence.

Dependency pairs. In some cases, the noun/verb pairs may not provide sufficient information for traceability prediction. For example, the verb pair feature (*delete*, *delete*) is suggestive of a positive instance, but the instance may turn out to be negative if one requirement concerns deleting messages and the other concerns deleting folders. As another example, the noun pair feature (*folder*, *folder*) is suggestive of a positive instance, but the instance may turn out to be negative if one requirement concerns creating folders and the other concerns deleting folders.

In other words, we need to develop features that encode the relationship between verbs and nouns. To do so, we first parse each requirement using the Stanford dependency parser (de Marneffe et al., 2006), and collect each noun-verb pair (n_i, v_j) connected by a dependency relation. We then create binary features by pairing each related noun-verb pair found in a high-level training requirement with each related noun-verb pair found in a low-level training requirement. The feature value is 1 if the two noun-verb pairs appear in the pair of requirements under consideration. To enable the learner to focus on learning from relevant verbs and nouns, only verbs and nouns that appear in the ontology are used to create these features.

7.2 Learning the Ontology

An interesting question is: is it possible to learn an ontology rather than hand-building it? This question is of practical relevance, as hand-constructing the ontology is a time-consuming and error-prone process. Below we describe the steps we propose for ontology learning.

Step 1: Verb/Noun selection. We select the nouns, noun phrases (NPs) and verbs in the training set to be clustered. Specifically, we select a verb/noun/NP if (1) it appears more than once in the training data; (2) it contains at least three characters (thus avoiding verbs such as *be*); and (3) it appears in the high-level but not the low-level requirements and vice versa.

Step 2: Verb/Noun representation. We represent each noun/NP/verb as a feature vector. Each verb v is represented using the set of nouns/NPs collected in Step 1. The value of each feature is binary: 1 if the corresponding noun/NP occurs as the direct or indirect object of v in the training data (as determined by the Stanford dependency parser), and 0 otherwise. Similarly, each noun n is represented using the set of verbs collected in Step 1. The value of each feature is binary: 1 if n serves as the direct or indirect object of the corresponding verb in the training data, and 0 otherwise.

Step 3: Clustering. To produce a verb clustering and a noun clustering, we cluster the verbs and the nouns/NPs separately using the single-link algorithm. Single-link is an agglomerative algorithm where each object to be clustered is initially in its own cluster. In each iteration, it merges the two most similar clusters and stops when the desired number of clusters is reached. Since we are using single-link clustering, the similarity between two clusters is the similarity between the two most similar objects in the two clusters. We compute the similarity between two objects by taking the dot product of their feature vectors.

Since we do not know the number of clusters to be produced *a priori*, for Pine we produce three noun clusterings and three verb clusterings (with 10, 15, and 20 clusters each). For WorldVistA, given its larger size, we produce five noun clusterings and five verb clusterings (with 10, 20, 30, 40, and 50 clusters each). We then select the combination of noun clustering, verb clustering, and C value that maximizes F-score on the dev set, and apply the resulting combination on the test set.

To compare the usefulness of the hand-built and induced ontologies, in our evaluation we will perform separate experiments in which each ontology is used to derive the features from Section 7.1.

8 Evaluation

8.1 Experimental Setup

We employ as our evaluation measure F-score, which is the unweighted harmonic mean of recall and precision. Recall (R) is the percentage of links in the gold standard that are recovered by our system. Precision (P) is the percentage of links recovered by our system that are correct. We preprocess each document by removing stopwords and stemming the remaining words. All results are obtained via five-fold cross validation.

8.2 Results and Discussion

Results on Pine and WorldVistA are shown in Table 4(a) and Table 4(b), respectively.

8.2.1 No Pseudo-instances

The "No pseudo" column of Table 4 shows the results when the learner learns from only real training instances (i.e., no pseudo-instances). Specifically, rows 1 and 2 show the results of the two unsupervised baselines, *tf-idf* and LDA, respectively.

Recall from Section 5.1 that in both baselines, we compute the cosine similarity between a pair of requirements, positing them as having a traceability link if and only if their similarity score exceeds a threshold that is tuned based on the *test* set. By doing so, we are essentially giving both unsupervised baselines an unfair advantage in the evaluation. As we can see from rows 1 and 2 of the table, *tf-idf* achieves F-scores of 54.5% on Pine and 46.5% on WorldVistA. LDA performs significantly worse than *tf-idf*, achieving F-scores of 34.2% on Pine and 15.1% on WorldVistA.[9]

Row 3 shows the results of the supervised baseline described in Section 5.2. As we can see, this baseline achieves F-scores of 57.5% on Pine and 63.3% on WorldVistA, significantly outperforming the better unsupervised baseline (*tf-idf*) on both datasets. When this baseline is augmented with features derived from manual clusters (row 4), the resulting system achieves F-scores of 62.6% on Pine and 64.2% on WorldVistA, outperforming the supervised baseline by 5.1% and 0.9% in F-score on these datasets. These results represent significant improvements over the supervised baseline on both datasets, suggesting the usefulness of the features derived from manual clusters for traceability link prediction. When employing features derived from induced rather than manual clusters (row 5), the resulting system achieves F-scores of 61.7% on Pine and 64.6% on WorldVistA, outperforming the supervised baseline by 4.2% and 1.3% in F-score on these datasets. These results also represent significant improvements over the supervised baseline on both datasets. In addition, the results obtained using manual clusters (row 4) and induced clusters (row 5) are statistically indistinguishable. This result suggests that the ontologies we induced can potentially be used in lieu of the manually constructed ontologies for traceability link prediction.

8.2.2 Using Positive Pseudo-instances

The "Pseudo pos only" column of Table 4 shows the results when each of the systems is trained with additional positive pseudo-instances.

Comparing the first two columns, we can see that employing positive pseudo-instances increases performance on Pine (F-scores rise by 0.7–1.1%) but decreases performance on WorldVistA (F-scores drop by 0.3–2.1%). Nevertheless, the corresponding F-scores in all but one case (Pine, induced) are statistically indistinguishable. These results seem to suggest that the addition of positive pseudo-instances is not useful for traceability link prediction.

Note that the addition of features derived from manual/induced clusters to the supervised baseline no longer consistently improves its performance: while F-scores still rise significantly by 4.6–5.5% on Pine, they drop insignificantly by 0.1–0.5% on WorldVistA.

8.2.3 Using Positive and Negative Pseudo-instances

The "Pseudo pos+neg" column of Table 4 shows the results when each of the systems is trained with additional positive *and* negative pseudo-instances.

Comparing these results with the corresponding "Pseudo pos only" results, we can see that

[9] All significance tests are paired t-tests ($p < 0.05$).

		No pseudo			Pseudo pos only			Pseudo pos+neg			Pseudo residual		
	System	R	P	F	R	P	F	R	P	F	R	P	F
1	*Tf-idf* baseline	73.6	43.3	54.5	–	–	–	–	–	–	–	–	–
2	LDA baseline	30.4	39.2	34.2	–	–	–	–	–	–	–	–	–
3	Supervised baseline	50.4	67.0	57.5	51.2	67.3	58.2	53.9	73.8	62.3	31.6	68.6	43.2
4	+ manual clusters	54.4	73.9	62.6	55.6	74.7	63.7	57.6	77.0	65.9	30.0	72.1	42.3
5	+ induced clusters	53.6	72.8	61.7	54.8	73.6	62.8	55.2	75.0	63.6	30.0	73.5	42.6

(a) Pine

		No pseudo			Pseudo pos only			Pseudo pos+neg			Pseudo residual		
	System	R	P	F	R	P	F	R	P	F	R	P	F
1	*Tf-idf* baseline	60.4	37.8	46.5	–	–	–	–	–	–	–	–	–
2	LDA baseline	25.9	10.6	15.1	–	–	–	–	–	–	–	–	–
3	Supervised baseline	52.5	79.9	63.3	52.2	79.2	63.0	55.9	80.6	66.0	49.2	71.5	58.3
4	+ manual clusters	52.5	82.8	64.2	51.5	80.8	62.9	57.1	83.0	67.6	47.7	76.1	58.6
5	+ induced clusters	52.8	83.2	64.6	51.0	80.7	62.5	57.1	82.1	67.4	47.7	76.4	58.7

(b) WorldVistA

Table 4: Results of supervised systems on the Pine and WorldVistA datasets.

additionally employing negative pseudo-instances consistently improves performance: F-scores rise by 0.8–4.1% on Pine and 3.0–4.9% on WorldVistA. In particular, the improvements in F-score in three of the six cases (Pine/Baseline, WorldVistA/manual, WorldVistA/induced) are statistically significant. These results suggest that the additional negative pseudo-instances provide useful information for traceability link prediction.

In addition, the use of features derived from manual/induced clusters to the supervised baseline consistently improves its performance: F-scores rise significantly by 1.3–3.6% on Pine and significantly by 1.4–1.6% on WorldVistA.

Finally, the best results in our experiments are achieved when both positive and negative pseudo-instances are used in combination with manual/induced clusters: F-scores reach 63.6–65.9% on Pine and 67.4–67.6% on WorldVistA. These results translate to significant improvements in F-score over the supervised baseline by 6.1–8.4% on Pine and 4.1–4.3% on WorldVistA, or relative error reductions of 14.3–19.7% on Pine and 11.1–11.7% on WorldVistA.

8.2.4 Pseudo-instances from Residuals

Recall that Zaidan et al. (2007) created pseudo-instances from the text fragments that remain after the rationales are removed. In Section 6.3, we argued that their method of creating positive pseudo-instances for our requirements traceability task is problematic. In this subsection, we empirically verify the correctness of this claim.

Specifically, the "Pseudo residual" column of Table 4 shows the results when each of the "No pseudo" systems is additionally trained on the positive pseudo-instances created using Zaidan et al.'s method. Comparing these results with the corresponding "Pseudo pos+neg" results, we see that replacing our method of creating positive pseudo-instances with Zaidan et al.'s method causes the F-scores to drop significantly by 7.7–23.6% in all cases. In fact, comparing these results with the corresponding "No pseudo" results, we see that except for the baseline system, employing positive pseudo-instances created from Zaidan et al.'s method yields significantly worse results than not employing pseudo-instances at all. These results provide suggestive evidence for our claim.

9 Conclusion

We investigated a knowledge-rich approach to an important yet under-studied SE task that presents a lot of challenges to NLP researchers: traceability prediction. Experiments on two evaluation datasets showed that (1) in comparison to a supervised baseline, this method reduces relative error by 11.1–19.7%; and (2) results obtained using induced clusters were competitive with those obtained using manual clusters. To stimulate research on this task, we make our annotated resources publicly available.

Acknowledgments

We thank the three anonymous reviewers for their insightful comments on an earlier draft of the paper. This research was supported in part by the U.S. Department of Defense Systems Engineering Research Center (SERC) new project incubator fund RT-128 and the U.S. National Science Foundation (NSF Awards CNS-1126747 and IIS-1219142).

References

David M. Blei, Andrew Y. Ng, and Michael I. Jordan. 2003. Latent Dirichlet Allocation. *Journal of Machine Learning Research*, 3:993–1022.

Chih-Chung Chang and Chih-Jen Lin. 2011. LIBSVM: a library for support vector machines. *ACM Transactions on Intelligent Systems and Technology*, 2(3):27.

Jane Cleland-Huang, Raffaella Settimi, Chuan Duan, and Xuchang Zou. 2005. Utilizing supporting evidence to improve dynamic requirements traceability. In *Proceedings of the 13th IEEE International Conference on Requirements Engineering*, pages 135–144.

Jane Cleland-Huang, Adam Czauderna, Marek Gibiec, and John Emenecker. 2010. A machine learning approach for tracing regulatory codes to product specific requirements. In *Proceedings of the 32nd ACM/IEEE International Conference on Software Engineering (Volume 1)*, pages 155–164.

Johan Natt Dag, Björn Regnell, Pär Carlshamre, Michael Andersson, and Joachim Karlsson. 2002. A feasibility study of automated natural language requirements analysis in market-driven development. *Requirements Engineering*, 7(1):20–33.

Andrea De Lucia, Fausto Fasano, Rocco Oliveto, and Genoveffa Tortora. 2007. Recovering traceability links in software artifact management systems using information retrieval methods. *ACM Transactions on Software Engineering and Methodology*, 16(4):13.

Andrea De Lucia, Rocco Oliveto, and Genoveffa Tortora. 2009. Assessing IR-based traceability recovery tools through controlled experiments. *Empirical Software Engineering*, 14(1):57–92.

Marie-Catherine de Marneffe, Bill MacCartney, and Christopher D. Manning. 2006. Generating typed dependency parses from phrase structure parses. In *Proceedings of the 5th International Conference on Language Resources and Evaluation*, pages 449–454.

Justin Jackson. 1991. A keyphrase based traceability scheme. In *IEEE Colloquium on Tools and Techniques for Maintaining Traceability During Design*, pages 2/1–2/4. IET.

Marco Lormans and Arie Van Deursen. 2006. Can LSI help reconstructing requirements traceability in design and test? In *Proceedings of the 10th European Conference on Software Maintenance and Reengineering*, pages 47–56.

Robert A Pierce. 1978. A requirements tracing tool. *ACM SIGSOFT Software Engineering Notes*, 3(5):53–60.

Daniel Port, Allen Nikora, Jane Huffman Hayes, and LiGuo Huang. 2011. Text mining support for software requirements: Traceability assurance. In *Proceedings of the 44th Hawaii International Conference on System Sciences*, pages 1–11.

Hakim Sultanov and Jane Huffman Hayes. 2010. Application of swarm techniques to requirements engineering: Requirements tracing. In *Requirements Engineering Conference (RE), 2010 18th IEEE International*, pages 211–220.

Senthil Karthikeyan Sundaram, Jane Huffman Hayes, and Alexander Dekhtyar. 2005. Baselines in requirements tracing. *ACM SIGSOFT Software Engineering Notes*, 30(4):1–6.

Omar Zaidan, Jason Eisner, and Christine Piatko. 2007. Using "annotator rationales" to improve machine learning for text categorization. In *Human Language Technologies 2007: The Conference of the North American Chapter of the Association for Computational Linguistics; Proceedings of the Main Conference*, pages 260–267.

Structural and lexical factors in adjective placement in complex noun phrases across Romance languages

Kristina Gulordava
University of Geneva
Kristina.Gulordava@unige.ch

Paola Merlo
University of Geneva
Paola.Merlo@unige.ch

Abstract

One of the most common features across all known languages is their variability in word order. We show that differences in the prenominal and postnominal placement of adjectives in the noun phrase across five main Romance languages is not only subject to heaviness effects, as previously reported, but also to subtler structural interactions among dependencies that are better explained as effects of the principle of dependency length minimisation. These effects are almost purely structural and show lexical conditioning only in highly frequent collocations.

1 Introduction

One of the most widely observed characteristics of all languages is the variability in the linear order of their words, both across and within a single language. In this study, we concentrate on word order alternations where one structure can be linearised in two different ways. Consider, for example, the case when a phrasal verb (V + particle) has a direct object (NP), in English. Two alternative orders are possible: VP_1 = V NP Prt, and VP_2 = V Prt NP. If the NP is heavy, as defined in number of words or number of syllables, it will be frequently placed after the Prt, yielding the V-Prt-NP order. Compare, for instance *Call me up!* to *Call up the customer who called yesterday.* This tendency is also formulated as a Principle of End Weight, where phrases are presented in order of increasing weight (Wasow, 2002). Cases of heavy NP-shift (Stallings et al., 1998), dative alternation (Bresnan et al., 2007) and other alternation preferences among verbal dependents are traditionally evoked to argue in favour of the "heaviness" effect.

In this work, we study the alternations in the noun-phrase domain, much less investigated in connection with the heaviness effect. Abeillé and Godard (2000) introduce the heaviness of adjective phrases as a principle explaining their postnominal placement compared to 'light' adjectives in French. Their observations have been recently confirmed in a corpus study by Thuilier (2012). Cross-linguistically, the data that we have collected across many languages and several families, presented in Figure 1, confirm the heaviness effect for adjectives[1]. By extracting relevant statistics from gold dependency annotated corpora, we can observe that heavy adjectives (adjective phrases of at least two words) appear more frequently postnominally than simple adjectives.

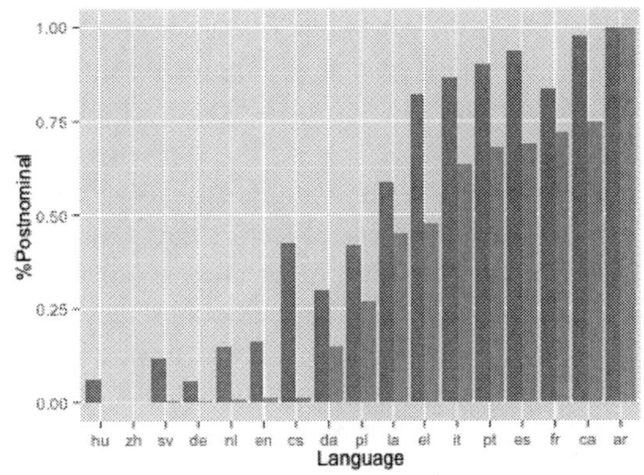

Figure 1: Percent of postnominal simple (green) and heavy (red) adjectives across seventeen languages.

While the effect of size or heaviness is well-documented, this statistics is very coarse and it confounds various linguistic factors, such as types

[1]We use the following languages and treebanks: English, Czech, Spanish, Chinese, Catalan, German, Italian (Hajič et al., 2009), Danish, Dutch, Portuguese, Swedish (Buchholz and Marsi, 2006), Latin, Ancient Greek (Haug and Jøhndal, 2008), Hungarian (Csendes et al., 2005), Polish (Woliński et al., 2011), Arabic (Zeman et al., 2012), French (McDonald et al., 2013). The extraction is based on the conversion to the universal part-of-speech tags (Petrov et al., 2012).

Proceedings of the 19th Conference on Computational Language Learning, pages 247–257,
Beijing, China, July 30-31, 2015. ©2015 Association for Computational Linguistics

of adjectives, and annotation conventions of different corpora. From a typological perspective, the formulation needs to be refined from a preference of end weight to a preference for all elements being closer to the governing head: languages with Verb-Object dominant order tend to put constituents in 'short before long' order, while Object-Verb languages, like Japanese or Korean, do the reverse (Hawkins, 1994; Wasow, 2002). A more general explanation for the weight effect has been sought in a general tendency to minimise the length of the dependency between two related words, called Dependency Length Minimisation (DLM, Temperley (2007), Gildea and Temperley (2007)).

In this paper, we look at the structural factors, such as DLM, and lexical factors that play a role in adjective-noun word order alternations in Romance languages and the predictions they make on prenominal or postnominal placement of adjectives. We concentrate on a smaller set of languages than those shown in Figure 1 to be able to study finer-grained effects than what can be observed at a very large scale and across many different corpus annotation schemes. We choose Romance languages because they show a good amount of variation in the word order of the noun phrase.

The DLM principle can be stated as follows: if there exist possible alternative orderings of a phrase, the one with the shortest overall dependency length (DL) is preferred.

Consider, again, the case when a phrasal verb (verb + particle) has a direct object (NP). Two alternative orders are possible: VP_1 = V NP Prt, whose length is DL_1 and VP_2 = V Prt NP, whose length is DL_2. DL_1 is $DL(\text{V-NP})+DL(\text{V-Prt}) = |\text{NP}| + 1$; DL_2 is $DL(\text{V-NP}) + DL(\text{V-Prt}) = |\text{Prt}| + 1$. If DL_1 is bigger than DL_2, then VP_2 is preferred over VP_1. Unlike the principle of End Weight, this explanation applies also to languages with a different word order than English.

The observation that human languages appear to minimise the distance between related words is well documented in sentence processing (Gibson, 1998; Hawkins, 1994; Hawkins, 2004), in corpus properties of treebanks (Gildea and Temperley, 2007; Futrell et al., 2015), in diachronic language change (Tily, 2010). It is usually interpreted as a means to reduce memory load and support efficient communication. Dependency length minimisation has been demonstrated on a large scale in the verbal domain and at the sentence level, but has not yet been investigated in the more limited nominal domain, where dependencies are usually shorter and might create lighter processing loads that do not need to be minimised. In applying the general principle of DLM to the dependency structure of noun phrases, our goal is to test to what extent the DLM principle predicts the observed adjective-noun word order alternation patterns.

In this paper, we develop and discuss a more complex variant of a model described previously (Gulordava et al., 2015) and extend its analysis. First, we investigate whether the more complex DLM principle is necessary to explain our findings or if the simpler heaviness effect demonstrated for many languages in Figure 1 is sufficient. The answer is positive: the complexity introduced by DLM is necessary. Then, we develop a more detailed analysis of the only prediction of the model that is only weakly confirmed, showing that this result still holds under different definitions of dependency length. We also present an in-depth study to show that the DLM effect is structural, as assumed, and not lexical. While it is well-known that in French prenominal and post-nominal placement of adjectives is sometimes lexically-specific and meaning-dependent, this is not often the case in other languages like Italian, and does not explain the extent of the variation.

2 Dependency length minimisation in the noun phrase

In this section, we summarise the model in Gulordava et al. (2015). In the next section we propose a more complex model and study some factors in depth. Gulordava et al. (2015) consider a prototypical noun phrase with an adjective phrase as a modifier. They assume a simplified noun phrase with only one adjective modifier adjacent to the noun and two possible placements for an adjective phrase: post-nominal and prenominal. The adjective modifier can be a complex phrase with both left and right dependents (α and β, respectively). The noun phrase can have parents and right modifiers (X and Y, respectively). The structures for the possible cases are shown in Figure 2.

These structures correspond to examples like those shown in (1), in Italian (X='vede', Adj='bella', N='casa', Y= 'al mare').

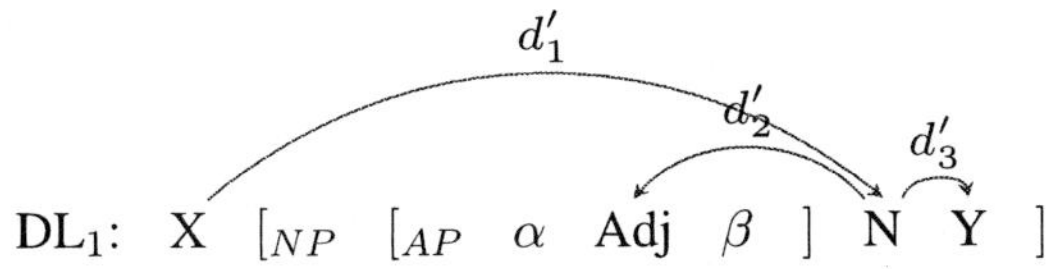

(a) Left external dependent, prenominal adjective

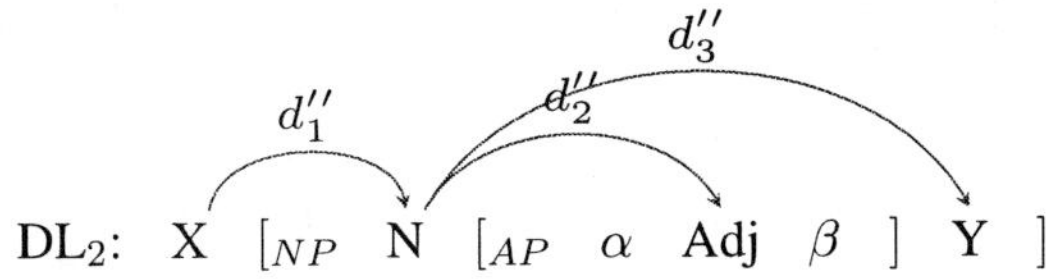

(b) Left external dependent, postnominal adjective

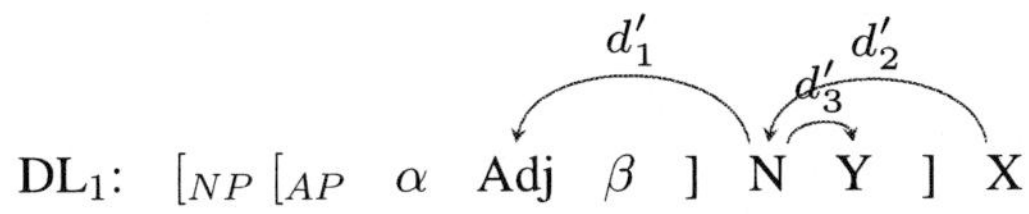

(c) Right external dependent, prenominal adjective

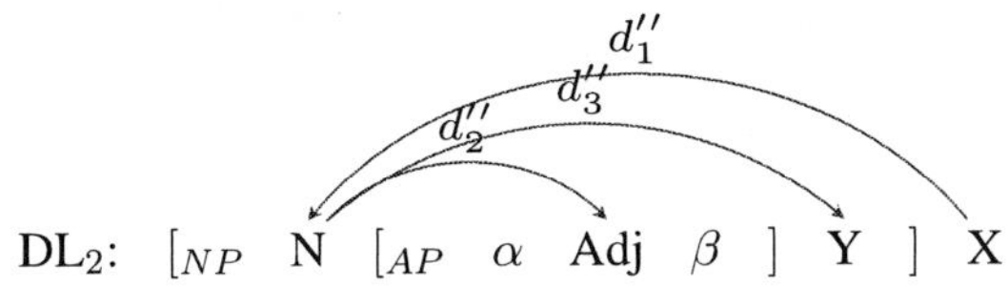

(d) Right external dependent, postnominal adjective

Figure 2: Noun phrase structure variants and the dependencies relevant for the DLM calculation with right noun dependent Y.

	RightNP=Yes	RightNP=No
X=Left	$\lvert\beta\rvert - \lvert\alpha\rvert$	$2\lvert\beta\rvert + 1$
X=Right	$-3\lvert\alpha\rvert - 2$	$-2\lvert\alpha\rvert - 1$

Table 1: Dependency length difference for different types of noun phrases. By convention, we always calculate $DL_1 - DL_2$.

(1) a. ...vede la bella casa al mare.
('..sees the beautiful house at the sea')

b. ...vede la casa bella al mare.
('..sees the house beautiful at the sea')

c. La bella casa al mare è vuota.
('the beautiful house at the sea is empty.')

d. La casa bella al mare è vuota.
('the house beautiful at the sea is empty.')

The differences in dependency lengths predicted by DLM are summarized in Table 1. DLM makes predictions on adjective placement with respect to the noun —prenominal or postnominal— given the dependents of the adjectives, α and β, and given the dependent of the noun Y.

The column RightNP=No shows the dependency length difference for the two cases where the noun does not have a right dependent Y. Given that the calculation of DL differences is always calculated as $DL_1 - DL_2$, the fact that the cell (X=Left, RightNP=No) holds a positive value indicates that $DL_1 > DL_2$ and that the difference in length depends only on β and not on α. Conversely, the negative value of (X=Right, RightNP=No) shows that $DL_1 < DL_2$ and that the difference in length does not depend on β, but only on α. This is not intuitive: intuitively, one would expect that whether the Adjective is left or right of the Noun depends on the relative lengths of α and β, but instead if we look at all the dependencies that come into play for a noun phrase in a larger structure, the adjective position depends on only one of the two dependents. The table also shows that, on average, across all the cells, the weights of α are less than zero while the weights of β are greater than zero. This indicates that $DL_1 < DL_2$, which means that globally the prenominal adjective order is preferred.

DLM also makes predictions on adjective placement with respect to the noun given the dependents of the noun. Here the predictions of DLM are not intuitive. DLM predicts that when the external dependency is right (the dependency from the noun to its parent, X=right), then the adjective is prenominal, else it is postnominal. To spell this out, DLM predicts that, for example, we should find more prenominal adjectives in subject NPs than in NPs in object position. We discuss this odd prediction below.

Another prediction that will be investigated in detail is that when the noun has a right dependent, the prenominal adjective position is more preferred than when there is no right dependent, as evinced by the fact that the RightNP = Yes column is always greater than the RightNP = No column.

Gulordava et al. (2015) develop a mixed-effects model to test which of the fine-grained predictions derived from DLM are confirmed by the data provided by the dependency annotated corpora of five main Romance languages. The different elements in the DLM configuration are encoded as four factors: corresponding to the factors illustrated in Figure 2 and example (1), represented as binary or real-valued variables: *LeftAP* - the cumulative length (in words) of all left dependents of the adjective, indicated as α in Figure 2; *RightAP* - the cumulative length (in words) of all right dependents of the adjective, indicated as β in Figure 2; *ExtDep* - the direction of the arc from the noun to its parent X, an indicator variable; *RightNP* - the indicator variable representing the presence or absence of the right dependent of the noun, indicated as Y in Figure 2. [2]

Their findings partly confirm the predictions about adjective placement with respect to the noun given the adjective dependents. The DLM predictions about the position of the noun with respect to its parent are instead not confirmed. Finally, the prediction related to the presence of a right dependent of the noun on the placement of the adjective are confirmed.

In the next two sections, we replicate and investigate in more detail these results. First, we develop and discuss a more detailed model, where not only the factors, but also their interactions are taken into account. Then, we compare the predictions of the DLM model to the predictions of a simpler heaviness account, and confirm that the complexity of DLM is needed, as a simpler model based on heaviness of the adjective does not yield the same effects. Then, we discuss the external dependency factor, which, in the more complex model with interactions, is a significant factor. Finally, the RightNP factor is significant in the fitted model. The presence of a noun dependent on the right of the noun favours a prenominal placement, as predicted by DLM. We investigate the lexical aspects of this result in a more detailed case study.

3 Analysis of Dependency Minimisation Factors

The analysis that we develop here is based on the assumption that DLM is exhibited by the dependencies in the avalailable dependency-annotated corpora for the five Romance languages.

3.1 Materials: Dependency treebanks

The dependency annotated corpora of five Romance languages are used: Catalan, Spanish, Italian (Hajič et al., 2009), French (McDonald et al., 2013), and Portuguese (Buchholz and Marsi, 2006).

Noun phrases containing adjectives are extracted using part-of-speech information and dependency arcs from the gold annotation. Specifically, all treebanks are converted to coarse universal part-of-speech tags, using existing conventional mappings from the original tagset to the universal tagset (Petrov et al., 2012). All adjectives are identified using the universal PoS tag 'ADJ', whose dependency head is a noun, tagged using the universal PoS tag 'NOUN'. All elements of the dependency subtree, the noun phrase, rooted in this noun are collected. For all languages where this information is available, we extract lemmas of adjective and noun tokens. The only treebank without lemma annotation is French, for which we extract token forms.[3] A total of around 64'000 instances of adjectives in noun phrases is collected, ranging from 2'800 for Italian to 20'000 for Spanish.

3.2 Method: Mixed-Effects models

The interactions of several dependency factors are analysed using a logit mixed effect models (Bates et al., 2014). Mixed-effect logistic regression models (logit models) are a type of Generalized Linear Mixed Models with the logit link function and are designed for binomially distributed outcomes such as $Order$, in our case.

3.3 Factors and their interactions

While the original model in Gulordava et al. (2015) represents the four main factors involved in DLM in the noun phrase — α, β, RightNP and ExtDep — the predictions described above often mention interactions, which are not directly modelled in the original proposal. We introduce interactions, so that the model is more faithful to the DLM predictions, as shown in (2) and in Table 2. We do not take directly represent the interaction between the LeftAP and RightAP because in our corpora these two factors were both greater than zero in only 1% of the cases.

[2]In addition, to account for lexical variation, they include adjective tokens (or lemmas when available) as grouping variables introducing random effects. For example, the instances of adjective-noun order for a particular adjective will share the same weight value γ for the adjective variable, but across different adjectives this value can vary.

[3]During preprocessing, we exclude all adjectives and nouns with non-lower case and non-alphabetic symbols which can include common names. Compounds (in Spanish and Catalan treebanks), and English borrowings are also excluded. Neither do we include in our analysis noun phrases which have their elements separated by punctuation (for example, commas or parentheses) to ensure that the placement of the adjective is not affected by an unusual structure of the noun phrase.

Predictor	β	SE	Z	p
Intercept	-0.157	0.117	-1.33	0.182
LeftAP	2.129	0.183	11.63	$< .001$
RightAP	0.887	0.091	9.79	$< .001$
RightNP	-0.794	0.056	-14.24	$< .001$
ExtDep	-0.243	0.118	-2.06	0.039
RightNP:ExtDep	0.296	0.149	1.98	0.047
RightAP:RightNP:ExtDep	-0.639	0.353	-1.81	0.070

Random effects	Var
Adjective	1.989
Language	0.023

Table 2: Summary of the fixed and random effects in the mixed-effects logit model with interactions ($N = 15842$), shown in (2). Non-significant factors are not shown.

Model	Df	AIC	BIC	logLik	deviance	χ^2	Df	p
Without interactions	7	12137	12190	-6061.3	12123			
With interactions	14	12134	12241	-6052.9	12106	16.847	7	0.018*

Table 3: Comparison of the fits of two models: the model with interactions (2) and a simpler model without any interactions between the factors RightAP, LeftAP, RightNP and ExtDep.

(2) $$y_{ij} = (LeftAP + RightAP) \cdot RightNP \cdot \cdot ExtDep \times \boldsymbol{\beta} + \gamma_{Adj_i} + \gamma_{Lang_j}$$

Contrary to the model without interactions (Gulordava et al., 2015), both the ExtDep factor and its interaction with the RightNP factor are significant. This interaction corresponds to the four different NP contexts presented in Table 1. Its significance, then, can be taken as preliminary confirming evidence for the distinction of these contexts, as predicted by DLM. A direct comparison of the two models, with and without interactions, shows, however, that the effects of these interactions are rather small (Table 3). The log-likelihood test shows that the model with interactions fits the data significantly better ($\chi^2 = 16.8, p = 0.02$), but the comparison of the Bayesian Information Criterion scores of the two models — criterion which strongly penalises the number of parameters — suggests that the model without interactions should be preferred.

3.4 Comparison of DLM and heaviness model

Dependency length minimisation was introduced, as mentioned in the introduction, to better explain processing effects at the sentence level for which heaviness accounts were inadequate. However, noun phrases are small and relatively simple domains. We ask, then, if a model is sufficient where the AP is not divided into LeftAP and RightAP, but holistically represented by the size of the whole AP.

Specifically, a simpler Heaviness model does not make a difference between left and right dependent of adjectives: all heavy adjectives are predicted to move post-nominally. Heaviness would also not predict the interaction between placement and the existence of a noun dependent to the right.

We compare, then, two minimally different models. Since neither the external dependency factor nor the interactions were shown to be highly significant, we compare a simplified DLM model shown in (3) to a model where AP is represented only by its heaviness (number of words) as in (4).

(3) $$y_{ij} = LeftAP \cdot \beta_{LAP} + RightAP \cdot \beta_{RAP} + RightNP \cdot \beta_{RNP} + \gamma_{Adj_i} + \gamma_{Lang_j}$$

(4) $$y_{ij} = SizeAP \cdot \beta_{HV} + RightNP \cdot \beta_{RNP} + \gamma_{Adj_i} + \gamma_{Lang_j}$$

The DLM model that distinguishes LeftAP from RightAP in (3) fits the data better than a model where AP is represented only by its heaviness as in (4), as can be seen in Table 4 and from the difference in AIC values of two models ($\Delta AIC = 146$). This result confirms that the complexity introduced by DLM minimisation is needed, and confirms DLM as a property of language, also in noun phrases. The main conceptual difference between heaviness accounts and DLM

	Df	AIC	BIC	logLik	deviance	χ^2	Df	p
Model with *SizeAP*	5	12518	12557	-6254.1	12508			
Model with *LeftAP*, *RightAP*	6	12372	12418	-6179.8	12360	148.5	1	$< .001$

Table 4: Comparison of the simplified DLM model in (3) and the heaviness model in (4).

accounts resides in the fact that the former do not take into account the structure and the nature of the context of the heavy element, while DLM does. This model comparison shows that adjective placement is not independent of its context.

Prediction for External Dependencies The expected effect of the external dependency of the noun predicted by the DLM is borne out only marginally. This factor predicts a difference between noun phrases that precede their head, for example subjects, and noun phrases that follow their head, for example objects. The prediction is unexpected, while the result that the factor is not highly significant less so, as it is not immediately clear why nouns preceding heads should behave differently from nouns that follow heads.

A possible explanation for this mismatch of the predictions and the observed data patterns lies in the assumptions underlying the DLM principle. We have assumed a definition of dependency length as the number of words between the head and the dependent, as found in the corpus annotation. Our data are annotated using a content-head rule, which assumes that the noun is the head of the noun phrase. Hawkins (1994), in his well-developed variant of DLM, postulates that minimisation occurs on the dependencies between the head and the *edge* of the dependent phrase. For noun phrases, the relevant dependencies will span between the determiner which unambiguously defines the left edge of the noun phrase and the head of NP (e.g., a verb). The predictions of Hawkins' theory for adjective placement will therefore differ from the DLM predictions based on our definition. As can be observed from Figure 2, the d'_1 and d''_1 dependencies to the left edge of the NP will be of equal length in cases (a) and (b) (similarly to d'_2 and d''_2 in cases (c) and (d)). The external dependency is predicted therefore not to affect the resulting adjective placement, as observed in the data. This result lends weak support to a theory where in this case the relevant dependency is between the parent and the edge of the dependent.

A question remains of what dependencies are minimised when the noun phrase does not have a determiner and the left edge of the noun phrase is ambiguous.[4] This issue is difficult to test in practice in our corpora. First, there are many more cases (84% versus 16%) with left ExtDep (X is on the right, e.g. for object NPs) than with right ExtDep (X is on the left, e.g. for subjects) in Romance languages. This is because all of them, except French, can optionally omit subjects. Moreover, the function of the NP, subject or object, and therefore the ExtDep variable, correlates with the definiteness of the NP. NPs in object position take an article 75% of time while NPs in subject position take an article 96% of time. Consequently, NPs without articles and on the left of the head are observed only 135 times in our data sample (across all languages). This small number of cases did not allow us to develop a model.

4 In-depth study of the RightNP dependency factor

The most novel result of the model in Gulordava et al. (2015), extended here to the more complex model (2) concerns the interaction between the adjective position and the RightNP. This effect would not be predicted by a heaviness explanation and even in the DLM framework it is surprising that minimisation should apply to such a short dependency. We investigate this interaction in more detail and ask two questions: is this effect evenly spread across different nouns and adjectives or is it driven by some lexical outliers? what are the lexical effects of the noun and its dependent? We analyse a large amount of data constructed to be a representative sample of adjective variation for several nouns (around thirty for each language) and very many adjectives and investigate noun phrases with a right dependent introduced by the preposition 'de/di'[5].

[4]In one of his analyses, Hawkins claims that adjectives define unambiguously the left edge of the NP, but this assumption is controversial.

[5]For Italian, the preposition is 'di', while for other three languages it is 'de'. We do not consider complex prepositions such as 'du' in French or 'do' in Portuguese.

4.1 Data extracted from large PoS-tagged corpora

We extract the data by querying automatically a collection of corpora brought together by the SketchEngine project (Kilgarriff et al., 2014). This web-interface-based collection allows partially restricted access to billion-word corpora of Italian (4 billions of words), French (11 billions), Spanish (8.7 billions) and Portuguese (4.5 billions). The corpora are collected by web-crawling and automatically PoS-tagged. A similar Catalan corpus was not available through this service.

First, we define the set of seed nouns that will be queried. For each language, we use our treebanks to find the list of the two-hundred most frequent nouns which take the 'di/de' preposition as a complement. A noun has 'di/de' as its right dependent if there is a direct head-dependent link between these elements in the gold annotation. Nouns in the list which could be ambiguous between different types of parts of speech are replaced manually. We randomly sample around thirty nouns, based on the percentage of their co-occurrence with 'di/de'. Given the list of seed nouns, we automatically queried the four corpora with simple regular patterns containing these nouns to extract cases of prenominal and postnominal noun-adjective co-occurrences.[6]

For each noun, we collected a maximum of 100'000 matches for each of the two patterns, which is the SketchEngine service limit. These matches include left and right contexts of the pattern and allow to extract the token following the pattern, which can be 'di/de' or nothing.

We modeled the data using the Logit mixed effect models, with the $Order$ as a response variable, one fixed effect (Di) and nouns and adjectives as random effects. We fit the maximal model with both slope and intercept parameters, as shown in model (5).

$$(5)\quad \begin{aligned} y = Di \cdot (\beta_{Di} + \beta_{Adj_i} + \beta_{Noun_j}) \\ + \gamma_{Adj_i} + \gamma_{Noun_j} \end{aligned}$$

We fit our models on a sample of data of around 200'000 instances of adjective-noun alternations for each language, equally balanced for noun phrases with $Di = True$ and $Di = False$.

[6]Our patterns were of the type '[tag="ADJ"] *noun*' and '*noun* [tag="ADJ"]', where the tag field is specified for the PoS tag of a token. In our case, 'A.' was the tag for adjectives in , and 'ADJ' in Italian, French and Spanish.

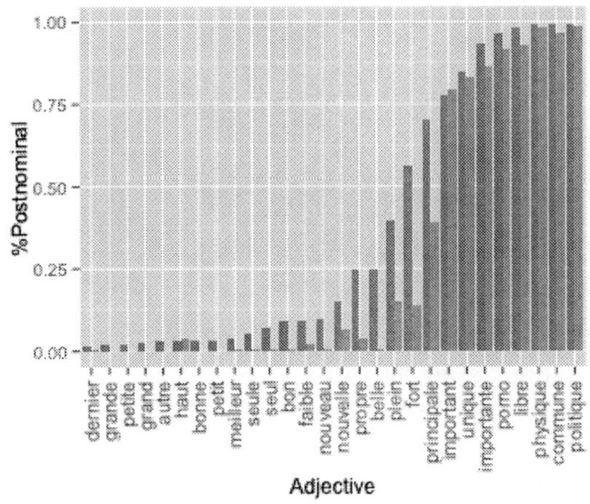

Figure 3: Percent postnominal placement for the thirty most frequent adjectives in French. (Noun phrase has a right 'de'-complement (green) and it does not (red).

4.2 Results

The data shows that the Di effect is small, but highly significant for all languages. The resulting values are similar: for French $\beta_{Di} = -0.84$, Portuguese $\beta_{Di} = -0.95$, Italian $\beta_{Di} = -1.14$ and Spanish $\beta_{Di} = -1.65$ (all $p < 0.001$).

Figure 3 illustrates the Di effect for French (cumulative for all nouns). We observe that most of the adjectives appear more frequently prenominally in noun phrases with a 'de' complement than in noun phrases without a 'de' complement (green columns are smaller than corresponding red columns). Importantly, we observe a very similar picture cross-linguistically for all four languages and for the adjective alternation across the majority of the nouns (if considered independently), as shown in Figure 4.

This result agrees with our predictions, and shows that DLM effects show up even in short spans, where they are not necessarily expected. If a postnominal adjective intervenes between the noun and the dependent, the dependency length increases only by one word (with respect to the noun phrase with the prenominal adjective). Our results nevertheless suggest that even such short dependencies are consistently minimised. This effect is confirmed in all languages.

4.3 Lexical effects on adjective placement

One of the lexical factors that could play a confounding role for the prenominal placement of ad-

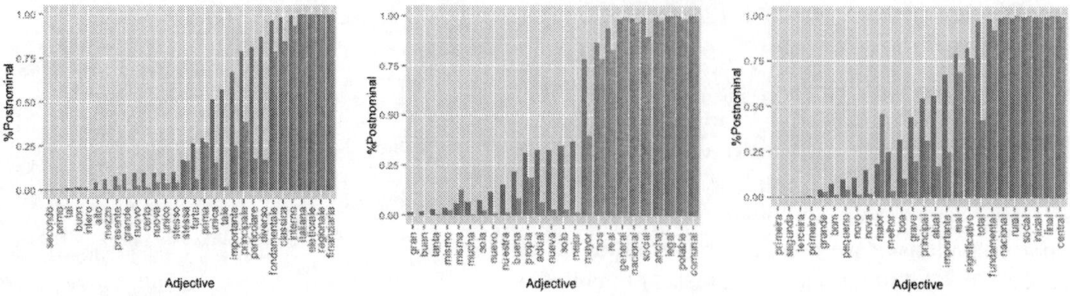

Figure 4: Percent postnominal placement for the thirty most frequent adjectives in Italian, Spanish, and Portuguese (in this order). (Noun phrase has a right 'de/di'-complement (green) and it does not (red).

jectives in *Di* constructions is the strength of the 'Noun + di/de + Complement' collocation. For example, in the French compound 'taux de chomage' ('unemployement rate') the placement of an adjective after the compound — 'taux de chomage important' — is preferred in our corpora to the adjacent postnominal placement ('taux important de chomage'). In our analysis, we do not extract these types of post-NP adjectives. From this perspective, a drop in the percentage of postnominal adjectives in 'di' cases could indicate that adjectives prefer not to intervene between nouns and their complements. We hypothesize that this dependency is more strongly minimised than other dependencies in the noun phrase because of this strong lexical link.

We confirm that the *Di* effect is an interaction of the DLM principle and lexical properties of compounds by a further preliminary analysis of collocations. From the French data, we selected a subset with the most frequent 'Noun + de + Complement' sequences (10 for each seed noun) and a subset with infrequent sequences (100 random de-complements for each seed noun). We assume that the frequency of the sequence is an indicator of the collocational strength, so that highly frequent sequences are collocations while low frequency sequences are non-collocational combinations. The first subset has a proportion of 78% prenominal and 22% postnominal adjectives, while the second subset has 61% prenominal and 39% postnominal adjectives. We confirm, then, that in the frequent collocations there is a substantial lexical effect in adjective placement. However, we also observe a preference of prenominal placement for the infrequent 'Noun + de + Complement' sequences that are not collocational combinations, since prenominal placement is still much higher than what is observed for French adjectives, on average (46% prenominal and 54% postnominal in our sample of data). These numbers suggest that the *Di* effect reported in the previous section is not a result of mere lexical collocation effects and that, for low frequency combinations at least, DLM is at play.

A different kind of lexical effect is shown in Figure 5. Here we plot the percent postnominal placement of the adjective, if the noun has a complement introduced by *di (of), che (that), per (for),* in Italian. We notice that adjective placement is no longer as majoritarily prenominal for the right dependent introduced by *che* and *per* as it is for *di*. The main difference between *di* (of) and *che* (that), *per* (for) is that the former introduces a PP that is inside the NP that selects it, while *che* and *per* usually do not, they are adjuncts, or infinitivals or clauses. In the linguistic literature, this is a distinction between arguments and adjuncts of the noun and it is represented structurally. This distinction is, then, a lexically-induced structural distinction, and not simply a collocation.

5 Related work

Our work occupies the middle ground between detailed linguistic investigations of weight effect in chosen constructions of well-studied languages and large scale demonstrations of the dependency length minimisation principle.

Gildea and Temperley (2007) demonstrated that DLM applies for the dependency annotated corpora in English and German. They calculate random and optimal dependency lengths for each sentence given its unordered dependency tree and compare these values to actual dependency lengths. English lengths are shown to be close to optimal, but for German this tendency is not as clear. A recent study of Futrell et al. (2015) applies

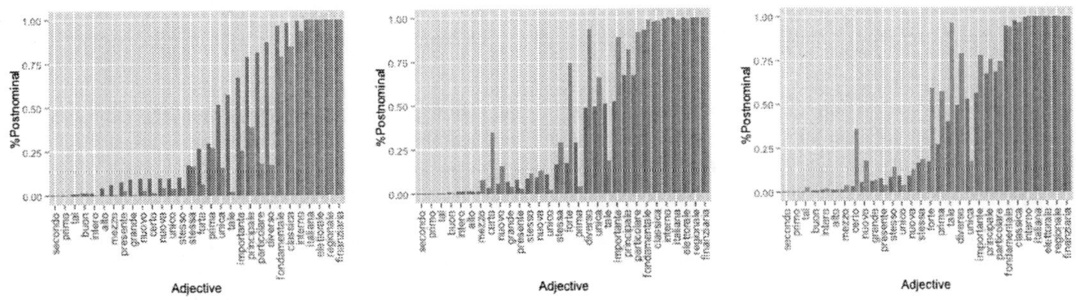

Figure 5: Percent postnominal placement for thirty most frequent adjectives in Italian, followed by function word *di, che, per*, in this order. (Noun phrase has a right 'di/per/che'-complement (green) and it does not (red)).

this analysis on a large-scale, for more than thirty languages that have dependency treebanks. Their results also confirm the correspondence between the dependency annotation and the experimental data, something that has been reported previously (Merlo, 1994; Roland and Jurafsky, 2002).

Much work in theoretical linguistics addresses the adjective-noun order in Romance languages. Such work typically concentrates on lexico-semantic aspects of adjective placement (Cinque, 2010; Alexiadou, 2001). In our work, we account for the strong lexical prenominal or postnominal preferences of adjectives by including them as random effects in our models.

Closest to our paper is the theoretical work of Abeillé and Godard (2000) on the placement of adjective phrases in French and recent corpus-based work by Fox and Thuilier (2012) and Thuilier (2012). Fox and Thuilier (2012) use a dependency annotated corpus of French to extract cases of adjective-noun variation and their syntactic contexts. They model the placement of an adjective as a lexical, syntactic and semantic multifactorial variation. They find, for example, that phonologically heavy simple adjectives tend to be postnominal. This result highlights the distinction between phonological weight and syntactic weight, a topic which we do not address in the current work.

6 Conclusion

In this paper, we have shown that differences in the prenominal and postnominal placement of adjectives in the noun phrase across five main Romance languages is not only subject to heaviness effects, but to subtler dependency length minimisation effects. These effects are almost purely structural and show lexical conditioning only in highly frequent collocations.

The subtle interactions found in this work raise questions about the exact definition of what dependencies are minimised and to what extent a given dependency annotation captures these distinctions. Future work will investigate more refined definitions of dependency length minimisation, that distinguish different kinds of dependencies with different weights.

Acknowledgements

We gratefully acknowledge the partial funding of this work by the Swiss National Science Foundation, under grant 144362. Part of this work was conducted during the visit of The first author to the Labex EFL in Paris and Alpage INRIA group. We thank Benoit Crabbé for the fruitful discussions during this period.

References

Anne Abeillé and Daniele Godard. 2000. French word order and lexical weight. In Robert D. Borsley, editor, *The nature and function of Syntactic Categories*, volume 32 of *Syntax and Semantics*, pages 325–360. BRILL.

Artemis Alexiadou. 2001. Adjective syntax and noun raising: word order asymmetries in the DP as the result of adjective distribution. *Studia linguistica*, 55(3):217–248.

Douglas Bates, Martin Maechler, Ben Bolker, and Steven Walker, 2014. *lme4: Linear mixed-effects models using Eigen and S4*. R package version 1.1-7.

Joan Bresnan, Anna Cueni, Tatiana Nikitina, and Harald Baayen. 2007. Predicting the dative alternation. In G. Boume, I. Kraemer, and J. Zwarts, editors,

Cognitive Foundations of Interpretation, pages 69–94. Royal Netherlands Academy of Science, Amsterdam.

Sabine Buchholz and Erwin Marsi. 2006. CoNLL-X Shared Task on Multilingual Dependency Parsing. In *Proceedings of the Tenth Conference on Computational Natural Language Learning*, CoNLL-X '06, pages 149–164, Stroudsburg, PA, USA. Association for Computational Linguistics.

Guglielmo Cinque. 2010. *The Syntax of Adjectives: A Comparative Study*. MIT Press.

Dóra Csendes, János Csirik, Tibor Gyimóthy, and András Kocsor. 2005. The Szeged treebank. In *Text, Speech and Dialogue*, pages 123–131. Springer.

Gwendoline Fox and Juliette Thuilier. 2012. Predicting the Position of Attributive Adjectives in the French NP. In Daniel Lassiter and Marija Slavkovik, editors, *New Directions in Logic, Language and Computation*, Lecture Notes in Computer Science, pages 1–15. Springer, April.

Richard Futrell, Kyle Mahowald, and Edward Gibson. 2015. Large-Scale Evidence of Dependency Length Minimization in 37 Languages. (Submitted to Proceedings of the National Academy of Sciences of the United States of America).

Edward Gibson. 1998. Linguistic complexity: Locality of syntactic dependencies. *Cognition*, 68(1):1–76.

Daniel Gildea and David Temperley. 2007. Optimizing Grammars for Minimum Dependency Length. In *Proceedings of the 45th Annual Conference of the Association for Computational Linguistics (ACL'07)*, pages 184–191, Prague, Czech Republic.

Kristina Gulordava, Paola Merlo, and Benoit Crabbé. 2015. Dependency length minimisation effects in short spans: a large-scale analysis of adjective placement in complex noun phrases. In *Proceedings of the 53rd Annual Meeting of the Association for Computational Linguistics: Short Papers (ACL'15)*.

Jan Hajič, Massimiliano Ciaramita, Richard Johansson, Daisuke Kawahara, Maria Antònia Martí, Lluís Màrquez, Adam Meyers, Joakim Nivre, Sebastian Padó, Jan Štěpánek, Pavel Straňák, Mihai Surdeanu, Nianwen Xue, and Yi Zhang. 2009. The CoNLL-2009 shared task: syntactic and semantic dependencies in multiple languages. In *Proceedings of the Thirteenth Conference on Computational Natural Language Learning: Shared Task*, CoNLL '09, pages 1–18, Stroudsburg, PA, USA. Association for Computational Linguistics.

Dag T. T. Haug and Marius L. Jøhndal. 2008. Creating a Parallel Treebank of the Old Indo-European Bible Translations. In *Proceedings of the 2nd Workshop on Language Technology for Cultural Heritage Data*, pages 27–34, Marrakech, Morocco.

John A Hawkins. 1994. *A performance theory of order and constituency*. Cambridge University Press, Cambridge.

John A. Hawkins. 2004. *Efficiency and Complexity in Grammars*. Oxford linguistics. Oxford University Press, Oxford, UK.

Adam Kilgarriff, Vít Baisa, Jan Bušta, Miloš Jakubíček, Vojtěch Kovář, Jan Michelfeit, Pavel Rychlý, and Vít Suchomel. 2014. The sketch engine: ten years on. *Lexicography*, 1(1):7–36.

Ryan McDonald, Joakim Nivre, Yvonne Quirmbach-Brundage, Yoav Goldberg, Dipanjan Das, Kuzman Ganchev, Keith Hall, Slav Petrov, Hao Zhang, Oscar Täckström, Claudia Bedini, Núria Bertomeu Castelló, and Jungmee Lee. 2013. Universal dependency annotation for multilingual parsing. In *Proceedings of the 51st Annual Meeting of the Association for Computational Linguistics (Volume 2: Short Papers)*, pages 92–97. Association for Computational Linguistics.

Paola Merlo. 1994. A corpus-based analysis of verb continuation frequencies for syntactic processing. *Journal of Psycholinguistic Research*, 23(6):435–457.

Slav Petrov, Dipanjan Das, and Ryan T. McDonald. 2012. A Universal Part-of-Speech Tagset. In *Proceedings of the Eight International Conference on Language Resources and Evaluation (LREC'12)*, pages 2089–2096, Istanbul, Turkey.

Douglas Roland and Daniel Jurafsky. 2002. Verb sense and verb subcategorization probabilities. In Paola Merlo and Suzanne Stevenson, editors, *The lexical basis of sentence processing: Formal, computational, and experimental issues*. John Benjamins.

Lynne M Stallings, Maryellen C MacDonald, and Padraig G O'Seaghdha. 1998. Phrasal ordering constraints in sentence production: Phrase length and verb disposition in heavy-NP shift. *Journal of Memory and Language*, 39(3):392–417.

David Temperley. 2007. Minimization of dependency length in written English. *Cognition*, 105(2):300–333.

Juliette Thuilier. 2012. *Contraintes préférentielles et ordre des mots en français*. Ph.D. Thesis, Université Paris-Diderot - Paris VII, Sep.

Harry Joel Tily. 2010. *The role of processing complexity in word order variation and change*. Ph.D. Thesis, Stanford University.

Thomas Wasow. 2002. *Postverbal Behavior*. CSLI Publications.

Marcin Woliński, Katarzyna Głowińska, and Marek Świdziński. 2011. A Preliminary Version of Skladnica—a Treebank of Polish. In Zygmunt Vetulani, editor, *Proceedings of the 5th Language & Technology Conference: Human Language Technologies as a Challenge for Computer Science and Linguistics*, pages 299–303, Poznan, Poland.

Daniel Zeman, David Mareček, Martin Popel, Loganathan Ramasamy, Jan Štěpánek, Zdeněk Žabokrtský, and Jan Hajič. 2012. HamleDT: To Parse or Not to Parse? In *Proceedings of the Eight International Conference on Language Resources and Evaluation (LREC'12)*, pages 23–25, Istanbul, Turkey, may. European Language Resources Association (ELRA).

Symmetric Pattern Based Word Embeddings for Improved Word Similarity Prediction

Roy Schwartz,[1] **Roi Reichart,**[2] **Ari Rappoport**[1]
[1]Institute of Computer Science, The Hebrew University
[2]Technion, IIT
{roys02|arir}@cs.huji.ac.il roiri@ie.technion.ac.il

Abstract

We present a novel word level vector representation based on *symmetric patterns (SPs)*. For this aim we automatically acquire SPs (e.g., "X *and* Y") from a large corpus of plain text, and generate vectors where each coordinate represents the co-occurrence in SPs of the represented word with another word of the vocabulary. Our representation has three advantages over existing alternatives: First, being based on symmetric word relationships, it is highly suitable for word similarity prediction. Particularly, on the SimLex999 word similarity dataset, our model achieves a Spearman's ρ score of 0.517, compared to 0.462 of the state-of-the-art word2vec model. Interestingly, our model performs exceptionally well on verbs, outperforming state-of-the-art baselines by 20.2–41.5%. Second, pattern features can be adapted to the needs of a target NLP application. For example, we show that we can easily control whether the embeddings derived from SPs deem antonym pairs (e.g. (*big,small*)) as similar or dissimilar, an important distinction for tasks such as word classification and sentiment analysis. Finally, we show that a simple combination of the word similarity scores generated by our method and by word2vec results in a superior predictive power over that of each individual model, scoring as high as 0.563 in Spearman's ρ on SimLex999. This emphasizes the differences between the signals captured by each of the models.

1 Introduction

In the last decade, vector space modeling *(VSM)* for word representation (a.k.a word embedding), has become a key tool in NLP. Most approaches to word representation follow the distributional hypothesis (Harris, 1954), which states that words that co-occur in similar contexts are likely to have similar meanings.

VSMs differ in the way they exploit word co-occurrence statistics. Earlier works (see (Turney et al., 2010)) encode this information directly in the features of the word vector representation. More Recently, Neural Networks have become prominent in word representation learning (Bengio et al., 2003; Collobert and Weston, 2008; Collobert et al., 2011; Mikolov et al., 2013a; Pennington et al., 2014, inter alia). Most of these models aim to learn word vectors that maximize a language model objective, thus capturing the tendencies of the represented words to co-occur in the training corpus. VSM approaches have resulted in highly useful word embeddings, obtaining high quality results on various semantic tasks (Baroni et al., 2014).

Interestingly, the impressive results of these models are achieved despite the shallow linguistic information most of them consider, which is limited to the tendency of words to co-occur together in a pre-specified context window. Particularly, very little information is encoded about the syntactic and semantic relations between the participating words, and, instead, a bag-of-words approach is taken.[1]

This bag-of-words approach, however, comes with a cost. As recently shown by Hill et al. (2014), despite the impressive results VSMs that take this approach obtain on modeling word *association*, they are much less successful in modeling word *similarity*. Indeed, when evaluating these VSMs with datasets such as wordsim353 (Finkelstein et al., 2001), where the word pair scores re-

[1]A few recent VSMs go beyond the bag-of-words assumption and consider deeper linguistic information in word representation. We address this line of work in Section 2.

Proceedings of the 19th Conference on Computational Language Learning, pages 258–267,
Beijing, China, July 30-31, 2015.

flect association rather than similarity (and therefore the (*cup,coffee*) pair is scored higher than the (*car,train*) pair), the Spearman correlation between their scores and the human scores often crosses the 0.7 level. However, when evaluating with datasets such as SimLex999 (Hill et al., 2014), where the pair scores reflect similarity, the correlation of these models with human judgment is below 0.5 (Section 6).

In order to address the challenge in modeling word similarity, we propose an alternative, pattern-based, approach to word representation. In previous work patterns were used to represent a variety of semantic relations, including hyponymy (Hearst, 1992), meronymy (Berland and Charniak, 1999) and antonymy (Lin et al., 2003). Here, in order to capture similarity between words, we use *Symmetric patterns (SPs)*, such as "X *and* Y" and "X *as well as* Y", where each of the words in the pair can take either the *X* or the *Y* position. Symmetric patterns have shown useful for representing similarity between words in various NLP tasks including lexical acquisition (Widdows and Dorow, 2002), word clustering (Davidov and Rappoport, 2006) and classification of words to semantic categories (Schwartz et al., 2014). However, to the best of our knowledge, they have not been applied to vector space word representation.

Our representation is constructed in the following way (Section 3). For each word w, we construct a vector v of size V, where V is the size of the lexicon. Each element in v represents the co-occurrence in SPs of w with another word in the lexicon, which results in a sparse word representation. Unlike most previous works that applied SPs to NLP tasks, we do not use a hard coded set of patterns. Instead, we extract a set of SPs from plain text using an unsupervised algorithm (Davidov and Rappoport, 2006). This substantially reduces the human supervision our model requires and makes it applicable for practically every language for which a large corpus of text is available.

Our SP-based word representation is flexible. Particularly, by exploiting the semantics of the pattern based features, our representation can be adapted to fit the specific needs of target NLP applications. In Section 4 we exemplify this property through the ability of our model to control whether its word representations will deem antonyms similar or dissimilar. *Antonyms* are words that have opposite semantic meanings (e.g., (*small,big*)), yet, due to their tendency to co-occur in the same context, they are often assigned similar vectors by co-occurrence based representation models (Section 6). Controlling the model judgment of antonym pairs is highly useful for NLP tasks: in some tasks, like word classification, antonym pairs such as (*small,big*) belong to the same class (size adjectives), while in other tasks, like sentiment analysis, identifying the difference between them is crucial. As discussed in Section 4, we believe that this flexibility holds for various other pattern types and for other lexical semantic relations (e.g. hypernymy, the *is-a* relation, which holds in word pairs such as (*dog,animal*)).

We experiment (Section 6) with the SimLex999 dataset (Hill et al., 2014), consisting of 999 pairs of words annotated by human subjects for similarity. When comparing the correlation between the similarity scores derived from our learned representation and the human scores, our representation receives a Spearman correlation coefficient score (ρ) of 0.517, outperforming six strong baselines, including the state-of-the-art *word2vec* (Mikolov et al., 2013a) embeddings, by 5.5–16.7%. Our model performs particularly well on the verb portion of SimLex999 (222 verb pairs), achieving a Spearman score of 0.578 compared to scores of 0.163–0.376 of the baseline models, an astonishing improvement of 20.2–41.5%. Our analysis reveals that the antonym adjustment capability of our model is vital for its success.

We further demonstrate that the word pair scores produced by our model can be combined with those of word2vec to get an improved predictive power for word similarity. The combined scores result in a Spearman's ρ correlation of 0.563, a further 4.6% improvement compared to our model, and a total of 10.1–21.3% improvement over the baseline models. This suggests that the models provide complementary information about word semantics.

2 Related Work

Vector Space Models for Lexical Semantics. Research on vector spaces for word representation dates back to the early 1970's (Salton, 1971). In traditional methods, a vector for each word w is generated, with each coordinate representing the co-occurrence of w and another context item of interest – most often a word but possibly also a sentence, a document or other items. The feature representation generated by this basic construction is sometimes post-processed using techniques such as Positive Pointwise Mutual Information (PPMI) normalization and dimensionality reduction. For recent surveys, see (Turney et al., 2010; Clark, 2012; Erk, 2012).

Most VSM works share two important characteristics. First, they encode co-occurrence statistics from an input corpus directly into the word vector features. Second, they consider very little information on the syntactic and semantic relations between the represented word and its context items. Instead, a bag-of-words approach is taken.

Recently, there is a surge of work focusing on Neural Network (NN) algorithms for word representations learning (Bengio et al., 2003; Collobert and Weston, 2008; Mnih and Hinton, 2009; Collobert et al., 2011; Dhillon et al., 2011; Mikolov et al., 2013a; Mnih and Kavukcuoglu, 2013; Lebret and Collobert, 2014; Pennington et al., 2014). Like the more traditional models, these works also take the bag-of-words approach, encoding only shallow co-occurrence information between linguistic items. However, they encode this information into their objective, often a language model, rather than directly into the features.

Consider, for example, the successful word2vec model (Mikolov et al., 2013a). Its continuous-bag-of-words architecture is designed to predict a word given its past and future context. The resulted objective function is:

$$\max \sum_{t=1}^{T} \log p(w_t | w_{t-c}, \ldots, w_{t-1}, w_{t+1}, \ldots, w_{t+c})$$

where T is the number of words in the corpus, and c is a pre-determined window size. Another word2vec architecture, skip-gram, aims to predict the past and future context given a word. Its objective is:

$$\max \sum_{t=1}^{T} \sum_{-c \leq j \leq c, j \neq 0} \log p(w_{t+j} | w_t)$$

In both cases the objective function relates to the co-occurrence of words within a context window.

A small number of works went beyond the bag-of-words assumption, considering deeper relationships between linguistic items. The Strudel system (Baroni et al., 2010) represents a word using the clusters of lexico-syntactic patterns in which it occurs. Murphy et al. (2012) represented words through their co-occurrence with other words in syntactic dependency relations, and then used the Non-Negative Sparse Embedding (NNSE) method to reduce the dimension of the resulted representation. Levy and Goldberg (2014) extended the skip-gram word2vec model with negative sampling (Mikolov et al., 2013b) by basing the word co-occurrence window on the dependency parse tree of the sentence. Bollegala et al. (2015) replaced bag-of-words contexts with various patterns (lexical, POS and dependency).

We introduce a symmetric pattern based approach to word representation which is particularly suitable for capturing word similarity. In experiments we show the superiority of our model over six models of the above three families: (a) bag-of-words models that encode co-occurrence statistics directly in features; (b) NN models that implement the bag-of-words approach in their objective; and (c) models that go beyond the bag-of-words assumption.

Similarity vs. Association Most recent VSM research does not distinguish between association and similarity in a principled way, although notable exceptions exist. Turney (2012) constructed two VSMs with the explicit goal of capturing either similarity or association. A classifier that uses the output of these models was able to predict whether two concepts are associated, similar or both. Agirre et al. (2009) partitioned the wordsim353 dataset into two subsets, one focused on similarity and the other on association. They demonstrated the importance of the association/similarity distinction by showing that some VSMs perform relatively well on one subset while others perform comparatively better on the other.

Recently, Hill et al. (2014) presented the SimLex999 dataset consisting of 999 word pairs judged by humans for similarity only. The participating words belong to a variety of POS tags and concreteness levels, arguably providing a more realistic sample of the English lexicon. Using their dataset the authors show the tendency of VSMs that take the bag-of-words approach to capture association much better than similarity. This observation motivates our work.

Symmetric Patterns. Patterns (*symmetric* or not) were found useful in a variety of NLP tasks, including identification of word relations such as hyponymy (Hearst, 1992), meronymy (Berland and Charniak, 1999) and antonymy (Lin et al., 2003). Patterns have also been applied to tackle sentence level tasks such as identification of sarcasm (Tsur et al., 2010), sentiment analysis (Davidov et al., 2010) and authorship attribution (Schwartz et al., 2013).

Symmetric patterns (SPs) were employed in various NLP tasks to capture different aspects of word similarity. Widdows and Dorow (2002) used SPs for the task of lexical acquisition. Dorow et al. (2005) and Davidov and Rappoport (2006) used them to perform unsupervised clustering of words. Kozareva et al. (2008) used SPs to classify proper names (e.g., fish names, singer names). Feng et al. (2013) used SPs to build a connotation lexicon, and Schwartz et al. (2014) used SPs to perform minimally supervised classification of words into semantic categories.

While some of these works used a hand crafted set of SPs (Widdows and Dorow, 2002; Dorow et al., 2005; Kozareva et al., 2008; Feng et al., 2013), Davidov and Rappoport (2006) introduced a fully unsupervised algorithm for the extraction of SPs. Here we apply their algorithm in order to reduce the required human supervision and demonstrate the language independence of our approach.

Antonyms. A useful property of our model is its ability to control the representation of antonym pairs. Outside the VSM literature several works identified antonyms using word co-occurrence statistics, manually and automatically induced patterns, the WordNet lexicon and thesauri (Lin et al., 2003; Turney, 2008; Wang et al., 2010; Mohammad et al., 2013; Schulte im Walde and Koper, 2013; Roth and Schulte im Walde, 2014). Recently, Yih et al. (2012), Chang et al. (2013) and Ono et al. (2015) proposed word representation methods that assign dissimilar vectors to antonyms. Unlike our unsupervised model, which uses plain text only, these works used the WordNet lexicon and a thesaurus.

3 Model

In this section we describe our approach for generating pattern-based word embeddings. We start by describing symmetric patterns (SPs), continue to show how SPs can be acquired automatically from text, and, finally, explain how these SPs are used for word embedding construction.

3.1 Symmetric Patterns

Lexico-syntactic patterns are sequences of words and wildcards (Hearst, 1992). Examples of patterns include "X *such as* Y", "X *or* Y" and "X *is a* Y". When patterns are instantiated in text, wildcards are replaced by words. For example, the pattern "**X** *is a* **Y**", with the **X** and **Y** wildcards, can be instantiated in phrases like "**Guffy** *is a* **dog**".

Candidate	Examples of Instances
"X *of* Y"	"point *of* view", "years *of* age"
"X *the* Y"	"around *the* world", "over *the* past"
"X *to* Y"	"nothing *to* do", "like *to* see"
"X *and* Y"	"men *and* women", "oil *and* gas"
"X *in* Y"	"keep *in* mind", "put *in* place"
"X *of the* Y"	"rest *of the* world", "end *of the* war"

Table 1:
The six most frequent pattern candidates that contain exactly two wildcards and 1-3 words in our corpus.

Symmetric patterns are a special type of patterns that contain exactly two wildcards and that tend to be instantiated by wildcard pairs such that each member of the pair can take the **X** or the **Y** position. For example, the symmetry of the pattern "**X** *or* **Y**" is exemplified by the semantically plausible expressions "cats *or* dogs" and "dogs *or* cats".

Previous works have shown that words that co-occur in SPs are semantically similar (Section 2). In this work we use symmetric patterns to represent words. Our hypothesis is that such representation would reflect word similarity (i.e., that similar vectors would represent similar words). Our experiments show that this is indeed the case.

Symmetric Patterns Extraction. Most works that used SPs manually constructed a set of such patterns. The most prominent patterns in these works are "X *and* Y" and "X *or* Y" (Widdows and Dorow, 2002; Feng et al., 2013). In this work we follow (Davidov and Rappoport, 2006) and apply an unsupervised algorithm for the automatic extraction of SPs from plain text.

This algorithm starts by defining an SP template to be a sequence of 3-5 tokens, consisting of exactly two wildcards, and 1-3 words. It then traverses a corpus, looking for frequent pattern candidates that match this template. Table 1 shows the six most frequent pattern candidates, along with common instances of these patterns.

The algorithm continues by traversing the pattern candidates and selecting a pattern p if a large portion of the pairs of words w_i, w_j that co-occur in p co-occur both in the ($X = w_i$,$Y = w_j$) form and in the ($X = w_j$,$Y = w_i$) form. Consider, for example, the pattern candidate "X *and* Y", and the pair of words "cat","dog". Both pattern instances "cat *and* dog" and "dog *and* cat" are likely to be seen in a large corpus. If this property holds for a large portion[2] of the pairs of words that co-occur in this pattern, it is selected as symmetric. On the other hand, the pattern candidate "X *of* Y" is in fact asymmetric: pairs of words such as "point", "view" tend to come only in the (X = "point",Y = "view") form and not the other way around. The reader is referred to (Davidov and Rappoport, 2006) for a more formal description of this algorithm. The resulting pattern set we use in this paper is "X *and* Y", "X *or* Y", "X *and the* Y", "*from* X *to* Y", "X *or the* Y", "X *as well as* Y", "X *or a* Y","X *rather than* Y", "X *nor* Y", "X *and one* Y", "*either* X *or* Y".

3.2 SP-based Word Embeddings

In order to generate word embeddings, our model requires a large corpus C, and a set of SPs P. The model first computes a symmetric matrix M of size $V \times V$ (where V is the size of the lexicon). In this matrix, $M_{i,j}$ is the co-occurrence count of both w_i,w_j and w_j,w_i in all patterns $p \in P$. For example, if w_i,w_j co-occur 1 time in p_1 and 3 times in p_5, while w_j,w_i co-occur 7 times in p_9, then $M_{i,j} = M_{j,i} = 1 + 3 + 7 = 11$. We then compute the Positive Pointwise Mutual Information (PPMI) of M, denoted by M^*.[3] The vector representation of the word w_i (denoted by v_i) is the ith row in M^*.

Smoothing. In order to decrease the sparsity of our representation, we apply a simple smoothing technique. For each word w_i, W_i^n denotes the top n vectors with the smallest cosine-distance from v_i. We define the word embedding of w_i to be

$$v_i' = v_i + \alpha \cdot \sum_{v \in W_i^n} v$$

where α is a smoothing factor.[4] This process reduces the sparsity of our vector representation. For example, when $n = 0$ (i.e., no smoothing), the average number of non-zero values per vector is only 0.3K (where the vector size is $\sim$250K). When $n = 250$, this number reaches $\sim$14K.

[2] We use 15% of the pairs of words as a threshold.

[3] PPMI was shown useful for various co-occurrence models (Baroni et al., 2014).

[4] We tune n and α using a development set (Section 5). Typical values for n and α are 250 and 7, respectively.

4 Antonym Representation

In this section we show how our model allows us to adjust the representation of pairs of antonyms to the needs of a subsequent NLP task. This property will later be demonstrated to have a substantial impact on performance.

Antonyms are pairs of words with an opposite meaning (e.g., (*tall,short*)). As the members of an antonym pair tend to occur in the same context, their word embeddings are often similar. For example, in the skip-gram model (Mikolov et al., 2013a), the score of the (*accept,reject*) pair is 0.73, and the score of (*long,short*) is 0.71. Our SP-based word embeddings also exhibit a similar behavior.

The question of whether antonyms are similar or not is not a trivial one. On the one hand, some NLP tasks might benefit from representing antonyms as similar. For example, in word classification tasks, words such as "big" and "small" potentially belong to the same class (size adjectives), and thus representing them as similar is desired. On the other hand, antonyms are very dissimilar by definition. This distinction is crucial in tasks such as search, where a query such as "tall buildings" might be poorly processed if the representations of "tall" and "short" are similar.

In light of this, we construct our word embeddings to be *controllable* of antonyms. That is, our model contains an antonym parameter that can be turned on in order to generate word embeddings that represent antonyms as dissimilar, and turned off to represent them as similar.

To implement this mechanism, we follow (Lin et al., 2003), who showed that two patterns are particularly indicative of antonymy – "*from* X *to* Y" and "*either* X *or* Y" (e.g., "*from* **bottom** *to* **top**", "*either* **high** *or* **low**"). As it turns out, these two patterns are also symmetric, and are discovered by our automatic algorithm. Henceforth, we refer to these two patterns as *antonym patterns*.

Based on this observation, we present a variant of our model, which is designed to assign dissimilar vector representations to antonyms. We define two new matrices: M^{SP} and M^{AP}, which are computed similarly to M^* (see Section 3.2), only with different SP sets. M^{SP} is computed using the original set of SPs, excluding the two antonym patterns, while M^{AP} is computed using the two antonym patterns only.

Then, we define an antonym-sensitive, co-occurrence matrix M^{+AN} to be

$$M^{+AN} = M^{SP} - \beta \cdot M^{AP}$$

where β is a weighting parameter.[5] Similarly to M^*, the antonym-sensitive word representation of the ith word is the ith row in M^{+AN}.

Discussion. The case of antonyms presented in this paper is an example of one relation that a pattern based representation model can control. This property can be potentially extended to additional word relations, as long as they can be identified using patterns. Consider, for example, the hypernymy relation (is-a, as in the (*apple,fruit*) pair). This relation can be accurately identified using patterns such as "X *such as* Y" and "X *like* Y" (Hearst, 1992). Consequently, it is likely that a pattern-based model can be adapted to control its predictions with respect to this relation using a method similar to the one we use to control antonym representation. We consider this a strong motivation for a deeper investigation of pattern-based VSMs in future work.

We next turn to empirically evaluate the performance of our model in estimating word similarity.

5 Experimental Setup

5.1 Datasets

Evaluation Dataset. We experiment with the SimLex999 dataset (Hill et al., 2014),[6] consisting of 999 pairs of words. Each pair in this dataset was annotated by roughly 50 human subjects, who were asked to score the similarity between the pair members. SimLex999 has several appealing properties, including its size, part-of-speech diversity, and diversity in the level of concreteness of the participating words.

We follow a 10-fold cross-validation experimental protocol. In each fold, we randomly sample 25% of the SimLex999 word pairs (~250 pairs) and use them as a development set for parameter tuning. We use the remaining 75% of the pairs (~750 pairs) as a test set. We report the average of the results we got in the 10 folds.

Training Corpus. We use an 8G words corpus, constructed using the word2vec script.[7] Through this script we also apply a pre-processing step which employs the word2phrase tool (Mikolov et al., 2013c) to merge common word pairs and triples to expression tokens. Our corpus consists of four datasets: (a) The 2012 and 2013 crawled news articles from the ACL 2014 workshop on statistical machine translation (Bojar et al., 2014);[8] (b) The One Billion Word Benchmark of Chelba et al. (2013);[9] (c) The UMBC corpus (Han et al., 2013);[10] and (d) The September 2014 dump of the English Wikipedia.[11]

5.2 Baselines

We compare our model against six baselines: one that encodes bag-of-words co-occurrence statistics into its features (model 1 below), three NN models that encode the same type of information into their objective function (models 2-4), and two models that go beyond the bag-of-words assumption (models 5-6). Unless stated otherwise, all models are trained on our training corpus.

1. BOW. A simple model where each coordinate corresponds to the co-occurrence count of the represented word with another word in the training corpus. The resulted features are re-weighted according to PPMI. The model's window size parameter is tuned on the development set.[12]

2-3. word2vec. The state-of-the-art *word2vec* toolkit (Mikolov et al., 2013a)[13] offers two word embedding architectures: continuous-bag-of-words (**CBOW**) and **skip-gram**. We follow the recommendations of the word2vec script for setting the parameters of both models, and tune the window size on the development set.[14]

4. GloVe. GloVe (Pennington et al., 2014)[15] is a global log-bilinear regression model for word embedding generation, which trains only on the nonzero elements in a co-occurrence matrix. We use the parameters suggested by the authors, and tune the window size on the development set.[16]

[5] We tune β using a development set (Section 5). Typical values are 7 and 10.

[6] `www.cl.cam.ac.uk/~fh295/simlex.html`

[7] `code.google.com/p/word2vec/source/browse/trunk/demo-train-big-model-v1.sh`

[8] `http://www.statmt.org/wmt14/training-monolingual-news-crawl/`

[9] `http://www.statmt.org/lm-benchmark/1-billion-word-language-modeling-benchmark-r13output.tar.gz`

[10] `http://ebiquity.umbc.edu/redirect/to/resource/id/351/UMBC-webbase-corpus`

[11] `dumps.wikimedia.org/enwiki/latest/enwiki-latest-pages-articles.xml.bz2`

[12] The value 2 is almost constantly selected.

[13] `https://code.google.com/p/word2vec/`

[14] Window size 2 is generally selected for both models.

[15] `nlp.stanford.edu/projects/glove/`

[16] Window size 2 is generally selected.

5. NNSE. The NNSE model (Murphy et al., 2012). As no full implementation of this model is available online, we use the off-the-shelf embeddings available at the authors' website,[17] taking the *full document and dependency* model with 2500 dimensions. Embeddings were computed using a dataset about twice as big as our corpus.

6. Dep. The modified, dependency-based, skip-gram model (Levy and Goldberg, 2014). To generate dependency links, we use the Stanford POS Tagger (Toutanova et al., 2003)[18] and the MALT parser (Nivre et al., 2006).[19] We follow the parameters suggested by the authors.

5.3 Evaluation

For evaluation we follow the standard VSM literature: the score assigned to each pair of words by a model m is the cosine similarity between the vectors induced by m for the participating words. m's quality is evaluated by computing the Spearman correlation coefficient score (ρ) between the ranking derived from m's scores and the one derived from the human scores.

6 Results

Main Result. Table 2 presents our results. Our model outperforms the baselines by a margin of 5.5–16.7% in the Spearman's correlation coefficient (ρ). Note that the capability of our model to control antonym representation has a substantial impact, boosting its performance from $\rho = 0.434$ when the antonym parameter is turned off to $\rho = 0.517$ when it is turned on.

Model Combination. We turn to explore whether our pattern-based model and our best baseline, skip-gram, which implements a bag-of-words approach, can be combined to provide an improved predictive power.

For each pair of words in the test set, we take a linear combination of the cosine similarity score computed using our embeddings and the score computed using the skip-gram (SG) embeddings:

$$f^{+}(w_i, w_j) = \gamma \cdot f_{SP}(w_i, w_j) + (1-\gamma) \cdot f_{SG}(w_i, w_j)$$

In this equation $f_{<m>}(w_i, w_j)$ is the cosine similarity between the vector representations of words w_i and w_j according to model m, and γ is a weighting parameter tuned on the development set (a common value is 0.8).

As shown in Table 2, this combination forms the top performing model on SimLex999, achieving a Spearman's ρ score of 0.563. This score is 4.6% higher than the score of our model, and a 10.1–21.3% improvement compared to the baselines.

Model	Spearman's ρ
GloVe	0.35
BOW	0.423
CBOW	0.43
Dep	0.436
NNSE	0.455
skip-gram	0.462
SP$^{(-)}$	0.434
SP$^{(+)}$	**0.517**
Joint (SP$^{(+)}$, skip-gram)	**0.563**
Average Human Score	0.651

Table 2: Spearman's ρ scores of our SP-based model with the antonym parameter turned on ($SP^{(+)}$) or off ($SP^{(-)}$) and of the baselines described in Section 5.2. *Joint ($SP^{(+)}$, skip-gram)* is an interpolation of the scores produced by *skip-gram* and our $SP^{(+)}$ model. *Average Human Score* is the average correlation of a single annotator with the average score of all annotators, taken from (Hill et al., 2014).

wordsim353 Experiments. The wordsim353 dataset (Finkelstein et al., 2001) is frequently used for evaluating word representations. In order to be compatible with previous work, we experiment with this dataset as well. As our word embeddings are designed to support word similarity rather than relatedness, we focus on the similarity subset of this dataset, according to the division presented in (Agirre et al., 2009).

As noted by (Hill et al., 2014), the word pair scores in both subsets of wordsim353 reflect word association. This is because the two subsets created by (Agirre et al., 2009) keep the original wordsim353 scores, produced by human evaluators that were instructed to score according to association rather than similarity. Consequently, we expect our model to perform worse on this dataset compared to a dataset, such as SimLex999, whose annotators were guided to score word pairs according to similarity.

Contrary to SimLex999, wordsim353 treats antonyms as similar. For example, the similarity score of the (*life,death*) and (*profit,loss*) pairs are 7.88 and 7.63 respectively, on a 0-10 scale. Consequently, we turn the antonym parameter off for this experiment.

Table 3 presents the results. As expected, our

[17] http://www.cs.cmu.edu/~bmurphy/NNSE/
[18] nlp.stanford.edu/software/
[19] http://www.maltparser.org/index.html

Model	Spearman's ρ
GloVe	0.677
Dep	0.712
BOW	0.729
CBOW	0.734
NNSE	0.78
skip-gram	**0.792**
$SP^{(-)}$	0.728
Average Human Score	0.756

Table 3:
Spearman's ρ scores for the similarity portion of wordsim353 (Agirre et al., 2009). $SP^{(-)}$ is our model with the antonym parameter turned off. Other abbreviations are as in Table 2.

Model	Adj.	Nouns	Verbs
GloVe	0.571	0.377	0.163
Dep	0.54	0.449	0.376
BOW	0.548	0.451	0.276
CBOW	0.579	0.48	0.252
NNSE	0.594	0.487	0.318
skip-gram	0.604	**0.501**	0.307
$SP^{(+)}$	**0.663**	0.497	**0.578**

Table 4:
A POS-based analysis of the various models. Numbers are the Spearman's ρ scores of each model on each of the respective portions of SimLex999.

model is not as successful on a dataset that doesn't reflect pure similarity. Yet, it still crosses the $\rho = 0.7$ score, a quite high performance level.

Part-of-Speech Analysis. We next perform a POS-based evaluation of the participating models, using the three portions of the SimLex999: 666 pairs of nouns, 222 pairs of verbs, and 111 pairs of adjectives. Table 4 indicates that our $SP^{(+)}$ model is exceptionally successful in predicting verb and adjective similarity. On verbs, $SP^{(+)}$ obtains a score of $\rho = 0.578$, a 20.2–41.5% improvement over the baselines. On adjectives, $SP^{(+)}$ performs even better ($\rho = 0.663$), an improvement of 5.9–12.3% over the baselines. On nouns, $SP^{(+)}$ is second only to *skip-gram*, though with very small margin (0.497 vs. 0.501), and is outperforming the other baselines by 1–12%. The lower performance of our model on nouns might partially explain its relatively low performance on wordsim353, which is composed exclusively of nouns.

Analysis of Antonyms. We now turn to a qualitative analysis, in order to understand the impact of our modeling decisions on the scores of antonym word pairs. Table 5 presents examples of antonym pairs taken from the SimLex999 dataset, along with their relative ranking among all pairs in the set, as judged by our model ($SP^{(+)}$ with $\beta = 10$ or $SP^{(-)}$ with $\beta = -1$) and by the best

Pair of Words	*SP* +AN	*SP* -AN	*skip-gram*
new - old	1	6	6
narrow - wide	1	7	8
necessary - unnecessary	2	2	9
bottom - top	3	8	10
absence - presence	4	7	9
receive - send	1	9	8
fail - succeed	1	8	6

Table 5:
Examples of antonym pairs and their decile in the similarity ranking of our *SP* model with the antonym parameter turned on (+AN, β=10) or off (-AN, β=-1), and of the skip-gram model, the best baseline. All examples are judged in the lowest decile (1) by SimLex999's annotators.

baseline representation (skip-gram). Each pair of words is assigned a score between 1 and 10 by each model, where a score of M means that the pair is ranked at the M'th decile. The examples in the table are taken from the first (lowest) decile according to SimLex999's human evaluators. The table shows that when the antonym parameter is off, our model generally recognizes antonyms as similar. In contrast, when the parameter is on, ranks of antonyms substantially decrease.

Antonymy as Word Analogy. One of the most notable features of the skip-gram model is that some geometric relations between its vectors translate to semantic relations between the represented words (Mikolov et al., 2013c), e.g.:

$$v_{woman} - v_{man} + v_{king} \approx v_{queen}$$

It is therefore possible that a similar method can be applied to capture antonymy – a useful property that our model was demonstrated to have.

To test this hypothesis, we generated a set of 200 analogy questions of the form "X - Y + Z = ?" where X and Y are antonyms, and Z is a word with an unknown antonym.[20] Example questions include: "*stupid - smart + life = ?*" (*death*) and "*huge - tiny + arrive = ?*" (*leave*). We applied the standard word analogy evaluation (Mikolov et al., 2013c) on this dataset with the skip-gram embeddings, and found that results are quite poor: 3.5% accuracy (compared to an average 56% accuracy this model obtains on a standard word analogy dataset (Mikolov et al., 2013a)). Given these results, the question of whether skip-gram is capa-

[20]Two human annotators selected a list of potential antonym pairs from SimLex999 and wordsim353. We took the intersection of their selections (26 antonym pairs) and randomly generated 200 analogy questions, each containing two antonym pairs. The dataset can be found in `www.cs.huji.ac.il/~roys02/papers/sp_embeddings/antonymy_analogy_questions.zip`

ble of accounting for antonyms remains open.

7 Conclusions

We presented a symmetric pattern based model for word vector representation. On SimLex999, our model is superior to six strong baselines, including the state-of-the-art word2vec skip-gram model by as much as 5.5–16.7% in Spearman's ρ score. We have shown that this gain is largely attributed to the remarkably high performance of our model on verbs, where it outperforms all baselines by 20.2–41.5%. We further demonstrated the adaptability of our model to antonym judgment specifications, and its complementary nature with respect to word2vec.

In future work we intend to extend our pattern-based word representation framework beyond symmetric patterns. As discussed in Section 4, other types of patterns have the potential to further improve the expressive power of word vectors. A particularly interesting challenge is to enhance our pattern-based approach with bag-of-words information, thus enjoying the provable advantages of both frameworks.

Acknowledgments

We would like to thank Elad Eban for his helpful advice. This research was funded (in part) by the Intel Collaborative Research Institute for Computational Intelligence (ICRI-CI) and the Israel Ministry of Science and Technology Center of Knowledge in Machine Learning and Artificial Intelligence (Grant number 3-9243).

References

Eneko Agirre, Enrique Alfonseca, Keith Hall, Jana Kravalova, Marius Pasca, and Aitor Soroa. 2009. A study on similarity and relatedness using distributional and wordnet-based approaches. In *Proc. of HLT-NAACL*.

Marco Baroni, Brian Murphy, Eduard Barbu, and Massimo Poesio. 2010. Strudel: A corpus-based semantic model based on properties and types. *Cognitive Science*.

Marco Baroni, Georgiana Dinu, and Germán Kruszewski. 2014. Don't count, predict! a systematic comparison of context-counting vs. context-predicting semantic vectors. In *Proc. of ACL*.

Yoshua Bengio, Réjean Ducharme, Pascal Vincent, and Christian Jauvin. 2003. A neural probabilistic language model. *JMLR*.

Matthew Berland and Eugene Charniak. 1999. Finding parts in very large corpora. In *Proc. of ACL*.

Ondřej Bojar, Christian Buck, Christian Federmann, Barry Haddow, Philipp Koehn, Christof Monz, Matt Post, and Lucia Specia, editors. 2014. *Proc. of the Ninth Workshop on Statistical Machine Translation*.

Danushka Bollegala, Takanori Maehara, Yuichi Yoshida, and Ken ichi Kawarabayashi. 2015. Learning word representations from relational graphs. In *Proc. of AAAI*.

Kai-wei Chang, Wen-tau Yih, and Christopher Meek. 2013. Multi-Relational Latent Semantic Analysis. In *Proc. of EMNLP*.

Ciprian Chelba, Tomas Mikolov, Mike Schuster, Qi Ge, Thorsten Brants, and Phillipp Koehn. 2013. One billion word benchmark for measuring progress in statistical language modeling. *CoRR*.

Stephen Clark. 2012. Vector space models of lexical meaning. *Handbook of Contemporary Semanticssecond edition*, pages 1–42.

Ronan Collobert and Jason Weston. 2008. A unified architecture for natural language processing: Deep neural networks with multitask learning. In *Proc. of ICML*.

Ronan Collobert, Jason Weston, Léon Bottou, Michael Karlen, Koray Kavukcuoglu, and Pavel Kuksa. 2011. Natural language processing (almost) from scratch. *JMLR*, 12:2493–2537.

Dmitry Davidov and Ari Rappoport. 2006. Efficient unsupervised discovery of word categories using symmetric patterns and high frequency words. In *Proc. of ACL-Coling*.

Dmitry Davidov, Oren Tsur, and Ari Rappoport. 2010. Enhanced sentiment learning using twitter hashtags and smileys. In *Proc. of Coling*.

Paramveer Dhillon, Dean P Foster, and Lyle H Ungar. 2011. Multi-view learning of word embeddings via cca. In *Proc. of NIPS*.

Beate Dorow, Dominic Widdows, Katarina Ling, Jean-Pierre Eckmann, Danilo Sergi, and Elisha Moses. 2005. Using Curvature and Markov Clustering in Graphs for Lexical Acquisition and Word Sense Discrimination.

Katrin Erk. 2012. Vector Space Models of Word Meaning and Phrase Meaning: A Survey. *Language and Linguistics Compass*, 6(10):635–653.

Song Feng, Jun Seok Kang, Polina Kuznetsova, and Yejin Choi. 2013. Connotation lexicon: A dash of sentiment beneath the surface meaning. In *Proc. of ACL*.

Lev Finkelstein, Evgeniy Gabrilovich, Yossi Matias, Ehud Rivlin, Zach Solan, Gadi Wolfman, and Eytan Ruppin. 2001. Placing search in context: The concept revisited. In *Proc. of WWW*.

Lushan Han, Abhay L. Kashyap, Tim Finin, James Mayfield, and Jonathan Weese. 2013. Umbc_ebiquity-core: Semantic textual similarity systems. In *Proc. of *SEM*.

Zellig Harris. 1954. Distributional structure. *Word*.

Marti A. Hearst. 1992. Automatic acquisition of hyponyms from large text corpora. In *Proc. of Coling – Volume 2*.

Felix Hill, Roi Reichart, and Anna Korhonen. 2014. Simlex-999: Evaluating semantic models with (genuine) similarity estimation. *arXiv:1408.3456 [cs.CL]*.

Zornitsa Kozareva, Ellen Riloff, and Eduard Hovy. 2008. Semantic class learning from the web with hyponym pattern linkage graphs. In *Proc. of ACL-HLT*.

Rémi Lebret and Ronan Collobert. 2014. Word embeddings through hellinger pca. In *Proc. of EACL*.

Omer Levy and Yoav Goldberg. 2014. Dependency-based word embeddings. In *Proc. of ACL (Volume 2: Short Papers)*.

Dekang Lin, Shaojun Zhao, Lijuan Qin, and Ming Zhou. 2003. Identifying synonyms among distributionally similar words. In *Proc. of IJCAI*.

Tomas Mikolov, Kai Chen, Greg Corrado, and Jeffrey Dean. 2013a. Efficient estimation of word representations in vector space. *arXiv preprint arXiv:1301.3781*.

Tomas Mikolov, Ilya Sutskever, Kai Chen, Greg S Corrado, and Jeff Dean. 2013b. Distributed representations of words and phrases and their compositionality. In *Proc. of NIPS*.

Tomas Mikolov, Wen-tau Yih, and Geoffrey Zweig. 2013c. Linguistic regularities in continuous space word representations. In *Proc. of NAACL-HLT*.

Andriy Mnih and Geoffrey E Hinton. 2009. A scalable hierarchical distributed language model. In *Proc. of NIPS*.

Andriy Mnih and Koray Kavukcuoglu. 2013. Learning word embeddings efficiently with noise-contrastive estimation. In *Proc. of NIPS*.

Saif M. Mohammad, Bonnie J. Dorr, Graeme Hirst, and Peter D. Turney. 2013. Computing lexical contrast. *Computational Linguistics*, 39(3):555–590.

Brian Murphy, Partha Pratim Talukdar, and Tom Mitchell. 2012. Learning Effective and Interpretable Semantic Models using Non-Negative Sparse Embedding. In *Proc. of Coling*.

Joakim Nivre, Johan Hall, and Jens Nilsson. 2006. Maltparser: A data-driven parser-generator for dependency parsing. In *Proc. of LREC*.

Masataka Ono, Makoto Miwa, and Yutaka Sasaki. 2015. Word embedding-based antonym detection using thesauri and distributional information. In *Proc. of NAACL*.

Jeffrey Pennington, Richard Socher, and Christopher D. Manning. 2014. Glove: Global vectors for word representation. In *Proc. of EMNLP*.

Michael Roth and Sabine Schulte im Walde. 2014. Combining Word Patterns and Discourse Markers for Paradigmatic Relation Classification. In *Proc. of ACL*.

Gerard Salton. 1971. *The SMART Retrieval System: Experiments in Automatic Document Processing*. Prentice-Hall, Inc., Upper Saddle River, NJ, USA.

Sabine Schulte im Walde and Maximilian Koper. 2013. Pattern-based distinction of paradigmatic relations for german nouns, verbs, adjectives. *Language Processing and Knowledge in the Web*, pages 184–198.

Roy Schwartz, Oren Tsur, Ari Rappoport, and Moshe Koppel. 2013. Authorship attribution of micro-messages. In *Proc. of EMNLP*.

Roy Schwartz, Roi Reichart, and Ari Rappoport. 2014. Minimally supervised classification to semantic categories using automatically acquired symmetric patterns. In *Proc. of Coling*.

Kristina Toutanova, Dan Klein, Christopher D Manning, and Yoram Singer. 2003. Feature-rich part-of-speech tagging with a cyclic dependency network. In *Proc. of NAACL*.

Oren Tsur, Dmitry Davidov, and Ari Rappoport. 2010. Icwsm–a great catchy name: Semi-supervised recognition of sarcastic sentences in online product reviews. In *Proc. of ICWSM*.

Peter D. Turney, Patrick Pantel, et al. 2010. From frequency to meaning: Vector space models of semantics. *Journal of Artificial Intelligence research*.

Peter D. Turney. 2008. A uniform approach to analogies, synonyms, antonyms, and associations. In *Proc. of Coling*.

Peter D. Turney. 2012. Domain and function: A dual-space model of semantic relations and compositions. *Journal of Artificial Intelligence Research*, pages 533–585.

Wenbo Wang, Christopher Thomas, Amit Sheth, and Victor Chan. 2010. Pattern-based synonym and antonym extraction. In *Proc. of ACM*.

Dominic Widdows and Beate Dorow. 2002. A graph model for unsupervised lexical acquisition. In *Proc. of Coling*.

Wen-tau Yih, Geoffrey Zweig, and John C. Platt. 2012. Polarity inducing latent semantic analysis. In *Proc. of EMNLP-CoNLL*.

Task-Oriented Learning of Word Embeddings for Semantic Relation Classification

Kazuma Hashimoto[†], **Pontus Stenetorp**[‡], **Makoto Miwa**[§], **and Yoshimasa Tsuruoka**[†]
†The University of Tokyo, 3-7-1 Hongo, Bunkyo-ku, Tokyo, Japan
{hassy,tsuruoka}@logos.t.u-tokyo.ac.jp
‡University College London, London, United Kingdom
pontus@stenetorp.se
§Toyota Technological Institute, 2-12-1 Hisakata, Tempaku-ku, Nagoya, Japan
makoto-miwa@toyota-ti.ac.jp

Abstract

We present a novel learning method for word embeddings designed for relation classification. Our word embeddings are trained by predicting words between noun pairs using lexical relation-specific features on a large unlabeled corpus. This allows us to explicitly incorporate relation-specific information into the word embeddings. The learned word embeddings are then used to construct feature vectors for a relation classification model. On a well-established semantic relation classification task, our method significantly outperforms a baseline based on a previously introduced word embedding method, and compares favorably to previous state-of-the-art models that use syntactic information or manually constructed external resources.

1 Introduction

Automatic classification of semantic relations has a variety of applications, such as information extraction and the construction of semantic networks (Girju et al., 2007; Hendrickx et al., 2010). A traditional approach to relation classification is to train classifiers using various kinds of features with class labels annotated by humans. Carefully crafted features derived from lexical, syntactic, and semantic resources play a significant role in achieving high accuracy for semantic relation classification (Rink and Harabagiu, 2010).

In recent years there has been an increasing interest in using *word embeddings* as an alternative to traditional hand-crafted features. Word embeddings are represented as real-valued vectors and capture syntactic and semantic similarity between words. For example, *word2vec*[1] (Mikolov et al., 2013b) is a well-established tool for learning word embeddings. Although word2vec has successfully been used to learn word embeddings, these kinds of word embeddings capture only co-occurrence relationships between words (Levy and Goldberg, 2014). While simply adding word embeddings trained using window-based contexts as additional features to existing systems has proven valuable (Turian et al., 2010), more recent studies have focused on how to tune and enhance word embeddings for specific tasks (Bansal et al., 2014; Boros et al., 2014; Chen et al., 2014; Guo et al., 2014; Nguyen and Grishman, 2014) and we continue this line of research for the task of relation classification.

In this work we present a learning method for word embeddings specifically designed to be useful for relation classification. The overview of our system and the embedding learning process are shown in Figure 1. First we train word embeddings by predicting each of the words between noun pairs using lexical relation-specific features on a large unlabeled corpus. We then use the word embeddings to construct lexical feature vectors for relation classification. Lastly, the feature vectors are used to train a relation classification model.

We evaluate our method on a well-established semantic relation classification task and compare it to a baseline based on word2vec embeddings and previous state-of-the-art models that rely on either manually crafted features, syntactic parses or external semantic resources. Our method significantly outperforms the word2vec-based baseline, and compares favorably with previous state-of-the-art models, despite relying only on lexi-

[1] https://code.google.com/p/word2vec/.

Proceedings of the 19th Conference on Computational Language Learning, pages 268–278,
Beijing, China, July 30-31, 2015.

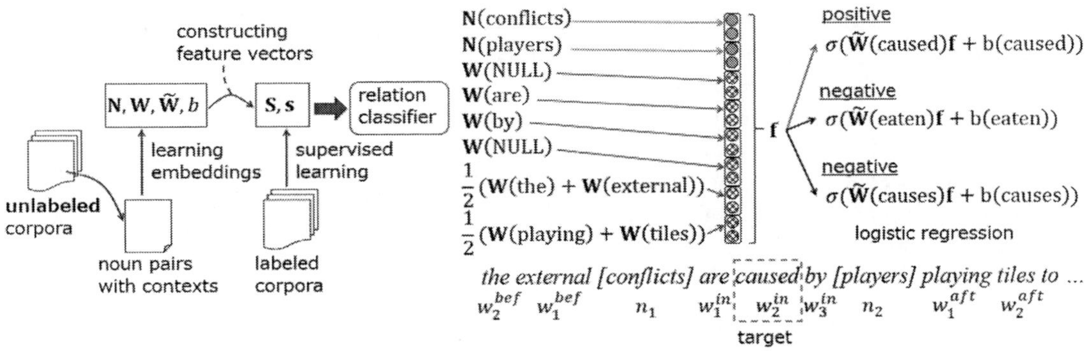

(a) Overall system

(b) Learning embeddings for relation classification

Figure 1: The overview of our system (a) and the embedding learning method (b). In the example sentence, each of *are*, *caused*, and *by* is treated as a target word to be predicted during training.

cal level features and no external annotated resources. Furthermore, our qualitative analysis of the learned embeddings shows that n-grams of our embeddings capture salient syntactic patterns similar to semantic relation types.

2 Related Work

A traditional approach to relation classification is to train classifiers in a supervised fashion using a variety of features. These features include lexical bag-of-words features and features based on syntactic parse trees. For syntactic parse trees, the paths between the target entities on constituency and dependency trees have been demonstrated to be useful (Bunescu and Mooney, 2005; Zhang et al., 2006). On the shared task introduced by Hendrickx et al. (2010), Rink and Harabagiu (2010) achieved the best score using a variety of hand-crafted features which were then used to train a Support Vector Machine (SVM).

Recently, word embeddings have become popular as an alternative to hand-crafted features (Collobert et al., 2011). However, one of the limitations is that word embeddings are usually learned by predicting a target word in its context, leading to only local co-occurrence information being captured (Levy and Goldberg, 2014). Thus, several recent studies have focused on overcoming this limitation. Le and Mikolov (2014) integrated paragraph information into a word2vec-based model, which allowed them to capture paragraph-level information. For dependency parsing, Bansal et al. (2014) and Chen et al. (2014) found ways to improve performance by integrating dependency-based context information into their embeddings. Bansal et al. (2014) trained embeddings by defining parent and child nodes in dependency trees as contexts. Chen et al. (2014) introduced the concept of feature embeddings induced by parsing a large unannotated corpus and then learning embeddings for the manually crafted features. For information extraction, Boros et al. (2014) trained word embeddings relevant for event role extraction, and Nguyen and Grishman (2014) employed word embeddings for domain adaptation of relation extraction. Another kind of task-specific word embeddings was proposed by Tang et al. (2014), which used sentiment labels on tweets to adapt word embeddings for a sentiment analysis tasks. However, such an approach is only feasible when a large amount of labeled data is available.

3 Relation Classification Using Word Embedding-based Features

We propose a novel method for learning word embeddings designed for relation classification. The word embeddings are trained by *predicting each word between noun pairs*, given the corresponding low-level features for relation classification. In general, to classify relations between pairs of nouns the most important features come from the pairs themselves and the words between and around the pairs (Hendrickx et al., 2010). For example, in the sentence in Figure 1 (b) there is a *cause-effect* relationship between the two nouns *conflicts* and *players*. To classify the relation, the most common features are the noun pair (*conflicts, players*), the words between the noun pair (*are, caused, by*), the words before the pair (*the, external*), and the words after the pair (*playing, tiles, to, ...*). As shown by Rink and Harabagiu (2010), the words between the noun pairs are the most effective among these features. Our main idea is to treat the most important features (the words between the noun pairs) as the targets to be predicted and other lexical features (noun pairs, words outside them) as their contexts. Due to this, we expect our embeddings to capture relevant features for relation classification better than previous models which only use window-based contexts.

In this section we first describe the learning process for the word embeddings, focusing on lexical features for relation classification (Figure 1 (b)). We then propose a simple and powerful technique to construct features which serve as input for a softmax classifier. The overview of our proposed system is shown in Figure 1 (a).

3.1 Learning Word Embeddings

Assume that there is a noun pair $\mathbf{n} = (n_1, n_2)$ in a sentence with M_{in} words between the pair and M_{out} words before and after the pair:

- $\mathbf{w}_{in} = (w_1^{in}, \ldots, w_{M_{in}}^{in})$,
- $\mathbf{w}_{bef} = (w_1^{bef}, \ldots, w_{M_{out}}^{bef})$, and
- $\mathbf{w}_{aft} = (w_1^{aft}, \ldots, w_{M_{out}}^{aft})$.

Our method predicts each target word $w_i^{in} \in \mathbf{w}_{in}$ using three kinds of information: $\mathbf{n}$, words around w_i^{in} in $\mathbf{w}_{in}$, and words in $\mathbf{w}_{bef}$ and $\mathbf{w}_{aft}$. Words are embedded in a d-dimensional vector space and we refer to these vectors as word embeddings. To discriminate between words in $\mathbf{n}$ from those in $\mathbf{w}_{in}$, $\mathbf{w}_{bef}$, and $\mathbf{w}_{aft}$, we have two sets of word embeddings: $\mathbf{N} \in \mathbb{R}^{d \times |\mathcal{N}|}$ and $\mathbf{W} \in \mathbb{R}^{d \times |\mathcal{W}|}$. $\mathcal{W}$ is a set of words and $\mathcal{N}$ is also a set of words but contains only nouns. Hence, the word *cause* has two embeddings: one in $\mathbf{N}$ and another in $\mathbf{W}$. In general *cause* is used as a noun and a verb, and thus we expect the noun embeddings to capture the meanings focusing on their noun usage. This is inspired by some recent work on word representations that explicitly assigns an independent representation for each word usage according to its part-of-speech tag (Baroni and Zamparelli, 2010; Grefenstette and Sadrzadeh, 2011; Hashimoto et al., 2013; Hashimoto et al., 2014; Kartsaklis and Sadrzadeh, 2013).

A feature vector $\mathbf{f} \in \mathbb{R}^{2d(2+c) \times 1}$ is constructed to predict w_i^{in} by concatenating word embeddings:

$$\mathbf{f} = [\mathbf{N}(n_1); \mathbf{N}(n_2); \mathbf{W}(w_{i-1}^{in}); \ldots; \mathbf{W}(w_{i-c}^{in}); \mathbf{W}(w_{i+1}^{in}); \ldots; \mathbf{W}(w_{i+c}^{in}); \frac{1}{M_{out}} \sum_{j=1}^{M_{out}} \mathbf{W}(w_j^{bef}); \frac{1}{M_{out}} \sum_{j=1}^{M_{out}} \mathbf{W}(w_j^{aft})] . \quad (1)$$

$\mathbf{N}(\cdot)$ and $\mathbf{W}(\cdot) \in \mathbb{R}^{d \times 1}$ corresponds to each word and c is the context size. A special *NULL* token is used if $i-j$ is smaller than 1 or $i+j$ is larger than M_{in} for each $j \in \{1, 2, \ldots, c\}$.

Our method then estimates a conditional probability $p(w|\mathbf{f})$ that the target word is a word w given the feature vector $\mathbf{f}$, using a logistic regression model:

$$p(w|\mathbf{f}) = \sigma(\tilde{\mathbf{W}}(w) \cdot \mathbf{f} + b(w)) , \quad (2)$$

where $\tilde{\mathbf{W}}(w) \in \mathbb{R}^{2d(2+c) \times 1}$ is a weight vector for w, $b(w) \in \mathbb{R}$ is a bias for w, and $\sigma(x) = \frac{1}{1+e^{-x}}$ is the logistic function. Each column vector in $\tilde{\mathbf{W}} \in \mathbb{R}^{2d(c+1) \times |\mathcal{W}|}$ corresponds to a word. That is, we assign a logistic regression model for each word, and we can train the embeddings using the one-versus-rest approach to make $p(w_i^{in}|\mathbf{f})$ larger than $p(w'|\mathbf{f})$ for $w' \neq w_i^{in}$. However, naively optimizing the parameters of those logistic regression models would lead to prohibitive computational cost since it grows linearly with the size of the vocabulary.

When training we employ several procedures introduced by Mikolov et al. (2013b), namely, *negative sampling*, a modified unigram noise distribution and *subsampling*. For negative sampling the model parameters $\mathbf{N}$, $\mathbf{W}$, $\tilde{\mathbf{W}}$, and b are learned by maximizing the objective function $J_{unlabeled}$:

$$\sum_{\mathbf{n}} \sum_{i=1}^{M_{in}} \left(\log(p(w_i^{in}|\mathbf{f})) + \sum_{j=1}^{k} \log(1 - p(w'_j|\mathbf{f})) \right) , \quad (3)$$

where w'_j is a word randomly drawn from the unigram noise distribution weighted by an exponent of 0.75. Maximizing $J_{unlabeled}$ means that our method can discriminate between each target word and k noise words given the target word's context. This approach is much less computationally expensive than the one-versus-rest approach and has proven effective in learning word embeddings.

To reduce redundancy during training we use subsampling. A training sample, whose target word is w, is discarded with the probability $P_d(w) = 1 - \sqrt{\frac{t}{p(w)}}$, where t is a threshold which is set to 10^{-5} and $p(w)$ is a probability corresponding to the frequency of w in the training corpus. The more frequent a target word is, the more likely it is to be discarded. To further emphasize infrequent words, we apply the subsampling approach not only to target words, but also to noun pairs; concretely, by drawing two random numbers r_1 and r_2, a training sample whose noun pair is (n_1, n_2) is discarded if $P_d(n_1)$ is larger than r_1 or $P_d(n_2)$ is larger than r_2.

Since the feature vector $\mathbf{f}$ is constructed as defined in Eq. (1), at each training step, $\tilde{\mathbf{W}}(w)$ is updated based on information about what pair of nouns surrounds w, what word n-grams appear in a small window around w, and what words appear outside the noun pair. Hence, the weight vector $\tilde{\mathbf{W}}(w)$ captures rich information regarding the target word w.

3.2 Constructing Feature Vectors

Once the word embeddings are trained, we can use them for relation classification. Given a noun pair $\mathbf{n} = (n_1, n_2)$ with its context words $\mathbf{w}_{in}$, $\mathbf{w}_{bef}$, and $\mathbf{w}_{aft}$, we construct a feature vector to classify the relation between n_1 and n_2 by concatenating three kinds of feature vectors:

$\mathbf{g}_{\text{n}}$ the word embeddings of the noun pair,

$\mathbf{g}_{\text{in}}$ the averaged n-gram embeddings between the pair, and

$\mathbf{g}_{\text{out}}$ the concatenation of the averaged word embeddings in $\mathbf{w}_{bef}$ and $\mathbf{w}_{aft}$.

The feature vector $\mathbf{g}_{\text{n}} \in \mathbb{R}^{2d \times 1}$ is the concatenation of $\mathbf{N}(n_1)$ and $\mathbf{N}(n_2)$:

$$\mathbf{g}_{\text{n}} = [\mathbf{N}(n_1); \mathbf{N}(n_2)] \,. \tag{4}$$

Words between the noun pair contribute to classifying the relation, and one of the most common ways to incorporate an arbitrary number of words is treating them as a bag of words. However, word order information is lost for bag-of-words features such as averaged word embeddings. To incorporate the word order information, we first define n-gram embeddings $\mathbf{h}_i \in \mathbb{R}^{4d(1+c)\times 1}$ between the noun pair:

$$\begin{aligned} \mathbf{h}_i = [&\mathbf{W}(w^{in}_{i-1}); \ldots; \mathbf{W}(w^{in}_{i-c}); \\ &\mathbf{W}(w^{in}_{i+1}); \ldots; \mathbf{W}(w^{in}_{i+c}); \tilde{\mathbf{W}}(w^{in}_i)] \,. \end{aligned} \tag{5}$$

Note that $\tilde{\mathbf{W}}$ can also be used and that the value used for n is $(2c+1)$. As described in Section 3.1, $\tilde{\mathbf{W}}$ captures meaningful information about each word and after the first embedding learning step we can treat the embeddings in $\tilde{\mathbf{W}}$ as features for the words. Mnih and Kavukcuoglu (2013) have demonstrated that using embeddings like those in $\tilde{\mathbf{W}}$ is useful in representing the words. We then compute the feature vector $\mathbf{g}_{\text{in}}$ by averaging $\mathbf{h}_i$:

$$\mathbf{g}_{\text{in}} = \frac{1}{M_{in}} \sum_{i=1}^{M_{in}} \mathbf{h}_i \,. \tag{6}$$

We use the averaging approach since M_{in} depends on each instance. The feature vector $\mathbf{g}_{\text{in}}$ allows us to represent word sequences of arbitrary lengths as fixed-length feature vectors using the simple operations: concatenation and averaging.

The words before and after the noun pair are sometimes important in classifying the relation. For example, in the phrase "pour n_1 into n_2", the word *pour* should be helpful in classifying the relation. As with Eq. (1), we use the concatenation of the averaged word embeddings of words before and after the noun pair to compute the feature vector $\mathbf{g}_{\text{out}} \in \mathbb{R}^{2d\times 1}$:

$$\mathbf{g}_{\text{out}} = \frac{1}{M_{out}} [\sum_{j=1}^{M_{out}} \mathbf{W}(w^{bef}_j); \sum_{j=1}^{M_{out}} \mathbf{W}(w^{aft}_j)] \,. \tag{7}$$

As described above, the overall feature vector $\mathbf{e} \in \mathbb{R}^{4d(2+c)\times 1}$ is constructed by concatenating $\mathbf{g}_{\text{n}}$, $\mathbf{g}_{\text{in}}$, and $\mathbf{g}_{\text{out}}$. We would like to emphasize that we only use simple operations: averaging and concatenating the learned word embeddings. The feature vector $\mathbf{e}$ is then used as input for a softmax classifier, without any complex transformation such as matrix multiplication with non-linear functions.

3.3 Supervised Learning

Given a relation classification task we train a softmax classifier using the feature vector $\mathbf{e}$ described in Section 3.2. For each k-th training sample with a corresponding label l_k among L predefined labels, we compute a conditional probability given its feature vector $\mathbf{e}_k$:

$$p(l_k|\mathbf{e}_k) = \frac{\exp(\mathbf{o}(l_k))}{\sum_{i=1}^{L}\exp(\mathbf{o}(i))}, \quad (8)$$

where $\mathbf{o} \in \mathbb{R}^{L\times 1}$ is defined as $\mathbf{o} = \mathbf{S}\mathbf{e}_k + \mathbf{s}$, and $\mathbf{S} \in \mathbb{R}^{L\times 4d(2+c)}$ and $\mathbf{s} \in \mathbb{R}^{L\times 1}$ are the softmax parameters. $\mathbf{o}(i)$ is the i-th element of $\mathbf{o}$. We then define the objective function as:

$$J_{labeled} = \sum_{k=1}^{K} \log(p(l_k|\mathbf{e}_k)) - \frac{\lambda}{2}\|\theta\|^2 . \quad (9)$$

K is the number of training samples and λ controls the L-2 regularization. $\theta = (\mathbf{N}, \mathbf{W}, \tilde{\mathbf{W}}, \mathbf{S}, \mathbf{s})$ is the set of parameters and $J_{labeled}$ is maximized using AdaGrad (Duchi et al., 2011). We have found that *dropout* (Hinton et al., 2012) is helpful in preventing our model from overfitting. Concretely, elements in $\mathbf{e}$ are randomly omitted with a probability of 0.5 at each training step. Recently dropout has been applied to deep neural network models for natural language processing tasks and proven effective (Irsoy and Cardie, 2014; Paulus et al., 2014).

In what follows, we refer to the above method as **RelEmb**. While RelEmb uses only low-level features, a variety of useful features have been proposed for relation classification. Among them, we use dependency path features (Bunescu and Mooney, 2005) based on the untyped binary dependencies of the Stanford parser to find the shortest path between target nouns. The dependency path features are computed by averaging word embeddings from $\mathbf{W}$ on the shortest path, and are then concatenated to the feature vector $\mathbf{e}$. Furthermore, we directly incorporate semantic information using word-level semantic features from Named Entity (NE) tags and WordNet hypernyms, as used in previous work (Rink and Harabagiu, 2010; Socher et al., 2012; Yu et al., 2014). We refer to this extended method as **RelEmb$_{\text{FULL}}$**. Concretely, RelEmb$_{\text{FULL}}$ uses the same binary features as in Socher et al. (2012). The features come from NE tags and WordNet hypernym tags of target nouns provided by a sense tagger (Ciaramita and Altun, 2006).

4 Experimental Settings

4.1 Training Data

For pre-training we used a snapshot of the English Wikipedia[2] from November 2013. First, we extracted 80 million sentences from the original Wikipedia file, and then used *Enju*[3] (Miyao and Tsujii, 2008) to automatically assign part-of-speech (POS) tags. From the POS tags we used *NN*, *NNS*, *NNP*, or *NNPS* to locate noun pairs in the corpus. We then collected training data by listing pairs of nouns and the words between, before, and after the noun pairs. A noun pair was omitted if the number of words between the pair was larger than 10 and we consequently collected 1.4 billion pairs of nouns and their contexts [4]. We used the 300,000 most frequent words and the 300,000 most frequent nouns and treated out-of-vocabulary words as a special *UNK* token.

4.2 Initialization and Optimization

We initialized the embedding matrices $\mathbf{N}$ and $\mathbf{W}$ with zero-mean gaussian noise with a variance of $\frac{1}{d}$. $\tilde{\mathbf{W}}$ and b were zero-initialized. The model parameters were optimized by maximizing the objective function in Eq. (3) using stochastic gradient ascent. The learning rate was set to α and linearly decreased to 0 during training, as described in Mikolov et al. (2013a). The hyperparameters are the embedding dimensionality d, the context size c, the number of negative samples k, the initial learning rate α, and M_{out}, the number of words outside the noun pairs. For hyperparameter tuning, we first fixed α to 0.025 and M_{out} to 5, and then set d to $\{50,\ 100,\ 300\}$, c to $\{1,\ 2,\ 3\}$, and k to $\{5,\ 15,\ 25\}$.

At the supervised learning step, we initialized $\mathbf{S}$ and $\mathbf{s}$ with zeros. The hyperparameters, the learning rate for AdaGrad, λ, M_{out}, and the number of iterations, were determined via 10-fold cross validation on the training set for each setting. Note that M_{out} can be tuned at the supervised learning step, adapting to a specific dataset.

5 Evaluation

5.1 Evaluation Dataset

We evaluated our method on the SemEval 2010 Task 8 data set[5] (Hendrickx et al., 2010), which involves predicting the semantic relations between

[2] http://dumps.wikimedia.org/enwiki/.

[3] Despite Enju being a syntactic parser we only use the POS tagger component. The accuracy of the POS tagger is about 97.2% on the WSJ corpus.

[4] The training data, the training code, and the learned model parameters used in this paper are publicly available at http://www.logos.t.u-tokyo.ac.jp/~hassy/publications/conll2015/

[5] http://docs.google.com/View?docid=dfvxd49s_36c28v9pmw.

noun pairs in their contexts. The dataset, containing 8,000 training and 2,717 test samples, defines nine classes (*Cause-Effect, Entity-Origin, etc.*) for ordered relations and one class (*Other*) for other relations. Thus, the task can be treated as a 19-class classification task. Two examples from the training set are shown below.

(a) Financial $[\text{stress}]_{E_1}$ is one of the main causes of $[\text{divorce}]_{E_2}$

(b) The $[\text{burst}]_{E_1}$ has been caused by water hammer $[\text{pressure}]_{E_2}$

Training example (a) is classified as *Cause-Effect*(E_1, E_2) which denotes that E_2 is an effect caused by E_1, while training example (b) is classified as *Cause-Effect*(E_2, E_1) which is the inverse of *Cause-Effect*(E_1, E_2). We report the official macro-averaged F1 scores and accuracy.

5.2 Models

To empirically investigate the performance of our proposed method we compared it to several baselines and previously proposed models.

5.2.1 Random and word2vec Initialization

Rand-Init. The first baseline is RelEmb itself, but without applying the learning method on the unlabeled corpus. In other words, we train the softmax classifier from Section 3.3 on the labeled training data with randomly initialized model parameters.

W2V-Init. The second baseline is RelEmb using word embeddings learned by word2vec. More specifically, we initialize the embedding matrices $\mathbf{N}$ and $\mathbf{W}$ with the word2vec embeddings. Related to our method, word2vec has a set of weight vectors similar to $\tilde{\mathbf{W}}$ when trained with negative sampling and we use these weight vectors as a replacement for $\tilde{\mathbf{W}}$. We trained the word2vec embeddings using the *CBOW* model with subsampling on the full Wikipedia corpus. As with our experimental settings, we fix the learning rate to 0.025, and investigate several hyperparameter settings. For hyperparameter tuning we set the embedding dimensionality d to $\{50, 100, 300\}$, the context size c to $\{1, 3, 9\}$, and the number of negative samples k to $\{5, 15, 25\}$.

5.2.2 SVM-Based Systems

A simple approach to the relation classification task is to use SVMs with standard binary bag-of-words features. The bag-of-words features included the noun pairs and words between, before, and after the pairs, and we used LIBLINEAR[6] as our classifier.

5.2.3 Neural Network Models

Socher et al. (2012) used Recursive Neural Network (RNN) models to classify the relations. Subsequently, Ebrahimi and Dou (2015) and Hashimoto et al. (2013) proposed RNN models to better handle the relations. These methods rely on syntactic parse trees.

Yu et al. (2014) introduced their novel Factor-based Compositional Model (FCM) and presented results from several model variants, the best performing being FCM_{EMB} and FCM_{FULL}. The former only uses word embedding information and the latter relies on dependency paths and NE features, in addition to word embeddings.

Zeng et al. (2014) used a Convolutional Neural Network (CNN) with WordNet hypernyms. Noteworthy in relation to the RNN-based methods, the CNN model does not rely on parse trees. More recently, dos Santos et al. (2015) have introduced CR-CNN by extending the CNN model and achieved the best result to date. The key point of CR-CNN is that it improves the classification score by omitting the noisy class "Other" in the dataset described in Section 5.1. We call CR-CNN using the "Other" class $\text{CR-CNN}_{\text{Other}}$ and CR-CNN omitting the class $\text{CR-CNN}_{\text{Best}}$.

5.3 Results and Discussion

The scores on the test set for SemEval 2010 Task 8 are shown in Table 1. RelEmb achieves 82.8% of F1 which is better than those of almost all models compared and comparable to that of the previous state of the art, except for $\text{CR-CNN}_{\text{Best}}$. Note that RelEmb does not rely on external semantic features and syntactic parse features[7]. Furthermore, $\text{RelEmb}_{\text{FULL}}$ achieves 83.5% of F1. We calculated a confidence interval (82.0, 84.9) ($p < 0.05$) using bootstrap resampling (Noreen, 1989).

5.3.1 Comparison with the Baselines

RelEmb significantly outperforms not only the Rand-Init baseline, but also the W2V-Init baseline.

[6]http://www.csie.ntu.edu.tw/~cjlin/liblinear/.

[7]While we use a POS tagger to locate noun pairs, RelEmb does not explicitly use POS features at the supervised learning step.

	Features for classifiers	F1 / ACC (%)
RelEmb$_{\mathrm{FULL}}$	embeddings, dependency paths, WordNet, NE	83.5 / 79.9
RelEmb	embeddings	82.8 / 78.9
RelEmb (W2V-Init)	embeddings	81.8 / 77.7
RelEmb (Rand-Init)	embeddings	78.2 / 73.5
SVM	bag of words	76.5 / 72.0
SVM (Rink and Harabagiu, 2010)	bag of words, POS, dependency paths, WordNet, paraphrases, TextRunner, Google n-grams, etc.	82.2 / 77.9
CR-CNN$_{\mathrm{Best}}$ (dos Santos et al., 2015)	embeddings, word position embeddings	84.1 / n/a
FCM$_{\mathrm{FULL}}$ (Yu et al., 2014)	embeddings, dependency paths, NE	83.0 / n/a
CR-CNN$_{\mathrm{Other}}$ (dos Santos et al., 2015)	embeddings, word position embeddings	82.7 / n/a
CRNN (Ebrahimi and Dou, 2015)	embeddings, parse trees, WordNet, NE, POS	82.7 / n/a
CNN (Zeng et al., 2014)	embeddings, WordNet	82.7 / n/a
MVRNN (Socher et al., 2012)	embeddings, parse trees, WordNet, NE, POS	82.4 / n/a
FCM$_{\mathrm{EMB}}$ (Yu et al., 2014)	embeddings	80.6 / n/a
RNN (Hashimoto et al., 2013)	embeddings, parse trees, phrase categories, etc.	79.4 / n/a

Table 1: Scores on the test set for SemEval 2010 Task 8.

These results show that our task-specific word embeddings are more useful than those trained using window-based contexts. A point that we would like to emphasize is that the baselines are unexpectedly strong. As was noted by Wang and Manning (2012), we should carefully implement strong baselines and see whether complex models can outperform these baselines.

5.3.2 Comparison with SVM-Based Systems

RelEmb performs much better than the bag-of-words-based SVM. This is not surprising given that we use a large unannotated corpus and embeddings with a large number of parameters. RelEmb also outperforms the SVM system of Rink and Harabagiu (2010), which demonstrates the effectiveness of our task-specific word embeddings, despite our only requirement being a large unannotated corpus and a POS tagger.

5.3.3 Comparison with Neural Network Models

RelEmb outperforms the RNN models. In our preliminary experiments, we have found some undesirable parse trees when computing vector representations using RNN-based models and such parsing errors might hamper the performance of the RNN models.

FCM$_{\mathrm{FULL}}$, which relies on dependency paths and NE features, achieves a better score than that of REIEmb. Without such features, RelEmb outperforms FCM$_{\mathrm{EMB}}$ by a large margin. By incorporating external resources, RelEmb$_{\mathrm{FULL}}$ outperforms FCM$_{\mathrm{FULL}}$.

RelEmb compares favorably to CR-CNN$_{\mathrm{Other}}$, despite our method being less computationally expensive than CR-CNN$_{\mathrm{Other}}$. When classifying an instance, the number of the floating number multiplications is $4d(2 + c)L$ in our method since our method requires only one matrix-vector product for the softmax classifier as described in Section 3.3. c is the window size, d is the word embedding dimensionality, and L is the number of the classes. In CR-CNN$_{\mathrm{Other}}$, the number is $(Dc(d + 2d')N + DL)$, where D is the dimensionality of the convolution layer, d' is the position embedding dimensionality, and N is the average length of the input sentences. Here, we omit the cost of the hyperbolic tangent function in CR-CNN$_{\mathrm{Other}}$ for simplicity. Using the best hyperparameter settings, the number is roughly 3.8×10^4 in our method, and 1.6×10^7 in CR-CNN$_{\mathrm{Other}}$ assuming N is 10. dos Santos et al. (2015) also boosted the score of CR-CNN$_{\mathrm{Other}}$ by omitting the noisy class "Other" by a ranking-based classifier, and achieved the best score (CR-CNN$_{\mathrm{Best}}$). Our results may also be improved by using the same technique, but the technique is dataset-dependent, so we did not incorporate the technique.

5.4 Analysis on Training Settings

We perform analysis of the training procedure focusing on RelEmb.

5.4.1 Effects of Tuning Hyperparameters

In Tables 2 and 3, we show how tuning the hyperparameters of our method and word2vec affects

c	d	$k = 5$	$k = 15$	$k = 25$
1	50	80.5	81.0	80.9
	100	80.9	81.3	81.2
2	50	80.9	81.3	81.3
	100	81.3	81.6	81.7
3	50	81.0	81.0	81.5
	100	81.3	81.9	**82.2**
	300	-	-	82.0

Table 2: Cross-validation results for RelEmb.

c	d	$k = 5$	$k = 15$	$k = 25$
1	50	80.5	80.7	80.9
	100	81.1	81.2	81.0
	300	81.2	**81.3**	81.2
3	50	80.4	80.7	80.8
	100	81.0	81.0	80.9
9	50	80.0	79.8	80.2
	100	80.3	80.4	80.1

Table 3: Cross-validation results for the W2V-Init.

the classification results using 10-fold cross validation on the training set. The same split is used for each setting, so all results are comparable to each other. The best settings for the cross validation are used to produce the results reported in Table 1.

Table 2 shows F1 scores obtained by RelEmb. The results for $d = 50, 100$ show that RelEmb benefits from relatively large context sizes. The n-gram embeddings in RelEmb capture richer information by setting c to 3 compared to setting c to 1. Relatively large numbers of negative samples also slightly boost the scores. As opposed to these trends, the score does not improve using $d = 300$. We use the best setting ($c = 3$, $d = 100$, $k = 25$) for the remaining analysis. We note that RelEmb$_{\text{FULL}}$ achieves an F1-score of 82.5.

We also performed similar experiments for the W2V-Init baseline, and the results are shown in Table 3. In this case, the number of negative samples does not affect the scores, and the best score is achieved by $c = 1$. As discussed in Bansal et al. (2014), the small context size captures the syntactic similarity between words rather than the topical similarity. This result indicates that syntactic similarity is more important than topical similarity for this task. Compared to the word2vec embeddings, our embeddings capture not only local context information using word order, but also long-range co-occurrence information by being tailored for the specific task.

$\mathbf{g}_{\text{n}}$	$\mathbf{g}_{\text{in}}$	$\mathbf{g}'_{\text{in}}$	$\mathbf{g}_{\text{n}}, \mathbf{g}_{\text{in}}$	$\mathbf{g}_{\text{n}}, \mathbf{g}_{\text{in}}, \mathbf{g}_{\text{out}}$
61.8	70.2	68.2	81.1	82.2

Table 4: Cross-validation results for ablation tests.

Method	Score
RelEmb **N**	0.690
RelEmb **W**	0.599
W2V-Init	0.687

Table 5: Evaluation on the WordSim-353 dataset.

5.4.2 Ablation Tests

As described in Section 3.2, we concatenate three kinds of feature vectors, $\mathbf{g}_{\text{n}}$, $\mathbf{g}_{\text{in}}$, and $\mathbf{g}_{\text{out}}$, for supervised learning. Table 4 shows classification scores for ablation tests using 10-fold cross validation. We also provide a score using a simplified version of $\mathbf{g}_{\text{in}}$, where the feature vector $\mathbf{g}'_{\text{in}}$ is computed by averaging the word embeddings $[\mathbf{W}(w_i^{in}); \tilde{\mathbf{W}}(w_i^{in})]$ of the words between the noun pairs. This feature vector $\mathbf{g}'_{\text{in}}$ then serves as a bag-of-words feature.

Table 4 clearly shows that the averaged n-gram embeddings contribute the most to the semantic relation classification performance. The difference between the scores of $\mathbf{g}_{\text{in}}$ and $\mathbf{g}'_{\text{in}}$ shows the effectiveness of our averaged n-gram embeddings.

5.4.3 Effects of Dropout

At the supervised learning step we use dropout to regularize our model. Without dropout, our performance drops from 82.2% to 81.3% of F1 on the training set using 10-fold cross validation.

5.4.4 Performance on a Word Similarity Task

As described in Section 3.1, we have the noun-specific embeddings $\mathbf{N}$ as well as the standard word embeddings $\mathbf{W}$. We evaluated the learned embeddings using a word-level semantic evaluation task called *WordSim-353* (Finkelstein et al., 2001). This dataset consists of 353 pairs of nouns and each pair has an averaged human rating which corresponds to a semantic similarity score. Evaluation is performed by measuring Spearman's rank correlation between the human ratings and the cosine similarity scores of the embeddings. Table 5 shows the evaluation results. We used the best settings reported in Table 2 and 3 since our method

Cause-Effect(E_1,E_2)				Content-Container(E_1,E_2)				Message-Topic(E_1,E_2)			
resulted	poverty	caused	the	inside	was	inside	a	discuss	magazines	relating	to
caused	stability	caused	the	in	was	in	a	explaining	to	discuss	aspects
generated	coast	resulted	in	hidden	hidden	in	a	discussing	concerned	about	NULL
cause	fire	caused	due	was	was	inside	the	relating	interview	relates	to
causes	that	resulted	in	stored	was	hidden	in	describing	to	discuss	the
Cause-Effect(E_2,E_1)				**Content-Container(E_2,E_1)**				**Message-Topic(E_2,E_1)**			
after	caused	by	radiation	full	NULL	full	of	subject	were	related	in
from	caused	by	infection	included	was	full	of	related	was	related	in
caused	stomach	caused	by	contains	a	full	NULL	discussed	been	discussed	in
triggered	caused	by	genetic	contained	a	full	and	documented	is	related	through
due	anger	caused	by	stored	a	full	forty	received	the	subject	of

Table 6: Top five unigrams and trigrams with the highest scores for six classes.

is designed for relation classification and it is not clear how to tune the hyperparameters for the word similarity task. As shown in the result table, the noun-specific embeddings perform better than the standard embeddings in our method, which indicates the noun-specific embeddings capture more useful information in measuring the semantic similarity between nouns. The performance of the noun-specific embeddings is roughly the same as that of the word2vec embeddings.

5.5 Qualitative Analysis on the Embeddings

Using the n-gram embeddings $\mathbf{h}_i$ in Eq. (5), we inspect which n-grams are relevant to each relation class after the supervised learning step of RelEmb. When the context size c is 3, we can use at most 7-grams. The learned weight matrix $\mathbf{S}$ in Section 3.3 is used to detect the most relevant n-grams for each class. More specifically, for each n-gram embedding $(n = 1, 3)$ in the training set, we compute the dot product between the n-gram embedding and the corresponding components in $\mathbf{S}$. We then select the pairs of n-grams and class labels with the highest scores. In Table 6 we show the top five n-grams for six classes. These results clearly show that the n-gram embeddings capture salient syntactic patterns which are useful for the relation classification task.

6 Conclusions and Future Work

We have presented a method for learning word embeddings specifically designed for relation classification. The word embeddings are trained using large unlabeled corpora to capture lexical features for relation classification. On a well-established semantic relation classification task our method significantly outperforms the baseline based on word2vec. Our method also compares favorably to previous state-of-the-art models that rely on syntactic parsers and external semantic resources, despite our method requiring only access to an unannotated corpus and a POS tagger. For future work, we will investigate how well our method performs on other domains and datasets and how relation labels can help when learning embeddings in a semi-supervised learning setting.

Acknowledgments

We thank the anonymous reviewers for their helpful comments and suggestions.

References

Mohit Bansal, Kevin Gimpel, and Karen Livescu. 2014. Tailoring Continuous Word Representations for Dependency Parsing. In *Proceedings of the 52nd Annual Meeting of the Association for Computational Linguistics (Volume 2: Short Papers)*, pages 809–815.

Marco Baroni and Roberto Zamparelli. 2010. Nouns are Vectors, Adjectives are Matrices: Representing Adjective-Noun Constructions in Semantic Space. In *Proceedings of the 2010 Conference on Empirical Methods in Natural Language Processing*, pages 1183–1193.

Emanuela Boros, Romaric Besançon, Olivier Ferret, and Brigitte Grau. 2014. Event Role Extraction using Domain-Relevant Word Representations. In *Proceedings of the 2014 Conference on Empirical Methods in Natural Language Processing (EMNLP)*, pages 1852–1857.

Razvan Bunescu and Raymond Mooney. 2005. A Shortest Path Dependency Kernel for Relation Extraction. In *Proceedings of Human Language Technology Conference and Conference on Empirical Methods in Natural Language Processing*, pages 724–731.

Wenliang Chen, Yue Zhang, and Min Zhang. 2014. Feature Embedding for Dependency Parsing. In

Proceedings of COLING 2014, the 25th International Conference on Computational Linguistics: Technical Papers, pages 816–826.

Massimiliano Ciaramita and Yasemin Altun. 2006. Broad-Coverage Sense Disambiguation and Information Extraction with a Supersense Sequence Tagger. In *Proceedings of the 2006 Conference on Empirical Methods in Natural Language Processing*, pages 594–602.

Ronan Collobert, Jason Weston, Léon Bottou, Michael Karlen, Koray Kavukcuoglu, and Pavel Kuksa. 2011. Natural Language Processing (Almost) from Scratch. *Journal of Machine Learning Research*, 12:2493–2537.

Cicero Nogueira dos Santos, Bing Xiang, and Bowen Zhou. 2015. Classifying Relations by Ranking with Convolutional Neural Networks. In *Proceedings of the Joint Conference of the 53rd Annual Meeting of the Association for Computational Linguistics and the 7th International Joint Conference on Natural Language Processing of the Asian Federation of Natural Language Processing*. to appear.

John Duchi, Elad Hazan, and Yoram Singer. 2011. Adaptive Subgradient Methods for Online Learning and Stochastic Optimization. *Journal of Machine Learning Research*, 12:2121–2159.

Javid Ebrahimi and Dejing Dou. 2015. Chain Based RNN for Relation Classification. In *Proceedings of the 2015 Conference of the North American Chapter of the Association for Computational Linguistics: Human Language Technologies*, pages 1244–1249.

Lev Finkelstein, Gabrilovich Evgenly, Matias Yossi, Rivlin Ehud, Solan Zach, Wolfman Gadi, and Ruppin Eytan. 2001. Placing Search in Context: The Concept Revisited. In *Proceedings of the Tenth International World Wide Web Conference*.

Roxana Girju, Preslav Nakov, Vivi Nastase, Stan Szpakowicz, Peter Turney, and Deniz Yuret. 2007. SemEval-2007 Task 04: Classification of Semantic Relations between Nominals. In *Proceedings of the Fourth International Workshop on Semantic Evaluations (SemEval-2007)*, pages 13–18.

Edward Grefenstette and Mehrnoosh Sadrzadeh. 2011. Experimental Support for a Categorical Compositional Distributional Model of Meaning. In *Proceedings of the 2011 Conference on Empirical Methods in Natural Language Processing*, pages 1394–1404.

Jiang Guo, Wanxiang Che, Haifeng Wang, and Ting Liu. 2014. Revisiting Embedding Features for Simple Semi-supervised Learning. In *Proceedings of the 2014 Conference on Empirical Methods in Natural Language Processing (EMNLP)*, pages 110–120.

Kazuma Hashimoto, Makoto Miwa, Yoshimasa Tsuruoka, and Takashi Chikayama. 2013. Simple Customization of Recursive Neural Networks for Semantic Relation Classification. In *Proceedings of the 2013 Conference on Empirical Methods in Natural Language Processing*, pages 1372–1376.

Kazuma Hashimoto, Pontus Stenetorp, Makoto Miwa, and Yoshimasa Tsuruoka. 2014. Jointly Learning Word Representations and Composition Functions Using Predicate-Argument Structures. In *Proceedings of the 2014 Conference on Empirical Methods in Natural Language Processing (EMNLP)*, pages 1544–1555.

Iris Hendrickx, Su Nam Kim, Zornitsa Kozareva, Preslav Nakov, Diarmuid Ó Séaghdha, Sebastian Padó, Marco Pennacchiotti, Lorenza Romano, and Stan Szpakowicz. 2010. SemEval-2010 Task 8: Multi-Way Classification of Semantic Relations between Pairs of Nominals. In *Proceedings of the 5th International Workshop on Semantic Evaluation*, pages 33–38.

Geoffrey E. Hinton, Nitish Srivastava, Alex Krizhevsky, Ilya Sutskever, and Ruslan Salakhutdinov. 2012. Improving neural networks by preventing co-adaptation of feature detectors. *CoRR*, abs/1207.0580.

Ozan Irsoy and Claire Cardie. 2014. Deep Recursive Neural Networks for Compositionality in Language. In *Advances in Neural Information Processing Systems 27*, pages 2096–2104.

Dimitri Kartsaklis and Mehrnoosh Sadrzadeh. 2013. Prior Disambiguation of Word Tensors for Constructing Sentence Vectors. In *Proceedings of the 2013 Conference on Empirical Methods in Natural Language Processing*, pages 1590–1601.

Quoc Le and Tomas Mikolov. 2014. Distributed Representations of Sentences and Documents. In *Proceedings of the 31st International Conference on Machine Learning (ICML-14)*, ICML '14, pages 1188–1196.

Omer Levy and Yoav Goldberg. 2014. Neural Word Embedding as Implicit Matrix Factorization. In *Advances in Neural Information Processing Systems 27*, pages 2177–2185.

Tomas Mikolov, Kai Chen, Greg Corrado, and Jeffrey Dean. 2013a. Efficient Estimation of Word Representations in Vector Space. In *Proceedings of Workshop at the International Conference on Learning Representations*.

Tomas Mikolov, Ilya Sutskever, Kai Chen, Greg S Corrado, and Jeff Dean. 2013b. Distributed Representations of Words and Phrases and their Compositionality. In *Advances in Neural Information Processing Systems 26*, pages 3111–3119.

Yusuke Miyao and Jun'ichi Tsujii. 2008. Feature Forest Models for Probabilistic HPSG Parsing. *Computational Linguistics*, 34(1):35–80, March.

Andriy Mnih and Koray Kavukcuoglu. 2013. Learning word embeddings efficiently with noise-contrastive estimation. In *Advances in Neural Information Processing Systems 26*, pages 2265–2273.

Thien Huu Nguyen and Ralph Grishman. 2014. Employing Word Representations and Regularization for Domain Adaptation of Relation Extraction. In *Proceedings of the 52nd Annual Meeting of the Association for Computational Linguistics (Volume 2: Short Papers)*, pages 68–74.

Eric W. Noreen. 1989. *Computer-Intensive Methods for Testing Hypotheses: An Introduction*. Wiley-Interscience.

Romain Paulus, Richard Socher, and Christopher D Manning. 2014. Global Belief Recursive Neural Networks. In *Advances in Neural Information Processing Systems 27*, pages 2888–2896.

Bryan Rink and Sanda Harabagiu. 2010. UTD: Classifying Semantic Relations by Combining Lexical and Semantic Resources. In *Proceedings of the 5th International Workshop on Semantic Evaluation*, pages 256–259.

Richard Socher, Brody Huval, Christopher D. Manning, and Andrew Y. Ng. 2012. Semantic Compositionality through Recursive Matrix-Vector Spaces. In *Proceedings of the 2012 Joint Conference on Empirical Methods in Natural Language Processing and Computational Natural Language Learning*, pages 1201–1211.

Duyu Tang, Furu Wei, Nan Yang, Ming Zhou, Ting Liu, and Bing Qin. 2014. Learning Sentiment-Specific Word Embedding for Twitter Sentiment Classification. In *Proceedings of the 52nd Annual Meeting of the Association for Computational Linguistics (Volume 1: Long Papers)*, pages 1555–1565.

Joseph Turian, Lev-Arie Ratinov, and Yoshua Bengio. 2010. Word Representations: A Simple and General Method for Semi-Supervised Learning. In *Proceedings of the 48th Annual Meeting of the Association for Computational Linguistics*, pages 384–394.

Sida Wang and Christopher Manning. 2012. Baselines and Bigrams: Simple, Good Sentiment and Topic Classification. In *Proceedings of the 50th Annual Meeting of the Association for Computational Linguistics (Volume 2: Short Papers)*, pages 90–94.

Mo Yu, Matthew R. Gormley, and Mark Dredze. 2014. Factor-based Compositional Embedding Models. In *Proceedings of Workshop on Learning Semantics at the 2014 Conference on Neural Information Processing Systems*.

Daojian Zeng, Kang Liu, Siwei Lai, Guangyou Zhou, and Jun Zhao. 2014. Relation Classification via Convolutional Deep Neural Network. In *Proceedings of COLING 2014, the 25th International Conference on Computational Linguistics: Technical Papers*, pages 2335–2344.

Min Zhang, Jie Zhang, Jian Su, and GuoDong Zhou. 2006. A Composite Kernel to Extract Relations between Entities with Both Flat and Structured Features. In *Proceedings of the 21st International Conference on Computational Linguistics and 44th Annual Meeting of the Association for Computational Linguistics*, pages 825–832.

Temporal Information Extraction from Korean Texts

Young-Seob Jeong, Zae Myung Kim, Hyun-Woo Do, Chae-Gyun Lim, and Ho-Jin Choi
School of Computing
Korea Advanced Institute of Science and Technology
291 Daehak-ro, Yuseong-gu, Daejeon 305-701, South Korea
{pinode,zaemyung,realstorm103,rayote,hojinc}@kaist.ac.kr

Abstract

As documents tend to contain temporal information, extracting such information is attracting much research interests recently. In this paper, we propose a hybrid method that combines machine-learning models and hand-crafted rules for the task of extracting temporal information from unstructured Korean texts. We address Korean-specific research issues and propose a new probabilistic model to generate complementary features. The performance of our approach is demonstrated by experiments on the TempEval-2 dataset, and the Korean TimeBank dataset which we built for this study.

1 Introduction

Due to the increasing number of unstructured documents available on the Web and from other sources, developing techniques that automatically extract knowledge from the documents has been of paramount importance. Among many aspects of extracting knowledge from documents, the extraction of temporal information is recently drawing much attention, since the documents usually incorporate temporal information that is useful for further applications such as Information Retrieval (IR) and Question Answering (QA) systems. Given a simple question, "who was the president of the U.S. 8 years ago?", for example, a QA system may have a difficulty in finding the right answer without the correct temporal information about when the question is posed and what '8 years ago' refers to.

There have been many studies for temporal information extraction, but most of them are applicable only to their target languages. The main reason for this limitation is that some parts of temporal information are difficult to predict without the use of language-specific processing. For example, the normalized value '1983-03-08' can be represented by 'March 8, 1983' in English, while it can be represented by '1983년삼월8일' in Korean. The order of date representation in Korean is usually different from that of English, and the digit expression in Korean is more complex than that of English. This implies that it is necessary to investigate language-specific difficulties for developing a method to extract temporal information.

In this paper, we propose a method for temporal information extraction from Korean texts. The contributions of this paper are as follows: we (1) show how the Korean-specific issues (e.g., morpheme-level tagging, various ways of digit expression, uses of lunar calendar, and so on) are addressed, (2) propose a hybrid method that combines a set of hand-crafted rules and machine-learning models, (3) propose a data-driven probabilistic model to generate complementary features, and (4) create a new dataset, the Korean TimeBank, that consists of more than 3,700 manually annotated sentences.

The rest of the paper is organized as follows. Section 2 describes the background of the research. Section 3 presents the details of the proposed method, the Korean TimeBank dataset, and how we apply the probabilistic model for generating features. Section 4 shows experimental results, and Section 5 concludes the paper.

2 Background

TempEval is a series of shared tasks for temporal information extraction (Verhagen et al., 2009; Verhagen et al., 2010; UzZaman et al., 2013). There have been many studies related to the shared tasks (Chambers et al., 2007; Yoshikawa et al., 2009; UzZaman and Allen, 2010; Ling and Weld, 2010; Mirroshandel and Ghassem-Sani, 2012; Bethard, 2013b), which are based on the Time Mark-up Language (TimeML) (Pustejovsky et al., 2003).

Proceedings of the 19th Conference on Computational Language Learning, pages 279–288,
Beijing, China, July 30-31, 2015.

The shared tasks can be summarized into three extraction tasks: (1) extraction of *timex3* tags, (2) extraction of *event* and *makeinstance* tags, and (3) extraction of *tlink* tags. The *timex3* tag is associated with expressions of temporal information such as 'May 1973' and 'today'. The *event* tag and *makeinstance* tag represent some eventual expressions which can be related to temporal information. The *makeinstance* tag is an instance of the *event* tag. For example, the sentence, "I go to school on Mondays and Tuesdays", contains one *event* tag on 'go' and two *makeinstance* tags as the action 'go' occurs twice on Mondays and Tuesdays. The *tlink* tag represents a linkage between two tags. The *tlink* can be a linkage between two *timex3* tags (TT *tlink*), two *makeinstance* tags (MM *tlink*), a *timex3* tag and a *makeinstance* tag (TM *tlink*), or Document Creation Time and a *makeinstance* tag (DM *tlink*). Note that the *tlink* takes *makeinstance* tags as arguments, but not the *event* tags, as the *event* tags are merely templates for them. For the above sentence, there will be two TM *tlinks*: go-Tuesdays and go-Mondays. The TT *tlink* is assumed to be easy to extract, so TempEval does not incorporate the TT *tlink* into the task of extracting *tlink* tags.

Among many related studies, there are several leading ones. HeidelTime is proposed for extraction of *timex3* tags (Strotgen and Gertz, 2010). It strongly depends on hand-crafted rules, and showed the best performance in TempEval-2. Llorens et al. (2010) proposed TIPSem for all of the three extraction tasks. It employs Conditional Random Fields (CRF) (Lafferty et al., 2001) for capturing patterns of texts, and defines a set of hand-crafted rules for determining several attributes of the tags. ClearTK is another work proposed for all three extraction tasks (Bethard, 2013a); it utilizes machine-learning models such as Support Vector Machines (SVM) (Boser et al., 1992; Cortes and Vapnik, 1995) and Logistic Regressions (LR), and shows the best performance in TempEval-3.

Although the existing approaches show good results, most of them are applicable only to their target languages. The first reason is that there are several attributes which are difficult to predict without the use of language-specific processing. For instance, the attribute *value* of *timex3* tag has a normalized form of time (e.g., 1999-04-12) following ISO-8601. This is not accurately predictable by relying solely on data-driven approaches. The second reason is that they depend on some language-specific resources (e.g., WordNet) or tools. Unless the same quality of resources or tools is achieved for other languages, the existing works would not be available to the other languages. To alleviate this limitation, a language independent parser for extracting *timex3* tags is proposed (Angeli and Uszkoreit, 2013). Its portability is demonstrated by experiments with TempEval-2 dataset of six languages: English, Spanish, Italian, Chinese, Korean, and French. However, the performance in English and Spanish datasets are about twice as high as the other languages, since the method highly depends on the feature definition and language-specific preprocessing (e.g., morphological analysis). This implies that it is necessary to address language-specific difficulties in order to achieve high performance.

Korean language has many subtle rules and exceptions on word spacing. Korean is an agglutinative language, where verbs are formed by attaching various endings to the stem. There are usually multiple morphemes for each token, and empty elements appear very often because subjects and objects are dropped to avoid duplication. Temporal expressions often take the lunar calendar representation as a tradition. Moreover, the same temporal information can have various forms due to a complex system of digit expression. For instance, a digit 30 can be represented as '30', '삼십[sam-sib]', or '서른[seo-run]'. Most of these issues stem from the Chinese language, as a large number of Chinese words and letters have become an integral part of Korean vocabulary due to historical contact. All these issues hinder the performance of the existing approaches when applied to Korean documents.

In this paper, we show how these issues are addressed in our Korean-specific hybrid method. To the best of our knowledge, this is the first Korean-specific study which addresses all of the three extraction tasks.

3 Proposed Method

3.1 Korean TimeBank

Although there is a Korean dataset provided by TempEval-2, we chose not to use it because it is small in size and has many annotation errors. In TempEval-2 Korean dataset, there are missing values of *timex3* tags, and multiple tags that must be

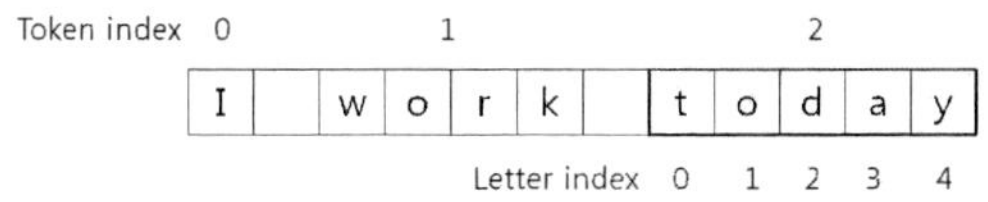

Figure 1: Example of extent representation by token indices and letter indices.

merged into one. Please refer to the examples in the 11th sentence of the 2nd training document of the TempEval-2 Korean dataset. Thus, we constructed a new dataset called Korean TimeBank.

The new dataset is based on TimeML but with several differences. The tags of the new dataset are represented using a stand-off scheme, keeping the original sentences unharmed. As there are often multiple morphemes within each token in Korean, the tags are annotated in letter-level. The letter-level annotation allows multiple annotations to appear within a single token. This also makes the dataset independent of morphological analysis, so it is not required to update the dataset when the morphological analyzer is updated. To enable the letter-level annotation, we introduce several attributes for *timex3* tag and *event* tag: *text*, *begin*, *end*, *e_begin*, and *e_end*. The attributes *e_begin* and *e_end* indicate token indices, while *begin* and *end* indicate letter indices of the extent. The attribute *text* contains the string of the extent. For example, the sentence, "I work today" in Fig. 1, contains one *timex3* tag whose *text* is 'today', where *e_begin*=2, *e_end*=2, *begin*=0, and *end*=4.

Since temporal expressions following the lunar calendar representation appear often in Korean, we add an attribute *calendar*. The value of the *calendar* can be LUNAR or other types of calendar, and its default value is GREGORIAN when it is not explicitly clarified. We also add two values for the attribute *mod* of *timex3* tag: START_OR_MID and MID_OR_END, as these expressions appear often in Korean. For example, '초중반[cho-joong-ban]' represents beginning or middle phase of a period, and '중후반[joong-hoo-ban]' represents middle or ending phase of a period.

The source of the Korean TimeBank includes Wikipedia documents and hundreds of manually generated question-answer pairs. The domains of the Wikipedia documents are personage, music, university, and history. The documents are annotated by two trained annotators and a supervisor, all majoring in computer science. The annotated tags of each document is saved in an XML file.

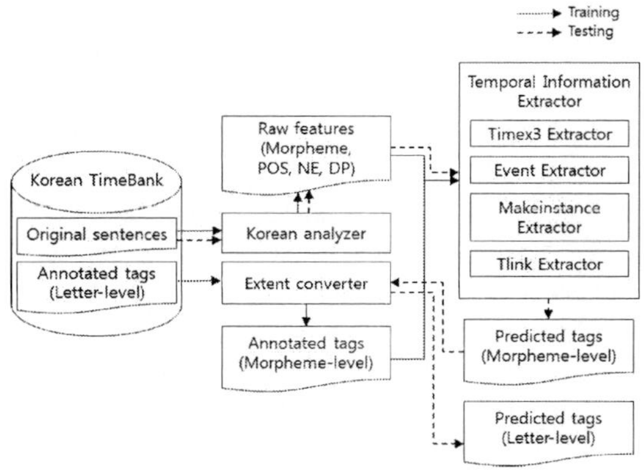

Figure 2: Overall process of temporal information extraction from Korean texts.

3.2 Temporal Information Extraction from Korean Texts

Our proposed method addresses all of the three tasks: (1) extraction of *timex3* tags, (2) extraction of *event* and *makeinstance* tags, and (3) extraction of *tlink* tags. The proposed method also extracts additional attributes of *timex3* tag, such as *freq*, *beginPoint*, *endPoint*, *mod*, and *calendar*. The overall process is depicted in Fig. 2, where the solid line represents training process and the dotted line represents testing process. The Korean analyzer at the center of the figure takes Korean texts as an input and generates several raw features as an output, such as results of morphological analysis, Part-Of-Speech (POS) tags, Named-Entity (NE) tags, and results of dependency parsing (Lim et al., 2006). The number of possible POS tags is 45, which follows the definition of Sejong Treebank[1]. The number of possible NE tags is 178, where each of them belongs to one of 15 super NE tags.

The generated raw features are used to define a set of features for machine-learning models and a set of hand-crafted rules. The rules are designed by examining the training dataset and the errors that the proposed method generates with the validation dataset. We employ several machine-learning methods that have shown the best performance in the TempEval shared tasks, such as Maximum Entropy Model (MEM), Support Vector Machine (SVM), Conditional Random Fields (CRF), and Logistic Regression (LR).

Fig. 2 introduces Temporal Information Extractor (TIE) which consists of four sub-extractors:

[1] Korean Language Institute, http://www.sejong.or.kr

timex3 extractor, *event* extractor, *makeinstance* extractor, and *tlink* extractor. The *timex3* extractor and the *event* extractor work independently, and the *makeinstance* extractor uses the predicted *event* tags. The *tlink* extractor makes use of the predicted *makeinstance* tags and predicted *timex3* tags. Thus, the performance of *timex3* extractor and *event* extractor will strongly influence the performance of *makeinstance* extractor and *tlink* extractor. These four sub-extractors as a whole give predicted tags as an output, where the tags are represented in morpheme-level. The extent converter at the center of the figure changes the morpheme-level tags into letter-level and vice versa by checking ASCII values of each letter and each morpheme. In training process, the annotated tags of Korean TimeBank are converted into morpheme-level through the extent converter, and used to train the TIE.

3.2.1 Timex3 extractor

The goal of *timex3* extractor is to predict whether each morpheme belongs to the extent of a *timex3* tag or not, and finds appropriate attributes of the tag. There are five *type*s of *timex3* tag: DATE, TIME, DURATION, SET, and NONE. The NONE represents that the corresponding morpheme does not belong to the extent of a *timex3* tag, and the other four types follow the same definition of TimeML. This is essentially a morpheme-level classification over 5 classes.

We basically take two approaches: a set of 100 hand-crafted rules and machine-learning models. Examples of the rules for extent and *type* are listed in Table 1. In the second rule of the table, the first condition is satisfied when the sequence of two morphemes is a digit followed by a morpheme '월[wol]'(month), '일[il]'(day), or '주[joo]'(week). The various ways of digit expressions are also considered. The second condition is satisfied when the morpheme next to the extent is '에[eh]'(at) or '마다[ma-da]'(every) followed by '번[beon]'(times) or '회[hoi]'(times), and there must be no other tags between the two morphemes. If these two conditions are satisfied, then the sequence of morphemes becomes the extent of *timex3* tag whose *type* is SET. If one of the rules is satisfied, then the remaining rules are skipped for the target morpheme.

We compare two machine-learning models, CRF and MEM, for *timex3* tag by experiments. We defined a set of features based on the raw features

Table 1: Examples of the rules for extent and *type* of *timex3* tags.

Type	Conditions
DATE	Extent=(digit,년)
SET	Extent=(digit,월∨일∨주), Next morps= (에∨마다,no other tags,번∨회)

Table 2: Examples of the rules for *value* of *timex3* tag.

Operations	Conditions
Month=digit Context updated	Type=DATE∨TIME Surrounding morps= (digit,월)
Year=context	Type=DATE∨TIME Surrounding morps= (올해∨이번해)

obtained from the Korean analyzer. The defined features include morphemes, POS tags, NE tags, morpheme-level features of dependency parsing, given a particular window size. The morpheme-level features of dependency parsing are generated by following approaches in Sang and Buchholz (2000).

To predict other attributes of each predicted *timex3* tag, we also define sets of rules: 112 rules for *value*, 7 rules for *beginPoint*/*endPoint*, 9 rules for *freq*, 10 rules for *mod*, and 1 rule for *calendar*. Especially, the rules for *value* and *freq* take a temporal context into account. For instance, the sentence "We go there tomorrow", makes it hard to predict *value* of 'tomorrow' without considering the temporal context. We assume that the temporal context of each sentence depends on the previous sentence. For each document, the temporal context is initialized with Document Creation Time (DCT), and the context is updated when a normalized *value* appears in a certain condition.

Examples of the rules are described in Table 2. If the first rule in the table is satisfied, then the month of *value* is changed to the corresponding digit and the temporal context is updated.

As there can be multiple clues for determining *value* within an extent, all of the rules are checked for each *timex3* tag. To avoid overwriting *value* by multiple satisfied rules, the rules are listed in ascending order of temporal unit. That is, the rules for seconds or minutes are listed before the rules for hours or days. This allows *value* to be changed from smaller temporal unit to bigger unit, thereby avoiding overwriting wrong *value*. The rules for different attributes are listed in separate files, and are written in a systematic way similar to regular expressions. Such format enables rules to be easily manipulated.

3.2.2 Event extractor

The goal of *event* extractor is to predict whether each morpheme belongs to the extent of an *event* tag or not, and finds appropriate *class* of the tag. There are 7 *class*es of *event* tag: OCCURRENCE, PERCEPTION, REPORTING, STATE, I_STATE, I_ACTION, and NONE. The NONE represents that the corresponding morpheme does not belong to the extent, and the other *class*es follow the same definition of TimeML. Similar to the *timex3* extractor, we take two approaches: a set of 26 rules and machine-learning models (e.g., CRF and MEM), based on the set of features used in the *timex3* extractor.

There are several verbs that often appear within the extents of *event* tags, although they do not carry any meaning. For example, in the sentence, "나는 공부를 하다"(I study), the verb '하[ha]'(do) has no meaning while the noun '공부[gong-bu]'(study) has eventual meaning. We define a set of such verbal morphemes (e.g., '위하[wi-ha]'(for), and '통하[tong-ha]'(through)), to avoid generating meaningless *event* tags.

3.2.3 Makeinstance extractor

The goal of *makeinstance* extractor is to generate at least one *makeinstance* tag for each *event* tag, and find appropriate attributes. As we observed that there is only one *makeinstance* tag for each *event* tag in most cases, the *makeinstance* extractor simply generates one *makeinstance* tag for each *event* tag. For the attribute *POS*, we simply take the POS tags obtained from the Korean analyzer. We define a set of 5 rules for the attribute *tense*, and 2 rules for the attribute *polarity*.

3.2.4 Tlink extractor

The goal of *tlink* extractor is to make a linkage between two tags, and find appropriate types of the links. For each pair of tags, it determines whether there must be a linkage between them, and finds the most appropriate *relType*. There are 11 *relTypes*: BEFORE, AFTER, INCLUDES, DURING, DURING_INV, SIMULTANEOUS, IDENTITY, BEGINS, ENDS, OVERLAP, and NONE. The NONE represents that there is no linkage between the two argument tags, and the OVERLAP means that the temporal intervals of two tags are overlapping. The other *relTypes* follow the same definition of TimeML. Thus, it is essentially a classification over 11 classes for each pair of two argument tags.

Table 3: Features in the two kinds of classifiers.

Features for TM *tlink*
Surrounding morphemes of the argument tags
Linear order of the argument tags
Attribute *type* of *timex3* tag
Attribute *class* of *event* tag
Attribute *polarity* of *makeinstance* tag
Attribute *tense* of *makeinstance* tag
Whether *tlink* tag is non-consuming tag or not
Does *timex3* tag exist between argument tags?
Does *event* tag exist between argument tags?
Is *event* tag an objective of other *event* tag in dependency tree?
Features for MM *tlink*
Surrounding morphemes of *event* tags
Linear order of *event* tags
Attribute *class* of *event* tags
Attribute *polarity* of *makeinstance* tags
Attribute *tense* of *makeinstance* tags
Does *timex3* tag exist between *event* tags?
Does *event* tag exist between *event* tags?

The *tlink* extractor generates intra-sentence *tlink*s and inter-sentence *tlink*s. For the intra-sentence *tlink*s, we take two approaches: a set of 19 rules and machine-learning models (e.g., SVM and LR). Among the four kinds of *tlink*s (e.g., TT *tlink*, TM *tlink*, MM *tlink*, and DM *tlink*), our *tlink* extractor generates the first three kinds of *tlink*s. The reason for excluding DM *tlink* is that we maintain the temporal context initialized with DCT in the *timex3* extractor, so it is not necessary to generate DM *tlink*s. The TT *tlink*s are extracted by comparing normalized *values* of two *timex3* tags. Two models are independently trained for predicting TM *tlink*s and MM *tlink*s, respectively. We tried many possible combinations of features to reach better performance, and obtained sets of features as described in Table 3.

Given a pair of two *makeinstance* tags, it is straight forward to derive *relType* when the two *event* tags are linked with *timex3* tags. Thus, firstly we predict TT *tlinks*, and thereafter predict TM *tlinks* and MM *tlinks*. For the inter-sentence *tlinks*, we generate MM *tlinks* between adjacent sentences when there is a particular expression at the beginning of a sentence, such as '그 후[geu-hoo]'(afterward), '그 전[geu-jeon]'(beforehand), or '그 다음[geu-da-eum]'(thereafter).

3.3 Online LIFE

As the performance of the Korean analyzer is not stable, we need complementary features to make better classifiers. Jeong and Choi (2015) proposed Language Independent Feature Extractor (LIFE) which generates a pair of class label and topic label for each Letter-Sequence (LS), where LS represents frequently appeared letter sequence. The class labels can be used as syntactic features, while the topic labels can be used as semantic features. The concept of LS makes it language independent, so it is basically applicable to any language. This is especially helpful to some languages that have no stable feature extractors. Korean is one of such languages, so we employ the LIFE to generate complementary features.

The temporal information extractor must work online because it usually takes a stream of documents as an input. However, as the LIFE is originally designed to work offline, we propose an extended version of the LIFE, namely, Online LIFE (O-LIFE), whose parameters are estimated incrementally. When we design O-LIFE, the LS concept of LIFE becomes a problem because the LS dictionary changes. For example, if the LS dictionary has only one LS *goes* and a new token *go* comes in, then the LS dictionary may contain *go* and *es*. Note that the LS *goes* does not exist in the new dictionary. This issue is addressed by our proposed algorithm which basically distributes the values of previously estimated parameters to new prior parameters of overlapping LSs. For the above example, $\phi_{k,\text{'}goes\text{'}}$ will be distributed to $\beta_{k,\text{'}go\text{'}}$ and $\beta_{k,\text{'}es\text{'}}$, where k is a topic index.

The formal algorithm of O-LIFE is shown in Algorithm 1, where C is the number of classes and T is the number of topics. S_{stream} is the number of streams, and S^s is s-th stream of D^s documents. The four parameters a, b_t, g and b_c are default values of the priors α, β, γ and δ. The three threshold parameters t_1, t_2, and t_3 are used to generate LS dictionary.

Algorithm 1 Online LIFE

1: INPUT: $a;b_t;g;b_c;w^p;S^s;t_1;t_2;t_3$
2: **for** s=1 to S_{stream} **do**
3: $\mathbf{Dic^s}$ = DictionaryGenerator(t_1,t_2,t_3)
4: **if** s=1 **then**
5: $\beta^s_t=b_t,\ 1\leq t\leq T$
6: $\delta^s_c=b_c,\ 1\leq c\leq C$
7: **else**
8: $\beta^s_{t,w}=b_t,\ w\in\mathbf{Dic^s}$
9: $\delta^s_{c,w}=b_c,\ w\in\mathbf{Dic^s}$
10: **for** each item $w_i\in\mathbf{Dic^{s-1}}$ **do**
11: **if** $w_i\in\mathbf{Dic^s}$ **then**
12: β^s_{t,w_i}+=$\mathbf{B}^{s-1}_{t,w_i}w^p,\ 1\leq t\leq T$
13: δ^s_{c,w_i}+=$\mathbf{D}^{s-1}_{c,w_i}w^p,\ 1\leq c\leq C$
14: **end if**
15: **for** each $w'_i\in\mathbf{Dic^s}$ **do**
16: β^s_{t,w'_i}+=$\mathbf{B}^{s-1}_{t,w_i}w^p,\ 1\leq t\leq T$
17: δ^s_{c,w'_i}+=$\mathbf{D}^{s-1}_{c,w_i}w^p,\ 1\leq c\leq C$
18: **end for**
19: **for** each $w''_i\in\mathbf{Dic^s}$ **do**
20: $r=|w_{overlap}|/|w_i|$
21: β^s_{t,w''_i}+=$\mathbf{B}^{s-1}_{t,w_i}rw^p,\ 1\leq t\leq T$
22: δ^s_{c,w''_i}+=$\mathbf{D}^{s-1}_{c,w_i}rw^p,\ 1\leq c\leq C$
23: **end for**
24: **end for**
25: **end if**
26: $\alpha^s_d=a,\ 1\leq d\leq D^s$
27: $\gamma^s_c=g,\ 1\leq c\leq C$
28: initilize ϕ^s, η^s, π^s, and θ^s to zeros
29: initilize class/topic assignments
30: $[\phi^s,\eta^s,\pi^s,\theta^s]$ =
31: ParameterEstimation(S^s,α^s,β^s,γ^s,δ^s)
32: $\mathbf{B}^s_t=\mathbf{B}^{s-1}_t\cup\phi^s_t,\ 1\leq t\leq T$
33: $\mathbf{D}^s_t=\mathbf{D}^{s-1}_t\cup\eta^s_c,\ 1\leq c\leq C$
34: **end for**

The LS dictionary of O-LIFE is updated as it reads data. That is, $|\mathbf{Dic^{prev}}|\leq|\mathbf{Dic^{cur}}|$ and $\mathbf{Dic^{prev}}\not\subseteq\mathbf{Dic^{cur}}$, where $\mathbf{Dic^{prev}}$ is the previous dictionary and $\mathbf{Dic^{cur}}$ is the current dictionary. To handle this change in dictionary, the two parameters (e.g., β, δ) are updated by four steps, based on an assumption that every unique LS w_i of the previous dictionary should contribute to the new dictionary as much as possible. Firstly, as described in 8th line of the algorithm, the two parameters are initialized with default values. Secondly, if a particular LS w_i of the previous dictioanry exists in the new dictionary, then the two parameters increase by $\mathbf{B}^{s-1}_{t,w_i}w^p$ and $\mathbf{D}^{s-1}_{c,w_i}w^p$, re-

Table 4: The statistics of Korean TimeBank, where the digits represent the number of corresponding items.

	Training	Validation	Test
documents	536	131	173
sentences	2357	466	879
timex3	1245	253	494
event	6594	1145	2609
makeinstance	6615	1155	2613
tlink	1295	374	674

spectively. $\mathbf{B}_t^{s-1}$ denotes an evolutionary matrix whose columns are LS-topic distribution ϕ_t^{s-1}, and $\mathbf{D}_c^{s-1}$ means an evolutionary matrix whose columns are LS-class distribution η_t^{s-1}. By multiplying them with the weight vector w^p, the contribution in initializing priors is determined for each time slice. We call this value, the *weighted contribution*. Thirdly, for every w_i' which contains w_i, the two parameters increase by the weighted contribution. Lastly, for every w_i'' which overlaps with w_i, the two parameters increase by r times of the weighted contribution, where $w_{overlap}$ is the overlapping part.

The class labels and topic labels are converted to morpheme-level features by concatenating labels of LSs overlapping with a given morpheme. We call these features as *LIFE features*, and these are used to train machine-learning models, together with the features based on the raw features.

4 Experiments

The Korean TimeBank is divided into a training dataset, a validation dataset, and a test dataset. The statistics of the dataset are described in Table 4. As shown in the table, only one *makeinstance* tag exists for each *event* tag in most cases, which follows the assumption of *makeinstance* extractor.

4.1 Timex3 prediction

For the extent and *type* prediction, only the exactly predicted extents and *types* are regarded as correct, and the results are summarized in Table 5, where MEM is trained only with the features generated from raw features, and MEM_L is trained with both of the features and LIFE features. We employ the CRF++ library[2] and MEM toolkit[3]. The optimal parameter settings are found by a grid search with the validation set. The optimal setting for CRF is as follows: L1-regularization, c=0.6, and f=1. The MEM shows its best performance without Gaussian prior smoothing. Both models give generally better performance when window size is 2. The parameter setting for O-LIFE is as follows: a=0.1, b_t=0.1, g=0.1, b_c=0.1, w^p=(1), C=10, T=10, t_1=0.4, t_2=0.4, t_3=0.7, and the number of iterations for estimation is 1000.

[2]http://crfpp.googlecode.com/svn/trunk/doc/index.html

[3]http://homepages.inf.ed.ac.uk/lzhang10/maxent_toolkit

As shown in the table, CRF gives generally better performance than MEM and rules. We tried a combination of the rules and machine-learning models, and the combination led to an increase in the performance. For example, the combination of CRF and rules gives better performance than using only CRF. This can be explained that there are some patterns that the machine-learning models could not capture, so the combination with the rules can deal with the patterns. Note that using the LIFE features dramatically increases the performance. We believe that this is due to the raw features of Korean (e.g., POS tagger) being unstable. The LIFE features complement these unstable features by capturing syntactic/semantic patterns that are inherent in the given documents. Furthermore, we observed that the combination of the rules and machine-learning models trained with LIFE features does not contribute to the performance. This implies that using LIFE features allows the machine-learning models to capture the patterns that could not be captured by the machine-learning models without LIFE features. The CRF_L is discovered to be the best, and the other remaining attributes are predicted using the rules. The performance is measured in a sequential manner, so the performance generally decreases from the top to bottom of the table.

Another experiments of *timex3* prediction using TempEval-2 Korean dataset are conducted to compare with the existing method of Angeli and Uszkoreit (2013). The existing method makes use of a latent parse conveying a language-flexible representation of time, and extract features over both the parse and associated temporal semantics. The results of comparison are shown in Table 6, where our method uses CRF_L for *type* and rules for *value*. For a fair comparison, both methods are trained and tested using only TempEval-2 Korean dataset. As mentioned before, TempEval-2 Korean dataset contained errors, so we corrected them and

Table 5: Timex3 prediction results, where P represents precision, R means recall, F represents F1 score, points represent *beginPoint/endPoint*, and cal represents *calendar*.

Attri-butes	Performances			
	Comb	**P**	**R**	**F**
extent	Rules	74.79	70.95	72.82
	MEM	31.79	25.1	28.05
	CRF	80.34	65.42	72.11
	MEM,Rules	70.61	70.75	70.68
	CRF,Rules	73.05	**72.33**	72.69
	$\mathrm{MEM_L}$	33.51	41.34	37.02
	$\mathbf{CRF_L}$	**81.15**	**72.33**	**76.49**
type	Rules	72.71	68.97	70.79
	MEM	30.26	23.89	26.7
	CRF	**78.88**	64.23	70.81
	MEM,Rules	68.64	68.77	68.71
	CRF,Rules	71.06	**70.36**	70.7
	$\mathrm{MEM_L}$	31.88	39.16	35.15
	$\mathbf{CRF_L}$	75.83	67.59	**71.47**
value	Rules	71.18	63.44	67.08
points	Rules	71.18	63.44	67.08
freq	Rules	71.18	63.44	67.08
mod	Rules	70.07	62.45	66.04
cal	Rules	70.07	62.45	66.04

Table 6: Results of *timex3* prediction with TempEval-2 Korean dataset, where the digits represent accuracy.

Attributes	Angeli's method	Our method
type	82.0	**100.0**
value	42.0	**100.0**

used for this experiment. As shown in the table, our method gives much better accuracy than the existing method.

4.2 Event prediction

The results of *event* prediction are summarized in Table 7, which are similar to the results of *timex3* prediction. By a grid search, the optimal parameter settings are found to be the same as that of the *timex3* extractor. Employing the LIFE features again increases the performance, and the $\mathrm{CRF_L}$ is discovered to be the best.

Table 7: Event prediction results.

Attri-butes	Performances			
	Comb	**P**	**R**	**F**
extent	Rules	75.62	44.0	55.63
	MEM	33.22	15.07	20.73
	CRF	45.33	35.72	39.96
	MEM,Rules	43.57	47.15	45.29
	CRF,Rules	72.67	64.32	68.24
	$\mathrm{MEM_L}$	37.49	56.34	45.02
	$\mathbf{CRF_L}$	**86.49**	**78.5**	**82.3**
class	Rules	63.97	37.22	47.06
	MEM	31.11	14.12	19.41
	CRF	34.63	27.29	30.53
	MEM,Rules	36.91	39.94	38.37
	CRF,Rules	61.15	54.12	57.42
	$\mathrm{MEM_L}$	34.74	51.46	41.48
	$\mathbf{CRF_L}$	**78.63**	**71.37**	**74.82**

Table 8: Makeinstance prediction results.

Attri-butes	Performances		
	P	**R**	**F**
eventID	86.28	78.19	82.03
polarity	93.59	73.17	82.13
tense	71.03	51.97	60.02

4.3 Makeinstance prediction

All the attributes of *makeinstance* tag are predicted through hand-crafted rules. The performance is summarized in Table 8. The measurement of the attribute *POS* is excluded because we simply take the results of the Korean analyzer.

4.4 Tlink prediction

By performing a grid search with the validation set, we found that Support Vector Machine (SVM) of C-SVC type with Radial Basis Function (RBF) gives the best performance when Γ of kernel function is 1/number of features. It is also found that the L1-regularized Logistic Regression (LR) with C=1 gives the best performance. We observed that both models give better performance when a window size is 1.

There are two cases of *tlink* prediction: (1) *tlink* prediction given correct other tags, and (2) *tlink* prediction given predicted other tags. The results of the first case are summarized in Table 9, where the performance is measured in a sequential manner. As shown in the table, we tried a combina-

Table 9: Tlink prediction results given correct *timex3*, *event*, and *makeinstance* tags.

Attributes	Performances			
	Comb	**P**	**R**	**F**
linkage	SVM	**63.84**	16.72	26.49
	LR	20.02	63.91	30.49
	Rules	39.11	59.76	47.28
	SVM,Rules	39.04	61.69	**47.82**
	LR,Rules	21.13	**77.22**	33.19
relType	SVM	**63.84**	16.72	26.49
	LR	19.18	61.24	29.22
	Rules	37.27	56.95	45.06
	SVM,Rules	37.27	58.88	**45.64**
	LR,Rules	20.2	**73.82**	31.72

Table 10: Tlink prediction results of the combination of SVM and rules, given *timex3*, *event*, and *makeinstance* tags which are predicted using LIFE features.

Attributes	Performances		
	P	**R**	**F**
linkage	34.39	38.46	36.31
relType	32.94	36.83	34.77

tion of the rules and machine-learning models, and the combination of SVM and rules performed the best. Note that we do not use the LIFE features for *tlink* prediction because we observed that the LIFE features do not contribute to the performance for *tlink* prediction. We believe that this is because the LIFE features represent only the syntactic/semantic patterns of the given terms, but not arbitrary relations between the terms.

The results of the second case are obtained using the best combination, and are shown in Table 10. Note that the *tlink* tags are predicted without the LIFE features, while the other tags (e.g., *timex3*, *event*, *makeinstance*) are obtained using the LIFE features. To measure the impact of the LIFE features, we also conduct the experiment of the second case given the predicted tags without using the LIFE features, and the results are shown in Table 11. As shown in Table 10 and Table 11, using the LIFE features increases the F1 score about 6 percents.

Table 11: Tlink prediction results of the combination of SVM and rules, given the tags predicted without using the LIFE features.

Attributes	Performances		
	P	**R**	**F**
linkage	25.41	36.69	30.02
relType	24.18	34.91	28.57

5 Conclusion

We introduced a new method for extracting temporal information from unstructured Korean texts. Korean language has a complex grammar, so there were many research issues to address prior to achieving our goal. We presented such issues and our solutions to them. Experimental results illustrated the effectiveness of our method, especially when we adopted the extended probabilistical model, Online LIFE (O-LIFE), to generate complementary features for training machine-learning models. In addition, as there were no sufficient data for this study, we have manually constructed the Korean TimeBank consisting of more than 3,700 annotated sentences. We will extend our study to interact with Knowledge-Base for achieving better prediction of temporal information.

Acknowledgments

This work was supported by ICT R&D program of MSIP/IITP. [R0101-15-0062, Development of Knowledge Evolutionary WiseQA Platform Technology for Human Knowledge Augmented Services] Many thanks to my family (HoYoun, YounSeo), and my parents.

References

Gabor Angeli and Jakob Uszkoreit. 2013. Language-independent discriminative parsing of temporal expressions. In *Proceedings of the 51th Annual Meeting of the Association for Computational Linguistics*, Sofia, Bulgaria.

Steven Bethard. 2013a. Cleartk-timeml: A minimalist approach to tempeval 2013. In *Proceedings of the Seventh International Workshop on Semantic Evaluation*, pages 10–14, Atlanta, Georgia, USA.

Steven Bethard. 2013b. A synchronous context free grammar for time normalization. In *Proceedings of the Conference on Empirical Methods in Natural Language Processing*, pages 821–826, Seattle, USA.

Bernhard E. Boser, Isabelle M. Guyon, and Vladimir N. Vapnik. 1992. A training algorithm for optimal margin classifiers. In *Proceedings of the fifth Annual Workshop on Computational Learning Theory*, pages 144–152, Pittsburgh, PA, USA.

Nathanael Chambers, Shan Wang, and Dan Jurafsky. 2007. Classifying temporal relations between events. In *Proceedings of the 45th Annual Meeting of the ACL on Interactive Poster and Demonstration Sessions*, pages 173–176, Prague, Czech Republic.

Corinna Cortes and Vladimir Vapnik. 1995. Support-vector networks. *Machine Learning*, 20(3):273–297.

Young-Seob Jeong and Ho-Jin Choi. 2015. Language independent feature extractor. In *Proceedings of the Twenty-Ninth AAAI Conference on Artificial Intelligence*, pages 4170–4171, Texas, USA.

John D. Lafferty, Andrew McCallum, and Fernando C. N. Pereira. 2001. Conditional random fields: Probabilistic models for segmenting and labeling sequence data. In *Proceedings of the Eighteenth International Conference on Machine Learning*, pages 282–289, Williamstown, USA.

Soojong Lim, ChangKi Lee, Jeong Hur, and Myoung-Gil Jang. 2006. Syntax analysis of enumeration type and parallel type using maximum entropy model. In *Proceedings of the Korea Human-Computer Interaction Conference*, pages 1240–1245.

Xiao Ling and Daniel S. Weld. 2010. Temporal information extraction. In *Proceedings of the Twenty-Fourth AAAI Conference on Artificial Intelligence*, Atlanta, Georgia, USA.

Hector Llorens, Estela Saquete, and Borja Navarro. 2010. Tipsem (english and spanish): Evaluating crfs and semantic roles in tempeval-2. In *Proceedings of the Fifth International Workshop on Semantic Evaluation*, pages 284–291, Uppsala, Sweden.

Seyed Abolghasem Mirroshandel and Gholamreza Ghassem-Sani. 2012. Towards unsupervised learning of temporal relations between events. *Journal of Artificial Intelligence Research*, 45(1):125–163.

James Pustejovsky, Jose Castano, Robert Ingria, Roser Sauri, Robert Gaizauskas, Andrea Setzer, and Graham Katz. 2003. Timeml: Robust specification of event and temporal expressions in text. In *New Directions in Question Answering*, pages 28–34, Stanford, USA.

Erik F. Tjong Kim Sang and Sabine Buchholz. 2000. Introduction to the conll-2000 shared task: chunking. In *Proceedings of the 2nd workshop on Learning language in logic and the 4th conference on Computational natural language learning*, pages 127–132, Lisbon, Portugal.

Jannik Strotgen and Michael Gertz. 2010. Heideltime: High quality rule-based extraction and normalization of temporal expressions. In *Proceedings of the Fifth International Workshop on Semantic Evaluation*, pages 321–324, Uppsala, Sweden.

Naushad UzZaman and James Allen. 2010. Event and temporal expression extraction from raw text: First step towards a temporally aware system. *International Journal of Semantic Computing*, 4(4):487–508.

Naushad UzZaman, Hector Llorens, Leon Derczynski, Marc Verhagen, James Allen, and James Pustejovsky. 2013. Semeval-2013 task 1: Tempeval-3: Evaluating time expressions, events, and temporal relations. In *Proceedings of the Seventh International Workshop on Semantic Evaluation*, pages 1–9, Atlanta, Georgia, USA.

Marc Verhagen, Robert J. Gaizauskas, Frank Schilder, Mark Hepple, Jessica Moszkowicz, and James Pustejovsky. 2009. The tempeval challenge: Identifying temporal relations in text. *Language Resources and Evaluation*, 43(2):161–179.

Marc Verhagen, Roser Sauri, Tommaso Caselli, and James Pustejovsky. 2010. Semeval-2010 task 13: Tempeval-2. In *Proceedings of the Fifth International Workshop on Semantic Evaluation*, pages 57–62, Uppsala, Sweden.

Katsumasa Yoshikawa, Sebastian Riedel, Masayuki Asahara, and Yuji Matsumoto. 2009. Jointly identifying temporal relations with markov logic. In *Proceedings of the Joint Conference of the 47th Annual Meeting of the ACL and the 4th International Joint Conference on Natural Language Processing of the AFNLP*, pages 405–413, Suntec, Singapore.

Transition-based Spinal Parsing

Miguel Ballesteros[1,2] **Xavier Carreras**[3]
[1]NLP Group, Pompeu Fabra University [2]Carnegie Mellon University
[3]Xerox Research Centre Europe
miguel.ballesteros@upf.edu xavier.carreras@xrce.xerox.com

Abstract

We present a transition-based arc-eager model to parse spinal trees, a dependency-based representation that includes phrase-structure information in the form of constituent spines assigned to tokens. As a main advantage, the arc-eager model can use a rich set of features combining dependency and constituent information, while parsing in linear time. We describe a set of conditions for the arc-eager system to produce valid spinal structures. In experiments using beam search we show that the model obtains a good trade-off between speed and accuracy, and yields state of the art performance for both dependency and constituent parsing measures.

1 Introduction

There are two main representations of the syntactic structure of sentences, namely constituent and dependency-based structures. In terms of statistical modeling, an advantage of dependency representations is that they are naturally lexicalized, and this allows the statistical model to capture a rich set of lexico-syntactic features. The recent literature has shown that such lexical features greatly favor the accuracy of statistical models for parsing (Collins, 1999; Nivre, 2003; McDonald et al., 2005). Constituent structure, on the other hand, might still provide valuable syntactic information that is not captured by standard dependencies.

In this work we investigate transition-based statistical models that produce *spinal trees*, a representation that combines dependency and constituent structures. Statistical models that use both representations jointly were pioneered by Collins (1999), who used constituent trees annotated with head-child information in order to define lexicalized PCFG models, i.e. extensions of classic constituent-based PCFG that make a central use of lexical dependencies.

An alternative approach is to view the combined representation as a dependency structure augmented with constituent information. This approach was first explored by Collins (1996), who defined a dependency-based probabilistic model that associates a triple of constituents with each dependency. In our case, we follow the representations proposed by Carreras et al. (2008), which we call spinal trees. In a spinal tree (see Figure 1 for an example), each token is associated with a *spine* of constituents, and head-modifier dependencies are attached to nodes in the spine, thus combining the two sources of information in a tight manner. Since spinal trees are inherently dependency-based, it is possible to extend dependency models for such representations, as shown by Carreras et al. (2008) using a so-called graph-based model. The main advantage of such models is that they allow a large family of rich features that include dependency features, constituent features and conjunctions of the two. However, the consequence is that the additional spinal structure greatly increases the number of dependency relations. Even though a graph-based model remains parseable in cubic time, it is impractical unless some pruning strategy is used (Carreras et al., 2008).

In this paper we propose a transition-based parser for spinal parsing, based on the arc-eager strategy by Nivre (2003). Since transition-based parsers run in linear time, our aim is to speed up spinal parsing while taking advantage of the rich representation it provides. Thus, the research question underlying this paper is whether we can accurately learn to take greedy parsing decisions for rich but complex structures such as spinal trees. To control the trade-off, we use beam search for transition-based parsing, which has been shown to be successful (Zhang and Clark, 2011b). The main contributions of this paper are

Proceedings of the 19th Conference on Computational Language Learning, pages 289–299,
Beijing, China, July 30-31, 2015. ©2015 Association for Computational Linguistics

the following:

- We define an arc-eager statistical model for spinal parsing that is based on the triplet relations by Collins (1996). Such relations, in conjunction with the partial spinal structure available in the stack of the parser, provide a very rich set of features.

- We describe a set of conditions that an arc-eager strategy must guarantee in order to produce valid spinal structures.

- In experiments using beam search we show that our method obtains a good trade-off between speed and accuracy for both dependency-based attachment scores and constituent measures.

2 Background

2.1 Spinal Trees

A spinal tree is a generalization of a dependency tree that adds constituent structure to the dependencies in the form of *spines*. In this section we describe the spinal trees used by Carreras et al. (2008). A spine is a sequence of constituent nodes associated with a word in the sentence. From a linguistic perspective, a spine corresponds to the projection of the word in the constituent tree. In other words, the spine of a word consists of the constituents whose head is the word. See Figure 1 for an example of a sentence and its constituent and spinal trees. In the example the spine of each token is the vertical sequence on top of it.

Formally a spinal tree for a sentence $x_{1:n}$ is a pair (V, E), where V is a sequence of n spinal nodes and E is a set of n spinal dependencies. The i-th node in V is a pair (x_i, σ_i), where x_i is the i-th word of the sentence and σ_i is its spine.

A spine σ is a vertical sequence of constituent nodes. We denote by $\mathcal{N}$ the set of constituent nodes, and we use $\star \notin \mathcal{N}$ to denote a special *terminal* node. We denote by $l(\sigma)$ the length of a spine. A spine σ is always non-empty, $l(\sigma) \geq 1$, its first node is always $\star$, and for any $2 \leq j \leq l(\sigma)$ the j-th node of the spine is an element of $\mathcal{N}$.

A spinal dependency is a tuple $\langle h, d, p \rangle$ that represents a directed dependency from the p-th node of σ_h to the d-th node of V. Thus, a spinal dependency is a regular dependency between a head token h and a dependent token d augmented with a position p in the head spine. It must be that $1 \leq h, d \leq n$ and that $1 < p \leq l(\sigma_h)$.

The set of spinal dependencies E satisfies the standard conditions of forming a rooted directed projected tree (Kübler et al., 2009). Plus, E satisfies that the dependencies are correctly nested with respect to the constituent structure that the spines represent. Formally, let (h, d_1, p_1) and (h, d_2, p_2) be two spinal dependencies associated with the same head h. For left dependencies, correct nesting means that if $d_1 < d_2 < h$ then $p_1 \geq p_2$. For right dependents, if $h < d_1 < d_2$ then $p_1 \leq p_2$.

In practice, it is straightforward to obtain spinal trees from a treebank of constituent trees with head-child annotations in each constituent (Carreras et al., 2008): starting from a token, its spine consists of the non-terminal labels of the constituents whose head is the token; the parent node of the top of the spine gives information about the lexical head (by following the head children of the parent) and the position where the spine attaches to. Given a spinal tree it is trivial to recover the constituent and dependency trees.

2.2 Arc-Eager Transition-Based Parsing

The arc-eager transition-based parser (Nivre, 2003) parses a sentence from left to right in linear time. It makes use of a stack that stores tokens that are already processed (partially built dependency structures) and it chooses the highest-scoring parsing action at each point. The arc-eager algorithm adds every arc at the earliest possible opportunity and it can only parse projective trees.

The training process is performed with an oracle (a set of transitions to a parse for a given sentence, (see Figure 2)) and it learns the best transition given a configuration. The SHIFT transition removes the first node from the buffer and puts it on the stack. The REDUCE transition removes the top node from the stack. The LEFT-ARC$_t$ transition introduces a labeled dependency edge between the first element of the buffer and the top element of the stack with the label t. The top element is removed from the stack (reduce transition). The RIGHT-ARC$_t$ transition introduces a labeled dependency edge between the top element of the stack and the first element in the buffer with a label d, and it performs a shift transition. Each action can have constraints (Nivre et al., 2014), Figure 2 and Section 3.2 describe the constraints of the spinal parser.

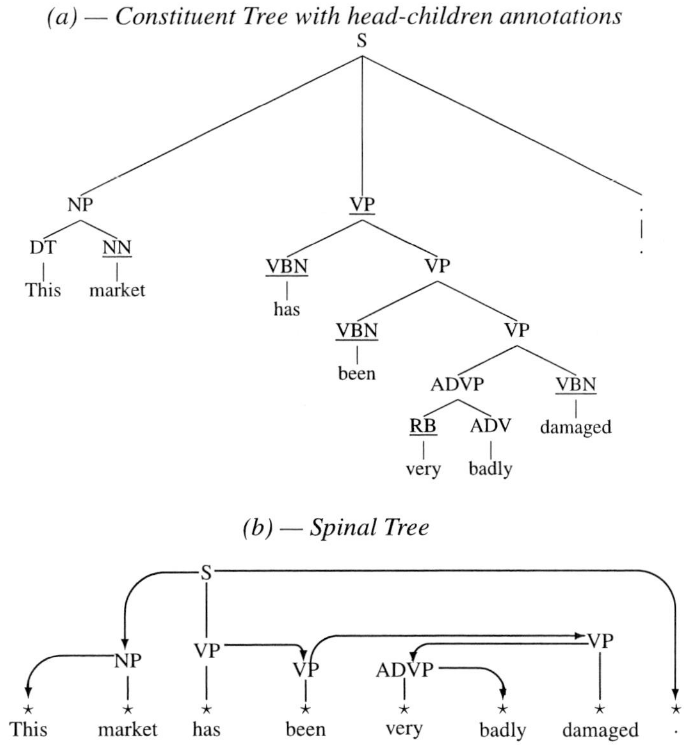

Figure 1: (a) A constituent tree for *This market has been very badly damaged*. For each constituent, the underlined child annotates the head child of the constituent. (b) The corresponding spinal tree.

In this paper, we took the already existent implementation of arc-eager from ZPar[1] (Zhang and Clark, 2009) which is a beam-search parser implemented in C++ focused on efficiency. ZPar gives competitive accuracies, yielding state-of-the-art results, and very fast parsing speeds for dependency parsing. In the case of ZPar, the parsing process starts with a root node at the top of the stack (see Figure 3) and the buffer contains the words/tokens to be parsed.

3 Transition-based Spinal Parsing

In this section we describe an arc-eager transition system that produces spinal trees. Figure 3 shows a parsing example. In essence, the strategy we propose builds the spine of a token by pieces, by adding a piece of spine each time the parser produces a dependency involving such token.

We first describe a labeling of dependencies that encodes a triplet of constituent labels, and it is the basis for defining an arc-eager statistical model. Then we describe a set of constraints that guarantees that the arc-eager derivations we produce correspond to spinal trees. Finally we discuss how to map arc-eager derivations to spinal trees.

3.1 Constituent Triplets

We follow Collins (1996) and define a labeling for dependencies based on constituent triplets.

Consider a spinal tree (V, E) for a sentence $x_{1:n}$. A *constituent triplet* of a spinal dependency $(h, d, p) \in E$ is a tuple $\langle a, b, c\rangle$ where:

- $a \in \mathcal{N}$ is the node at position p of σ_h (parent label)
- $b \in \mathcal{N} \cup \{\star\}$ is the node at position $p-1$ of σ_h (head label)
- $c \in \mathcal{N} \cup \{\star\}$ is the top node of σ_d (dependent label)

For example, a dependency labeled with $\langle \text{S}, \text{VP}, \text{NP}\rangle$ is a subject relation, while the triplet $\langle \text{VP}, \star, \text{NP}\rangle$ represents an object relation. Note that a constituent triplet, in essence, corresponds to a context-free production in a head-driven PCFG (i.e. $a \rightarrow bc$, where b is the head child of a).

[1] http://sourceforge.net/projects/zpar/

$$
\begin{array}{ll}
\textbf{Initial configuration } C_i = \langle [\,], [x_1 \ldots x_n], \emptyset, \rangle & \\
\textbf{Terminal configuration } C_f \in \{C \,|\, C = \langle \Sigma, [\,], A\rangle\} & \\
\textsc{Shift} & \langle \Sigma, i|B, A\rangle \Rightarrow \langle \Sigma|i, B, A\rangle \\
\textsc{Reduce} & \langle \Sigma|i, B, A\rangle \Rightarrow \langle \Sigma, B, A\rangle \\
 & \textbf{if } \exists j, t : \{j \xrightarrow{t} i\} \in A \\
\textsc{Left-Arc}(\langle a,b,c\rangle) & \langle \Sigma|i, j|B, A\rangle \Rightarrow \langle \Sigma, j|B, A \cup \{j \overset{\langle a,b,c\rangle}{\rightarrow} i\}\rangle \\
 & \textbf{if } \neg\exists k, t : \{i \xrightarrow{t} k\} \in A \\
 & \textbf{(1) if } (c \neq \star) \lor \neg(\exists k : \{i \xrightarrow{t} k\} \in A) \\
 & \textbf{(3) if } b = \star \Rightarrow \forall \{i \overset{\langle a',b',c'\rangle}{\rightarrow} k\} \in A,\ a = a' \land b = b' \\
\textsc{Right-Arc}(\langle a,b,c\rangle) & \langle \Sigma|i, j|B, A\rangle \Rightarrow \langle \Sigma|i|j, B, A \cup \{i \overset{\langle a,b,c\rangle}{\rightarrow} j\}\rangle \\
 & \textbf{(1) if } (c \neq \star) \lor \neg(\exists k : \{j \xrightarrow{t} k\} \in A) \\
 & \textbf{(2) if } \neg(\exists k, \langle a',b',c'\rangle : \{k \overset{\langle a',b',c'\rangle}{\rightarrow} i\} \in A \land c' = \star) \\
 & \textbf{(4) if } b = \star \Rightarrow \forall \{j \overset{\langle a',b',c'\rangle}{\rightarrow} k\} \in A \text{ such that } j < k,\ a = a' \land b = b' \\
 & \textbf{(5) if } b = \star \Rightarrow \forall \{j \overset{\langle a',b',c'\rangle}{\rightarrow} k\} \in A \text{ such that } k < j \land b' = \star,\ a = a'
\end{array}
$$

Figure 2: Arc-eager transition system with spinal constraints. Σ represents the stack, B represents the buffer, A represents the set of arcs, t represents a given triplet when its components are not relevant, $\langle a, b, c\rangle$ represents a given triplet when its components are relevant and i, j and k represent tokens of the sentence. The constraints labeled with (1) ... (5) are described in Section 3.2. The constraints that are not labeled are standard constraints of the arc-eager parsing algorithm (Nivre, 2003).

In the literature, these triplets have been shown to provide very rich parameterizations of statistical models for parsing (Collins, 1996; Collins, 1999; Carreras et al., 2008).

For our purposes, we associate with each spinal dependency $(h, d, p) \in E$ a *triplet dependency* $(h, d, \langle a, b, c\rangle)$, where the triplet is defined as above. We then define a standard statistical model for arc-eager parsing that uses constituent triplets as dependency labels. An important advantage of this model is that left-arc and right-arc transitions can have feature descriptions that combine standard dependency features with phrase-structure information in the form of constituent triplets. As shown by Carreras et al. (2008), this rich set of features can obtain significant gains in parsing accuracy.

3.2 Spinal Arc-Eager Constraints

We now describe constraints that guarantee that any derivation produced by a triplet-based arc-eager model corresponds to a spinal structure.

Let us make explicit some properties that relate a derivation D with a token i, the arcs in D involving i, and its spine σ_i:

- D has at most a single arc $(h, i, \langle a, b, c\rangle)$ where i is in the dependent position. The dependent label c of this triplet defines the top of σ_i. If $c = \star$ then $\sigma_i = \star$, and i can not have dependants.
- Consider the subsequence of D of left arcs with head i, of the form $(i, j, \langle a, b, c\rangle)$. In an arc-eager derivation this subsequence follows a head-outwards order. Each of these arcs has in its triplet a pair of contiguous nodes $b{-}a$ of σ_i. We call such pairs *spinal edges*. The subsequence of spinal edges is ordered bottom-up, because arcs appear head-outwards. In addition, sibling arcs may attach to the same position in σ_i. Thus, the subsequence of left spinal edges of i in D is a subsequence with repeats of the sequence of edges of σ_i.
- Analogously, the subsequence of right spinal

Transition	Stack	Buffer	Added Arc
	[Root]	[This, market, has, been, very, badly, damaged, .]	
SHIFT	[Root, This]	[market, has, been, very, badly, damaged, .]	
L-A($\langle$NP, $\star$, $\star\rangle$)	[Root]	[market, has, been, very, badly, damaged, .]	market $\overset{\langle NP,\star,\star\rangle}{\longrightarrow}$ This
SHIFT	[Root, market]	[has, been, very, badly, damaged, .]	
L-A($\langle$S, VP, NP$\rangle$)	[Root]	[has, been, very, badly, damaged, .]	has $\overset{\langle S,VP,NP\rangle}{\longrightarrow}$ market
R-A($\langle$TOP, $\star$, S$\rangle$)	[Root, has]	[been, very, badly, damaged, .]	Root $\overset{\langle TOP,\star,S\rangle}{\longrightarrow}$ has
R-A($\langle$VP, $\star$, VP$\rangle$)	[Root, has, been]	[very, badly, damaged, .]	has $\overset{\langle VP,\star,VP\rangle}{\longrightarrow}$ been
SHIFT	[Root, has,been, very]	[badly, damaged, .]	
R-A($\langle$ADVP, $\star$, $\star\rangle$)	[Root, has, been, very, badly]	[damaged, .]	very $\overset{\langle ADVP,\star,\star\rangle}{\longrightarrow}$ badly
REDUCE	[Root, has, been, very]	[damaged, .]	
L-A($\langle$VP, $\star$, ADVP$\rangle$)	[Root, has, been]	[damaged, .]	damaged $\overset{\langle VP,\star,ADVP\rangle}{\longrightarrow}$ very
R-A($\langle$VP, $\star$, VP$\rangle$)	[Root, has, been, damaged]	[.]	been $\overset{\langle VP,\star,VP\rangle}{\longrightarrow}$ damaged
REDUCE	[Root, has, been]	[.]	
REDUCE	[Root, has]	[.]	
R-A($\langle$S, VP, $\star\rangle$)	[Root, has, .]	[ ]	has $\overset{\langle S,VP,\star\rangle}{\longrightarrow}$.

Figure 3: Transition sequence for *This market has been very badly damaged.*

edges of i in D is a subsequence with repeats of the edges of σ_i. In D, right spinal edges appear after left spinal edges.

We constrain the arc-eager transition process such that these properties hold. Recall that a well-formed spine starts with a terminal node $\star$, and so does the first edge of the spine and only the first. Let C be a configuration, i.e. a partial derivation. The constraints are:

(1) An arc $(h, i, \langle a, b, \star\rangle)$ is not valid if i has dependents in C.

(2) An arc $(i, j, \langle a, b, c\rangle)$ is not valid if C contains a dependency of the form $(h, i, \langle a', b', \star\rangle)$.

(3) A left arc $(i, j, \langle a, \star, c\rangle)$ is only valid if all sibling left arcs in C are of the form $(i, j', \langle a, \star, c'\rangle)$.

(4) Analogous to (3) for right arcs.

(5) If C has a left arc $(i, j, \langle a, \star, c\rangle)$, then a right arc $(i, j', \langle a', \star, c\rangle)$ is not valid if $a \neq a'$.

In essence, constraints 1-2 relate the top of a spine with the existence of descendants, while constraints 3-5 enforce that the bottom of the spine is well formed. We enforce no further constraints looking at edges in the middle of the spine. This means that left and right arc operations can add spinal edges in a free manner, without explicitly encoding how these edges relate to each other. In other words, we rely on the statistical model to correctly build a spine by adding left and right spinal edges along the transition process in a bottom-up fashion.

It is easy to see that these constraints do not prevent the transition process from ending. Specifically, even though the constraints invalidate arc operations, the arc-eager process can always finish by leaving tokens in the buffer without any head assigned, in which case the resulting derivation is a forest of several projective trees.

3.3 Mapping Derivations to Spinal Trees

The constrained arc-eager derivations correspond to spinal structures, but not necessarily to single spinal trees, for two reasons. First, from the derivation we can extract two subsequences of left and right spinal edges, but the derivation does not encode how these sequences should merge into a spine. Second, as in the basic arc-eager process, the derivation might be a forest rather than a single tree. Next we describe processes to turn a spinal arc-eager derivation into a tree.

Forming spines. For each token i we depart from the top of the spine t, a sequence L of left spinal edges, and a sequence R of right spinal edges. The goal is to form a spine σ_i, such that its top is t, and that L and R are subsequences with repeats of the edges of σ_i. We look for the shortest spine satisfying these properties. For example, consider the derivation in Figure 3 and the third token *has*:

- Top t: S
- Left edges L: VP $-$ S
- Right edges R: $\star-$VP, VP $-$ S

In this case the shortest spine that is consistent with the edges and the top is $\star - VP - S$. Our method runs in two steps:

1. Collapse. Traverse each sequence of edges and replace any contiguous subsequence of identical edges by a single occurrence. The assumption is that identical contiguous edges correspond to sibling dependencies that attach to the same node in the spine.[2]

2. Merge the left L and right R sequences of edges overlapping them as much as possible, i.e. looking for the shortest spine. We do this in $\mathcal{O}(nm)$, where n and m are the lengths of the two sequences. Whenever multiple shortest spines are compatible with the left and right edge sequences, we give preference to the spine that places left edges to the bottom.

The result of this process is a spine σ_i with left and right dependents attached to positions of the spine. Note that this strategy has some limitations: (a) it can not recover non-terminal spinal nodes that do not participate in any triplet; and (b) it flattens spinal structures that involve contiguous identical spinal edges. [3]

Rooting Forests. The arc-eager transition system is not guaranteed to generate a single root in a derivation (though see (Nivre and Fernández-González, 2014) for a solution). Thus, after mapping a derivation to a spinal structure, we might get a forest of projective spinal trees. In this case, to produce a constituent tree from the spinal forest, we promote the last tree and place the rest of trees as children of its top node.

4 Experiments

In this section we describe the performance of the transition-based spinal parser by running it with different sizes of the beam and by comparing it with the state-of-the-art. We used the ZPar implementation modified to incorporate the constraints for spinal arc-eager parsing. We used the exact same features as Zhang and Nivre (2011), which extract a rich set of features that encode higher-order interactions betwen the current action and elements of the stack. Since our dependency labels are constituent triplets, these features encode a mix of constituent and dependency structure.

4.1 Data

We use the WSJ portion of the Penn Treebank[4], augmented with head-dependant information using the rules of Yamada and Matsumoto (2003). This results in a total of 974 different constituent triplets, which we use as dependency labels in the spinal arc-eager model. We use predicted part-of-speech tags[5].

4.2 Results in the Development Set

In Table 1 we show the results of our parser for the dependency trees, the table shows unlabeled attachment score (UAS) , triplet accuracy (TA, which would be label accuracy, LA) and triplet attachment score (TAS), and spinal accuracy (SA) (the spinal accuracy is the percentage of complete spines that the parser correctly predicts). In order to be fully comparable, for the dependency-based metrics we report results including and excluding punctuation symbols for evaluation. The table also shows the speed (sentences per second) in standard hardware. We trained the parser with different beam values, we run a number of iterations until the model converges and we report the results of the best iteration.

As it can be observed the best model is the one trained with beam size 64, and greater sizes of the beam help to improve the results. Nonetheless, it also makes the parser slower. This result is expected since the number of dependency labels, i.e. triplets, is 974 so a higher size of the beam allows to test more of them when new actions are included in the agenda. This model already provides high results over 92.34% UAS and it can also predict most of the triplets that label the dependency

[2] However, this is not always the case. For example, in the Penn Treebank adjuncts create an additional constituent level in the verb-phrase structure, and this can result in a series of contiguous VP spinal nodes. The effect of flattening such structures is mild, see below.

[3] These limitations have relatively mild effects on recovering constituent trees in the style of the Penn Treebank. To measure the effect, we took the correct spinal trees of the development section and mapped them to the corresponding arc-eager derivation. Then we mapped the derivation back to a spinal tree using this process and recovered the constituent tree. This process obtained 98.4% of bracketing recall, 99.5% of bracketing precision, and 99.0 of F_1 measure.

[4] We use the standard partition: sections 02-21 for training, section 22 for development, and section 23 for testing.

[5] We use the same setting as in (Carreras et al., 2008) by training over a treebank with predicted part-of-speech tags with mxpost (Ratnaparkhi, 1996) (accuracy: 96.5) and we test on the development set and test set with predicted part-of-speech tags of Collins (1997) (accuracy: 96.8).

	Dep. (incl punct)				Dep. (excl punct)			Const			Speed
Beam-size	UAS	TA	TAS	SA	UAS	TA	TAS	LR	LP	F1	Sent/Sec
8	91.39	90.47	88.78	95.60	92.32	91.21	89.73	88.6	88.4	88.5	7.8
16	91.81	90.95	89.28	95.84	92.70	91.65	90.21	89.0	89.1	89.1	3.9
32	92.08	91.14	89.52	95.96	92.91	91.77	90.38	89.4	89.5	89.5	1.7
64	92.34	91.45	89.84	96.13	93.12	92.04	90.65	89.5	89.7	89.7	0.8

Table 1: UAS with predicted part-of-speech tags for the dev.set including and excluding punctuation symbols. Constituent results for the development set. Parsing speed in sentences per second (an estimate that varies depending on the machine). TA and TAS refer to label accuracy and labeled attachment score where the labels are the different constituent triplets described in Section 3. SA is the spinal accuracy.

arcs (91.45 TA and 89.84 TAS) (including punctuation symbols for evaluation).

Table 1 also shows the results of the parser in the development set after transforming the dependency trees by following the method described in Section 3. The result even surpasses 89.5% F1 which is a competitive accuracy. As we can see, the parser also provides a good trade-off between parsing speed and accuracy.[6]

In order to test whether the number of dependency labels is an issue for the parser, we also trained a model on dependency trees labeled with Yamada and Matsumoto (2003) rules, and the results are comparable to ours. For a beam of size 64, the best model with dependency labels provides 92.3% UAS for the development set including punctuation and 93.0% excluding punctuation, while our spinal parser for the same beam size provides 92.3% UAS including punctuation and 93.1% excluding punctuation. This means that the beam-search arc-eager parser is capable of coping with the dependency triplets, since it even provides slightly better results for unlabeled attachment scores. However, unlike (Carreras et al., 2008), the arc-eager parser does not substantially benefit of using the triplets during training.

4.3 Final Results and State-of-the-art Comparison

Our best model (obtained with beam=64) provides 92.14 UAS, 90.91 TA and 89.32 TAS in the test set including punctuation and 92.78 UAS, 91.53 TA and 90.11 TAS excluding punctuation. Table 2 compares our results with the state-of-the-art. Our model obtains comptetitive dependency accuracies when compared to other systems.

Parser	UAS
McDonald et al. (2005)	90.9
McDonald and Pereira (2006)	91.5
Huang and Sagae (2010)	92.1
Zhang and Nivre (2011)	92.9
Koo and Collins (2010)*	93.0
Bohnet and Nivre (2012)	93.0
Koo et al. (2008) †*	93.2
Martins et al. (2010)	93.3
Ballesteros and Bohnet (2014)	93.5
Carreras et al. (2008) †*	93.5
Suzuki et al. (2009) †*	93.8
this work (beam 64) †*	92.1
this work (beam 64) †	92.8

Table 2: State-of-the-art comparison for unlabeled attachment score for WSJ-PTB with Y&M rules. Results marked with † use other kind of information, and are not directly comparable. Results marked with * include punctuation for evaluation.

In terms of constituent structure, our best model (beam=64) obtains 88.74 LR, 89.21 LP and 88.97 F1. Table 3 compares our model with other constituent parsers, including shift-reduce parsers as ours. Our best model is competitive compared with the rest.

5 Related Work

Collins (1996) defined a statistical model for dependency parsing based on using constituent triplets in the labels, which forms the basis of our arc-eager model. In that work, a chart-based algorithm was used for parsing, while here we use greedy transition-based parsing.

[6] However, in absolute terms, our running times are slower than typical shift-reduce parsers. Our purpose is to show a relation between speed and accuracy, and we opted for a simple implementation rather than an engineered one. As one example, our parser considers all dependency triplets (974) in all cases, which is somehow absurd since most of these can be ruled out given the parts-of-speech of the candidate dependency. Incorporating a filtering strategy of this kind would result in a speedup factor constant to all beam sizes.

Beam-size	LR	LP	F1
Sagae and Lavie (2005)*	86.1	86.0	86.0
Ratnaparkhi (1999)	86.3	87.5	86.9
Sagae and Lavie (2006)*	87.8	88.1	87.9
Collins (1999)	88.1	88.3	88.2
Charniak (2000)	89.5	89.9	89.5
Zhang and Clark (2009)*	90.0	89.9	89.9
Petrov and Klein (2007)	90.1	90.2	90.1
Zhu et al. (2013)-1*	90.2	90.7	90.4
Carreras et al. (2008)	90.7	91.4	91.1
Zhu et al. (2013)-2†*	91.1	91.5	91.3
Huang (2008)	91.2	91.8	91.5
Charniak (2000)	91.2	91.8	91.5
Huang et al. (2010)	91.2	91.8	91.5
McClosky et al. (2006)	91.2	91.8	91.5
this work (beam 64)*	88.7	89.2	89.0

Table 3: State-of-the-art comparison in the test set for phrase structure parsing. Results marked with † use additional information, such as semi-supervised models, and are not directly comparable to the others. Results marked with * are shift-reduce parsers.

Carreras et al. (2008) was the first to use spinal representations to define an arc-factored dependency parsing model based on the Eisner algorithm, that parses in cubic time. Our work can be seen as the transition-based counterpart of that, with a greedy parsing strategy that runs in linear time. Because of the extra complexity of spinal structures, they used three probabilistic non-spinal dependency models to prune the search space of the spinal model. In our work, we show that a single arc-eager model can obtain very competitive results, even though the accuracies of our model are lower than theirs.

In terms of parsing spinal structures, Rush et al. (2010) introduced a dual decomposition method that uses constituent and dependency parsing routines to parse a combined spinal structure.

In a similar style to our method Hall et al. (2007), Hall and Nivre (2008) and Hall (2008) introduced an approach for parsing Swedish and German, in which MaltParser (Nivre et al., 2007) is used to predict dependency trees, whose dependency labels are enriched with constituency labels. They used tuples that encode dependency labels, constituent labels, head relations and the attachment. The last step is to make the inverse transformation from a dependency graph to a constituent structure.

Recently Kong et al. (2015) proposed a structured prediction model for mapping dependency trees to constituent trees, using the CKY algorithm. They assume a fixed dependency tree used as a hard constraint. Also recently, Fernández-González and Martins (2015) proposed an arc-factored dependency model for constituent parsing. In that work dependency labels encode the constituent node where the dependency arises as well as the position index of that node in the head spine. In contrast, we use constituent triplets as dependency labels.

Our method is based on constraining a shift-reduce parser using the arc-eager strategy. Nivre (2003) and Nivre (2004) establish the basis for arc-eager algorithm and arc-standard parsing algorithms, which are central to most recent transition-based parsers (Zhang and Clark, 2011b; Zhang and Nivre, 2011; Bohnet and Nivre, 2012). These parsers are very fast, because the number of parsing actions is linear in the length of the sentence, and they obtain state-of-the-art-performance, as shown in Section 4.3.

For shift-reduce constituent parsing, Sagae and Lavie (2005; 2006) presented a shift-reduce phrase structure parser. The main difference to ours is that their models do not use lexical dependencies. Zhang and Clark (2011a) presented a shift-reduce parser based on CCG, and as such is lexicalized. Both spinal and CCG representations are very expressive. One difference is that spinal trees can be directly obtained from constituent treebanks with head-child information, while CCG derivations are harder to obtain.

More recently, Zhang and Clark (2009) and the subsequent work of Zhu et al. (2013) described a beam-search shift-reduce parsers obtaining very high results. These models use dependency information via stacking, by running a dependency parser as a preprocess. In the literature, stacking is a common technique to improve accuracies by combining dependency and constituent information, in both ways (Wang and Zong, 2011; Farkas and Bohnet, 2012). Our model differs from stacking approaches in that it natively produces the two structures jointly, in such a way that a rich set of features is available.

6 Conclusions and Future Work

There are several lessons to learn from this paper. First, we show that a simple modification to the arc-eager strategy results in a competitive greedy spinal parser which is capable of predicting dependency and constituent structure jointly. In order to make it work, we introduce simple constraints to the arc-eager strategy that ensure well-formed spinal derivations. Second, by doing this, we are providing a good trade-off between speed and accuracy, while at the same time we are providing a dependency structure which can be really useful for downstream applications. Even if the dependency model needs to cope with a huge amount of dependency labels (in the form of constituent triplets), the unlabeled attachment accuracy does not drop and the labeling accuracy (for the triplets) is good enough for getting a good phrase-structure parse. Overall, our work shows that greedy strategies to dependency parsing can be successfuly augmented to include constituent structure.

In the future, we plan to explore spinal derivations in new transition-based dependency parsers (Chen and Manning, 2014; Dyer et al., 2015; Weiss et al., 2015; Zhou et al., 2015). This would allow to explore the spinal derivations in new ways and to test their potentialities.

Acknowledgements

We thank Noah A. Smith and the anonymous reviewers for their very useful comments. Miguel Ballesteros is supported by the European Commission under the contract numbers FP7-ICT-610411 (project MULTISENSOR) and H2020-RIA-645012 (project KRISTINA).

References

Miguel Ballesteros and Bernd Bohnet. 2014. Automatic feature selection for agenda-based dependency parsing. In *Proc. COLING*.

Bernd Bohnet and Joakim Nivre. 2012. A transition-based system for joint part-of-speech tagging and labeled non-projective dependency parsing. In *Proceedings of the 2012 Joint Conference on Empirical Methods in Natural Language Processing and Computational Natural Language Learning*, pages 1455–1465, Jeju Island, Korea, July. Association for Computational Linguistics.

Xavier Carreras, Michael Collins, and Terry Koo. 2008. TAG, Dynamic Programming, and the Perceptron for Efficient, Feature-Rich Parsing. In *CoNLL 2008: Proceedings of the Twelfth Conference on Computational Natural Language Learning*, pages 9–16, Manchester, England, August. Coling 2008 Organizing Committee.

Eugene Charniak. 2000. A maximum-entropy-inspired parser. In *Proceedings of the 1st North American Chapter of the Association for Computational Linguistics Conference*, NAACL 2000, pages 132–139, Stroudsburg, PA, USA. Association for Computational Linguistics.

Danqi Chen and Christopher D. Manning. 2014. A fast and accurate dependency parser using neural networks. In *Proc. EMNLP*.

Michael John Collins. 1996. A new statistical parser based on bigram lexical dependencies. In *Proceedings of the 34th Annual Meeting of the Association for Computational Linguistics*, pages 184–191, Santa Cruz, California, USA, June. Association for Computational Linguistics.

Michael Collins. 1997. Three generative, lexicalised models for statistical parsing. In *Proceedings of the eighth conference on European chapter of the Association for Computational Linguistics*, pages 16–23. Association for Computational Linguistics.

Michael Collins. 1999. *Head-Driven Statistical Models for Natural Language Parsing*. Ph.D. thesis, University of Pennsylvania.

Chris Dyer, Miguel Ballesteros, Wang Ling, Austin Matthews, and Noah A. Smith. 2015. Transition-based dependency parsing with stack long short-term memory. In *Proceedings of ACL*.

Richárd Farkas and Bernd Bohnet. 2012. Stacking of dependency and phrase structure parsers. In *COLING*, pages 849–866.

Daniel Fernández-González and André F. T. Martins. 2015. Parsing as reduction. *CoRR*, abs/1503.00030.

Johan Hall and Joakim Nivre. 2008. A dependency-driven parser for german dependency and constituency representations. In *Proceedings of the Workshop on Parsing German*, PaGe '08, pages 47–54, Stroudsburg, PA, USA. Association for Computational Linguistics.

Johan Hall, Joakim Nivre, and Jens Nilsson. 2007. A Hybrid Constituency-Dependency Parser for Swedish. In *Proceedings of the 16th Nordic Conference of Computational Linguistics (NODALIDA)*.

Johan Hall. 2008. Transition-based natural language parsing with dependency and constituency representations. Master's thesis, Växjö University.

Liang Huang and Kenji Sagae. 2010. Dynamic programming for linear-time incremental parsing. In *Proceedings of the 48th Annual Meeting of the Association for Computational Linguistics (ACL)*, pages 1077–1086.

Zhongqiang Huang, Mary Harper, and Slav Petrov. 2010. Self-training with products of latent variable grammars. In *Proceedings of the 2010 Conference on Empirical Methods in Natural Language Processing*, pages 12–22. Association for Computational Linguistics.

Liang Huang. 2008. Forest reranking: Discriminative parsing with non-local features. In *ACL*, pages 586–594.

Lingpeng Kong, Alexander M. Rush, and Noah A. Smith. 2015. Transforming dependencies into phrase structures. In *Proceedings of the 2015 Conference of the North American Chapter of the Association for Computational Linguistics – Human Language Technologies*. Association for Computational Linguistics.

Terry Koo and Michael Collins. 2010. Efficient third-order dependency parsers. In *Proceedings of the 48th Annual Meeting of the Association for Computational Linguistics (ACL)*, pages 1–11.

Terry Koo, Xavier Carreras, and Michael Collins. 2008. Simple semi-supervised dependency parsing. In *Proceedings of the 46th Annual Meeting of the Association for Computational Linguistics (ACL)*, pages 595–603.

Sandra Kübler, Ryan McDonald, and Joakim Nivre. 2009. *Dependency Parsing*. Morgan and Claypool.

Andre Martins, Noah Smith, Eric Xing, Pedro Aguiar, and Mario Figueiredo. 2010. Turbo parsers: Dependency parsing by approximate variational inference. In *Proceedings of the Conference on Empirical Methods in Natural Language Processing (EMNLP)*, pages 34–44.

David McClosky, Eugene Charniak, and Mark Johnson. 2006. Effective self-training for parsing. In *Proceedings of the Main Conference on Human Language Technology Conference of the North American Chapter of the Association of Computational Linguistics*, HLT-NAACL '06, pages 152–159, Stroudsburg, PA, USA. Association for Computational Linguistics.

Ryan McDonald and Fernando Pereira. 2006. Online learning of approximate dependency parsing algorithms. In *Proceedings of the 11th Conference of the European Chapter of the Association for Computational Linguistics (EACL)*, pages 81–88.

Ryan McDonald, Koby Crammer, and Fernando Pereira. 2005. Online large-margin training of dependency parsers. In *Proceedings of the 43rd Annual Meeting of the Association for Computational Linguistics (ACL)*, pages 91–98.

Joakim Nivre and Daniel Fernández-González. 2014. Arc-eager parsing with the tree constraint. *Computational Linguistics*, 40(2):259–267.

Joakim Nivre, Johan Hall, Jens Nilsson, Atanas Chanev, Gülşen Eryiğit, Sandra Kübler, Svetoslav Marinov, and Erwin Marsi. 2007. Maltparser: A language-independent system for data-driven dependency parsing. *Natural Language Engineering*, 13:95–135.

Joakim Nivre, Yoav Goldberg, and Ryan T. McDonald. 2014. Constrained arc-eager dependency parsing. *Computational Linguistics*, 40(2):249–527.

Joakim Nivre. 2003. An efficient algorithm for projective dependency parsing. In *Proceedings of the 8th International Workshop on Parsing Technologies (IWPT)*, pages 149–160.

Joakim Nivre. 2004. Incrementality in deterministic dependency parsing. In *Proceedings of the Workshop on Incremental Parsing: Bringing Engineering and Cognition Together (ACL)*, pages 50–57.

Slav Petrov and Dan Klein. 2007. Improved inference for unlexicalized parsing. In *HLT-NAACL*, volume 7, pages 404–411.

Adwait Ratnaparkhi. 1996. A maximum entropy part-of-speech tagger. In *Proceedings of the Conference on Empirical Methods in Natural Language Processing*.

Adwait Ratnaparkhi. 1999. Learning to parse natural language with maximum entropy models. *Machine Learning*, 34(1-3):151–175.

Alexander M Rush, David Sontag, Michael Collins, and Tommi Jaakkola. 2010. On dual decomposition and linear programming relaxations for natural language processing. In *Proceedings of the 2010 Conference on Empirical Methods in Natural Language Processing*, pages 1–11. Association for Computational Linguistics.

Kenji Sagae and Alon Lavie. 2005. A classifier-based parser with linear run-time complexity. In *Proceedings of the Ninth International Workshop on Parsing Technology*, Parsing '05, pages 125–132, Stroudsburg, PA, USA. Association for Computational Linguistics.

Kenji Sagae and Alon Lavie. 2006. Parser combination by reparsing. In *Proceedings of the Human Language Technology Conference of the NAACL, Companion Volume: Short Papers*, NAACL-Short '06, pages 129–132, Stroudsburg, PA, USA. Association for Computational Linguistics.

Jun Suzuki, Hideki Isozaki, Xavier Carreras, and Michael Collins. 2009. An empirical study of semi-supervised structured conditional models for dependency parsing. In *Proceedings of EMNLP*, pages 551–560.

Zhiguo Wang and Chengqing Zong. 2011. Parse reranking based on higher-order lexical dependencies. In *IJCNLP*, pages 1251–1259.

David Weiss, Christopher Alberti, Michael Collins, and Slav Petrov. 2015. Structured training for neural network transition-based parsing. In *Proc. ACL*.

Hiroyasu Yamada and Yuji Matsumoto. 2003. Statistical dependency analysis with support vector machines. In *Proceedings of the 8th International Workshop on Parsing Technologies (IWPT)*, pages 195–206.

Yue Zhang and Stephen Clark. 2009. Transition-based parsing of the chinese treebank using a global discriminative model. In *Proceedings of the 11th International Conference on Parsing Technologies*, pages 162–171. Association for Computational Linguistics.

Yue Zhang and Stephen Clark. 2011a. Shift-reduce ccg parsing. In *Proceedings of the 49th Annual Meeting of the Association for Computational Linguistics: Human Language Technologies-Volume 1*, pages 683–692. Association for Computational Linguistics.

Yue Zhang and Stephen Clark. 2011b. Syntactic processing using the generalized perceptron and beam search. *Computational Linguistics*, 37(1):105–151.

Yue Zhang and Joakim Nivre. 2011. Transition-based dependency parsing with rich non-local features. In *Proceedings of the 49th Annual Meeting of the Association for Computational Linguistics (ACL)*, pages 188–193, Portland, Oregon, USA.

Hao Zhou, Yue Zhang, Shujian Huang, and Jiajun Chen. 2015. A Neural Probabilistic Structured-Prediction Model for Transition-Based Dependency Parsing. In *ACL*.

Muhua Zhu, Yue Zhang, Wenliang Chen, Min Zhang, and Jingbo Zhu. 2013. Fast and accurate shift-reduce constituent parsing. In *Proceedings of the 51st Annual Meeting of the Association for Computational Linguistics (Volume 1: Long Papers)*, pages 434–443. Association for Computational Linguistics.

Accurate Cross-lingual Projection between Count-based Word Vectors by Exploiting Translatable Context Pairs

Shonosuke Ishiwatari[♣], **Nobuhiro Kaji**[◇♡], **Naoki Yoshinaga**[◇♡],
♣ Graduate School of Information Science and Technology, the University of Tokyo
◇ Institute of Industrial Science, the University of Tokyo
♡ National Institute of Information and Communications Technology, Japan
{ishiwatari, kaji, ynaga}@tkl.iis.u-tokyo.ac.jp

Masashi Toyoda[◇], **Masaru Kitsuregawa**[◇♠]
◇ Institute of Industrial Science, the University of Tokyo
♠ National Institute of Informatics, Japan
{toyoda, kitsure}@tkl.iis.u-tokyo.ac.jp

Abstract

We propose a method that learns a cross-lingual projection of word representations from one language into another. Our method utilizes translatable context pairs as bonus terms of the objective function. In the experiments, our method outperformed existing methods in three language pairs, (English, Spanish), (Japanese, Chinese) and (English, Japanese), without using any additional supervisions.

1 Introduction

Vector-based representations of word meanings, hereafter *word vectors*, have been widely used in a variety of NLP applications including synonym detection (Baroni et al., 2014), paraphrase detection (Erk and Padó, 2008), and dialogue analysis (Kalchbrenner and Blunsom, 2013). The basic idea behind those representation methods is the distributional hypothesis (Harris, 1954; Firth, 1957) that similar words are likely to co-occur with similar context words.

A problem with the word vectors is that they are not meant for capturing the similarity between words in different languages, *i.e.*, translation pairs such as "*gato*" and "*cat*." The meaning representations of such word pairs are usually dissimilar, because the vast majority of the context words are from the same language as the target words (*e.g.*, Spanish for "*gato*" and English for "*cat*"). This prevents using word vectors in multi-lingual applications such as cross-lingual information retrieval and machine translation.

Several approaches have been made so far to address this problem (Fung, 1998; Klementiev et al., 2012; Mikolov et al., 2013b). In particular, Mikolov et al. (2013b) recently explored learning a linear transformation between word vectors of different languages from a small amount of training data, *i.e.*, a set of bilingual word pairs.

This study explores incorporating prior knowledge about the correspondence between dimensions of word vectors to learn more accurate transformation, when using count-based word vectors (Baroni et al., 2014). Since the dimensions of count-based word vectors are explicitly associated with context words, we can partially be aware of the cross-lingual correspondence between the dimensions of word vectors by diverting the training data. Also, word surface forms present noisy yet useful clues on the correspondence when targeting the language pairs that have exchanged their vocabulary (*e.g.*, "*cocktail*" in English and "*cóctel*" in Spanish). Although apparently useful, how to exploit such knowledge within the learning framework has not been addressed so far.

We evaluated the proposed method in three language pairs. Compared with baselines including a method that uses vectors learned by neural networks, our method gave better results.

2 Related Work

Neural networks (Mikolov et al., 2013a; Bengio et al., 2003) have recently gained much attention as a way of inducing word vectors. Although the scope of our study is currently limited to the count-based word vectors, our experiment demonstrated that the proposed method performs significantly better than strong baselines including neural networks. This suggests that count-based word vectors have a great advantage when learning a cross-lingual projection. As a future work, we are also

Proceedings of the 19th Conference on Computational Language Learning, pages 300–304,
Beijing, China, July 30-31, 2015.

interested in extending the method presented here to apply word vectors learned by neural networks.

There are also methods that directly inducing meaning representations shared by different languages (Klementiev et al., 2012; Lauly et al., 2014; Xiao and Guo, 2014; Hermann and Blunsom, 2014; Faruqui and Dyer, 2014; Gouws and Søgaard, 2015), rather than learning transformation between different languages (Fung, 1998; Mikolov et al., 2013b; Dinu and Baroni, 2014). However, the former approach is unable to handle words not appearing in the training data, unlike the latter approach.

3 Proposed Method

3.1 Learning cross-lingual projection

We begin by introducing the previous method of learning a linear transformation from word vectors in one language into another, which are hereafter referred to as source and target language.

Suppose we have a training data of n examples $\{(\boldsymbol{x}_1, \boldsymbol{z}_1), (\boldsymbol{x}_2, \boldsymbol{z}_2), \ldots (\boldsymbol{x}_n, \boldsymbol{z}_n)\}$, where $\boldsymbol{x}_i$ is the count-based vector representation of a word in the source language (*e.g.*, "*gato*"), and $\boldsymbol{z}_i$ is the word vector of its translation in the target language (*e.g.*, "*cat*"). Then, we seek for a translation matrix, $\boldsymbol{W}$, such that $\boldsymbol{W}\boldsymbol{x}_i$ approximates $\boldsymbol{z}_i$, by solving the following optimization problem.

$$\boldsymbol{W}^{\star} = \operatorname*{argmin}_{\boldsymbol{W}} \sum_{i=1}^{n} \|\boldsymbol{W}\boldsymbol{x}_i - \boldsymbol{z}_i\|^2 + \frac{\lambda}{2}\|\boldsymbol{W}\|^2. \quad (1)$$

The second term is the L_2 regularizer. Although the regularization term does not appear in the original formalization (Mikolov et al., 2013b), we take this as a starting point of our investigation because the regularizer can prevent over-fitting and generally helps learn better models.

3.2 Exploiting translatable context pairs

Within the learning framework above, we propose exploiting the fact that dimensions of count-based word vectors are associated with context words, and some dimensions in the source language are translations of those in the target language.

For illustration purpose, suppose count-based word vectors of Spanish and English. The Spanish word vectors would have dimensions associated with context words such as "*amigo*," "*comer*," "*importante*," while the dimensions of the English word vectors are associated with "*eat*," "*run*," "*small*" and "*importance*," and so on. Since, for example, "*friend*" is a English translation of "*amigo*," the Spanish dimension associated with "*amigo*" is likely to be mapped to the English dimension associated with "*friend*." Such knowledge about the cross-lingual correspondence between dimensions is considered beneficial for learning accurate translation matrix.

We take two approaches to obtaining such correspondence. Firstly, since we have already assumed that a small amount of training data is available for training the translation matrix, it can also be used for finding the correspondence between dimensions (referred to as $\mathcal{D}_{train}$). Note that it is natural that some words in a language have many translations in another language. Thus, for example, $\mathcal{D}_{train}$ may include ("*amigo*", "*friend*"), ("*amigo*", "*fan*") and ("*amigo*", "*supporter*").

Secondly, since languages have evolved over the years while often deriving or borrowing words (or concepts) from those in other languages, those words have similar or even the same spelling. We take advantage of this to find the correspondence between dimensions. We specifically define function $\text{DIST}(r, s)$ that measures the surface-level similarity, and regard all context word pairs (r, s) having smaller distance than a threshold[1] as translatable ones (referred to as $\mathcal{D}_{sim}$).

$$\text{DIST}(r, s) = \frac{Levenshtein(r, s)}{\min(len(r), len(s))}$$

where function $Levenshtein(r, s)$ represents the Levenshtein distance between the two words, and $len(r)$ represents the length of the word.

3.3 New objective function

We incorporate the knowledge about the correspondence between the dimensions into the learning framework. Since the correspondence obtained by the methods presented above can be noisy, we want to treat it as a soft constraint. This consideration leads us to develop the following new objective function:

$$\boldsymbol{W}^{\star} = \operatorname*{argmin}_{\boldsymbol{W}} \sum_{i=1}^{n} \|\boldsymbol{W}\boldsymbol{x}_i - \boldsymbol{z}_i\|^2 + \frac{\lambda}{2}\|\boldsymbol{W}\|^2 - \beta_{train} \sum_{(j,k)\in\mathcal{D}_{train}} w_{jk} - \beta_{sim} \sum_{(j,k)\in\mathcal{D}_{sim}} w_{jk}.$$

The third and fourth terms are newly added to guide the learning process to strengthen w_{jk} when

[1] The threshold was fixed to 0.5.

k-th dimension in the source language corresponds to j-th dimension in the target language. $\mathcal{D}_{train}$ and $\mathcal{D}_{sim}$ are sets of dimension pairs found by the two methods. β_{train} and β_{sim} are parameters representing the strength of the new terms, and are tuned on held-out development data.

3.4 Optimization

We use Pegasos algorithm (Shalev-Shwartz et al., 2011), an instance of the stochastic gradient descent (Bottou, 2004), to optimize the new objective. Given τ-th learning sample $(\boldsymbol{x}_\tau, \boldsymbol{z}_\tau)$, we update translation matrix $\boldsymbol{W}$ as follows:

$$\boldsymbol{W} \leftarrow \boldsymbol{W} - \eta_\tau \nabla E_\tau(\boldsymbol{W})$$

where η_τ represents the learning rate and is set to $\eta_\tau = \frac{1}{\lambda \tau}$, and $\nabla E_\tau(\boldsymbol{W})$ is the gradient which is calculated from τ-th sample $(\boldsymbol{x}_\tau, \boldsymbol{z}_\tau)$:

$$2(\boldsymbol{W}\boldsymbol{x}_\tau - \boldsymbol{z}_\tau)\boldsymbol{x}_\tau^{\mathrm{T}} - \beta_{train}\boldsymbol{A} - \beta_{sim}\boldsymbol{B} + \lambda\boldsymbol{W}.$$

$\boldsymbol{A}$ and $\boldsymbol{B}$ are gradients corresponding to the two new terms. $\boldsymbol{A}$ is a matrix in which $a_{jk} = 1$ if $(j, k) \in \mathcal{D}_{train}$ otherwise 0. $\boldsymbol{B}$ is defined similarly.

4 Experiments

We evaluate our method on translation among word vectors in four languages: English (En), Spanish (Es), Japanese (Jp) and Chinese (Cn). We have chosen three language pairs: (En, Es), (Jp, Cn) and (En, Jp), for the translation, so that we can examine the impact of each type of translatable context pairs integrated into the learning objective.

4.1 Setup

First, we prepared source text in the four languages from Wikipedia[2] dumps following (Baroni et al., 2014). We extracted plain text from the XML dumps by using wp2txt.[3] Since words are concatenated in Japanese and Chinese, we used MeCab[4] and Stanford Word Segmenter[5] to tokenize the text. Since inflection occurs in English, Spanish, and Japanese, we used Stanford POS tagger,[6] Pattern,[7] and MeCab to lemmatize the text.

Next, we induced count-based word vectors from the obtained text. We considered context windows of five words to both sides of the target word. The function words are then excluded from the extracted context words. Since the count vectors are very high-dimensional and sparse, we selected top-10k frequent words as contexts words (in other words, the number of dimensions of the word vectors). We converted the counts into positive point-wise mutual information (Church and Hanks, 1990) and normalized the resulting vectors to remove the bias that is introduced by the difference of the word frequency.

Then, we compiled a seed bilingual dictionary (a set of bilingual word pairs) for each language pair that is used to learn and evaluate the translation matrix. We utilized cross-lingual synsets in the Open Multilingual Wordnet[8] to obtain bilingual pairs.

Since our method aims to be used in expanding bilingual dictionaries, we designed datasets assuming such a situation. Considering that more frequent words are likely to be registered in a dictionary, we sorted words in the source language by frequency and used the top-11k words and their translations in the target language as a training/development data, and used the subsequent 1k words and their translations as a test data.

We have compared our method with the following three methods:

Baseline learns a translation matrix using Eq. 1 for the same count-based word vectors as the proposed method. Comparison between the proposed method and this method reveals the impact of incorporating the cross-lingual correspondences between dimensions.

CBOW learns a translation matrix using Eq. 1 for word vectors learned by a neural network (specifically, continuous bag-of-words (CBOW)) (Mikolov et al., 2013b). Comparison between this method and the above baseline reveals the impact of the vector representation. Note that the CBOW-based word vectors take rare context words as well as the top-10k frequent words into account. We used word2vec[9] to obtain the vectors for each language.[10] Since Mikolov et al. (2013b)

[2]http://dumps.wikimedia.org/
[3]https://github.com/yohasebe/wp2txt/
[4]http://taku910.github.io/mecab/
[5]http://nlp.stanford.edu/software/segmenter.shtml
[6]http://nlp.stanford.edu/software/tagger.shtml
[7]http://www.clips.ua.ac.be/pages/pattern
[8]http://compling.hss.ntu.edu.sg/omw/
[9]https://code.google.com/p/word2vec/
[10]The threshold of sub-sampling of words was set to 1e-3 to reduce the effect of very frequent words, *e.g.*, "*a*" or "*the*."

Table 1: Experimental results: the accuracy of the translation.

Testset	Baseline		CBOW		Direct Mapping		Proposed$_{\text{w/o surface}}$		Proposed	
	P@1	P@5	P@1	P@5	P@1	P@5	P@1	P@5	P@1	P@5
Es → En	0.1%	0.5%	7.5%	22.0%	45.7%	61.1%	46.6%	62.4%	**54.7%**	**67.6%**
Es ← En	0.1%	0.6%	7.1%	18.9%	11.9%	26.1%	28.7%	45.7%	**31.3%**	**49.6%**
Jp → Cn	0.6%	1.6%	5.4%	13.8%	9.3%	22.2%	11.1%	26.2%	**15.5%**	**34.0%**
Jp ← Cn	0.3%	1.2%	2.9%	11.3%	11.6%	26.8%	7.8%	21.6%	**13.1%**	**27.9%**
En → Jp	0.3%	1.1%	4.9%	13.3%	5.4%	13.9%	18.5%	36.4%	**19.3%**	**37.1%**
En ← Jp	0.2%	1.0%	6.5%	19.1%	22.3%	37.4%	32.3%	51.0%	**32.5%**	**51.9%**

reported the accurate translation can be obtained when the vectors in the source language is 2-4x larger than that in the target language, we prepared m-dimensional ($m = 100, 200, 300$) vectors for the target language and n-dimensional ($n = 2m, 3m, 4m$) vectors for the source language, and optimized their combinations on the development data.

Direct Mapping exploits the training data to map each dimension in a word vector in the source language to the corresponding dimension in a word vector in the target language, referring to the bilingual pairs in the training data (Fung, 1998). To deal with words that have more than one translation, we weighted each translation by a reciprocal rank of its frequency among the translations in the target language, as in (Prochasson et al., 2009).

Note that all methods, including the proposed methods, use the same amount of supervision (training data) and thereby they are completely comparable with each other.

Evaluation procedure For each word vector in the source language, we translate it into the target language and evaluate the quality of the translation as in (Mikolov et al., 2013b): i) measure the cosine similarity between the resulting word vector and all the vectors in the test data (in the target language), ii) next choose the top-n ($n = 1, 5$) word vectors that have the highest similarity against the resulting vector, and iii) then examine whether the chosen vectors include the correct one.

4.2 Results

Table 1 shows results of the translation between word vectors in each language pair. **Proposed** significantly improved the translation quality against **Baseline**, and performed the best among all of the methods. Although the use of CBOW-based word vectors (**CBOW**) has improved the translation quality against **Baseline**, the performance

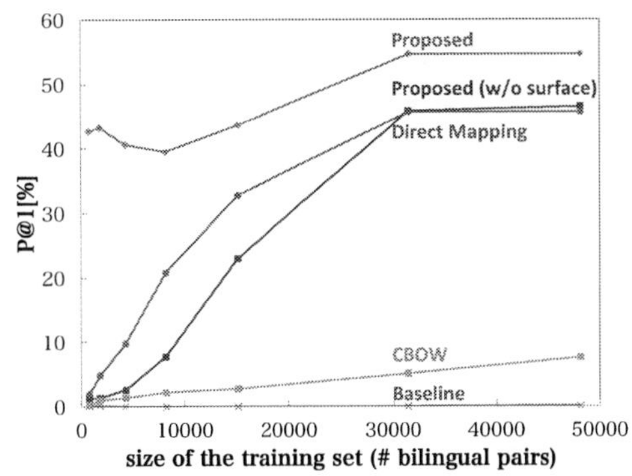

Figure 1: The impact of the size of training data (Es → En).

gain is smaller than that obtained by our new objective. **Proposed$_{\text{w/o surface}}$** uses only the training data to find translatable context pairs by setting $\beta_{sim} = 0$. Thus, its advantage over **Direct Mapping** confirms the importance of learning a translation matrix. In addition, the greater advantage of **Proposed** over **Proposed$_{\text{w/o surface}}$** in the translation between (En, Es) or (Jp, Cn) conforms to our expectation that surface-level similarity is more useful for translation between the language pairs which have often exchanged their vocabulary.

Figure 1 shows P@1 (Es → En) plotted against the size of training data. Remember that the training data is not only used to learn a translation matrix in the methods other than **Direct Mapping** but also is used to map dimensions in **Direct Mapping** and the proposed methods. **Proposed** performs the best among all methods regardless the size of training data. Comparison between **Direct Mapping** and **Proposed$_{\text{w/o surface}}$** reveals that learning a translation matrix is not always effective when the size of the training data is small, since it may be suffered from over-fitting (the size of the translation matrix is too large for the size of training data). We can see that surface-level similarity is beneficial especially when the size of training data is small.

5 Conclusion

We have proposed the use of prior knowledge in accurately translating word vectors. We have specifically exploited two types of translatable context pairs, which are taken from the training data and guessed by surface-level similarity, to design a new objective function in learning the translation matrix. Experimental results confirmed that our method significantly improved the translation among word vectors in four languages, and the advantage was greater than that obtained by the use of a word vector learned by a neural network.

Acknowledgments

This work was partially supported by JSPS KAKENHI Grant Number 25280111.

References

Marco Baroni, Georgiana Dinu, and Germán Kruszewski. 2014. Don't count, predict! a systematic comparison of context-counting vs. context-predicting semantic vectors. In *Proceedings of ACL*, pages 238–247.

Yoshua Bengio, Réjean Ducharme, Pascal Vincent, and Christian Janvin. 2003. A neural probabilistic language model. *The Journal of Machine Learning Research*, 3:1137–1155.

Léon Bottou. 2004. Stochastic learning. In *Advanced lectures on machine learning*, pages 146–168. Springer.

Kenneth Ward Church and Patrick Hanks. 1990. Word association norms, mutual information, and lexicography. *Computational linguistics*, 16(1):22–29.

Georgiana Dinu and Marco Baroni. 2014. How to make words with vectors: Phrase generation in distributional semantics. In *Proceedings of ACL*, pages 624–633.

Katrin Erk and Sebastian Padó. 2008. A structured vector space model for word meaning in context. In *Proceedings of EMNLP*, pages 897–906.

Manaal Faruqui and Chris Dyer. 2014. Improving vector space word representations using multilingual correlation. In *Proceedings of EACL*, pages 462–471.

John R. Firth. 1957. A synopsis of linguistic theory. *Studies in Linguistic Analysis*, pages 1–32.

Pascale Fung. 1998. A statistical view on bilingual lexicon extraction: from parallel corpora to non-parallel corpora. In *Machine Translation and the Information Soup*, pages 1–17. Springer.

Stephan Gouws and Anders Søgaard. 2015. Simple task-specific bilingual word embeddings. In *Proceedings of NAACL-HLT*, pages 1386–1390.

Zellig S. Harris. 1954. Distributional structure. *Word*, 10:146–162.

Karl Moritz Hermann and Phil Blunsom. 2014. Multilingual models for compositional distributed semantics. In *Proceedings of ACL*, pages 58–68.

Nal Kalchbrenner and Phil Blunsom. 2013. Recurrent convolutional neural networks for discourse compositionality. In *Proceedings of ACL Workshop on Continuous Vector Space Models and their Compositionality*, pages 119–126.

Alexandre Klementiev, Ivan Titov, and Binod Bhattarai. 2012. Inducing crosslingual distributed representations of words. In *Proceedings of COLING*, pages 1459–1474.

Stanislas Lauly, Hugo Larochelle, Mitesh Khapra, Balaraman Ravindran, Vikas C Raykar, and Amrita Saha. 2014. An autoencoder approach to learning bilingual word representations. In *Advances in NIPS*, pages 1853–1861.

Tomas Mikolov, Kai Chen, Greg Corrado, and Jeffrey Dean. 2013a. Efficient estimation of word representations in vector space. In *Proceedings of Workshop at ICLR*.

Tomas Mikolov, Quoc V. Le, and Ilya Sutskever. 2013b. Exploiting similarities among languages for machine translation. *arXiv preprint*.

Emmanuel Prochasson, Emmanuel Morin, and Kyo Kageura. 2009. Anchor points for bilingual lexicon extraction from small comparable corpora. In *Proceedings of MT Summit XII*, pages 284–291.

Shai Shalev-Shwartz, Yoram Singer, Nathan Srebro, and Andrew Cotter. 2011. Pegasos: Primal estimated sub-gradient solver for SVM. *Mathematical programming*, 127(1):3–30.

Min Xiao and Yuhong Guo. 2014. Distributed word representation learning for cross-lingual dependency parsing. In *Proceedings of CoNLL*, pages 119–129.

Deep Neural Language Models for Machine Translation

Minh-Thang Luong **Michael Kayser** **Christopher D. Manning**
Computer Science Department, Stanford University, Stanford, CA, 94305
{lmthang, mkayser, manning}@stanford.edu

Abstract

Neural language models (NLMs) have been able to improve machine translation (MT) thanks to their ability to generalize well to long contexts. Despite recent successes of deep neural networks in speech and vision, the general practice in MT is to incorporate NLMs with only one or two hidden layers and there have not been clear results on whether having more layers helps. In this paper, we demonstrate that deep NLMs with three or four layers outperform those with fewer layers in terms of both the perplexity and the translation quality. We combine various techniques to successfully train deep NLMs that jointly condition on both the source and target contexts. When reranking n-best lists of a strong web-forum baseline, our deep models yield an average boost of 0.5 TER / 0.5 BLEU points compared to using a shallow NLM. Additionally, we adapt our models to a new sms-chat domain and obtain a similar gain of 1.0 TER / 0.5 BLEU points.[1]

1 Introduction

Deep neural networks (DNNs) have been successful in learning more complex functions than shallow ones (Bengio, 2009) and exceled in many challenging tasks such as in speech (Hinton et al., 2012) and vision (Krizhevsky et al., 2012). These results have sparked interest in applying DNNs to natural language processing problems as well. Specifically, in machine translation (MT), there has been an active body of work recently in utilizing neural language models (NLMs) to improve translation quality. However, to the best of our knowledge, work in this direction only makes use of NLMs with either one or two hidden layers. For example, Schwenk (2010, 2012) and Son et al. (2012) used shallow NLMs with a single hidden layer for reranking. Vaswani et al. (2013) considered two-layer NLMs for decoding but provided no comparison among models of various depths. Devlin et al. (2014) reported only a small gain when decoding with a two-layer NLM over a single layer one. There have not been clear results on whether adding more layers to NLMs helps.

In this paper, we demonstrate that deep NLMs with three or four layers are better than those with fewer layers in terms of the perplexity and the translation quality. We detail how we combine various techniques from past work to successfully train deep NLMs that condition on both the source and target contexts. When reranking n-best lists of a strong web-forum MT baseline, our deep models achieve an additional improvement of 0.5 TER / 0.5 BLEU compared to using a shallow NLM. Furthermore, by fine-tuning general in-domain NLMs with out-of-domain data, we obtain a similar boost of 1.0 TER / 0.5 BLEU points over a strong domain-adapted sms-chat baseline compared to utilizing a shallow NLM.

2 Neural Language Models

We briefly describe the NLM architecture and training objective used in this work as well as compare our approach to other related work.

Architecture. Neural language models are fundamentally feed-forward networks as described in (Bengio et al., 2003), but not necessarily limited to only a single hidden layer. Like any

[1] Our code and related materials are publicly available at http://stanford.edu/~lmthang/nlm.

Proceedings of the 19th Conference on Computational Language Learning, pages 305–309,
Beijing, China, July 30-31, 2015.

other language model, NLMs specify a distribution, $p(w|c)$, to predict the next word w given a context c. The first step is to lookup embeddings for words in the context and concatenate them to form an input, $h^{(0)}$, to the first hidden layer. We then repeatedly build up hidden representations as follows, for $l = 1, \ldots, n$:

$$h^{(l)} = f\left(W^{(l)}h^{(l-1)} + b^{(l)}\right) \quad (1)$$

where f is a non-linear fuction such as $\tanh$. The predictive distribution, $p(w|c)$, is then derived using the standard softmax:

$$\begin{aligned} s &= W^{(sm)}h^{(n)} + b^{(sm)} \\ p(w|c) &= \frac{\exp(s_w)}{\sum_{w \in V} \exp(s_w)} \end{aligned} \quad (2)$$

Objective. The typical way of training NLMs is to maximize the training data likelihood, or equivalently, to minimize the cross-entropy objective of the following form: $\sum_{(c,w) \in T} - \log p(w|c)$.

Training NLMs can be prohibitively slow due to the computationally expensive softmax layer. As a result, past works have tried to use a more efficient version of the softmax such as the hierarchical softmax (Morin, 2005; Mnih and Hinton, 2007; Mnih and Hinton, 2009) or the class-based one (Mikolov et al., 2010; Mikolov et al., 2011). Recently, the noise-contrastive estimation (NCE) technique (Gutmann and Hyvärinen, 2012) has been applied to train NLMs in (Mnih and Teh, 2012; Vaswani et al., 2013) to avoid explicitly computing the normalization factors.

Devlin et al. (2014) used a modified version of the cross-entropy objective, the *self-normalized* one. The idea is to not only improve the prediction, $p(w|c)$, but also to push the normalization factor per context, Z_c, close to 1:

$$\mathbb{J} = \sum_{(c,w) \in T} - \log p(w|c) + \alpha \log^2(Z_c) \quad (3)$$

While self-normalization does not lead to speed up in training, it allows trained models to be applied efficiently at test time without computing the normalization factors. This is similar in flavor to NCE but allows for flexibility (through α) in how hard we want to "squeeze" the normalization factors.

Training deep NLMs. We follow (Devlin et al., 2014) to train self-normalized NLMs, conditioning on both the source and target contexts. Unlike (Devlin et al., 2014), we found that using the rectified linear function, $\max\{0, x\}$, proposed in (Nair and Hinton, 2010), works better than $\tanh$. The rectified linear function was used in (Vaswani et al., 2013) as well. Furthermore, while these works use a fixed learning rate throughout, we found that having a simple learning rate schedule is useful in training well-performing deep NLMs. This has also been demonstrated in (Sutskever et al., 2014; Luong et al., 2015) and is detailed in Section 3. We do not perform any gradient clipping and notice that learning is more stable when short sentences of length less than or equal to 2 are removed. Bias terms are used for all hidden layers as well as the softmax layer as described earlier, which is slightly different from other work such as (Vaswani et al., 2013). All these details contribute to our success in training deep NLMs.

For simplicity, the same vocabulary is used for both the embedding and the softmax matrices.[2] In addition, we adopt the standard softmax to take advantage of GPUs in performing large matrix multiplications. All hyperparameters are given later.

3 Experiments

3.1 Data

We use the Chinese-English bitext in the DARPA BOLT (Broad Operational Language Translation) program, with 11.1M parallel sentences (281M Chinese words and 307M English words). We reserve 585 sentences for validation, i.e., choosing hyperparameters, and 1124 sentences for testing.[3]

3.2 NLM Training

We train our NLMs described in Section 2 with SGD, using: (a) a source window of size 5, i.e., 11-gram source context[4], (b) a 4-word target history, i.e., 5-gram target LM, (c) a self-normalized weight $\alpha = 0.1$, (d) a mini-batch of size 128, and (e) a learning rate of 0.1 (training costs are normalized by the mini-batch size). All weights are uniformly initialized in $[-0.01, 0.01]$. We train our models for 4 epochs (after 2 epochs, the learning rate is halved every 0.5 epoch). The vocabularies are limited to the top 40K frequent words for both Chinese and English. All words not in

[2] Some work (Schwenk, 2010; Schwenk et al., 2012) utilize a smaller softmax vocabulary, called short-list.

[3] The test set is from BOLT and labeled as p1r6_dev.

[4] We used an alignment heuristic similar to Devlin et al. (2014) but applicable to our phrase-based MT system.

Models	Valid	Test	$\lvert \log Z \rvert$
1 layer	9.39	8.99	0.51
2 layers	9.20	8.96	0.50
3 layers	8.64	8.13	0.43
4 layers	**8.10**	**7.71**	**0.35**

Table 1: **Training NLMs** – validation and test perplexities achieved by self-normalized NLMs of various depths. We report the $\lvert \log Z \rvert$ value (base e), similar to Devlin et al. (2014), to indicate how good each model is in pushing the log normalization factors towards 0. All perplexities are derived by explicitly computing the normalization factors.

these vocabularies are replaced by a universal unknown symbol. Embeddings are of size 256 and all hidden layers have 512 units each. Our training speed on a single Tesla K40 GPU device is about 1000 target words per second and it generally takes about 10-14 days to fully train a model.

We present the NLM training results in Table 1. With more layers, the model succeeds in learning more complex functions; the prediction, hence, becomes more accurate as evidenced by smaller perplexities for both the validation and test sets. Interestingly, we observe that deeper nets can learn self-normalized NLMs better: the mean log normalization factor, $\lvert \log Z \rvert$ in Eq. (3), is driven towards 0 as the depth increases.[5]

3.3 MT Reranking with NLMs

Our MT models are built using the Phrasal MT toolkit (Cer et al., 2010). In addition to the standard dense feature set[6], we include a variety of sparse features for rules, word pairs, and word classes, as described in (Green et al., 2014). Our decoder uses three language models.[7] We use a tuning set of 396K words in the newswire and web domains and tune our systems using online expected error rate training as in (Green et al., 2014). Our tuning metric is (BLEU-TER)/2.

We run a discriminative reranker on the 1000-best output of a decoder with MERT. The features used in reranking include all the dense features, an aggregate decoder score, and an NLM score. We learn the reranker weights on a second tuning set, different from the decoder tuning set, to make the reranker less biased towards the dense features. This second tuning set consists of 33K words of web-forum text and is important to obtain good improvements with reranking.

System	*dev*		*test1*		*test2*	
	T↓	B↑	T↓	B↑	T↓	B↑
baseline	53.7	33.1	55.1	31.3	63.5	16.5
Reranking						
1 layer	52.9	34.3	54.5	32.0	63.1	16.7
2 layers	52.7	34.1	54.3	31.9	63.0	16.8
3 layers	**52.5**	34.5	54.3	32.3	**62.5**	**17.3**
4 layers	52.6	**34.7**	**54.1**	**32.4**	62.7	17.2
vs. baseline	+1.2†	+1.6†	+1.0†	+1.1†	+1.0†	+0.8†
vs. 1 layer	+0.4†	+0.4†	+0.4†	+0.4†	+0.6†	+0.6†

Table 2: **Web-forum Results** – TER (T) and BLEU (B) scores on both the dev set (dev10wb_dev), used to tune reranking weights, and the test sets (dev10wb_syscomtune and p1r6_dev accordingly). Relative improvements between the best system and the baseline as well as the 1-layer model are **bolded**. † marks improvements that are statistically significant ($p < 0.05$).

3.4 Results

As shown in Table 2, it is not obvious if the depth-2 model is better than the single layer one, both of which are what past work used. In contrast, reranking with deep NLMs of three or four layers are clearly better, yielding average improvements of 1.0 TER / 1.0 BLEU points over the baseline and 0.5 TER / 0.5 BLEU points over the system reranked with the 1-layer model, all of which are statisfically significant according to the test described in (Riezler and Maxwell, 2005).

The fact that the improvements in terms of the intrinsic metrics listed in Table 1 do translate into gains in translation quality is interesting. It reinforces the trend reported in (Luong et al., 2015) that better source-conditioned perplexities lead to better translation scores. This phenomon is a useful result as in the past, many intrinsic metrics, e.g., alignment error rate, do not necessarily correlate with MT quality metrics.

3.5 Domain Adaptation

For the sms-chat domain, we use a tune set of 260K words in the newswire, web, and sms-chat domains to tune the decoder weights and a sepa-

[5]As a reference point, though not directly comparable, Devlin et al. (2014) achieved 0.68 for $\lvert \log Z \rvert$ on a different test set with the same self-normalized constant $\alpha = 0.1$.

[6]Consisting of forward and backward translation models, lexical weighting, linear distortion, word penalty, phrase penalty and language model.

[7]One is trained on the English side of the bitext, one is trained on a 16.3-billion-word monolingual corpus taken from various domains, and one is a class-based language model trained on the same large monolingual corpus.

System		*dev*		*test*	
		T↓	B↑	T↓	B↑
baseline		62.2	18.7	57.3	23.3
Reranking					
1 layer	*(5.42, 0.51)*	60.1	**22.0**	56.2	25.9
2 layers	*(5.50, 0.51)*	60.7	21.5	56.3	26.0
3 layers	*(5.34 0.43)*	**59.9**	21.4	**55.2**	**26.4**
vs. baseline		+2.3‡	+3.3‡	+2.1‡	+3.1‡
vs. 1 layer		+0.2	-0.6	+1.0‡	+0.5

Table 3: **Domain-adaptation Results** – translation scores for the sms-chat domain similar to Table 2. We use p2r2smscht_dev for *dev* and p2r2smscht_syscomtune for *test*. The test perplexities and the $|\log Z|$ values of our domain-adapted NLMs are shown in *italics*. ‡ marks improvements that are statistically significant ($p < 0.01$).

rate small, 8K words set to tune reranking weights. To train adapted NLMs, we use models previously trained on general in-domain data and further fine-tune with out-domain data for about 4 hours.[8]

Similar to the web-forum domain, for sms-chat, Table 3 shows that on the test set, our deep NLM with three layers yields a significant gain of 2.1 TER / 3.1 BLEU points over the baseline and 1.0 TER / 0.5 BLEU points over the 1-layer reranked system. It is worth pointing out that for such a small amount of out-domain training data, depth becomes less effective as exhibited through the insignificant BLEU gain in *test* and a drop in *dev* when comparing between the 1- and 3-layer models. We exclude the 4-layer NLM as it seems to have overfitted the training data. Nevertheless, we still achieve decent gains in using NLMs for MT domain adaptation.

4 Analysis

4.1 NLM Training

We show in Figure 1 the learning curves for various NLMs, demonstrating that deep nets are better than the shallow NLM with a single hidden layer. Starting from minibatch 20K, the ranking is generally maintained that deeper NLMs have better cross-entropies. The gaps become less discernible from minibatch 30K onwards, but numerically, as the model becomes deeper, the average gaps, in perplexities, are consistently 40.1, 1.1, and 2.0.

[8] Our sms-chat corpus consists of 146K sentences (1.6M Chinese and 1.9M English words). We randomly select 3000 sentences for validation and 3000 sentences for test. Models are trained for 8 iterations with the same hyperparameters.

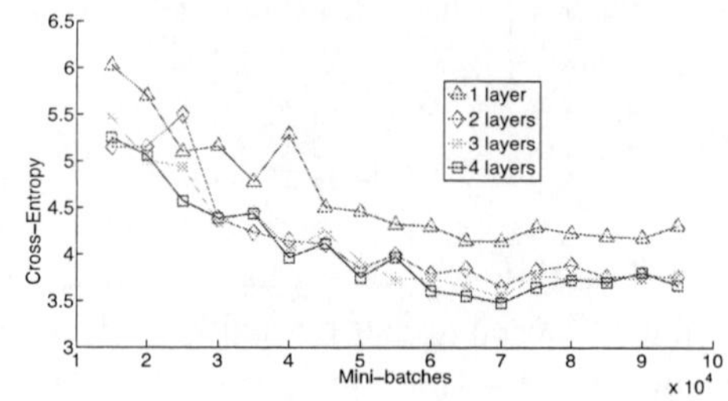

Figure 1: **NLM Learning Curve** – test cross-entropies ($\log_e$ perplexities) for various NLMs.

4.2 Reranking Settings

In Table 4, we compare reranking using all dense features (*All*) to conditions which use only dense LM features (*LM*) and optionally, include a word penalty (WP) feature. All these settings include an NLM score and an aggregate decoder score. As shown, it is best to include *all* dense features at reranking time.

	All	**LMs + WP**	**LMs**
1 layer	11.3	11.3	11.4
2 layers	11.2	11.4	11.5
3 layers	11.0	11.1	11.4
4 layers	10.9	11.2	11.3

Table 4: **Reranking Conditions** – (TER-BLEU)/2 scores when reranking the web-forum baseline.

5 Related Work

It is worth mentioning another active line of research in building end-to-end neural MT systems (Kalchbrenner and Blunsom, 2013; Sutskever et al., 2014; Bahdanau et al., 2015; Luong et al., 2015; Jean et al., 2015). These methods have not yet demonstrated success on challenging language pairs such as English-Chinese. Arsoy et al. (2012) have preliminarily examined deep NLMs for speech recognition, however, we believe, this is the first work that puts deep NLMs into the context of MT.

6 Conclusion

In this paper, we have bridged the gap that past work did not show, that is, neural language models with more than two layers can help improve translation quality. Our results confirm the trend reported in (Luong et al., 2015) that source-conditioned perplexity strongly correlates with MT performance. We have also demonstrated the use of deep NLMs to obtain decent gains in out-of-domain conditions.

Acknowledgment

We gratefully acknowledge support from a gift from Bloomberg L.P. and from the Defense Advanced Research Projects Agency (DARPA) Broad Operational Language Translation (BOLT) program under contract HR0011-12-C-0015 through IBM. Any opinions, findings, and conclusions or recommendations expressed in this material are those of the author(s) and do not necessarily reflect the view of DARPA, or the US government. We thank members of the Stanford NLP Group as well as the annonymous reviewers for their valuable comments and feedbacks.

References

Ebru Arsoy, Tara N. Sainath, Brian Kingsbury, and Bhuvana Ramabhadran. 2012. Deep neural network language models. In *NAACL WLM Workshop*.

D. Bahdanau, K. Cho, and Y. Bengio. 2015. Neural machine translation by jointly learning to align and translate. In *ICLR*.

Y. Bengio, R. Ducharme, P. Vincent, and C. Janvin. 2003. A neural probabilistic language model. *JMLR*, 3:1137–1155.

Yoshua Bengio. 2009. Learning deep architectures for ai. *Foundations and Trends in Machine Learning*, 2(1):1–127, January.

D. Cer, M. Galley, D. Jurafsky, and C. D. Manning. 2010. Phrasal: A statistical machine translation toolkit for exploring new model features. In *ACL, Demonstration Session*.

J. Devlin, R. Zbib, Z. Huang, T. Lamar, R. Schwartz, and J. Makhoul. 2014. Fast and robust neural network joint models for statistical machine translation. In *ACL*.

S. Green, D. Cer, and C. D. Manning. 2014. An empirical comparison of features and tuning for phrase-based machine translation. In *WMT*.

Michael Gutmann and Aapo Hyvärinen. 2012. Noise-contrastive estimation of unnormalized statistical models, with applications to natural image statistics. *JMLR*, 13:307–361.

G. Hinton, L. Deng, D. Yu, G. Dahl, A. Mohamed, N. Jaitly, A. Senior, V. Vanhoucke, P. Nguyen, T. Sainath, and B. Kingsbury. 2012. Deep neural networks for acoustic modeling in speech recognition. *IEEE Signal Processing Magazine*.

Sébastien Jean, Kyunghyun Cho, Roland Memisevic, and Yoshua Bengio. 2015. On using very large target vocabulary for neural machine translation. In *ACL*.

N. Kalchbrenner and P. Blunsom. 2013. Recurrent continuous translation models. In *EMNLP*.

A. Krizhevsky, I. Sutskever, and G. E. Hinton. 2012. ImageNet classification with deep convolutional neural networks. In *NIPS*.

M.-T. Luong, I. Sutskever, Q. V. Le, O. Vinyals, and W. Zaremba. 2015. Addressing the rare word problem in neural machine translation. In *ACL*.

Tomas Mikolov, Martin Karafiát, Lukas Burget, Jan Cernocký, and Sanjeev Khudanpur. 2010. Recurrent neural network based language model. In *Interspeech*.

Tomas Mikolov, Stefan Kombrink, Lukas Burget, Jan Cernocký, and Sanjeev Khudanpur. 2011. Extensions of recurrent neural network language model. In *ICASSP*.

Andriy Mnih and Geoffrey Hinton. 2007. Three new graphical models for statistical language modelling. In *ICML*.

Andriy Mnih and Geoffrey Hinton. 2009. A scalable hierarchical distributed language model. In *NIPS*.

Andriy Mnih and Yee Whye Teh. 2012. A fast and simple algorithm for training neural probabilistic language models. In *ICML*.

Frederic Morin. 2005. Hierarchical probabilistic neural network language model. In *AISTATS*.

Vinod Nair and Geoffrey E. Hinton. 2010. Rectified linear units improve restricted boltzmann machines. In *ICML*.

Stefan Riezler and T. John Maxwell. 2005. On some pitfalls in automatic evaluation and significance testing for MT. In *ACL Workshop, Intrinsic/Extrinsic Evaluation Measures for MT and Summarization*.

H. Schwenk, A. Rousseau, and M. Attik. 2012. Large, pruned or continuous space language models on a gpu for statistical machine translation. In *NAACL WLM workshop*.

H. Schwenk. 2010. Continuous space language models for statistical machine translation. *The Prague Bulletin of Mathematical Linguistics*, (93):137–146.

Le Hai Son, Alexandre Allauzen, and François Yvon. 2012. Continuous space translation models with neural networks. In *NAACL-HLT*.

I. Sutskever, O. Vinyals, and Q. V. Le. 2014. Sequence to sequence learning with neural networks. In *NIPS*.

Ashish Vaswani, Yinggong Zhao, Victoria Fossum, and David Chiang. 2013. Decoding with large-scale neural language models improves translation. In *EMNLP*.

Finding Opinion Manipulation Trolls in News Community Forums

Todor Mihaylov
FMI
Sofia University
tbmihailov@gmail.com

Georgi D. Georgiev
Ontotext AD
Sofia, Bulgaria
georgiev@ontotext.com

Preslav Nakov
Qatar Computing Research Institute
HBKU, Qatar
pnakov@qf.org.qa

Abstract

The emergence of user forums in electronic news media has given rise to the proliferation of *opinion manipulation trolls*. Finding such trolls automatically is a hard task, as there is no easy way to recognize or even to define what they are; this also makes it hard to get training and testing data. We solve this issue pragmatically: we assume that a user who is called a troll by several people is likely to be one. We experiment with different variations of this definition, and in each case we show that we can train a classifier to distinguish a likely troll from a non-troll with very high accuracy, 82–95%, thanks to our rich feature set.

1 Introduction

With the rise of social media, it became normal for people to read and follow other users' opinion. This created the opportunity for corporations, governments and others to distribute rumors, misinformation, speculation and to use other dishonest practices to manipulate user opinion (Derczynski and Bontcheva, 2014a). They could consistently use trolls (Cambria et al., 2010), write fake posts and comments in public forums, thus making veracity one of the challenges in digital social networking (Derczynski and Bontcheva, 2014b).

The practice of using opinion manipulation trolls has been reality since the rise of Internet and community forums. It has been shown that user opinions about products, companies and politics can be influenced by posts by other users in online forums and social networks (Dellarocas, 2006). This makes it easy for companies and political parties to gain popularity by paying for "reputation management" to people or companies that write in discussion forums and social networks fake opinions from fake profiles.

In Europe, the problem has emerged in the context of the crisis in Ukraine.[1][2] There have been a number of publications in news media describing the behavior of organized trolls that try to manipulate other users' opinion.[3][4][5] Still, it is hard for forum administrators to block them as trolls try not to violate the forum rules.

2 Related Work

Troll detection and offensive language use are understudied problems (Xu and Zhu, 2010). They have been addressed using analysis of the semantics and sentiment in posts to filter out trolls (Cambria et al., 2010); there have been also studies of general troll behavior (Herring et al., 2002; Buckels et al., 2014). Another approach has been to use lexico-syntactic features about user's writing style, structure and specific cyber-bullying content (Chen et al., 2012); cyber-bullying was detected using sentiment analysis (Xu et al., 2012); graph-based approaches over signed social networks have been used as well (Ortega et al., 2012; Kumar et al., 2014). A related problem is that of trustworthiness of statements on the Web (Rowe and Butters, 2009). Yet another related problem is Web spam detection, which has been addressed as a text classification problem (Sebastiani, 2002), e.g., using spam keyword spotting (Dave et al., 2003), lexical affinity of arbitrary words to spam content (Hu and Liu, 2004), frequency of punctuation and word co-occurrence (Li et al., 2006). See (Castillo and Davison, 2011) for an overview on adversarial web search.

[1] http://www.forbes.com/sites/peterhimler/2014/05/06/russias-media-trolls/

[2] http://www.theguardian.com/commentisfree/2014/may/04/pro-russia-trolls-ukraine-guardian-online

[3] http://www.washingtonpost.com/news/the-intersect/wp/2014/06/04/hunting-for-paid-russian-trolls-in-the-washington-post-comments-section/

[4] http://www.theguardian.com/world/2015/apr/02/putin-kremlin-inside-russian-troll-house

[5] http://www.theguardian.com/commentisfree/2014/may/04/pro-russia-trolls-ukraine-guardian-online

Proceedings of the 19th Conference on Computational Language Learning, pages 310–314,
Beijing, China, July 30-31, 2015.

Object	Count
Publications	34,514
Comments	1,930,818
-of which replies	897,806
User profiles	14,598
Topics	232
Tags	13,575

Table 1: Statistics about our dataset.

3 Data

We crawled the largest Internet community forum of a Bulgarian media, that of Dnevnik.bg,[6] a daily newspaper that requires users to be signed in in order to comment, which makes it easy to track them. The platform allows users to comment on news, to reply to other users' comments and to vote on them with thumbs up or thumbs down. In the forum, the official language is Bulgarian and all comments are written in Bulgarian.

Each publication has a category, a subcategory, and a list of manually selected tags (keywords). We crawled all publications in the *Bulgaria*, *Europe*, and *World* categories, which turned out to be mostly about politics, for the period 01-Jan-2013 to 01-Apr-2015, together with the comments and the corresponding user profiles as seen in Table 1.

We considered as *trolls* users who were called such by at least n distinct users, and *non-trolls* if they have never been called so. Requiring that a user should have at least 100 comments in order to be interesting for our experiments left us with 317 trolls and 964 non-trolls. Here are two examples (translated):

"To comment from "Historama": Murzi[7], you know that you cannot manipulate public opinion, right?"

"To comment from "Rozalina": You, trolls, are so funny :) I saw the same signature under other comments:)"

[6]http://dnevnik.bg

[7]*Murzi* is the short for *murzilka*. According to series of recent publications in Bulgarian media, Russian Internet users reportedly use the term *murzilka* to refer to Internet trolls. As a result, this term was adopted by some pro-Western Bulgarian forum users as a way to refer to users that they perceive as pro-Russian opinion manipulation trolls. Despite the term being now in circulation in Bulgaria, it is not really in use in Russia. In fact, the vast majority of Russian Internet users have never heard that *murzilka*, the name of a cute monkey-like children's toy and of a popular Soviet-time children's journal, could possibly be used to refer to Internet trolls.

4 Method

Our features are motivated by several publications about troll behavior mentioned above.

For each user, we extract statistics such as number of comments posted, number of days in the forum, number of days with at least one comment, and number of publications commented on. All (other) features are scaled with respect to these statistics, which makes it possible to handle users that registered only recently. Our features can be divided in the following groups:

Vote-based features. We calculate the number of comments with positive and negative votes for each user. This is useful as we assume that non-trolls are likely to disagree with trolls, and to give them negative votes. We use the sum from all comments as a feature. We also count separately the comments with high, low and medium positive to negative ratio. Here are some example features: the number of comments where (positive/negative) < 0.25, and the number of comments where (positive/negative) < 0.50.

Comment-to-publication similarity. These features measure the similarity between comments and publications. We use cosine and TF.IDF-weighted vectors for the comment and for the publication. The idea is that trolls might try to change or blurr the topic of the publication if it differs from his/her views or agenda.

Comment order-based features. We count how many user comments the user has among the first k. The idea is that trolls might try to be among the first to comment to achieve higher impact.

Top loved/hated comments. We calculate the number of times the user's comments were among the top 1, 3, 5, 10 most loved/hated comments in some thread. The idea is that in the comment thread below many publications there are some trolls that oppose all other users, and usually their comments are among the most hated.

Comment replies-based features. These are features that count how many user comments are replies to other comments, how many are replies to replies, and so on. The assumption here is that trolls try to post the most comments and want to dominate the conversation, especially when defending a specific cause. We further generate complex features that mix comment reply features and vote counts-based features, thus generating even more features that model the relationship between replies and user agreement/disagreement.

Time-based features. We generate features from the number of comments posted during different time periods on a daily or on a weekly basis. We assume that users that write comments on purpose could be paid, or could be activists of political parties, and they probably have some usual times to post, e.g., maybe they do it as a full-time job. On the other hand, most non-trolls work from 9:00 to 18:00, and thus we could expect that they should probably post less comments during this part of the day. We have time-based features that count the number of comments from 9:00 to 9:59, from 12:00 to 12:59, during working hours 9:00-18:00, etc.

All the above features are scaled, i.e., divided by the number of comments, the number of days in the forum, the number of days with more than one comment. Overall, we have a total of 338 such scaled features. In addition, we define a new set of features, which are non-scaled.

Non-scaled features. The non-scaled features are features based on the same statistics as above, but just not divided by the number of comments / number of days in the forum / number of days with more that one comment, etc. For example, one non-scaled feature is the number of times a comment by the target user was voted negatively, i.e., as thumbs down, by other users. As a non-scaled feature, we would use this number directly, while above we would scale it by dividing it by the total number of user's comments, by the total number of publications the user has commented on, etc. Obviously, there is a danger in using non-scaled features: older users are likely to have higher values for them compared to recently-registered users.

5 Experiments and Evaluation

As we mentioned above, in our experiments, we focus on users with at least 100 comments. This includes 317 trolls and 964 non-trolls. For each user, we extract the above-described features, scaled and non-scaled, and we normalize them in the -1 to 1 interval. We then use a support vector machine (SVM) classifier (Chang and Lin, 2011) with an RBF kernel with C=32 and g=0.0078125 as this was the best-performing configuration. In order to avoid overfitting, we used 5-fold cross-validation. The results are shown in Tables 2 and 3, where the *Accuracy* column shows the cross-validation accuracy and the *Diff* column shows the improvement over the majority class baseline.

Features	Accuracy	Diff
AS + Non-scaled	94.37(+3.74)	19.13
AS – total comments	91.17(+0.54)	15.93
AS – comment order	91.10(+0.46)	15.85
AS – similarity	91.02(+0.39)	15.77
AS – time day of week	90.78(+0.15)	15.53
AS – trigg rep range	90.78(+0.15)	15.53
AS – time all	90.71(+0.07)	15.46
All scaled (AS)	**90.63**	**15.38**
AS – top loved/hated	90.55(-0.07)	15.30
AS – time hours	90.47(-0.15)	15.22
AS – vote u/down rep	90.47(-0.15)	15.22
AS – similarity top	90.32(-0.31)	15.07
AS – triggered cmnts	90.32(-0.31)	15.07
AS – is rep to has rep	90.08(-0.54)	14.83
AS – vote up/down all	89.69(-0.93)	14.44
AS – is reply	89.61(-1.01)	14.36
AS – up/down votes	88.29(-2.34)	13.04

Table 2: Results for classifying 317 mentioned trolls vs. 964 non-trolls for *All Scaled (AS)* '–' (minus) some scaled feature group. The *Accuracy* column shows the cross-validation accuracy, and the *Diff* column shows the improvement over the majority class baseline.

Table 2 presents the results when using all features, as well as when using all features but excluding/adding one feature group. Here *All scaled (AS)* refers to the features from all groups except for those in the *non-scaled features* group described last in the previous section.

We can see that the best feature set is the one that includes all features, including the *Non-scaled* features group: adding this group contributes +3.74 to accuracy. We further see that excluding features based on time, e.g., *AS – time day of week* and *AS – time all*, improves the accuracy, which means that time of posting is not so important as a feature. Similarly, we see that it hurts accuracy to use as features the total number or the order of comments. Finally, the most important features turn out to be those based on replies and on thumbs up/down votes.

Next, Table 3 shows results of experiments when using different feature groups in isolation. As expected, the features that hurt most when excluded from the *All scaled* feature set, perform best when used alone. Here, the *similarity* features perform worst, which suggests that trolls tend not to change the topic.

Features	Accuracy	Diff
All Non-scaled	93.21	17.95
Only vote up/down	87.67	12.41
Only vote up/down totals	87.20	11.94
Only reply up/down voted	86.10	10.85
Only time hours	84.93	9.68
Only time all	84.31	9.06
Only is reply with rep	82.83	7.57
Only triggered rep range	82.83	7.57
Only day of week	82.28	7.03
Only total comments	82.28	7.03
Only reply status	80.72	5.46
Only triggered replies	80.33	5.07
Only comment order	80.09	4.84
Only top loved/hated	79.39	4.14
Only pub similarity top	75.25	0.00
Only pub similarity	75.25	0.00

Table 3: Results for classifying 317 mentioned trolls vs. 964 non-trolls for individual feature groups (all scaled, except for line 1). The *Accuracy* column shows the cross-validation accuracy, and the *Diff* column shows the improvement over the majority class baseline.

6 Discussion

We considered as trolls people who try to manipulate other users' opinion. Our positive and negative examples are based on trolls having been called such by at least n other users (we used $n = 5$).

However, this is much of a witch hunt and despite our good overall results, the data needs some manual checking in future work. We are also aware that some trolls can actually accuse non-trolls of being trolls, and we cannot be sure whether this is true or not unless we have someone to check it manually. In fact, we do have a list of trolls that are known to have been paid (as exposed in Bulgarian media), but there are only 15 of them, and we could not build a good classifier using only them due to the severe class imbalance.

As the choice of a minimum number of accusations for a user of being a troll that we used to define a troll, namely $n = 5$, might be seen as arbitrary, we also experimented with n = 3, 4, 5, 6, while keeping the required minimum number of comments per user to be 100 as before. The results are shown in Table 4. We can see that as the number of troll mentions/accusations increases, so does the cross-validation accuracy.

min mentions	3	4	5	6
trolls	545	419	317	260
non-troll	964	964	964	964
Accuracy	85.49	87.85	90.87	92.32
Diff	+21.60	+18.15	+15.61	+13.56

Table 4: Results for classifying mentioned trolls vs. non-trolls, using different numbers of minimum troll accusations to define a troll (users with 100 comments or more only). The *Accuracy* column shows the cross-validation accuracy, and the *Diff* column shows the improvement over the majority class baseline.

However, this is partly due to the increased class imbalance of trolls vs. non-trolls, which can be seen by the decrease in the improvement of our classifier compared to the majority class baseline.

We also ran experiments with a fixed number of minimum mentions for the trolls (namely 5 as before), but with varying minimum number of comments per user: 10, 25, 50, 100. The results are shown in Figure 1. We can see that as the minimum number of comments increases, the cross-validation accuracy for both the baseline and for our classifier decreases (as the troll-vs-non-troll ratio becomes more balanced); yet, the improvement of our classifier over the baseline increases, which means that the more we know about a user, the better we can predict whether s/he will be seen as a troll by other users.

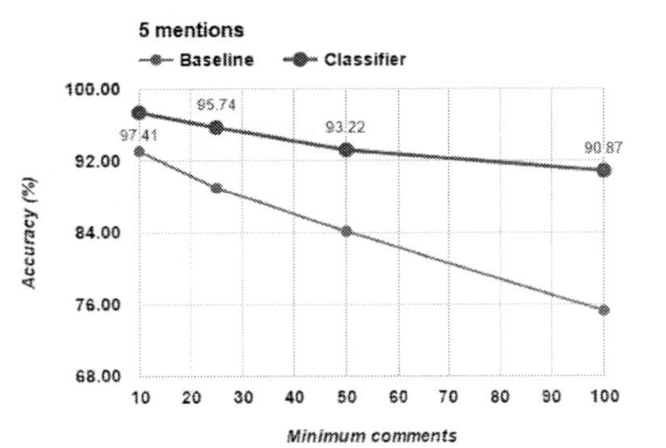

Figure 1: Results for classifying mentioned trolls vs. non-trolls for users with a different minimal number of comments (trolls were accused of being such by 5 or more different users). Shown are results for our classifier and for the majority class baseline.

7 Conclusion and Future Work

We have presented experiments in trying to distinguish trolls vs. non-trolls in news community forums. We have experimented with a large number of features, both scaled and non-scaled, and we have achieved very strong overall results using statistics such as number of comments, of positive and negative votes, of posting replies, activity over time, etc. The nature of our features means that our troll detection works best for "elder trolls" with at least 100 comments in the forum. In future work, we plan to add content features such as keywords, topics, named entities, part of speech, and named entities, which should help detect "fresh" trolls. Our ultimate objective is to be able to find and expose *paid* opinion manipulation trolls.

Acknowledgments

We would like to thank the anonymous reviewers for their constructive comments, which have helped us to improve the paper.

References

Erin E Buckels, Paul D Trapnell, and Delroy L Paulhus. 2014. Trolls just want to have fun. *Personality and individual Differences*, 67:97–102.

Erik Cambria, Praphul Chandra, Avinash Sharma, and Amir Hussain. 2010. Do not feel the trolls. In *Proceedings of the 3rd International Workshop on Social Data on the Web*, SDoW '10, Shanghai, China.

Carlos Castillo and Brian D. Davison. 2011. Adversarial web search. *Found. Trends Inf. Retr.*, 4(5):377–486, May.

Chih-Chung Chang and Chih-Jen Lin. 2011. LIBSVM: A library for support vector machines. *ACM Transactions on Intelligent Systems and Technology*, 2:27:1–27:27.

Ying Chen, Yilu Zhou, Sencun Zhu, and Heng Xu. 2012. Detecting offensive language in social media to protect adolescent online safety. In *Proceedings of the 2012 International Conference on Privacy, Security, Risk and Trust and of the 2012 International Conference on Social Computing*, PASSAT/SocialCom '12, pages 71–80, Amsterdam, Netherlands.

Kushal Dave, Steve Lawrence, and David M Pennock. 2003. Mining the peanut gallery: Opinion extraction and semantic classification of product reviews. In *Proceedings of the 12th international World Wide Web conference*, WWW '03, pages 519–528, Budapest, Hungary.

Chrysanthos Dellarocas. 2006. Strategic manipulation of internet opinion forums: Implications for consumers and firms. *Management Science*, 52(10):1577–1593.

Leon Derczynski and Kalina Bontcheva. 2014a. Pheme: Veracity in digital social networks. In *Proceedings of the UMAP Project Synergy workshop*.

Leon Derczynski and Kalina Bontcheva. 2014b. Spatio-temporal grounding of claims made on the web, in pheme. In *Proceedings of the 10th Joint ISO-ACL SIGSEM Workshop on Interoperable Semantic Annotation*, ISA '14, page 65, Reykjavik, Iceland.

Susan Herring, Kirk Job-Sluder, Rebecca Scheckler, and Sasha Barab. 2002. Searching for safety online: Managing "trolling" in a feminist forum. *The Information Society*, 18(5):371–384.

Minqing Hu and Bing Liu. 2004. Mining and summarizing customer reviews. In *Proceedings of the tenth ACM SIGKDD international conference on Knowledge discovery and data mining*, KDD '04, pages 168–177, Seattle, WA, USA.

Srijan Kumar, Francesca Spezzano, and VS Subrahmanian. 2014. Accurately detecting trolls in slashdot zoo via decluttering. In *Proceedings of the 2014 IEEE/ACM International Conference on Advances in Social Network Analysis and Mining*, ASONAM '14, pages 188–195, Beijing, China.

Wenbin Li, Ning Zhong, and Chunnian Liu. 2006. Combining multiple email filters based on multivariate statistical analysis. In *Foundations of Intelligent Systems*, pages 729–738. Springer.

F. Javier Ortega, José A. Troyano, Fermín L. Cruz, Carlos G. Vallejo, and Fernando Enríquez. 2012. Propagation of trust and distrust for the detection of trolls in a social network. *Computer Networks*, 56(12):2884 – 2895.

Matthew Rowe and Jonathan Butters. 2009. Assessing Trust: Contextual Accountability. In *Proceedings of the First Workshop on Trust and Privacy on the Social and Semantic Web*, SPOT '09, Heraklion, Greece.

Fabrizio Sebastiani. 2002. Machine learning in automated text categorization. *ACM computing surveys (CSUR)*, 34(1):1–47.

Zhi Xu and Sencun Zhu. 2010. Filtering offensive language in online communities using grammatical relations. In *Proceedings of the Seventh Annual Collaboration, Electronic Messaging, Anti-Abuse and Spam Conference*.

Jun-Ming Xu, Xiaojin Zhu, and Amy Bellmore. 2012. Fast learning for sentiment analysis on bullying. In *Proceedings of the First International Workshop on Issues of Sentiment Discovery and Opinion Mining*, WISDOM '12, pages 10:1–10:6, New York, NY, USA.

Do dependency parsing metrics correlate with human judgments?

Barbara Plank,[⋆] **Héctor Martínez Alonso,**[⋆] **Željko Agić,**[⋆] **Danijela Merkler,**[†] **Anders Søgaard**[⋆]
[⋆]Center for Language Technology, University of Copenhagen, Denmark
[†]Department of Linguistics, University of Zagreb, Croatia
bplank@cst.dk

Abstract

Using automatic measures such as labeled and unlabeled attachment scores is common practice in dependency parser evaluation. In this paper, we examine whether these measures correlate with human judgments of overall parse quality. We ask linguists with experience in dependency annotation to judge system outputs. We measure the correlation between their judgments and a range of parse evaluation metrics across five languages. The human-metric correlation is lower for dependency parsing than for other NLP tasks. Also, inter-annotator agreement is sometimes higher than the agreement between judgments and metrics, indicating that the standard metrics fail to capture certain aspects of parse quality, such as the relevance of root attachment or the relative importance of the different parts of speech.

1 Introduction

In dependency parser evaluation, the standard accuracy metrics—labeled and unlabeled attachment scores—are defined simply as averages over correct attachment decisions. Several authors have pointed out problems with these metrics; they are both sensitive to annotation guidelines (Schwartz et al., 2012; Tsarfaty et al., 2011), and they fail to say anything about how parsers fare on rare, but important linguistic constructions (Nivre et al., 2010). Both criticisms rely on the intuition that some parsing errors are more important than others, and that our metrics should somehow reflect that. There are sentences that are hard to annotate because they are ambiguous, or because they contain phenomena peripheral to linguistic theory, such as punctuation, clitics, or fragments. Manning (2011) discusses similar issues for part-of-speech tagging.

To measure the variable relevance of parsing errors, we present experiments with human judgment of parse output quality across five languages: Croatian, Danish, English, German, and Spanish. For the human judgments, we asked professional linguists with dependency annotation experience to judge which of two parsers produced the better parse. Our stance here is that, insofar experts are able to annotate dependency trees, they are also able to determine the quality of a predicted syntactic structure, which we can in turn use to evaluate parser evaluation metrics. Even though downstream evaluation is critical in assessing the usefulness of parses, it also presents non-trivial challenges in choosing the appropriate downstream tasks (Elming et al., 2013), we see human judgments as an important supplement to extrinsic evaluation.

To the best of our knowledge, no prior study has analyzed the correlation between dependency parsing metrics and human judgments. For a range of other NLP tasks, metrics have been evaluated by how well they correlate with human judgments. For instance, the standard automatic metrics for certain tasks—such as BLEU in machine translation, or ROUGE-N and NIST in summarization or natural language generation—were evaluated, reaching correlation coefficients well above .80 (Papineni et al., 2002; Lin, 2004; Belz and Reiter, 2006; Callison-Burch et al., 2007).

We find that correlations between evaluation metrics and human judgments are weaker for dependency parsing than other NLP tasks—our correlation coefficients are typically between .35 and .55—and that inter-annotator agreement is sometimes higher than human-metric agreement. Moreover, our analysis (§5) reveals that humans have a preference for attachment over labeling decisions, and that attachments closer to the root are more important. Our findings suggest that the currently employed metrics are not fully adequate.

Proceedings of the 19th Conference on Computational Language Learning, pages 315–320,
Beijing, China, July 30-31, 2015.

Contributions We present i) a systematic comparison between a range of available dependency parsing metrics and their correlation with human judgments; and ii) a novel dataset[1] of 984 sentences (up to 200 sentences for each of the 5 languages) annotated with human judgments for the preferred automatically parsed dependency tree, enabling further research in this direction.

2 Metrics

We evaluate seven dependency parsing metrics, described in this section.

Given a labeled gold tree $G = \langle V, E_G, l_G(\cdot)\rangle$ and a labeled predicted tree $P = \langle V, E_P, l_P(\cdot)\rangle$, let $E \subset V \times V$ be the set of directed edges from dependents to heads, and let $l : V \times V \rightarrow L$ be the edge labeling function, with L the set of dependency labels.

The three most commonly used metrics are those from the CoNLL 2006–7 shared tasks (Buchholz and Marsi, 2006): unlabeled attachment score (UAS), label accuracy (LA), both introduced by Eisner (1996), and labeled attachment score (LAS), the pivotal dependency parsing metric introduced by Nivre et al. (2004).

$$\text{UAS} = \frac{|\{e \mid e \in E_G \cap E_P\}|}{|V|}$$

$$\text{LAS} = \frac{|\{e \mid l_G(e) = l_P(e), e \in E_G \cap E_P\}|}{|V|}$$

$$\text{LA} = \frac{|\{v \mid v \in V, l_G(v,\cdot) = l_P(v,\cdot)\}|}{|V|}$$

We include two further metrics—namely, labeled (LCP) and unlabeled (UCP) complete predications—to give account for the relevance of correct predicate prediction for parsing quality.

LCP is inspired by the *complete predicates* metric from the SemEval 2015 shared task on semantic parsing (Oepen et al., 2015).[2] LCP is triggered by a verb (i.e., set of nodes V_{verb}) and checks whether all its core arguments match, i.e., all outgoing dependency edges except for punctuation. Since LCP is a very strict metric, we also evaluate UCP, its unlabeled variant. Given a function $c_X(v)$ that retrieves the set of child nodes of a node v from a tree X, we first define UCP as follows, and then incorporate the label matching for LCP:

$$\text{UCP} = \frac{|\{v \mid V_{verb}, c_G(v) = c_P(v)\}|}{|V_{verb}|}$$

$$\text{LCP} = \frac{|\{v \mid V_{verb}, c_G(v) = c_P(v) \wedge l_G(v,\cdot) = l_P(v,\cdot)\}|}{|V_{verb}|}$$

For the final figure of seven different parsing metrics, on top of the previous five, in our experiments we also include the neutral edge direction metric (NED) (Schwartz et al., 2011), and tree edit distance (TED) (Tsarfaty et al., 2011; Tsarfaty et al., 2012).[3]

3 Experiment

In our analysis, we compare the metrics with human judgments. We examine how well the automatic metrics correlate with each other, as well as with human judgments, and whether inter-annotator agreement exceeds annotator-metric agreement.

LANG	TYPE	SENT	$\overline{SL}$	$\overline{TD}$	ANN	RAW	κ
da	CDT	200	22.7	8.1	2-3	.77	.53
de	UD	200	18.0	4.4	2	.67	.33
en	UD	200	23.4	5.4	4	.73	.45
es	UD	184	32.5	6.7	4	.60	.20
hr	PDT	200	28.5	7.8	2	.80	.59

Table 1: Data characteristics and agreement statistics. TD: tree depth; SL: sentence length.

Data In our experiments we use data from five languages: The English (en), German (de) and Spanish (es) treebanks from the Universal Dependencies (UD v1.0) project (Nivre et al., 2015), the Copenhagen Dependency Treebank (da) (Buch-Kromann, 2003), and the Croatian Dependency Treebank (hr) (Agić and Merkler, 2013). We keep the original POS tags for all datasets (17 tags in case of UD, 13 tags for Croatian, and 23 for Danish). Data characteristics are in Table 1.

For the parsing systems, we follow McDonald and Nivre (2007) and use the second order MST (McDonald et al., 2005), as well as Malt parser with pseudo-projectivization (Nivre and Nilsson, 2005) and default parameters. For each language, we train the parsers on the canonical training section. We randomly select 200 sentences from the test sections, where our two de-

[1] The dataset is publicly available at https://bitbucket.org/lowlands/release

[2] http://alt.qcri.org/semeval2015/

[3] http://www.tsarfaty.com/unipar/

LANG	PARSER	LAS	UAS	LA	NED	TED	LCP	UCP
en	Malt	**79.17**	82.31	87.88	84.34	85.20	41.27	47.17
	MST	78.30	82.91	86.80	84.72	83.49	36.05	45.58
es	Malt	78.72	82.85	87.34	82.90	84.20	34.00	43.00
	MST	**79.51**	84.97	86.95	85.00	83.16	31.83	44.00
da	Malt	79.28	83.40	85.92	83.39	77.50	47.69	55.23
	MST	**82.75**	87.00	88.42	87.01	78.39	52.31	62.31
de	Malt	69.09	75.70	82.05	75.54	80.37	19.72	30.45
	MST	**72.07**	80.29	82.22	80.13	78.94	19.38	33.22
hr	Malt	63.21	72.34	76.66	71.94	71.64	23.18	31.03
	MST	**65.98**	76.20	79.01	75.89	72.82	24.71	34.29
Avg	Malt	73.84	79.32	83.97	76.62	**79.78**	**33.17**	43.18
	MST	**75.72**	**82.27**	**84.68**	**82.55**	79.36	32.86	**44.08**

Table 2: Parsing performance of Malt and MST.

pendency parsers do not agree on the correct analysis, after removing punctuation.[4] We do not control for predicted trees matching the gold standard.

Annotation task A total of 7 annotators were involved in the annotation task. All the annotators are either native or fluent speakers, and well-versed in dependency syntax analysis.

For each language, we present the selected 200 sentences with their two predicted dependency structures to 2–4 annotators and ask them to rank which of the two parses is better. They see graphical representations of the two dependency structures, visualized with the *What's Wrong With My NLP?* tool.[5] The annotators were not informed of what parser produced which tree, nor had they access to the gold standard. The dataset of 984 sentences is available at: `https://bitbucket.org/lowlands/release` (folder `CoNLL2015`).

4 Results

First, we perform a standard evaluation in order to see how the parsers fare, using our range of dependency evaluation measures. In addition, we compute correlations between metrics to assess their similarity. Finally, we correlate the measures with human judgements, and compare average annotator and human-system agreements.

Table 2 presents the parsing performances with respect to the set of metrics. We see that using LAS, Malt performs better on English, while MST performs better on the remaining four languages.

Table 3 presents Spearman's ρ between metrics across the 5 languages. Some metrics are strongly

[4]For Spanish, we had fewer analyses where the two parsers disagreed, i.e., 184.

[5]`https://code.google.com/p/whatswrong/`

ρ	UAS	LA	NED	TED	LCP	UCP
LAS	.755	.622	.743	.556	.236	.286
UAS	–	.436	.869	.512	.211	.342
LA	–	–	.436	.419	.206	.154
NED	–	–	–	.499	.216	.339
TED	–	–	–	–	.175	.219
LCP	–	–	–	–	–	.352

Table 3: Correlations between metrics.

ρ	en	es	da	de	hr	All
LAS	**.547**	**.478**	.297	.466	**.540**	**.457**
UAS	.541	.437	**.331**	.453	.397	.425
LA	.387*	.250*	.232	.310	.467	.324*
NED	.541	.469	.318	**.501**	.446	.448
TED	.372*	.404	.323	.331	.405*	.361*
LCP	.022*	.230*	.171	.120*	.120*	.126*
UCP	.249*	.195*	.223	.190*	.143*	.195*

Table 4: Correlations between human judgments and metrics (micro avg). * means significantly different from LAS ρ using Fisher's z-transform. Bold: highest correlation per language.

correlated, e.g., LAS and LA, and UAS and NED, but some exhibit very low correlation coefficients.

Next we study correlations with human judgments (Table 4). In order to aggregate over the annotations, we use an item-response model (Hovy et al., 2013). The correlations are relatively weak compared to similar findings for other NLP tasks. For instance, ROUGE-1 (Lin, 2004) correlates strongly with perceived summary quality, with a coefficient of 0.99. The same holds for BLEU and human judgments of machine translation quality (Papineni et al., 2002).

We find that, overall, LAS is the metric that correlates best with human judgments. It is closely followed by UAS, which does not differ significantly from LAS, albeit the correlations for UAS are slightly lower on average. NED is in turn highly correlated with UAS. The correlations for the predicate-based measures (LCP, UCP) are the lowest, as they are presumably too strict, and very different to LAS.

Motivated by the fact that people prefer the parse that gets the overall structure right (§5), we experimented with weighting edges proportionally to their log-distance to root. However, the signal was fairly weak; the correlations were only slightly higher for English and Danish: .552 and .338, respectively.

Finally, we compare the mean agreement be-

	ANN	LAS	UAS	LA	NED	TED	LCP	UCP
da	.768	.838	**.848**	.808	.828	.828	.745	.765
de	.670	**.710**	.690	.635	.710	.630	.575	.565
en	**.728**	.715	.705	.660	.700	.658	.525	.600
es	.601	**.663**	.644	.603	.652	.635	.581	.554
hr	**.800**	.755	.700	.735	.730	.705	.570	.580

Table 5: Average mean agreement between annotators, and between annotators and metrics.

tween humans with the mean agreement between humans and standard metrics, cf. Table 5. For two languages (English and Croatian), humans agree more with each other than with the standard metrics, suggesting that metrics are not fully adequate. The mean agreement between humans is .728 for English, with slightly lower scores for the metrics (LAS: .715, UAS: .705, NED: .660). The difference between mean agreement of annotators and human-metric was higher for Croatian: .80 vs .755. For Danish, German and Spanish, however, average agreement between metrics and human judgments is higher than our inter-annotator agreement.

5 Analysis

In sum, our experiments show that metrics correlate relatively weakly with human judgments, suggesting that some errors are more important to humans than others, and that the relevance of these errors are not captured by the metrics.

To better understand this, we first consider the POS-wise correlations between human judgments and LAS, cf. Table 6. In English, for example, the correlation between judgments and LAS is significantly stronger for content words[6] ($\rho_c = 0.522$) than for function words ($\rho_f = 0.175$). This also holds for the other UD languages, namely German ($\rho_c = 0.423$ vs $\rho_f = 0.263$) and Spanish ($\rho_c = 0.403$ vs $\rho_f = 0.228$). This is not the case for the non-UD languages, Croatian and Danish, where the difference between content-POS and function-POS correlations is not significantly different. In Danish, function words head nouns, and are thus more important than in UD, where content-content word relations are annotated, and function words are leaves in the dependency tree. This difference in dependency formalism is shown by the higher correlation for ρ_f for Danish.

The greater correlation for content words for English, German and Spanish suggests that errors

ρ	content	function
en	.522	.175
de	.423	.263
es	.403	.228
da	.148	.173
hr	.340	.306

Table 6: Correlations between human judgements and POS-wise LAS (content ρ_c vs function ρ_f poswise LAS correlations).

in attaching or labeling content words mean more to human judges than errors in attaching or labeling function words. We also observe that longer sentences do not compromise annotation quality, with a ρ between -0.07 and 0.08 across languages regarding sentence length and agreement.

For the languages for which we had 4 annotators, we analyzed the subset of trees where humans and system (by LAS) disagreed, but where there was majority vote for one tree. We obtained 35 dependency instances for English and 27 for Spanish (cf. Table 7). Two of the authors determined whether humans preferred labeling over attachment, or otherwise.

	attachment	labeling	items
en	86%	14%	35
es	67%	33%	27

Table 7: Preference of attachment or labeling for items where humans and system disagreed and human agreement ≥ 0.75.

Table 7 shows that there is a prevalent preference for attachment over labeling for both languages. For Spanish, there is proportionally higher label preference. Out of the attachment preferences, 36% and 28% were related to root/main predicate attachments, for English and Spanish respectively. The relevance of the root-attachment preference indicates that attachment is more important than labeling for our annotators.

Figure 5 provides three examples from the data where human and system disagree. Parse i) involves a coordination as well as a (local) adverbial, where humans voted for correct coordination (red) and thus unanimously preferred attachment over labeling. Yet, LAS was higher for the analysis in blue because "certainly" is attached to "Europeans" in the gold standard. Parse ii) is another

[6] Tagged as ADJ, NOUN, PROPN, VERB.

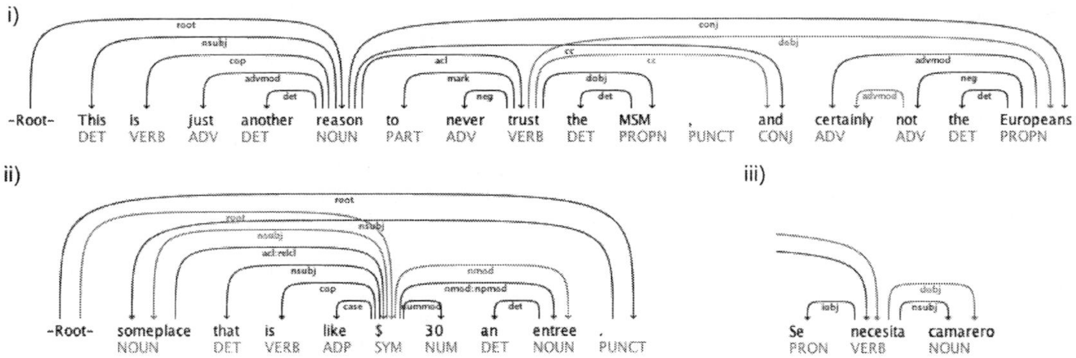

Figure 1: Examples where human and system (LAS) disagree. Human choice: i) red; ii) red; iii) blue.

example where humans preferred attachment (in this case root attachment), while iii) shows a Spanish example ("waiter is needed") where the subject label (*nsubj*) of "camarero" ("waiter") was the decisive trait.

6 Related Work

Parsing metrics are sensitive to the choice of annotation scheme (Schwartz et al., 2012; Tsarfaty et al., 2011) and fail to capture how parsers fare on important linguistic constructions (Nivre et al., 2010). In other NLP tasks, several studies have examined how metrics correlate with human judgments, including machine translation, summarization and natural language generation (Papineni et al., 2002; Lin, 2004; Belz and Reiter, 2006; Callison-Burch et al., 2007). Our study is the first to assess the correlation of human judgments and dependency parsing metrics. While previous studies reached correlation coefficients over 0.80, this is not the case for dependency parsing, where we observe much lower coefficients.

7 Conclusions

We have shown that out of seven metrics, LAS correlates best with human jugdments. Nevertheless, our study shows that there is an amount of human preference that is not captured with LAS. Our analysis on human versus system disagreement indicates that attachment is more important than labeling, and that humans prefer a parse that gets the overall structure right. For some languages, inter-annotator agreement is higher than annotator-metric (LAS) agreement, and content-POS is more important than function-POS, indicating there is an amount of human preference that is not captured with our current metrics. These observations raise the important question on how to incorporate our observations into parsing metrics that provide a better fit to human judgments. We do not propose a better metric here, but simply show that while LAS seems to be the most adequate metric, there is still a need for better metrics to complement downstream evaluation.

We outline a number of extensions for future research. Among those, we would aim at augmenting the annotations by obtaining more detailed judgments from human annotators. The current evaluation would ideally encompass more (diverse) domains and languages, as well as the many diverse annotation schemes implemented in various publicly available dependency treebanks that were not included in our experiment.

Acknowledgments

We thank Muntsa Padró and Miguel Ballesteros for their help and the three anonymous reviewers for their valuable feedback.

References

Željko Agić and Danijela Merkler. 2013. Three Syntactic Formalisms for Data-Driven Dependency Parsing of Croatian. In *Text, Speech, and Dialogue*. Springer.

Anja Belz and Ehud Reiter. 2006. Comparing Automatic and Human Evaluation of NLG Systems. In *EACL*.

Matthias Buch-Kromann. 2003. The Danish Dependency Treebank and the DTAG Treebank Tool. In *TLT*.

Sabine Buchholz and Erwin Marsi. 2006. CoNLL-X Shared Task on Multilingual Dependency Parsing. In *CoNLL*.

Chris Callison-Burch, Cameron Fordyce, Philipp Koehn, Christof Monz, and Josh Schroeder. 2007. (meta-) evaluation of machine translation. In *Proceedings of the Second Workshop on Statistical Machine Translation*.

Jason Eisner. 1996. Three new probabilistic models for dependency parsing. In *COLING*.

Jakob Elming, Anders Johannsen, Sigrid Klerke, Emanuele Lapponi, Héctor Martínez Alonso, and Anders Søgaard. 2013. Down-stream effects of tree-to-dependency conversions. In *NAACL*.

Dirk Hovy, Taylor Berg-Kirkpatrick, Ashish Vaswani, and Eduard Hovy. 2013. Learning whom to trust with MACE. In *NAACL*.

Chin-Yew Lin. 2004. ROUGE: a package for automatic evaluation of summaries. In *Text summarization branches out: Proceedings of the ACL-04 workshop*.

Christopher D Manning. 2011. Part-of-speech tagging from 97% to 100%: is it time for some linguistics? In *Computational Linguistics and Intelligent Text Processing*. Springer.

Ryan McDonald and Joakim Nivre. 2007. Characterizing the errors of data-driven dependency parsers. In *EMNLP-CoNLL*.

Ryan McDonald, Koby Crammer, and Fernando Pereira. 2005. Online large-margin training of dependency parsers. In *ACL*.

Joakim Nivre and Jens Nilsson. 2005. Pseudo-projective dependency parsing. In *ACL*.

Joakim Nivre, Johan Hall, and Jens Nilsson. 2004. Memory-based dependency parsing. In *CoNLL*.

Joakim Nivre, Laura Rimell, Ryan McDonald, and Carlos Gomez-Rodriguez. 2010. Evaluation of dependency parsers on unbounded dependencies. In *COLING*.

Joakim Nivre, Cristina Bosco, Jinho Choi, Marie-Catherine de Marneffe, Timothy Dozat, Richárd Farkas, Jennifer Foster, Filip Ginter, Yoav Goldberg, Jan Hajič, Jenna Kanerva, Veronika Laippala, Alessandro Lenci, Teresa Lynn, Christopher Manning, Ryan McDonald, Anna Missilä, Simonetta Montemagni, Slav Petrov, Sampo Pyysalo, Natalia Silveira, Maria Simi, Aaron Smith, Reut Tsarfaty, Veronika Vincze, and Daniel Zeman. 2015. Universal dependencies 1.0.

Stephan Oepen, Marco Kuhlmann, Yusuke Miyao, Daniel Zeman, Silvie Cinkova, Dan Flickinger, Jan Hajic, and Zdenka Uresova. 2015. Semeval 2015 task 18: Broad-coverage semantic dependency parsing. In *Proceedings of the 9th International Workshop on Semantic Evaluation (SemEval 2015)*.

Kishore Papineni, Salim Roukus, Todd Ward, and Wei-Jing Zhu. 2002. BLEU: a method for automatic evaluation of machine translation. In *ACL*, Philadelphia, Pennsylvania.

Roy Schwartz, Omri Abend, Roi Reichart, and Ari Rappoport. 2011. Neutralizing linguistically problematic annotations in unsupervised dependency parsing evaluation. In *ACL*.

Roy Schwartz, Omri Abend, and Ari Rappoport. 2012. Learnability-based syntactic annotation design. In *COLING*.

Reut Tsarfaty, Joakim Nivre, and Evelina Andersson. 2011. Evaluating dependency parsing: robust and heuristics-free cross-annotation evaluation. In *EMNLP*.

Reut Tsarfaty, Joakim Nivre, and Evelina Andersson. 2012. Cross-framework evaluation for statistical parsing. In *EACL*.

Feature Selection for Short Text Classification using Wavelet Packet Transform

Anuj Mahajan
Indian Institute of Technology, Delhi
Hauz Khas, New Delhi 110016
India
anujmahajan.iitd@gmail.com

Sharmistha, Shourya Roy
Xerox Research Centre India
Bangalore - 560103
India
{sharmistha.jat,shourya.roy}@xerox.com

Abstract

Text classification tasks suffer from curse of dimensionality due to large feature space. Short text data further exacerbates the problem due to their sparse and noisy nature. Feature selection thus becomes an important step in improving the classification performance. In this paper, we propose a novel feature selection method using Wavelet Packet Transform. Wavelet Packet Transform (WPT) has been used widely in various fields due to its efficiency in encoding transient signals. We demonstrate how short text classification task can be benefited by feature selection using WPT due to their sparse nature. Our technique chooses the most discriminating features by computing inter-class distances in the transformed space. We experimented extensively with several short text datasets. Compared to well known techniques our approach reduces the feature space size and improves the overall classification performance significantly in all the datasets.

1 Introduction

Text classification task consists of assigning a document to one or more classes. This can be done using machine learning techniques by training a model with labelled documents. Documents are usually represented as vectors with a variety of techniques like bag-of-words(unigram, bigram), TFIDF representation, etc. Typically, text corpora have very high dimensional document representation equal to the size of vocabulary. This leads to curse of dimensionality[1] in machine learning models, thereby degrading the performance.

Short text corpora, like SMS, tweets, etc., in particular suffer from sparse high dimensional feature space, due to large vocabulary and short document length. To give an idea as to how these factors affect the size of the feature space we compare Reuters with Twitter data corpus. In Reuters-21578 corpus there are approximately 2.5 Million words in total and 14506 unique vocabulary entries after standard preprocessing steps (which is the dimensionality of the feature space). However, Twitter 1 corpus, we used for experiments has approximately 15,000 words in total and feature space size of 7423 words. Additionally, the average length of an English tweet is 10-12 words whereas the average length of a document in Reuters-21578 news classification corpus is 200 words. Therefore, the dimensionality is extremely high even for small corpora with short texts. In addition, the average number of words in a document is significantly less in short text data leading to higher sparsity of feature space representation of documents.

Owing to this high dimensionality problem, one of the important steps in text classification workflows is feature selection. Feature selection techniques for traditional documents have been aplenty and a few seminal survey articles have been written on this topic (Blitzer, 2008). In contrast, for short text there is much less work on statistical feature selection but more focus has gone to feature engineering towards word normalization, canonicalization etc. (Han and Baldwin, 2011).

In this paper, we propose a dimensionality reduction technique for short text using Wavelet packet transform called Improvised Adaptive Discriminant Wavelet Packet Transform (IADWPT). IAWDPT does dimensionality reduction by selecting discriminative features (wavelet coefficients) from the Wavelet Packet Transform (WPT) representation. Short text data resembles transient signals in vector representation and WPT encodes transient signals (signals lasting for very short duration) well (Learned and Willsky, 1995), using very few coefficients. This leads to considerable decrease in the dimensionality of the feature space along with increase in classification accuracy. Additionally, we optimise the procedure to select the most discriminative features from WPT representation. To the best of our knowledge this is the first attempt to apply an algorithm based on wavelet packet transform to the feature selection in short text classification.

2 Related Work

Feature selection has been widely adopted for dimensionality reduction of text datasets in the past. Yiming Yang et al. (Yang and Pedersen, 1997) performed a comparative study of some of these methods including, document frequency, information gain(IG), mutual

[1] `https://en.wikipedia.org/wiki/Curse_of_dimensionality`

Proceedings of the 19th Conference on Computational Language Learning, pages 321–326,
Beijing, China, July 30-31, 2015.

information(MI), χ^2-test(CHI) and term strength(TS). They concluded that IG and CHI are the most effective in aggressive dimensionality reduction. The mRMR technique proposed by (Peng et al., 2005) selects the best feature subset by increasing relevancy of feature with target class and reducing redundancy between chosen features.

Wavelet transform provides time-frequency representation of a given signal. The time-frequency representation is useful for describing signals with time varying frequency content. Detailed explanation of wavelet transform theory is beyond the scope of this paper. For detailed theory, refer to Daubechies (Daubechies, 2006; Daubechies, 1992; Coifman and Wickerhauser, 2006) and Robi Polikar (Polikar,). First use of wavelet transform for compression was proposed by Ronald R Coifman et al. (Coifman et al., 1994). Hammad Qureshi et al. (Qureshi et al., 2008) proposed an adaptive discriminant wavelet packet transform(ADWPT) for feature reduction.

In past wavelet transform has been applied to natural language processing tasks. A survey on wavelet applications in data mining (Li et al., 2002), discusses the basics and properties of wavelets which make it a very effective technique in Data Mining. CC Aggarwal (Aggarwal, 2002) uses wavelets for strings classification. He notes that wavelet technique creates a hierarchical decomposition of the data which can capture trends at varying levels of granularity and thus helps classification task with the new representation. Geraldo Xexeo et al. (Xexeo et al., 2008) used wavelet transform to represent documents for classification.

3 Wavelet Packet Transform for Short-text Dimensionality Reduction

Feature selection performs compression of feature space to preserve maximum discriminative power of features for classification. We use this analogy to do compression of document feature space using Wavelet Packet Transform. Vector format(e.g. dictionary encoded vector) representation of a document is equivalent to a digital representation. This vector format can then be processed using wavelet transform to get a compressed representation of the document in terms of wavelet coefficients. Document features are transformed into wavelet coefficients. Wavelet coefficients are ranked and selected based on their discrimination power between classes. Classification model is trained on these highly informative coefficients. Results show a considerable improvement in model accuracy using our dimensionality reduction technique.

Typically, vector representation of short text will have very few non-zero entries due to short length of the documents. If we plot count of each word in the dictionary on y-axis v/s distinct words on x-axis. Just like transient signals, the resulting graph will have very few spikes. Transient signals last for a very little time in the whole duration of the observation. (Learned and Willsky, 1995) show the efficacy of wavelet packet transform in representing transient signal. This motivates our use of Wavelet Packet Transform to encode short text.

Wavelet transform is a popular choice for feature representation in image processing. Our approach is inspired by a related work by (Qureshi et al., 2008). They propose Adaptive Discriminant Wavelet Packet Transform (ADWPT) based representation for meningioma subtype classfication. ADWPT obtains a wavelet based representation by optimising the discrimination power of the various features. Proposed technique IADWPT differs from ADWPT in the way discriminative feature are selected. Next section provides details about the proposed approach IADWPT.

4 IADWPT - Improvised Adaptive Discriminant Wavelet Packet Transform

This section presents the proposed short text feature selection technique IADWPT. IADWPT uses wavelet packet transform of the data to extract useful discriminative features from the sub-bands at various depths.

Natural language processing tasks usually represent their documents in dictionary encoded bag-of-words representation. This numerical vector representation of a document is equivalent to signal representation. In order to get IADWPT representation of the document following steps should be computed:

1) Compute full wavelet packet transform of the document vector representation.

2) Compute the discrimination power of each coefficient in wavelet packet transform representation.

3) Select the most discriminative coefficients to represent all the documents in the corpus.

Once the 1-D wavelet transform is computed at a desired level l, wavelet packet transform (WPT) produces 2^l different sets of coefficients (nodes in WPT tree). These coefficients represent the magnitude of various frequencies present in the signal at a given time. We select the most discriminative coefficients to represent all the documents in the corpus by calculating the discriminative power of each coefficient.

The classification task consists of c classes with d documents. 1-D Wavelet Packet Transform of the d_k^{th} document yields l levels with f sub bands consisting of m coefficients in each sub band. $x_{m,f,l}$ represent the coefficients of Wavelet Packet Transform. Following terms are defined for Algorithm 1.

- probability density estimates ($S_{m,f,l}$) of a particular sub-band in a level l a training sample document d_k^i of a given Class c_i is given by:

  $$S^k_{m,f,l} = \frac{(x^k_{m,f,l})^2}{\sum_j (x^k_{j,f,l})^2}$$

  Here, $x_{m,f,l}$ is the mth coefficient in f^{th} sub-band of lth level of document d_k. Where, j varies

Algorithm 1 IADWPT Algorithm for best discriminative feature selection

for all classes C **do**
  Calculate Wavelet Packet Transform for all the documents d_k in class c_i
  for all Documents d_k **do**
    Calculate probability density estimates $S^k_{m,f,l}$
  end for
  for all Levels of WPT l and their sub bands f **do**
    for all Wavelet Packet Transform Coefficients m in subband f **do**
      Calculate average probability density $A^{c_i}_{m,f,l}$
    end for
  end for
end for
for all Class Pairs c_a, c_b **do**
  Calculate discriminative power $D^{a,b}_{m,f,l}$
end for
Select top m' coefficients for representing documents in corpus

over the length of sub-band. Wavelet supports vary with the bands, Normalization ensures that the feature selection done gives uniform weightage to the features from different bands. This step calculates the normalised value of coefficients in a sub-band.

- Average probability density ($A^{c_i}_{m,f,l}$) estimates are derived using all the training samples $d_k$in a given class c_i.

  $A^{c_i}_{m,f,l} = \frac{\sum_k S^k_{m,f,l}}{d}$

  for, coefficient m in sub-band f for class c_i and d is the total number of documents in the class. k varies over the number of documents in the class. It measures the average value of a coefficient in all the documents belonging to a class.

- Discriminative power ($D^{a,b}_{m,f,l}$) of each coefficient in l^{th} level's f^{th} sub band's m^{th} coefficient, between classes a and b is defined as follows:

  $D^{a,b}_{m,f,l} = |\sqrt{A^a_{m,f,l}} - \sqrt{A^b_{m,f,l}}|$

  Discriminative power is the hellinger distance between the average probability density estimates of a coefficient for the two classes. It quantifies the difference in the average value of a coefficient between a pair of classes. More the difference, better the discriminative power of the coefficient. Thus discriminative features tend to have a higher average probability density in one of the classes whereas redundant features cancel out in taking the difference in computing the distance. (Rajpoot, 2003) have shown efficacy of Hellinger distance applied to ADWPT.

Selecting coefficients with greater discriminative power helps the classifier perform well. Full algorithm is mentioned in algorithm 1.

Multi class classification can then be handled in this framework using one-vs-one classification. We select the top m' features from the wavelet representation for representing the data in the classification task. Time complexity of the algorithm is polynomial. The method is based on adaptive discriminant wavelet packet transform (ADWPT) (Qureshi et al., 2008). Therefore, we name it as improvised adaptive discriminant wavelet packet transform (IADWPT). ADWPT uses best basis for classification which is a union of the various subbands selected that can span the transformed space, so noise is still retained in the signal whereas IADWPT selects coefficients from the sub-band having maximal discriminative power thus improving the classification results. As opposed to ADWPT, IADWPT is a one way transform, original signal cannot be recovered from the transform domain. Experimental results confirm that IADWPT performs better than ADWPT in short text datasets.

4.1 IADWPT Example

Figure 1 Gives intuition of the workings of IADWPT transform. Uppermost graph displays the Average probability density in positive class samples. Middle graph in the Figure 1 shows the Average probability density in negative class samples. These two energy values are then subtracted, resulting values are shown in the bottom most component of Figure 1. Peak positive and negative values in the bottommost graph represent the most discriminant features. Absolute value of the discriminative power can then be used to select the most discriminative features to represent each document in corpus.

5 Experiments and Results

We used multiple short text datasets to prove efficacy of proposed algorithm against state of the art algorithms for feature selection.

1) **Twitter_1**: This dataset is a part of the SemEval 2013 task B dataset (Nakov et al.,) for two class sentiment classification. We gathered 624 examples in positive and negative class each for our experiments.

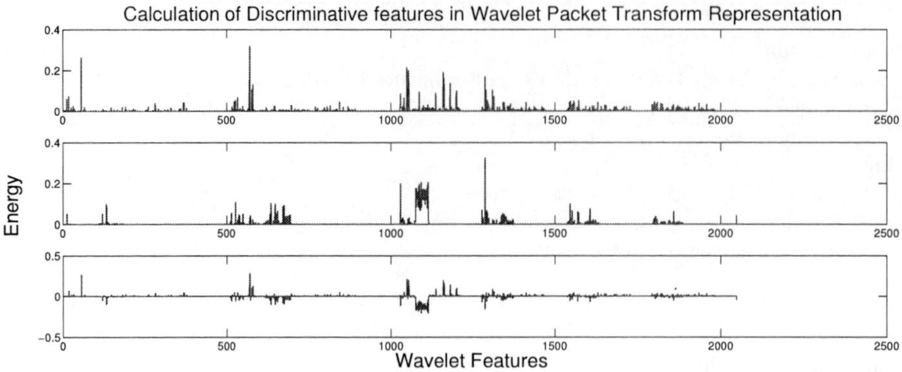

Figure 1: x-axis represents the wavelet packet transform coefficients, y-axis represents amplitude. From top to bottom, 1) Average probability density $A^a_{m,f,l}$value of coefficients in positive class a), 2) Average probability density $A^b_{m,f,l}$value of coefficients in negative class (b), 3) Difference between $A^a_{m,f,l}$ and $A^b_{m,f,l}$

Table 1: CLASSIFICATION RESULTS - SUPPORT VECTOR MACHINE (SVM) AND LOGISTIC REGRESSION (LR)

Dataset	Baseline	MI-avg	χ^2	PCA	ADWPT	IADWPT
Classification accuracy - SVM						
Twitter 1	47.04	47.57	45.62	59.28	46	**63.44**
SMS Spam 1 - HAM Accuracy	99.82	99.71	99.77	99.87	99.63	**99.94**
SMS Spam 1 - SPAM Accuracy	83.10	83.32	82.96	83.81	83.57	**83.92**
SMS Spam 2 - HAM Accuracy	55.2	56.31	55.62	81.12	54.1	**87.7**
SMS Spam 2 - SPAM Accuracy	46.6	46.7	46.49	92.39	47.3	**99.42**
Total dimensions in best classification accuracy result - SVM						
Twitter 1	7423	2065	515	540	7423	23
SMS Spam 1	9394	3540	550	750	9394	815
SMS Spam 2	10681	2985	490	855	1068	250
Classification accuracy - Logistic Regression						
Twitter 1	75.8	74.97	75.21	76.28	68.2	**76.72**
SMS Spam 1 - HAM Accuracy	97.91	94.67	95.28	98.71	98.03	**99.61**
SMS Spam 1 - SPAM Accuracy	**95.48**	85.34	86.37	91.37	82.2	87.54
SMS Spam 2 - HAM Accuracy	96.02	89.54	92.76	71.21	95.09	**98.5**
SMS Spam 2 - SPAM Accuracy	91.2	88.37	91.38	89.15	92.2	**94.51**
Total dimensions in best classification accuracy result - Logistic Regression						
Twitter 1	7423	5600	3250	3575	7423	2749
SMS Spam 1	9394	7545	1755	2350	9394	1680
SMS Spam 2	10681	6550	3000	3050	10681	9981

2) **SMS_Spam_1**: UCI spam dataset (Almeida,) consists of 5,574 instances of SMS classified into SPAM and HAM classes. SPAM class is defined as messages which are not useful and HAM is the class of useful messages. We compare our results with the results they published in their paper (Almeida et al., 2013). Therefore, we followed the same experiment procedure as cited in the paper. First 30% samples were used in train and the rest in test set as reported in the paper.

3) **SMS_Spam_2**: The dataset was published by Yadav et al. (Yadav et al., 2011). It consists of 2000 SMS, 1000 SPAM and 1000 HAM messages. Experiment settings are same as that of dataset SMS_Spam_1.

The goal of our experiments is to examine the effectiveness of the proposed algorithm in feature selection for short text datasets. We measure the effectiveness of the feature selection technique with respect to the increase in accuracy in the final machine learning task. Our method does not depend on a specific classifier used in the final classification. Therefore, we used

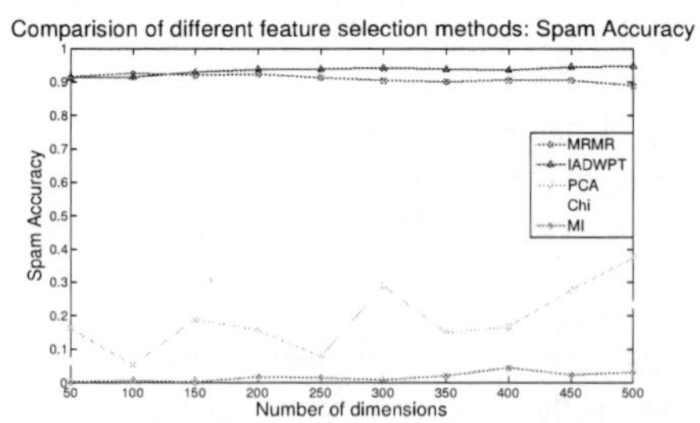

Figure 2: Spam Classification Accuracy comparison across various feature selection algorithm for SMS Spam 2 dataset

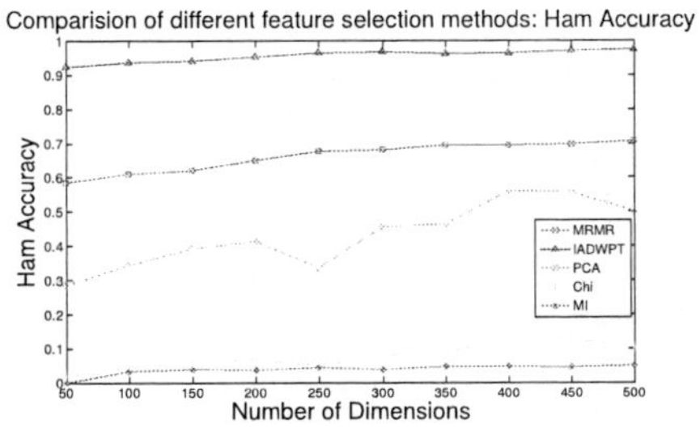

Figure 3: Ham Classification Accuracy comparison across various feature selection algorithm for SMS Spam 2 dataset

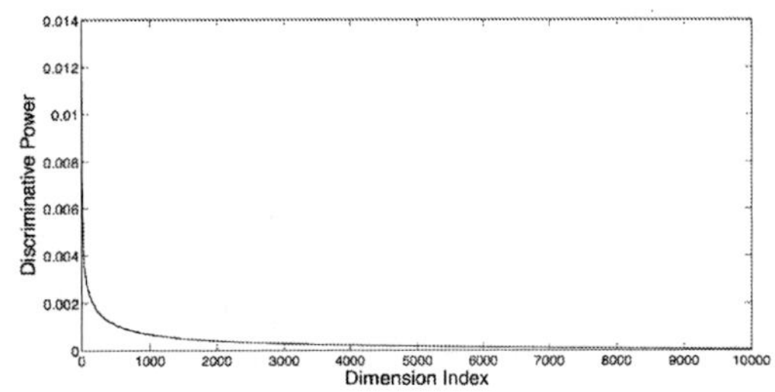

Figure 4: Plot of Discriminative Power ($D^{a,b}_{m,f,l}$) arranged in descending order

popular classifiers like Support Vector Machine (RBF kernel with grid search) (Cortes and Vapnik, 1995) and Logistic Regression with and without dimensionality reduction for unigram representation to benchmark the performance. All the experiments were done with 10 fold cross validation and grid search on C parameter. We report results with respect to classification accuracy which is measured as $\frac{\#correctly\ classified\ datapoints}{\#total\ datapoints}$.

We conducted detailed experiments comparing IADWPT using Coiflets of order 2 with other feature selection techniques such as PCA, Mutual Information, χ^2, mRMR (Peng et al., 2005) and ADWPT (Qureshi et al., 2008). Results are reported in Table 1. The table reports best accuracy values and respective feature set size selected by the technique. It can be observed that IADWPT gives best accuracy in most of the cases with very few features.

We compared performance of our algorithm with mRMR. Results for SMS_Spam_2 dataset are shown in Figure 2 and Figure 3. The plots prove efficacy of our algorithm versus state of the art mRMR algorithm. mRMR technique could not finish execution for the rest of the datasets. It can also be observed from results in Table 1 and Figure 1,2 that performance of feature selection algorithms follow consistent pattern in short text. Following is observed order of performance of algorithms in decreasing order, IADWPT, mRMR, PCA, Chi Square, MI. Further, it is observed that IADWPT performs well at feature selection without losing discriminative information, even when the dimensionality of feature space is reduced to as far as 1/40th of original feature space and steadily maintains the accuracy as dimensionality is reduced, which makes it a suitable technique for aggressive dimensionality reduction. This also helps in learning ML (machine learning) models faster due to reduced dimensionality. We plotted the discrimination power of coefficients in each dataset. Plot suggested that very few coefficients contained most of the discriminative power. And, therefore just working with these coefficients can help in getting good accuracies resulting in aggressive dimensionality reduction. Results establish the effectiveness of IADWPT for applicability in compressing short text feature representation and reducing noise to improve classification accuracy.

5.1 IADWPT Effectiveness

Short text data is noisy and consists of many features which are irrelevant to the task of classification of data. IADWPT effectively gets rid of the noise in approximations(as Signal strength is greater than the noise), the feature selection step at the sub-band level as described in Algorithm 1, it enforces selection of good discriminative features and thus improves classifier accuracy, reducing feature space dimensionality at the same time. Features from sub-bands of the signal are chosen based on their discriminative power, therefore, the original signal information is lost and the transform is not reversible.

IADWPT gives good compression of data and without losing discriminative information, even when the dimensionality of space is reduced to as far as 1/40th of original feature space and is thus steadily maintaining the accuracy as dimensionality is reduced, which makes it a suitable technique for dimensionality reduction. This also helps learning machine learning models faster due to reduced dimensionality. Figure 4 shows the plot of Discriminative Power $D^{a,b}_{m,f,l}$ values for coefficients arranged in descending order for SMS_Spam_2 dataset. Other datasets displayed similar graph for Discriminative Power. From the figure it can be observed that few coefficients hold most of the discriminative power, and thus aggressive dimensionality reduction is possible with IADWPT algorithm. Results establish the effectiveness of IADWPT for applicability in compressing short text feature representation and reducing noise.

6 Conclusion and Future Work

In this paper, we have proposed IADWPT algorithm for effective dimensionality reduction for short text corpus. The algorithm can be used in a number of scenarios where high dimensionality and sparsity pose challenge. Experiments prove efficacy of IADWPT based dimensionality reduction for short text data. This technique can prove useful to a number of social media data analysis applications. In future, we would like to explore theoretical bounds on best number of dimensions to choose from wavelet representation.

References

Charu C. Aggarwal. 2002. On effective classification of strings with wavelets.

Tiago A Almeida. Sms spam collection v.1. `http://www.dt.fee.unicamp.br/~tiago/smsspamcollection/`,[Online; accessed 10-September-2014].

T. Almeida, J. M. G. Hidalgo, and T. P. Silva. 2013. Towards sms spam filtering: Results under a new dataset. *International Journal of Information Security Science*.

John Blitzer. 2008. A survey of dimensionality reduction techniques for natural language. `http://john.blitzer.com/papers/wpe2.pdf`,[Online; accessed 10-September-2014].

R. R. Coifman and M. V. Wickerhauser. 2006. Entropy-based algorithms for best basis selection. *IEEE Trans. Inf. Theor.*, 38(2):713–718, September.

RonaldR. Coifman, Yves Meyer, Steven Quake, and M.Victor Wickerhauser. 1994. Signal processing and compression with wavelet packets. In J.S. Byrnes, JenniferL. Byrnes, KathrynA. Hargreaves, and Karl Berry, editors, *Wavelets and Their Applications*, volume 442 of *NATO ASI Series*, pages 363–379. Springer Netherlands.

Corinna Cortes and Vladimir Vapnik. 1995. Support-vector networks. *Mach. Learn.*, 20(3):273–297, September.

Ingrid Daubechies. 1992. *Ten Lectures on Wavelets*. Society for Industrial and Applied Mathematics, Philadelphia, PA, USA.

I. Daubechies. 2006. The wavelet transform, time-frequency localization and signal analysis. *IEEE Trans. Inf. Theor.*, 36(5):961–1005, September.

Bo Han and Timothy Baldwin. 2011. Lexical normalisation of short text messages. In *Proceedings of the 49th Annual Meeting of the Association for Computational Linguistics: Human Language Technologies - Volume 1*, HLT '11, pages 368–378, Stroudsburg, PA, USA. Association for Computational Linguistics.

Rachel E. Learned and Alan S. Willsky. 1995. A wavelet packet approach to transient signal classification. *Applied and Computational Harmonic Analysis*, 2(3):265 – 278.

Tao Li, Qi Li, Shenghuo Zhu, and Mitsunori Ogihara. 2002. A survey on wavelet applications in data mining. *SIGKDD Explor. Newsl.*, 4(2):49–68, December.

Preslav Nakov, Zornitsa Kozareva, Alan Ritter, Sara Rosenthal, Veselin Stoyanov, and Theresa Wilson. Semeval-2013 task 2: Sentiment analysis in twitter.

Hanchuan Peng, Fuhui Long, and Chris Ding. 2005. Feature selection based on mutual information: criteria of max-dependency, max-relevance, and min-redundancy. *IEEE Transactions on Pattern Analysis and Machine Intelligence*, 27:1226–1238.

Robi Polikar. Wavelet Tutorial. `http://users.rowan.edu/~polikar/wavelets/wttutorial.html`,[Online; accessed 10-January-2015].

Hammad Qureshi, Olcay Sertel, Nasir Rajpoot, Roland Wilson, and Metin Gurcan. 2008. Adaptive discriminant wavelet packet transform and local binary patterns for meningioma subtype classification. In Dimitris N. Metaxas, Leon Axel, Gabor Fichtinger, and Gbor Szkely, editors, *MICCAI (2)*, volume 5242 of *Lecture Notes in Computer Science*, pages 196–204. Springer.

NM Rajpoot. 2003. Local discriminant wavelet packet basis for texture classification. In *SPIE Wavelets X*, pages 774–783. SPIE.

Geraldo Xexeo, Jano de Souza, Patricia F. Castro, and Wallace A. Pinheiro. 2008. Using wavelets to classify documents. *Web Intelligence and Intelligent Agent Technology, IEEE/WIC/ACM International Conference on*, 1:272–278.

Kuldeep Yadav, Ponnurangam Kumaraguru, Atul Goyal, Ashish Gupta, and Vinayak Naik. 2011. Smsassassin: Crowdsourcing driven mobile-based system for sms spam filtering. In *Proceedings of the 12th Workshop on Mobile Computing Systems and Applications*, HotMobile '11, pages 1–6, New York, NY, USA. ACM.

Yiming Yang and Jan O. Pedersen. 1997. A comparative study on feature selection in text categorization. In *Proceedings of the Fourteenth International Conference on Machine Learning*, ICML '97, pages 412–420, San Francisco, CA, USA. Morgan Kaufmann Publishers Inc.

Learning Adjective Meanings with a Tensor-Based Skip-Gram Model

Jean Maillard
University of Cambridge
Computer Laboratory
jean@maillard.it

Stephen Clark
University of Cambridge
Computer Laboratory
sc609@cam.ac.uk

Abstract

We present a compositional distributional semantic model which is an implementation of the tensor-based framework of Coecke et al. (2011). It is an extended skip-gram model (Mikolov et al., 2013) which we apply to adjective-noun combinations, learning nouns as vectors and adjectives as matrices. We also propose a novel measure of adjective similarity, and show that adjective matrix representations lead to improved performance in adjective and adjective-noun similarity tasks, as well as in the detection of semantically anomalous adjective-noun pairs.

1 Introduction

A number of approaches have emerged for combining compositional and distributional semantics. Some approaches assume that all words and phrases are represented by vectors living in the same semantic space, and use mathematical operations such as vector addition and element-wise multiplication to combine the constituent vectors (Mitchell and Lapata, 2008). In these relatively simple methods, the composition function does not typically depend on its arguments or their syntactic role in the sentence.

An alternative which makes more use of grammatical structure is the recursive neural network approach of Socher et al. (2010). Constituent vectors in a phrase are combined using a matrix and non-linearity, with the resulting vector living in the same vector space as the inputs. The matrices can be parameterised by the syntactic type of the combining words or phrases (Socher et al., 2013; Hermann and Blunsom, 2013). Socher et al. (2012) extend this idea by representing the meanings of words and phrases as both a vector and a matrix, introducing a form of lexicalisation into the model.

A further extension, which moves us closer to formal semantics (Dowty et al., 1981), is to build a semantic representation in step with the syntactic derivation, and have the embeddings of words be determined by their syntactic type. Coecke et al. (2011) achieve this by treating relational words such as verbs and adjectives as functions in the semantic space. The functions are assumed to be multilinear maps, and are therefore realised as tensors, with composition being achieved through tensor contraction.[1] While the framework specifies the "shape" or semantic type of these tensors, it makes no assumption about how the values of these tensors should be interpreted (nor how they can be learned).

A proposal for the case of adjective-noun combinations is given by Baroni and Zamparelli (2010) (and also Guevara (2010)). Their model represents adjectives as matrices over noun space, trained via linear regression to approximate the "holistic" adjective-noun vectors from the corpus.

In this paper we propose a new solution to the problem of learning adjective meaning representations. The model is an implementation of the tensor framework of Coecke et al. (2011), here applied to adjective-noun combinations as a starting point. Like Baroni and Zamparelli (2010), our model also learn nouns as vectors and adjectives as matrices, but uses a skip-gram approach with negative sampling (Mikolov et al., 2013), extended to learn matrices.

We also propose a new way of quantifying adjective similarity, based on the action of adjectives on nouns (consistent with the view that adjectives are functions). We use this new measure instead of the naive cosine similarity function applied to matrices, and obtain competitive performance compared to the baseline skip-gram vectors (Mikolov et al., 2013) on an adjective similarity task. We also perform competitively on the

[1] Baroni et al. (2014) have developed a similar approach.

Proceedings of the 19th Conference on Computational Language Learning, pages 327–331,
Beijing, China, July 30-31, 2015. ©2015 Association for Computational Linguistics

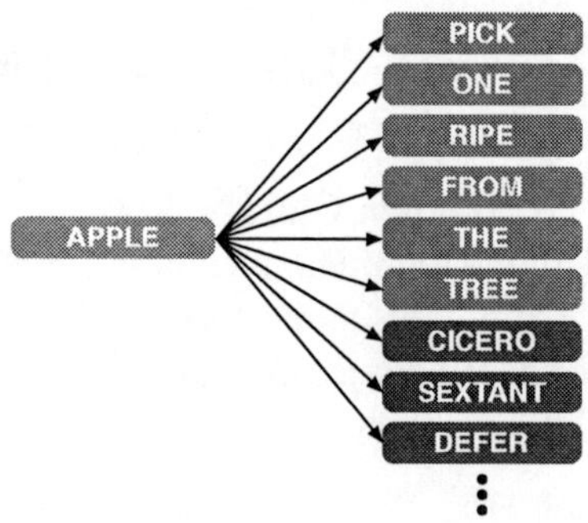

Figure 1: Learning the vector for *apple* in the context *pick one ripe apple from the tree*. The vector for *apple* is updated in order to increase the inner product with green vectors and decrease it with red ones, which are negatively sampled.

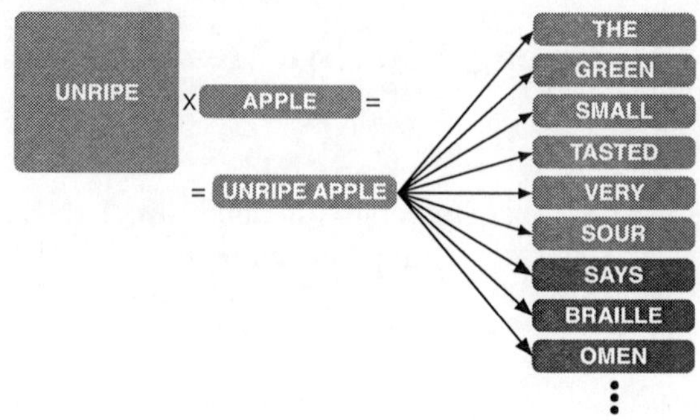

Figure 2: Learning the matrix for *unripe* in the context *the green small unripe apple tasted very sour*. The matrix for *unripe* is updated to increase the inner product of the vector for *unripe apple* with green vectors and decrease it with red ones.

adjective-noun similarity dataset from Mitchell and Lapata (2010). Finally, the tensor-based skip-gram model also leads to improved performance in the detection of semantically anomalous adjective-noun phrases, compared to previous work.

2 A tensor-based skip-gram model

Our model treats adjectives as linear maps over the vector space of noun meanings, encoded as matrices. The algorithm works in two stages: the first stage learns the noun vectors, as in a standard skip-gram model, and the second stage learns the adjective matrices, given fixed noun vectors.

2.1 Training of nouns

To learn noun vectors, we use a skip-gram model with negative sampling (Mikolov et al., 2013). Each noun n in the vocabulary is assigned two d-dimensional vectors: a *content* vector $\boldsymbol{n}$, which constitutes the embedding, and a *context* vector $\boldsymbol{n}'$. For every occurrence of a noun n in the corpus, the embeddings are updated in order to maximise the objective function

$$\sum_{c' \in C} \log \sigma(\boldsymbol{n} \cdot \boldsymbol{c}') + \sum_{\overline{c}' \in \overline{C}} \log \sigma(-\boldsymbol{n} \cdot \overline{\boldsymbol{c}}'), \qquad (1)$$

where C is a set of contexts for the current noun, and $\overline{C}$ is a set of negative contexts. The contexts are taken to be the vectors of words in a fixed window around the noun, while the negative contexts are vectors for k words sampled from a unigram distribution raised to the power of $3/4$ (Goldberg, 2014). In our experiments, we have set $k = 5$.

After each step, both content and context vectors are updated via back-propagation. This procedure leads to noun embeddings (content vectors) which have a high inner product with the vectors of words in the context of the noun, and a low inner product with vectors of negatively sampled words. Fig. 1 shows this intuition.

2.2 Training of adjectives

Each adjective a in the vocabulary is assigned a matrix $\mathbf{A}$, initialised to the identity plus uniform noise. First, all adjective-noun phrases (a, n) are extracted from the corpus. For each (a, n) pair, the corresponding adjective matrix $\mathbf{A}$ and noun vector $\boldsymbol{n}$ are multiplied to compute the adjective-noun vector $\mathbf{A}\boldsymbol{n}$. The matrix $\mathbf{A}$ is then updated to maximise the objective function

$$\sum_{c' \in C} \log \sigma(\mathbf{A}\boldsymbol{n} \cdot \boldsymbol{c}') + \sum_{\overline{c}' \in \overline{C}} \log \sigma(-\mathbf{A}\boldsymbol{n} \cdot \overline{\boldsymbol{c}}'). \qquad (2)$$

The contexts C are taken to be the vectors of words in a window around the adjective-noun phrase, while the negative contexts $\overline{C}$ are again vectors of randomly sampled words. Matrices are initialised to the identity, while the context vectors C are the results of Section 2.1.

Finally, the matrix $\mathbf{A}$ is updated via back-propagation. Equation 2 means that the induced matrices will have the following property: when multiplying the matrix with a noun vector, the resulting adjective-noun vector will have a high inner product with words in the context window of the adjective-noun phrase, and low inner product for negatively sampled words. This is exemplified in Figure 2.

2.3 Similarity measure

The similarity of two vectors $\boldsymbol{n}$ and $\boldsymbol{m}$ is generally measured using the cosine similarity function (Turney and Pantel, 2010; Baroni et al., 2014),

$$\mathrm{vecsim}(\boldsymbol{n}, \boldsymbol{m}) = \frac{\boldsymbol{n} \cdot \boldsymbol{m}}{\|\boldsymbol{n}\| \, \|\boldsymbol{m}\|}.$$

Based on tests using a development set, we found that using cosine to measure the similarity of adjective matrices leads to no correlation with gold-standard similarity judgements. Cosine similarity, while suitable for vectors, does not capture any information about the function of matrices as linear maps. We postulate that a suitable measure of the similarity of two adjectives should be related to how similarly they transform nouns.

Consider two adjective matrices $\mathbf{A}$ and $\mathbf{B}$. If $\mathbf{A}\boldsymbol{n}$ and $\mathbf{B}\boldsymbol{n}$ are similar vectors for every noun vector $\boldsymbol{n}$, then we deem the adjectives to be similar. Therefore, one possible measure involves calculating the cosine distance between the images of all nouns under the two adjectives, and taking the average or median of these distances. Rather than working on every noun in the vocabulary, which is expensive, we instead take the most frequent nouns, cluster them, and use the cluster centroids (obtained in our case using k-means). The resulting distance function is given by

$$\mathrm{matsim}(\mathbf{A}, \mathbf{B}) = \operatorname*{median}_{\boldsymbol{n} \in \mathcal{N}} \mathrm{vecsim}(\mathbf{A}\boldsymbol{n}, \mathbf{B}\boldsymbol{n}), \tag{3}$$

where the median is taken over the set of cluster centroids $\mathcal{N}$.[2]

3 Evaluation

The model is trained on a dump of the English Wikipedia, automatically parsed with the C&C parser (Clark and Curran, 2007). The corpus contains around 200 million noun examples, and 30 million adjective-noun examples. For every context word in the corpus, 5 negative words are sampled from the unigram distribution. Subsampling is used to decrease the number of frequent words (Mikolov et al., 2013). We train 100-dimensional noun vectors and 100×100-dimensional adjective matrices.

3.1 Word Similarity

First we test word, rather than phrase, similarity on the MEN test collection (Bruni et al., 2014), which contains a set of POS-tagged word pairs together with gold-standard human similarity judgements. We use the POS tags to select all noun-noun and adjective-adjective pairs, leaving us with a set of 643 noun-noun pairs and 96 adjective-adjective pairs. For the noun-noun dataset, we are testing the quality of the 100-dimensional noun vectors from the first stage of the tensor-based skip-gram model (TBSG), which is essentially `word2vec` applied to just learning noun vectors. These are compared to the 300-dimensional SKIPGRAM vectors available from the `word2vec` page (which have been trained on a very large news corpus).[3]

MODEL	CORRELATION
SKIPGRAM-300	**0.776**
TBSG-100	0.769

Table 1: Spearman rank correlation on noun similarity task.

MODEL	CORRELATION
TBSG-100×100	**0.645**
SKIPGRAM-300	0.638

Table 2: Spearman rank correlation on adjective similarity task.

The adjective-adjective pairs are used to test the 100×100 matrices obtained from our TBSG model, again compared to the 300-dimensional SKIPGRAM vectors. The Spearman correlations between human judgements and the similarity of vectors are reported in Tables 1 and 2. Note that for adjectives we used the similarity measure described in Section 2.3. Table 1 shows that the noun vectors we use are of a high quality, performing comparably to the SKIPGRAM noun vectors on the noun-noun similarity data. Table 2 shows our TBSG adjective matrices, plus new similarity measure, to also perform comparably to the SKIPGRAM adjective vectors on the adjective-adjective similarity data.

3.2 Phrase Similarity

The TBSG model aims to learn matrices that act in a compositional manner. Therefore, a more interesting evaluation of its performance is to test how well the matrices combine with noun vectors.

[2]We chose the median instead of the average as it is more resistant to outliers in the data.

[3]`http://word2vec.googlecode.com/`

MODEL	CORRELATION
TBSG-100	**0.50**
SKIPGRAM-300 (add)	0.48
SKIPGRAM-300 (N only)	0.43
TBSG-100 (N only)	0.42
REG-600	0.37
humans	*0.52*

Table 3: Spearman rank correlation on adjective-noun similarity task.

	COSINE		DENSITY	
MODEL	t	sig.	t	sig.
TBSG-100	**5.16**	$***$	**5.72**	$***$
ADD-300	0.31		2.63	$**$
MUL-300	-0.56		2.68	$**$
REG-300	0.48		3.12	$**$

Table 4: Correlation on test data for semantic anomalies. Significance levels are marked $***$ for $p < 0.001$, $**$ for $p < 0.01$.

We use the Mitchell and Lapata (2010) adjective-noun similarity dataset, which contains pairs of adjective-noun phrases such as *last number – vast majority* together with gold-standard human similarity judgements. For the evaluation, we calculate the Spearman correlation between non-averaged human similarity judgements and the cosine similarity of the vectors produced by various compositional models.

The results in Table 3 show that TBSG has the best correlation with human judgements of the other models tested. It outperforms SKIPGRAM vectors with both addition and element-wise multiplication as composition functions (the latter not shown in that table, as it is worse than addition). Also reported is the baseline performance of SKIPGRAM and TBSG when using only nouns to compute similarity (ignoring the adjectives). It is interesting to note that TBSG also outperforms the result of the matrix-vector linear regression method (REG-600) of Baroni and Zamparelli (2010) as reported by Vecchi et al. (2015) on the same dataset. Their method trains a matrix for every adjective via linear regression to approximate corpus-extracted "holistic" adjective-noun vectors, and is therefore similar in spirit to TBSG.

3.3 Semantic Anomaly

Finally, we use the model to distinguish between semantically acceptable and anomalous adjective-noun phrases, using the data from Vecchi et al. (2011). The data consists of two sets: a set of unobserved acceptable phrases (e.g. *ethical statute*) and one of deviant phrases (e.g. *cultural acne*). Following Vecchi et al. (2011) we use two indices of semantic anomaly. The first, denoted COSINE, is the cosine between the adjective-noun vector and the noun vector. This is based on the hypothesis that deviant adjective-noun vectors will form a wider angle with the noun vector. The second index, denoted DENSITY, is the average cosine distance between the adjective-noun vector and its 10 nearest noun neighbours. This measure is based on the hypothesis that nonsensical adjective-nouns should not have many neighbours in the space of (meaningful) nouns.[4] These two measures are computed for the acceptable and deviant sets, and compared using a two-tailed Welch's t-test.

Table 4 compares the performance of TBSG with the results of count-based vectors using addition (ADD) and element-wise multiplication (MUL) reported by Vecchi et al. (2011), as well as the matrix-vector linear regression method (REG-300) of Baroni and Zamparelli (2010). TBSG obtains the highest scores with both measures.

4 Conclusions

In this paper we have implemented the tensor-based framework of Coecke et al. (2011) in the form of a skip-gram model extended to learn higher-order embeddings, in this case adjectives as matrices. While adjectives and nouns are learned separately in this study, an obvious extension is to learn embeddings jointly. We find the tensor-based skip-gram model particularly attractive for the obvious ways in which it can be extended to other parts-of-speech (Maillard et al., 2014). For example, in this framework transitive verbs are third-order tensors which yield a sentence vector when contracted with subject and object vectors. Assuming contextual representations of sentences, these could be learned by the tensor-based skip-gram as a straghtforward extension from second-order (matrices) to third-order tensors (and potentially beyond for words requiring even higher order tensors).

[4] Vecchi et al. (2011) also use a third index of semantic anomaly, based on the length of adjective-noun vectors. We omit this measure as we deem it unsuitable for models not based on context counts and elementwise vector operations.

Acknowledgements

Jean Maillard is supported by an EPSRC Doctoral Training Grant and a St John's Scholarship. Stephen Clark is supported by ERC Starting Grant DisCoTex (306920) and EPSRC grant EP/I037512/1. We would like to thank Tamara Polajnar, Laura Rimell, and Eva Vecchi for useful discussion.

References

Marco Baroni, Roberto Zamparelli 2010. *Nouns are vectors, adjectives are matrices: representing adjective-noun constructions in semantic space. Proceedings of EMNLP*, 1183–1193.

Marco Baroni, Raffaela Bernardi, Roberto Zamparelli 2014 *Frege in space: A program for compositional distributional semantics. Linguistic Issues in Language Technologies* 9(6), 5–110.

Marco Baroni, Georgiana Dinu, Germán Kruszewski 2014 *Don't count, predict! A systematic comparison of context-counting vs. context-predicting semantic vectors. Proceedings of ACL*, 238–247.

Elia Bruni, Nam Khanh Tran, Marco Baroni 2014 *Multimodal Distributional Semantics. Journal of Artificial Intelligence Research* 49, 1–47.

Stephen Clark, James R. Curran 2007 *Wide-coverage efficient statistical parsing with CCG and log-linear models. Computational Linguistics* 33(4), 493–552.

Bob Coecke, Mehrnoosh Sadrzadeh, Stephen Clark 2011. *Mathematical Foundations for a Compositional Distributional Model of Meaning. Linguistic Analysis* 36 (Lambek Festschrift), 345–384.

David R. Dowty, Robert E. Wall, Stanley Peters 1981 *Introduction to Montague semantics. Dordrecht.*

Yoav Goldberg, Omer Levy 2014 *word2vec Explained: deriving Mikolov et al.'s negative-sampling word-embedding method. arXiv preprint* 1402.3722.

Emiliano Guevara 2010 *A regression model of adjective-noun compositionality in distributional semantics. Proceedings of the ACL GEMS workshop*, 33–37.

Karl Moritz Hermann and Phil Blunsom. 2013 *The role of syntax in vector space models of compositional semantics. Proceedings of ACL*, 894–904.

Jean Maillard, Stephen Clark, Edward Grefenstette 2014. *A Type-Driven Tensor-Based Semantics for CCG. Proceedings of the EACL 2014 Type Theory and Natural Language Semantics Workshop*, 46–54.

Tomas Mikolov, Ilya Sutskever, Kai Chen, Greg Corrado, Jeff Dean 2013. *Distributed representations of words and phrases and their compositionality. Proceedings of NIPS*, 3111–3119.

Jeff Mitchell, Mirella Lapata 2008 *Vector-based models of semantic composition. Proceedings of ACL 08*, 263–244.

Jeff Mitchell, Mirella Lapata 2010 *Composition in Distributional Models of Semantics. Cognitive science* 34(8), 1388–1439.

Richard Socher, Christopher D. Manning, Andrew Y. Ng 2010 *Learning continuous phrase representations and syntactic parsing with recursive neural networks. Proceedings of the NIPS Deep Learning and Unsupervised Feature Learning Workshop*, 1–9.

Richard Socher, Brody Huval, Christopher D. Manning, Andrew Y. Ng 2012 *Semantic compositionality through recursive matrix-vector spaces. Proceedings of EMNLP*, 1201–1211.

Richard Socher, John Bauer, Christopher D. Manning, Andrew Y. Ng 2013 *Parsing with Compositional Vector Grammars. Proceedings of ACL*, 455-465.

Mark Steedman 2000 *The Syntactic Process. MIT Press.*

Peter D. Turney, Patrick Pantel 2010. *From frequency to meaning: vector space models of semantics. Journal of Artificial Intelligence Research* 37, 141–188.

Eva M. Vecchi, Marco Baroni, Roberto Zamparelli 2011 *(Linear) maps of the impossible: Capturing semantic anomalies in distributional space. Proceedings of ACL DISCo Workshop*, 1–9.

Eva M. Vecchi, Marco Marelli, Roberto Zamparelli, Marco Baroni 2015 *Spicy adjectives and nominal donkeys: Capturing semantic deviance using compositionality in distributional spaces. Accepted for publication.*

Model Selection for Type-Supervised Learning with Application to POS Tagging

Kristina Toutanova
Microsoft Research
Redmond, WA, USA

Waleed Ammar*
School of Computer Science
Carnegie Mellon University

Pallavi Chourdhury **Hoifung Poon**
Microsoft Research
Redmond, WA, USA

Abstract

Model selection (picking, for example, the feature set and the regularization strength) is crucial for building high-accuracy NLP models. In supervised learning, we can estimate the accuracy of a model on a subset of the labeled data and choose the model with the highest accuracy. In contrast, here we focus on type-supervised learning, which uses constraints over the possible labels for word types for supervision, and labeled data is either not available or very small. For the setting where no labeled data is available, we perform a comparative study of previously proposed and one novel model selection criterion on type-supervised POS-tagging in nine languages. For the setting where a small labeled set is available, we show that the set should be used for semi-supervised learning rather than for model selection only – using it for model selection reduces the error by less than 5%, whereas using it for semi-supervised learning reduces the error by 44%.

1 Introduction

Fully supervised training of NLP models (e.g., part-of-speech taggers, named entity recognizers, relation extractors) works well when plenty of labeled examples are available. However, manually labeled corpora are expensive to construct in many languages and domains, whereas an alternative, if weaker, supervision is often readily available. For example, corpora labeled with POS tags at the token level are only available for around 35 languages, while tag dictionaries of the form displayed in Fig. 1 are available for many more languages, either in commercial dictionaries or community created resources such as Wiktionary. Tag dictionaries provide type-level supervision for word types in the lexicon. Similarly, while sentences labeled with named entities are scarce, gazetteers and databases are more readily available (Bollacker et al., 2008).

There has been substantial research on how best to build models using such type-level supervision, for POS tagging, super sense tagging, NER, and relation extraction (Craven et al., 1999; Smith and Eisner, 2005; Carlson et al., 2009; Mintz et al., 2009; Johannsen et al., 2014), *inter alia*, focussing on parametric forms and loss functions for model training. However, there has been little research on the practically important aspect of model selection for type-supervised learning. While some previous work used criteria based on the type-level supervision only (Smith and Eisner, 2005; Goldwater and Griffiths, 2007), much prior work used a labeled set for model selection (Vaswani et al., 2010; Soderland and Weld, 2014). We are not aware of any prior work aiming to compare or improve existing type-supervised model selection criteria.

For POS tagging, there is also work on using both type-level supervision from lexicons, and projection from another language (Täckström et al., 2013). Methods for training with a small labeled set have also been developed (Søgaard, 2011; Garrette and Baldridge, 2013; Duong et al., 2014), but there have not been studies on the utility of a small labeled set for model selection versus model training. Our contributions are: 1) a simple and generally applicable model selection criterion for type-supervised learning, 2) the first multi-lingual systematic evaluation of model selection criteria for type-supervised models, 3) empirical evidence that, if a small labeled set is available, the set should be used for semi-supervised

*This research was conducted during the author's internship at Microsoft Research.

Proceedings of the 19th Conference on Computational Language Learning, pages 332–337,
Beijing, China, July 30-31, 2015.

Greek tag dictionary

αυτούς	det., pron.	train lexicon
σταθερά	adj., adv., noun	
μετέδωσα	verb	
ανάπαυση	noun	
παλιά	adj., adv.	
ενός	det., num.	dev lexicon
γαλακτικέ	adj.	

Figure 1: A tag dictionary (lexicon) for Greek. The splits into lex_{train} and lex_{dev} are discussed in §2.

learning and not only for model selection.

2 Model selection and training for type-supervised learning

Notation. In type-supervised learning, we have unlabeled text $\mathcal{T} = \{\mathbf{x}\}$ of token sequences, and a lexicon lex which lists possible labels for word types. Model training finds the model parameters θ which minimize a training loss function $L(\theta; lex, \mathcal{T}, \mathbf{h})$. We use $\mathbf{h}$ to represent the configurations and modeling decisions (also known as *hyperparameters*). Examples include the dependency structure between variables, feature templates, and regularization strengths. Given a set of fully-specified hyperparameter configurations $\{\mathbf{h}_1, \ldots, \mathbf{h}_M\}$, model selection aims to find the configuration $\mathbf{h}_{\hat{m}}$ that maximizes the expected performance of the corresponding model $\theta_{\hat{m}}$ according to a suitable accuracy measure. $\mathbf{x}$ is a token sequence, $\mathbf{y}$ is a label sequence, and $lex[\mathbf{x}]$ is the set of label sequences compatible with token sequence $\mathbf{x}$ according to lex.

Task. For the application in this paper, the task is type-supervised POS tagging, and the parametric model family we consider is that of featurized first order HMMs (Berg-Kirkpatrick et al., 2010). The hyperparameters specify the feature set used and the strength of an L_2 regularizer on the parameters.

Evaluation function. The evaluation function used in model selection is the main focus of this work. We use a function $eval(m, \mathcal{T}_{dev})$ to estimate the performance of the model trained with hyperparameters $\mathbf{h}_m$ on a development set $\mathcal{T}_{dev}$. In the following subsections, we discuss definitions of $eval$ when the development set $\mathcal{T}_{dev}$ is labeled and when it is unlabeled, respectively.

2.1 $\mathcal{T}_{dev}$ is labeled

When the development set $\mathcal{T}_{dev}$ is labeled, a natural choice of $eval$ is token-level prediction accuracy:

$$eval_{sup}(m, \mathcal{T}_{dev}) = \sum_{i=1}^{|\mathcal{T}_{dev}|} \frac{\mathbb{1}(\mathbf{y}_m[i] = \mathbf{y}_{gold}[i])}{|\mathcal{T}_{dev}|}$$

Here, we use i to index all tokens in $\mathcal{T}_{dev}$; $\mathbf{y}_{gold}[i]$ denotes the *correct* POS tag, and $\mathbf{y}_m[i]$ denotes the *predicted* POS tag of the i-th token obtained with hyperparameters $\mathbf{h}_m$.

2.2 $\mathcal{T}_{dev}$ is unlabeled

When token-supervision is not available, we cannot compute $eval_{sup}$. Instead, previous work on POS tagging with type supervision (Smith and Eisner, 2005) used:

$$eval_{cond}(m, \mathcal{T}_{dev}) = \sum_{\mathbf{x} \in \mathcal{T}_{dev}} \log \sum_{\mathbf{y} \in lex[\mathbf{x}]} p_{\theta_m}(\mathbf{y} \mid \mathbf{x}),$$

$$eval_{joint}(m, \mathcal{T}_{dev}) = \sum_{\mathbf{x} \in \mathcal{T}_{dev}} \log \sum_{\mathbf{y} \in lex[\mathbf{x}]} p_{\theta_m}(\mathbf{x}, \mathbf{y})$$

$eval_{cond}$ estimates the conditional log-likelihood of "lex-compatible" labels *given* token sequences, while $eval_{joint}$ estimates the joint log-likelihood of lex-compatible labels *and* token sequences.

The held-out lexicon criterion. We propose a new model selection criterion which estimates prediction accuracy more directly and is applicable to any model type, without requiring that the model define conditional or joint probabilities of label sequences. The idea behind this proposed criterion is simple: we hold out a portion of the lexicon entries and use it to estimate model performance as follows:

$$eval_{devlex}(m, \mathcal{T}) = \sum_{i=1 : x_i \in lex_{dev}}^{|\mathcal{T}|} \frac{\mathbb{1}(\mathbf{y}_m[i] \in lex[x_i])}{|lex[x_i]| \times |\mathcal{T}_{x \in lex_{dev}}|}$$

where lex_{dev} is the held-out portion of the lexicon entries, and x_i is the i-th token in $\mathcal{T}$.

The remainder of this section details the theory behind this criterion. The expected token-level accuracy of a model trained with hyperparameters $\mathbf{h}_m$ is defined as $\mathbb{E}_{(x, y_{gold}, y_m) \sim \mathcal{D}} [\mathbb{1}(y_m = y_{gold})]$; where $\mathcal{D}$ is a joint distribution over tokens x (in context), their gold labels y_{gold}, and the predicted labels y_m (for the configuration $\mathbf{h}_m$). Since when no labeled data is available we do not have access to samples from $\mathcal{D}$, we derive an approximation to this distribution using lex and $\mathcal{T}$.

We first split the full lexicon into a training lexicon lex_{train} and a held-out (or development) lexicon lex_{dev} (see Fig. 1), by sampling words according to their token frequency $c(x)$ in $\mathcal{T}$, and placing them in the development or training portions of the lexicon such that lex_{dev} covers 25% of the tokens in $\mathcal{T}$. The goal of the sampling process is to make the distribution of word tags for words in the development lexicon representative of the tag distribution for all words.

Given $\mathbf{h}_m$, we train a tagging model using lex_{train} and use it to predict labels y_m for all tokens in $\mathcal{T}$. We then use the word tokens covered by the development lexicon and their predicted tags y_m to approximate $\mathcal{D}$ by letting $P(y_{gold} \mid x)$ be a uniform distribution over gold labels consistent with the lexicon for x, resulting in the following approximation $P_{\mathcal{D}}(x, y_{gold}, y_m) \propto$

$$\frac{c(x, y_m) \times \mathbb{1}(x \in lex_{dev}, y_{gold} \in lex_{dev}[x])}{|lex_{dev}[x]|}$$

We then compute the expected accuracy as $eval_{devlex} = \mathbb{E}_{\mathcal{D}}\left[\mathbb{1}(y_{gold} = y_m)\right]$, and select the hyperparameter configuration $\hat{m}$ which maximizes this criterion, then re-train the model with the full lexicon lex.[1]

3 How to best use a small labeled set $\mathcal{T}_L$?

Several prior works used a labeled set for supervised hyper-parameter selection even when only type-level supervision is assumed to be available for training (Vaswani et al., 2010; Soderland and Weld, 2014). In this section, we want to answer the question: if a small labeled set is available, what are the potential gains from using it for model selection only, versus using it for both model training and model selection?

A simple way to use a small labeled set for parameter training together with a larger unlabeled set in our type-supervised learning setting, is to do semi-supervised model training as follows (Nigam et al., 2000): Starting with our training loss function defined using a lexicon lex and unlabeled set $\mathcal{T}_U$ $L(\theta; lex, \mathcal{T}_U, \mathbf{h}_m)$, we define a combined loss function using both the unlabeled set $\mathcal{T}_U$ and the labeled set $\mathcal{T}_L$: $L(\theta; lex, \mathcal{T}_U, \mathbf{h}_m) + \lambda L(\theta; lex, \mathcal{T}_L, \mathbf{h}_m)$. We then select parameters θ_m to minimize the new loss function, where λ is now an additional hyperparameter that usually gives more weight to the labeled set. An advantage of this method is that it can be applied to any type-supervised model using less than 100 lines of code.[2] We implement this method for semi-supervised training, and we use the labeled set both for semi-supervised model training and for hyper-parameter selection using a standard five-fold cross-validation approach.[3]

4 Experiments

We evaluate the introduced methods for model selection and training with type supervision in two type-supervised settings: when no labeled examples are available, and when a small number of labeled examples are available.

We use a feature-rich first-order HMM model (Berg-Kirkpatrick et al., 2010) with an L_2 prior on feature weights.[4] Instead of using a multinomial distribution for the local emissions and transitions, this model uses a log-linear distribution (i.e., $p(x_i \mid y_i) \propto \exp \lambda^\top f(x_i, y_i)$) with a feature vector f and a weight vector λ. We use the feature set described in (Li et al., 2012): transition features, word-tag features ($\langle y_i, x_i \rangle$) (lowercased words with frequency greater than a threshold), whether the word contains a hyphen and/or starts with a capital letter, character suffixes, and whether the word contains a digit. We initialize the transition and emission distributions of the HMM using unambiguous words as proposed by (Zhang and DeNero, 2014). **Data.** We use the Danish, Dutch, German, Greek, English, Italian, Portuguese, Spanish and Swedish datasets from CoNLL-X and CoNLL-2007 shared tasks (Buchholz and Marsi, 2006; Nivre et al., 2007). We map the POS labels in the CoNLL datasets to the universal POS tagset (Petrov et al., 2012). We use the tag dictionaries provided by Li et al. (2012). **Model configurations.** For each

[1] Note that this criterion underestimates the performance of all models in consideration by virtue of evaluating model versions trained using a subset of the full lexicon, but it can still be useful for ranking the models.

[2] The labeled data loss is the negative joint log-likelihood of the observed token sequences and labels: $-\sum_{\mathbf{x},\mathbf{y} \in \mathcal{T}_L} \log p_\theta(\mathbf{x}, \mathbf{y})$.

[3] We split the labeled set into five folds, and for each setting of the hyper-parameters train five different models on $\frac{4}{5}$-ths of the data, estimating accuracy on the remaining $\frac{1}{5}$-th. We average the accuracy estimates from different folds and use this as a combined estimate of the accuracy of a model trained using the full labeled and unlabeled set, given these hyperparameters. After selecting a configuration of hyperparameters using cross-validation, we then use this configuration and retrain the model on all available data.

[4] We used a first-order HMM for simplicity, but it is possible to obtain better results using a second-order HMM (Li et al., 2012).

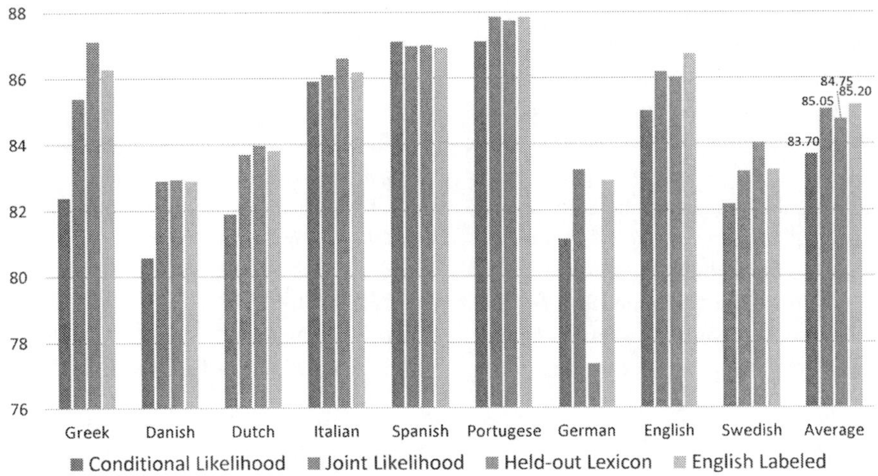

Figure 2: Token-level accuracy when doing training and model selection with no labeled data. Model selection with different criteria (left to right): conditional log-likelihood, joint log-likelihood, held-out lexicon, and English-labeled.

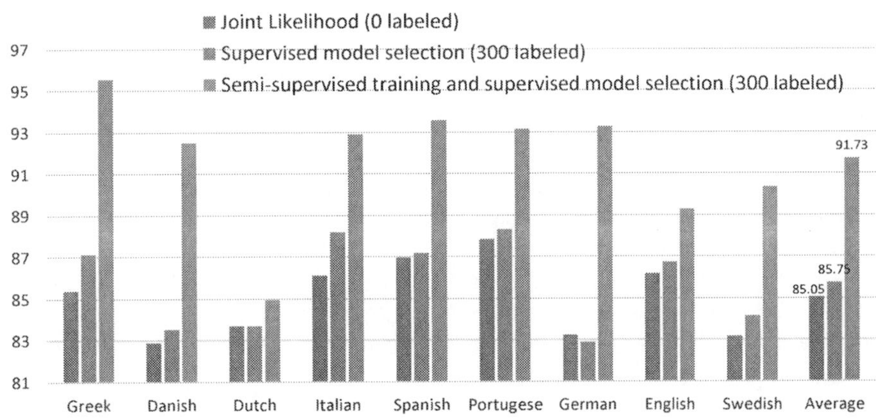

Figure 3: Token-level accuracy with (left to right): no labeled data, model selection on labeled data (300 sentences), semi-supervised training + model selection on labeled data (300 sentences).

language, we consider $M = 15$ configurations of the hyperparameters which vary in the L_2 regularization strength (5 values), and the minimum word frequency for word-tag features (3 values). When a small labeled set is available we additionally choose one of 3 values for the weight of the labeled set (see Section 3). We report final performance of models selected using different criteria using token-level accuracy on an unseen test set.

No labeled examples. When no labeled examples are available, we do model training and selection using only unlabeled text $\mathcal{T}$ and a tagging lexicon lex. We compare three type-supervised model selection criteria: conditional likelihood, joint likelihood, and the held-out lexicon criterion $eval_{devlex}$. Additionally, we include the performance of a method which selects the hyperparameters using labeled data in English and uses these (same) hyperparameters for English and all other languages (we call this method "English Labeled"). Fig. 2 shows the accuracy of the models chosen by each of the four criteria on nine languages, as well as the average accuracy across languages. The lower (upper) bounds on average performance obtained by always choosing the worst (best) hyperparameters is 82.77 (85.83). $eval_{joint}$ outperformed $eval_{cond}$ on eight out of the nine languages and achieved a significantly higher average accuracy (85.05 vs 83.70). $eval_{devlex}$ outperformed $eval_{joint}$ on six out of nine languages, but did significantly worse on one language (German), which resulted in a slightly lower average accuracy. Choosing the hyper-parameters using English labeled data and using the same hyper-parameters for all languages performed comparably to $eval_{joint}$, with slightly higher average accuracy even when limited to the non-English languages (85.0 vs 84.9). Overall the results showed that the conditional log-likelihood criterion was dominated by the other three, which were comparable in average accuracy. Looking at the eight languages excluding English (since one criterion uses labeled data for English), the newly proposed held-out lexicon criterion was the winning method on five out of eight languages, $eval_{cond}$ was best on one language, $eval_{joint}$ was best (or tied for best) on two, and English-labeled was tied for best on one language.

Few labeled examples. We consider two ways of leveraging the labeled examples: (*i*) type-supervised model training + supervised model selection: only use unlabeled examples to optimize model parameters, then use the labeled examples for supervised model selection with $eval_{sup}$, and (*ii*) semi-supervised model training + supervised model selection (see Section 3 for details). Fig. 3 shows how much we can improve on the method with highest average accuracy from Figure 2 ($eval_{joint}$), when a small number of examples is available. Using the 300 labeled sentences for semi-supervised training and model selection reduced the error by 44.6% (comparing to the model with best average accuracy using only type-level supervision with average performance of 85.05, the semi-supervised average is 91.8). In contrast, using the 300 sentences to select hyper-parameters only reduced the error by less than 5% (the average accuracy was 85.75). Even when only 50 labeled sentences are used for semi-supervised training and supervised model selection, we still see a boost to average accuracy of 89% (results not shown in the Figure).

5 Conclusion

We presented the first comparative evaluation of model selection criteria for type-supervised POS-tagging on many languages. We introduced a novel, generally applicable model selection criterion which outperformed previously proposed ones for a majority of languages. We evaluated the utility of a small labeled set for model selection versus model training, and showed that when such labeled set is available, it should not be used solely for supervised model selection, because using it additionally for model parameter training provides strikingly larger accuracy gains.

Acknowledgments

We thank Nathan Schneider and the anonymous reviewers for helpful suggestions.

References

Taylor Berg-Kirkpatrick, Alexandre Bouchard-Côté, John DeNero, and Dan Klein. 2010. Painless unsupervised learning with features. In *Proc. of NAACL.*

Kurt Bollacker, Colin Evans, Praveen Paritosh, Tim Sturge, and Jamie Taylor. 2008. Freebase: A collaboratively created graph database for structuring human knowledge. In *Proceedings of the 2008 ACM SIGMOD International Conference on Management of Data*, SIGMOD '08, pages 1247–1250.

Sabine Buchholz and Erwin Marsi. 2006. CoNLL-X shared task on multilingual dependency parsing. In *CoNLL-X.*

Andrew Carlson, Scott Gaffney, and Flavian Vasile. 2009. Learning a named entity tagger from gazetteers with the partial perceptron. In *AAAI Spring Symposium: Learning by Reading and Learning to Read*, pages 7–13.

Mark Craven, Johan Kumlien, et al. 1999. Constructing biological knowledge bases by extracting information from text sources. In *ISMB*, volume 1999, pages 77–86.

Long Duong, Trevor Cohn, Karin Verspoor, Steven Bird, and Paul Cook. 2014. What can we get from 1000 tokens? a case study of multilingual pos tagging for resource-poor languages. In *Proc. of EMNLP.*

Dan Garrette and Jason Baldridge. 2013. Learning a part-of-speech tagger from two hours of annotation. In *Proc. of NAACL-HLT*, pages 138–147.

Sharon Goldwater and Tom Griffiths. 2007. A fully bayesian approach to unsupervised part-of-speech tagging. In *Annual meeting-association for computational linguistics.*

Anders Johannsen, Dirk Hovy, Héctor Martınez Alonso, Barbara Plank, and Anders Søgaard. 2014. More or less supervised supersense tagging of twitter. *Proc. of* SEM*, pages 1–11.

Shen Li, João Graça, and Ben Taskar. 2012. Wiki-ly supervised part-of-speech tagging. In *Proc. of EMNLP*.

Mike Mintz, Steven Bills, Rion Snow, and Dan Jurafsky. 2009. Distant supervision for relation extraction without labeled data. In *Proceedings of the Joint Conference of the 47th Annual Meeting of the ACL and the 4th International Joint Conference on Natural Language Processing of the AFNLP: Volume 2-Volume 2*, pages 1003–1011. Association for Computational Linguistics.

Kamal Nigam, Andrew Kachites McCallum, Sebastian Thrun, and Tom Mitchell. 2000. Text classification from labeled and unlabeled documents using em. *Machine learning*, 39.

Joakim Nivre, Johan Hall, Sandra Kubler, Ryan McDonald, Jens Nilsson, Sebastian Riedel, and Deniz Yuret. 2007. The CoNLL 2007 shared task on dependency parsing. In *Proc. of CoNLL*.

Slav Petrov, Dipanjan Das, and Ryan McDonald. 2012. A universal part-of-speech tagset. In *Proc. of LREC*, May.

Noah A. Smith and Jason Eisner. 2005. Contrastive estimation: Training log-linear models on unlabeled data. In *Proc. of ACL*.

Mitchell Koch John Gilmer Stephen Soderland and Daniel S Weld. 2014. Type-aware distantly supervised relation extraction with linked arguments. In *Proc. of EMNLP*.

Anders Søgaard. 2011. Semisupervised condensed nearest neighbor for part-of-speech tagging. In *Proceedings of the 49th Annual Meeting of the Association for Computational Linguistics: Human Language Technologies: Short Papers - Volume 2*, HLT '11, pages 48–52, Stroudsburg, PA, USA. Association for Computational Linguistics.

Oscar Täckström, Dipanjan Das, Slav Petrov, Ryan McDonald, and Joakim Nivre. 2013. Token and type constraints for cross-lingual part-of-speech tagging. *Transactions of the Association for Computational Linguistics*, 1:1–12.

Ashish Vaswani, Adam Pauls, and David Chiang. 2010. Efficient optimization of an mdl-inspired objective function for unsupervised part-of-speech tagging. In *Proceedings of the ACL 2010 Conference Short Papers*, pages 209–214. Association for Computational Linguistics.

Hui Zhang and John DeNero. 2014. Observational initialization of type-supervised taggers. In *Proceedings of the Association for Computational Linguistics (Short Paper Track)*.

One Million Sense-Tagged Instances for Word Sense Disambiguation and Induction

Kaveh Taghipour
Department of Computer Science
National University of Singapore
13 Computing Drive
Singapore 117417
kaveh@comp.nus.edu.sg

Hwee Tou Ng
Department of Computer Science
National University of Singapore
13 Computing Drive
Singapore 117417
nght@comp.nus.edu.sg

Abstract

Supervised word sense disambiguation (WSD) systems are usually the best performing systems when evaluated on standard benchmarks. However, these systems need annotated training data to function properly. While there are some publicly available open source WSD systems, very few large annotated datasets are available to the research community. The two main goals of this paper are to extract and annotate a large number of samples and release them for public use, and also to evaluate this dataset against some word sense disambiguation and induction tasks. We show that the open source IMS WSD system trained on our dataset achieves state-of-the-art results in standard disambiguation tasks and a recent word sense induction task, outperforming several task submissions and strong baselines.

1 Introduction

Identifying the meaning of a word automatically has been an interesting research topic for a few decades. The approaches used to solve this problem can be roughly categorized into two main classes: Word Sense Disambiguation (WSD) and Word Sense Induction (WSI) (Navigli, 2009). For word sense disambiguation, some systems are based on supervised machine learning algorithms (Lee et al., 2004; Zhong and Ng, 2010), while others use ontologies and other structured knowledge sources (Ponzetto and Navigli, 2010; Agirre et al., 2014; Moro et al., 2014).

There are several sense-annotated datasets for WSD (Miller et al., 1993; Ng and Lee, 1996; Passonneau et al., 2012). However, these datasets either include few samples per word sense or only cover a small set of polysemous words. To overcome these limitations, automatic methods have been developed for annotating training samples. For example, Ng et al. (2003), Chan and Ng (2005), and Zhong and Ng (2009) used Chinese-English parallel corpora to extract samples for training their supervised WSD system. Diab (2004) proposed an unsupervised bootstrapping method to automatically generate a sense-annotated dataset. Another example of automatically created datasets is the semi-supervised method used in (Kübler and Zhekova, 2009), which employed a supervised classifier to label instances.

The two main contributions of this paper are as follows. First, we employ the same method used in (Ng et al., 2003; Chan and Ng, 2005) to *semi-automatically* annotate one million training samples based on the WordNet sense inventory (Miller, 1995) and release the annotated corpus for public use. To our knowledge, this annotated set of sense-tagged samples is the largest publicly available dataset for word sense disambiguation. Second, we train an open source supervised WSD system, IMS (Zhong and Ng, 2010), using our data and evaluate it against standard WSD and WSI benchmarks. We show that our system outperforms other state-of-the-art systems in most cases.

As any WSD system is also a WSI system when we treat the pre-defined sense inventory of the WSD system as the induced word senses, a WSD system can also be evaluated and used for WSI. Some researchers believe that, in some cases, WSI methods may perform better than WSD systems (Jurgens and Klapaftis, 2013; Wang et al., 2015). However, we argue that WSI systems have few advantages compared to WSD methods and according to our results, disambiguation systems consistently outperform induction systems. Although there are some cases where WSI systems can be useful (e.g., for resource-poor languages), in most cases WSD systems are preferable because

Proceedings of the 19th Conference on Computational Language Learning, pages 338–344,
Beijing, China, July 30-31, 2015.

of higher accuracy and better interpretability of output.

The rest of this paper is composed of the following sections. Section 2 explains our methodology for creating the training data. We evaluate the extracted data in Section 3 and finally, we conclude the paper in Section 4.

2 Training Data

In order to train a supervised word sense disambiguation system, we extract and sense-tag data from a freely available parallel corpus, in a *semi-automatic* manner. To increase the coverage and therefore the ultimate performance of our WSD system, we also make use of existing sense-tagged datasets. This section explains each step in detail.

Since the main purpose of this paper is to build and release a publicly available training set for word sense disambiguation systems, we selected the MultiUN corpus (MUN) (Eisele and Chen, 2010) produced in the EuroMatrixPlus project[1]. This corpus is freely available via the project website and includes seven languages. An automatically sentence-aligned version of this dataset can be downloaded from the OPUS website[2] and therefore we decided to extract samples from this sentence-aligned version.

To extract training data from the MultiUN parallel corpus, we follow the approach described in (Chan and Ng, 2005) and select the Chinese-English part of the MultiUN corpus. The extraction method has the following steps:

1. Tokenization and word segmentation: The English side of the corpus is tokenized using the Penn TreeBank tokenizer[3], while the Chinese side of the corpus is segmented using the Chinese word segmenter of (Low et al., 2005).

2. Word alignment: After tokenizing the texts, GIZA++ (Och and Ney, 2000) is used to align English and Chinese words.

3. Part-of-speech (POS) tagging and lemmatization: After running GIZA++, we use the OpenNLP POS tagger[4] and then the WordNet lemmatizer to obtain POS tags and word lemmas of the English sentence.

4. Annotation: In order to assign a WordNet sense tag to an English word w_e in a sentence, we make use of the aligned Chinese translation w_c of w_e, based on the automatic word alignment formed by GIZA++. For each sense i of w_e in the WordNet sense inventory (WordNet 1.7.1), a list of Chinese translations of sense i of w_e has been manually created. If w_c matches one of these Chinese translations of sense i, then w_e is tagged with sense i.

The average time needed to manually assign Chinese translations to the word senses of one word type for noun, adjective, and verb is 20, 25, and 40 minutes respectively (Chan, 2008). The above procedure annotates the top 60% most frequent word types (nouns, verbs, and adjectives) in English, selected based on their frequency in the Brown corpus. This set of selected word types includes 649 nouns, 190 verbs, and 319 adjectives.

Since automatic sentence and word alignment can be noisy, and a Chinese word w_c can occasionally be a valid translation of more than one sense of an English word w_e, the senses tagged using the above procedure may be erroneous. To get an idea of the accuracy of the senses tagged with this procedure, we manually evaluated a subset of 1,000 randomly selected sense-tagged instances. Although the sense inventory is fine-grained (WordNet 1.7.1), the sense-tag accuracy achieved is 83.7%. We also performed an error analysis to identify the sources of errors. We found that only 4% of errors are caused by wrong sentence or word alignment. However, 69% of erroneous sense-tagged instances are the result of a Chinese word associated with multiple senses of a target English word. In such cases, the Chinese word is linked to multiple sense tags and therefore, errors in sense-tagged data are introduced. Our results are similar to those reported in (Chan, 2008).

To speed up the training process, we perform random sampling on the sense tags with more than 500 samples and limit the number of samples *per sense* to 500. However, all samples of senses with fewer than 500 samples are included in the training data. This sampling method ensures that rare sense tags also have training samples during the selection process.

In order to improve the coverage of the training set, we augment it by adding samples from SEMCOR (SC) (Miller et al., 1993) and the DSO cor-

[1] http://www.euromatrixplus.eu/multi-un
[2] http://opus.lingfil.uu.se/MultiUN.php
[3] http://www.cis.upenn.edu/~treebank/tokenization.html
[4] http://opennlp.apache.org

	Avg. # samples per word type
MUN (before sampling)	19,837.6
MUN	852.5
MUN+SC	55.4
MUN+SC+DSO	63.7

Table 3: Average number of samples per word type (WordNet 1.7.1)

pus (Ng and Lee, 1996). We only add the 28 most frequent adverbs from SEMCOR because we observe almost no improvement when adding all adverbs. We notice that the DSO corpus generally improves the performance of our system. However, since the annotated DSO corpus is copyrighted, we are unable to release a dataset including the DSO corpus. Therefore, we experiment with two different configurations, one with the DSO corpus and one without, although the released dataset will not include the DSO corpus.

Since some shared tasks use newer WordNet versions, we convert the training set sense labels using the sense mapping files provided by WordNet[5]. As replicating our results requires WordNet versions 1.7.1, 2.1, and 3.0, we release our sense-tagged dataset in all three versions. Some statistics about the sense-tagged training set can be found in Table 1 to Table 3.

3 Evaluation

For the WSD system, we use IMS (Zhong and Ng, 2010) in our experiments. IMS is a supervised WSD system based on support vector machines (SVM). This WSD system comes with out-of-the-box pre-trained models. However, since the original training set is not released, we use our own training set (see Section 2) to train IMS and then evaluate it on standard WSD and WSI benchmarks. This section presents the results obtained on four WSD and one WSI shared tasks. The four all-words WSD shared tasks are SensEval-2 (Edmonds and Cotton, 2001), SensEval-3 task 1 (Snyder and Palmer, 2004), and both the fine-grained task 17 and coarse-grained task 7 of SemEval-2007 (Pradhan et al., 2007; Navigli et al., 2007). These all-words WSD shared tasks provide no training data to the participants. The selected word sense induction task in our experiments is SemEval-2013 task 13 (Jurgens and Klapaftis, 2013).

[5]http://wordnet.princeton.edu/wordnet/download/current-version/

3.1 WSD All-Words Tasks

The results of our experiments on WSD tasks are presented in Table 4. For the SensEval-2 and SensEval-3 test sets, we use the training set with the WordNet 1.7.1 sense inventory and for the SemEval-2007 test sets, we use training data with the WordNet 2.1 sense inventory.

In Table 4, IMS (original) refers to the IMS system trained with the original training instances as reported in (Zhong and Ng, 2010). We also compare our systems with two other configurations obtained from training IMS on SEMCOR, and SEMCOR plus DSO datasets. In Table 4, these two settings are shown by IMS (SC) and IMS (SC+DSO), respectively. Finally, Rank 1 and Rank 2 are the top two participating systems in the respective all-words tasks.

As shown in Table 4, our systems (both with and without the DSO corpus as training instances) perform competitively with and in some cases even better than the original IMS and also the best shared task submissions. This shows that our training set is of high quality and training a supervised WSD system using our training data achieves state-of-the-art results on the all-words tasks. Since the MUN dataset does not cover all target word types in the all-words shared tasks, the accuracy achieved with MUN alone is lower than the SC and SC+DSO settings. However, the evaluation results show that IMS trained on MUN alone often performs better than or is competitive with the WordNet Sense 1 baseline. Finally, it can be seen that adding the training instances from MUN (that is, IMS (MUN+SC) and IMS (MUN+SC+DSO)) often achieves higher accuracy than without MUN instances (IMS (SC) and IMS (SC+DSO)).

3.2 SemEval-2013 Word Sense Induction Task

In order to evaluate our system on a word sense induction task, we selected SemEval-2013 task 13, the latest WSI shared task. Unlike most other tasks that assume a single sense is sufficient for representing word senses, this task allows each instance to be associated with multiple sense labels with their applicability weights. This WSI task considers 50 lemmas, including 20 nouns, 20 verbs, and 10 adjectives, annotated with the WordNet 3.1

	noun	verb	adjective	adverb	total
MUN (before sampling)	649	190	319	0	1,158
MUN	649	190	319	0	1,158
MUN+SC	11,446	4,705	5,129	28	21,308
MUN+SC+DSO	11,446	4,705	5,129	28	21,308

Table 1: Number of word types in each part-of-speech (WordNet 1.7.1)

	number of training samples					
	noun	verb	adjective	adverb	total	size
MUN (before sampling)	14,492,639	4,400,813	4,078,543	0	22,971,995	17.7 GB
MUN	503,408	265,785	218,046	0	987,239	745 MB
MUN+SC	582,028	341,141	251,362	6,207	1,180,738	872 MB
MUN+SC+DSO	687,871	412,482	251,362	6,207	1,357,922	939 MB

Table 2: Number of training samples in each part-of-speech (WordNet 1.7.1). The size column shows the total size of each dataset in megabytes or gigabytes.

sense inventory. We use WordNet 3.0 in our experiments on this task.

We evaluated our system using all measures used in the shared task. The results are presented in Table 5. The columns in this table denote the scores of the various systems according to the different evaluation metrics used in the WSI shared task, which are Jaccard Index, K_{δ}^{sim}, WNDCG, Fuzzy NMI, and Fuzzy B-Cubed. See (Jurgens and Klapaftis, 2013) for details of the evaluation metrics.

This table also includes the top two systems in the shared task, `AI-KU` (Baskaya et al., 2013) and `Unimelb` (Lau et al., 2013), as well as `Wang-15` (Wang et al., 2015). `AI-KU` uses a language model to find the most likely substitutes for a target word to represent the context. The clustering method used in `AI-KU` is K-means and the system gives good performance in the shared task. `Unimelb` relies on Hierarchical Dirichlet Process (Teh et al., 2006) to identify the sense of a target word using positional word features. Finally, `Wang-15` uses Latent Dirichlet Allocation (LDA) (Blei et al., 2003) to model the word sense and topic jointly. This system obtains high scores, according to Fuzzy B-Cubed and Fuzzy NMI measures. The last three rows are some baseline systems: grouping all instances into one cluster, grouping each instance into a cluster of its own, and assigning the most frequent sense in SEMCOR to all instances. As shown in Table 5, training IMS on our training data outperforms all other systems on three out of five evaluation metrics, and performs competitively on the remaining two metrics.

IMS trained on MUN alone (IMS (MUN)) outperforms IMS (SC) and IMS (SC+DSO) in terms of the first three evaluation measures, and achieves comparable Fuzzy NMI and Fuzzy B-Cubed scores. Moreover, the evaluation results show that IMS (MUN) often performs better than the SEMCOR most frequent sense baseline. Finally, it can be observed that in most cases, adding training instances from MUN significantly improves IMS (SC) and IMS (SC+DSO).

4 Conclusion

One of the major problems in building supervised word sense disambiguation systems is the training data acquisition bottleneck. In this paper, we semi-automatically extracted and sense-tagged an English corpus containing one million sense-tagged instances. This large sense-tagged corpus can be used for training any supervised WSD systems. We then evaluated the performance of IMS trained on our sense-tagged corpus in several WSD and WSI shared tasks. Our sense-tagged dataset has been released publicly[6]. We believe our dataset is the largest publicly available annotated dataset for WSD at present.

After training a supervised WSD system using our training set, we evaluated the system using standard benchmarks. The evaluation results show that our sense-tagged corpus can be used to build a WSD system that performs competitively with the

[6]http://www.comp.nus.edu.sg/~nlp/corpora.html

	SensEval-2	SensEval-3	SemEval-2007	
	Fine-grained	Fine-grained	Fine-grained	Coarse-grained
IMS (MUN)	64.5	60.6	52.7	78.7
IMS (MUN+SC)	68.2	67.4	58.5	81.6
IMS (MUN+SC+DSO)	68.0	66.6	58.9	82.3
IMS (original)	68.2	**67.6**	58.3	**82.6**
IMS (SC)	66.1	67.0	58.7	81.9
IMS (SC+DSO)	66.5	67.0	57.8	81.6
Rank 1	**69.0**	65.2	**59.1**	82.5
Rank 2	63.6	64.6	58.7	81.6
WordNet Sense 1	61.9	62.4	51.4	78.9

Table 4: Accuracy (in %) on all-words word sense disambiguation tasks

	Jac. Ind.	K_{δ}^{sim}	WNDCG	Fuzzy NMI	Fuzzy B-Cubed
IMS (MUN)	24.6	64.9	33.0	6.9	57.1
IMS (MUN+SC)	25.0	**65.4**	34.2	9.1	55.9
IMS (MUN+SC+DSO)	**25.5**	**65.4**	35.1	**9.7**	55.4
IMS (original)	23.4	64.5	34.0	8.6	59.0
IMS (SC)	22.9	63.5	32.4	6.8	57.3
IMS (SC+DSO)	23.4	63.6	32.9	7.1	57.6
Wang-15 (ukWac)	-	-	-	**9.7**	54.5
Wang-15 (actual)	-	-	-	9.4	59.1
AI-KU (base)	19.7	62.0	**38.7**	6.5	39.0
AI-KU (add1000)	19.7	60.6	21.5	3.5	32.0
AI-KU (remove5-add1000)	24.4	64.2	33.2	3.9	45.1
Unimelb (5p)	21.8	61.4	36.5	5.6	45.9
Unimelb (50k)	21.3	62.0	37.1	6.0	48.3
all-instances-1cluster	19.2	60.9	28.8	0.0	**62.3**
each-instance-1cluster	0.0	0.0	0.0	7.1	0.0
SEMCOR most freq sense	19.2	60.9	28.8	0.0	**62.3**

Table 5: Supervised and unsupervised evaluation results (in %) on SemEval-2013 word sense induction task

top performing WSD systems in the SensEval-2, SensEval-3, and SemEval-2007 fine-grained and coarse-grained all-words tasks, as well as the top systems in the SemEval-2013 WSI task.

Acknowledgments

This research is supported by the Singapore National Research Foundation under its International Research Centre @ Singapore Funding Initiative and administered by the IDM Programme Office. We are also grateful to Christian Hadiwinoto and Benjamin Yap for assistance with performing the error analysis, and to the anonymous reviewers for their helpful comments.

References

Eneko Agirre, Oier López de Lacalle, and Aitor Soroa. 2014. Random walks for knowledge-based word sense disambiguation. *Computational Linguistics*, 40(1):57–84.

Osman Baskaya, Enis Sert, Volkan Cirik, and Deniz Yuret. 2013. AI-KU: using substitute vectors and co-occurrence modeling for word sense induction and disambiguation. In *Proceedings of the Seventh International Workshop on Semantic Evaluation (SemEval 2013)*, pages 300–306.

David M. Blei, Andrew Y. Ng, and Michael I. Jordan. 2003. Latent Dirichlet allocation. *Journal of Machine Learning Research*, 3:993–1022.

Yee Seng Chan and Hwee Tou Ng. 2005. Scaling up word sense disambiguation via parallel texts. In

Proceedings of the 20th National Conference on Artificial Intelligence, pages 1037–1042.

Yee Seng Chan. 2008. *Word Sense Disambiguation: Scaling up, Domain Adaptation, and Application to Machine Translation*. Ph.D. thesis, National University of Singapore.

Mona Diab. 2004. Relieving the data acquisition bottleneck in word sense disambiguation. In *Proceedings of the 42nd Annual Meeting of the Association for Computational Linguistics*, pages 303–310.

Philip Edmonds and Scott Cotton. 2001. SENSEVAL-2: Overview. In *Proceedings of the Second International Workshop on Evaluating Word Sense Disambiguation Systems*, pages 1–5.

Andreas Eisele and Yu Chen. 2010. MultiUN: A multilingual corpus from United Nation documents. In *Proceedings of the Seventh International Conference on Language Resources and Evaluation*, pages 2868–2872.

David Jurgens and Ioannis Klapaftis. 2013. Semeval-2013 task 13: Word sense induction for graded and non-graded senses. In *Proceedings of the Seventh International Workshop on Semantic Evaluation (SemEval 2013)*, pages 290–299.

Sandra Kübler and Desislava Zhekova. 2009. Semi-supervised learning for word sense disambiguation: Quality vs. quantity. In *Proceedings of the International Conference on Recent Advances in Natural Language Processing*, pages 197–202.

Jey Han Lau, Paul Cook, and Timothy Baldwin. 2013. unimelb: topic modelling-based word sense induction. In *Proceedings of the Seventh International Workshop on Semantic Evaluation (SemEval 2013)*, pages 307–311.

Yoong Keok Lee, Hwee Tou Ng, and Tee Kiah Chia. 2004. Supervised word sense disambiguation with support vector machines and multiple knowledge sources. In *Senseval-3: Third International Workshop on the Evaluation of Systems for the Semantic Analysis of Text*, pages 137–140.

Jin Kiat Low, Hwee Tou Ng, and Wenyuan Guo. 2005. A maximum entropy approach to Chinese word segmentation. In *Proceedings of the Fourth SIGHAN Workshop on Chinese Language Processing*, pages 161–164.

George A. Miller, Claudia Leacock, Randee Tengi, and Ross T. Bunker. 1993. A semantic concordance. In *Proceedings of the Workshop on Human Language Technology*, pages 303–308.

George A. Miller. 1995. WordNet: a lexical database for English. *Communications of the ACM*, 38(11):39–41.

Andrea Moro, Alessandro Raganato, and Roberto Navigli. 2014. Entity linking meets word sense disambiguation: a unified approach. *Transactions of the Association for Computational Linguistics*, 2:231–244.

Roberto Navigli, Kenneth C. Litkowski, and Orin Hargraves. 2007. Semeval-2007 task 07: Coarse-grained English all-words task. In *Proceedings of the Fourth International Workshop on Semantic Evaluations (SemEval-2007)*, pages 30–35.

Roberto Navigli. 2009. Word sense disambiguation: A survey. *ACM Computing Surveys*, 41(2):10:1–10:69.

Hwee Tou Ng and Hian Beng Lee. 1996. Integrating multiple knowledge sources to disambiguate word sense: An exemplar-based approach. In *Proceedings of the 34th Annual Meeting of the Association for Computational Linguistics*, pages 40–47.

Hwee Tou Ng, Bin Wang, and Yee Seng Chan. 2003. Exploiting parallel texts for word sense disambiguation: An empirical study. In *Proceedings of the 41st Annual Meeting of the Association for Computational Linguistics*, pages 455–462.

Franz Josef Och and Hermann Ney. 2000. Improved statistical alignment models. In *Proceedings of the 38th Annual Meeting of the Association for Computational Linguistics*, pages 440–447.

Rebecca Passonneau, Collin Baker, Christiane Fellbaum, and Nancy Ide. 2012. The MASC word sense sentence corpus. In *Proceedings of the Eighth International Conference on Language Resources and Evaluation*, pages 3025–3030.

Simone Paolo Ponzetto and Roberto Navigli. 2010. Knowledge-rich word sense disambiguation rivaling supervised systems. In *Proceedings of the 48th Annual Meeting of the Association for Computational Linguistics*, pages 1522–1531.

Sameer Pradhan, Edward Loper, Dmitriy Dligach, and Martha Palmer. 2007. Semeval-2007 task-17: English lexical sample, SRL and all words. In *Proceedings of the Fourth International Workshop on Semantic Evaluations (SemEval-2007)*, pages 87–92.

Benjamin Snyder and Martha Palmer. 2004. The English all-words task. In *Proceedings of the Third International Workshop on the Evaluation of Systems for the Semantic Analysis of Text*, pages 41–43.

Yee Whye Teh, Michael I Jordan, Matthew J Beal, and David M Blei. 2006. Hierarchical Dirichlet processes. *Journal of the American Statistical Association*, 101(476):1566–1581.

Jing Wang, Mohit Bansal, Kevin Gimpel, Brian D. Ziebart, and Clement T. Yu. 2015. A sense-topic model for word sense induction with unsupervised data enrichment. *Transactions of the Association for Computational Linguistics*, 3:59–71.

Zhi Zhong and Hwee Tou Ng. 2009. Word sense disambiguation for all words without hard labor. In *Proceedings of the Twenty-First International Joint Conference on Artificial Intelligence*, pages 1616–1621.

Zhi Zhong and Hwee Tou Ng. 2010. It Makes Sense: A wide-coverage word sense disambiguation system for free text. In *Proceedings of the 48th Annual Meeting of the Association for Computational Linguistics System Demonstrations*, pages 78–83.

Reading behavior predicts syntactic categories

Maria Barrett and Anders Søgaard
University of Copenhagen
Njalsgade 140
DK-2300 Copenhagen S
{dtq912,soegaard}@hum.ku.dk

Abstract

It is well-known that readers are less likely to fixate their gaze on closed class syntactic categories such as prepositions and pronouns. This paper investigates to what extent the syntactic category of a word in context can be predicted from gaze features obtained using eye-tracking equipment. If syntax can be reliably predicted from eye movements of readers, it can speed up linguistic annotation substantially, since reading is considerably faster than doing linguistic annotation by hand. Our results show that gaze features do discriminate between most pairs of syntactic categories, and we show how we can use this to annotate words with part of speech across domains, when tag dictionaries enable us to narrow down the set of potential categories.

1 Introduction

Eye movements during reading is a well-established proxy for cognitive processing, and it is well-known that readers are more likely to fixate on words from open syntactic categories (verbs, nouns, adjectives) than on closed category items like prepositions and conjunctions (Rayner, 1998; Nilsson and Nivre, 2009). Generally, readers seem to be most likely to fixate and re-fixate on nouns (Furtner et al., 2009). If reading behavior is affected by syntactic category, maybe reading behavior can, conversely, also tell us about the syntax of words in context.

This paper investigates to what extent gaze data can be used to *predict* syntactic categories. We show that gaze data can effectively be used to discriminate between a wide range of part of speech (POS) pairs, and gaze data can therefore be used to significantly improve type-constrained POS taggers. This is potentially useful, since eye-tracking data becomes more and more readily available with the emergence of eye trackers in mainstream consumer products (San Agustin et al., 2010). With the development of robust eye-tracking in laptops, it is easy to imagine digital text providers storing gaze data, which could then be used to improve automated analysis of their publications.

Contributions We are, to the best of our knowledge, the first to study reading behavior of syntactically annotated, natural text across domains, and how gaze correlates with a complete set of syntactic categories. We use logistic regression to show that gaze features discriminate between POS pairs, even across domains. We then show how gaze features can improve a cross-domain supervised POS tagger. We show that gaze-based predictions are robust, not only across domains, but also across subjects.

2 Experiment

In our experiment, 10 subjects read syntactically annotated sentences from five domains.

Data The data consists of 250 sentences: 50 sentences (min. 3 tokens, max. 120 characters), randomly sampled from each of five different, manually annotated corpora: Wall Street Journal articles (WSJ), Wall Street Journal headlines (HDL), emails (MAI), weblogs (WBL), and Twitter (TWI). WSJ and HDL syntactically annotated sentences come from the OntoNotes 4.0 release of the English Penn Treebank.[1] The MAI and WBL sections come from the English Web Treebank.[2]

[1] catalog.ldc.upenn.edu/LDC2011T03
[2] catalog.ldc.upenn.edu/LDC2012T13

Proceedings of the 19th Conference on Computational Language Learning, pages 345–349,
Beijing, China, July 30-31, 2015.

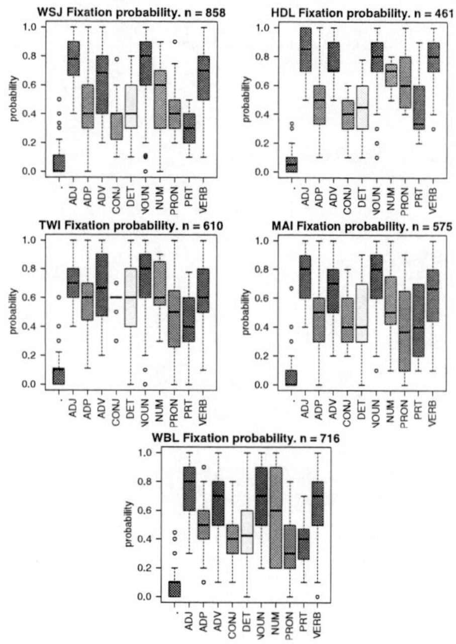

Figure 1: Fixation probability boxplots across five domains

The TWI data comes from the work of Foster et al. (2011). We mapped the gold labels to the 12 Universal POS (Petrov et al., 2011), but discarded the category X due to data sparsity.

Experimental design The 250 items were read by all 10 participants, but participants read the items in one of five randomized orders. Neither the source domain for the sentence, nor the POS tags were revealed to the participant at any time. One sentence was presented at a time in black on a light gray background. Font face was Verdana and font size was 25 pixels. Sentences were centered vertically, and all sentences could fit into one line. All sentences were preceded by a fixation cross. The experiment was self-paced. To switch to a new sentence and to ensure that the sentence was actually processed by the participant, participants rated the immediate interest towards the sentence on a scale from 1-6 by pressing the corresponding number on the numeric keypad. Participants were instructed to read and continue to the next sentence as quickly as possible. The actual experiment was preceded by 25 practice sentences to familiarize the participant with the experimental setup.

Our apparatus was a Tobii X120 eye tracker with a 15" monitor. Sampling rate was 120 Hz binocular. Participants were seated on a chair approximately 65 cm from the display. We recruited 10 participants (7 male, mean age 31.30 $\pm$4.74)) from campus. All were native English speakers. Their vision was normal or corrected to normal, and none were diagnosed with dyslexia. All were skilled readers. Minimum educational level was an ongoing MA. Each session lasted around 40 minutes. One participant had no fixations on a few sentences. We believe that erroneous key strokes caused the participant to skip a few sentences.

Features There are many different features for exploring cognitive load during reading (Rayner, 1998). We extracted a broad selection of cognitive effort features from the raw eye-tracking data in order to determine which are more fit for the task. The features are inspired by Salojärvi et al. (2003), who used a similarly exploratory approach. We wanted to cover both oculomotor features, such as fixations on previous and subsequent words, and measures relating to early (e.g. first fixation duration) and late processing (e.g. regression destinations / departure points and total fixation time). We also included reading speed and reading depth features, such as fixation probability and total fixation time per word. In total, we have 32 gaze features, where some are highly correlated (such as number of fixations on a word and total fixation time per sentence).

Dundee Corpus The main weakness of the experiment is the small dataset. As future work, we plan to replicate the experiment with a $99 eye tracker for subjects to use at home. This will make it easy to collect thousands of sentences, leading to more robust gaze-based POS models. Here, instead, we include an experiment with the Dundee corpus (Kennedy and Pynte, 2005). The Dundee corpus is a widely used dataset in research on reading and consists of gaze data for 10 subjects reading 20 newswire articles (about 51,000 words). We extracted the same word-based features as above, except probability for 1st and 2nd fixation, and sentence-level features (in the Dundee corpus, subjects are exposed to multiple sentences per screen window), and used them as features in our POS tagging experiments (§3).

Learning experiments In our experiments, we used type-constrained logistic regression with L2-regularization and type-constrained (averaged) structured perceptron (Collins, 2002; Täckström et al., 2013). In all experiments, unless otherwise stated, we trained our models on four domains and evaluated on the fifth to avoid over-fitting to the

Rank	Feature	% of votes
0	Fixation prob	19.0
1	Previous word fixated binary	13.7
2	Next word fixated binary	13.2
3	nFixations	12.2
4	First fixation duration on every word	9.1
5	Previous fixation duration	7.0
6	Mean fixation duration per word	6.6
7	Re-read prob	5.7
8	Next fixation duration	2.0
9	Total fixation duration per word	2.0

Table 1: 10 most used features by stability selection from logistic regression classification of all POS pairs on all domains, 5-fold cross validation.

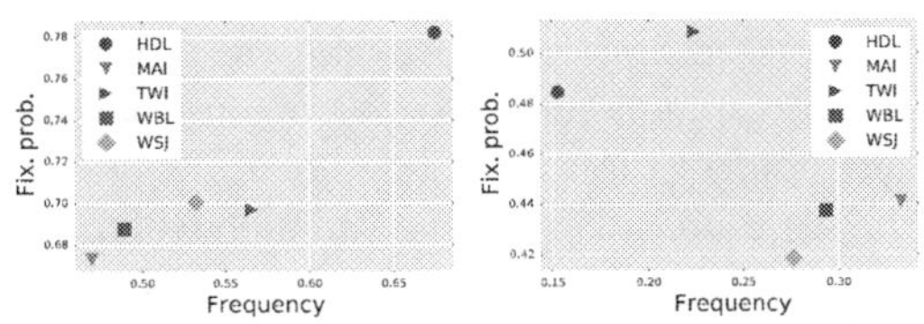

(a) Content words (b) Function words

Figure 2: Scatter plot of frequency and fixation probability for content words (NOUN, VERB, ADJ, NUM) and function words (PRON, CONJ, ADP, DET, PRT)

characteristics of a specific domain. Our tag dictionary is from Wiktionary[3] and covers 95% of all tokens.

3 Results

Domain differences Our first observation is that the gaze characteristics differ slightly across domains, but more across POS. Figure 1 presents the

[3]`https://code.google.com/p/wikily-supervised-pos-tagger/downloads/list`

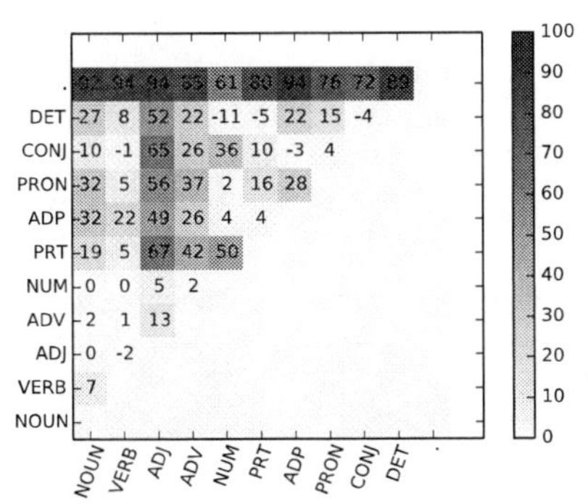

Figure 3: Error reduction of logistic regression over a majority baseline. All domains

fixation probabilities across the 11 parts of speech. While the overall pattern is similar across the five domains (open category items are more likely to be fixated), we see domain differences. For example, pronouns are more likely to be fixated in headlines. The explanation could lie in the different distributions of function words and content words. It is established and unchallenged that function words are fixated on about 35% of the time and content words are fixated on about 85% of the time (Rayner and Duffy, 1988). In our data, these numbers vary among the domains according to frequency of that word class, see Figure 2. Figure 2a shows that there is a strong linear correlation between content word frequency and content word fixation probability among the different domains: Pearson's $\rho = 0.909$. From Figure 2b, there is a negative correlation between function word frequency and function word fixation probability: Pearson's $\rho = -0.702$.

Predictive gaze features To investigate which gaze features were more predictive of part of speech, we used stability selection (Meinshausen and Bühlmann, 2010) with logistic regression classification on all binary POS classifications. Fixation probability was the most informative feature, but also whether the words around the word is fixated is important along with number of fixations. In our binary discrimination and POS tagging experiments, using L2-regularization or averaging with all features was superior (on Twitter data) to using stability selection for feature selection. We also asked a psycholinguist to select a small set of relatively independent gaze features fit for the task (first fixation duration, fixation probability and re-read probability), but again, using all features with L2-regularization led to better performance on the Twitter data.

Binary discrimination First, we trained L2-regularized logistic regression models to discriminate between all pairs of POS tags only using gaze features. In other words, for example we selected all words annotated as NOUN or VERB, and trained a logistic regression model to discriminate between the two in a five-fold cross validation setup. We report error reduction $\frac{acc-baseline}{1-baseline}$ in Figure 3.

POS tagging We also tried evaluating our gaze features directly in a supervised POS tagger.[4] We

[4]`https://github.com/coastalcph/rungsted`

	SP	+GAZE	+DGAZE	+FREQLEN	+DGAZE+FREQLEN
HDL	0.807	0.822	0.822	0.826	**0.843**
MAI	0.791	0.831	**0.834**	0.795	0.831
TWI	0.771	0.787	**0.800**	0.772	0.793
WBL	0.836	0.854	0.858	0.850	**0.861**
WSJ	0.831	0.837	0.838	0.831	**0.859**
Macro-av	0.807	0.826	0.830	0.815	**0.837**

Table 2: POS tagging results on different test sets using 200 out-of-domain sentences for training. DGAZE is using gaze features from Dundee. Best result for each row in bold face

trained a type-constrained (averaged) perceptron model with drop-out and a standard feature model (from Owoputi et al. (2013)) augmented with the above gaze features. The POS tagger was trained on a very small seed of data (200 sentences), doing 20 passes over the data, and evaluated on out-of-domain test data; training on four domains, testing on one. For the gaze features, instead of using token gaze features, we first built a lexicon with average word type statistics from the training data. We normalize the gaze matrix by dividing with its standard deviation. This is the normalizer in Turian et al. (2010) with $\sigma = 1.0$. We condition on the gaze features of the current word, only. We compare performance using gaze features to using only word frequency, estimating from the (unlabeled) English Web Treebank corpus, and word length (FREQLEN).

The first three columns in Table 2 show, that gaze features help POS tagging, at least when trained on very small seeds of data. Error reduction using gaze features from the Dundee corpus (DGAZE) is 12%. We know that gaze features correlate with word frequency and word length, but using these features directly leads to much smaller performance gains. Concatenating the two features sets leads to the best performance, with an error reduction of 16%.

In follow-up experiments, we observe that averaging over 10 subjects when collecting gaze features does not seem as important as we expected. Tagging accuracies on raw (non-averaged) data are only about 1% lower. Finally, we also tried running logistic regression experiments across subjects rather than domains. Here, tagging accuracies were again comparable to our set-up, suggesting that gaze features are also robust across subjects.

4 Related work

Matthies and Søgaard (2013) present results that suggest that individual variation among (academically trained) subjects' reading behavior was not a greater source of error than variation within subjects, showing that it is possible to predict fixations across readers. Our work relates to such work, studying the robustness of reading models across domains and readers, but it also relates in spirit to research on using weak supervision in NLP, e.g., work on using HTML markup to improve dependency parsers (Spitkovsky, 2013) or using click-through data to improve POS taggers (Ganchev et al., 2012).

5 Conclusions

We have shown that it is possible to use gaze features to discriminate between many POS pairs across domains, even with only a small dataset and a small set of subjects. We also showed that gaze features can improve the performance of a POS tagger trained on small seeds of data.

References

Michael Collins. 2002. Discriminative training methods for Hidden Markov Models. In *EMNLP*.

Jennifer Foster, Ozlem Cetinoglu, Joachim Wagner, Josef Le Roux, Joakim Nivre, Deirde Hogan, and Josef van Genabith. 2011. From news to comments: Resources and benchmarks for parsing the language of Web 2.0. In *IJCNLP*.

Marco R Furtner, John F Rauthmann, and Pierre Sachse. 2009. Nomen est omen: Investigating the dominance of nouns in word comprehension with eye movement analyses. *Advances in Cognitive Psychology*, 5:91.

Kuzman Ganchev, Keith Hall, Ryan McDonald, and Slav Petrov. 2012. Using search-logs to improve query tagging. In *ACL*.

Alan Kennedy and Joël Pynte. 2005. Parafoveal-on-foveal effects in normal reading. *Vision research*, 45(2):153–168.

Franz Matthies and Anders Søgaard. 2013. With blinkers on: Robust prediction of eye movements across readers. In *EMNLP*, Seattle, Washington, USA.

Nicolai Meinshausen and Peter Bühlmann. 2010. Stability selection. *Journal of the Royal Statistical Society: Series B (Statistical Methodology)*, 72(4):417–473.

Matthias Nilsson and Joakim Nivre. 2009. Learning where to look: Modeling eye movements in reading. In *CoNLL*.

Olutobi Owoputi, Brendan O'Connor, Chris Dyer, Kevin Gimpel, Nathan Schneider, and Noah A Smith. 2013. Improved part-of-speech tagging for online conversational text with word clusters. In *NAACL*.

Slav Petrov, Dipanjan Das, and Ryan McDonald. 2011. A universal part-of-speech tagset. *arXiv preprint arXiv:1104.2086*.

K.; Rayner and S. A. Duffy. 1988. On-line comprehension processes and eye movements in reading. In G. E. MacKinnon M. Daneman and T. G. Waller, editors, *Reading research: Advances in theory and practice*, pages 13–66. Academic Press, New York.

Keith Rayner. 1998. Eye movements in reading and information processing: 20 years of research. *Psychological bulletin*, 124(3):372.

Jarkko Salojärvi, Ilpo Kojo, Jaana Simola, and Samuel Kaski. 2003. Can relevance be inferred from eye movements in information retrieval. In *Proceedings of WSOM*, volume 3, pages 261–266.

Javier San Agustin, Henrik Skovsgaard, Emilie Mollenbach, Maria Barret, Martin Tall, Dan Witzner Hansen, and John Paulin Hansen. 2010. Evaluation of a low-cost open-source gaze tracker. In *Proceedings of the 2010 Symposium on Eye-Tracking Research & Applications*, pages 77–80. ACM.

Valentin Ilyich Spitkovsky. 2013. *Grammar Induction and Parsing with Dependency-and-Boundary Models*. Ph.D. thesis, STANFORD UNIVERSITY.

Oscar Täckström, Dipanjan Das, Slav Petrov, Ryan McDonald, and Joakim Nivre. 2013. Token and type constraints for cross-lingual part-of-speech tagging. *TACL*, 1:1–12.

Joseph Turian, Lev Ratinov, and Yoshua Bengio. 2010. Word representations: a simple and general method for semi-supervised learning. In *ACL*.

Author Index